The Network Society

The Network Society

A Cross-cultural Perspective

Edited by

Manuel Castells

*Wallis Annenberg Chair Professor of Communication Technology and Society,
University of Southern California, Los Angeles
and Research Professor, Open University of Catalonia, Barcelona*

Edward Elgar
Cheltenham, UK • Northampton, MA, USA

Published by
Edward Elgar Publishing Limited
The Lypiatts
15 Lansdown Road
Cheltenham
Glos GL50 2JA
UK

Edward Elgar Publishing, Inc.
William Pratt House
9 Dewey Court
Northampton
Massachusetts 01060
USA

This book has been printed on demand to keep the title in print.

A catalogue record for this book
is available from the British Library

Library of Congress Cataloguing in Publication Data
The network society : a cross-cultural perspective / edited by Manuel Castells.
    p. cm.
  1. Information society —Cross-cultural studies. I. Castells, Manuel.

HD851.N475 2004
303.48'33—dc22

2004043491

ISBN 978 1 84376 505 9 (cased)
     978 1 84542 435 0 (paperback)

Printed and bound in Great Britain by
Marston Book Services Limited, Didcot

Contents

List of figures   viii
List of tables   ix
Notes on contributors   xi
Acknowledgments   xvi
Editor's preface   xvii

PART I THE THEORY OF THE NETWORK SOCIETY

1 Informationalism, Networks, and the Network Society:
   A Theoretical Blueprint   3
   Manuel Castells

PART II THE CULTURAL AND INSTITUTIONAL DIVERSITY
         OF THE NETWORK SOCIETY

2 Institutional Models of the Network Society: Silicon Valley
   and Finland   49
   Pekka Himanen and Manuel Castells
3 The Russian Network Society   84
   Elena Vartanova
4 The Internet in China: Technologies of Freedom in a Statist
   Society   99
   Jack Linchuan Qiu
5 Reflexive Internet? The British Experience of New Electronic
   Technologies   125
   Steve Woolgar

PART III THE NETWORK ECONOMY

6 Why Information Should Influence Productivity   145
   Marshall Van Alstyne and Nathaniel Bulkley
7 Labor in the Network Society: Lessons from Silicon Valley   174
   Chris Benner
8 Time, Space, and Technology in Financial Networks   198
   Caitlin Zaloom

vi	*Contents*

PART IV SOCIABILITY AND SOCIAL STRUCTURE IN THE AGE OF
        THE INTERNET

 9 Networked Sociability Online, Off-line	217
    Keith N. Hampton
10 Social Structure, Cultural Identity, and Personal Autonomy in the
    Practice of the Internet: The Network Society in Catalonia	233
    Manuel Castells, Imma Tubella, Teresa Sancho,
    Maria Isabel Díaz de Isla, and Barry Wellman
11 Racial Segregation and the Digital Divide in the Detroit
    Metropolitan Region	249
    Wayne E. Baker and Kenneth M. Coleman

PART V THE INTERNET IN THE PUBLIC INTEREST

12 The Promise and the Myths of e-Learning in Post-secondary
    Education	271
    Tony Bates
13 e-Health Networks and Social Transformations: Expectations of
    Centralization, Experiences of Decentralization	293
    James E. Katz, Ronald E. Rice, and Sophia K. Acord
14 Narrowing the Digital Divide: The Potential and Limits of the US
    Community Technology Movement	319
    Lisa J. Servon and Randal D. Pinkett

PART VI NETWORKED SOCIAL MOVEMENTS AND
         INFORMATIONAL POLITICS

15 Networked Social Movements: Global Movements for Global
    Justice	341
    Jeffrey S. Juris
16 From Media Politics to Networked Politics: The Internet and the
    Political Process	363
    Araba Sey and Manuel Castells

PART VII THE CULTURE OF THE NETWORK SOCIETY

17 Television, the Internet, and the Construction of Identity	385
    Imma Tubella
18 Globalization, Identity, and Television Networks: Community
    Mediation and Global Responses in Multicultural India	402
    Anshu Chatterjee

19   The Hacker Ethic as the Culture of the Information Age   420
       Pekka Himanen

Afterword: An Historian's View on the Network Society   432
Rosalind Williams

Index   449

Figures

2.1   Technological development measured by the UN Technology
      Achievement Index, 2001   51
2.2   Economic competitiveness measured by the World Economic
      Forum Growth Competitiveness Index, 2002   52
2.3   Labor productivity in manufacturing based on the OECD STAN
      database   52
2.4   Social inequality and exclusion in the US and Finland,
      1950–1990   54
2.5   Share of public funding in private research and development,
      1987–1999   58
2.6   The Silicon Valley model of the new economy   62
2.7   Level of start-up activity, 2001   63
2.8   National R&D investment as a percentage of GDP,
      1985–2001   64
2.9   The Finnish model of the information society   68
2.10 An example of Nokia project networking   71
2.11 Share of Tekes funding in Nokia's R&D   72
2.12 Private R&D investment as a share of the total (%),
      1981–2001   73
2.13 Entrepreneurial motivation (scale 1–5)   77
2.14 Venture capital market in Europe as a whole and in selected
      European countries   78
2.15 Labor productivity growth in Finland (1985 = 100)   79
4.1   The concentration of Internet resources in the core region of
      Beijing, Shanghai, and Guangdong Province   105
6.1   Moving along the efficient production frontier (e.g. resource
      substitution)   149
6.2   (a) Moving to the frontier (e.g. better decisions);
      (b) Shifting the frontier (e.g. new processes)   152
12.1 The continuum of e-learning in formal education   274

Tables

2.1	Production of technology and social inclusion	53
2.2	Top five Silicon Valley information technology companies	55
2.3	Top five Finnish information technology companies	66
3.1	Dynamics of the Russian Internet audience	88
3.2	Areas of residence of Runet visitors	89
4.1	Demographic comparison: Internet users vis-à-vis average Chinese	104
7.1	Dimensions of flexible labor	177
7.2	Indicators of flexible employment in Silicon Valley	182
9.1	Seeking advice from family	224
10.1	Distribution of Internet users according to Internet use	240
10.2	Results of factor analysis of variables indicative of projects of autonomy	245
11.1	Black–white segregation and black isolation in top metropolitan areas in the United States	252
11.2	Patterns of computer and Internet use by race, gender, age, education, household income, employment status, family structure, and location	254
11.3	OLS and logistic coefficients from the regression of computer and Internet use on income, education, age, race, gender, employment status, location, and family	257
11.4	Activities done on the Internet in the past 12 months by race and location	260
11.5	Logistic coefficients from regression of inter-neighborhood and inter-racial socializing on income, education, age, race, gender, employment status, location, family structure, and computer and Internet usage	262
12.1	Rough estimate of e-learners globally, 2002–2003	279
13.1	Use of the Internet and Internet healthcare resources by the US public, 1997–2002	295
13.2	Comparison of features of Internet patient decision-support tools of some leading providers	301
13.3	Use of online resources by physicians in the United States	307

13.4 Physician reports of the percentage of their patients who talked to them in person about information that the patient has obtained from the Internet 308

13.5 Physician assessment of effect on physician/patient relationship of patient presenting Internet-derived information 309

14.1 Dimensions of the digital divide 322

16.1 Internet use for political purposes in the US, 1998–2002 369

18.1 Community language channels, 1990–2002 405

18.2 Audience share of major channels in three states, 1999 407

Notes on contributors

Sophia K. Acord is a PhD candidate in Sociology and the Philosophy of Culture at the University of Exeter in the United Kingdom. Her research interests include applied drama as well as issues of social hierarchy in the culture of contemporary art.

Wayne E. Baker is Professor of Management and Organizations and Professor of Sociology at the University of Michigan, and Faculty Associate at the Institute for Social Research. He is the Principal Investigator for the 2003 Detroit Area Study and Principal Investigator and Team Leader for the Detroit Arab American Study. His research interests include economic sociology, networks and social capital, organizations, and culture.

Tony Bates is a private consultant specializing in the planning and management of e-learning in higher education. Between 1995 and 2003 he was Director of Distance Education and Technology at the University of British Columbia, following five years as Executive Director, Strategic Planning, at the Open Learning Agency, Vancouver, Canada. He was a founding staff member of the British Open University, working there from 1969 to 1989, becoming Professor of Educational Media Research. He is the author of eight books on educational media, distance education, and the management of learning technologies. He has been a consultant to the World Bank, OECD, UNESCO, Ministries of Education in several countries, and state higher education commissions in the USA, as well as to many universities and colleges. He is currently advising the Open University of Catalonia on research into e-learning. He has a PhD in educational administration from the University of London, and has honorary degrees from Laurentian University and the Open University of Portugal.

Chris Benner is an Assistant Professor of Geography at Pennsylvania State University. His work focuses on labor markets and regional development in the information economy, paying particular attention to the relationship between the diffusion of information technologies and the transformation of work and employment patterns. His book *Work in the New Economy* was published in 2002. He received his doctorate in City and Regional Planning from the University of California, Berkeley.

Nathaniel Bulkley is a PhD student at the University of Michigan School of Information. His dissertation work focuses on the relationship between information management practices and productivity in the context of executive recruiting.

Manuel Castells is the Wallis Annenberg Chair Professor of Communication Technology and Society at the Annenberg School of Communication, University of Southern California, Los Angeles. He is also Research Professor of Information Society at the Open University of Catalonia (UOC) in Barcelona, Professor Emeritus of Sociology and of Planning, at the University of California at Berkeley, and Distinguished Visiting Professor of Technology and Society at the Massachusetts Institute of Technology.

Anshu Chatterjee is a Research Fellow at the Center for South Asian Studies of the University of California, Berkeley. She received her PhD from the Asian Studies Department of the University of California, Berkeley. She has been a recipient of the MacArthur Multilateralism Fellowship and University of California, Berkeley, Chancellor's Fellowship. Among her publications is "Global Compulsions and National Objectives: Shifting Media Terms in Multicultural India," in Patrick Brunet (ed.), *Valeurs et éthique des médias: une approche internationale* (2004). She is currently studying the interaction between transnational and community media and cross-border political activities in South Asia.

Kenneth M. Coleman is a Senior Research Analyst with Market Strategies, Inc., in Livonia, Michigan, USA, and a Faculty Associate of the Center for Political Studies in the Institute for Social Research at the University of Michigan. He has written extensively on public opinion in Latin America.

Maria Isabel Díaz de Isla is a doctoral student in the Information and Knowledge Society PhD program at the Open University of Catalonia (UOC), Barcelona. Her doctoral research interest is in the impact of the Internet and other information and communication technologies on health systems. She is a co-author of the research report *The Network Society in Catalonia* (July 2002) with Manuel Castells, Imma Tubella, Teresa Sancho, and Barry Wellman.

Keith N. Hampton is Assistant Professor of Technology, Urban and Community Sociology in the Department of Urban Studies and Planning at Massachusetts Institute of Technology. His research interests focus on the relationship between information and communication technologies, social networks, and the urban environment.

Pekka Himanen divides his time between the Helsinki Institute for Information Society and the University of California at Berkeley . He has also acted as an adviser on the information society to the Finnish president, government, and parliament. His books on the network society have been published in twenty languages. They include *The Hacker Ethic and the Spirit of the Information Age* (2001) and (with Manuel Castells) *The Information Society and the Welfare State: The Finnish Model* (2001).

Jeffrey S. Juris is a postdoctoral fellow at the Annenberg School of Communication, University of Southern California. He received his PhD in anthropology from the University of California, Berkeley, where his research focused on globalization, social movements, and transnational activism. He is currently writing on the culture and politics of transnational networking among anti-corporate globalization activists. He is also conducting comparative ethnographic research on the utopian use of new information technologies and digitial collaboration among media activists in Europe and Latin America.

James E. Katz is Professor of Communication at Rutgers University. Currently, he is investigating how personal communication technologies, such as mobile phones and the Internet, affect social relationships. Among his books are *Connections: Social and Cultural Studies of the Telephone in American Life* (1999) and *Social Consequences of Internet Use: Access, Involvement, Expression* (2002), co-authored with Ronald E. Rice.

Jack Linchuan Qiu is a post-doctoral research fellow at the Annenberg School for Communication at the University of Southern California. He researches on the development of new media, late capitalism, and social transformations in the Asian Pacific. He co-founded and moderates the China Internet Research e-Group, while serving as policy consultant for various international organizations.

Randal D. Pinkett is the President and CEO of BCT Partners, a management, technology, and policy consulting firm that improves organizational effectiveness and supports strategies for change. BCT specializes in the following industries/sectors: housing and community development, community and nonprofit technology, e-government, education, pharmaceuticals, financial services, and telecommunications.

Ronald E. Rice is Arthur N. Rupe Chair in Communication of the Department of Communication at the University of California, Santa Barbara. He has co-authored or co-edited *The New Media* (1984), *Managing Organizational Innovation* (1987), *Research Methods and the New Media* (1988), *Accessing* *and Browsing Information and Communication* (2001), *The Internet and Health Communication* (2001), *Public Communication Campaigns* (3rd edn, 2001), and *Social Consequences of Internet Use: Access, Involvement, Expression* (2002).

Teresa Sancho gained her PhD in Electronic Engineering from Ramon Llull University in Barcelona. She is the academic coordinator of the doctoral program at the Open University of Catalonia (UOC), Barcelona. She has also taught at the La Salle School of Engineering in Barcelona. At the UOC, her research includes e-learning processes, as well as the study of the network society in Catalonia for quantitative subjects. She is a co-author of *La societat xarxa a Catalunya* (2003).

Lisa J. Servon is Associate Professor and Associate Director of the Community Development Research Center at the Milano Graduate School of Management and Policy, New School University, New York. She works on urban poverty, community economic development, and issues of gender and race.

Araba Sey is a doctoral student and the Wallis Annenberg Graduate Student Fellow at the Annenberg School of Communication, University of Southern California.

Imma Tubella is Professor of Communication Theory and Vice-rector for Research at the Open University of Catalonia (UOC), Barcelona. Her research interests concern the relationship between media and identity. She a member of the Board of the Catalan Broadcasting Corporation. Among other publications, she is a co-author of *La societat xarxa a Catalunya* (2003).

Marshall Van Alstyne teaches information economics, computer modeling, e-commerce, and statistics at the University of Michigan. His research focuses on the economics of information, its value, production, property rights, and effects on firms and social systems. This research has received an NSF Career Award, best paper award, and has appeared in *Science* and the popular press. He received his bachelor's degree in computer science from Yale University, and MS and PhD degrees in information technology from Massachusetts Institute of Technology.

Elena Vartanova is Professor and Deputy Dean in the Faculty of Journalism, Moscow State University, as well as Director of the Center for Finnish Russian Studies. Her research interests include Nordic media systems, the information society, the post-Soviet transformation of the Russian media, and media economics. She is the author of three monographs, co-editor of the *Russian Media Challenge* (2001, 2002), and author of seventy articles in Russian and foreign academic journals.

Barry Wellman is a sociologist who directs NetLab at the University of Toronto's Center for Urban and Community Studies. He founded the International Network for Social Network Analysis in 1976. In addition to more than two hundred articles, he has co-edited *Social Structures: A Network Approach* (1988), *Networks in the Global Village* (1999), and *The Internet in Everyday Life* (2002).

Rosalind Williams is Metcalfe Professor of Writing and Director of the Program in Science, Technology, and Society at the Massachusetts Institute of Technology. In 2005 she will be President of the Society for the History of Technology. A cultural historian of technology, her most recent work is *Retooling: A Historian Confronts Technological Change* (2002).

Steve Woolgar is a sociologist who holds the Chair of Marketing and is Director of Research at the Saïd Business School of the University of Oxford. He is also a member of the Management Board of the Oxford Internet Institute. From 1997 to 2002 he was Director of the ESRC Programme *Virtual Society? The Social Science of Electronic Technologies*, comprising twenty-two research projects throughout the United Kingdom. He was formerly Professor of Sociology and Director of CRICT at Brunel University. He has published widely in social studies of science and technology, social problems, and social theory. He is the editor of *Virtual Society? Technology, Cyberbole, Reality* (2002).

Caitlin Zaloom is Assistant Professor and Faculty Fellow in the Metropolitan Studies Program at New York University. Her work on technologies of finance and risk-taking has appeared in *American Ethnologist* and *Cultural Anthropology*. Her book *The Discipline of Speculators: Trading and Technology from Chicago to London* is forthcoming from the University of Chicago Press.

Acknowledgments

This book is the result of a networked project of cooperation undertaken by 26 researchers from Universities around the world. Therefore, it would not exist without the efficient management of this network by the coordinator of the book project: Ms. Anna Sanchez-Juarez, from the Internet Interdisciplinary Institute of the Open University of Catalonia (UOC).

As with all academic endeavors, this project is endebted to the material and intellectual support of the research institutions that constitute the daily working environment of the authors. We wish to express our gratitude to our universities and research centers for this support. The editor wishes also to acknowledge specially the support received from the Annenberg School of Communication, University of Southern California, Los Angeles, and from the Internet Interdisciplinary Institute, Open University of Catalonia, Barcelona. More specifically, the work leading to this book has benefited fom the research environments established around the Annenberg Research Network on International Communication at USC, and around the Project Internet Catalonia (PIC) at the Open University of Catalonia.

A special word deserves our publishing editor, Ms. Francine O'Sullivan, from Edward Elgar, who initiated the project of this book and supported it throughout its evolution. The copy editor of this book, Ms. Sue Ashton, is, once again, as in several projects led by the book's editor, the indispensable communicating links between our analysis and you the reader. Specific acknowledgements to colleagues who have commented and helped the substance of the book are included by the authors in each chapter.

Editor's preface

This volume explores the patterns and dynamics of the network society in its cultural and institutional diversity. By network society, we refer to the social structure that results from the interaction between social organization, social change, and a technological paradigm constituted around digital information and communication technologies. We start from a rejection of technological determinism, as technology cannot be considered independently of its social context. But we also emphasize the importance of technology as material culture by focusing on the specific social processes related to the emergence of this new technological paradigm. Thus, while several chapters focus on the social uses of the Internet, this is not a study of the Internet. Instead, observation of the practices of the Internet is our entry point to understand the diffusion of networking as an organizational form and to examine the complex interaction between technology and society in our world. Using an historical parallel, the equivalent would be to study the diffusion and uses of the electrical engine and the electric grid to understand the development of industrial society.

What defines the collective research effort presented in this book is the conviction that the network society, while presenting some fundamental, common features in all contexts, takes very different forms depending on the cultural and institutional environments in which it evolves. We would like, as our contribution to the understanding of a world in the making, to break with the ethnocentrism of many visions of the network society (or information and knowledge society in another terminology), which often assimilate the rise of this society to the cultural and organizational unification of a globalized world, usually reproducing the social forms and values of the United States or Western Europe.

Furthermore, there is an implicit assumption that this convergence in the ways of producing, living, and thinking is a necessary condition to access the promise of the new technological power. The more a new society emerges, the more the analytical effort to understand it reproduces the historical error made in the study of industrialism and postindustrialism: societies that did not look like the United States, England, France, or Germany were considered to be exceptions to or variations of the basic model of industrial or postindustrial society. We would like to introduce, in the early stages of the development of the network society, the notion of its diversity, as a result of the differential interaction between new socio-technical processes and the culture and history of each society. Thus, our comparative study of Silicon Valley and Finland (chapter 2) provides support for the proposition that similarly technologically advanced and economically competitive societies can be rooted in very different institutions and guided by sharply divergent public policies. We go on to show how, in various contexts around the world, the diffusion of the Internet, the adoption of digital technology in the production process, or the relationship between cultural identity and electronic media is treated in different ways.

But we also contend that there are some common features to the network society, and that they are related to the socio-technical specificity of the informational paradigm. This volume analyzes, along the main dimensions of economy, society, and culture, the interaction between structural commonality and cultural singularity in the deployment of a new social structure on a planetary scale.

The perspective of this volume is cross-cultural. To be sure, there are many cultures, and societies, that are not studied here. Our purpose was not to create an encyclopedia of the network society by accumulating information and analysis on a large number of countries. Our objective is analytical; it is to suggest a method of inquiry on a variety of key themes in a diversity of cultural and institutional contexts. We hope that this effort will stimulate specific studies in countries around the world, so that we can learn from each other, and build, cumulatively, the human cross-cultural map of the emerging network society.

The volume starts with an attempt to present, in tentative terms, the theory of the network society. I want to emphasize that this is not the common theoretical framework of this volume. Neither do the chapters in this volume represent an application of the conceptual framework presented in the first chapter. Each author has built the results of his or her research on his or her own conceptual system. However, there is a common approach in trying to comprehend the autonomous interaction between technology and social structure, emphasizing the importance of networking as an organizational form. So, to some extent, the theoretical blueprint presented here (elaborated and written after the analytical chapters were completed) tries to relate to the issues and findings permeating the whole volume. However, I do not feel that it is necessary, or possible, to systematically integrate the empirical record in the categories of the theoretical scheme presented here. The empirical evidence for this theoretical chapter must be looked for in my own analytical work, as referred to in the notes to the chapter. Nonetheless, it is my hope that by placing up front the theoretical discussion of the network society, we can clarify terms, define issues, and enhance the understanding of the meaning of findings presented in the rest of the volume.

The organization of the book is straightforward. After presenting a tentative theoretical discussion of the network society, we analyze, in part II, processes of technological transformation, in interaction with social structure, in five different cultural and institutional contexts: Silicon Valley, Finland, Russia, China, and the UK. Part of the approach is directly comparative (between Silicon Valley and Finland). Most analyses document the specific development of networking technology and organization in each society, leaving the interested reader with the task of considering the contrasting experiences of socio-technical transformation.

Part III of the volume analyzes the transformation of the economic dimension of the network society by focusing on the three major components of the economy: capital, labor, and the production process. We try to analyze the specificity of productivity growth in the new economy; the transformation of the process of valuation of capital, in terms of time and space, in the global financial networks; and the emergence of flexible labor as the form of labor characteristic of the network economy on the basis of observation of the original site of the transformation, Silicon Valley.

The fourth part of the book looks at patterns of social structuration and social relationships, comparing the findings of research conducted in North America and in Catalonia, with a particular emphasis on the new patterns of socio-spatial segregation as observed in the Detroit Metropolitan Area.

We then undertake, in part V, the study of the transformation of the public sector, and its related public policies, by organizational networking and communication technologies. We summarize and discuss some of the knowledge available in the key areas of e-learning, e-health, and community development, trying to assess the social and institutional limits that exist on the use of Internet in the public interest.

Next, part VI analyzes the sociopolitical implications of networking and the Internet by studying, on the one hand, the reconfiguration of social movements, and particularly the so-called "anti-globalization movement," and, on the other hand, shortcomings in the use of the Internet in formal politics, which is, by and large, still organized in hierarchical terms, while providing a hint on the potential of grassroots networking on the condition of the enhancement of political autonomy in civil society.

Part VII explores the crucial question of culture in the network society, with particular emphasis on the interaction between the construction of identity and the dynamics of television, contrasting the experiences of Catalonia and India. There is also the presentation of a novel hypothesis which tries to find the cultural matrix of the new society in the materials provided by the "hacker ethic," in an historical transposition of Weber's attempt to propose the Protestant ethic as the spirit of capitalism.

Finally, a distinguished historian of technology and culture provides an historical perspective to relativize even further our relativism on the process of socio-technical transformation that we have identified as the multicultural formation of the network society in this early twenty-first century.

In ending these introductory remarks, I would like to emphasize the practical consequences of our analytical perspective. If, indeed, the new technological modernity comes in a variety of sociocultural formats, societies – and their representatives – would be ill advised to copy successful models which will likely operate as implants and be rejected by the people at large. Instead, it is by opening up the ability of societies to experiment for themselves with the new socio-technical paradigm that home-grown network societies will emerge, rooted in their identities and open to the social forms of other cultures. The networking process will then allow the cross-fertilization of human experience, so that a global network society may be the result of identity-based, specific forms of network society communicating with each other. Communication, rather than replication, seems to be the historical horizon for societies in the information age.

PART I

The Theory of the Network Society

1. Informationalism, networks, and the network society: a theoretical blueprint

Manuel Castells

NETWORKS, SOCIETY, AND COMMUNICATION TECHNOLOGY

A network society is a society whose social structure is made of networks powered by microelectronics-based information and communication technologies. By social structure, I understand the organizational arrangements of humans in relations of production, consumption, reproduction, experience, and power expressed in meaningful communication coded by culture. A network is a set of interconnected nodes. A node is the point where the curve intersects itself. A network has no center, just nodes. Nodes may be of varying relevance for the network. Nodes increase their importance for the network by absorbing more relevant information, and processing it more efficiently. The relative importance of a node does not stem from its specific features but from its ability to contribute to the network's goals. However, all nodes of a network are necessary for the network's performance. When nodes become redundant or useless, networks tend to reconfigure themselves, deleting some nodes, and adding new ones. Nodes only exist and function as components of networks. The network is the unit, not the node.

"Communication networks are the patterns of contact that are created by flows of messages among communicators through time and space" (Monge and Contractor, 2003: 39). So, networks process flows. Flows are streams of information between nodes circulating through the channels of connection between nodes. A network is defined by the program that assigns the network its goals and its rules of performance. This program is made up of codes that include valuation of performance and criteria for success or failure. To alter the outcomes of the network, a new program (a set of compatible codes) will have to be installed in the network – from outside the network. Networks cooperate or compete with each other. Cooperation is based on the ability to communicate between networks. This ability depends on the existence of codes of translation and inter-operability between the networks (protocols of communication), and on access to connection points (switches). Competition

3

depends on the ability to outperform other networks by superior efficiency in performance or in cooperation capacity. Competition may also take a destructive form by disrupting the switches of competing networks and/or interfering with their communication protocols.

Networks work on a binary logic: inclusion/exclusion. Within the network, distance between nodes tends to zero, as networks follow the logic of small worlds' properties: they are able to connect to the entire network and communicated networks from any node in the network by sharing protocols of communication. Between nodes in the network and those outside the network distance is infinite, since there is no access unless the program of the network is changed. Thus, networks are self-reconfigurable, complex structures of communication that ensure, at the same time, unity of purpose and flexibility of its execution by the capacity to adapt to the operating environment.

Networks, however, are not specific to twenty-first century societies or, for that matter, to human organization. Networks constitute the fundamental pattern of life, of all kinds of life. As Fritjof Capra writes "the network is a pattern that is common to all life. Wherever we see life, we see networks" (2002: 9). In social life, social networks analysts have for a long time investigated the dynamic of social networks at the heart of social interaction and the production of meaning, leading to the formulation of a systematic theory of communication networks (Monge and Contractor, 2003). Furthermore, in terms of social structure, archaeologists and historians of antiquity have forcefully reminded us that the historical record shows the pervasiveness and relevance of networks as the backbone of societies, thousands of years ago, in the most advanced ancient civilizations in several regions of the planet. Indeed, if we transfer the notion of globalization to the geography of the ancient world, as determined by available transportation technologies, there was globalization of a sort in antiquity, as societies depended for their livelihood, resources, and power on the connectivity of their main activities to networks transcending the limits of their locality (La Bianca, forthcoming).

This observation of the actual historical record runs counter to the predominant vision of the evolution of society that has focused on a different type of organization: hierarchical bureaucracies based on the vertical integration of resources and subjects as the expression of the organized power of a social elite, legitimized by mythology and religion. This is to some extent a distorted vision as historical and social analysis has been built, more often than not, on ethnocentrism and apology rather than on the scholarly investigation of the complexity of a multicultural world. But the relative indifference of our historical representation to the importance of networks in the structure and dynamics of society may also be linked to the actual subordination of these networks to the logic of vertical organizations, whose power was inscribed in the institutions of society and distributed in one-directional flows of information and resources (Colas, 1992).

My hypothesis for the historical superiority of vertical-hierarchical organizations over networks is that the networked form of social organization had material limits to overcome, limits that were fundamentally linked to available technology. Indeed, networks have their strength in their flexibility, adaptability, and self-reconfiguring capacity. Yet, beyond a certain threshold of size, complexity, and volume of exchange, they become less efficient than vertically organized command and control structures, *under the conditions of pre-electronic communication technology* (Mokyr, 1990). Yes, wind-powered vessels could build sea-crossing, and even transoceanic, networks of trade and conquest. And horse-riding emissaries or fast-running messengers could maintain communication from the center to the periphery of vast territorial empires. But the time lag of the feedback loop in the communication process was such that the logic of the system amounted to a one-way flow of information and instruction. Under such conditions, networks were an extension of power concentrated at the top of the vertical organizations that shaped the history of humankind: states, religious apparatuses, war lords, armies, bureaucracies, and their subordinates in charge of production, trade, and culture.

The ability of networks to introduce new actors and new contents in the process of social organization, with relative independence of the power centers, increased over time with technological change, and, more precisely, with the evolution of communication technologies. This was particularly the case with the possibility of relying on a distributed energy network that characterized the advent of the industrial revolution: railways, ocean liners, and the telegraph constituted the first infrastructure for a quasi-global network with self-reconfiguring capacity. However, industrial society (both in its capitalist and its statist versions) was predominantly structured around large-scale, vertical production organizations and extremely hierarchical state apparatuses, in some instances evolving into totalitarian systems. This is to say that early, electrically based communication technologies were not powerful enough to equip networks with autonomy in all their nodes, as this autonomy would have required multidirectionality and a continuous flow of interactive information processing. But it also means that the availability of proper technology is a necessary, but not sufficient condition for the transformation of the social structure. It was only under the conditions of a mature industrial society that autonomous projects of organizational networking could emerge. When they did, they could use the potential of microelectronics-based communication technologies.

Networks became the most efficient organizational form as a result of three major features of networks that benefited from the new technological environment: flexibility, scalability, and survivability.

- *Flexibility*: networks can reconfigure according to changing environments, keeping their goals while changing their components. They go
  around blocking points in communication channels to find new connections.
- *Scalability*: they can expand or shrink in size with little disruption.
- *Survivability*: because they have no center, and can operate in a wide
  range of configurations, networks can resist attacks on their nodes and
  codes because the codes of the network are contained in multiple nodes
  that can reproduce the instructions and find new ways to perform. So,
  only the physical ability to destroy the connecting points can eliminate
  the network.

At the core of the technological change that unleashed the power of networks
was the transformation of information and communication technologies, based
on the microelectronics revolution that took place in the 1940s and 1950s. It
constituted the foundation of a new technological paradigm, consolidated in the
1970s, mainly in the United States, and rapidly diffused throughout the world,
ushering in what I have characterized, descriptively, as the information age.

William Mitchell, in an important and well-documented book (Mitchell,
2003), has retraced the evolving logic of information and communication
technology throughout history as a process of expansion and augmentation of
the human body and the human mind; a process that, in the early twenty-first
century, is characterized by the explosion of portable machines that provide
ubiquitous wireless communication and computing capacity. This enables
social units (individuals or organizations) to interact anywhere, anytime, while
relying on a support infrastructure that manages material resources in a distributed information power grid. With the advent of nanotechnology and the
convergence between microelectronics and biological processes and materials,
the boundaries between human life and machine life are blurred, so that
networks extend their interaction from our inner self to the whole realm of
human activity, transcending barriers of time and space. Neither Mitchell nor
I indulge in science fiction scenarios as a substitute for analysis of the techno-
social transformation process. But it is essential, precisely for the sake of
analysis, to emphasize the role of technology in the process of social transformation, particularly when we consider the central technology of our time,
communication technology, which relates to the heart of the specificity of the
human species: conscious, meaningful communication (Capra, 1996, 2002).

It is because of available electronic information and communication technologies that the network society can deploy itself fully, transcending the
historical limits of networks as forms of social organization and interaction.
This approach is different from the conceptual framework that defines our
societies as information or knowledge societies. To be blunt, I believe that this

is an empirical and theoretical error, as I will elaborate in the conclusion to this chapter. But let me advance the argument.

The reason, very simply, is that, as far as we can trust the historical record, all known societies are based on information and knowledge as the source of power, wealth, and meaning (Mokyr, 1990; Mazlish, 1993). Information has not much value per se without the knowledge to recombine it for a purpose. And knowledge is, of course, relative to each culture and society. So, knowledge of metallurgy or the technology of sailing or Roman law were the essential means of information and knowledge on which military power, administrative efficiency, the control of resources, and, ultimately, wealth and the rules for its distribution were based. So, if information and knowledge are the key factors for power and wealth in *all* societies, it is misleading to conceptualize our society as such, even if, for the practical reason of making communication easier, I gave in to the fashion of the times in my labels by characterizing our historical period as the "information age." What we actually mean, and what I always meant, is that our society is characterized by the power embedded in information technology, at the heart of an entirely new technological paradigm, which I called informationalism. Yet printing is also a most important information technology, and it has been around for quite a while, particularly in China. And we do not usually consider the post-printing societies as information societies.

So, what is actually new, both technologically and socially, is a society built around microelectronics-based information technologies. To which I add biological technologies based on genetic engineering, as they also refer to the decoding and recoding of the information of living matter. Furthermore, information technologies can be more properly labeled as communication technologies, since information that is not communicated ceases to be relevant. The early emphasis on information technology, semantically separated from communication, reflected, in fact, the logic of stand-alone electronic devices and computers. This is outdated, at least since the deployment of the Arpanet, more than three decades ago. It is also a reflection of the division of the world of communication technology between computers, telecommunications, and the broadcast media. Again, this is a distinction that has a relative justification in the business and institutions that organize each domain, but is senseless in technological terms. Thus, what is specific to our world is the extension and augmentation of the body and mind of human subjects in networks of interaction powered by microelectronics-based, software-operated, communication technologies. These technologies are increasingly diffused throughout the entire realm of human activity by growing miniaturization. They are converging with new genetic engineering technologies able to reprogram the communication networks of living matter. It is on this basis that a new social structure is expanding as the foundation of our society: the network society.

INFORMATIONALISM: THE TECHNOLOGICAL PARADIGM OF THE NETWORK SOCIETY

Technology, understood as material culture, is a fundamental dimension of social structure and social change (Fischer, 1992: 1–32). Technology is usually defined as the use of scientific knowledge to set procedures for performance in a reproducible manner. It evolves in interaction with other dimensions of society, but it has its own dynamics, linked to the conditions of scientific discovery, technological innovation, and application and diffusion in society at large. Technological systems evolve incrementally, but this evolution is punctuated by major discontinuities, as Stephen J. Gould (1980) has convincingly argued for the history of life. These discontinuities are marked by technological revolutions that usher in a new technological paradigm. The notion of paradigm was proposed by Thomas Kuhn (1962) to explain the transformation of knowledge by scientific revolutions, and imported into the social and economic formations of technology by Christopher Freeman (1982) and Carlota Perez (1983). A paradigm is a conceptual pattern that sets the standards for performance. It integrates discoveries into a coherent system of relationships characterized by its synergy; that is, by the added value of the system vis-à-vis its individual components. A technological paradigm organizes a series of technological discoveries around a nucleus and a system of relationships that enhance the performance of each specific technology.

Informationalism is the technological paradigm that constitutes the material basis of early twenty-first century societies. Over the last quarter of the twentieth century of the Common Era it replaced and subsumed industrialism as the dominant technological paradigm. Industrialism, associated with the industrial revolution, is a paradigm characterized by the systemic organization of technologies based on the capacity to generate and distribute energy by human-made machines without depending on the natural environment – albeit they use natural resources as an input for the generation of energy. Energy is a primary resource for all activities, and by transforming energy generation, and the ability to distribute it to any location and to portable applications, humankind became able to increase its power over nature, taking charge of the conditions for its own existence (not necessarily a good thing, as the historical record of the twentieth-century shows). Around the energy nucleus of the industrial revolution, technologies clustered and converged in various fields, from chemical engineering and metallurgy to transportation, telecommunications, and, ultimately, life sciences and their applications.

A similar structuration of scientific knowledge and technological innovation is taking place under the new paradigm of informationalism. To be sure, industrialism does not disappear. It is subsumed by informationalism. Informationalism presupposes industrialism, as energy, and its associated technologies are still a fundamental component of all processes. Informationalism is a technological paradigm based on the augmentation of the human capacity of information processing and communication made possible by the revolutions in microelectronics, software, and genetic engineering. Computers and digital communications are the most direct expressions of this revolution. Indeed, microelectronics, software, computation, telecommunications, and digital communication as a whole, are all components of the same integrated system. Thus, in strict terms, the paradigm should be called "electronic informational-communicationalism." Reasons of clarity and economy suggest, however, that it is better to keep the concept of informationalism, as it is already widely employed and resonates in close parallel to industrialism. As information and communication are the most fundamental dimensions of human activity and organization, a revolutionary change in the material conditions of their performance affects the entire realm of human activity.

However, what is specific to this new system of information and communication technologies that sets it apart from historical experience? I propose that what makes this paradigm unique in relation to previous historical developments of information and communication technologies (such as printing, the telegraph, or the non-digital telephone) are, in essence, three major, distinctive features of the technologies at the heart of the system:

- their self-expanding processing and communicating capacity in terms of volume, complexity, and speed;
- their ability to recombine on the basis of digitization and recurrent communication;
- their distributing flexibility through interactive, digitized networking.

Let me elaborate on these features. I will do it separately for the two fundamental, and originally distinct, fields – digital electronics and genetic engineering – before considering their interaction.

Digital electronics technologies allow for an historically unprecedented increase in the capacity to process information, not only in the volume of information, but in the complexity of the operations involved, and in the speed of processing, including the speed of communication. However, how much is "much more" compared with previous information-processing technologies? How do we know that there is a revolution characterized by a giant leap forward in processing capacity?

One factor in the answer to this fundamental question is empirical. The history of electronics information and communication technologies in the past three decades shows an exponential increase in processing power, coupled with an equally dramatic decrease in the cost per operation, precisely the mark of a technological revolution, as documented by Paul David (1975) for the industrial revolution. Whatever measures we take in terms of integration of circuitry in microelectronics, of speed and volume in telecommunications, in computing power measured from megabytes to terabytes, and in the management of complex operations per lines of software code, they all show an unprecedented rate of technological change in the information and communication field.

But I advance the hypothesis that there is something else, not only quantitative but qualitative: the capacity of these technologies to self-expand their processing power because of their recurrent, communicative ability. This is because of the continuous feedback effect on technological innovation produced by the knowledge generated with the help of these technologies. In other words, these technologies hold emergent properties; that is, the ability to derive new, unforeseen processes of innovation by their endless reconfiguration (Johnson, 2001). This is a risky hypothesis because processing power may find the physical limits to the further integration of microchips, and the complexity of networked computation may overwhelm the programming power of software developers under the conditions of proprietary software. However, every doomsday prediction of the limits of integration has been belied by manufacturing research. Continuing research into biological materials, and other new materials, may yield new possibilities, including chemically processed DNA-chips. Open source software is overcoming the barriers of technological oligopoly and unleashing waves of new applications and development breakthroughs, in an increasing virtuous circle created by thousands of free programmers networked around the world. And, most significantly, the networking capacity of distributed processing power and software development escapes the limits of stand-alone machines, and creates a global, digitized system of human–machine interaction, always ready for action.

Thus, a formal version of the hypothesis presented above is the following: in the first three decades of the information and communication technology revolution we have observed the self-generated, expansive capacity of new technologies to process information; current limits of integration, programming, and networking capacity are likely to be superseded by new waves of innovation in the making; and if and when the limits of the processing power of these technologies are reached, a new technological paradigm will emerge – under forms and with technologies that we cannot imagine today, except in science fiction scenarios, or in the innovative dreams of the usual suspects.

Secondly, digital technologies are also characterized by their ability to recombine information on the basis of recurrent, interactive communication. This is what I call the hypertext, in the tradition of Ted Nelson and Tim Berners-Lee. One of the key contributions of the Internet is its potential ability to link up everything digital from everywhere and to recombine it. Indeed, the original design of the World Wide Web by Berners-Lee had two functions: a browser and an editor (Berners-Lee, 1999). The commercial and bureaucratic practice of the World Wide Web has largely reduced its use, for most people, to a browser and information provider, connected to an e-mail system. Yet, from shared art creation to the political agora of the anti-globalization movement, and to joint engineering of networked corporate labs, the Internet is quickly becoming a medium of interactive communication beyond the cute, but scarcely relevant practice of chat rooms (increasingly made obsolete by SMSs and other wireless, instant communication systems). The added value of the Internet over other communication media is its capacity to recombine in chosen time information products and information processes to generate a new output, which is immediately processed in the Net, in an endless process of production of information, communication, and feedback in real time or chosen time (Castells, 2001). This is crucial because recombination is the source of innovation, and innovation is at the root of economic productivity, cultural creativity, and political power-making. Indeed, while the generation of new knowledge always required the application of theory to recombined information, the ability to experiment in real time with the results of the recombination, coming from a multiplicity of sources, considerably extends the realm of knowledge generation. It also allows increasing connections between different fields of knowledge and their applications – precisely the source of knowledge innovation in Kuhn's theory of scientific revolutions.

The third feature of new information and communication technologies is their flexibility, which allows the distribution of processing power in various contexts and applications, such as business firms, military units, the media, public services (such as health or distance education), political activity, and personal interaction. Software developments, such as Java and Jini languages, powered the distributive networks. And wireless communications made the multiplication of points of communication possible almost at the level of each individual – except, of course, for the majority of the population of the planet on the other side of the digital divide, a major social issue to which I will return in my analysis of the network society. So, it is not only a matter of the density of the communication network, but also of its flexibility, and of its ability to be integrated in all the sites and contexts of the human environment. As Mitchell (2003: 144) writes "wireless connections and portable access devices create continuous fields of presence that may extend throughout buildings, outdoors, and into public space as well as private. This has profound implications for the locations and spatial distributions of all human activities that depend, in some way, upon access to information." It is this spatial transformation that I have tried to capture under the concept of the space of flows, which interacts with the traditional space of places, so that the new spatial structure associated with informationalism, is not placeless, but is made up of networks connecting places by information and communication flows, as I will elaborate below.

Under the informational paradigm, the capacity for any communicating subject to act on the communication network gives people and organizations the possibility of reconfiguring the network according to their needs, desires, and projects. Yet (and this is fundamental) the reconfiguring capacity for each subject depends on the pattern of power present in the configuration of the network.

I will elaborate more succinctly on the second component of the information and communication technology revolution: *genetic engineering*. I consider its potential consequences as more far reaching than those already induced by the digital revolution in the structure and dynamics of society. This is because it affects the programs of life, and therefore the basis of our existence. However, its effects have been less diffused throughout the entire social structure because of the nature of its implications which have led to institutional resistance to their application; and also because its true breakthroughs required further advancements in the digital revolution, whose technologies are essential for the qualitative development of biological research (as was shown by the decisive role played by massive, parallel computing in the elaboration of the Human Genome Project).

While genetic engineering is often considered as an independent process from the information technology revolution, it is not. First, from an analytical perspective, these technologies are obviously information technologies, focused on the decoding and actual reprogramming of DNA, the code of living matter. And since biologists know that cells do not work in isolation, the real issue is to understand their networks of communication. Thus, genetic engineering is both an information and a communication technology, very much as digital electronics.

Secondly, there is a direct, methodological connection between the two revolutions. Computer models, and computing power, are the tools of trade in genetic engineering nowadays, so that microbiologists, bio-engineers, electrical engineers, chemical engineers, and computer scientists are all essential components of the daring teams attempting to unearth the secrets of life – and in some cases to play God. On the other hand, bio-chips and DNA-based chemically operated computing processes are the foundations of a new form of digital processing and molecular electronics, leading the way to the diffusion of nanotechnology, and, eventually, to the spread of nanobots, in a whole range of applications, including the repair and maintenance of the human body.

Thirdly, there is a theoretical convergence between the two technological fields around the analytical paradigm based on networking, complexity, self-organization, and emergent properties, as illustrated some time ago by the work of visionary teams of researchers at the Santa Fe Institute and as theorized by Fritjof Capra.

Genetic engineering technologies are also characterized by their self-expanding processing capacity, by their ability to recombine through communication networks, and by the flexibility of their distributive power. To be more specific, the existence of the Human Genome Map, and, increasingly, of genetic maps of specific parts of our body, as well as of a number of species and subspecies, raises the possibility of cumulative knowledge in the field of genetic engineering, leading to the understanding of processes that were beyond the realm of observation. In other words, better targeted, new, meaningful experiments become possible as knowledge progresses and fills the empty spaces of the model.

Secondly, the recombining ability of genetic engineering technologies is critical, as it is in the uses of digital communication and information processing. The first generation of genetic engineering applications largely failed because cells were manipulated as isolated entities, without a full understanding of their context, and of their place in the networks of life. Research has shown that cells are defined in their function by their relationship to others. Their DNA structure is meaningless outside the context of their specific interactions. So, interacting networks of cells, communicating through their codes, rather than isolated sets of instructions, are the object of genetic recombination strategies. Emergent properties are associated with networks of genes, and are identified by simulation models, only later validated by clinical experiments.

Finally, the promise of genetic engineering is precisely its ability to reprogram different codes and their protocols of communication in different areas of different bodies (or systems) of different species. Transgenic research and self-regenerative processes in living organisms are the frontiers of genetic engineering. Genetic drugs, which will at some time be delivered by nanotechnology-produced devices, are intended to induce in the body the capability of self-programming by living organisms: this is the ultimate expression of distributed information-processing power by communication networks.

It was on the foundations of informationalism that the network society gradually emerged as a new form of social organization of human activity in the last lap of the twentieth century. Without the capacity provided by this new technological paradigm, the network society would not be able to operate, just as industrial society could not fully expand without the use of electricity. But the network society was not the consequence of the technological revolution. Rather, it was the serendipitous coincidence, in a particular time and space, of economic, social, political, and cultural factors that led to the emergence of new forms of social organization which, when they had the historical chance of harnessing the power of informationalism, prevailed and expanded. So, I now turn, succinctly, to the genesis of the network society.

THE RISE OF THE NETWORK SOCIETY

Every new social structure has its own genesis, dependent on spatiotemporal contexts. Naturally, there is a relationship between the historical process of production of a given social structure and its characteristics. However, it is possible to analyze this social structure as a given, without considering in detail the processes that led to its formation. In fact, this is the option taken in this chapter, which is focused on the theory of the network society rather than on its history. Nonetheless, I will summarize some of the analysis of the genesis of the network society, presented in my earlier writings (Castells, 2000b, c), with one specific purpose: to dispel the notion that either technology or social evolution led inevitably to the network society, as the later incarnation of modernity, in the form of postmodernity, or as the information/knowledge society as a natural outcome in the long evolution of the human species. We have ample evidence that there is no predetermined sense of history, and that every age and every power claims ethnocentrically and historocentrically its right to be the supreme stage of human evolution. What we observe throughout history is that different forms of society come and go by accident, internal self-destruction, serendipitous creation, or, more often, as the outcome of largely undetermined social struggles.

True, there has been a long-term trend toward technological development that has increased the mental power of humankind over its environment. But the jury is still out on the outcome of such a process measured in terms of progress, unless we consider as minor issues the highly rational process of mass murder that led to the Holocaust, the management of large-scale incarceration that created gulags out of the hopes for workers' liberation, the nuclear destruction of Hiroshima and Nagasaki to finish off an already vanquished nation, or the spread of AIDS in Africa while pharmaceutical companies and their parent governments discuss payment for their intellectual property rights.

And, to remain in the realm of analysis, nothing predetermined the trajectory taken by the information and communication technology revolution. Personal computers were not in the mind of governments and corporations at the onset of the revolution: it was done by people. And the crucial technology of the network society, the Internet, would have never come to be a global network of free communication if ATT had accepted in 1970 the offer of the American Defense Department to give it free to that corporation; or if Vint Cerf and Robert Kahn had not diffused over the Net the source code of the IP/TCP protocols on which the Internet is still based. Historical evolution is an open-ended, conflictive process, enacted by subjects and actors who try to make society according to their interests and values, or, more often, produce social forms of organization by resisting the domination of those who identify social life with their own desires enforced through violence.

So, how did the network society come about? At its source there was the *accidental coincidence, in the 1970s, of three independent processes*, whose interaction constituted a new technological paradigm, informationalism, and a new social structure, the network society, which are inseparably intertwined. These three processes were: the crisis and restructuring of industrialism and its two associated modes of production, capitalism and statism; the freedom-oriented, cultural social movements of the late 1960s and early 1970s; and the revolution in information and communication technologies, as described above. Given the analytical purpose of this chapter, I will not enter into the detail of the analysis of these three complex historical processes, but take the liberty of referring the reader to my earlier writings (Castells, 1980, 2000b, c, 2001, 2004; Castells and Kiselyova, 2003). Yet, I will summarize the essence of the analysis as it relates to understanding the formation of the network society.

First, the industrial model of development hit the buffers of its limits to increase productivity growth as the organizations, values, and policies of the industrial society could not manage the transition to knowledge-based productivity growth by using the potential unleashed by information and communication technologies. However, a crisis in the mode of development is translated specifically into a crisis in the model of accumulation that is dominant in each time and space. In the case of capitalism, this meant the calling into question of the Keynesian model that had characterized the period of high productivity increase and steady economic growth after World War II. That model was based on the ability to increase both profits and social redistribution through government guidance and funding, largely in a controlled, domestic policy environment. Productivity growth and market expansion were based on a social contract that ensured social stability, improved living conditions, and mass consumption of mass-produced goods and services. Declining productivity resulted in declining surplus, thus in declining profits, and declining private investment. The model was sustained by increasing public spending and private indebtedness. Public borrowing and increased money supply led to rampant inflation. Under conditions of fiscal stress and inflationary pressures, the sudden rise in oil prices of 1973–5 by OPEC and its associated multinational corporations both increased inflation and provided the opportunity to declare a crisis, and the ensuing search for corrective policies. The worldwide crisis of the 1970s prompted a debate, in the United States as in the rest of the world, on the future of capitalism. Corporations responded by shedding labor, putting pressure on wages, benefits, and job security, globalizing production and markets, stepping up research and development, investing in technology, and finding more flexible, efficient forms of management.

But the decisive shift to a different model of accumulation came from governments, albeit in harmony with corporations. It can be related to the twin victories of Thatcher in the UK in 1979 and Reagan in the USA in 1980. They were both political conservatives. They came to government with a mission: to recapitalize capitalism, thus ushering in the era of economic liberal policies that by successive waves took over the world, in different political-ideological versions, over the next two decades. The crushing of organized labor politically, the cutting of taxes for the rich and the corporations, and widespread deregulation and liberalization of markets, both nationally and internationally, were crucial strategic initiatives that reversed the Keynesian policies that had dominated capitalism in the previous twenty-five years.

Balancing the budget and reducing government intervention was part of the ideology but not of the practice. Indeed, Reagan presided over the largest increase in budget deficit in peace time because of the combination of tax cuts and large military expenditures. He practiced what we called at that time "military Keynesianism," although the term is provocative but incorrect because Keynesianism was not just about inducing outlets, but about integrating people into the consumption process (Carnoy and Castells, 1984). What was important was that, directly through deregulation and privatization policies, and indirectly by the signals sent from government to companies, the rules of the game changed, first in the US, second in the UK, and then in the rest of the world. Market liberalization and the disengagement of government from social spending and income redistribution became a generalized practice, either by ideological choice or by the need to adapt to the rules of the world market, which was imposed by the most powerful players, followed by global flows of investment, and enforced when necessary by the IMF. A new orthodoxy was established throughout the world. We call this process globalization. It is, to be sure, unfettered capitalist globalization, spearheaded by the liberalization of financial markets (the Big Bang of the City of London in October 1987), and enshrined in asymmetrical trade globalization represented by the new managing authority, the World Trade Organization. Under the new conditions, global capitalism recovered its dynamism, and increased profits, investment, and economic growth, at least in its core countries and in the networks that connected areas of prosperity around the world, in the midst of a sea of poverty and marginalization.

I want to emphasize that this was not an historical necessity, nor the only policy that could have restructured capitalism, and ensured its dynamic transition from industrial capitalism to informational capitalism. Indeed, in my book on the economic crisis in America (Castells, 1980), I stressed the coherence of the strategy proposed by Reagan, but I also analyzed the possibilities offered by other political programs in America, for instance the platform represented by Senator Edward Kennedy, a potential president until the Chappaquidik affair, based on a rekindling of government-led policy adapted to the new economic and social conditions. In fact, if one of the key elements of the underlying structural crisis in Western capitalism was the necessity to adapt to a knowledge-based economy, it seemed logical that a strategy of deepening and reforming the welfare state, to provide the human capital necessary for this economy, in terms of education, health, and modernization of the public sector, would have been a better bet in the long term.

Yet, the urgency of restoring profitability to business, and the outcome of the political process, led to the victory of Reaganomics, in Europe to Thatcherism, and in developing countries to the model elaborated by the Chicago boys, disciples of Milton Friedman, which was imposed by dictatorships and the IMF's budgetary discipline. In other words, the crisis of industrialism was also the crisis of the specific model of capitalist accumulation of the mature stage of industrialism, and it was this latter crisis that was addressed as a priority according to the interests and values of the political actors that seized power in the main economies. The political muscle of the US in the global economy, and ideological hegemony, linked to the bankruptcy of statism and to the short-sighted pragmatism of social democracy, did the rest.

This is to say that the institutional conditions for globalization and business flexibility were concomitant with a weakening of the power of labor and a retrenchment of the welfare state. However, they were not the necessary outcome of the crisis of industrialism and of Keynesian capitalism, but one of the options to restructure the system. It just happened to be the winning option. Its victory, on a global scale, created the conditions for the structural transformations that induced not only a new model of capitalism, but also contributed to the emergency of a new social structure.

The shape of this transformation was also influenced by the collapse of statism, as a result of the failure of the restructuring policies that had tried to address its economic and technological crisis. Indeed, precisely in the 1970s, the Soviet economy reached the point of quasi-stagnation, reversing decades of fast economic growth, and its technological development lost pace in relation to the West, particularly in the critical area of information and communication technologies. Our study on the matter (Castells and Kiselyova, 2003) has documented the direct relationship between the features of Soviet statism, based on the control of information and of the capture of technology in the military complex, and the economic and technological crisis of the Soviet Union. Both crises decisively undermined Soviet military power, and prompted the need for reform, opening the way to Gorbachev's *perestroika*. The depth of the crisis was such that Gorbachev had to go outside the channels of the party to call for support for his *perestroika* from civil society. The ensuing process spiraled out of control and led to the unexpected demise of the Soviet empire, in one of the most extraordinary courses of events in history.

Without the backbone provided by the Soviet Union, most statist countries in the Third World gravitated toward Western influence and accepted the formal and informal leadership of the IMF and its liberal economic policies, opening the way for the rapid spread of capitalist globalization. Chinese Communists undertook their own reform in the hope of keeping state power while joining global capitalism. The experiment is still underway, but, whatever its outcome, it has sharply departed from the logic of statism, and has substantially expanded the space of global capitalism. In the early twenty-first century, while global capitalism is far from being a stable system, it has become the only game on the planet, albeit increasingly challenged by activist minorities, and burdened with the marginalization of the majority of humankind.

There was a second social trend, quite independent from the crises of industrialism, Keynesian capitalism, and Soviet statism: the alternative projects and values emerging from the *cultural social movements of the 1960s and 1970s*. These movements (whose first symbolic manifestations can be traced back to the free speech movement in Berkeley in 1964 and to the May movement in Paris in 1968) were, fundamentally, freedom-oriented. They were the affirmation of a culture of personal freedom and social autonomy, both vis-à-vis capitalism and statism, challenging the conservative establishment as well as the traditional left. They were profoundly political in their implications, but they were not oriented toward the state or preoccupied with the seizing of state power. They did have various formats and ideologies, in interaction with the societies in which they took place: they connected with the civil rights movement in the United States; they called upon the working class and reignited the old tradition of the street barricade in France; they became "imagined proletarians" in Italy (mainly under the mantra of a Maoist ideology that would have prompted Mao to shoot them); they opposed dictatorships in Spain, Portugal, Greece, and throughout Latin America; and they combined with the critique of the industrial work ethic and with the conservatism of society in Germany, The Netherlands, and Japan.

In all cases they opposed war, at the time symbolized by the Vietnam War, but their influence was mainly felt in the assertion of the principle of the autonomy of the individual, in direct challenge to the cultural foundations of societies, starting with the family, the church, the state, and the corporate world. They, of course, failed politically because accessing government was never their goal. Most of their young militants became corporate managers, respected politicians, publishers, academics, new philosophers, consultants, and web designers. Yet, their ideas permeated the entire society of the developed, capitalist world, and reached to the cultural elites of most of the world.

Perhaps the most significant outcome of the 1960s' movements was their productive dissolution into the forms of the more articulate movements that emerged from their demise in the 1970s. Such was the case of feminism. Of course, women's struggles have a long history, way before the Commune of

Paris, the American suffragists, the Glasgow general strike of 1915, or the followers of Alexandra Kollontai.They go back to the origins of humankind, and they left their mark in the unofficial history of resistance to patriarchal oppression, as in the many women tortured and burned as witches. But the women's movement, which has spread throughout most of the world since the 1970s, amounting to a mass insurrection of women against their submissive condition, actually succeeded in a real revolution: changing the minds of women about themselves and about their role in family and in society. The movement originated, by and large, in the reaction of militant women in the 1960s' movements against the sexism they experienced from their male comrades, and led to the formation of autonomous feminist movements in the 1970s, and then to pervasive feminist interventions in all realms of society thereafter.

A similar story can be told about the environmental movement: the first Earth Day mobilization in the United States was in May 1970, as an outcome of the debates that had taken place in the social movements of the 1960s after the exhaustion of their explicit political agenda, and their degeneration into a variety of political sects. To save the earth – and my neighborhood in the process – seemed like a good idea, appealing to everybody and connecting with the vitalist, anti-consumption ethics that characterized the young idealists who were participants in the movement. It turned out to be far more subversive of the values and interests of industrialism than the obsolete ideologies of the left. It went on – in the US, in Canada, in Germany, in the UK, in Northern and Western Europe, and, later on, in most of the world – to take on the self-destructive logic of global capitalist development. It eventually connected with the critique of poverty and exploitative economic growth in the world at large, laying the ground for what would become, two decades later, the anti-globalization movement.

For the analytical purpose of this chapter, what must be remembered is that *these social movements were cultural; that is, oriented toward a transformation of the values of society*. And the key values that were put forward, and that ultimately created a new culture around the world, were three: the value of freedom and individual autonomy vis-à-vis the institutions of society and the power of corporations; the value of cultural diversity and the affirmation of the rights of minorities, ultimately expressed in terms of human rights; and the value of ecological solidarity; that is, the reunification of the interest of the human species as a common good, in opposition to the industrial values of material growth and consumption at all costs.

From the combination of these cultural threads arose the challenge to patriarchalism, the challenge to productivism, the challenge to cultural uniformity, and, ultimately, the challenge to state power and to militarism, as expressed in the peace movement.

Thus, while the movements of the 1960s, and the diverse cultural-political expressions that they induced in the 1970s, took place in the ideological and political vacuum related to the crisis of industrialism and of Keynesian capitalism, they were not a response to the crisis; nor were they the harbingers of the new policies and strategies that eventually restarted the engines of capitalism in its new incarnation. However, the values, ideas, and projects that they invented or rediscovered were essential materials in the reconstitution of society, as I will argue below.

There was a third component of the process of multidimensional transformation that took place in the 1970s. This was the *revolution in information and communication technologies* that led to the constitution of informationalism as a new technological paradigm, as presented earlier in this chapter. I will add three comments concerning the relationship between this technological revolution and the processes of capitalist restructuring and cultural social movements that, together, constituted the crucible from which the network society originated.

The first refers to the independence of the origins of this technological revolution from both the other two processes. The invention of the microprocessor, the personal computer, the digital switch, the Internet, and recombinant DNA were not a response to business demands or the needs of capitalism. Military funding and sponsorship was essential, as technological superiority was seen, appropriately, as the means to win the Cold War without actual fighting between the superpowers. But even this dependence on the military was generic to the whole process of technological innovation, not specific to some of the critical technologies that were developed. Miniaturization and advanced telecommunications were essential for missile-based warfare, and they were deliberately targeted by companies under defense contracts. But computer networking, and therefore the Internet, was a byproduct of experimentation by computer scientists for their own scientific curiosity, as the Internet did not have military applications until everybody began to use it in the 1990s. The personal computer was a serendipitous invention of the computer counter-culture, and the best software development was based on open source, and so was produced outside the corporate world, in the universities and in freelance ventures.

The whys and wherefores of this technological revolution have been chronicled numerous times, and their presentation is beyond the scope of this chapter. But it was an autonomous process of research, innovation, and application which developed not as a response to the crisis of industrial capitalism but as the work of a community of practice that emerged at the unlikely crossroads of military-sponsored, big science and university-based, counter-cultural networks (Castells, 2001).

The second comment is that, while the three processes were independent in their origins, they interacted extensively in their development. Thus, the culture of personal freedom that originated in the university-based social movements inhabited the minds of the innovators who designed the actual shape of the technology revolution. Thus the personal computer was contemplated, in direct contradiction to the programmed trajectory of the corporate industry. And the tradition of proprietary invention was challenged, by asserting the right to diffuse, at no cost, the protocols at the source of the Internet or the software programs that constituted the bulk of applications of the new computing world. The university tradition of sharing discovery and communicating with peers was relied upon, in the hope of seeing invention improved by the collective work of the network, in sharp contrast to the world of corporations and government bureaucracies that had made secrecy and intellectual property rights the source of their power and wealth.

One had to be imbued with the ideals and values of the cultural movements of the 1960s and 1970s, oriented toward free expression, personal autonomy, and challenge to the establishment, in order to imagine the set of inventions that constituted the information technology revolution. Microsoft was, of course, the exception to the rule, and this is reflected in the animosity that still arises among the cutting-edge innovators of the information age. So, while most of the processes of technological innovation, and informationalism, originated independently of the corporate world (except for the invention of the transistor, which was, in fact, rapidly diffused into the public domain by Bell Labs), the shape and content of technology was culturally influenced by the social movements of the time. Not that the inventors were social activists (they were not, they were too busy inventing), but they breathed the same air of individual freedom and personal autonomy that was sustaining the movement, and was sustained by the movement (Levy, 2001).

On the other hand, when business engaged in its own restructuring process, it took advantage of the extraordinary range of technologies that were available from the new revolution, thus stepping up the process of technological change, and hugely expanding the range of its applications. Thus, the decision to go global in a big way, while being facilitated by government policies of deregulation, liberalization, and privatization, would not have been possible without computer networking, telecommunications, and information technology-based transportation systems. The network enterprise became the most productive and efficient form of doing business, replacing the Fordist organization of industrialism (see below). While it is true that the internal decentralization of companies and networks of firms began earlier, based on the fax, telephone, and electronic exchange systems, the full networking of companies, the digitalization of manufacturing, the networked computerization of services and office work, could only take place, from the 1980s onwards, on the basis of the new information and communication technologies.

In sum, the culture of freedom was decisive in inducing network technologies which, in turn, were the essential infrastructure for business to operate its restructuring in terms of globalization, decentralization, and networking. Only then could the knowledge-based economy function at is full potential because data, minds, bodies, and material production could be related globally and locally, in real time, in a continuous interactive network.

From the restructuring of business emerged the global, networked economy. From its success, and the simultaneous demise of statism, a new model of informational capitalism was constituted. From the opposition to its social, cultural, and political consequences emerged new forms of social movement. From the globalization and networking of both business and social movements arose the crisis of the nation-state of the industrial era. In sum, from the interaction between three originally independent processes (the crisis of industrialism, the rise of freedom-oriented social movements, and the revolution in information and communication technologies) there emerged a new form of social organization, the network society.

THE NETWORK SOCIETY: STRUCTURE, DIMENSIONS, DYNAMICS

A Global Society

Digital networks are global, as they know no boundaries in their capacity to reconfigure themselves. So, a social structure whose infrastructure is based on digital networks is by definition global. Thus, the network society is a global society. However, this does not mean that people everywhere are included in these networks. In fact, for the time being, most are not. But everybody is affected by the processes that take place in the global networks of this dominant social structure. This is because the core activities that shape and control human life in every corner of the planet are organized in these global networks: financial markets; transnational production, management, and the distribution of goods and services; highly skilled labor; science and technology; communication media, culture, art, sports; international institutions managing the global economy and intergovernmental relations; religion; the criminal economy; and the transnational NGOs that assert the rights and values of a new, global civil society (Castells, 2000a, b; Held and McGrew, 1999; Volkmer, 1999; Stiglitz, 2002; Juris, 2004).

However, the network society diffuses selectively throughout the planet, working on the pre-existing sites, organizations, and institutions that still make up most of the material environment of people's lives. The social structure is global, but most human experience is local, both in territorial and cultural terms (Borja and Castells, 1997). Specific societies, as defined by the current boundaries of nation-states, or by the cultural boundaries of their historical identities, are deeply fragmented by the double logic of inclusion and exclusion in the global networks that structure production, consumption, communication, and power. I propose the hypothesis that this fragmentation is not simply the expression of the time lag required by the gradual incorporation of previous social forms into the new dominant logic. It is, in fact, a structural feature of the network society. This is because the reconfiguring capacity inscribed in the process of networking allows the programs governing every network to search for valuable additions everywhere and to incorporate them, while bypassing and excluding those territories, activities, and people that have little or no value for the performance of the tasks assigned to the network. Indeed, as Geoff Mulgan observed, "networks are created not just to communicate, but also to gain position, to outcommunicate" (1991: 21). The network society works on the basis of a binary logic of inclusion/exclusion, whose boundaries change over time, both with the changes in the network's programs and with the conditions of performance of these programs.

It also depends on the ability of social actors, in various contexts, to act on these programs, modifying them according to their interests. The global network society is a dynamic structure, it is highly malleable to social forces, to culture, to politics, to economic strategies. But what remains in all instances is its dominance over activities and people who are external to the networks. In this sense, the global overwhelms the local, unless the local becomes a node in alternative global networks, as is the case with the incorrectly labelled "antiglobalization movement," which is a global movement for global justice according to its participants.

Thus, the imperfect globalization of the network society is, in fact, a highly significant feature of its social structure. The coexistence of the network society, as a global structure, with industrial, rural, communal or survival societies, characterizes the reality of all countries, albeit with a different share of population and territory on both sides of the divide, depending on the relevance of each segment for the dominant logic of each network. This is to say that various networks will have different geometries and geographies of inclusion and exclusion. The map of the global criminal economy is not the same as the map of the international location of high-technology industry, although they both have points of connection: drug lords depend on computers and the Internet, and quite a few Silicon Valley engineers invent with the help of cocaine.

Thus, in theoretical terms, the network society must be analyzed, first, as a global architecture of self-reconfiguring networks constantly programmed and reprogrammed by the powers that be in each dimension; second, as the result of the interaction between the various geometries and geographies of the networks that include the core activities, that is, the activities shaping life and work in society; and, third, as the result of a second-order interaction between these dominant networks and the geometry and geography of disconnection of social forms left outside the global networking logic.

Two theoretical comments are necessary to complete this analysis. First, structures do not live by themselves; they always express, in a contradictory and conflictive pattern, the interests, values, and projects of the actors who produce the structure while being conditioned by it. Second, inclusion/exclusion in the network society cannot be assimilated to the so-called "digital divide" as the use of the Internet and connection to telecommunication networks do not guarantee actual incorporation into the dominant networks or counter-domination networks that shape society. Yet, exclusion from the operative infrastructure of the network society is a good indicator of deeper structural subordination and irrelevance.

What is Value in the Network Society?

What constitutes value in this kind of social structure? What moves the production system? What motivates the appropriators of value and controllers of society? No change here: value is what the dominant institutions of society decide is value. So, if capitalism still dominates the world, and capital accumulation is the supreme value, then this will be value in every instance, as, under capitalism, money can ultimately buy everything else. The critical fact is that, in a social structure organized in global networks, whatever is the hierarchy between the networks will become the rule in the entire grid of networks organizing/dominating the planet. If, for instance, we say that capital accumulation is what moves the system, and the return on capital is fundamentally realized in the global financial market, the global financial market will assign value to every act in every country, as no economy is independent of financial valuation decided in the global financial markets. But if we consider that the supreme value is military power, the technological and organizational capacity of powerful military machines will structure, through their global networks of domination, their surrogate power in armed forces of different kinds, operating in every social setting. Block the transmission of technology, information, and knowledge to a particular armed organization, and it becomes irrelevant in the world context. To give another illustration: we may say that the most important influence in today's world is the transformation of people's minds. If so, then, the media are the key networks, as the media, organized in global oligopolies and their distributive networks, are the primary source of messages and images that reach people's minds.

Thus, given the variety of the potential origins of network domination, the network society is a multidimensional social structure in which networks of different kinds have different logics of value making. The definition of what constitutes value depends on the specificity of the network, and of its program. Any attempt to reduce all value to a common standard comes up against insurmountable methodological and practical difficulties. If money making is the supreme value under capitalism, military power ultimately conditions state power and the capacity of the state to decide and enforce new rules (ask the Russian oligarchs about Putin). At the same time, state power, even in non-democratic contexts, largely depends on the beliefs of people, on their capacity to accept the rules or, alternatively, on their willingness to resist. Then, the media system and other means of communication, such as the Internet, could precede state power, which, in turn, would condition the rules of money making, and thus would supersede the value of money as supreme value. Thus, value is, in fact, an expression of power: whoever holds power (often different from who is in government) decides what is valuable.

In this sense, the network society does not innovate. What is new, however, is its global reach, along with its networked architecture. This means, on the one hand, that relations of domination between networks are critical. They are characterized by constant, flexible interaction: for instance, between global financial markets, geopolitical processes, and media strategies. On the other hand, because the logic of value making, as an expression of domination, is global, those instances that have a structural impediment to existing globally are at a disadvantage with regard to others whose logic is inherently global.

This has considerable practical importance because it is at the root of the crisis of the nation-state of the industrial era (not of the state as such because every social structure generates its own form of state). Since the nation-state can only enforce its rules in its own territory, except in the case of alliances or invasion, it has to become either imperial or networked to relate to other networks in the definition of value. This is why, for instance, the US state, in the early twenty-first century, has made a point of defining security against terrorism as the overarching value for the entire world, as a way of building a military-based network that would assure its hegemony by placing security over money making or lesser goals (such as human well-being) as the supreme value. On the other hand, capital has always enjoyed a world without boundaries, as David Harvey has repeatedly reminded us, so that global financial networks have a head start as the defining instances of value in the global network society (Harvey, 1990).

Yet human thought is probably the most rapidly growing element, under conditions of relying on global/local, chosen-time, interactive communication – which is exactly what we have nowadays, for the first time in history (Mitchell, 2003). Thus, ideas, or specific sets of ideas, could assert themselves as the truly supreme value (such as preserving our planet, our species) as a precondition for everything else.

In sum, the old question of industrial society – indeed, the cornerstone of classical political economy – namely, "what is value?" has no definite answer in the network society. Value is what is processed in every dominant network at every moment in every space according to the hierarchy programmed into the network by the actors acting upon the network. Capitalism has not disappeared, but it is not – against ideologically inspired perception – the only source of value in the global town.

Work, Labor, and Class: The Network Enterprise and the New Social Division of Labor

This helps us understand the new division of labor, and therefore work, productivity, and exploitation. People work, they always have. In fact, people work more (in terms of total working hours in a given society) than they ever have, since most of women's work was previously not counted as socially recognized (paid) work (Guillemard, 2003). The crucial matter has always been how this work is organized and compensated. The division of labor was, and still is, a measure of what is valued and what is not in labor contribution. This judgment is organized in a particular form in the process of production, and is assigned a position in the sharing of the product, determining differential consumption and social stratification.

The most fundamental divide in the network society is what I have conceptualized, schematically, as "self-programmable labor" and "generic labor." Self-programmable labor has the autonomous capacity to focus on the goal assigned to it in the process of production, find the relevant information, recombine it into knowledge, using the available knowledge stock, and apply it in the form of tasks oriented toward the goals of the process. The more our information systems are complex, and interactively connected to databases and information sources, the more labor needs the ability to use this searching and recombining capacity. This requires appropriate training, not in terms of skills, but in terms of creative capacity, and the ability to evolve with organizations and with the addition of knowledge in society.

On the other hand, tasks that are not valued are assigned to "generic labor," eventually being replaced by machines or decentralized to low-cost production sites, depending on a dynamic cost–benefit analysis. The overwhelming mass of working people on the planet, and still the majority in advanced countries, are generic labor. They are disposable, except if they assert their right to exist as humans and citizens through their collective action. But in terms of value making (in finance, in manufacturing, in research, in sports, in military action, or in political capital) it is the self-programmable worker that counts for any organization in control of the resources. Thus, labor organization in the network society also acts on a binary logic, dividing self-programmable labor from generic labor. Furthermore, the flexibility and adaptability of both kinds of labor to a constantly changing environment is a precondition for their use as labor.

This specific division of labor is gendered to some extent. The rise of flexible labor is directly related to the feminization of the paid labor force, a fundamental trend in the social structure of the past three decades (Carnoy, 2000). The patriarchal organization of the family forces women to value the flexible organization of their professional work as the only way to cope with family and job duties. This is why more than 70 percent of temporary workers and part-time workers in most countries are women. Furthermore, while most women are employed as generic labor, their educational level has risen considerably compared with men, while their wages and working conditions have not changed at the same pace. Thus, women became the ideal workers of the networked, global economy: able to work efficiently, and adapt to the changing requirements of business, while receiving less compensation for the same work, and having fewer chances of promotion because of the ideology and practice of the gender division of labor under patriarchalism.

However, reality is, to use an old word, dialectical. While the mass incorporation of women into the paid labor force, partly because of their condition of patriarchal subordination, has been a decisive factor in the expansion of global, informational capitalism, the very transformation of women's condition as salaried women has ultimately undermined patriarchalism. The feminist ideas that emerged from the cultural social movements of the 1970s found a fertile ground in the experience of working women exposed to discrimination. But, even more importantly, the economic power won by women in the family strengthened their position vis-à-vis the male head of the family, while undermining the ideological justification of their subordination on the grounds of the respect due to the authority of the male bread-winner. Thus, the division of labor in the new organization of work is gendered, but this is a dynamic process, in which women are reversing dominant structural trends and inducing business to bring men into the same patterns of flexibility, job insecurity, downsizing, and offshoring of their jobs that used to be the lot of women. Thus, rather than women workers rising to the level of male workers, most male workers are being downgraded to the level of most women workers. This long-term trend has profound implications for both the class structure of society and the relationship between men and women at work and at home.

Autonomy and self-programmable capacity in labor would not yield its productivity pay-off if it were not able to be combined with the networking of labor. Indeed, the fundamental reason for the structural need for flexibility and autonomy is the transformation of the organization of the production process. This transformation is represented by the *rise of the network enterprise*. This new organizational business form is the historical equivalent under informationalism of the so-called Fordist organization of industrialism (both capitalist and statist); that is, the organization characterized by high-volume, standard-ized mass production, and vertical control of the labor process according to a top-down rationalized scheme ("scientific management" and Taylorism, the methods that prompted Lenin's admiration, leading to its imitation in the Soviet Union). Under Fordism, consumers were supposed to like all cars according to the Ford model T – and in black. And workers just had to follow the instructions of engineers to improve the efficiency of their physical move-ments on the assembly line, as immortalized by Charles Chaplin in *Modern Times*. Although there are still hundreds of thousands of workers in similarly run factories, the value-producing activities in the commanding heights of the production process (research and development, innovation, design, marketing, management, and high volume, customized flexible production) depend on an entirely different type of firm, and, therefore, of a different type of work process, and of labor: the network enterprise.

This is not a network of enterprises. It is a network made from either firms or segments of firms, and/or from the internal segmentation of firms. Thus, large corporations are internally decentralized as networks. Small and medium businesses are connected in networks, thus ensuring the critical mass of their contribution, while keeping their main asset: their flexibility. Small and medium business networks are often ancillary to large corporations, in most cases to several of them, except in the Japanese *keiretsu* and Korean *chaebol*. Large corporations, and their subsidiary networks, usually form networks of cooperation, called, in business parlance, strategic alliances or partnerships. But these alliances are rarely permanent cooperative structures. This is not a process of oligopolistic cartelization. These complex networks link up on specific business projects, and reconfigure their cooperation in different networks with each new project.

The usual business practice in this networked economy is one of alliances, partnerships, and collaborations that are specific to a given product, process, time, and space. These collaborations are based on sharing capital and labor, but most fundamentally information and knowledge, in order to win market share. So these are primarily information networks, which link suppliers and customers through the networked firm. The unit of the production process is not the firm but the business project, enacted by a network, the network enter-prise. The firm continues to be the legal unit of capital accumulation. But since the value of the firm ultimately depends on its financial valuation in the stock market, the unit of capital accumulation, the firm, becomes itself a node in a global network of financial flows. Thus, in the network economy, the dominant layer is the global financial market, the mother of all valuations. This global financial market works only partly according to market rules. It is also shaped and moved by information turbulences of various origins, processed and communicated by the computer networks that constitute the nerve system of the global, informational, capitalist economy (Hutton and Giddens, 2000).

Financial valuation determines the dynamics of the economy in the short term. But in the long run, everything depends on productivity growth. This is why the source of productivity constitutes the cornerstone of economic growth, and therefore of profits, wages, accumulation, and investment. And the key factor for productivity growth in this knowledge-intensive, networked economy is innovation (Lucas, 1999). Innovation is the capacity to recombine factors of production in a more efficient way, and/or produce higher value added in process or in product. Chapter 6 in this volume reminds us of this basic fact. Innovation depends on innovators. And innovators, as analyzed in chapter 2, depend on cultural creativity, on institutional openness to entrepreneurialism, on labor autonomy in the labor process, and on the adequate financing of this innovation-driven economy.

The new economy of our time is certainly capitalist, but it is a new brand of capitalism. It depends on innovation as the source of productivity growth, on computer-networked global financial markets, whose criteria for valuation are influenced by information turbulences, on the networking of production and management, internally and externally, locally and globally, and on labor that is flexible and adaptable in all cases. The creators of value have to be self-programmable, and able to autonomously process information into specific knowledge. Generic workers, reduced to their role as underlings, must be ready to adapt to the needs of the firm, or else face displacement by machines or alternative labor forces.

In this system, rather than exploitation in the traditional sense, the key issue for labor is the differentiation between three categories: those who are the source of innovation and value; those who merely carry out instructions; and whose who are structurally irrelevant, either as workers (not enough education, living in areas without the proper infrastructure and institutional environment for global production) or as consumers (too poor to be part of the market). For the mass of the world population their primary concern is how to avoid irrelevance, and, instead, to engage in a meaningful relationship, such as the relationship we used to call exploitation. Because exploitation does have a meaning for the exploited. The danger is, rather, for those who become invisible to the programs commanding the global networks of production, distribution, and valuation.

Communication, Media, and the Public Space

In the realm of communication, the network society is characterized by a pattern of networking, flexibility, the recombination of codes, and ephemeral symbolic communication. This is a culture primarily organized around and integrated by a diversified system of electronic media, including the Internet. Cultural expressions of all kinds are enclosed and shaped by this interlinked, electronic hypertext, formed by television, radio, print media, film, video, art, and Internet communication in the so-called "multimedia system" (Croteau and Hoynes, 2000).

This multimedia system, even in its current state of oligopolistic business concentration, is not characterized by one-way messages to a mass audience. This was the mass culture of the industrial society. Media in the network society present a large variety of channels of communication, with increasing interactivity. And they do not constitute the global village of a unified, Hollywood-centered culture. They are inclusive of a wide range of cultures and social groups, and send targeted messages to selected audiences or to specific moods of an audience. The media system is characterized by global business concentration, by diversification of the audience (including cultural diversification), by technological versatility and channel multiplicity, and by the growing autonomy of an audience that is equipped with the Internet and has learned the rules of the game: namely, everything that is a collective mental experience is virtual, but this virtuality is a fundamental dimension of everybody's reality.

The enclosure of communication in the space of flexible, interactive, electronic hypertext has a decisive effect on politics. Media have become the public space (Volkmer, 2003). The Habermasian vision of the constitution and democratic political institutions as the common ground of society, or the Chicago School vision (unwittingly revived by Henri Lefebvre and Richard Sennett) of the city as the public space of communication and social integration, has faded away. The commons of society are made of electronic networks, be it the media inherited from the mass media age, but deeply transformed by digitalization, or the new communication systems built in and around the Internet. This is not to say that cities disappear or that face-to-face interaction is a relic of the past. In fact, we observe the opposite trend: the more communication happens in the electronic space, the more people assert their own culture and experience in their localities (Borja, 2003).

However, local experience remains fragmented, customized, individualized. The socialization of society – the construction of a shared cultural practice that allows individuals and social groups to live together (even in a conflictive togetherness) – takes place nowadays in the networked, digitized, interactive space of communication, centered around mass media and the Internet. Thus, the relationship between citizens and politicians, between the represented and the representative, depends essentially on what happens in this media-centered communication space. Not that the media dictate politics and policies. But it is in the media space that political battles of all kinds are fought, won, and lost. Here, again, media politics works, as other instances of the network society, in a binary mode: to be or not to be on television. Or, as chapter 16 in this volume documents, on the Internet, as an alternative form of sociopolitical presence, using the input of grassroots power. Therefore, the language of politics and media tactics are essential in shaping the public mind, and therefore the capacity of societies to manage themselves. Which takes us to the fundamental question in social theory: the question of power.

Power in the Networks

Where does power lie in the network society? I have already analyzed the power of the networks that make up the network society over human communities or individuals who are *not* integrated into these networks. In this case, power operates by exclusion/inclusion. But who has power in the dominant networks? This depends on how we define power. Power is the structural capacity to impose one's will over another's will. There can be bargaining, but, in the last resort, power is exercised when, regardless of the will of someone (a person, a social group, a category of people, an organization, a country, and the like), that actor must submit to the will of the power-holder – or else be exposed to violence of different forms. Under these conditions, the question of power-holding in the networks of the network society could be either very simple or impossible to answer.

The very simple answer: each network defines its own power system depending on its programmed goals. Thus, in global capitalism, the global financial market has the last word, and the IMF is its authoritative interpreter for ordinary mortals. The word is usually spoken in the language of the United States Treasury Department and the Federal Reserve Board, with the occasional German, French, Japanese, or Oxbridge accent, depending upon times and spaces. Or else, in terms of state military power, there is just the power of the United States, or, in more analytical terms, the power of any apparatus able to harness technological innovation in the pursuit of military power, which has the material resources and know-how to invest in technology without gravely hampering its social and economic equilibrium.

On the other hand, the question could become an analytical dead-end if we try to answer one-dimensionally: the source of power as a single entity. Military power could not prevent a catastrophic financial crisis; in fact, it could provoke it under certain conditions of irrational, defensive paranoia. Alternatively, the global financial market can be seen as an automaton, out of the control of any major financial institution, because of the size, volume, and complexity of the flows of capital that circulate in its networks, and because of the dependence of its valuation criteria on unpredictable information turbulences. Political decision-making is said to be dependent on the media, and the media constitute a plural ground, however biased in ideological and political terms. As for the capitalist class, it does have some power, but not *the* power, as it is highly dependent on both the autonomous dynamics of global markets and on the decisions of governments in terms of regulations and policies. Finally, governments themselves are linked in complex networks of imperfect global governance, indirectly submitted to their citizenry, and periodically assailed by social movements and expressions of resistance that do not recede easily in the back room of the end of history (Nye and Donahue, 2000). So, perhaps the question of power, as traditionally formulated, does not make sense in the network society. But other forms of domination and determination are critical in shaping people's lives against their will. Let me elaborate.

In a world of networks, the ability to exercise control over others depends on two basic mechanisms: the ability to program/reprogram the network(s) in terms of the goals assigned to the network; and the ability to connect different networks to ensure their cooperation by sharing common goals and increasing resources. I call the holders of the first power position the "programmers," and the holders of the second power position the "switchers." It is important to consider that these programmers and switchers are certainly social actors, but are not necessarily identified with one particular group or individual. More often than not these mechanisms operate at the interface between various social actors, defined in terms of their position in the social structure, and in the organizational framework of society. Thus, I suggest that the power-holders are networks themselves. Not abstract, unconscious networks, not automata: they are humans organized around their projects and interests. But they are not single actors (individuals, groups, classes, religious leaders, political leaders) since the exercise of power in the network society requires a complex set of joint action that goes beyond alliances to become a new form of subject, akin to what Bruno Latour (1993) brilliantly theorized as the action-network actor.

Let us examine the workings of these two mechanisms. The capacity to program the goals of the network (as well as the reprogramming capacity) is, of course, decisive because, once programmed, the network will perform efficiently and reconfigure itself in terms of structure and nodes to achieve its goals. ICT-powered, global/local networks are efficient machines; they have no values other than performing what they are ordered to do. They kill or kiss – nothing personal. How actors of different kinds achieve the programming of the network is a process specific to each network. It is not the same in global finance as it is in military power, in scientific research, in organized crime, or in professional sports. However, all these networks do have something in common: ideas, visions, projects generate the programs. These are cultural materials. In the network society, culture is by and large embedded in the processes of communication, in the electronic hypertext, with the media and the Internet at its core. So, ideas may be generated from a variety of origins, and linked to specific interests and subcultures (for example, neoclassical economics, religious fundamentalism of various kinds, the cult of individual freedom, and the like). Yet, they are processed in society through their treatment in the realm of communication. And, ultimately, they reach the constituencies of each network on the basis of the exposure of these constituencies to the processes of communication. Thus, control of, or influence on, the apparatuses of communication, the ability to create an effective process of communication and persuasion along lines that favor the projects of the would-be programmers, is the key asset in the ability to program each network. In other words, the process of communication in society, and the organizations of this process of communication (often, but not only, the media), are the key fields in which programming projects are formed, and where constituencies are built for these projects. They are the fields of power in the network society.

There is, however, a second source of power, probably more decisive, although this is a matter for research to decide. This is to be found in the controllers of the connecting points between various strategic networks: the "switchers;" for instance, the connection between political leadership networks, media networks, scientific and technology networks, and military and security networks in asserting a geopolitical strategy. Or the connection between business networks and media networks, by using, for instance, the control of regulatory institutions on behalf of the business interests. Or the relationship between religious networks and political networks to advance a religious agenda in a secular society. Or between academic networks and business networks to exchange knowledge and accreditation for resources for the learning institutions and jobs for their products (meaning graduates).

This is not the old boys' network. These are specific interface systems that are set on a relatively stable basis as a way to articulate the operating system of society beyond the formal self-presentation of institutions and organizations. However, I am not resurrecting the idea of a power elite. There is no power elite. This is a caricatural image of power in society, whose analytical value is limited to some extreme cases of personalized dictatorship, as in Pinochet's Chile. It is precisely because there is no power elite capable of keeping under its control the programming and switching operations of all important networks that more subtle, complex, and negotiated systems of power enforcement have to be established, so that the dominant networks of society have compatible goals and are able, through the switching processes enacted by actor-networks, to communicate with each other, inducing synergy and limiting contradiction. This is why it is so important that media tycoons do not become political leaders, as in the case of Berlusconi in Italy. The more the switchers are crude expressions of single-purpose domination, the more the network society suffocates the dynamism and creativity of its multiple sources of social structuration and social change. Switchers are not persons, but they are made up of persons. They are actors, but made up of networks of actors, engaging in dynamic interfaces that are specifically operated in each particular process of connection. *Programmers and switchers* are those actors and networks of actors that, because of their position in the social structure, *exercise power in the network society.*

Power and Counter-power in the Network Society

Processes of power-making must be seen from two perspectives: on the one hand, seizing and/or enforcing power; on the other hand, resisting power, on behalf of interests, values, and projects that are excluded or under-represented in the programs of the networks. Analytically, both processes ultimately configure power structures through their interaction. But they are distinct. They do, however, operate on the same logic. This means that resistance to power is effected through the same two mechanisms that constitute power in the network society: the programs of the networks, and the switches between networks. Thus, the collective action of social movements, in their different forms, aims to introduce new instructions and new codes into the networks' programs. For instance, new instructions in the global financial networks mean that under conditions of extreme poverty debt should be condoned for some countries, as demanded, and partially obtained, by the Jubilee Movement. Another example of a new code in the global financial networks is the project of evaluating company stocks according to the company's environmental ethics in the hope that this will ultimately impact on the attitude of investors and shareholders vis-à-vis companies deemed to be bad citizens of the planet. Under these conditions, the code of economic calculation shifts from growth potential to sustainable growth potential.

More radical reprogramming comes from resistance movements aimed at altering the fundamental principle of a network – or the kernel of the program code, to maintain the parallel with software language. For instance, if God's will must prevail under all conditions (as stated by Christian fundamentalists), the institutional networks that constitute the legal and judicial systems must be reprogrammed, not to follow the political constitution, legal prescriptions, or government decisions (for example, in letting women decide about their own bodies and pregnancies), but to submit them to the interpretation of God's will by his earthly bishops. In another example, when the movement for global justice claims that trade agreements managed by the World Trade Organization should be re-written to include environmental conservation, social rights, and respect for indigenous minorities, it is acting to modify the programs under which the networks of the global economy work.

The second mechanism of resistance consists in blocking the switches of connection between networks that allow the control of these networks by the meta-program of shared values expressing structural domination. Hence, blocking control of the media by oligopolistic business by challenging the rules of the US Federal Communication Commission that allow greater concentration of ownership. Or blocking the networking between corporate business and the political system by regulating campaign finance or by enforcing the conflict of interests between being a vice-president and receiving income from your former company, which has benefited from military contracts. Or by denouncing intellectual servitude to the powers-that-be by academics using their chairs as platforms for propaganda.

More radical disruption of the switchers affects the material infrastructure of the network society: the physical and psychological attacks on air transportation, on computer networks, on information systems, and on the networks of facilities on which the livelihood of society depends in the highly complex, interdependent system that characterizes the informational world. The challenge of terrorism is precisely predicated on this capacity to target strategic material switches so that their disruption or the threat of their disruption disorganizes people's daily lives, and forces them to live in a state of emergency – thus feeding the growth of other power networks, the security networks, that extend to every domain of life. There is, indeed, a symbiotic relationship between the disruption of strategic switches by resistance actions, and the reconfiguration of power networks towards a new set of switches organized around security networks.

Resistance to power programmed in the networks also takes place through and by networks, and these are also information networks powered by information and communication technologies (Arquilla and Ronfeldt, 2001). The so-called "anti-globalization movement" is a global/local network organized and debated on the Internet, and structurally switched on with the media network. *Al-Qaeda*, and its related organizations, is a network made up of multiple nodes, with little central coordination, and also directly aimed at its switching with the media networks, through which they hope to inflict fear among the infidels and raise hope among the oppressed masses of believers (Gunaratna, 2002).

It is characteristic of the network society that both the dynamics of domination and of resistance to domination rely on network formation and network strategies of offense and defense. Indeed, this is consistent with the historical experience of previous types of society, such as the industrial society. The factory and the large, vertically organized industrial corporation were the material basis for the development of both the industrial bourgeoisie and the labor movement. Nowadays, computer networks perform the same function for global financial markets, transnational production systems, "smart" armed forces with a global reach, terrorist resistance networks, and networked social movements struggling for a better world. All of them aim to reach their constituencies and target audiences through the decisive switch to the media networks. In the network society, power is redefined, but it does not vanish. Nor do social struggles. Domination and resistance to domination change in character according to the specific social structure from which they originate and which they modify by their action. Power rules, counter-powers fight. Networks process their contradictory programs while people try to make sense of the sources of their fears and hopes.

Space of Flows and Timeless Time

As with all historical transformations, the emergence of a new social structure is linked to the redefinition of the material foundations of our existence, space and time, as Giddens (1984), Thrift (1986), Adams (1990), Harvey (1990), Lash and Urry (1994), and Graham and Marvin (2000), among others, have argued. Two emergent social forms of time and space characterize the network society, while coexisting with prior forms. They are the space of flows and timeless time. Space and time are related, in nature as in society. In social theory, space can be defined as the material support of time-sharing social practices. The development of communication technologies can be understood as the gradual decoupling of contiguity and time-sharing. The space of flows refers to the technological and organizational possibility of practicing simultaneity (or chosen time in time-sharing) without contiguity. Most dominant functions in the network society (financial markets, transnational production networks, media networks, networked forms of global governance, global social movements) are organized around the space of flows.

However, the space of flows is not placeless. It is made of nodes and networks; that is, of places connected by electronically powered communication networks through which flows of information circulate and interact, which ensure the time-sharing of practices processed in such a space. While in the space of places, based on contiguity of practice, meaning, function, and locality are closely interrelated; in the space of flows, places receive their meaning and function from their nodal role in the specific networks to which they belong. Thus, the space of flows is not the same for financial activities or for science, for media networks or for political power networks. Space cannot be conceived as separate from social practices. Therefore, every dimension of the network society that we have analyzed in this chapter has a spatial manifestation. Because practices are networked, so is their space. Since networked practices are based on information flows processed between various sites by communication technologies, the space of the network society is made up of the articulation between three elements: the places where activities (and people enacting them) are located, the material communication networks linking these activities, and the content and geometry of the flows of information that perform the activities in terms of function and meaning. This is the space of flows.

Time, in social terms, used to be defined as the sequencing of practices. Biological time, characteristic of most of human existence (and still the lot of most people in the world) is defined by the sequence programmed in the life cycles of nature. Biological time was shaped throughout history by what I call bureaucratic time; that is, the organization of time, in institutions and in every-day life, by the codes of military-ideological apparatuses, working on the rhythms of biological time. In the industrial age, clock time gradually emerged; that is, the measure and organization of sequencing with enough precision to assign tasks and order to every moment of life, starting with stan-dardized industrial work and the calculation of the time horizon of financial transactions, two fundamental components of industrial capitalism that could not work without clock time. In the network society, the emphasis on sequenc-ing is reversed. The relationship to time is defined by the use of information and communication technologies in a relentless effort to annihilate time by negating sequencing. This is done, on the one hand, by compressing time (as in split-second global financial transactions or the effort to fight "instant wars"), and, on the other, by blurring the sequence of social practices, includ-ing past, present, and future, in a random order, as in the electronic hypertext, or in the blurring of life-cycle patterns, both in work and in parenting.

In industrial society, organized around the idea of progress and the devel-opment of productive forces, *becoming* structured *being*, time conformed to space. In the network society, the space of flows dissolves time by disordering the sequence of events and making them simultaneous, thus installing society in structural ephemerality: *being* cancels *becoming*.

The construction of space and time is socially differentiated. The multiple space of places, fragmented and disconnected, displays diverse temporalities, from the most traditional domination of biological rhythms to the control of clock time. Selected functions and individuals transcend time, while devalued activities and subordinate people endure life as time goes by. There are, however, alternative projects of structuration of time and space, as an expres-sion of social movements that aim at modifying the dominant programs of the network society. Thus, instead of accepting timeless time as the time of automata, the environmental movement proposes to live time in a *longue durée* cosmological perspective, seeing our lives as part of the evolution of our species, and feeling solidarity with future generations, and with our cosmo-logical belonging. This is what Lash and Urry (1994) conceptualized as glacial time.

Communities around the world also fight to preserve the meaning of local-ity, and to assert the space of places, based on experience, over the logic of the space of flows, based on instrumentality, in the process that I label as the "grassrooting" of the space of flows. Indeed, the space of flows does not disappear, since it is the spatial form of the network society, but its logic can be transformed. Instead of enclosing meaning and function in the programs of the networks, it could provide material support for the global connection of local experience.

Space and time are redefined at the same time by the emergence of a new social structure and by the struggles over the shape and programs of this social structure. In a sense, space and time express the culture(s) of the network society.

Culture in the Network Society

All societies are cultural constructs, if we understand culture as the set of values and beliefs that inform and motivate people's behavior. So, if there is a specific network society, we should be able to identify the culture of the network society as its historical marker. Here again, however, the complexity and novelty of the network society suggest caution. First of all, because the network society is global, it works with and integrates a multiplicity of cultures, linked to the history and geography of each area of the world. In fact, industrialism, and the culture of the industrial society, did not make cultures disappear around the world. The industrial society had many different, and indeed contradictory, manifestations (from the United States to the Soviet Union, and from Japan to the United Kingdom). There were also industrialized cores in otherwise largely rural and traditional societies. Not even capitalism unified its realm of historical existence culturally. Yes, the market ruled in every capitalist country, but under such specific rules, and with such a variety of cultural forms, that identifying a culture as capitalist is of little analytical help, unless we actually mean by that American or Western culture: it then becomes empirically wrong.

So, in the same way, the network society develops in a multiplicity of cultural settings, produced by the differential history of each context. It materializes in specific forms, leading to the formation of highly diverse institutional systems, as the studies presented in this volume demonstrate. There is still a common core to the network society, as there was to industrial society, but there is an additional layer of unity in the network society. It exists globally in real time. It is global in its structure. Thus, not only does it deploy its logic in the whole world, but it keeps its networked organization at the global level at the same time as it makes itself specific in every society.

This double movement of commonality and singularity has two main consequences at the cultural level. On the one hand, specific cultural identities become the trenches of autonomy, and sometimes of resistance, for collectives and individuals who refuse to fade away in the logic of dominant networks. To be French becomes, again, as relevant as to be a citizen. To be Catalan, or Irish, or Basque, or Quebecois, or Kurd, or Tibetan, or Aymara, becomes a rallying point of self-identification vis-à-vis the domination of imposed nation-states. In contrast to the ideologies of the end of history, which propose the merger of all cultures in the cosmopolitan melting pot of the citizens of the world, resistance identities have exploded in the early stages of the development of the global network society, and have produced the most dramatic social and political conflicts in recent times.

Respectable theorists and less respectable ideologists may warn of the dangers of such a development. But we cannot ignore it. Observation must inform theory, not the other way around. Thus, what characterizes the global network society is the contraposition of the logic of the global Net and the affirmation of a multiplicity of local selves, as I tried to argue and document in my trilogy on the information age (Castells, 2000a, c, 2004). Rather than the rise of a homogeneous global culture, what we observe as the main common trend is historical cultural diversity: fragmentation rather than convergence. The key question that then arises is whether these specific cultural identities (made with the materials inherited from singular histories and reworked in the new context) have the capacity to communicate with each other (Touraine, 1997). Otherwise, the sharing of a social structure, while not being able to speak a common language of values and beliefs, leads to systemic misunderstanding, at the roots of destructive violence against the other. Thus, protocols of communication between different cultures are the cornerstone of the network society, as, without them, there is no society, just dominant networks and resisting communes.

The Habermasian–Beckian project of a cosmopolitan culture to create a constitution for the citizens of the world, laying the foundations for democratic global governance, identifies correctly the central cultural-institutional issue of the network society (Habermas, 1998; Beck, 2003). Unfortunately, this vision proposes the solution without being able to identify the process by which these protocols of communication could be created, given the fact that the cosmopolitan culture, according to empirical research, is present only in a very small part of the population, including in Europe (Norris, 2000). There is, indeed, no real European identity in the minds of most Europeans.

To determine, even hypothetically, what these protocols of communication are, or could be, requires an empirical analysis that, although possible, exceeds the limits of this theoretical text. But, in terms of the theory, this is my proposition: *the culture of the global network society is a culture of protocols of communication enabling communication between different cultures on the basis, not necessarily of shared values, but of sharing the value of communication.* This is to say: the new culture is not made of content but of process. It is a culture of communication for the sake of communication. It is an open-ended network of cultural meanings that can not only coexist, but also interact and modify each other on the basis of this exchange.

I will illustrate the meaning of this admittedly abstract statement by re-interpreting one of the most original hypotheses that have been proposed to identify the culture of the information age: the "hacker ethic," in the terms conceptualized by Pekka Himanen in his influential book (Himanen, 2001), and summarized by him in chapter 19 of this volume. The hacker ethic (as exemplified in the networks of innovators that created the Internet, its applications, and much of the essential technologies of the information age) can be understood in two versions, both correct, and complementary in my view. The first, which has received broad acceptance in intellectual and business circles alike, refers to the culture of innovation for the sake of innovation. The passion to create replaces capital accumulation as a means of salvation. Playing is producing. Instead of the deferred gratification pattern of the Protestant (and capitalist) ethic, there is affirmation of an instant gratification pattern: the joy of creating and the immediate use of the creation.

But there is a second, fundamental dimension in the practice of hackers and in the theory of Himanen that has been overlooked: sharing. The free sharing of knowledge and discovery is the essential mechanism by which innovation takes place in the information age (and probably in earlier societies). And since innovation is the source of productivity, wealth and power, there is a direct relationship between the power of sharing and the sharing of power. So, networking for the sake of networking, being ready to learn from others and to give them what you have, could be the culture of the network society: a belief in the power of the network, in your empowerment by being open to others, and in the joy of diversity. In the example of hacker networks, network-ing is practiced on the basis of one common value: the value of creativity, the feeling of self-realization by the exercise of the capacity of the mind to chal-lenge and invent.

So, this is my hypothesis: the culture of the network society is a culture of protocols of communication between all cultures in the world, developed on the basis of a common belief in the power of networking and of the synergy obtained by giving to others and receiving from others. A process of material construction of the culture of the network society is underway. But it is not the diffusion of the capitalist mind through the power exercised in the global networks by the dominant elites inherited from industrial society. Nor is it the idealistic proposals of philosophers dreaming of a world of abstract, cosmopolitan citizens. It is the process by which conscious social actors of multiple origins bring to others their resources and beliefs, expecting in return to receive the same, and even more: sharing a diverse world, and thus ending the ancestral fear of the other.

CONCLUSION: THE PRACTICAL CONSEQUENCES OF THEORETICAL MISTAKES

At this point in the analysis presented here, this conclusion will not come as a shock: we are not in the information or knowledge society. At least, no more than we have been in other historical periods. Knowledge and information have always been essential sources of productivity and power. If, by emphasizing the knowledge component of our world, we imply that we know now and were ignorant in earlier times, a little modesty would be welcome. Knowledge is always historically relative. We certainly know more than a few centuries ago, and we can even say that the growth of knowledge has been exponential, although in many fields of science, without these earlier discoveries, we would still be in the dark. But we certainly know very little in some basic dimensions of nature or human life. I will just mention the brain, which is the source of who we are, and whose structure and functions are ignored for the most part. As for society and the economy, I will simply remind the reader that the analysis of the aggregate production function underlying productivity growth as a result of factors others than capital, labor, or raw materials was originally established by Robert Solow in 1957, on the basis of statistical data concerning the United States for the period 1909–49, the heyday of the industrial society (Solow, 1957). Never mind: information society apologists invariably start with Solow's analysis of productivity to found their claims on the role of information as the basis of the new society.

As I have analyzed in various works, and in this volume, information and knowledge are indeed essential, in the economy and in society at large. But they are not specific as dominant components of our kind of society. What is specific is that, on the basis of a new technological paradigm (informationalism), a new social structure has emerged, a structure made up of electronic communication technologies – powered, social networks. So, what is different? It is the technology, of course. But it is also the networked social structure, and the specific set of relationships implied in the networking logic.

Therefore, in my view, we must let the notion of an information society or of a knowledge society wither, and replace it with the concept of the network society, as presented in this chapter, and researched throughout this volume, from a variety of theoretical perspectives. I contend that this reconceptualization matters because it carries practical consequences.

If we were now in an information society, as a direct consequence of the invention and diffusion of electronic information and communication technologies, the economic and social development of a country would depend, for instance, on installing computers everywhere, and pushing everybody to be on the Internet or not to be. Studies on the uses of information and communication technologies demonstrate, again, what historians of technology established long since: that technology can only yield its promise in the framework of cultural, organizational, and institutional transformations. Computers in school are only as good as the teachers are. And teachers cannot do much unless the organizational set-up of the school transcends the disciplinary bureaucracies of the information age. Or, alternatively, the Internet in universities cannot do much in the context of a cultural and academic setting that, in many cases, has changed little since the pre-industrial theological schools.

Furthermore, computers and the Internet do little to help economic productivity and business competitiveness in the absence of the diffusion of the organizational form represented by the network enterprise. The dot-com bust was provoked by the fantasies of business consultants and futurologists who forgot that the key role of the Internet is to power the real economy, rather than to escape into the domain of a new, virtual economy. And electronic democracy must start with the redefinition of citizen participation and political participation.

In broader terms of social evolution, the notion of the information society reproduces the myth of the historical continuum from nomadic to agricultural societies, then to industrial society, to culminate in the apogee, obviously in our time, of the information society. Human history is then assimilated to the long march of progress under the guidance of reason (with occasional prayers to God just in case), as exemplified by the wonders of computers, clean toilets, and smart weapons. No conflict, no contradiction, just technologically predetermined change, and resistance to change. And since resistance to reason is irrational, it must be obliterated to clear the shining path toward our promised star.

If, instead, we identify our society as a network society, in the precise sense defined and elaborated in this chapter, we must place at the center of the analysis the networking capacity of institutions, organizations, and social actors, both locally and globally. Connectivity and access to networks become essential. The right combination of information and communication technology, development of human capacity to take advantage of the full potential of these technologies, and organizational restructuring based on networking becomes the key to ensuring productivity, competitiveness, innovation, creativity, and, ultimately, power and power sharing. If we conceive of the global network society as something other than telecommunication networks, if we recall the interactive, multinodal logic of the Internet, then it is possible to design communication systems for inclusion and collaboration. If all cultures have their relevance as nodes of a networked system of cultural dialogue, there is no opposition between hypermodernity and tradition, but complementarity and reciprocal learning.

In sum, the notion of the information or knowledge society is simply a technological extrapolation of the industrial society, usually assimilated to the

Western culture of modernization. The concept of the network society shifts the emphasis to organizational transformation, and to the emergence of a globally interdependent social structure, with its processes of domination and counter-domination. It also helps us to define the terms of the fundamental dilemma of our world: the dominance of the programs of a global network of power without social control or, alternatively, the emergence of a network of interacting cultures, unified by a common belief in the use value of sharing.

REFERENCES

Adams, Barbara (1990) *Time and Social Theory*. Cambridge: Polity Press.
Arquilla, John and Ronfeldt, David (eds) (2001) *Networks and Netwars: The Future of Terror, Crime, and Militancy*. Santa Monica, CA: RAND Corporation.
Beck, Ulrich (2003) "Las instituciones de gobernanza mundial en la sociedad global de riesgo," in Manuel Castells and Narcis Serra (eds), *Guerra y paz en el siglo XXI*, pp. 53–66. Barcelona: Tusquets.
Berners-Lee, Tim, with Frischetti, Mark (1999) *Waving the Web*. San Francisco: HarperCollins.
Borja, Jordi (2003) *La ciudad conquistada*. Madrid: Alianza.
— — and Castells, Manuel (1997) *Local and Global*. London: Earthscan.
Capra, Fritjof (1996) *The Web of Life*. New York: Random House.
— — (2002) *Hidden Connections: Integrating the Biological, Cognitive, and Social Dimensions of Life into a Science of Sustainability*. New York: Random House.
Carnoy, Martin (2000) *Sustaining the New Economy: Work, Family and Community in the Information Age*. Cambridge, MA: Harvard University Press.
— — and Castells, Manuel (1984) "After the Crisis?," *World Policy Journal* (Fall).
Castells, Manuel (1980) *The Economic Crisis and American Society*. Princeton, NJ: Princeton University Press.
— — (2000a) *End of Millennium*, 2nd edn. Oxford: Blackwell.
— — (2000b) "Materials for an Exploratory Theory of the Network Society," *British Journal of Sociology* 51: 1 (January–March), 5–24.
— — (2000c) *The Rise of the Network Society*, 2nd edn. Oxford: Blackwell.
— — (2001) *The Internet Galaxy*. Oxford: Oxford University Press.
— — (2004) *The Power of Identity*, 2nd edn. Oxford: Blackwell.
— — and Kiselyova, Emma (2003) *The Collapse of the Soviet Union: The View from the Information Society*. Los Angeles: Figueroa Press/USC Bookstore.
Colas, Dominique (1992) *La Glaive et le fleau: généalogie du fanatisme et de la société civile*. Paris: Bernard Grasset.
Croteau, David and Hoynes, William (2000) *Media/Society: Industries, Images, and Audiences*, 2nd edn. Thousand Oaks, CA: Pine Forge.
David, Paul (1975) *Technical Choice, Innovation and Economic Growth: Essays on American and British Experience in the Nineteenth Century*. London: Cambridge University Press.
Fischer, Claude (1992) *America Calling: A Social History of the Telephone to 1940*. Berkeley, CA: University of California Press.
Freeman Christopher (1982) *The Economics of Industrial Innovation*. London: Frances Pinter.

Giddens, Anthony (1984) *The Constitution of Society: Outline of a Theory of Structuration*. Cambridge: Polity Press.

Gould, Stephen J. (1980) *The Panda's Thumb: More Reflections on Natural History*. New York: W. W. Norton.

Graham, Stephen and Marvin, Simon (2000) *Splintering Networks, Fragmenting Cities: Urban Infrastructure in Global Local Age*. London: Routledge.

Guillemard, Anne-Marie (2003) *L'Age de l'emploi*. Paris: Armand Colin.

Gunaratna, Rohan (2002) *Inside Al-Qaeda: Global Network of Terror*. New York: Columbia University Press.

Habermas, Jurgen (1998) *Die Postnationale Konstellation*. Frankfurt: Suhrkamp.

Harvey, David (1990) *The Condition of Postmodernity*. Oxford: Blackwell.

Held, David and McGrew, Anthony (1999) *Global Transformations*. Stanford, CA: Stanford University Press.

Himanen, Pekka (2001) *The Hacker Ethic and the Spirit of the Information Age*. New York: Random House.

Hutton, Will and Giddens, Anthony (eds) (2000) *On the Edge: Living in Global Capitalism*. London: Jonathan Cape.

Johnson, Steve (2001) *Emergence: The Connected Lives of Ants, Brains, Cities, and Software*. New York: Scribner.

Juris, Jeff (2004) "Transnational Activism and the Cultural Logic of Networking," unpublished PhD thesis in anthropology, University of California, Berkeley, California.

Kuhn, Thomas (1962) *The Structure of Scientific Revolutions*. Chicago, IL: University of Chicago Press.

La Bianca, Oystein (ed.) (forthcoming) *Connectivity in Antiquity*.

Lash, Scott and Urry, John (1994) *Economies of Signs and Space*. London: Sage.

Latour, Bruno (1993) *We Have Never Been Modern*. Cambridge, MA: Harvard University Press.

Levy, Steve (2001) *Hackers: Heroes of the Computer Revolution*, 2nd edn. New York: Penguin.

Lucas, Henry (1999) *Information Technology and the Productivity Paradox*. New York: Oxford University Press.

Mazlish, Bruce (1993) *The Fourth Discontinuity: The Co-evolution of Men and Machines*. New Haven, CT: Yale University Press.

Mitchell, William J. (2003) *ME ++: The Cyborg Self and the Networked City*. Cambridge, MA: MIT Press.

Mokyr, Joel (1990) *The Lever of Riches: Technological Creativity and Economic Progress*. Oxford: Oxford University Press.

Monge, Peter R. and Contractor, Noshir S. (2003) *Theories of Communication Networks*. Oxford: Oxford University Press.

Mulgan, Geoff J. (1991) *Communication and Control: Networks and the New Economies of communication*. New York: Guilford Press.

Norris, Pippa (2000) "Global Governance and Cosmopolitan Citizens," in Joseph Nye and John Donahue (eds), *Governance in a Globalizing World*, pp. 155–77. Washington, DC: Brookings Institution Press.

Nye, Joseph and Donahue, John (eds) (2000) *Governance in a Globalizing World*. Washington, DC: Brookings Institution Press.

Perez, Carlota (1983) "Structural Change and the Assimilation of New Technologies in the Economic and Social Systems," *Futures* 15: 357–75.

Solow, Robert M. (1957) "Technical Change and the Aggregate Production Function," *Revue of Economics and Statistics* 39 (August): 214–31.

Stiglitz, Joseph (2002) *Globalization and its Discontents*. New York: W. W. Norton.

Thrift, Nigel (1986) "The Fixers: The Urban Geography of International Financial Capital," Department of Geography, University of Wales, Lampeter.

Touraine, Alain (1997) *Pourrons-nous vivre ensemble? Egaux et différents*. Paris: Fayard.

Volkmer, Ingrid (1999) *News in the Global Sphere: A Study of CNN and its Impact on Global Communication*. Luton: Luton University Press.

—— (2003) "The Global Network Society and the Global Public Sphere," *Journal of Development* 46: 9–16.

PART II

The cultural and institutional diversity of the network society

2. Institutional models of the network society: Silicon Valley and Finland

Pekka Himanen and Manuel Castells

This chapter emphasizes the institutional and cultural diversity of network societies around the world. It focuses on a comparison of the two network societies that have for many years topped the global rankings in technological advancement and economic competitiveness. What makes the comparison especially interesting is the fact that their dynamic performance has been based on very different social and institutional models. The model of the United States – which we call the "Silicon Valley model" as this region is its most dynamic area and, indeed, its symbol – is based on unfettered capitalism. There is widespread belief among leading political and business circles that an advanced information economy is only possible by replicating the successful Silicon Valley model. Therefore, whether by competition or design, it is the Californian experience that has shaped public perception of the global rise of the network society.

However, the Finnish model factually contradicts this belief. Finland occupies the leading position in the United Nations index of technological development, and it was ranked as the most competitive economy in the world by the World Economic Forum in 2003. It is also a trendsetter in some of the key technologies, such as mobile telecommunications (in which Nokia has roughly 40 percent of the world market) and open-source software (in which the Linux operating system runs the largest part of the World Wide Web). Yet the process of technological development and economic growth in Finland has been actively steered by the government. And Finland, in sharp contrast with Silicon Valley, features a comprehensive welfare state, which includes free, public, and high-quality education, including student grants for university; a mostly free, public, and high-quality health care system, which is open to everyone regardless of employment status; universal unemployment and pension protection; and a universal right to low-cost, public child care run by child-care specialists with college-level education.

At a time characterized by the tension between the rise of the global network society and social movements attempting to re-establish social control over market forces, a comparison of the Silicon Valley model and the

Finnish model has political relevance both for these countries and for the world at large. Suddenly, the European tradition of government guidance and concern for social protection is no longer necessarily sentenced to historical oblivion. And, for the developing world, the transformation of Finland from a relatively poor country in 1950, mostly making a living from agriculture and forestry with 50 percent of its population employed in the primary sector, to a leading global economy fifty years later provides cause for reflection for countries trying to "leapfrog" into the information age.

As for the Silicon Valley model, the region around the San Francisco Bay Area has been the seedbed of the information technology revolution since the late 1950s. It has been at the forefront of the successive waves of entrepreneurial and technological innovation that have constituted the infrastructure of the information age: the microelectronics revolution of the 1960s and 1970s, the development of personal computers and recombinant DNA in the 1970s, the adoption and development of UNIX and open-source software (together with the Massachusetts Institute of Technology) in the 1980s, the explosion of Internet applications and businesses in the 1990s, and, in the early twenty-first century, nanotechnology, advanced genetic engineering, and the convergence between microelectronics, computing, and biological technologies.

As so much of the innovation system and so many businesses in the "new economy" of the US are based on the replication and expansion of the experience of the Silicon Valley innovation complex, we use the notion of "Silicon Valley" as a proxy for the underlying model of innovation that has induced economic productivity, organizational networking, and cultural change in the United States as a whole. Our observations will focus on the specific processes of Silicon Valley's innovation model, although the aggregate data on the performance of economic and technological processes will refer to the United States, as statistical sources for comparisons and rankings use countries as the accounting unit.

However, when we refer to the Silicon Valley or Finnish "model," we do not in either case mean a normative model to be followed by other societies: a simple imitation would not, of course, be possible as societies have to transform themselves on the basis of their own history, institutions, and culture. Our purpose here is purely analytical. The fact that the "Finnish model" has performed technologically and economically as well as the "Silicon Valley model," albeit on a vastly smaller scale, means that there is not just one way inherent in the dynamics of information technology for it to be the lever of a successful information economy. Thus, there is political choice and there are policy alternatives in the ways in which institutions shape the network society. Yet, in the context of this book, we will resist normative judgments and leave the debate on political decisions to people and governments.

PATHS OF TECHNOLOGICAL, ECONOMIC, AND SOCIAL DEVELOPMENT: A STATISTICAL COMPARISON

Let us start by looking at some basic indicators of the Silicon Valley and Finnish models that have created two of the most dynamic information technology milieux of innovation in the world. The United Nations Technology Achievement Index ranks Finland and the United States as the first and second countries, based on such measures as technology innovation, diffusion of the Internet, technology exports, and human skills (see figure 2.1). The World Economic Forum ranked the United States and Finland the first and second most competitive economies in the world in 2002 (figure 2.2). In 2003, they topped the chart in the reverse order. This reflected such traditional criteria of economic performance as productivity in which the United States has, for a

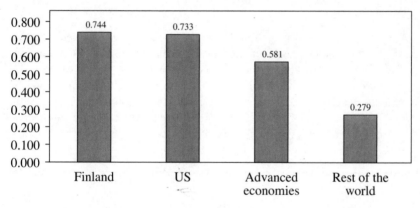

Notes:
The index is based on four components: creation of technology (the number of patents granted per capita, the receipts of royalty and license fees from abroad per capita), diffusion of recent innovations (the diffusion of the Internet, exports of high- and medium-technology products as a share of all exports), diffusion of old innovations (telephones, electricity), and human skills (mean years of schooling, gross enrolment ratio of tertiary students enrolled in science, mathematics, and engineering).

By "advanced economies" we mean largely the same as the International Monetary Fund; that is, the Western economies (United States, Canada, Australia, New Zealand, Israel, United Kingdom, Ireland, Germany, France, Austria, Switzerland, Italy, Spain, Portugal, Greece, Norway, Denmark, Sweden, Finland) and the strongest Asian economies (Japan, Korea, Singapore; Hong Kong and Taiwan are not included here because they are not counted independently in all statistics).

Source: UNDP (2001)

Figure 2.1   Technological development measured by the UN Technology Achievement Index, 2001

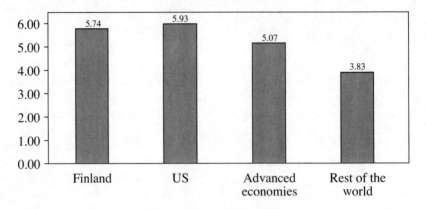

*Figure 2.2   Economic competitiveness measured by the World Economic
Forum Growth Competitiveness Index, 2002*

long period, been the world leader. Figure 2.3 shows the development of labor
productivity in manufacturing in the United States and Finland; the productivity level in Finland has recently even exceeded that of the United States.

However, these two technologically and economically dynamic models
have led to very different social outcomes. While the US and Finland come top
in all the usual comparisons of information economies (being innovative
producers of technology), Finland also comes top in a comparison of social

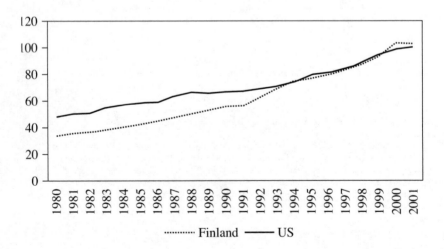

*Figure 2.3   Labor productivity in manufacturing based on the OECD STAN
database (US 2001 = 100)*

Table 2.1   Production of technology and social inclusion

	US	Finland	Advanced economies
Production of technology			
innovation (measured by receipts of royalties and license fees US$ per 1,000 pop.)	130 (4)	126 (5)	56
High-tech exports (%)	32 (4)	27 (8)	18
Social inclusion			
Richest 20% to poorest 20% (ratio)	9.0 (–3)	3.6 (3)	5.8
People below the poverty line (%)	14.1 (–4)	3.8 (4)	10.6

The figures in parentheses mark position on a ranking of the advanced economies (the minus sign counting from the bottom).

Source: UNDP (2001)

inclusion (low level of poverty and income inequality), while the US comes at the bottom of these lists (see table 2.1). In fact, in the US, the information technology-led economic revolution which began in the 1970s has put the levels of social inequality (measured by the Gini index) and exclusion (measured by the incarceration rate which reflects how many people are left with only crime as a means of survival) on a dramatic rise. In Finland, the information technology revolution has been accompanied by a fall, and then a continued low level, of social inequality and exclusion, as we can see in figure 2.4.

Let us now analyze the dynamics behind these results which are very similar on technological and economic measures but very dissimilar on social measures. We will start with the Silicon Valley model and then contrast it with the Finnish model.

THE SILICON VALLEY MODEL

The history of the development of Silicon Valley as the world's premier milieu of technological and entrepreneurial innovation of the information technology revolution is well known (Castells and Hall, 1994; Saxenian, 1994). The beginning of Silicon Valley can be traced back to the founding of Hewlett-Packard

Pekka Himanen and Manuel Castells

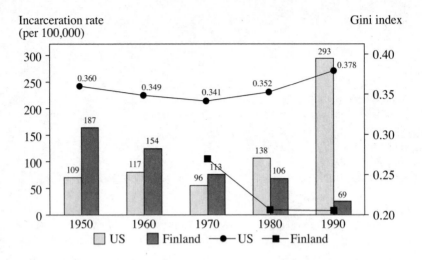

Source: UNDP (2001)

*Figure 2.4   Social inequality and exclusion in the US and Finland,
            1950–1990*

in a Palo Alto garage in 1938. The company was started by two Stanford
University students, William Hewlett and David Packard, who were encouraged and supported with 1,062 dollars by their professor, Frederick Terman,
later to become Dean of Engineering and Provost. To advance this kind of
entrepreneurship further, in 1951 Terman created the Stanford Industrial
Park where technology companies could interact with the university and
with each other. They paid an annual fee of 1 dollar for this prime real-estate
location. They were carefully selected by a committee, which considered,
above all other criteria, the potential of the company as a technological innovator.

   Terman also encouraged William Shockley, the inventor of the transistor, to
start his company Shockley Transistors in Palo Alto in 1956, recruiting a group
of talented engineers. However, seeing the potential of using silicon for integrating transistors, eight young engineers decided to leave after a year and
start their own company, Fairchild Semiconductors, with venture capital organized by Arthur Rock. Thus, Fairchild was the company that started the Silicon
Valley model of turning innovations into business with the help of venture
capital. It was also the company that developed the integrated circuit with the
planar manufacturing process and began the microelectronics revolution in
Silicon Valley.

   Because of the option included in Fairchild's venture capital agreement that the financier could acquire the whole company at a low set price after three years, the engineers left the company to spin-off their own businesses to develop the new technology and reap the financial rewards. Bob Noyce, Gordon Moore, and Andy Grove started Intel, again with venture capital organized by Arthur Rock, but without the earlier option so that the innovator-owners would be fully rewarded for their risk-taking. In fact, half of the largest American semiconductor companies, such as Advanced Micro Devices, can be traced back to a round of spin-offs from Fairchild. The same is also true of many of the leading venture capital and business services companies in Silicon Valley. For example, in addition to Arthur Rock, who was behind Fairchild itself, Intel and Apple, two Fairchild employees Donald Valentine and Eugene Kleiner started two of the biggest venture capital firms in Silicon Valley: Sequoia (e.g. Apple) and Kleiner, Perkins, Caufield, and Byers. The leading high-tech marketing firm McKenna Group, which made global brands of Intel and Apple, for example, is also rooted in one of the Fairchild spin-offs when Regis McKenna decided to start his own company.

In 1971, Intel engineers Ted Hoff and Federico Faggin developed the first microprocessor, an invention that Steve Wozniak took advantage of when he started the personal computer revolution by building the Apple Computer and founding the company with Steve Jobs in 1976. Sun Microsystems and Cisco Systems spearheaded the computer networking revolution in the 1980s. The mass breakthrough of the Internet also began in Silicon Valley, with the Netscape graphical web browser in 1994 and the creation of companies like Yahoo! Since the start of the revolution with Fairchild, Silicon Valley has become the world's leading information technology cluster, which has diversified from semiconductors to computers, data storage, networking (including the Internet), and a whole array of information and communication technologies. Table 2.2 presents the revenue figures for the five biggest companies in Silicon Valley.

Table 2.2 Top five Silicon Valley information technology companies (revenues for 2003)

Company	Industry	Revenues (US$ billion)
1 Hewlett-Packard	Computers	73.1
2 Intel	Semiconductors	30.1
3 Cisco Systems	Networking	18.9
4 Solectron	EMS	11.7
5 Sun Microsystems	Computers	11.4

Source: Based on *Fortune 500* (2004)

In a parallel, but related development, recombinant DNA technology was developed at Stanford University and at the University of California, San Francisco, in 1973–5, leading to the growth of early, leading biotechnology companies in the Bay Area, such as Cetus and Genentech. The process continued over the next three decades and made the Bay Area the site of the largest concentration of the most advanced genetic engineering companies in the world. Similarly, in the 1990s, when computer graphics and the Internet revolution created the multimedia industry, it was also in San Francisco, in the South of Market area, that some of the most advanced start-up companies were located. They later connected with the much larger Los Angeles multimedia complex, forming what in the Californian jargon is called "Siliwood" (a combination of Hollywood and Silicon Valley). Thus, there is something in Silicon Valley (a region that, in fact, includes the entire San Francisco Bay Area, beyond its original South Bay location between Stanford and San Jose) that has made it the seedbed of innovation for over half a century. What is it?

Silicon Valley as a Milieu of Innovation

A milieu of innovation appears when there is synergy emerging from a specific production complex (Castells, 1989) A production complex is formed, as in all production systems, by the combination of capital, labor, and raw material to process inputs into outputs. What studies on Silicon Valley show is that the synergy resulting from this production system was linked to the geographical coincidence of specific raw material, specific capital, and specific labor (Castells and Hall, 1994; Saxenian, 1994). The specific raw material was new knowledge on information technologies. It came, to some extent, from leading universities in the area, particularly Stanford and Berkeley. But it also resulted from the extraordinary talent that was attracted to the area, and this was somewhat serendipitous, as the case of William Shockley shows, a Nobel Prize winner for his invention of the transistor and the grandfather of the semiconductors revolution in the valley, who relocated there, from Bell Laboratories in New Jersey, partly because his mother was living in Palo Alto. Furthermore, the innovative culture, and a critical mass of highly educated young population in the area, provided the basis for the raw material in the form of young minds interacting with each other, for example in the Homebrew Computer Club, the source of the personal computer and related software development.

The specific labor were the high-quality engineers, computer scientists, and scientists that the Bay Area universities were mass producing from the 1960s, overtaking the leading East Coast universities in quantity with similar quality. In addition, as soon as the industry expanded, young engineers from all over America, and the world, came to work in Silicon Valley. A vast pool of talent provided the basis for the growth of the milieu of innovation.

There was still a need for a specific kind of capital, capital ready to take high risks in the expectation of high pay-offs. The first round of financing came from the US Defense Department, in the 1950s and 1960s. Sputnik in 1957 motivated the US government to fund technological development so that it would remain the world's leading superpower. For example, the main market for Fairchild, begun with venture capital, was the military, which was in the process of digitalizing its systems. It was originally the tough military avionics requirements for reliability that forced Fairchild to develop the new revolutionary planar process that protected the transistors and the integrated circuit (Lécuyer, 2000). The military remained the main market for the integrated circuits industry in the 1960s, and semiconductor manufacturers like Intel still sold a fifth of their production to military contractors in the late 1990s.

In addition to providing a safe market for high-tech production, the military also directly funded university research and development. For this purpose, the Department of Defense founded the Advanced Research Projects Agency (ARPA) in 1958. Michael Dertouzos of the Massachusetts Institute of Technology (MIT) has estimated that between a third and a half of all computer science and technology innovations have been at least partly funded by ARPA. The most famous example is, of course, the ARPAnet which later became the Internet, in which MIT, Stanford, UCLA, UC Santa Barbara, and Berkeley all had an important role. If we look at the five top companies in table 2.2, they have all had key ARPA-funded projects. Sun is an especially good example of the dynamics. Sun was created to commercialize two technologies funded by ARPA: one was the workstation developed by Andy Bechtolsheim at Stanford, and the other was the BSD Unix operating system developed by Bill Joy at Berkeley. For the first year, 80 percent of Sun's market was ARPA-related and, in 2001, Sun still announced a $1billion deal with the US Air Force. Stanford-related institutes are still among the leading recipients of this money: for example, the funding of SRI is three-quarters military.

Of course, it should be stressed that most people in Silicon Valley are not motivated by military goals but by an interest in technological innovation, mainly with civilian applications. And the Silicon Valley model has been run predominantly with private finance since the 1970s. Venture capital companies have emerged from the industry itself, with inside knowledge of the processes of innovation, and they have also moved to the area, given the importance of closely following the work of the innovators they are betting on (Zook, 2004). But in the original development of private funding, the government's push had a critical role and it has not totally disappeared in the early twenty-first century. In fact, the public contribution to private research and development projects, at least until 1999, was higher than in Finland, for example (see figure 2.5). Therefore, although Silicon Valley is known as a business-driven model of the information society, the state has had a very significant role in financing some of the key technological innovations.

In this way, the spatial interaction between a specific raw material (knowledge), specific labor (highly skilled scientists and engineers), and specific capital (defense funding first, then venture capital), concentrated in a given area, led to the formation of Silicon Valley as a milieu of innovation. But the location in this particular area and the formation of the milieu were a function of the initiative of an institutional entrepreneur, Stanford University, which played the role that public sector development agencies have played in other countries. Thus, Stanford University and the Defense Department, as a source of funding and markets, show that non-profit and public sector institutions are also essential in the United States, as in other countries, in inducing technological innovation and economic growth.

It is also important to note that Silicon Valley, as all production complexes, relies on a vast array of local supporting services, something that many imitators of the Silicon Valley model have not understood. As important as financial services are business services, such as legal and marketing services. In fact, one of the most influential players in Silicon Valley is the law firm Wilson, Sonsini, Goodrich, and Rosati, whose clients include, among others, Intel. Like all other service companies, law firms also go beyond legal assistance in intellectual property rights and high-tech deals: they are also business advisers who often establish the initial contacts between start-up entrepreneurs, venture capitalists, and partner companies. Equally important are the marketing services for making technology products into global brands. In the

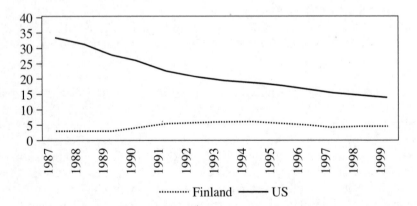

Figure 2.5   Share of public funding in private research and development
projects (OECD Main Science and Technology Indicators),
1987–1999

informational economy, the symbolic level of products has become more and more important. In fact, increasingly, people buy the symbolic experience related to a product. Silicon Valley marketing companies, such as the McKenna Group, realized this before others and understood how to make brands of such complicated products as high-tech information technology. The McKenna Group was the company that made Intel and Apple into global brands.

Silicon Valley is also based on its social fabric. Once the milieu was constituted, in the 1960s, the role of social networks of engineers and entrepreneurs was essential in consolidating it and in assuring its internal mobility and the cross-fertilization of innovation, as research by Anna Lee Saxenian (1994) has shown. A triple supporting structure for new entrepreneurs – high-tech partner companies, an inheritance of the experience of successful entrepreneurs, and the actual services for turning ideas into businesses – makes Silicon Valley an efficient machine. The result is a very fast transformation from an idea to a business with venture capital, legal and marketing capabilities, ready to link to the global financial markets through an initial public offering.

As Richard Gordon (1984) has analyzed in his pioneer research on Silicon Valley, around this territorially concentrated milieu, global networks of innovation linked up with Silicon Valley, making it a node in a global system of innovation. The ability of Silicon Valley companies to tap into the vast technological and labor resources of the entire planet came from their capacity to use networking and networking technologies earlier than any other firms, for the simple reason that they were inventing and producing these technologies. The production of network technologies favored the networking of the production process around the world. Once synergy was assured, the process kept feeding itself, as greater speed of innovation led to increased capital, labor, and knowledge embodied in talent attracted to Silicon Valley.

A final important element must be added to explain why Silicon Valley is so powerful, and that is its ability to be open to ideas from around the world. None of the "Fairchild Eight" was from California. Of the Eight, Jean Hoerni who made the breakthrough innovation of the planar process – the cornerstone of modern semiconductors manufacturing – was from Switzerland, and Eugene Kleiner, one of the key people in establishing the Valley venture capital market, was Austrian. Andy Grove, one of the founders of Intel, was from Hungary. Of the inventors of the microprocessor, Ted Hoff was born on the East Coast and Federico Faggin was Italian. The four founders of Sun Microsystems were from Germany (Andreas Bechtolsheim), India (Vinod Khosla), and elsewhere in the US (Bill Joy and Scott McNealy). Jerry Yang, the co-founder of Yahoo!, is Taiwanese. Solectron's two key people were Roy Kusumoto and Winston Chen, the former of Japanese heritage and the latter from Taiwan.

People from around the world have come to Silicon Valley because it is such an open environment within which ideas can flourish. This should not be understood to mean that Silicon Valley just turns the ideas of others into business. This would be quite untrue. Much of the innovation still takes place among the "locals." Nor is it the case that immigrant innovators had their ideas in place before they came to Silicon Valley and came here just to realize them. That is not the situation either. It is Silicon Valley's open culture of innovation that nurtures people's ideas. Often, they have also gone through the innovation-encouraging education of universities such as Stanford or Berkeley. But the role of immigrants is clearly increasing. In the 1990s, the United States granted, on average, 215,000 H1 special visas to highly qualified professionals every year. Anna Lee Saxenian has shown that almost a third of Silicon Valley engineers are immigrants and a quarter of Valley companies are run by Indian or Chinese chief executives alone (Saxenian, 1999, 2002). Nowadays it is still said that the success of Silicon Valley is based on ICs: not integrated circuits but Indians and Chinese. If we focus on new companies that have been created recently, and include other immigrants, we probably come to a figure close to 40 percent of companies in Silicon Valley run by immigrants.

Let us try now to analyze the process from the point of view of the firm, the key unit in the Silicon Valley model of innovation.

The Process of Innovation and the New Economy in Silicon Valley

What came to be labeled the "new economy," first in Silicon Valley, and then in the world, was not the dot-com business. This new economy, as all new economies in history, is characterized by a new process of production that underlies a substantial and sustained increase in the rate of productivity growth. This has clearly been the case in Silicon Valley and in the United States since the mid-1990s. From 1996 to 2002, labor productivity in the US grew at an annual average of 2.8 percent, doubling the performance of 1985–1995. Furthermore, productivity growth continued in 2001–2003 during the downturn of the cycle, and increased at a whopping 6.8 percent annual rate in the second quarter of 2003.

Productivity measured by output per man hour grew by 4.1 percent from mid-2002 to mid-2003. Productivity growth was much higher in the information technology industries. A number of studies, including those of the Federal Reserve Board, have pinpointed the critical role played by investment in information and communication technologies in the surge of productivity (Sichel, 1997; Jorgenson and Stiroh, 2000; Jorgenson and Yip, 2000). However, some of these studies also show that it is only under the conditions of organizational change (networking) and the development of human resources (talented labor) that ICTs can yield their full potential (Brynjolfsson and Hitt, 2000). For a full discussion of the analysis of productivity growth and its relationship to information technology, see chapter 6 of this volume.

Both productivity and competitiveness are key indicators of performance for business firms. At the macro level, it is only under conditions of sustained, high productivity growth that a given economy can experience high growth and high employment with low inflation. At the micro level, it is the productivity-based competitiveness of firms (as well as of regions and countries) that ensures a dynamic presence in global markets, the source of wealth in our time.

But where does this growth in productivity and enhanced competitiveness come from? Building on case studies from Silicon Valley and on a review of the literature, we hypothesize that innovation is the most important source of both productivity and competitiveness at the level of the firm (Castells, 2001). In figure 2.6 we represent the process that links innovation to the performance of firms, as well as the sources of innovation, in the specific case of Silicon Valley. Let us comment briefly on the process charted in this figure.

Innovation operates in three dimensions: technology, process, and product. By process, we mean organizational networking, both intra-firm and in the relationships with other firms, providers, and clients. Technology refers to microelectronics-based information and communication technologies. Product innovation refers to the specific production line of each firm. We contend that, for innovation to enhance productivity and competitiveness, the three dimensions of innovation must proceed together, and interact in a positive feedback loop. The question then becomes: what are the sources of innovation?

Entrepreneurialism
With reference to Silicon Valley firms, the first condition is entrepreneurship; that is, the transforming of a business project into business practice. The development of a business firm requires an entrepreneur (individual or collective) who brings together specific knowledge and talented labor. And for entrepreneurs to exist, an entrepreneurial culture is needed, as well as a supportive entrepreneurial institutional environment. A strong entrepreneurial culture is the element that distinguishes the Silicon Valley model most clearly from other models.

Although the big companies dominate the Silicon Valley economy, the essence of Silicon Valley consists in new start-ups that grow big fast. In many European countries, the main innovators in information technology industries are often large companies with a history going back more than a hundred years. Silicon Valley constantly creates new companies that become world leaders, such as Intel in semiconductors in the 1960s, Apple in computers in the 1970s, Sun and Cisco in networking in the 1980s, and Netscape, Yahoo!,

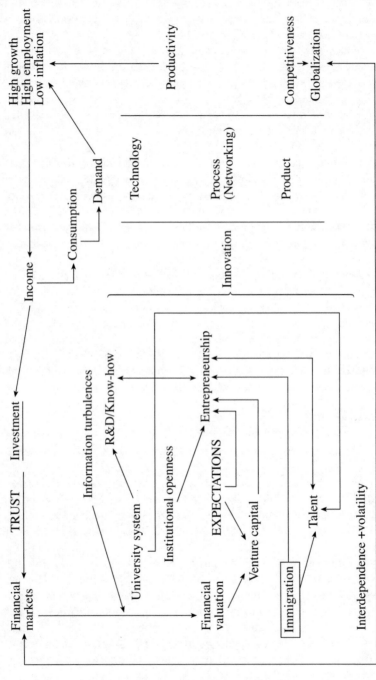

Figure 2.6   The Silicon Valley model of the new economy

EBay, and Google, in the Internet in the 1990s. Silicon Valley concentrates a significant part of the strong American entrepreneurial drive (figure 2.7).

There are also strong supporting structures for new entrepreneurs. They can specialize in quite narrow areas of expertise because there are many companies that have complementary skills. Silicon Valley is based on the network enterprise model where some companies focus on innovation and branding and others focus on subcontracting for these companies. Network enterprises reconfigure their networks of partners based on their changing needs, leaving much of the production to electronics manufacturing companies, such as Solectron. This dynamic adaptation of the network enterprise is possible because of the ready availability of flexible labor: only one-fifth of labor has long-term, non-flexible jobs (Benner, 2002).

The financial and business services of Silicon Valley are experienced in financing and advising new high-tech companies. The venture capitalists, for example, are used to helping dreamers who believe in a new idea turn it into a business reality because many of them are former successful technology entrepreneurs, such as Fairchild's Kleiner (Kleiner, Perkins, Caufield, and Byers) and Valentine (Sequoia) or, more recently, Sun's founder Vinod Khosla. Their help goes far beyond financial assistance: venture capitalists are business counselors who help in developing the business plan, participate on the board, and so on. However, even entrepreneurs need capital to start a business. So, there is still another essential component of the process leading to innovation: finance.

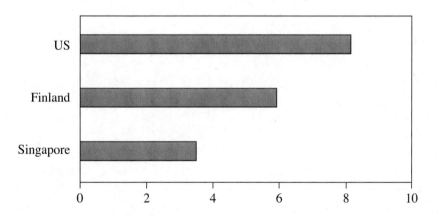

Source: Global Entrepreneurship Monitor 2001

Figure 2.7   Level of start-up activity (% of adult population trying to start a new business), 2001

The financing of innovation

The stock of knowledge depends on society's and firms' investment in research and development. Innovation is, by definition, risky. So, high-risk finance is a fundamental pre-requisite for start-up firms in Silicon Valley. One form of this investment is research and development (R&D) funding. The United States has always invested heavily in innovation. For years, its national R&D investment has topped the world and continues to be considerably above the average for the advanced economies (see figure 2.8). This funding has made the world's leading research in the technology fields possible, with the top universities producing highly talented innovators.

In Silicon Valley, a key innovative role has been played by the two top universities Stanford (private) and the University of California at Berkeley (the leading campus of the state's system). The graduate schools of these two universities, as well as their computer science programs, are consistently ranked among the top five in the United States. Business links with this public research and development. Universities and business have close relations along the lines of Terman's strategy: as leading researchers have joint projects with companies, knowledge about future key areas becomes shared. This knowledge goes in two directions: the top business leaders and engineers also share their knowledge with the universities. For instance, the former chairman of Intel, Andy Grove, has taught at Berkeley. Business also donates funding to universities to further develop human talent.

But the most important element in Silicon Valley is venture capital. Most of the innovative, highly productive firms were start-ups at some point in the past three decades. Venture capital is at the source of entrepreneurship that

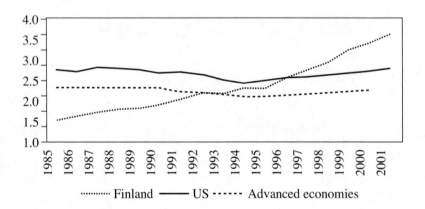

Source: OECD Main Science and Technology Indicators

*Figure 2.8	National R&D investment as a percentage of GDP, 1985–2001*

produces innovation in the practice of business. Venture capital operates on the basis of high expectations of return, so that the many projects that fail are more than compensated for by those that succeed.

The returns are essentially provided by the valuation in financial markets. Here lies both the strength and the weakness of the new economy model. Global, dynamic, interdependent financial markets offer a large pool of capital that can be channeled through venture capital firms into innovative projects, which, if rewarded by high market valuation, often in anticipation of performance, become the endless source of new funding for a high-flying economy. But this strength becomes a fundamental weakness if the valuation process devalues the anticipated performance of the firm.

How and why do financial markets reverse themselves? They are founded on two basic premises: (a) *trust* from investors in the relative stability of the market and in the reliability of the institutions overseeing the market; and (b) *expectation of a return* on investment. During the 1990s, there was a period of relative stability in the United States, in spite of financial crises in several emerging markets, and of widespread optimism after the end of the Cold War, along with the expansion of the global economy. Expectations of returns on technology stocks were high, first because of reasonable assumptions about the role of innovative industries in the new economy; later, because of unwarranted expectations fueled by futurologists and some Internet consultants. The shift of savings to investments in stocks, and new financial instruments assisted by new technologies and computer models, pushed the entire stock market upward. In some cases, since expectations of firms' performance were major sources of valuation, and then financing, some firms engaged in "creative accounting" (namely, "cooking the books"), and some accounting firms condoned these practices. Then, expectations reversed, when it became clear that the dot-com companies were based on a wrong business model, and they brought down with them, in their fall, all other technology stocks, regardless of the actual performance of each of the downgraded companies. Deflation of expectations followed an inflation of expectations.

Simultaneously, geopolitical stability was shattered and the exposure of business abuses (from Enron and Arthur Andersen to ABB and BBV) undermined trust in the institutions of the market. Investors withdrew, drying up the sources of finance for innovation. This prompted the crisis of the new economy and of the Silicon Valley model. The same virtuous circle represented graphically in figure 2.6 became a vicious circle of business failures.

However, *in the midst of the downturn, innovation continued to proceed and productivity growth was sustained*. This is a fundamental feature, both practically and analytically. Practically, while many Silicon Valley firms closed down or had to retrench, laying off tens of thousands of highly skilled workers, the heart of the high-technology industry survived, and seemed to be positioned for a new round of innovation and growth in new market lines and in new areas of the world. Analytically, the key question is why innovation continued, and why productivity growth kept rising at a high rate. The answers to this question may provide the key for the specificity of the Silicon Valley model, and thus we reserve them for our conclusion.

THE FINNISH MODEL

Let us now compare the Finnish model to the Silicon Valley model. At the beginning of this chapter we showed that Finland is one of the leading information economies in the world. Behind this feature there is a specific Finnish model of technological innovation, economic productivity, and social organization.

At the heart of Finnish information technology production is an information technology cluster that consists of approximately 3,000 companies (Ali-Yrkkö et al., 1999). In addition to Nokia, the Finnish information technology companies include tele-operators like TeliaSonera and Elisa, electronics manufacturing service companies like Elcoteq and Flextronics, electronics manufacturers like Tellabs, NK Cables, and Aspocomp, and system integrators like TietoEnator. Table 2.3 presents the top five information technology companies in Finland. There are also many innovative start-up companies, such as the security software houses F-Secure and SSH Communications, which do not yet make it onto the top five list.

Currently, Nokia is by far the biggest information technology company in Finland. It forms the core of the Finnish IT industry. In fact, Nokia's partner network includes three hundred Finnish IT companies. However, this figure also means that the Finnish IT cluster is by no means limited to, or only dependent on, Nokia. And being a partner of Nokia does not necessarily mean being

Table 2.3   *Top five Finnish information technology companies (revenues for 2003)*

Company	Industry	Revenues (EUR billion)
1 Nokia	Mobile phones and networks	29.5
2 TeliaSonera	Tele-operator	9.0
3 Elcoteq	EMS	2.2
4 Elisa	Tele-operator	1.5
5 TietoEnator	System integration	1.4

Source: Based on annual reports

wholly devoted to, or dependent on, Nokia. For example, it would be wrong to say that the growth of the tele-operators TeliaSonera and Elisa or the system integrator TietoEnator – all cooperating with Nokia in some projects – has been based on Nokia. The electronics manufacturing service companies Elcoteq and Flextronics also have other customers than Nokia, and so on.

Some 3 percent of the Finnish labor force work in these IT companies. Again, Nokia is the biggest employer, but it still has a limited role. In 2002, Nokia employed 24,000 workers in Finland, which represents approximately 1 percent of the total labor force. There are many others working in Nokia's network of partners but, as these companies also have other customers, their employment is mainly independent of Nokia.

Elements of the Finnish Model

In a simplified form, the main elements of the Finnish model can be represented graphically as figure 2.9. At the center of the Finnish model is innovation: technological, product, and process (organization) innovation. Ultimately, technological and product innovation combined with the new network form of organization have been behind the growth of Finnish productivity (Koski et al., 2002). This is especially true in mobile telecommunications where Finland is the world leader. Finnish innovativeness is also one of the highest in the world, as measured by the receipts of royalties and license fees per capita.

Innovation is based on talented people, the availability of finance for new risky projects, and a culture of innovation. The existence of these three conditions depends on the nature and connections between the university, business, and the state, as shown in figure 2.9.

The state has a double function both as a developmental and a welfare state. As a welfare state, Finnish policy has been to invest in a free, public, and high-quality education system that gives people equal opportunities to learn and thus incorporates the potential of the population more fully than in most other countries. The university system includes 70 percent of the young generation, with over a quarter of these students in technology fields, and thus forms the human talent needed to continue innovation in Finnish business. Because of universal health, unemployment, and pension protection, in addition to the system of collective bargaining that generates stable industrial relations (80 percent of the labor force remain unionized), people are better prepared for the big structural changes that the information economy requires.

In its role as a developer of the information economy (developmental state), the government's key actor is the Science and Technology Policy Council. Largely under its guidance, national R&D investment increased from 1 percent of GDP at the beginning of the 1980s to 3.6 percent of GDP by 2001.

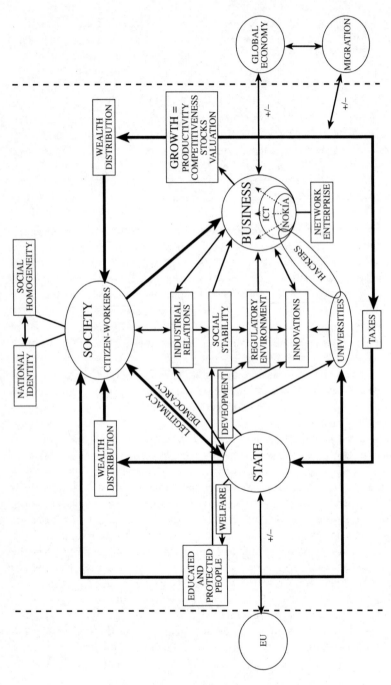

Figure 2.9 The Finnish model of the information society

68

The state has also encouraged a culture of innovation through its policy of an open regulatory environment. The Finnish state actively pushed the Finnish mobile telecommunications companies to develop an open transnational mobile phone network (first NMT, then GSM). From the beginning, the state also maintained an open market so that, unlike in most other countries, the equipment manufacturers had to compete with each other, which resulted in fast, competitive development. The state also liberalized mobile service provision earlier than other countries and thus also created rapid, competitive development in mobile phone services.

Although the state has played an active role, it has not led all the developments. Rather, the Science and Technology Policy Council, which consists of top representatives from government, industry, labor, and the university world, represents a wider Finnish view of technology needs and is thus also the vision of industry. For example, pressure from industry in the Council is also behind the growth of human talent in Finnish universities, and the close cooperation between business and the universities is at a higher level than the average for the advanced economies. In this way, information about new areas of innovation flows both ways, as well as the work and teaching talent.

Business is also the primary financier of innovation. In fact, business investment in R&D has grown even faster than investment by the state based on its own interests. Thus, the share of national R&D investment by the business sector is more than 70 percent, which is slightly more than in the "business-driven" United States. After the initial public push, the capital needed to finance the turning of innovations into products has come almost entirely from within companies and from private venture capitalists, which comprise 85 percent of Finnish venture capital investments.

Of course, ultimately, innovation turns into business through an entrepreneurial culture, which is the final element to be added to the Finnish field of innovation. Entrepreneurialism includes both start-up entrepreneurialism and the entrepreneurial spirit within a large company, as was witnessed in Nokia's rise from the brink of bankruptcy in the early 1990s. In Finland, the latter form of entrepreneurialism has been especially strong as we shall see.

However, the real core of the Finnish model is a virtuous circle between the welfare state and the information economy. The welfare state produces highly skilled people to continue to create growth in business and this growth makes it possible to continue to finance the welfare state, as well as the state and business investment in innovation. Another way of putting this is to say that the welfare state contributes a sustainable basis for growth (as shown in figure 2.9), both in an economic and in a social sense: the welfare state makes development socially more inclusive, and, as people feel more protected, they are more ready for the social restructuring that the information economy requires. Inclusion generates trust, which is ultimately the main requirement for the financial markets to prosper. In fact, in a highly socially contradictory world, people lose their faith in the future, and this undermines positive expectations about the future, which is the fundamental driver of the financial markets. Thus, the state can have a positive impact on expectations in the financial markets through the trust it generates when most people can see themselves included as beneficiaries of economic growth.

Let us analyze these connections in more detail. At the center of the Finnish model is innovation, growing in a "field of innovation." The key elements of this field are highly skilled people, finance, and the culture of innovation.

The Process of Innovation

Talented people

The Finnish Science and Technology Policy Council has always emphasized investment in human talent. Here, it has represented the view of the state, industry, and the education system itself. As a result, Finnish investment in R&D rose from a low 1 percent of GDP in the early 1980s to a leading 3.6 percent of GDP in 2001, which is almost double the average for the advanced economies (see figure 2.8).

The basis of the Finnish innovation system is a public, free, and high-quality education system. In the OECD PISA comparison of the performance of students, Finnish students topped all of the measured topics, from literacy to mathematics and science. The proportion of "excluded" or those who perform at a functionally uneducated level is the lowest in the world. In Finland, student performance is the least dependent on the school that the student attends.

The university system is also highly inclusive. The state has invested in a public, free, and high-quality university system, where students receive a student grant. Since the 1960s, the university system has expanded considerably to 56 institutions which now include 70 percent of the young generation. Financing has pushed education toward the technology fields and, as a result, 27 percent of Finnish university students graduate in mathematics, science, or engineering – which is about double the average for the advanced economies.

In addition, according to the OECD Science, Technology and Industry Scoreboard, there is also very close cooperation between universities and business, which share knowledge about future key areas more effectively than in the advanced economies in general. Nokia is a case in point that illustrates how this interaction in R&D works between universities and companies. Figure 2.10 presents the dynamics of one representative project which has included funding from the state (and therefore its information is publicly available). Although Nokia's R&D network is essentially global nowadays and includes such nodes as Stanford University, the University of California at Berkeley, the Massachusetts Institute of Technology, the University of Tokyo,

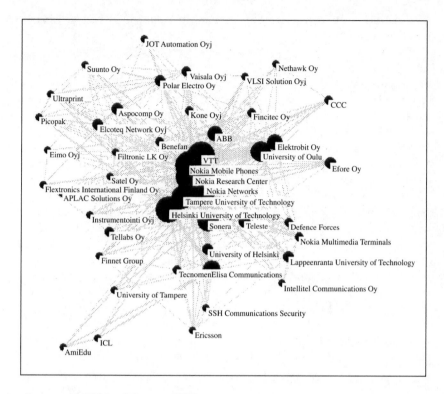

JOT Automation Oyj

Suunto Oy

Nethawk Oy

Vaisala Oyj
Polar Electro Oy

VLSI Solution Oyj

Ultraprint

CCC

Aspocomp Oy

Kone Oyj

Fincitec Oy

Picopak

Elcoteq Network Oyj

Benefan

ABB

Eimo Oyj

Filtronic LK Oy

Elektrobit Oy
University of Oulu

VTT

Efore Oy

Nokia Mobile Phones

Satel Oy

Nokia Research Center

Flextronics International Finland Oy

Nokia Networks

APLAC Solutions Oy

Tampere University of Technology

Helsinki University of Technology

Instrumentointi Oyj

Sonera   Teleste

Defence Forces

Tellabs Oy

Nokia Multimedia Terminals

Finnet Group

University of Helsinki

Lappeenranta University of Technology

TecnomenElisa Communications

University of Tampere

Intellitel Communications Oy

SSH Communications Security

Ericsson

ICL

AmiEdu

Source: Ali-Yrkkö and Hermans (2002)

Figure 2.10   An example of Nokia project networking

and Beijing University of Posts and Telecommunications, its core (more than half) is still the interaction in the Finnish innovation network between Nokia and universities like Helsinki University of Technology, Tampere University of Technology, the University of Oulu, VTT, and Nokia's partner companies.

Finally, the Finnish education system has not only produced highly skilled people to innovate and work in business, the state, and the education and research system itself, but it has also allowed individuals to be important technology innovators. There is an especially strong "hacker culture" in Finland, led by names like Linus Torvalds (the creator of the Linux operating system), Jarkko Oikarinen (the inventor of Internet chat), and Tatu Ylonen (the developer of encrypted Internet communication), who were all university students who played with new ideas and then networked with other like-minded individuals around the world. As there is no immediate financial pressure on students, they can afford the time to experiment. It took Linus Torvalds eight years to finish his masters thesis but, using this freedom, he created the Linux operating system.

Financing the process of innovation
The second key factor in the process of innovation is finance. The state has also invested in the financing of innovation, as reflected in the high level of national R&D investment. Two public agencies have been formed to take responsibility for finance: Tekes (the National Technology Agency) finances risky new R&D projects, and Sitra has proactively developed the Finnish venture capital market by setting an example as a "public capitalist." They have both been given an autonomous status so that, although they report to the Ministry of Trade and Industry and to Parliament, they are not directly part of the governmental bureaucracy and can thus make independent decisions to react more dynamically to changing needs. Internally, they are also more like network organizations: in all, they have only 260 employees and they network with other partners based on the needs of each project.

Nokia is a good example of how the state has helped Finnish companies to invest in longer-term innovation. At the beginning of the 1980s, the development of the GSM standard was started, and, as has been noted, the development of an open mobile phone standard was considered very critical by the Finnish state, which therefore invested heavily in its development. As can be seen in figure 2.11, the public Tekes support helped Nokia to take a

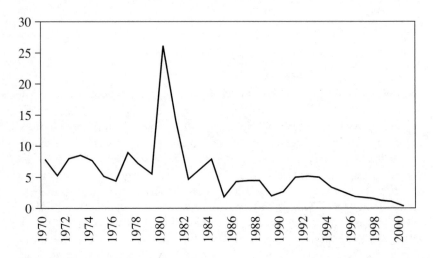

Source: Ali-Yrkkö and Hermans (2002)

Figure 2.11   Share of Tekes funding in Nokia's R&D (%)

risk in creating the new GSM standard. The figure also shows how public funding also helped Nokia to continue its R&D investment during the severe financial trouble it experienced that coincided with the Finnish recession of 1981–4. Still, as we can also see in figure 2.11, Nokia has always been responsible for most of its own R&D funding, and, excluding the exceptional public investment of the 1980s, the public share has on average been less than 5 percent, and in 2000 it constituted only 0.3 percent, of Nokia's total R&D investment.

In fact, Finnish financing of innovation has for decades been primarily led by the private sector. As can be seen in figure 2.12, private investment has, for a long time, been more than half of the total and has been a slightly larger share than in the "business-driven" United States. Figure 2.5 illustrates this fact from a different angle: the role of public funding in business R&D projects has always remained at the low level of about 5 percent, which is lower than in the United States.

Whereas Tekes has helped in the development of Finnish R&D financing, Sitra has done the same for the venture capital market. Until the early 1990s, Finland's venture capital market was very underdeveloped and Sitra started the push for the formation of this capital, which is critical for the financing of high-risk innovation. Gradually, the venture capital market has grown and is today led by the private sector, which now has an 85 percent share of total investments. However, compared to Silicon Valley, the venture capital market is not sufficiently advanced.

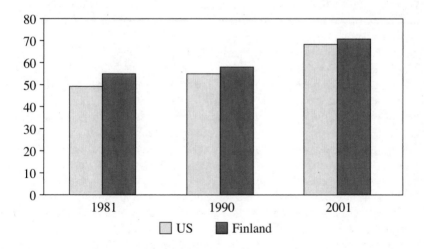

Figure 2.12   Private R&D investment as a share of the total (%), 1981–2001

The culture of innovation

The third key factor in the innovation field is the culture of innovation. A high level of knowledge turns into new innovations only if people are motivated to use their creativity. In Finland, a positive culture of innovation has encouraged people like Jorma Nieminen, the pioneer of the mobile phone at Nokia, or Linus Torvalds, the creator of the Linux operating system, to innovate both in business and in the university.

Again, the state, business, and people all contribute to the culture of innovation. On the government's part, one of the most critical developments for the Finnish breakthrough in mobile telecommunications was the push for an open Nordic mobile standard and market. At the turn of the 1960s, this resulted in cooperation between the Nordic national postal and telecommunication companies to create the NMT (Nordic Mobile Telephone) network. This became the world's first transnational automatic mobile communication network and, in fact, was the world's biggest market in the number of users at the beginning of the 1980s (Pulkkinen, 1997). More importantly, it was a network based on an open standard that was open to competition before others. From the beginning, it was open for all equipment manufacturers to compete, and Nokia had to take on such big challengers as Ericsson, Motorola, Mitsubishi, Panasonic, NET, and Siemens both in mobile network and phone technology. In the same way, when Finland liberalized mobile phone service provision in 1990, the Finnish company Radiolinja (part of Elisa Communications) became the world's first commercial GSM operator, and mobile tele-operators have had to compete based on their services. When the GSM mobile revolution began on a global scale, Nokia already had years of experience in transnational open competition and was especially well positioned to take the world leadership.

Fundamentally, the state has facilitated the innovation of highly educated people in the universities and business. In companies, innovativeness is based on a work and management culture of innovation. This is well illustrated by the case of Nokia. In the 1960s, a few innovators started to believe that in the future communications might be wireless, and they persisted in this vision so strongly that Nokia set up a special laboratory to develop this technology. The laboratory was full of young engineers who were enthusiastic about the new idea and joined forces to make it happen. The laboratory had close links with the research taking place at Helsinki University of Technology, so like-minded professors and students kept joining the lab.

There were also other places that gave their engineers the freedom and security to be creative, which ultimately became merged with the Nokia lab. One of these places was another big Finnish company called Salora, which invested in the development of mobile phones at the same time. In fact, its development, led by the pioneer innovator Jorma Nieminen, was in some respects more advanced than Nokia's but neither one was big enough to succeed globally on its own. Therefore, in 1979, Nokia and Salora saw that they had to join forces to compete in the new NMT network market and started a joint company called Mobira. Soon, Nokia was able to acquire the company entirely and thus concentrated the innovators and the culture of innovation in mobile phones in Finland. Nokia's first successful product was the Mobira Talkman phone for the NMT network and the global "killer application" was the Nokia 2100 GSM phone series in 1992–3.

A work and management culture of innovation is something that has been strongly emphasized by the new leadership at Nokia, which lifted Nokia from near-bankruptcy to be one of the most successful global companies. In the process of finding a way to survive the crisis of the old industrial conglomerate model that Nokia had become by the beginning of the 1990s, an analysis was made in order to define the key characteristics behind Nokia's earlier success. The result was the so-called "Nokia way," which very much summed up the spirit of the early innovators of Nokia lab, and was seen as the work and management culture for the dynamic network enterprise that Nokia wanted to become.

Beyond the rhetoric, the key content of this restructuring can be summed up in the following way. By the late 1980s, Nokia had become a hierarchical conglomerate of eleven largely unrelated industries in mature markets, led by an old industrial-patron style of management. This structure and management culture meant that Nokia had become very undynamic in reacting to, and even less in leading, its markets. The new CEO Jorma Ollila brought with him a new way of thinking about the company structure and its management. First, he determined that Nokia should become "telecom-oriented, global, focused, and value-added." Following this vision, Nokia gradually sold off all its divisions other than mobile telecommunications. Another key principle that Ollila introduced was "structure drives strategy." As a result, Nokia started to turn into a network enterprise that focused on the core innovation, branding, and production and networked with other companies for the rest of its needs. Nokia's market, production and R&D are global, so that, currently, the network includes thousands of partners from production and R&D partners to clients (mobile phone dealers and network buyers).

What differentiates Nokia from many other companies is the fact that, in production, it concentrates on the key mobile technology production and buys all the other components from its subcontractors. Nokia's own R&D is also much more product-oriented than is generally the case: Nokia leaves the basic research to universities and then cooperates with them closely (this is guaranteed by the fact that the Nokia Research Center has to earn 70 percent of its finance by selling its research to the business R&D units). But the main difference is in the management of the network enterprise. There are many companies now that have quite a similar external structure to Nokia's but they have faced severe problems in keeping the network together.

Behind Nokia's ability to use the networking model flexibly and effectively is a management culture that is suited to orchestrating a network enterprise. First, Nokia as a whole could be described as a dynamic network oriented toward picking up, realizing, and creating signals about future expectations. The key is "efficient logistics," which is much more than traditional logistics: it means transparent and rapid sharing of information about expectations within Nokia's network of customers, production, and R&D (increasingly through electronic networks). In fact, in addition to increasing flexibility, Nokia's main reason for networking with other producers and R&D institutions is the sharing of signals about future expectations. This efficient sharing of information makes it possible to reflect the changes in the markets immediately in R&D and production.

Secondly, Nokia is internally a network organization, offering a platform for innovators to network with each other and with production and branding based on the needs of each project. Nokia has mainly developed its innovation capacity based on an internal innovation culture, which attracts the best talent to join it, in contrast to the Cisco model that depends on an innovation strategy of acquisition which faces serious difficulties when the value of the company declines, limiting the financial margin for acquisitions. What drives the varying formation of Nokia's internal innovation networks, which then connect to external networks without internalizing them, is the "Nokia way" or the Nokia work and management culture. Its three main principles are "achievement" (forming networks based on shared ambitious goals), "respect" (trusting people and encouraging them to take risks in an environment where failing is permitted), and "continuous learning" (being ready to constantly challenge and change one's thinking and wanting to surpass earlier levels of achievement, both individually and collectively).

A critical part of an innovation culture, in addition to the state and business, is the intellectual ability of the population. Innovation requires an education system that encourages a culture of innovation, creativity, pursuing one's new ideas, thinking differently. Although, in a complete form, this is hardly the case in any country, the Finnish education system has proved to be supportive enough for people to begin creating and implementing their own ideas. The cases of Linux, Internet relay chat, and encrypted Internet communications are good examples of this. Behind all of these ideas were young university students who were passionate about their new creative idea and then networked with other like-minded individuals on the Net. Linus Torvalds has explained the driving force of Linux hackers like this: "The reason that Linux hackers do something is that they find it to be very interesting, and they like to share this interesting thing with others . . . This is how you have this fundamental Linux networking effect where you have a lot of hackers working together because they enjoy what they do." It is these kinds of people with creative passion working together that make the innovations.

Entrepreneurialism

The final key element to add to the field of innovation is entrepreneurialism: turning new ideas into practice. We can talk about business entrepreneurialism, public entrepreneurialism as well as citizen entrepreneurialism.

Business entrepreneurialism is about turning ideas into business. This means both within big companies and by starting up new companies. Nokia's transformation from the early 1990s is a good example of an entrepreneurial culture within a big company. In fact, in the Finnish case, this type of entrepreneurialism has been especially strong, as witnessed also by leading tele-operators such as TeliaSonera and Elisa.

However, start-up entrepreneurialism is also critical for a flourishing culture of entrepreneurialism and this has clearly been a problem in Finland. Figure 2.7 shows the low level of start-up activity in Finland; figure 2.13 shows that there is, additionally, a low level of motivation to become an entrepreneur. A prime example of this combination of a strong innovation culture with a low level of entrepreneurial motivation is the story of the first graphical Web browser, which was developed by Helsinki University of Technology students a good while before Netscape, but they were not interested in developing it into a product and starting a business. There is also a problem with expectations: people take

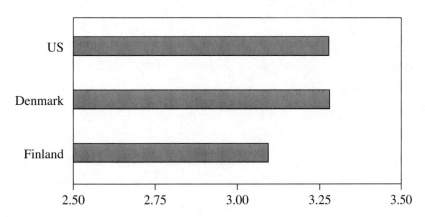

Source: Global Entrepreneurship Monitor 2001

Figure 2.13   Entrepreneurial motivation (scale 1–5)

personal risks to be entrepreneurs if there is an expectation of high rewards, but the Finnish state discourages this through high taxation.

The low level of start-up entrepreneurialism is clearly one of the biggest challenges for the Finnish model. However, figure 2.13 also shows that a low entrepreneurial culture is not a necessary consequence of the welfare state. For example, Denmark, which has a generous welfare state, equals the US level of entrepreneurial motivation. A related problem of entrepreneurialism is the fact that the venture capital market still lacks both resources and the kind of exper-tise that entrepreneurs turned venture capitalists bring in Silicon Valley to help start-ups in a rapid global breakthrough. Figure 2.14 shows how the venture capital market is smaller in Finland than in Europe in general. Again, this is not a necessary feature of the welfare state. One of the world's biggest venture capital markets is in Sweden (in relative terms) and the liberal Ireland is behind Finland.

Public entrepreneurialism refers to putting innovation into practice in the public services. However, although there has been some innovation to get the public services through the recession of the early 1990s, generally the public sector cannot be described as a "culture of innovation" or as having an "entre-preneurial spirit." This problem is much bigger for Finland than for the United States because of its large public sector and aging population.

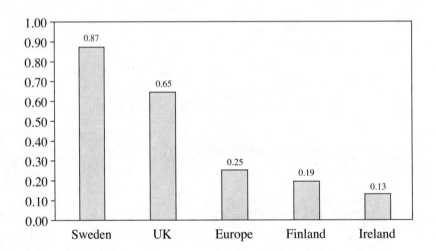

Source: European Private Equity and Venture Capital Association

Figure 2.14   Venture capital market in Europe as a whole and in selected European countries

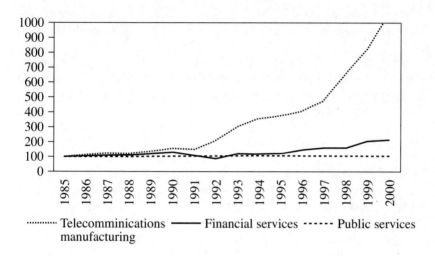

.... Telecomminications ——— Financial services ‑‑‑‑‑ Public services
manufacturing

Source: ETLA (The Research Institute of the Finnish Economy)

Figure 2.15   Labor productivity growth in Finland (1985 = 100)

So far, the state has invested in the Finnish capacity for innovation that has made high growth in manufacturing productivity possible. However, it has not been a two-way street. The state is not renewing its own structures or encouraging innovation to increase productivity and make totally new things possible also in the public services. Figure 2.15 shows this well. While productivity growth in telecommunications manufacturing has been phenomenal, there has been practically no growth at all in public services.

While it is more difficult to increase the productivity of services, the significant growth in productivity in the financial services sector shows that it is possible. The real issue about the low level of productivity in public services is not a lack of IT infrastructure: Finnish public-sector expenditure (administration) on ICT is already the third highest in the European Union. The main issue is that there can be no increase in productivity just by the addition of IT without organizational renewal, which is possible only through a new management culture. This has been shown for private companies, and we can safely assume that this is also the case for public services. In fact, what is needed is product innovation combined with organizational innovation which both require a culture of innovation and entrepreneurialism.

The low level of start-up entrepreneurialism and the low level of productivity in public services are linked problems. As the Finnish population ages, the costs of the welfare state will rise and become unbearable unless there is new innovation to increase productivity in the public services and new start-up entrepreneurialism to create economic growth. In fact, in the alternative case, this will become a trap: taxes will go up and decrease further entrepreneurialism.

Ultimately, the lack of entrepreneurialism in public services results not only from the weak culture of innovation but also from the fact that there are no positive incentives to create new ways of doing things. There are no rewards for public innovators for doing anything better.

Finland in the Global Networks

Another clear problem in the Finnish model is the asymmetrical connection between local and global flows of talent and finance. While the Finnish economy is well connected to the global flows of financing, the same is not true for the global flows of talent.

Even if one might argue that, from a purely technological point of view, Finland is, as the leader in the mobile revolution, as interesting a place as Silicon Valley for technology innovators to come to change the world, Finland's image is not even close to Silicon Valley's. Finns often think that the weather, language barriers, and a northern location discourage immigration. This is clearly in contradiction with the worldwide experience of immigration. Immigrants, and particularly immigrant entrepreneurs, are ready to go wherever opportunities arise, thinking of themselves and of their children. The reality is that Finland has a very restrictive immigration policy that has put the government at odds with companies in the high-technology sector, which have much need for foreign talent as they deplete the stock of top Finnish scientists and engineers. In addition, surveys in Finland show a negative attitude toward foreigners in a sizable proportion of the population (Castells and Himanen, 2002), thus undermining the chances of the Finnish network society becoming networked around the world: only 2.5 percent of Finland's residents are foreigners or foreign-born, which is one of the lowest percentages among the advanced economies.

For Finland, the process of attraction is largely working in reverse, which means that Finnish companies and talent are transferring their know-how to the rest of the world by locating production elsewhere, for instance in the United States or in China, and by establishing a global network, connected to multiple markets, while keeping a central node in Finland. Cultural identity and strong support from the Finnish government provide a good foundation for this specific model of globalization. However, the model is sustainable only as long as Finland continues to produce Finnish innovators who are willing to use their talent for industrial purposes and remain attached to Finland. The capacity of the Finnish state to generate loyalty to its culture and to its nation is the necessary antidote to counter the centrifugal force embedded in the Finnish model of networking. Otherwise, the networks will process outgoing flows of young people and incoming flows of capital.

CONCLUSION: CONTRASTING MODELS

Both Finland and Silicon Valley offer paths toward technological innovation, networking organization, and high economic productivity under the conditions of the informational paradigm. In both cases, government and non-profit institutional actors were critical in starting the process, and private business became the key actor of production, innovation, and competition. So a comparison of the two models should not be read as opposing the private and the public sectors as agencies of the development process. Neither is the role of universities different: they are central sources of knowledge and talent in both models, confirming the essential role of universities in the knowledge economy. Innovation is also a common factor, and it could not be otherwise because without innovation there is no information-driven economy. There are, however, two major differences. One concerns the sources of innovation. The other concerns the relationship between the world of innovation and entrepreneurship and society at large.

In Finland, the heart of the model is the welfare state and the legitimacy of government acting on behalf of the nation, a nation affirming its cultural identity in a rapidly globalizing world. Innovators come from the full support given by the government to a high-quality, public education system, to universities, and to research, in close partnership with business.

In Silicon Valley, in spite of the importance of the military connection at the outset, and its enduring strategic role, the source of innovation is the individual entrepreneur, tapping into the resources of knowledge, social networks, and the supporting services and firms that have accumulated in the region over half a century of relentless innovation. These individuals come to the Valley from all over the world. But many of them are a special kind of individual: they are innovators, this is why they come to Silicon Valley. And since they keep coming, the culture of the region is increasingly a culture of innovation, and a culture of entrepreneurialism. This is why immigration is crucial, and this is why Silicon Valley can thrive in the middle of the paradox of being the technology hub of the world while being dependent on the inferior public education system of California, which, for the most part, is not at the level of other advanced countries.

Not that all innovators are foreign immigrants. Most are American immigrants, and there are also thousands of California-grown innovators who find their place right where they are – or a little further away, in Silicon Valley, in the Bay Area, or in San Diego, and Los Angeles, around the various milieux of innovation of California. Because they are innovators, they keep innovating in the bad times as well as the good times. They expect to be rewarded, but this is not what drives them. In a very broad sense, it is the hacker culture, as defined in chapter 19 of this volume, that characterizes Silicon Valley and the universities, firms, and research centers around the Silicon Valley networks. It is creativity for the sake of creativity because innovation is enjoyment and empowerment, and the only way in which an individual, distrustful of the state, and affirmed in his or her own, chosen identity, can grasp life around them. This is why discoveries and innovation kept continuing in 2000–2003, in spite of dark economic prospects, political uncertainty, and a reduction in venture capital finance. And because innovation does not stop, the engine of wealth will eventually be restarted.

It does not happen without costs. This is the dark side of the Silicon Valley model. The moment of crisis, collective or personal, finds many individuals, and their families, unprotected. So, it is a winner's society that accumulates losers on its margins in growing numbers. And since there is a deep-seated distrust of government, the resources of the public sector keep dwindling, particularly in relation to the growing costs of public needs. This is the other paradox of California: the most dynamic economy in the world, submitted to a structural fiscal crisis of the state because of the model of individual accumulation of the wealth generated from individual entrepreneurialism.

Finland, of course, protects its people under all circumstances. But in order to generate wealth it has to induce innovation and entrepreneurialism in the hope that business will be able to channel the potential of young innovators. But innovation also requires freedom, and if young Finns decide to use their freedom and talent to innovate in culture and in the arts, it will be up to business to find a way of making this cultural content into a globally competitive industry.

Both models seem to have fundamental challenges, and interesting times, ahead. Silicon Valley will have to find ways to link up individual projects with the institutions of society, and induce solidarity among its members, to be socially sustainable. Finland will have to reconcile its national identity and welfare state with an opening up to the world, based on two-way channels of communication, and with a stimulus to entrepreneurship as a source of wealth creation to make the welfare state economically sustainable. Yet, both models share the distinction of having pioneered alternative ways of development of the knowledge economy and of the network society.

REFERENCES

Ali-Yrkkö, Jyrki and Hermans, Raine (2002) *Nokia in the Finnish Information System.* Helsinki: ETLA.

— —, Paija, Laura, Reilly, Catherine, and Ylä-Anttila, Pekka (2000) *Nokia: A Big Company in a Small Country*. Helsinki: Taloustieto.

Benner, Chris (2002) *Work in the New Economy: Flexible Labor Markets in Silicon Valley*. Oxford: Blackwell.

Brynjolfsson, Erik and Hitt, Lorin M. (2000) "Computing Productivity: Firm-level Evidence," Cambridge, MA: MIT–Sloan School Center for E-business, working paper.

Castells, Manuel (1989) *The Informational City: Information Technology, Economic Restructuring, and the Urban Regional Process*. Oxford: Blackwell.

— — (2001) *The Internet Galaxy*. Oxford: Oxford University Press.

— — and Hall, Peter (1994) *Technopoles of the World: The Making of Twenty-first Century Industrial Complexes*. London: Routledge.

— — and Himanen, Pekka (2002) *The Information Society and the Welfare State: The Finnish Model*. Oxford: Oxford University Press.

Gordon, Richard (1994) *Informationalization, Multinationalization, Globalization: Contradictory World Economies and New Spatial Divisions of Labor*. Santa Cruz, CA: University of California Center for the Study of Global Transformations, working paper no. 94.

Jorgenson, Dale and Stiroh, Kevin (2000) *Raising the Speed Limit: US Economic Growth in the Information Age*. Brookings Papers on Economic Activity, volume 2. Washington, DC: The Brookings Institution.

— — and Yip, Eric (2000) "Whatever Happened to Productivity? Investment and Growth in the G-7," in E. R. Dean et al. (2000) *New Developments in Productivity Analysis*. Chicago, IL: University of Chicago Press.

Koski, Heli, Rouvinen, Petri, and Ylä-Anttila, Pekka (2002) *Tieto & Talous: Mitä uudesta taloudesta jäi*. Helsinki: Edita.

Lécuyer, Christophe (2000) "Fairchild Semiconductor and its Influence," in Chong-Moon Lee, William F. Miller, Marguerite Gong Hancock, and Henry S. Rowen (eds), *The Silicon Valley Edge: A Habitat for Innovation and Entrepreneurship*. Stanford, CA: Stanford University Press.

Organization for Economic Co-operation and Development (OECD) (2001) *Knowledge and Skills for Life: First Results from PISA 2000*. Paris: OECD.

Pulkkinen, Matti (1997) *The Breakthrough of Nokia Mobile Phones*. Helsinki: Helsinki School of Economics and Business Administration.

Saxenian, Anna Lee (1994) *Regional Advantage: Culture and Competition in Silicon Valley and Route 128*. Cambridge, MA: Harvard University Press.

— — (1999) *Immigrant Entrepreneurs in Silicon Valley*. San Francisco: Public Policy Institute of California.

— — (2002) *Local and Global Networks of Immigrant Professionals in Silicon Valley*. San Francisco, CA: Public Policy Institute of California.

Sichel, Daniel (1997) *The Computer Revolution: An Economic Perspective*. Washington, DC: The Brookings Institution.

United Nations Development Programme (UNDP) (2001) *Human Development Report 2001*. Oxford: Oxford University Press.

Zook, Matthew (2004) *The Geography of the Internet Industry*. Oxford: Blackwell.

3. The Russian network society

Elena Vartanova

Recent decades have been marked by the emergence of much research on the information society which has put technological, economic, and media developments into the focus of international academic discourse (Webster, 1995). However, its ambiguity becomes evident, especially in comparison with already-existing theories of post-industrial, post-capitalist, globalized societies (Bell, 1960; Drucker, 1993; Giddens, 1993). The concept of the network society has brought a new perspective into academic discourse by focusing on the complexity and multiplicity of interrelations among a variety of social agents acting in a modern society, thus intertwining contradictory driving forces into an interconnected reality. Technology and telecommunications, a globalized economy and labor, nation-states and non-governmental civic organizations, new social and cultural movements, all have been reconsidered through their interrelations within a network structure that has become the backbone infrastructure of a modern globalized world (Castells, 1996–8). The concept of the network society applied in social research, as Castells and Kiselyova (2000) have shown, has become a universal characteristic of modern social reality and structures regardless of their national or economic origins.

For Russia, as for other countries of the former Soviet region, the concept of a network society has emerged as an academic challenge for several reasons. The collapse of the USSR led to a total change of intellectual paradigms and posed many new questions, especially in the field of social research. Although the antagonism between capitalism and socialism, or statism as Castells (1996–8) has termed it, is no longer a core element of the global system, the nature of present worldwide transformations is still approached by many Russian academics through a concept of dichotomy. Russia is often viewed as a society of clashing antagonisms: between East and West, understood first and foremost as Christian and technologically advanced Europe (Kara-Mourza, 2001), democracy and authoritarianism, industrialism and post-industrialism (Inozemtsev, 1999, 2001), center and periphery (Neklessa, 1999), national and global (Segbers, 1999; Delyagin, 2001; Neklessa, 2001; Rantanen, 2002). Some scholars, however, argue that present Russian society can no longer be described by a commonly shared definition, but should be characterized primarily as a mosaic and chaotic one (Pokrovsky, 2001).

There is an evident gap between theoretical knowledge and an empirical analysis of the transformations occurring in Russia, and it is impossible to analyze the Russian transition only through an opposition of conflicting driving forces. For contemporary Russia, the concept of a network society is especially valuable because it adds new perspectives to the analysis of continuing internal changes by placing them in a global environment and underlining the significance of changes in the economy, politics, the cultural milieu, and the social strategies of the states inspired by progress in information technology. For Russian scholars, the network society is also a concept that allows them to avoid the transitional specifics of the post-Soviet period and include Russia in the general context of globalization (Semenov, 2002).

The network society applied to Russian circumstances could promote better understanding of the existing complexity of modern Russian society. One of the key conflicts has emerged from a contradiction between the centralization of state governance and surveillance dictated by the size, economic inconsistencies, multi-dimensional structure, and multi-ethnicity of Russian society and the decentralizing tendencies of the country, brought on by the logic of contemporary economic life and technological development. From this point of view, a network society, understood by Russian intellectuals as an interaction of social and economic groups – clusters in a new telecommunications environment – permits us to reconsider the role of traditional centers of power (Semenov, 2002: 272).

The idea of decentralized and non-hierarchical societal communication implied in the concept of the network society might also help us to understand some national peculiarities, which have paved the way to the present reality. In this context it is worth remembering a particular Russian tradition of creating informal networks in the economy and in social life as a form of individual or group opposition to legitimate structures of the Soviet *nomenklatura* state. As a form of informal group unity, opposed to state bureaucracy and legal power constructions, unofficial networks represented a challenge, though semi-legal, to hierarchical institutions of the state or business. Paradoxically, the informal exchange of favors, known in the Soviet Union as *blat*, and other forms of informal arrangements popular among Soviet people (Ledeneva, 2000), promoted the philosophy of a horizontal society much wider than any recent political decisions by the Russian state or government on e-society. Certainly, there are no direct links between the informal networks for the exchange of favors and the concept of a network society, but the traditions of flexible social relations, the superiority of interpersonal contacts over established social links, allows Russians more easily to adapt to the new corporate and social mentality emerging within the framework of a network society.

Broadly speaking, for contemporary Russia, the concept of the network society remains an intellectual hypothesis, but at the same time it has particular value in describing recent trends.

THE INTERNET IN RUSSIA: FRAGMENTED GLOBALIZATION

Major driving forces behind the Russian transformation were "economic reforms," an uneasy combination of privatization, liberalization, and decentralization. However, widespread expectations of economic growth of the early 1990s have not been realized, and, compared to other former socialist economies of Eastern and Central Europe, and especially compared to the socialist economy of China, the Russian economy looks weak and unsuccessful.

The failure of the Russian transition has numerous explanations, and many of them are significant for understanding the progress of the new economy and network society in Russia. After a decade of change, the structure of the Russian economy has remained outdated and based on natural resource sectors which still play a decisive role in Russian exports; oil and gas account for over half of all exports. National industrial production felt by almost 60 percent. The magnitude of the decline in GDP is still unclear, but some sources approximate it at the level of 54 percent in the period 1990–2000 (Inozemtsev, 2000: 266–8, 272–3). Poverty and economic inequality have divided Russian society and produced political disappointment, moral depression, and social escapism. As a result, Russia has got the worst of all possible worlds – an enormous decline in output and an enormous increase in inequality.

While Russian financial and political elites have become increasingly involved in the globalized economy and in their everyday practices have benefited from progress in information technology and the global communication revolution, the national economy as a whole has been transformed from an industrial giant into an oil and gas supplier. Domestic consumption and investments are not yet strong enough, and as a result many industries experience a lack of finance to update their infrastructure and increase productivity. This is especially true for hi-tech industries where the general difficulties of the Russian economy are most visible. A low level of technology, and lack of production of competitive products and services for global markets, are often accompanied by high educational and intellectual potential among employees. Therefore, the outcomes of the Russian transition are economically unbalanced, and scholars stress that the Russian economy is far from being a knowledge-based or information economy, but continues to be an industrial and resource-based one (Castells and Kiselyova, 2001; Stiglitz, 2002).

All this has led to a drastic decline in living standards for the majority of Russians. In early 2003, about 60 percent of Russians were living below a minimum living standard, according to estimated data provided by the Russian media. New forms of employment – a combination of low-paid professional activity and additional salaries earned in leisure hours – have become the norm in the Russian labor market, thus hindering the restructuring of the national economy. As the result of under-investment in the national social system, many social institutions have lost their social significance and become marginalized. Decline of state-supported education, health care, and pension systems, and a crisis in the state financing of cultural institutions, have seriously damaged individual attitudes to outdated social institutions.

In these circumstances, many Russians associate the country's future with the progress of telecommunications and new media, first and foremost with the Internet and mobile telephony. The idea of the revolutionizing potential of information technology has been strongly accepted by Russian intellectuals. "Technological determinists" have accepted the leading role of the "West," the USA, and some advanced Asian states in hardware and software production, but remain convinced that Russia can benefit both socially and politically from the use of the Internet in social communication and interpersonal contact. Many expectations have been raised by the potential of the Internet to construct a new social reality, to support the creation of new democratic institutions in post-communist Russia instead of the outdated social and political structures still existing in the political environment. The idea of transparent online communication between state and citizens has given birth to naïve political aspirations about the possibility of Russia catching up with the "civilized world" and successfully implementing a Western European model of democracy, at least in the online domain (Ovchinnikov, 2002).

There is a strong rationale behind this approach. Even taking into account new Russian inequalities, the progress of the new media provides a clear case of the positive adaptation of global changes by modern Russian society, although this is a limited case of fragmented globalization which has involved a small, but advanced and flexible part of Russian society. A fraction of the Russian population, a group of urban dwellers, made up of comparatively young, rich professionals and middle-class intellectuals, the "intelligentsia," has become the core of the Russian network society.

Runet, the Russian-language sector of the Internet, has been defined by communication scholars as a new Russian miracle, especially in terms of the growth in number of users and increase in supply of Russian language resources and online services (Doctorov, 1999). The brief, but astonishing history of Runet provides some observations crucial to an understanding of the Russian network society.

Technically, the Internet first appeared in the Soviet Union as a purely scientific and academic computer network, with only a few academics having access to the evolving international network. The development of the Internet in Russia can be divided into three main periods. In the first period, from 1991 to 1993, the main users were academic institutions in the leading research centers, such as Moscow, St Petersburg, and Novosibirsk. In the second period, from 1993 to 1996, the Internet moved to business and spread mainly in Moscow and St Petersburg, two major cities which were telecommunication clusters and provided a model for spreading the Internet throughout Russia (Perfiliev, 2002b). Among the users were state officials, businessmen, and journalists employed by large media companies. In the present period (since 1996) growth has taken place in large academic centers (Novosibirsk, Samara, Ekaterinburg, Nizhny Novgorod, Irkutsk, Khabarovsk) outside Moscow and St Petersburg.

Although the progress of the Internet in the regions is apparent, its unevenness remains a crucial characteristic of the present situation. Of all Russian Internet users, almost one-third are residents of the Central and Northern regions, one-third are in Siberia and the Far East, but the southern areas have a much lower share: 8.8 per cent (Perfiliev, 2002a). The number of domains demonstrates the dominance of Moscow (35.5 per cent of domains in net.ru, com.ru, org.ru, pp.ru zones and 66.5 per cent in .ru zone), St Petersburg (6.3 per cent and 5.8 per cent), and foreign states, i.e. domain computers that are located outside Russia (32.9 per cent and 6.9 per cent), while the presence of other Russian regions and local contents is extremely low (Rumetrica, 2002).

Compared to many countries, public use of the Internet began slowly in Russia. However, from 1993 to 1997 the number of Russian Internet users doubled each year. In 1998, it survived the August crisis and the number of users exceeded 1 million (see table 3.1). The statistics show that the number of Russian Internet users ever connected to the Internet now stands at close to 18 million (about 25 percent of the population), and the number of frequent users is about 8 million (*Mezhdunarodnyi otraslevoi almanakh*, 2002: 13).

Patterns of Internet development in Russia resemble its global growth. The progress initially took place in big cities, primarily in Moscow. Internet penetration in the capital is still the highest compared to other cities, but the

Table 3.1   Dynamics of the Russian Internet audience (in millions)

Audience	1998	2000	2002
No. of frequent users	0.2	5.0	8
Maximum no. of users	1.1	9.2	18

Source: *Mezhdunarodnyi otraslevoi almanakh* 9 (2002): 12–13, 14–15

inequality of geographical regions has visibly decreased. While, in the summer of 1996, 85 percent of all Russian Internet users lived in big cities and 75 percent of them were Moscow residents, by the beginning of the twenty-first century there was a definite rise in the number of users among residents of the Russian regions. In 2002, 33.7 percent of Russian Internet users lived outside the two "capitals," Moscow and St Petersburg. However, Moscow (57.2 percent Internet users) and St Petersburg (9.1 percent) still represent the main areas of residence of Russian Internet users. However, another important indicator, the geographical representation of the number of Runet visitors, proves that the Runet audience is rather divergent and the largest segment of users is comprised by non-Muscovites (see table 3.2).

Runet has now enlarged in terms of geography, social and gender representation. Currently, the share of female users stands at almost 40 percent. However, a typical user is mostly an educated and/or high-income urban man (20–35 years of age) working as a state official, politician, businessman, journalist, or student. Another trend indicative of the Russian Internet is the increase in the number of individual users compared to corporate ones. However, the number of connections to the Net from homes remains comparatively low, and at present the correlation between access from individual apartments and corporate offices stand at the level of 33 percent to 65 percent (*Mezhdunarodnyi otraslevoi almanakh*, 2002: 13; Rumetrica, 2002). It should be noted, however, that within "corporate use" the Russian data do not specify either the number of schools connected to the Net or the use of the Internet by schoolchildren.

Table 3.2   Areas of residence of Runet visitors (2002)

Area	Share of Runet visitors (%)
Moscow	32.27
St Petersburg	5.83
Krasnodar region	1.78
Sverdlovsk region	1.46
Moscow region	1.24
Samara region	1.19
Rostov region	1.18
Other regions	21.79
Foreign countries	31.39
Residence not defined	1.87
Total	100

Source: http://rumetrica.rambler.ru/data/auditory/geo/

Recent data show that the Russian Internet is growing along the same lines as elsewhere in the developed world. Runet has become an important communication space and information channel used by certain groups of the Russian population. Intellectuals and academics have traditionally comprised the biggest group of users, but now young people go online most frequently due to investments made by the Soros Foundation, which financed a large-scale program to link 54 Russian universities to the Internet. The student Net community has produced extremely diverse, vivid, and informal resources for the Runet, and also maintained the use of the Internet during the economic crisis in August 1998. At the moment, students and schoolchildren form one of the most considerable groups of Runet users at 23 percent of all users.

The growth of the Internet in Russia has produced a number of expectations among Russian intellectuals, but, at the same time, it has also raised a number of concerns. The crucial point is that Russian statistics need to be assessed critically because the core audience, frequent regular users, actually represent only one-third of the audience at most, which is no more than 3–5 percent of the population. Consequently, the rapid expansion of the Internet in Russia and the steady growth in the number of users, which have exceeded indicators for many technologically advanced countries, involve only a minority of Russians; for example, elite groups including the most educated, highly paid urban residents, widely traveled in foreign countries, and normally with a good command of English. Two additional characteristics of frequent Russian Internet users are of particular significance. A high level of optimism about life and a low interest in politics have been revealed as important attitudes among those who regularly use the Internet (Ovchinnikov, 2002). Therefore, we witness the emergence of a new group within Russian society: "well-to-do urban optimists." For them, access to information and communication networks has become a criterion of social and intellectual wealth and the network society has become a reality. But is this network society open to all Russians?

THE NEW ECONOMY: INFRASTRUCTURE FOR THE FUTURE?

A traditional way of measuring the progress of the network society is to analyze the statistics of the new economy. In the Russian case, it is difficult to rely upon economic indicators simply because relevant and reliable data are often missing. Generally speaking, the Russian information-technology sector remains insignificant in the national economy, although its size is increasing constantly. In the early 2000s, it represented 4 percent (or 8.4 billion US$) of the GDP. The overall production of the information-technology sector was estimated at the level of 2.2 percent of GDP (4.7 billion US$). The number of employees was about 500,000, less than 1 percent of the labor force (*Issledovanije ID "Komp'juterra*, 2003).

The statistics are in many ways discouraging. They show the marginal role of the information-technology sector in Russia's economy and, in addition, demonstrate the gap between the industrial and new sectors of the Russian economy. Distance and technical backwardness hamper the all-Russian progress of interactive digital networks – the backbone of the new economy. As a rule, problems of the new Russian economy arise from the low level of the national telecommunications infrastructure (still using copper cables) and the long-term crisis in the economy. The monopoly position of *Rostelecom*, the key player in the regional telecom markets, hinders competition in the sector and prevents the resolution of the problem of the "last mile."

Access to the Internet has become an evident indicator of acute problems faced by the new economy. Low telephone penetration (no more than 180 lines per 1,000 inhabitants) and the poor quality of telephone lines (ISDN-lines are extremely rare even in big cities, and fiber optics almost inaccessible), along with low penetration of home computers (64 per 1,000 inhabitants in 2001) are the most critical obstacles to progress. Poor living standards make the rapid expansion of the telecommunications infrastructure (for example, broadband digital networks) into homes practically unrealistic. This also leads to the almost complete disconnection of rural areas both from fixed telephone and Internet networks.

Compared to other former Soviet countries, Russia maintains the biggest network of Internet hosts, but on a similar index for Western European countries it lags far behind, with only 105 hosts per 1,000 citizens. Russia is, of course, ahead of Moldavia, Armenia, Georgia, and the independent states of Central Asia where less than 1 per cent of the population has access to the Internet. It is worth noting that the level of telecommunications infrastructure in the country does not allow for a drastic improvement in the situation. The level of teledensity is 197 telephones per 1,000 citizens, still far behind the most advanced countries.

Nevertheless, at the beginning of the twenty-first century, the Russian information-technology sector has experienced an essential growth inspired by Internet progress. Investments have increased significantly and private companies have enthusiastically entered the market. In order to promote the Internet among the mass audience, small-scale access providers have invented a specifically Russian solution of a cheaper technology, so-called home networks, invented to avoid the "last mile" problem by connecting neighboring apartments and further switching them to the Internet. Home networks have evolved in the densely populated areas of big cities and linked private apartments into intranets with a further connection to the Internet. However, the majority of Russian access providers are secondary providers and technically unable to provide access to international networks. Only in Moscow and St Petersburg can Internet companies connect users directly with foreign networks. The dominance of the two megapolises in terms of content and service supply makes the prospect for significant spreading of the new economy into the regions fairly problematic.

Eventually, Russian private business, especially finance institutions and small firms, have become heavy users of the Internet, which enables them to overcome many of the existing defects in communication, transport, and administration. The Internet has made private business less dependent upon the assistance and cooperation of official authorities. Other advantages for small and medium Russian enterprises are based upon the fact that some popular electronic mail servers offer their facilities and services free of charge; in addition, local telephone operators provide their services mostly free. As a result, this technologically advanced, although small, sector of the Russian economy is characterized by active use of information technology and network corporate structures to guarantee greater efficiency in organizational communication within companies.

This uneasy progress of the new Russian economy is partly counterbalanced by the progress of mobile telephony. Its significance as an alternative technological infrastructure for a network society has grown enormously. With the increase in amount and volume of transmitted information, mobile telephone networks have radically changed the Russian communication landscape. The spread of cellular phones has responded not only to the demand for improved one-to-one communication. Almost 23 million Russians (15.5 percent of the population) who currently use mobile phones have shown an interest in various technological applications like SMS services, distribution of content, and so on. In general terms, the significance of mobile telephony for Russia is difficult to overestimate. It has created a competitive and economically viable market based on flexible pricing policies. As a result, three big companies operating in the sector constantly offer new services and the opportunity of lower prices. As a result, operators of fixed telephone networks have lost their monopoly, and Russians have received more mobility and independence in their everyday information consumption, business-to-business and multiple-to-multiple communication.

FROM VERTICAL PYRAMID TO NETWORKS: RUNET IN POLITICS AND LEISURE

The rapid spread of the Internet has created its own mythology. Among the most popular declarations is the one claiming greater than ever freedom of expression and democratic control provided by the Net. Improved access to information, greater selectivity, and non-hierarchical types of social and personal interaction afforded by information technology have been viewed by many scholars as key features of the new society which enable citizens to avoid the manipulative and misinforming effects of mass communication (Graham, 1999: 33–4, 62).

Approached from this angle, the Internet has been assessed by Russian intellectuals without any hesitation as an infrastructure for a network society and an alternative to the traditional mass media which were propagandistic cornerstones of the authoritarian and centralized Soviet empire. The Internet has also been seen as an imperative for transforming the ex-empire into a modern democratic society, a tool to decentralize patterns of political communication between power elites and ordinary citizens.

From this rather simplistic point of view, some experts declared that, at the grassroots level, there has already appeared a "professional reader," a frequent, regular Internet user characterized by increased independence and individuality in accessing and selecting content through Runet (Nosik, 2003: 158). Consequently, this observation has produced a belief that reorganized structures of social power would meet the expectations of a new citizen by establishing an open, online, individualized dialogue and inventing new forms of individual and group political participation in a digital format.

In contrast to this, Runet, mainly in its political information section, has been successfully transformed by the political elite into a national political medium, fulfilling many functions of the old mass media. Naturally, the Internet has played a substantial role in forming local and/or individual identities, and in connecting professional or interest groups dispersed over the vast Russian territory and even globally. However, online political communication in Russia remains under strict central control. Thus, at the beginning of this century, when Russia was divided into seven federal regions (*okrug*) with a view to reinforcing centralization of the Russian Federation, seven big Internet hubs and powerful content providers were set up around regional administrative centers following the creation of federal super-regions. Russian political leaders and "oligarchs," a particular group in the integrated Russian financial–political elite, have become the most influential gatekeepers of the market in information and have obviously benefited from the limited scope of the Runet audience convinced of the ultimate freedom of speech on the Internet.

The influence of the Internet on political communication was enforced in the parliamentary (1999) and presidential (2000) elections. Sites run by the government-supported *Fond Effectivnoi politiki* (The Foundation for Effective Politics) played a crucial propagandistic role in the creation of the public image of leading political parties and politicians. By releasing compromising material about some well-known politicians, Russian political image-makers appealed directly to those forming public opinion – journalists and party activists. The Internet served as a mediator between the political powers and intellectuals who, in turn, forwarded the information obtained through the Net to the bulk of the Russian population by means of traditional media, thus constructing a two-step communication system between the political elite and the mass audience. The apparent PR function of the Russian Internet was ensured by its non-open nature, which put the Net into the use only of well-paid, well-educated Russians who, by a large degree, shaped the decision-making elite. Quotations from online sites made by the traditional media during the election campaigns safeguarded the enormous popularity of the Net.

The Internet, the nervous system of the network society, has become a new means of political surveillance over internal flows of news information. Certainly, in a broad philosophical sense, one should emphasize that there exists a dialectics between surveillance and the potential to build autonomy and freedom. The network provides the possibility for both, and, in fact, particular national (or social, cultural, corporate, other) circumstances shape the social and cultural outcomes of network interaction within a specific organization or structure. Consequently, in Russia, by providing Russian opinion-makers with "free" online information, the political elite has demonstrated a shift to a principle of administrative rationalization and the scientific management of the public sphere of political information and communication. As Robin and Webster (1999: 106) argue, "if social control is to be effective, the control of information and communication channels is imperative."

The Russian state has made several attempts to put the Internet under its control by setting up a legal framework for its telecommunications policy. Since 1996, it has produced a number of political documents regarding information technology and online networks. The Concept of the State Information Policy (1998) for the first time introduced the building of the information society as a strategic goal of national development. The Concept of Building the Information Society in Russia (1999), adopted by the Ministry of Telecommunications and Informatization, proposed a Russian model for the transition to the information society. It pointed to the need to protect national identity, especially in culture and the media, and promoted national "values" as the strong state presence in the area of information technology, the subordination of the market to the state, and the slow liberalization of the Russian telecommunications sector. Information security and measures for its protection were mentioned among other priorities.

In 2001 the Russian government approved two federal programs: *Electronic Russia in the Years 2002–2010* and *The Development of the Unified Information and Educational Space in 2001–2005*, aimed at the development of information technology. The documents promoted a broader use of information technology in state governance and education, and an effective dialogue between the powers-that-be and the citizen. As a result, the level of computerization in Russian secondary schools should significantly increase.

Paradoxically, the Internet played an integrating role in the Russian context, providing simultaneous news coverage for the Russian elite (or for those with access) nationwide. In the decentralized Russian media system, where newspapers have increasingly become local and TV has become commercially oriented, the Internet took on the role of a political communicator which actively constructed the Russian "integrated information space." For the political elite, increased opportunities for manipulating information opened up, at least for a period, new possibilities to manage public opinion. And, here again, we face the well-known conflict between technology and its social uses highlighted by Williams (1974) and Winston (1998). What is important in today's Russia is the contradiction between the novelty of Internet communication and the structures emerging from it and the uses widely exercised by Russian politicians. In contrast to the old uses of the Internet as a political medium, Runet, as a leisure activity, demonstrates diverse models of individual innovative behavior significant in the network structure of postmodern societies.

One of the reasons why Russians have taken to the Internet so enthusiastically might be explained by its potential to increase the scope of personal liberation and the possibilities for individual choice, which have traditionally been very limited in Russian society. The significance of the Internet in the personal life of Russians has not been studied in depth as yet, but it is clear that Runet attracts a great number of users who spend their leisure time online. It has already been shown by many studies that Russians use the Internet for e-mail and also for the world's websites, although most users prefer Russian content in the Russian language. According to the statistics of *Rambler*, one of the largest Russian portals, the "Top Twenty" of the most popular Russian language sites includes *3Dnews.ru*, a webzine on computers, *Anekdot.ru*, a joke site, *Aport.ru*, a search engine, *Auto.ru*, a webzine on cars, and *Bankreferatov.ru*, a site containing educational materials. Among the other most popular services are online newspapers, free e-mail services, and the Russian tax authority.

It is well known that Russians have more sites devoted to humor on the Internet than any other nation, and this is online proof of the fact that, for many Russians, humor is a traditional means of lightening life burdens. Online humor and satirical sites have emerged as a domain for a new subculture, Russian online folklore. Compared to traditional folklore, online satire exists as an interactive, constantly updated, and limitlessly rich segment of Runet, providing users with a number of facts describing present Russian realities (Verner, 2003).

Current Runet subcultures vary from popular anecdotes and jokes sites to academic or literary magazines read by a few hi-brow intellectuals. With improvements in living standards, at least among those of the Runet audience, content preferences have begun to change. Polls have illustrated the shift of interest from sites devoted to light entertainment to sites containing information on information technology, science, practical economics, and cars. As a living organism, Runet constantly produces new myths and heroes. A modest flash cartoon, transmitting stories about Masyanya, an optimistic, friendly, but unlucky girl from St Petersburg, has become extremely popular since it reflects the philosophy of many Russians who have failed to achieve financial success but retain their optimistic attitude to life. More convincing than many off-line characters, Masyanya has turned into a popular image for TV news and cartoons, and an object of conversations and chats.

The language of Runet has become a particularly crucial area for present Russian cultural identity. Postmodernist experiments with Cyrillic and Latin characters, Russian and English words, and the integration of verbal and non-verbal forms of expression, have produced a new Internet language that has lexically reflected the new virtual reality. In addition, an innovative use of the Russian language by the Russian Internet community, migrating from site to site, has become the sign of a constant renewal and reconstruction of communication and its substance. The language of the Russian Internet is an area that helps users to quit the hierarchical world for a virtual network society.

CONCLUSIONS

Paradoxically, in Russia, a country still surviving economic crisis, the network society has got a comparatively good foundation. There exists a working system of satellite connections, considerable intellectual potential for researchers, engineers, and designers of software programs, as well as the necessary technological hardware. Telecommunications, information services, and content markets are rapidly developing, and the number of computers in offices and households is increasing. The level of education is still high, at least in administrative and industrial centers. Students, schoolchildren, and active professionals stand at the core of the new media universe. Private business, especially banking and service companies, is an active force in using and promoting information and communication technology. Even state agencies, at least formally, promote openness to e-democracy and e-governance, thus enforcing the use of the Internet in executive and legislative processes and laying down the foundations for a new political infrastructure of e-Russia.

On the other hand, in the Russian context, there exists an obvious lack of a "network culture," a specific type of interrelation between various social agents that provides a society with a new logic of economic and social interaction. Russian politicians and business elites have not demonstrated a willingness to move from authoritarian paternalistic structures to innovative and horizontal types of social and economic relations. The distribution of intellectual resources and social communication in Russia still follows old hierarchical patterns, and only a limited section of Russian society could be said to fall within the concept of a network society.

REFERENCES

Bell, D. (1960) *The End of Ideology*. New York: Free Press.
Castells, M. (1996–8) *The Information Age: Economy, Society and Culture*, 3 vols. Oxford: Blackwell.
— — and Kiselyova, E. (2000) "Rossija i setevoye obshestvo" (Russia and the Network Society), *Mir Rossiji* 1 (available at: http://NetHistory.Ru/biblio/1043176006.html).
— — and — (2001) "Rossija v informatsionnuyu epokhu" (Russia in the Information Age), *Mir Rossiji* 1 (available at: http://NetHistory.Ru/biblio/1043176006.html).
Delyagin, M. (2001) "Puti Rossiji v odnopolyarnom mire" (Russian Ways in a One-centered World), in M. Il'in and V. Inozemtsev (eds), *Megatrendy sovremennogo razvitija* (Mega Trends of Modern Development), pp. 94–103. Moscow: Ekonomika.
Doctorov, B. (1999) "Rossijiskiji Internet: novoye russkoye tchudo" (The Internet in Russia: New Russian Miracle), *Peterburgskiji Zhurnal sotsiologii* 2: 5–7.
Drucker, P. (1993) *Post-capitalist Society*. Oxford: Butterworth Heinemann.
Giddens, A. (1993) *The Consequences of Modernity*. Cambridge: Polity Press.
Graham, G. (1999) *The Internet: A Philosophical Inquiry*. New York: Routledge.
Inozemtsev, V. (1999) "Perspectivy postindustrial'noi teorii v menyayushemcya mir" (Perspectives of the Post-industrial Theory in the Changing World), in V. Inozemtsev (ed.), *Novaya postindustrial'naya volna na Zapade* (New Post-industrial Wave in the West), pp. 3–64. Moscow: Academia.
— — (2000) *Sovremennoye postindustrial'noye obshestvo: priroda, protivirachija, perspectivy* (Modern Post-industrial Society: Nature, Contradictions, Perspectives). Moscow: Logos.
Issledovanije ID "Komp'juterra" (2003) *Tendentsii razvitija IKY i ikh primenenije v sotsial'no-ekonomicheskoi spfere* (Trends of ICT Development and their Uses in the Social and Economic Sphere) (available at http://www.region2003.ru/tendency/).
Kara-Mourza, S. (2001) *Manipuljatzija soznaniem* (Manipulation of Conciseness). Moscow: EKSMO Press.
Ledeneva, A. (2000) "How Russia Really Works," *OpenDemocracy* (available at: http://www.opendemocracy.net/themes/article-6-253.jsp).
Lievrouw, L. and Livingstone, S. (eds) (2002) *Handbook of the New Media: Social Shaping and Consequences of ICTs*. London: Sage.
Mezhdunarodnyi otraslevoi almanakh (2002), no. 9. Moscow.
Neklessa, A. (1999) "Konetz tsivilizatsii, ili zigzag istorii" (The End of Civilization, or Zigzag of History), in *Postindustrial'nyi mir: tsentr, periferija, Rissija* (Post-industrial World: Center, Periphery, Russia), pp. 31–74. Moscow.
— — (2001) "Ordo quadro: prishetvije postsovremennogo mira" (Ordo Quadro: The Coming of the Post-modern World), in M. Il'in and V. Inozemtsev (eds),

Megatrendy sovremennogo razvitija (Mega Trends of Modern Development), pp. 127–51. Moscow: Ekonomika.

Nosik, A. (2003) "Samizdat, Internet and professional'nyi chitatel" (Samizdat, the Internet and the Professional Reader), *Otechestvennuje zapiski* 4 (13): 155–61.

Ovchinnikov, B. (2002) "Virtual'nuye nadezhdu: sostoyaniye I perspectivu politich-eskogo Runeta" (Virtual Expectations: The State and the Prospects for Political Runet), *Polis. Politicheskiye issledovanija* (available at: http://www.politstudies.ru/fulltext/2002/1/5.htm).

Perfiliev, Y. (2002a) "Internet v regionakh Rossii" (The Internet in the Russian Regions), *Regiony Rossii v 1999 godu* (available at: http://pubs.carnegie.ru/books/2001/01np/25yp.asp).

— — (2002b) "Territorial'naya organizatsija rossiiskogo internet-prostranstva" (The Territorial Organization of Russian Internet Space), in I. Semenov (ed.), *Internet i rossiiskoye obshestvo* (The Internet and Russian Society), pp. 21–46. Moscow: Gendalf.

Petrov, N. (2000) "Federalism po-russki" (Federalism Russian Style), *Pro et Contra* 1 (5): 7–33.

Pokrovsky, N. (2001) "Transit rossiyiskikh tsennostei: nerealisovannaya alternativa, anomiya, globalizatsija" (Transition of Russian Values: Unrealized Alternative, Anomie, Globalization), in A. Sogomonov and S. Kukhterin (eds), *Globalizatsija I postsovetskoye obshestvo* (Globalization and Post-Soviet Society), pp. 39–59. Moscow: Stovi.

Rantanen, T. (2002) *The Global and the National: Media and Communications in Post-communist Russia*. Lanham, MA: Rowman and Littlefield.

Robin, K. and Webster, F. (1999) *Times of the Technoculture: From Information Society to the Virtual Life*. New York: Routledge.

Rumetrica (2002) available at: http://www.rambler.ru/db/rumetrica.

Segbers, K. (1999) "Shivaya loskutnoye odeyalo" (Sewing Together the Patchwork Quilt), *Pro et Contra* 4 (4): 65–83.

Semenov, I. (ed.) (2002) *Internet i rossiiskoye obshestvo* (The Internet and Russian Society). Moscow: Gendalf.

Sparks, C., with Reading, A. (1998) *Communism, Capitalism and the Mass Media*. London: Sage.

Stiglitz, J. (2002) *Globalization and its Discontents*. London. Penguin.

Toffler, A. (1980) *The Third Wave*. New York: Bantam Books.

Vartanova, E. (2001) "Media Structures: Changed and Unchanged," in K. Nordenstreng, E. Vartanova and Y. Zassoursky (eds), *Russian Media Challenge*, pp. 21–72. Helsinki: Kikimora.

— — (2002) "Digital Divide and the Changing Political/Media Environment of Post-socialist Europe," *Gazette* 64 (5): 449–65.

Verner, D. (2003) " 'Anekdotu iz Rossiji' I folklore internetovskoji epokhi" ('Jokes from Russia' and the Folklore of the Internet Epoch), *Russkji Zhurnal/Net-kultura* (available at: www.russ.ru/netcult/20030617_verner.html).

Webster, F. (1995) *Theories of the Information Society*. New York: Routledge.

Williams, R. (1974) *Television, Technology and Cultural Form*. London: Fontana.

Winston, B. (1998) *Media Technology and Society: A History from the Telegraph to the Internet*. London: Routledge.

4. The Internet in China: technologies of freedom in a statist society

Jack Linchuan Qiu

This chapter considers the development of the Internet in the People's Republic of China (PRC): its diffusion, context, and institutional settings; its economic, political, and cultural components; its relationship with national and global actors; and its implications for the theorization of network societies around the globe.[1] For the purposes of comparison, the case of China is invaluable because, besides its obvious significance, Chinese business networks, as part of the dynamic East Asian economy, "have adapted more rapidly than other areas of the world to the new technologies and to the new forms of global competition" (Castells, 1996: 173). Most importantly, the continuing power of the Chinese Communist Party (CCP), juxtaposed with high growth rates in economic and technological sectors, calls into question many existing conceptions of the relations between technology and society formulated in the Western context of late capitalism. Is there a network society in China, as seen through the prism of China's Internet? If so, what is peculiar about this particular set of network formations – in its components, internal structure, and relation to the external environment? I will take an inductive approach to explore these questions.

THE SPIRIT OF CHINESE INFORMATIONALISM

Unlike Mao's experiments in creating a new social system, China's "information revolution" since the early 1990s has been discursively less flamboyant. On September 20, 1987, Professor Qian Tianbai sent the first e-mail from China.[2] But the event has been ignored and its slogan-like message – "Beyond the Great Wall, Joining the World (*yueguo changcheng, zouxiang shijie*)" – remained unpublicized until after 1994 when Beijing was mesmerized by Al Gore's speech on "Building the Information Superhighway."[3] Yet China was not far behind in the hi-tech domain. It established the first TCP/IP-capable academic network, the National Computing and Networking Facility of China (NCFC), in April 1994 (Qian, 1996), and opened the first public Internet service, ChinaNet, in January 1995.[4] These were more efforts of emulation than homegrown innovation, though: the World Bank provided partial funding for the NCFC; a foreign telecom firm, Sprint, operated the first international channels of both the NCFC and ChinaNet.[5] Global actors were instrumental in the genesis of the new technology in the PRC.

Since 1995, China's Internet has been developing rapidly, demonstrating the potential for the country to become a world leader in the Internet industry. According to the China Internet Network Information Center (CNNIC),[6] on average, the number of Internet users in China has been increasing by 262 percent every year from less than 40,000 in December 1995 to 59.1 million in June 2003.[7] By the end of 2002, there were more than 20.8 million online computers, 371,600 registered World Wide Web sites, and a total international connection capacity of 9,380 megabytes directly linking up China with other countries. Acknowledging that official statistics are flawed,[8] there is general agreement on the extraordinary rapidity of Internet growth in the country. Although China's huge population suggests that the scale of technology diffusion remains quite limited, the speed of development is remarkable considering that, when ChinaNet opened for business in 1995, the country had less than five telephone sets per hundred population, comparable to the US teledensity level of 1905.[9] China's Internet boom appeared to be little affected by the slowdown in the information technology (IT) industry worldwide at the turn of the millennium.

What accounts for this swift take-off? Although the dissemination of Western technologies was a key element from the beginning, the explanatory power of a diffusion model is no longer sufficient as the Internet materializes into the centerpiece of China's new economy and societal transformations. More causes therefore need to be sought in the peculiar sociohistorical context of China: from state policies to commercial rationale, from *guanxi* and family networks to the emergence of grassroots identities, to the competition of modernity projects, whether communist or capitalist, nationalist or globalist, and the alternative social movements arising. These factors all shape and become constituents of what might be called "informationalism with Chinese characteristics."

One thematic concern constantly accompanying the question of the Internet, which underlies most discourse on technology and globalization in the PRC, is a strong sense of humiliation for the atrocities inflicted upon the nation since the Opium War (1839–1842). The memory of China being the most technologically advanced nation on the planet lingers (Needham, 1981), so its fall from the throne hurts. As a result, restoring China's technical supremacy, and thereby reviving the Middle Kingdom, has been a constant goal for Chinese leaders since Dr Sun Yat-sen (who gave up his presidency of the Republic of China to become the Minister of Railways from a belief in the power of technology). The appeal of techno-nationalism greatly intensified after the communist takeover in 1949 when fanatical modernization projects such as the Great Leap Forward were implemented, emphasizing technology and engineering sectors. Of these attempts, many were too idealistic, poorly planned, and followed by disastrous consequences (Yang, 1998; Shapiro, 2001). Still, the PRC became a nuclear power in 1964, launched its first satellite in 1970, and sent a man into space in 2003.

Just as Maoist cadres aspired to emulate Soviet industrial statism, Chinese officials since the 1990s have been fully engaged in building a Chinese information society (Hachigian, 2001). Proponents of China's Internet often quote former President Jiang Zemin (a former Minister of the Electronics Industry), who said "Each of the Four Modernizations (of agriculture, industry, education, and the military) has to depend on informatization."[10] While addressing the Sixteenth National Congress of the CCP, Jiang also emphasized the need to "prioritize the information industry, and widely apply information technologies in economic and social domains."[11] Unlike the failed Maoist Great Leap Forward, this campaign, centered on the Internet, has succeeded by measures of growth indicators, sustainability (so far), and the capacity of the Chinese state to boost the new economy via investment, purchase, assistance in research and development, and the acquisition of foreign capital. China's successes are comparable to the developmental state model practiced in Japan and East Asian "tiger" economies for decades (Johnson, 1982, 1995; Castells, 1996: 172–90). However, China's advantage as a latecomer, its enormous market potential, and its relative independence from the capitalist world system enabled it to limit the damage of the Asian financial crisis as well as the global downturn in hi-tech industries.

The historical legacy and state sponsorship being the same, China's Internet would have developed differently had it occurred in the 1980s before Tiananmen, before the collapse of the Soviet Union in 1991, and Deng Xiaoping's call for all-out marketization in 1992 (Baum, 1994:119–368). The overlapping aftermath of these three interconnected events led to a fundamental paradox that characterizes contemporary Chinese society in general and the social construction of the Internet in particular: state agencies take new technologies as a means to improve people's living standards but not citizen participation. In short, China tries to reap economic benefits, while sustaining and reinforcing the political status quo. The policy-makers' objective is to cast computer networks primarily in the economic domain.[12] Nonetheless the post-hoc reaction of Chinese authorities to the many social, economic, and political challenges they face is becoming a major point of reference for the configuration of national information infrastructures in authoritarian countries worldwide (Kalathil and Boas, 2003).

That the party-state attempts to construct the new technology as an entirely economic instrument, however, is an incomplete characterization. Three issues add to the complexity of Chinese informationalism. First, it is difficult to esti-mate the extent to which the economic benefits of the Internet can be utilized to stabilize the current social structure. This is problematic because of the uneven pattern of Internet diffusion in China and the lack of attention to issues of information inequality until recently (Qiu, 2002a; Harwit, 2003; Giese, 2003). Second, despite its apparent unity, the Chinese state harbors multiple interest groups with competing and conflicting goals and rationales. They vie for dominance in China's cyberspace. Officials, especially at the level of local state, often form networks of "bureaucratic entrepreneurs" (Hsing, 1998) with members of the business community, including IT industry leaders,[13] from within and outside Mainland China. This makes it difficult to operationally define the boundary between politics and economy in the many localities, particularly in the coastal regions of Guangdong, Fujian, and Shanghai where trans-border commercial activities have been concentrated.

Finally, and most importantly, the role of grassroots user networks should be emphasized because their everyday activities not only ensure the continua-tion of China's Internet but also embody personal experiences that transform the new technology from an abstract cyberspace to meaningful places of social significance. User networks at the grassroots level constitute the most innov-ative source of change in China's virtual landscape, forming an unpredictable dimension imbued with tremendous potential for liberalization which is just beginning to be understood. The multitude of grassroots formations such as web-based nationalist movements, hacker alliances, youth culture, gay and lesbian groups, and dissident use of the Internet – via diverse channels such as chatrooms, online gaming, peer-to-peer technologies – have given rise to a kaleidoscope for the examination of the intricate interplay among a myriad of social forces in the networks of Chinese netizens, whose impact goes far beyond the online communities and beyond the borders of the People's Republic per se.

ACCESS, DEMOGRAPHICS, AND PROBLEMS OF DIFFUSION

Who is using the Internet in China? How do they connect to the World Wide Web, for what purposes, and how are Internet resources distributed throughout the country? Before reviewing the demography and geography of China's Internet, it is imperative to recognize that access to information and commu-nication technology is socially shaped (Dutton, 1999), and therefore reflects fundamental structures of a given society. In China, Internet access is largely limited to relatively affluent social groups in urban and urbanizing areas, especially those with a high demand for information and entertainment. The remarkable Internet boom within a limited social scope is a result of state-led telecom reform since 1993, characterized by the replacement of a national monopoly with a structure of semi-privatized and privatized oligopolies (Mueller and Tan, 1997; Harwit, 1998; Yan and Pitt, 2002).

The reform aimed at increasing market competition and enhancing the ability of domestic telecom firms to face the challenge of China's accession to the World Trade Organization (Horsley, 2001a, b). This strategy was useful in driving down prices and improving service quality, but telecom firms tended to shy away from the most deprived regions and populations. Reportedly, the Ministry of Information Industry (MII) and the Ministry of Finance only started to discuss the establishment of a Telecom Universal Service Fund, to be collected from major telecom companies to address the equality issue in rural and inland areas, in the second half of 2002 (Liu, 2003). The implementation and effects of this new measure, especially on Internet diffusion, remain unclear.

The 59.1 million Internet users in Mainland China at the end of 2002 is impressive, but accounts for only 4.5 percent of China's 1.3 billion population. The limited scope of dispersion is illustrated in table 4.1, which summarizes CNNIC user profiles since 1997 as compared to the average Chinese citizen, although the trend is also obvious that demographic gaps are narrowing at different speeds. Disparities along all four basic dimensions – income, education, gender, and age – are stunning. As expected, Internet users tend to be wealthy, educated, young males. The most prominent disparity is in educational attainment. Only 3.6 percent of the total population has gone to college, but the percentage of users with college education was still 57 percent in January 2003 (down from a peak of 89 percent in January 2001), indicating the critical importance of literacy and technical know-how. The user population is also predominantly young, with 72 percent being thirty or younger and 28 percent being students, according to the CNNIC report of January 2003. This shows that the current user group greatly represents the future of China.

At the same time, income discrepancy has gradually decreased since 2000, but still holds at a significant level with Internet users earning at least 60 percent more than an average Chinese citizen.[14] The most noteworthy movement toward equality is the narrowing down of gender discrepancy.[15] Yet, according to a study by Wei Bu (2003), although the gender gap is decreasing, women still tend to spend less time online, have a narrower scope of goals, and are more negative in evaluating the social impact of the Internet. Put another way, whereas more Chinese women have recently gained Internet access, they still lag behind in terms of their "connectedness" to the new technology (Jung et al., 2001).

The uneven spatial distribution of Internet resources is also notable. While

*Table 4.1   Demographic comparison: Internet users vis-à-vis average
            Chinese*

	Average income (US$)	College education (%)	Male (%)	30 years and under (%)
October 1997	116	_a	88	71
July 1998	177	_a	93	76
January 1999	152	70	86	79
July 1999	183	85	85	78
January 2000	221	84	79	78
July 2000	211	86	75	78
January 2001	176	89	70	75
July 2001	146	63	61	68
January 2002	158	60	60	68
July 2002	133	58	61	70
January 2003	134	57	59	72
Figures for average Chinese (2000)	84	3.6	51	51

[a] Data not available.
Sources: CNNIC *Survey Reports on China's Internet Development* (October 1997–January 2003);
China National Bureau of Statistics, *China Statistical Yearbook* (2000)

the rich coastal regions contain 21 percent of China's land and 40 percent of its population, they are home to more than 60 percent of Chinese Internet users and more than 80 percent of ".cn" domain names (Qiu, 2002a:165–9). Most disproportionate concentration is found in the urban centers of Beijing, Shanghai, and Guangdong Province, which collectively have only 8 percent of China's population, but account for 23 percent of users and more than half of the country's domain names and World Wide Web sites as of January 2003 (see figure 4.1). Although the concentration of users in the core region of these three urban centers has declined from its peak of 52 percent in 1997 to 20 percent in 2003, the concentration of online content providers in the areas remains little changed. The pattern that more regional disparity correlates with more sophisticated technology applies to the Internet as well as other communication resources such as mass media, landline and cellular phone subscriptions. The regional discrepancy also is parallel to a deep urban–rural split: although 69 percent of China's population is rural,[16] only 1 percent of Chinese Internet users work in "agriculture, forestry, husbandry, and fishery."[17]

According to the CNNIC January 2003 report, "seeking information" and

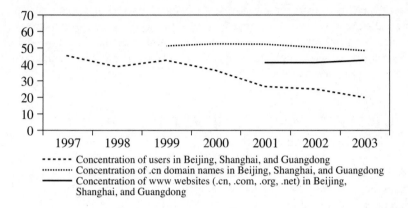

----- Concentration of users in Beijing, Shanghai, and Guangdong
·········· Concentration of .cn domain names in Beijing, Shanghai, and Guangdong
——— Concentration of www websites (.cn, .com, .org, .net) in Beijing,
Shanghai, and Guangdong

Source: CNNIC Survey Reports on China's Internet Development (October 1997–January 2003)

*Figure 4.1   The concentration of Internet resources in the core region of
Beijing, Shanghai, and Guangdong Province*

"entertainment" are the top two reasons people go online in China. The most frequently used online services are e-mail (92.6 percent), search engine (68.3 percent), chat (45.4 percent), and uploading/downloading software (45.3 percent). Of the online information accessed, 81 percent are in Chinese and 71 percent are domestic. Similarly, an independent survey conducted by the Chinese Academy of Social Sciences (Guo, 2003) found that users spent 80 percent of their online time viewing domestic websites, 13 percent time browsing Chinese websites outside China, and 6 percent time reading foreign language content on websites outside the country.

Most users (63 percent) access the Internet from their homes, 43 percent from offices, and 20 percent from Internet cafés.[18] Although broadband and wireless services have started to gain momentum in diffusion, the most robust growth was in Internet cafés. Only 3 percent of users accessed the Net from cybercafés in January 1999; the figure surged to 21 percent in January 2001. Since then the percentage has dropped to 15 percent and 17 percent probably because of restrictive state policies, especially after a fire in a Beijing cyber-café killed 25 people in June 2002.[19] Yet CNNIC still reported that 20 percent of users visited Internet cafés in January 2003.

Besides these official survey results, my fieldwork in south, west, and central China suggests the plausibility of continued cybercafé diffusion despite the national crackdown. Restraining state measures indeed devastated many small, private Internet cafés in metropolitan areas, but the effects have been less serious on large netbar chain stores with support from local authorities or underground operations outside urban centers. Internet cafés are most quickly proliferating in satellite towns surrounding big cities, where costs are low and regulations loosely enforced. Urban adolescents often travel in groups to these locations for online gaming, chatting, and to take part in a new youth subculture. Business people and migrant workers are also found seeking job-related information on the Net.

THE INTERNET AND THE DEVELOPMENTAL STATE: ENDOGENOUS AND EXOGENOUS CONDITIONS

The Chinese party-state is convinced that the Internet is essential to China's economic modernization. Therefore, the state has played a critical role in promoting and diffusing the new technology. Since 1992, major efforts have included the "Golden Projects" and "Government Online" (Harwit, 1998; Fries, 2000: 121–57). There have been ministerial reshuffles and focused use of foreign capital,[20] all for the purpose of building an advanced national information infrastructure. Government spending on the Internet has escalated. The State Council Informatization Steering Group (SCISC), established in 1996, included representatives from telecom regulators, key national economic planning commissions, and the People's Bank of China.[21] With mostly state investments and a combination of private funds, foreign loans, and venture capital, China's fiber-optic network had grown from 286,000 kilometers in 1995 to 1.25 million kilometers in 2000, forming a web of "eight horizontals and eight verticals (*bahengbazong*)" that covers most of the country.[22]

Beijing, in most of its economic policy-making, is emulating the developmental state model identified by Chalmers Johnson (1982, 1995) and defined by Manuel Castells in the East Asian context as a governance structure whose legitimacy resides in "its ability to promote and sustain development, understanding by development the combination of steady high rates of economic growth and structural change in the productive system" (Castells, 1998: 276). In the domain of the Internet, like the earlier processes of industrialization in neighboring East Asian "tigers," the Chinese enthusiasm for information technology should be understood as resulting from "the politics of survival" (Castells, 1998: 278). Internet expansion is part of an explicit effort to rebuild the nation via the acquisition of technological excellence. The early 1990s was a difficult time for Chinese leaders because of the conservative backlash following Tiananmen, continued problems in the state-owned sector, a plunge in international trade and foreign investment due to US-led sanctions, and, most important, the collapse of the Soviet Union which foreclosed any lingering idea of another world system. Although Deng Xiaoping issued a rallying call in 1992 in his famous Southern Tour Speeches, confirming to the nation and the world the continuation of China's reform and opening-up policy

(Baum, 1994: 341–68), the rhetoric was still emerging. It was not just a coincidence that Beijing officials were mesmerized by the hype of the Information Superhighway, whose Chinese version might induce sustainable development, strengthen national pride, and integrate China into the global economy.

The success story of the building of an Internet infrastructure in China should be told cautiously. Achievements in network construction since the mid-1990s are not a result of pro-Internet policies alone. They also arise from a host of institutional legacies and sociohistorical factors. The still centralized nature of national-level economic planning contributes to organizational efficiency in putting together a new technocratic state apparatus and mustering a formidable amount of resources. Moreover, the Internet boom is also the result of several decades of concentration in basic science and engineering research, which has been systematically furthered since 1978 (Bianchi et al., 1988; IDRC/SSTC, 1997).

Two other factors contributed to the shaping of China's Internet. First, the size and complexity of China made it more difficult for the state to implement policy than it was for the neighboring "tiger" economies, particularly at the local level, where everyday decision-making depends on "bureaucratic entrepreneurs" (Hsing, 1998) who have intricate ties to Chinese business networks that extend beyond the Chinese border. The tendency of local state authorities to form "local state corporatism" (Oi, 1995) or "quasi-autonomous local economic empires" (Baum and Schevchenko, 1999) has been an essential factor for Internet projects in South China's Pearl River Delta.[23] For example, in Nanhai, Guangdong Province, which hosts several national e-government model projects, the city government advocated the Internet as the key to economic growth, global competitiveness, and even an increase in local property value. The city invested heavily to connect all villages in Nanhai via fiber-optics and set up touch-screen computers in the main office of every administrative village. Similar enthusiasm was evident in the Taijiang District of Fuzhou City, Fujian Province (Damm, 2003), but was absent in other cities of the Pearl River Delta. This disparity reflects suspicion toward the informational model of modernization that characterizes most Chinese localities, where traditional industrialism holds as a more affordable route to economic growth. Thus, although informationalism, strongly advocated by the central government, has gained strongholds at the local level, the Internet is not yet universally recognized as an indispensable tool of governance and business in less-developed regions or localities with concentrated vested interest in agriculture and traditional industries.

While engaging in its project of national reinvigoration, the Chinese developmental state remains highly dependent on the global space of flows, technologically, financially, and in terms of personnel. Hardware and software transfers from Western countries, some of dubious legality, have been critical to the genesis and growth of China's Internet. Despite repeated official endeavors to regularize technology transfer and minimize intellectual property infringement, especially after China joined the World Trade Organization, success has been spotty. There still is more piracy in China than anywhere else, so the issue lingers (Yu, 2000, 2001). Another under-researched phenomenon is the fast growth of Linux (e.g. "Red Flag Linux") under the auspices of the Chinese state and as part of the global open source movement (*Asian Business*, 2002; Lohr, 2003).

Foreign direct investment (FDI) in China has also steadily increased. Although only a portion of the FDI has been used in computer network construction, the increase in FDI volume has facilitated the rapid diffusion of the Internet. In 2002, China attracted US$ 53 billion of FDI, surpassing that of the United States, although China's FDI would have been only a fraction of the US figure had there not been major financial scandals and the subsequent downturn of Western investment markets in 2001–2002 (*The Economist*, 2003). In addition, official policies limit foreign investors in China to network construction and the manufacture of hardware and software and ban them from more lucrative service provision sectors (Mueller and Lovelock, 2000). Still, the steady growth of FDI and the increasing integration between China's Internet industry and the global market was at least in part a response to China's development strategies. Since the 1990s, hi-tech industries using foreign resources have prospered in the Beijing–Tianjin region and the Pearl River Delta in South China. Especially notable is the re-positioning of Shanghai as the country's new economic center. Intel, Motorola, NEC, and other major firms established factories in Shanghai and adjacent areas (Fries, 2000: 95), as did many major Taiwanese microchip producers. Even though hi-tech production in the region is still in the take-off stage and only a few of the foreign enterprises are now profitable, it appears that the lower Yangtze Delta, with Shanghai as its dragonhead, will become an even more critical link between China and the world economy (Wu, 2000; Koehn, 2002).

Yet what percentage of China's FDI is actually foreign? Who is investing in China's Internet? These questions suggest a key but little publicized factor in the success of the Chinese developmental state – the networks of global Chinese diaspora that connect the Mainland with Hong Kong, Taiwan, Singapore, and Chinese communities around the world. Lawrence Ma estimated that the population of overseas Chinese was approximately 32.8 million in 1998 (Ma and Cartier, 2003: 19), more than one-quarter of the world's total migrant stock of 125 million (Gelbard et al., 1999). The diligence and high saving rates of many Chinese expatriates helped them accumulate formidable wealth, perhaps approaching US$ 600 billion (Brauchli and Biers, 1995), including more than half of Southeast Asia's top 1,000 companies (Kao, 1993). Most important, the Chinese expatriates often rely on family and native-place networks for business transactions and sociocultural association (Hamilton, 1996, 1999; Hsing, 1998; Liu, 1998; Olds and Yueng, 1999; Yueng, 1999). According to John Kao's (1993) survey of overseas Chinese entrepreneurs, 52 percent noted that more than half of their work relationships and 39 percent of their international business ties were with Chinese partners. Scholars understand that cultural synergy is attracting members of the Chinese diaspora to invest in Mainland China, particularly traditional origins of emigration in the southern provinces of Guangdong and Fujian (Lin, 1997; Hsing, 1998; Wei et al, 1999; Cartier, 2001). Although the role of returning expatriates is more prominent in manufacturing and trade than in Internet ventures, they have been critical to the globalization of China's economy and the dramatic increase in China's global informational links.

While older generation sojourners are returning to their ancestral home towns, a new school of Chinese engineers, business managers, and financial analysts are landing in the new airports of Beijing, Shanghai, and Guangzhou to form "the nucleus of a talented new generation of information technology entrepreneurs that is forging commercial links with China" (Gilley, 1999: 50). These are returning Chinese students sent offshore in the post-Mao era to study Western technology and business skills. Many have worked, or are still working, in Silicon Valley and other American or European hi-tech centers. These legendary IT entrepreneurs are like Edward Tian, who grew up in the Cultural Revolution, obtained advanced degrees in foreign universities, and then returned to staff China's top echelon of Internet entrepreneurs (Sheff, 2002: 1–10). This trend of "brain circulation" (Saxenian, 2002) accelerated after the burst of the technology bubble in the global IT industry because of massive lay-offs in the West, but also because they were lured by China's huge market potential, the temptation of going home, and, above all, the recognition that the developmental state could provide competitive jobs and good salaries.[24]

THE NETWORK OF CENSORS AND ITS ENEMIES

China's effort to adjust to a new mode of development is not unique. The same process is underway in neighboring countries and in economic sectors other than the Internet. The most intriguing idiosyncrasy about the Internet in China is that, despite the technology's liberalizing potential, its high speed of growth can be maintained within the framework of the current political system dominated by the Communist Party. The case is excellent for comparative purposes because the technology is fostered, shaped, and contested under more restrictive circumstances than in most parts of the world. Yet it developed rapidly, despite political factors that might have handicapped the Internet industry from the start. Since Internet control in China has been constantly challenged both domestically and from the outside (Hartford, 2000; Harwit and Clark, 2001; Zhao, 2004), it is premature to conclude who is likely to be the ultimate winner – the state control apparatus or those who challenge the political status quo. Still, the countless censorship battles fought in China's cyberspace may shed light on another restrictive aspect of the Chinese state, the internal conflicts among various state agencies, and the malleability of network technologies under politically restrictive circumstances.

Why does China control the Internet? Although the developmental state is loosening its grip on various economic and social aspects to promote globalization and the new economy, the attempt to control the Internet stems from an institutional legacy. The Chinese legal system has never paid more than lip service to the right of free speech. The demands of the authorities usually take precedence over the need for privacy protection. In the Chinese political culture, there is no distinction between "censorship" and "regulation." Hence, since officials think that the Internet should be controlled, it is difficult for many of them to imagine that there should be any limit on the power of the state.

Although much of the Chinese mediascape has been reformed to suit the goal of marketization, the very core of China's media control system is still guarded by Leninist principles (Zhao, 1998; Lee, 2000; Chan and Qiu, 2001) and governed by stakeholders who do not think like Ministry of Information Industry (MII) technocrats. Membership of the State Council Informatization Steering Group (SCISC), the nation's highest decision-making body for Internet affairs, is revealing. There are representatives from MII, the major economic, educational, and technological commissions, but also representatives of the CCP Central Propaganda Department, the State Council Information Office, the Ministry of Public Security (MPS), the State Secrecy Bureau (SSB), and the People's Liberation Army (PLA).[24] These agencies have policy priorities that differ from the logic of the developmental state. They care less about the national economy than the image of the CCP leaders, the maintaining and expanding of political power, and the ability to crush dissidents or opponents in future cyber-wars. They constitute a different "ecology of games" (Dutton, 1992, 1999), which does not share the goals of economic development and which operates with its own rationale of power maximization.

"The Temporary Measures for the Management of Computer Information Networks' International Connection" decree was announced in February 1996 and revised in May 1997. It mandated that (1) all international Internet traffic had to go through officially approved gateways; (2) all Internet service providers had to be licensed; (3) Internet users needed to be registered; and (4) "harmful information" which is "subversive" or "obscene" was banned. A second ordinance was issued by the MPS in December 1997 to improve "network security." It specified in broad terms the types of "harmful information" and "harmful activities," such as hacking and spreading computer viruses. In 1999, the State Encryption Management Commission, in cooperation with the SSB, promulgated the "Administration of Commercial Encryption Regulations" which required all network encryption products and equipment to be approved because they are regarded as state secret.

In 2000 alone, six major regulations regarding state secrets, online business operation, information and news services, and Internet security were issued (Cheung, 2003: 79–82). The new rules primarily targeted Internet content providers (ICPs). They required, among other measures, online news disseminators to get special licenses, prohibited foreign companies from being large shareholders of Chinese ICPs, and required bulletin board (BBS) and chatroom system operators to record user information (including content posted online, account name, duration online, Internet provider address, accessing phone number) for at least 60 days to facilitate police work. Regulations at the national level were reiterated, sometimes in stricter terms, in the management policies of regional networks and commercial websites (Qiu, 1999: 12), reflecting a "business culture of self-censorship" (Cheung, 2003: 85).

Administrative measures are used to ensure that the system of regulation has teeth (Cheung, 2003). The MPS and the SSB have set aside special task forces at national, provincial, and municipal levels, including full-time cyberpolice and "state information security liaison personnel (*guojia xinxi anquan lianluoyuan*)." Many of these cyber-cops are college students who are subsidized for computer and Internet access by working part-time for law enforcement.[26] There are also numerous system operators, webmasters, and BBS boardmasters who are required to share the labor. If they do not cooperate, penalties include temporary or permanent closure of their forums (Qiu, 1999).

On the technical front, China is known for its notorious "Great Firewall" which blocks access to harmful information, broadly defined, perhaps as many as 10 percent of the websites on the World Wide Web (Zittrain and Edelman, 2002). The state agencies also apply advanced intranet and tracking technologies, as well as content-filtering software, in the so-called "Golden Shield Project" (Walton, 2001). Since 1998, dozens of cyber-intruders have been tracked down and imprisoned on charges of disclosing state secrets, inciting subversion, Internet hacking, propagating Falun Gong, and, more recently, spreading rumors during the SARS epidemic. These men and women are mostly in their late teens to early 40s, and include private IT entrepreneurs, schoolteachers, college students, and unemployed urbanites. From September 2002, the blocking mechanisms became more sophisticated and aggressive. They specifically target certain online content (for example, an article at nytimes.com about Chinese corruption scandals, but not other sections of the electronic newspaper). Those who attempt to access outlawed information via the Internet may find their browser application or even the entire terminal disturbed (Zittrain and Edelman, 2002).

From an economic perspective, the censorship regime entails higher costs than justifiable for national development. Slower network speed and efficiency and the image of a fettered Internet structure may discourage foreign investment. Insiders would see the picture differently. The control efforts create jobs, generate profits, and bring opportunities for international collaboration for China's network censors. Surveillance and repressive control are a fast-growing global industry, particularly after 9/11. In China, domestic and foreign IT firms seek state contracts to provide security technologies such as "personal identification systems" for e-government projects.[27] Internet content providers (ICPs) with government background welcome more stringent censorship measures that apply to private start-ups with little official *guanxi*. Since 2000, private ICPs have become increasingly conservative due to new content regulations, frequently providing nothing more than clips from officially sanctioned sources. Meanwhile, ironically, netizen-based political debates (of corruption, WTO, international affairs and so on) migrate to online forums such as Qiangguo Luntan (www.qglt.com) hosted by the website of *People's Daily*.

Another aspect of censorship has to do with China's Internet cafés, a main point of access for children, migrant workers, and low-income Internet users.[28] Unlike large ISPs and ICPs, most cybercafés are small, private businesses, many run by laid-off or under-employed workers of state-owned enterprises.[29] In April 2001, the Measures for the Administration of Business Sites of Internet Access Services was promulgated by the MPS, the MII, the Ministry of Culture, the State Administration of Industry and Commerce, and the State Birth Planning Commission in response to Internet trespassing from the cafés and increasing parental complaints about the negative impact of cybercafés on schoolchildren. The measure formally prohibited Internet cafés from allowing patrons to access harmful information, required the special licensing of net-cafés, and prevented unaccompanied minors under the age of fourteen from entering. However, the regulation was poorly enforced until the fatal Beijing café fire of June 2002 (Murray, 2003). Even after the fire, there has been great geographical and temporal variation in the implementation of the Internet café regulations. Although officers in some municipalities confiscated equipment or collected heavy fines from the cafés during a crackdown campaign, others in neighboring towns were less predatory or turned a blind eye because the market demand for cybercafés was so huge.

As difficult as it is to control cybercafés, it is even more difficult to monitor individual users. It is most difficult to enforce the articles pertaining to user registration. There is no systematic way to ensure that each of China's 59 million Internet users is registered or that the registration information is verified.

Usually one can access the Net at a cybercafé without showing an ID card; and it is common practice for people to use "Get Online Cards (*shangwangka*)" that provide dial-up connections without asking for any personal information.[30] Although the censorship regime tries to block, filter, and track, most determined users in China can access outlawed information via encrypted messages, FTP, and, most recently, peer-to-peer technologies (Chase et al., forthcoming).

Moreover, China cannot extend its censorship overseas to disrupt human rights networks in the US, Falun Gong websites in Europe, multilingual list-servs about Tibet and Taiwan, or Western "hacktivist" groups whose members oppose Beijing's Internet strategies. The globally networked nature of such oppositional forces frustrates all national authorities trying to control the Internet. This is particularly so for the Chinese censors for they are unlikely to win public sympathy in liberal democracies where the anti-censorship networks are usually concentrated.

In sum, there are three discernible characteristics of China's Internet censorship system that deserve attention. First, regulatory measures are often post-hoc reactions to unpredictable conditions. The surge of content regulation in 2000 was driven by the official perception of threats arising from the 1999 anti-NATO demonstrations, in part organized by online forums, which followed the bombing of the Chinese embassy in Belgrade. It also resulted from the global dot-com fever that lured China's traditional media monopolies, which hoped to raise the entry barrier to the ICP market.

Second, although the censorship regime began as a hierarchy in the late 1990s (Qiu, 1999: 14–15), its internal redundancy has been increasing along legislative, administrative, and technological dimensions since 2000. This gives rise to a network of censors which includes multiple state agencies and commercial entities with relatively independent political and economic goals.[31] There is no single central control point, as evidenced in the unblocking of nytimes.com following the newspaper's interview with former president Jiang Zemin, when he praised *The New York Times* without knowing that its website was banned in China (Gittings, 2001; Wong, 2002b). The lack of a traditional censorship hierarchy was also shown in the blocking of Google in the fall of 2002. This fiasco reportedly involved multiple censorship agencies and China's domestic search-engine companies, which hoped to increase their market share by blocking Google.com (BBS News World Edition, 2002; Wong, 2002a). But the network of censors is not a flat assemblage of loose links either. It is enabled by new technologies to carry on the missions of various institutions: from the security/secrecy ministries to the CCP propaganda divisions at national and local levels, operating with compartmentalized interests in a way that differs from a traditional media control bureaucracy.

Finally, China's network of censors has entered into a covert alliance with the global IT industry (Zhao and Schiller, 2001), which enhances the capacity of the authoritarian state and necessitates a rethinking of the political role of the developmental state, and of economic globalization, in authoritarian countries. Many foreign IT firms, large and small, have provided material support for China's control efforts: Microsoft, CISCO, IBM, Sun, Nortel, and others in Europe and elsewhere (Qiu, 1999; Walton, 2001; Cheung, 2003). AC Nielsen/Net Ratings won China's first license to track consumer browsing behaviors, which many worry could be used against dissident activities (Cheung, 2003: 85). The dilemma is that, in China's increasingly globalized Internet politics, economics also matters. While promising to help China fight online piracy or learn to do standard American web-based consumer research, profit-seeking multinationals may also assist the regime of political control. Thus Internet censorship in China is not a purely political issue. It must be considered within the larger context of global capitalism.

THE FORMATION OF CULTURAL IDENTITIES

State agencies, IT firms, and activist groups interact to establish, transform, and control the fundamental parameters of China's cyberspace. Simultaneously, Chinese netizens are constructing their online identities in a peculiar Internet culture that bears both Chinese and universal characteristics. To a great extent, the forging of identities among Internet users is a process shaped by the uneven geographical distribution of the technology, the relative homogeneity of user demographics, the censorship regime, and the flourishing of consumerism fostered by the party-state and multinational corporations. Predictably, mainstream Chinese users care more about subjects that can be discussed and celebrated, generating instant gratification for mass consumption than the grand narratives of modernity: rationality, liberalism, or "socialist democracy." Two trends are essential to this process of collective identification: (1) the rise of consumerism throughout society and (2) the persistence of online nationalism with increasing affinity to state agendas. Both processes of cultural identification have been used by the state apparatus since the beginning of Deng Xiaoping's reform and opening-up period and are likely to remain central to the transformation of China. When the two bodies of discourse enter the virtual landscape, via keystrokes and mouse clicks, in images, sound bites, MP3s, and interactive Flash animations, they evolve into multiple inconsistent yet interrelated texts, infinite instances of representation, and a new media culture of the ephemeral.

First, the versatility of consumerism in subsuming other cultural elements is a familiar worldwide phenomenon. What is special about China is the astonishing speed at which such a massive society exchanged the Maoist puritan lifestyle of the 1970s for the periodic anti-materialism campaigns of the 1980s and then for the flourishing of hedonism today. In this sense, Chinese cyber-space, infused with symbols of money-making and pleasure-seeking, probably captures the most dazzling snapshots of consumerist culture in contemporary China. From the beginning, buying computers and going online have been advertised as fashionable entertainment, as "surfing," an imported (and there-fore pricey) pastime. Pop-up windows, flashy banner ads, and tinkling promo-tions sometimes occupy half of the browser space when one opens the home page of a major Internet service provider, probably because of users' remark-able tolerance of commercials.[32] Broadband service providers are now selling Japanese *hentai* cartoons and the latest Hollywood blockbusters to high-end users. Those with a more modest budget, including rural residents (Bolande, 2003), also demand online gaming, driving up the stock price for dot-coms like Netease, the biggest gainer of any company on the hi-tech Nasdaq in 2002, which climbed 1,500 percent from 75 cents to US$ 11.45 (Ghahremani, 2003).

To illustrate the seductive transience of China's consumption-oriented new media culture, consider the short messaging system (SMS), a new aspect of China's network society. Designed to enhance communication among China's 207 million cellular phone subscribers, SMS service relies on the Internet for fiber-optic channels and for content, including personal messages (for exam-ple, e-mails) as well as text, ring tones, and images provided by dot-coms (Clark, 2003). Like NTT Docomo in Japan, SMS has been a huge commercial success. This has special implications for China because, by allowing charges to be added to the phone bill, it bypasses the problem of online payment for the majority of Chinese who do not have credit cards. In 2002, the largest SMS carrier in the country, China Mobile, transmitted 80 billion short messages (Murphy, 2003), generating US$ 1 billion in revenue. Besides exchanges within existing personal networks, SMS dating applications, made possible by online clubs and QQ,[33] are popular. Instant messaging which links Internet and cell phone chatting is also a success. To increase SMS circulation, Chinese dot-coms like Netease have hired a team of "SMS authors (*duanxin xieshou*)" to write jokes, hoaxes, erotica, and congratulatory greetings that are crisp, condensed, and fleeting (Chen, 2002).

Just as the early diffusion of the telephone reinforced existing inclinations among Americans (Fischer, 1992), the rise of the Internet and new networked modes of communication is strengthening certain propensities in China's tran-sitional society. It also excludes alternative perceptions, such as the "hacker ethic" (Himanen, 2001), as most Chinese versions of Linux are sold for a fee and few in China protest.[34] The dominance of consumerism in shaping expe-riences with the Internet is only matched by the wide appeal of online nation-alism, the political discourse underlying everyday discussion among the netizens and of fundamental importance to the dynamics of social movements in China's cyberspace.

Reinstating China's historical glory has been a persistent goal for generations of Chinese leaders, including the current authorities who perceive the Internet as a tool in the larger project of national rejuvenation. However, it is still amazing to observe the intensity of relentless nationalistic sentiments during web-based grassroots movements. The first example was the protest against Japanese occupation of Diaoyu Island in September 1996 coordinated by Peking University's Untitled BBS Station (*weiming zhan*) (the first unauthorized student demonstration in Beijing since 1989). Since then, major online movements have targeted Indonesia (summer 1998), NATO (May 1999), Taiwan (July 1999), Japan (January 2000 and February–March 2001), and the United States (April–May 2001) (Qiu, 2001a). The outburst usually follows a critical event (for example, the 1999 NATO bombing of the Chinese embassy in Belgrade) which triggers heated discussion in Internet forums. This leads to web-based mobilization, online and off-line demonstrations (with or without official approval), and escalating cyber-violence which involves denial of access attacks, virus-sending, and hacking in a series of "patriotic net-wars (*wangluo weiguozhan*)" (Qiu, 2001a, b), culminating in the so-called "First World Hacker War" following the US–China spy plane stand-off in 2001, when thousands of websites on both sides of the Pacific fell victim (Smith, 2001).

Typically, visible groups or sites of organizers emerge within the first week of crisis to coordinate mobilization and aggressive efforts during the online movements. There is usually a distinctive form of organization which I term "Chinese hackerism" to highlight its collectivist tendencies and links to state and corporate establishments, which have been largely absent in Western "hacktivist" campaigns (Qiu, 2002b). More rapid than the formation of online patriotic alliances, however, was the speedy evaporation of the movements because of pressure from wary state authorities. This indicates that grassroots nationalism in China's cyberspace remains a short-term political spasm rather than an organized mode of citizen participation or a sustainable social force. Note also the absence of similar campaigns since the attacks in New York on September 11.

Nevertheless, a nationalist discourse permeates Chinese political arenas on the Internet and remains central to the shaping of cultural identity at the personal level because, unlike modernist ideologies on the left or the right, it is the only state-promoted narrative framework that appeals to the majority of netizens. The most important forum of this nature is Qianguo Luntan (i.e. "Strong Nation Forum") at the website peopledaily.com.cn. It began as an effort to spur discussion in the heat of the anti-NATO movement of 1999 but now hosts topics ranging from corruption to WTO to problems of unemployment, all under the explicit rubric of national rejuvenation.

To borrow from Roland Barthes (1972: 114), nationalism and consumerism in China's cyberspace are both "second-order semiological systems" that structure online experiences at a deeper level. Together, they reduce the spectrum of possibilities to a single core identity: *that of a Chinese consumer*. This nucleus of cultural identification is surrounded by an endless number of youth subcultures, hobby clubs, professional networks, and special-interest associations with varying degree of marginality, including faith-based movements (Zhao, 2004), gay and lesbian groups (Wang, 2003), and websites for the preservation of minority nationality cultures (Zhang, 2003). There are constraining effects of predominant cultural representations, but the plurality of online identities has surpassed the level of China's traditional media due to the interactivity of the medium and its ability to reach beyond boundaries. As elsewhere, there is a profound transformation into a new media culture which involves a readjustment of time and space coordinates, a shortening of attention span, a pastiche of global and local events, and an ever-increasing eclecticism under apparently fixed categories.

REFLECTIONS: CHINA AND THE NETWORKS

Central to an examination of the Internet in China is the classic contradiction between "technologies of freedom" (Pool, 1983) and hierarchical "statism" (Castells, 1996), which was rendered particularly acute by the scale and speed of development on both sides of the juxtaposition. Has the Internet liberalized China? Or has the Chinese state succeeded in creating an Internet in its own image? Empirical evidence is far more intricate than any framework of binary opposition, as network formations in the PRC are situated in a unique "communication action context" (Ball-Rokeach et al., 2001; Qiu, 2003) of legacies, institutions, social groups, and cultural identities.

Although the Chinese state remains robust and active in pursuing its economic, political, and ideological goals, the logic of profit maximization has also emerged as a predominant principle, particularly in large cities like Shanghai and the coastal South China region. Yet the phenomenal growth of the Internet occurred, together with a host of new or renewed social networks, largely owing to the developmental state and the entrepreneurial marketing of the multinationals. In this process, the social structure induced by technological growth is molded and substantiated by the global force of late capitalism, China's national institutional heritage, and by more diverse forms of system configuration in sub-national regions, cities, the countryside, and trans-boundary communities of all kinds.

In addition, beneath the network of fast growth is a series of interconnected conditions that are unfavorable to the expansion and integration of Internet networks in China. Despite their prominent role in creating both incentives and constraints, China's state agencies are usually reactors to unforeseen situations in the continuously evolving online environment. So far they have been fortunate. From the global space of flows to the emergence of a heavily commercialized cyber-culture, an overwhelming number of endogenous and exogenous factors are working to their benefit. Factors include China's market potential, the return of overseas Chinese, the popularity of nationalist and consumerist discourse, and collaboration with multinational corporations. However, many of these conditions are dynamic and their vicissitudes are beyond the control of any nation-state. This presents a risky situation given the flexible mode of production in late capitalism. Most important, the so-far favorable conditions are often coupled with serious challenges: information inequality, issues of piracy, conflicts of interests among major stakeholders, a low level of citizen participation, and the vulnerability of Beijing as excessively dependent on high economic growth rates, which will draw the country even further into the whirlwinds of global capitalism.

Finally, the promise of the Internet to bring more freedom to the Middle Kingdom remains because, concomitant with the technological boom, a fledging civil society is most decisively emerging in the online and off-line worlds of contemporary China. As political and economic constraints continue to proliferate, the sphere of unregulated communication keeps expanding in unexpected directions because, fundamentally, it is the information needs of millions of Chinese netizens that lead to creative modes of information attainment, media usage, and social formation.

"Every burned book enlightens the world." Rethinking this maxim from Ralph Waldo Emerson which captures a unique characteristic of information networks, one would realize that the Internet boom pertains directly to the general lack of information and entertainment in the PRC. If traditional media in the country had more diverse programming, or if Beijing had not banned the private ownership of satellite TV dishes in 1994, ordinary members of Chinese society would not have been so tempted to go online (Chan, 1994).[35] This is not a defense of the censorship regime but a reflection at a higher level of generality upon the paradox of rapid Internet growth under authoritarian circumstances. The Internet is not a superimposed agent of change. It is a conduit through which the existing propensities of the Chinese society itself are set free.

NOTES

1. The following discussions are informed by my research on China's Internet since 1996, which involves document analysis, participant observation, personal interview, focus group, and survey methods. The author is indebted to Manuel Castells, Jonathon Aronson, Carolyn

Cartier, and Rob Koepp for their input as well as institutional support from the Annenberg Research Network on International Communication and the Metamorphosis Project at the USC Annenberg School. Especially helpful were four months of fieldwork in the provinces of Guangdong and Sichuan during the summer of 2002, my involvement as moderator of the China Internet Research e-Group since 2000, and my experience as boardmaster of a popular university BBS in Shanghai during 1998–9. Also essential was the conference "China and the Internet: Technology, Economy, and Society in Transition," held at the USC Annenberg School in Los Angeles, May 30–31, 2003, which I co-organized with Peter Yu (Michigan State University), which exposed me to a wide range of empirical projects on the subject.

2. China Internet Network Information Center (CNNIC), "Evolution of the Internet in China" (available at www.cnnic.net.cn). The message was sent to Karlsruhe University in the former Western Germany.
3. This was reflected in newspaper articles and official speeches in the mid-1990s, as well as in interviews with IT analysts and government officials conducted by me in Beijing, Wuhan, Chengdu, and Guangdong during 1997–2002.
4. "China Logs on to the Internet," *The Economist* (January 7, 1995): 27.
5. CNNIC. "Evolution of the Internet in China."
6. Available at www.cnnic.net.cn. CNNIC is the organization authorized by the State Council to provide official statistics about the development of the Internet in China.
7. This is the world's third largest Internet population, tailing the United States (165.2 million, NetRatings, May 2002) and Japan (61.1 million, NetRatings, August 2002). Including Chinese Internet users in Hong Kong, Taiwan, Singapore, and the global Chinese diaspora, the total number was estimated to be 68.4 million by April 2002 (available at http://glreach.com/globstats/).
8. See the discussions on sampling problems prior to 2000 in Peter Weigang Lu, "Internet Development in China: An Analysis of the CNNIC Survey Report," *Virtual China* (2000) (http://www.virtualchina.com/infotech/analysis). See also CIIC, "How Many Internet Users Are There in China?" (2001) (www.china.org.cn/english/2001/Feb/7235.htm) for different definitions of Internet users in China.
9. China Ministry of Information Industry, *Annual Report on the Development of Telecommunications* (1995); US Department of Commerce, Bureau of the Census, *Historical Statistics of the United States: From Colonial Times to 1970.*
10. "*sige xiandaihua, nayihua yelibukai xinxihua.*" For more of Jiang's writing on the central role of informatization, see his prologue to Hu (2001).
11. Xinhua News Agency, November 17, 2002.
12. This is not to deny national efforts of e-government and multiple local experiments in e-democracy, which, however, are still mainly constructed to strengthen the CCP and the state instead of empower the disfranchised.
13. Interviews with local officials and IT entrepreneurs in Guangdong Province, summer 2002.
14. This, in part, has to do with a change in the CNNIC's survey instrument since 2001.
15. Although Chinese users were overwhelmingly male at one point (e.g. 93 percent in July 1998), the male proportion has been declining continuously to 59 percent in January 2003, i.e. only 8 percent higher than the national average of 51 males per 100 population.
16. *China Statistics Yearbook* (2000).
17. CNNIC Report (January, 2003).
18. Ibid. Users may log on from different locations so percentages exceed 100 percent.
19. "All Beijing Internet cafés closed for rectification to guarantee safety," Xinhua News Agency, June 16, 2002.
20. For major institutional reshuffles see Mueller and Tan (1997), Tan (1999), Yan and Pitt (2002: 91–115). For aspects of foreign investment, see Zhao (2000), Zhao and Schiller (2001), and Yan and Pitt (2002: 150–6).
21. *Telecommunications World* (*tongxin shijie*). "State Council Decision to Establish Informatization Steering Group (*guowuyuan jianli xinxihua gongzuo lingdao xiaozu jiasu xinxihua jincheng de zhongyao juece*)," July 1996. p. 4.
22. See China Ministry of Information Industry, "Statistical Report for the Development of Telecommunications in China (2001)" (available at www.mii.gov.cn).

23. Interviews with local officials and IT managers in the cities of Dongguan, Zhongshan, Foshan, and Nanhai, conducted during June and August 2002.
24. Interviews with computer scientists, electronic engineers, and home-returning IT businessmen in Beijing, Shanghai, Shenzhen, and Los Angeles, December 2000–summer 2003.
25. See China Ministry of Information Industry, "Statistical Report for the Development of Telecommunications in China (2001)" (available at www.mii.gov.cn).
26. "Internet Police Ranks Swell to 300,000," Hong Kong: *Ming Pao*, December 8, 2000.
27. Interviews with officials and entrepreneurs, and observations in IT industry conventions.
28. Personal observations. A survey I conducted in Guangzhou, Shenzhen, and Zhuhai also revealed that, compared to long-term urban residents, migrant workers are significantly more reliant on cybercafés for Internet access.
29. Personal interviews with cybercafé owners and managers in Sichuan and Guangdong, and online discussions regarding cybercafé management.
30. Participant observation in fieldtrips. This was my main way of Internet access in addition to cybercafés.
31. The Ministry of Public Security has been authorized to "supervise, inspect and guide the security protection work (of computer networking)" since 1994. But, since 2000, more ministries and CCP offices have started to claim power in regulating the Internet. These include the Ministry of Information Industry, the Ministry of State Secrecy, and the State Council Information Office, as well as less directly related bodies such as the State Administration of Film, Radio, and Television, the State Administration of Industry and Commerce, and the Ministry of Education, which have gained power in controlling specific types of Internet access, online content, or web-based transactions.
32. According to Guo (2003), only 33.9 percent of users surveyed in January and February 2003 supported the statement that online advertisements should be controlled.
33. QQ is the most popular online chat service in China. The name emulates ICQ, or "I seek you," the global Internet chat service.
34. Interviews with Internet researchers and industry leaders in Beijing and Guangdong, December 2000 to August 2002.
35. Those who purchased or planned to purchase private satellite dishes in 1994 were among the first to acquire Internet access in their households.

REFERENCES

Asian Business (2002) "A New Love Affair with Linux" (February) 38 (2), p. 43.

Ball-Rokeach, Sandra, Kim, Yong-Chan, and Matei, Sorin (2001) "Storytelling Neighborhood: Paths to Belonging in Diverse Urban Environments," *Communication Research* 28 (4): 392–428.

Barthes, Roland (1972) *Mythologies*, trans. Annette Lavers. New York: Hill and Wang.

Baum, Richard (1994) *Burying Mao*. Princeton, NJ: Princeton University Press.

— — and Schevchenko, Alexei (1999) "The State of the State," in Merle Goldman and Roderick MacFarquhar (eds), *The Paradox of China's Post-Mao Reforms*. Cambridge, MA: Harvard University Press.

BBS News World Edition (2002) "China Criticised for Ban on Google," September 5.

Bianchi, Patrizio, Carnoy, Martin, and Castells, Manuel (1988) *Economic Modernization and Technology Transfer in the People's Republic of China*. Stanford: CERAS, School of Education.

Bolande, H. Asher (2003) "Bored Residents of Rural China Flock to Web Games," *Wall Street Journal*, May 7, Eastern Edition, section B.6F.

Brauchli, Marcus and Biers, Dan (1995) "Green Lantern: Asia's Family Empires Change their Tactics for a Shrinking World," *Wall Street Journal*, April 19, p. 1.

Bu, Wei (2003) "Women and the Internet in the PRC," paper presented at the conference "China and the Internet: Technology, Economy, and Society in Transition," Los Angeles, May 30–31.

Cartier, Carolyn (2001) *Globalizing South China*. Oxford: Blackwell.

Castells, Manuel (1989) *The Informational City*. Oxford: Blackwell.

— — (1996) *The Rise of the Network Society*. Oxford: Blackwell.

— — (1997) *The Power of Identity*. Oxford: Blackwell.

— — (1998) *End of Millennium*. Oxford: Blackwell.

— — (2001) *The Internet Galaxy*. Oxford: Oxford University Press.

Chan, Joseph M. (1994) "National Responses and Accessibility to STAR TV in Asia," *Journal of Communication* 44 (3): 112–31.

— — and Qiu, Jack Linchuan (2001) "Media Liberalisation in China," in Monroe Price, Beata Rozumilowicz, and Stefaan Verhulst (eds), *Media Reform: Democratising the Media, Democratising the State*, pp. 27–46. London: Routledge.

Chase, Michael, Mulvenon, James, and Hachigian, Nina (forthcoming) "Comrade to Comrade Network: The Social and Political Implications of Peer-to-peer Networks in China," in Eberhard Sandschneider (ed.), *Chinese Cyberspaces: Technological Changes and Political Effects*. London: Routledge Curzon.

Chen, Long (2002) "I am a Backstage Manipulator of SMS Culture (*wojiushi duanxinwenhua de muhouheishou*)," Guangzhou: *New Weekly* (xinzhoukan), July 15, p. 39.

Cheung, Anne S.Y. (2003) "The Business of Governance: China's Legislation on Content Regulation in Cyberspace," paper presented at the conference "China and the Internet: Technology, Economy, and Society in Transition," Los Angeles, May 30–31.

Clark, Duncan (2003) "From the Web to Wireless," paper presented at the conference "China and the Internet: Technology, Economy, and Society in Transition," Los Angeles, May 30–31.

Damm, Jens (2003) "China's e-Policy: Examples of Local e-Government in Guangdong and Fujian," paper presented at the conference "China and the Internet: Technology, Economy, and Society in Transition," Los Angeles, May 30–31.

Dutton, William H. (1992) "The Ecology of Games Shaping Communication Policy," *Communication Theory* 2 (4): 303–28.

— — (1999) *Society on the Line*. Oxford: Oxford University Press.

The Economist (2003) "Is the wakening giant a monster?," February 13.

Fries, Manuel (2000) *China and Cyberspace: The Development of the Chinese National Information Infrastructure*. Bochum, Germany: Bochum University Press.

Gelbard, Alene, Haub, Carl, and Kent, Mary (1999) "World Population Beyond Six Billion," *Population Bulletin* 54: 17.

Ghahremani, Yasmin (2003) "Making Money On-line in China," *Far Eastern Economic Review* 166 (19) (May 15), 30–32.

Giese, Karsten (2003) "Internet Growth and the Digital Divide," in Christopher Hughes and Gudrun Wacker (eds), *China and the Internet: Politics of the Digital Leap Forward*, pp. 30–57. London: Routledge.

Gilley, Bruce (1999) "Looking Homeward," *Far Eastern Economic Review*, March 11, p. 50.

Gittings, John (2001) "In the Chinese Doghouse," *The Guardian*, September 27.

Guo, Liang (2003) "The Diffusion of the Internet in China," paper presented at the conference "China and the Internet: Technology, Economy, and Society in Transition," Los Angeles, May 30–31.

Hachigian, Nina (2001) "China's Cyber-strategy," *Foreign Affairs* 80 (2): 118–33.

Hamilton, Gary G. (ed.) (1996) *Asian Business Network*. New York: Walter de Gruyter.

— — (1999) *Cosmopolitan Capitalists: Hong Kong and the Chinese Diaspora at the End of the Twentieth Century*. Seattle: University of Washington Press.

Hartford, Kathleen (2000) "Cyberspace with Chinese Characteristics," *Current History* (September): 255–62.

Harwit, Eric (1998) "China's Telecommunications Industry: Development Patterns and Policies," *Pacific Affairs* 71 (2): 175–84.

— — (2003) "Understanding China's Digital Divide," paper presented at the conference "China and the Internet: Technology, Economy, and Society in Transition," Los Angeles, May 30–31.

— — and Clark, Duncan (2001) "Shaping the Internet in China: Evolution of Political Control over Network Infrastructure and Content," *Asian Survey* 41 (3): 377–408.

Himanen, Pekka (2001) *The Hacker Ethic and the Spirit of the Information Age*. New York: Random House.

Horsley, Jamie P. (2001a) "China's New Telecommunications Regulations and the WTO," *The China Business Review* 28 (4): 34–8.

— — (2001b) "PRC Regulation of Foreign Telecom Equipment and the WTO," *The China Business Review* 28 (5): 66–8.

Hsing, You-tien (1998) *Making Capitalism in China: The Taiwan Connection*. New York: Oxford University Press.

Hu, Qili (ed.) (2001) *Exploration and Practice for Informatization in China*. Beijing: Publishing House of Electronics Industry.

International Development Research Centre (IDSC-Canada) and State Science and Technology Commission (SSTC-PRC) (1997) *A Decade of Reform: Science and Technology Policy in China*. Ottawa, Canada: IDSC.

Johnson, Chalmers (1982) *MITI and the Japanese Miracle*. Stanford, CA: Stanford University Press.

— — (1995) *Japan: Who Governs? The Rise of the Developmental State*. New York: W. W. Norton.

Jung, Joo-yong, Qiu, Jack Linchuan, and Kim, Yong-chan (2001) "Internet Connectedness and Inequality: Beyond the 'Digital Divide'," *Communication Research* 28 (2): 507–35.

Kalathil, Shanthi and Boas, Taylor (2003) *Open Networks, Closed Regimes*. Washington, DC: Carnegie Endowment for International Peace.

Kao, John (1993) "The Worldwide Web of Chinese Business," *Harvard Business Review* (March/April): 24–36.

Koehn, Peter H. (2002) "The Shanghai Outlook on the WTO: Local Bureaucrats and Accession-related Reforms," *Pacific Affairs* 75 (3): 399–418.

Lee, Chin-chuan (ed.) (2000) *Power, Money, and Media: Communication Patterns and Bureaucratic Control in Cultural China*. Evanston, IL: Northwestern University Press.

Lin, George C. (1997) *Red Capitalism in South China: Growth and Development of the Pearl River Delta*. Vancouver: University of British Columbia Press.

Liu, Hong (1998) "Old Linkages, New Networks: The Globalization of Overseas Chinese Voluntary Associations and its Implications," *The China Quarterly* 155: 582–609.

Liu, Yuqi (2003) "Universal Service Fund Emerging, Equal Effective Competition Stressed (*dianxin pubianfuwu jijin chutai, yushi gongpinyouxiao jinzhengcheng jianguanzhongdian*)," Beijing: *Telecommunication Information* (tongxinxinxibao). February 19, p. 1.

Lohr, Steve (2002) "Microsoft to Give Governments Access to Code," *New York Times,* January 15, p. C10.

Ma, Laurence and Cartier, Carolyn (eds) (2003) *The Chinese Diaspora: Space, Place, Mobility, and Identity.* Lanham, MA: Rowman and Littlefield.

Mueller, Milton and Lovelock, Peter (2000) "The WTO and China's Ban on Foreign Investment in Telecommunication Services: A Game-theoretic Analysis," *Telecommunications Policy* 24 (8/9): 731–59.

— — and Tan, Zixiang (1997) *China in the Information Age: Telecommunications and the Dilemma of Reform.* Westport, CT: Praeger.

Murphy, David (2003) "He's No Techno Geek," *Far Eastern Economic Review* 166 (8) (February 27), 8.

Murray, Brendan (2003) "Policymaking for Internet Cafés in China," paper presented at the conference "China and the Internet: Technology, Economy, and Society in Transition," Los Angeles, May 30–31.

Needham, Joseph (1981) *Science in Traditional China.* Cambridge, MA: Harvard University Press.

Oi, Jean C. (1995) "The Role of the Local State in China's Transitional Economy," *The China Quarterly* 144: 1132–49.

Olds, Kris and Yeung, Henry W-C. (1999) "Reshaping 'Chinese' Business Networks in a Globalising Era," *Environment and Planning D: Society and Space* 17: 535–55.

Pool, Ithiel D. S. (1983) *Technologies of Freedom.* Cambridge, MA: Harvard University Press.

Qian, Tianbai (1996) "The Development of the Internet in China (*Internet zai zhongguo de fazhan*)," *Beijing: Computer World* (*jishuanji shijie*) (June 17): 131–3.

Qiu, Jack L. (1999) "Virtual Censorship in China: Keeping the Gates between the Cyber-spaces," *The International Journal of Communications Law and Policy* 4 (Winter): 1–25.

— — (2001a) "Chinese Opinions Collide Online: Civil Discussions Following the US–China Plane Collision," *Online Journalism Review* (April 12) (available at www.ojr.org./ojr/technology).

— — (2001b) "Online Nationalism in China: An Odd Myth with Normalcy," paper presented at the Annual Convention of National Communication. Atlanta, November 1–4.

— — (2002a) "Coming to Terms with Informational Stratification in the People's Republic of China," *Cardozo Arts and Entertainment Law Journal* 20 (1): 157–80.

— — (2002b) "Chinese Hackerism in Retrospect: The Legend of a New Revolutionary Army," *MFC Insight* (September 17) (available at www.mfcinsight.com).

— — (2003) "(Dis)connecting the Pearl River Delta: History of a Regional Telecommunications Infrastructure, 1978–2002," paper presented at the International Communication Association Annual Conference, San Diego, May 23–27.

Saxenian, Anna Lee (2002) "Brain Circulation," *The Brookings Review* 20 (1): 28–31.

Shapiro, Judith (2001) *Mao's War Against Nature.* Cambridge: Cambridge University Press.

Sheff, David (2002) *China Dawn: The Story of a Technology and Business Revolution.* New York: HarperCollins.

Smith, Craig S. (2001) "First World Hacker War," *New York Times,* May 13, p. 4.2.

Tan, Zixiang (1999) "Regulating China's Internet: Convergence toward a Coherent Regulatory Regime," *Telecommunications Policy* 23 (3): 261–76.

Walton, Greg (2001) *China's Golden Shield*. International Centre for Human Rights and Democratic Development (available at www.ichrdd.ca).

Wang, Ching-ning (2003) "The Formation of Tongzhi: Internet, Civil Society, and Information Economy in China," paper presented at the conference "China and the Internet: Technology, Economy, and Society in Transition," Los Angeles, May 30–31.

Wei, Yingqi, Liu, Xiaming, Parker, David, and Vaidya, Kirit (1999) "The Regional Distribution of Foreign Direct Investment in China," *Regional Studies* 33 (9): 857–67.

Weidendaum, Murray and Hughes, Samuel (1996) *The Bamboo Network*. New York: The Free Press.

Wong, Bobson (2002a) "Many Western Media Web Sites Now Accessible in China," Digital Freedom Network, May 20 (available at http://dfn.org/news/china/ban-lifted.htm).

— — (2002b) "China's Ban on Google Web Search Engine Lifted," Digital Freedom Network, September 12 (available at http://www.dfn.org/news/china/google2.htm).

Wu, Fulong (2000) "The Global and Local Dimensions of Place-making: Remaking Shanghai as a World City," *Urban Studies* 37 (8): 1359–78.

Yan, Xu and Pitt, Douglas (2002) *Chinese Telecommunications Policy*. Norwood, MA: Artech House.

Yang, Dali (1998) *Calamity and Reform in China*. Stanford, CA: Stanford University Press.

Yu, Peter (2000) "From Pirates to Partners: Protecting Intellectual Property in China in the Twenty-first Century," *American University Law Review* 50: 131–243.

— — (2001) "Piracy, Prejudice, and Perspectives: An Attempt to Use Shakespeare to Reconfigure the US–China Intellectual Property Debate," *Boston University International Law Journal* 19: 1–56.

Yueng, Henry W-C. (1999) "The Internationalization of Ethnic Chinese Business Firms from Southeast Asia," *International Journal of Urban and Regional Research* 23 (1): 103–27.

Zhang, Weidong (2003) "Displaying Culture, Voicing Identity: A Study of the Manchurian Web Site 'Eight Banners Descendant'," paper presented at the conference "China and the Internet: Technology, Economy, and Society in Transition," Los Angeles, May 30–31.

Zhao, Yuezhi (1998) *Media, Market, and Democracy in China: Between the Party Line and the Bottom Line*. Champaign, IL: University of Illinois Press.

— — (2000) "Caught in the Web: The Public Interest and the Battle for Control of China's Information Superhighway," *Info* 2 (1): 41–65.

— — (2004) "Falun Gong, Identity, and the Struggle over Meaning Inside and Outside China," in Nick Couldry and James Curran (eds), *Contesting Media Power*, pp. 209–224. Lanham, MA: Rowman and Littlefield.

— — and Schiller, Daniel (2001) "A Dance with Wolves? China's Integration into Digital Capitalism," *Info* 3 (2): 137–51.

Zittrain, Jonathan and Edelman, Benjamin (2002) *Empirical Analysis of Internet Filtering in China*. Cambridge, MA: Berkeman Center for Internet and Society, Harvard Law School (available at cyber.law.harvard.edu).

5. Reflexive Internet? The British experience of new electronic technologies

Steve Woolgar

A cartoon – well known to scholars in social studies of science – depicts a white-coated scientist holding a clipboard, intently taking notes on a group of baboons. Behind him, a sociologist holding a clipboard is intently taking notes on the scientist. The point of the joke is that no single set of observations occurs in a contextual vacuum, that "what the baboons are like" is not straight-forwardly, objectively available, but is the upshot of observations which always implicate layers of circumstance and context. Indeed, it is this same situation that gives rise to the oft-noted phenomenon that, for example, baboons observed by German scientists exhibit markedly German characteris-tics; that baboons observed by British scientists display remarkably "British" traits, and so on. Importantly, the effect is constitutive of the entity being observed; the baboons become British.

Applied to our understanding of the Internet, this general phenomenon suggests a reflexive connection between our ideas about "the Internet" and the circumstances of its apprehension and use. In particular, it is difficult to continue to think of the Internet as some kind of neutral technology around which there are simply differential responses. The nature and meaning of the technology is inseparably bound up with the circumstances of its use. This, in turn, has implications for our efforts to ask straightforward questions of the kind: is the Internet actually very different in different countries, regions, areas, organizations, groups, households?[1]

These observations are important and pertinent at this point in the evolution of Internet studies. The story to be told in this chapter is about a set of UK-based attempts to research the "social dimensions" of electronic technologies. But it is also a story about how to do such research while attempting to sustain a questioning attitude to the technologies under study. The first part of the chapter reviews some features of the evolution of Internet studies that now make a more reflexive appraisal of the Internet timely. In particular, it is argued, it is now time to take a hard analytic look at how we are using the concept of technology in our analyses. The second part of the chapter attempts to address these questions by reflecting more specifically on the experiences of the UK Economic and Social Research Council (ESRC) "Virtual Society?" research program.

RECENT TRENDS IN INTERNET STUDIES

We have now reached the stage in Internet studies where we might usefully turn our attention to key questions about the analytic status of our efforts to make sense of the Internet. A very large number of different theoretical perspectives have thus far been deployed. Yet there have been few attempts systematically to compare and contrast the main theoretical currents. On the basis of recent UK research, the following observations can be noted.

First, a notable feature of recent Internet studies is the very rich diversity of views, interests, perspectives, disciplines, assumptions, and methods being brought to bear on the topic. What accounts for this diversity? It seems the technology, the Internet, pulls us together. This is so, not just in the sense of enabling communication between us but also in providing a common focus. We are now used to conferences being organized around the topic of the Internet, where it is unlikely that many of us would be talking to each other but for the central unifying concept that ties our discussions together. As most facets of modern social life are inevitably related to or about the Internet, we enjoy a new set of interconnections and interactions with interests and perspectives we might not otherwise entertain. The social organization of our Internet research makes possible more of the connectedness that fascinates us about the Internet in the first place. In other words, the Internet is a classic "boundary object" (Star and Griesmer, 1989). It means a lot of different things to different people. Interpretively speaking, the Internet is a malleable, perhaps fluid object. We make sense of it from many different perspectives, and it allows us to do so together. We share an interest in the Internet even though this can mean profoundly different things to different people. This is, of course, a great benefit as a community holding mechanism, but we also need to reflect on the analytic status of the technology in our research.

So a second persistent and recurrent question of social research on tech-nology is what status we should give to the technology in our analyses. The classic framing of this issue is around technological determinism. The litera-ture exhibits an intriguing and enduring ambivalence on this question. Very few scholars now explicitly support the basic theses of raw technological determinism; for example, that the Internet straightforwardly causes social, economic, and political change. These processes are recognized to be subject to complex mediation by a range of variables. Yet the main thrust of much work is expressed in terms of trying to distinguish "the effects of the technology" from other relevant circumstances and conditions. How much, for example, is the possible success of e-democracy predicated on getting the networked technology right and how much is to do with broader social and political processes which would encourage the very idea of greater participation in the first place (Coleman, 2003)? More recently, researchers in Internet studies are using terms like "affordance" rather than determinism (for example, Livingstone, 2003; Wellman, 2003). But are affordances just a new kind of determinism smuggled in by the back door? What other aspects of our analyses implicitly deploy a form of technological determinism?

Third, a notable feature of many recent Internet studies is that they are primarily organized around familiar themes, issues, and concerns which occupied researchers before the advent of the new technology. This is reflected in book titles such as *The Governance of Cyberspace* (Loader, 1997), *The Politics of Cyberspace* (Toulouse and Luke, 1998), *Digital Democracy* (Hague and Loader, 1999), *Cyberpower* (Jordan, 1999), *Communities in Cyberspace* (Smith and Kollock, 1999), and *Digital Capitalism* (Schiller, 2000). Allowing for the fact that publishers often influence the marketing of academic research, this trend raises questions about the extent to which research on the Internet is merely following and reaffirming preconceived theoretical preferences. In the context of the history of science this situation has been caricatured as follows. Natural scientific activity is described as involving the fitting of square plugs (observations) into round holes (theories). When this does not work, the standard conventional assumption is that there must be something wrong with the plug (observation), not with the hole (theory). In other words, in the event of potentially unconfirming, non-fitting data, the conservative tendency of most research is to find fault with the methods rather than with the theory. The working injunction is to hang on to the theory at all costs! It is almost as if the new phenomenon to be explained and understood is somehow incidental to the renewed articulation of pre-existing analytic frameworks and perspectives.

Fourth, an appealing argument for maintaining pre-existing theoretical frameworks in the face of new technical phenomena is that the new technologies are massively overhyped. According to this point of view, it is important that we revert to the steady application of theories as a counterbalance to the hype. It is argued that we social scientists need to contribute good, solid, empirical work in the face of wild (unsupported) imaginings about the supposedly transformative qualities of the Internet. However, the downside of this point of view is that it can rather discourage theoretical change and development. The theory remains intact as it gets applied to the new (technological) phenomenon. This somewhat conservative (epistemologically speaking) strategy was caricatured in the caustic remark ascribed to Harold Garfinkel that sociology is, in the main, a "no news, no lose" enterprise. In other words, the kinds of finding we unearth are ultimately unsurprising, and our theoretical frameworks remain unchallenged. The alternative situation at which Garfinkel is hinting is one where our engagement with the new technology has a profound, destabilizing, challenging, and perhaps transforming effect on our theoretical assumptions.

Fifth, while much work comprises beautiful descriptions of social change, the defining question is, arguably, left hanging: what difference did the technologies make? Some recent work, looking at the detailed experience of Internet use in specific situations, offers the possibility that we need to recast the core question, that we can no longer ask it in such bald terms. Thus, writers like Hine (2000, 2003), Bakardjieva (2003), and Campbell (2003) stress the importance of disaggregation. Attention to the massive variation in the local conditions of Internet experience makes it no longer possible to speak in such synoptic terms. What difference does the Internet make? Their work shows that this question only makes sense on some occasions to some people in some parts of the organization. We are, of course, struggling here with our own implicit reliance on discourses of causality and determinism, fed in part by populistic, journalistic, and media usage. We need to unpack our use of "technology" and to try to find an alternative conception which allows us to ask the question differently. We need, in other words, to find ways of interrogating our reliance upon conventional descriptions of the technology at the heart of our research practice. These synoptic descriptions presume and perform aggregates and aggregate relationships. We need to beware of the clumping that goes with lack of disaggregation. At the same time, we do not want simply to ditch the core motivating question: what difference does technology make? The solution pursued by research programs like "Virtual Society?" (see below) is that we pursue the questions, but do so with caution and reflection and, in particular, with an eye to the audiences and contexts involved.

These aspects of recent Internet studies suggest that we now have an opportunity to reflect carefully on what we are assuming about technology. Everyone is "against" determinism, but are we not locked, at least to some large extent, into a determinist discourse, in the sense that our language depends on presumptions of essentialism and causality? What are the prospects for a form of social research that both informs us about the new technologies and simultaneously challenges our reliance upon traditional theoretical vehicles?

THE VIRTUAL SOCIETY? PROGRAM

The "Virtual Society?" program, a program of research funded by the UK

Economic and Social Research Council (ESRC), ran from 1997 to 2002. The 22 projects in the program were commissioned in 1997 and came on stream between October 1997 and February 1998. These 22 projects involved 76 researchers located at 25 universities throughout the UK (and, subsequently, at three overseas).[2]

The Virtual Society? program was set up to research the implications of the continued massive growth in new electronic technologies. It was felt that, although this growth is widely regarded as the impetus for radical changes, the social context of the development and use of the new technologies was still insufficiently understood. Accordingly, the program was organized around two key questions. First, are fundamental shifts taking place in how people behave, organize themselves, and interact as a result of the new technologies? Second, are electronic technologies bringing about significant changes in the nature and experience of interpersonal relations, in communications, social control, participation, inclusion and exclusion, social cohesion, trust, and identity?

It is important to note that these questions were not articulated as disinterested, solely academic matters of concern. They emerged and were articulated and organized in relation to a complex context of presumed relevance and interests. For example, it was recognized that answers to these questions were increasingly central to the policy agenda, and have a crucial bearing on commercial and business success, on the quality of life, and on the future of society. Whereas in the past the pursuit of answers to these questions had largely drawn upon technological expertise, it was clear we also needed a sophisticated appreciation of their social and human dimensions. In particular, it became clear, especially in communication with the varied range of potential "users" of this research (see below), that these core research questions needed careful articulation. For example, a common first response to these questions was "of course the technologies are making a difference" where this seemed to refer narrowly to the changed use of means of technical communication. Thus, for example, it was frequently pointed out that "people" were using e-mail massively more than they had done five years previously. It had to be explained that increases in technological use were not per se the interesting issue. The objective of the research was instead to find out if and to what extent such increases had made a significant difference to social and organizational features of our lives.

Although some social science researchers were already working in this area, much of the effort was spread across disciplines and deployed differing theoretical perspectives and methodologies. The Virtual Society? program aimed to draw together the disparate research efforts to form a UK sector in the strategic field of the social context of new electronic technologies. Much discussion about impacts was under way in initiatives such as the UK government Technology Foresight (later just Foresight) exercises but, especially in the early stages, rather little social science expertise was included. The research funded under the Virtual Society? program asked why electronic technologies take the form that they do. This series of investigations (22 projects) aimed to identify which social processes help shape new technology and what sorts of expectation are built into the development and implementation of these ICTs.

Accordingly, the main aims and objectives of the program were to:

- form a UK research community in the social context of new electronic technologies;
- help the ESRC fulfill its mission "to promote and support high-quality research which meets the needs of users and beneficiaries, thereby contributing to the economic competitiveness of the UK, the effectiveness of public service policy, and the quality of life; to provide advice on, and disseminate knowledge and promote public understanding of the social sciences;"
- help shape policy and practice through a better understanding of electronic technologies and information infrastructures in their development and use;
- enhance and promote new and better forms of interaction between different constituencies: technical and social scientific expertise, academics and journalists, researchers and the business and policy communities;
- and provide a key response to the UK Foresight exercise.

The research program and its questions thus emerged and were articulated in specific social and political contexts. The term "virtual society" stood as one expression of the more general problem of significant change resulting from the new electronic technologies.

RESEARCH HIGHLIGHTS

At the time of their first announcement, many of the program's research results were counter-intuitive. The research demonstrated that the new technologies were not being taken up at the rate we had been led to believe, nor by the people and groups we had anticipated, nor were they being used for the purposes envisaged. In a relatively short time, many of these outcomes became received wisdom, partly under the influence of the program.

In response to the changing environment of expectations and views about new technologies, the overall research findings were organized in terms of "Five Rules of Virtuality" (Woolgar, 2002). This way of organizing the results draws attention to the enduring tension between claims about the supposedly transforming character of the technologies ("virtuality") and the alleged actuality of their use ("reality"). The "rules" are intended as thematic research highlights, with results from projects each contributing to one or more theme. More importantly, this way of organizing the findings makes it possible to extrapolate the results to other technologies.

Rule 1 The uptake and use of the new technologies depend crucially on local social context

Different aspects of "context" bear upon the reception and deployment of electronic technologies. The importance of these "non-technical" circumstances is that they explain, for example, why the current rate of straightforward, rapid expansion may not continue; see, for example, Wyatt et al. (2002) on the discovery of large cohorts of teenage Internet drop-outs; or Swann and Watts (2002) on the lack of take-up of virtual reality technologies. Close social-psychological study of the comparison between computer-mediated communication and face-to-face communication shows that reduced bandwidth and increased anonymity can actually accentuate feelings of group belonging and identification (see, for example, Watt et al., 2002).

By taking specific senses of context into account, we glimpse the basis for an accentuated, perhaps even novel form of sociality arising from the use of Internet communications. Studies of the different kinds of "e-gateway" which promise access to and participation in the virtual world (cybercafés, telecottages) suggest that "third place" characteristics of local social context – a social setting separate from both domestic and economic spheres – provide a key to the successful integration of the real and the virtual (see, for example, Liff et al., 2002).

Rule 2 The fears and risks associated with new technologies are unevenly socially distributed

The research demonstrates that views about new technology – the anticipations, concerns, enthusiasm, and so on – are unevenly socially distributed. The research shows, for example, the transformative power of expectations about, and performances of, technological artifacts in social action (see, for example, Knights et al., 2002, on financial services); how views about technology are constantly "at stake" (for example, McGrail, 2002, on the use and reception of CCTV and related surveillance technologies in high-rise housing); and that a variety of counter-intuitive usages of technology at work are not easily classifiable as either conformity or resistance to surveillance-capable technologies. Thus, for example, Mason et al. (2002) find that, against expectation, their respondents accorded a markedly low priority to the question of privacy in relation to the impact of surveillance-capable technologies on social relations at work. Mason et al. (2002) use this finding as the basis for challenging some common assumptions about the privacy impacts of new technologies at work, especially in those literatures influenced by the labor process tradition. Instead of starting with the assumption that relations between management and employees are intrinsically oppositional, Mason et al. stress the importance of examining the actual usage and experience of new technologies in complex social situations.

Rule 3 Virtual technologies supplement rather than substitute for real activities

Our research showed that the virtual tends to sit alongside the real which, in much of the popular imagination, it is usually supposed to supplant. Thus, against the prospects for "virtual learning" (one part of the vision of "virtual universities"), our research found that the mere ability of students to access ICT failed to re-mediate the communal dimensions of learning (for example, Crook and Light, 2002); that virtual social life provides a further dimension to a person's real social life, not a substitution for it (for example, Nettleton et al., 2002); and that sources of virtual support via the Internet were used together with other resources and became enmeshed into people's social lives, in some cases thereby transcending the boundaries of real and virtual life.

Rule 4 The more virtual the more real!

This rule is an extension of the previous one. Not only do new virtual activities sit alongside existing "real" activities, but the introduction and use of new "virtual" technologies can actually stimulate more of the corresponding "real" activity. The Virtual Society? research documents the interplay of real and virtual connectivity (for example, Wittel et al., 2002, on the new media sector in London's "silicon alley") and the ways in which e-mail generates more real meetings, and even meetings to resolve disputes generated by e-mail communication (Brown and Lightfoot, 2002). This rule has important implications for business practice, specifically for the claim that networking computing can fundamentally change the nature and management of organizational memory.

Rule 5 The more global the more local!

Virtual technologies are famously implicated in the much-discussed phenomenon of globalization. In one of many possible interpretations of the term, globalization means the rapid movement and spread of symbolic and financial capital. Electronic technologies facilitate the rapid traffic in communication, the instantiation of activities and institutions at widespread locales, and the insinuation of standardized identities and imagery (especially brands) in multiple locations. Globalization is about the death of distance, and new technologies are claimed to be "space defying, boundary crossing and ubiquitously linking." Against this, our research found that the realization of the ideal of a "virtual organization" was actually set aside in favor of more trusted business solutions to the organizational problems of coordination. Workers' efforts are directed primarily at "making the new technology at home" within existing work practices. In so doing, it is local relevance that is crucial rather than global dimensions (Hughes et al., 2002). Relatedly, our research showed that the use of ICTs can reiterate spatial divisions and distinctiveness, rather than helping to ameliorate them (Agar et al., 2002). To a large extent this rule is a consequence of the preceding four rules.

REFLECTIONS ON THE VIRTUAL SOCIETY? PROGRAM

It was clear from the outset that the program should be built around strong networking both internally and externally, within academia and beyond, involving both researchers and "users." The program aimed to take full advantage of the new technologies so as to provide accessible and rapid electronic communication between and beyond the academic research communities. At its inception, intensive use of web technologies was a rarity. In 1997, I was told that the program should be seen as something of a flagship for the ESRC's use of new technologies.

The challenge of networking with non-academics, and using electronic technologies to do so, has three main consequences. First, it means that the majority of the repository of information about the program is available on the program website (www.virtualsociety.org.uk). The website provides a much fuller account of the activities and achievements of the Virtual Society? program than can the flat, textual structure of this chapter. Second, it means that the distinction between "internal networking arrangements" and "external communication with users," a key distinction in research council bureaucracy of the 1980s and 1990s, becomes blurred. Indeed, one clear lesson from the Virtual Society? program is the importance of rethinking some of the key categories and distinctions currently enshrined in processes of research organization and management. Third, this in turn provides a more general reminder that prevailing assumptions about the relations between "researchers" and "users" require re-evaluation.

By exploring some of the potential of enhanced networking and linkage, the Virtual Society? program was able to contribute to current debates about the prospects for a more "interactive" social science (Gibbons et al., 1994; Caswill and Shove, 2000; Gibbons, 2000; Woolgar, 2000). The work of directing this huge research effort was no longer just about intellectual leadership, it also involved strategic networking, a concerted effort to persuade "unsuspecting captains of industry" of the virtues of academic social science research. The researchers themselves had not only to carry out first-class scholarship, but also to exhibit good citizenship in willingly supporting the experiment of communicating with "users." Many outside the program had to be willing (or be persuaded) to adopt this "unicorn role."[3] Both constituencies were important in helping to shape and define the research agenda.

A notable feature of "dealings with users" was the marked change in the general context and environment in which the program operated over its lifetime. In summary terms, we moved from a general perception that the consequences of technologies were simply a matter for technologists; through breathless expectations about a world radically transformed by technology and the dawn of a virtual age; to the "busted flush" of sober realization in the wake of the dot-com crash. Throughout this whole period, it fell to the program to try to provide both a balanced consistency of perspective and a deeper understanding of what lies beneath these superficial judgments. Not only did the program manage relations with a bewildering variety of users – for in the final analysis there are few areas of social life potentially unaffected by concerns about new technology – it also engaged with users whose views were changing. As many of the program's publications point out, the central core of its research findings are "counter-intuitive." But this simple statement conceals a complexity in changes of ideas about the new technologies: we also had to consider for whom (which constituencies) the results were counter-intuitive.

The current state of our understanding of the new electronic technologies requires our attention to the form of the debate around claimed technological impacts. In particular, it is not enough, it certainly misses the point, and, perhaps, is even wrong-headed to attempt a straightforward evaluation of these claims. In simple terms, to set out to assess whether or not a virtual society is possible is already to accept the terms of reference of the debate. As Cooper et al. (2002) put it, we need some mutual contamination of the categories that make up the real–virtual opposition, and should proceed by neither endorsing nor debunking the concept of virtual society. Nettleton et al. (2002) similarly indicate that alignment with either extreme is inappropriate; they quote Wellman and Gulia's (1999: 167) observation that "statements of enthusiasm or criticism leave little room for moderate, mixed situations that may be the reality."[4]

The challenge is to find a way of interrogating the terms of the debate without disengaging from them altogether. This is an important aim both academically and strategically. The terms of the debate are themselves motivated; by which I mean that they are deeply imbued with relations, meanings, implied connections, and performed communities of associations. These claims thereby involve, give rise to, and sustain a form of social ordering. So, to undertake a straightforward evaluation of the claims is to align oneself with one or other constituency or version of (a particular) social order. On the other hand, the lofty disdain traditionally associated with an academic perspective is tantamount to the loss of engagement with these constituencies.

How, then, to give space to moderate assessments of the situation to be sustained alongside, and on an equal footing with, the cyberbole?[5] At an early stage of this research venture I was presented with the draft specification for the program. The opening rationale for the research program closely followed the points already listed. My immediate reaction was that the stated rationale both vastly exaggerated the likely effects of the new technologies and bought into an unsophisticated form of technological determinism. For example, it included the passage: "all these technologies are set to modify the nature and experience of interpersonal relations …" And my first instinct was to set about redrafting the text so as to introduce large doses of academic caution: "*we might anticipate that perhaps some* electronic technologies *might* have *some* impact on *certain* aspects of interpersonal relations …"?!

The dramatic effect of this introduction of modalities was to downgrade the confident facticity of declarations about technological impact (cf. Latour and Woolgar, 1986: 75ff). This progressively gave rise to my feeling, as the redraft became replete with modifiers and hedges, that the central urgency of the research was becoming lost. The production of such texts involves input from, and attention to, many different (and often competing) interests and views. The end result is a compromise, or better a composite, of elements designed for different constituencies. So a recurrent mistake of those who respond to calls for research proposals is to imagine that there is a single, straightforward objective and audience in mind. I realized that my attempt at redrafting was effectively an attempt to redefine the audience, to reorient the program toward a singular implied reader, captured perhaps in the persona of the cautious academic. The effect was to diminish the urgency, edge, and provocation of the original draft, clearly oriented to a variety of other audiences, not least those who should be sufficiently impressed by the drama of potential technological impacts to support the allocation of funding for research into the actual effects of these technologies.

At this point, my dilemma – how to make the draft more friendly to the cautious academic, while retaining the pragmatic value of its cyberbolic overtones – was effectively finessed by the ESRC. I was advised that extensive redrafting was not possible because the draft had by then already been approved by the appropriate committee. In other words, the text already carried some measure of institutional approval of the reader constituencies that it performed. The solution was to retain (in large part) the given form of words, but to inject a question mark into the title. From that moment the Virtual Society research program became the Virtual Society? research program. The question mark is meant to signal the spirit of analytic skepticism (cf. Woolgar, 1999) that needs to run in concert with balder depictions of technological impact. It signals, for example, that the very notion of "impact" needs critical attention, not least because it implies a separation of technology and the contexts that constitute it. This very separation should instead be brought into scrutiny as part and parcel – perhaps even the crucial central focus – of the phenomenon to be explained (cf. Agar et al., 2002).

Of course, no one could expect that the simple insinuation of a punctuation mark would by itself achieve the subtle and difficult goal of bringing audiences of diverse expectations into easy coexistence. The question mark acquired a seen, but unnoticed quality. It became apparent that some people close to the program only first noticed the question mark in the title after several months of dealing with its papers and committees. Frequently, the title of the program was transcribed without the question mark into public written statements such as announcements of conferences, acknowledgments in academic publications (for example, Castells, 2001: xi), and seminar reports. The question mark was either overlooked altogether or it was assumed to be a typographical error in the information supplied to the publisher. Perhaps most telling of all, it turned out that the protocol for website addresses does not allow the inclusion of a question mark. We had to make do with www.virtualsociety.org.uk not www.virtualsociety?.org.uk. Such observations are iconic of the extent of the challenge of sustaining analytic skepticism in a context characterized predominantly by definitive versions of the capacity and effect of new technologies. The extent of the challenge can be understood as the degree of effort required simultaneously to satisfy audiences with quite diverse expectations.

CONCLUSIONS

The preceding discussion could be read as rather emphasizing some of the key conditions of researching the British network society than reporting its "actual characteristics." It stresses the context in which the work is done rather than simply reporting the results, and so could be viewed as a "more epistemological than sociological" discussion.

It is important to recognize, however, that epistemology and sociology are much closer in many British academic circles than elsewhere, especially, for example, in mainstream sociology in the US. From a British perspective, the conditions of researching and knowing themselves provide potentially rich research insights; they cannot be divorced from putatively pure results. This reflexive sensibility partly reflects the legacy of hermeneutic and European interpretivist traditions. It is especially evident in the influence in Britain of epistemologically informed social studies of science. As a result, those of us trained in that tradition attach considerable weight to the view that the nature of scientific knowledge, the results born of natural science, are best understood as the upshot of the social circumstances of their production rather than as a simple reflection of the actual state of affairs. The same applies to social scientific knowledge. In Britain at least, there is considerable reluctance to accept the idea that the methodologies and technologies of research are neutral tools which afford objective results. Results can no longer be considered as just results, in a kind of transcendental isolation. Since the conditions of researching the network society are instead part and parcel of the "results," these results are always results for somebody, some organization or institution. In this closing section, I indicate how this distinctive feature of British social science perspectives is intertwined with the emerging characteristics of the British "network society."

The Virtual Society? program was a major program of empirical research examining the social implications of Internet technologies in a wide range of application areas across the UK. This revealed a series of strikingly counter-intuitive results as summarized in the five rules of virtuality above. In brief, we found that in the UK the new Internet technologies were not being used for the purposes anticipated, nor by the people and groups expected, nor in the ways predicted, nor at the rates widely trailed in the period leading up to the dot-com crash. The results are thus counter-intuitive in the precise sense that they are against expectation. But the point about the relativity of the results allows us to see that there are important additional dimensions to this insight.

It turns out, for example, that although many of the results were surprisingly counter-intuitive in some quarters, they were viewed as more or less commonsensical by others. For example, the discovery that clerical workers pay little heed to the supposed dangers of privacy intrusion, associated with electronic office systems, was of little news to the workers themselves (Mason et al., 2002). Rather, it turned out that this finding ran counter to the specific claims of researchers within the labor process tradition, to some trade union interests, and to some concerns voiced within the media. This differential distribution of responses thus underlines the relativity of the results. It also raises at least two further crucial research questions. First, to the extent that we are willing to accept that such insights are counter-intuitive we might legitimately inquire: what then has happened to our intuitions?! What processes, what sets of social relations and associations, what alliances between different social institutions have helped shape our expectations, such that research documenting the *absence* of a much-anticipated effect is greeted with surprise?

Secondly, it reminds us once again to beware the temptation, when speaking of new technologies, to engage in the forms of "clumping" that go with lack of disaggregation. "The new Internet technologies were not being used for the purposes anticipated"? Yes, but the really important question is by whom were they anticipated as having these purposes? This question directs us to a search for the structuring and distribution of views about Internet technologies which, we argue, is crucial to understanding the dynamics of their reception and use, and hence to an appreciation of the particular characteristics of the network society.

Discussions of access and problems of the "digital divide," which, already in the short time since their original enunciation, have a tired feel about them, centered on government policy moves in relation to enabling access to the digitally disadvantaged. Considerable optimism was invested in the new public access points. The disadvantaged would be able to access the Internet in public spaces through local libraries, kiosks, and at cybercafés and telecottages. Yet the research found that a surprisingly high percentage of people using these spaces were already hooked up at home. It seems that the new access points were not providing access to those who did not have access; instead, they were providing alternative spaces for those who were already on the "right side" of the digital divide. A number of the new access points failed because they were poorly supported in terms of resources for training and maintenance. But the widely varying success of different "access points" seems also to depend on the social, cultural, and physical arrangements in place. The difficulty with much early UK government policy on access to Internet technologies was their singular focus on the provision of equipment. Guided by an analytic skepticism about assumptions that "the kit" would itself be the main driver of network formation, our research was able to show the consequences of overlooking the relevant sociological circumstances of use. Access to and participation in the British network society requires fostering the conditions of meaningful use, not just the provision of the right equipment.

The theme of analytic skepticism is exactly in line with recent empirical studies which characterize reactions to new Internet technologies in terms of participants' efforts to "make the technology at home." For example, British social scientists Miller and Slater (2000) have shown how the Internet was absorbed into Trinidadian culture. Far from transforming or otherwise significantly changing the prevailing culture of communications, the Internet was appropriated to support and enhance the existing Trinidadian diaspora. Miller and Slater explicitly reject the idea of virtuality or cyberspace as spaces or places apart from the rest of social life. Again, at a different level, Hughes et al. (2002) show how the introduction of new electronic systems into banking led to great efforts by the clerical workers to make the technology at home. Far from "transforming banking," the new systems became the focus of clerical workers' considerable efforts to accommodate them to prevailing work routines and practices. It is not yet clear whether and to what extent these kinds of example are specific to British research on the Internet. Yet they capture a skepticism with regard to pronouncements about the Internet which informs and drives the research.

To the extent that they will endure as a distinctive feature of the British experience of Internet technologies, counter-intuition and analytic skepticism are likely to have important implications. We are often told that a "natural" and recurrent trajectory of all new technology is initial hype followed by disappointment (the dot-com crash) and then the gradual accommodation and absorption of the new technology into society and the economy. But could it be that in the future the British will exhibit a more sophisticated response to the onset of new technologies? Could the emerging tendency toward skepticism about the Internet lead to a more considered and less overblown debate about the prospects and pitfalls of the next network society?

In Britain in the 1990s, much public discussion about new electronic technologies took place as part of a series of (often government-sponsored) meetings and events organized around the idea of discussing likely future developments in technology. Some of this was the direct consequence of the UK government Technology Foresight (later renamed simply Foresight) initiatives established to develop strategies for exploiting future new technologies as they came on stream. These events brought together key technology developers, business interests, representatives of government, and academics.[6] Often they centered on presentations and discussion of likely "future scenarios." They predominantly featured the expression of speculative views about the kinds of new technologies that might come on the scene in the next 10, 15, or 20 years. The presentations typically comprised descriptions, usually offered by representatives of supply-side telecommunications companies, of electronic "gizmos," such devices as intelligent remote domestic monitors (it would be possible remotely to determine whether one had left the fridge open, or the oven on, or one could start warming the stove in advance of arriving home) or systems for expense claims (it would be possible to submit one's expense claims via satellite link while driving home from the airport). Overwhelmingly, one was struck by the ethnocentricity (the target users seemed always to be middle-class, white, business men) and lack of imagination embodied in these suggestions: key applications to meet the pressing needs of twenty-first century British society these were not!

However, on one memorable occasion, Richard Sykes, a former industrialist, made a quite different kind of presentation. The key characteristic of the British network society of 2015, he predicted, was one where the major and most striking change would be the attitude of the population at large to new technologies. They would by that time be entirely unimpressed by the overblown cyberbole associated with new technologies. They would resist the mad rush to invest (literally and metaphorically) in the views propagated by the collusion of government, supply-side industries, and the media. Instead, they would be ready and equipped with an army of analytic tools and perspectives, poised to undertake a cool and considered appraisal of the claims being presented to them.

How would this state of affairs come about? Through widespread education in the social dimensions of new technologies! By 2015, we would have implemented programs of learning and understanding throughout our schools, universities, and beyond such that any commentator failing to deploy a critical analytic skepticism would simply not be taken seriously.[7]

This vision nicely counterpoises the more familiar visions of societies radically transformed by new technology. It is significant for our purpose because it embodies what I suggest are some unique features of a growing British sensibility to new technologies. The specific feature of the British network society is that it reflects the inclination toward counter-intuition and analytic skepticism on the part of a growing number of its observers and analysts.

NOTES

1. Against the universalizing tendencies of much scholarship on the Internet – those that emphasize the common global (and globalizing) features of the new communication technologies – this chapter queries the extent to which we can understand uniquely local experiences in terms of national characteristics.
2. Three UK-based researchers obtained positions in overseas universities during the lifetime of the program.
3. Shove and Rip (2000) use the figure of the unicorn to describe the mythical attributes and properties accorded by research councils and others to the role of "the user."
4. Elsewhere (Woolgar and Cooper, 1999), it is argued that there are advantages to the position of ambivalence as an alternative to the reasonable middle ground that is appealed to here.
5. A neologism borrowed (with slightly adapted spelling) from Imken (1999: 102): "It is easy to make long-term predictions and spew cyperbole [sic] that has no relation to reality, whether virtual or actual." In the current chapter "cyberbole" denotes the exaggerated depiction (hyperbole) of the capacities of cyber-technologies.
6. They rather less frequently included many "user" or "consumer" interests.
7. It is important to emphasize that analytic skepticism is not the same as cynicism. The envisaged attitude to new technologies is one of critical appraisal, not outright rejection.

REFERENCES

Agar, J., Green, S., and Harvey, P. (2002) "Cotton to Computers: From Industrial to Information Revolutions," in S. Woolgar (ed.), *Virtual Society? Technology, Cyberbole, Reality*, pp. 264–85. Oxford: Oxford University Press.

Bakardjieva, M. (2003) "Dimensions of Empowerment: Criss-crossing the Political and the Mundane," paper presented to the iCS/OII conference, Oxford, September 17–20.

Brown, S. D. and Lightfoot, G. (2002) "Presence, Absence and Accountability: E-mail and the Mediation of Organizational Memory," in S. Woolgar (ed.), *Virtual Society? Technology, Cyberbole, Reality*, pp. 209–29. Oxford: Oxford University Press.

Campbell, H. (2003) "Using New Media as a Platform for Creating Spiritual Networks," paper presented to the iCS/OII conference, Oxford, September 17–20.

Castells, M. (2001) *The Internet Galaxy*. Oxford: Oxford University Press.

Caswill, C. and Shove, E. (eds) (2000) "Interactive Social Science," *Science and Public Policy*, 27 (3), special issue.

Coleman, S. (2003) "The Lonely Representative," paper presented to the iCS/OII conference, Oxford, September 17–20.

Cooper, G., Green, N., Murtagh, G. M., and Harper, R. (2002) "Mobile Society? Technology, Distance and Presence," in S. Woolgar (ed.), *Virtual Society? Technology, Cyberbole, Reality*, pp. 286–301. Oxford: Oxford University Press.

Crook, C. and Light, P. (2002) "Virtual Society and the Cultural Practice of Study," in S. Woolgar (ed.), *Virtual Society? Technology, Cyberbole, Reality*, pp. 153–75. Oxford: Oxford University Press.

Gibbons, Michael (2000) "Mode 2 Society and the Emergence of Context-sensitive Science," *Science and Public Policy*, 27 (3): 159–63.

— —, Limoges, C., Nowotny, Helga, Trow, M., Scott, P., and Schwartzman, S. (1994) *The New Production of Knowledge*. London: Sage.

Hague, B. and Loader, B. (eds) (1999) *Digital Democracy: Discourse and Decision Making in the Digital Age*. London: Routledge.

Hine, C. (2000) *Virtual Ethnography*. London: Sage.

— — (2003) "Systematics as Cyberscience: The Role of ICTs in the Working Practices of Taxonomy," paper presented to the iCS/OII conference, Oxford, September 17–20.

Hughes, J. A., Rouncefield, M., and Tolmie, P. (2002) "The Day-to-day Work of Standardisation: A Sceptical Note on the Reliance on IT in a Retail Bank," in S. Woolgar (ed.), *Virtual Society? Technology, Cyberbole, Reality*, pp. 247–63. Oxford: Oxford University Press.

Imken, O. (1999) "The Convergence of Virtual and Actual in the Global Matrix: Artificial Life, Geo-economics and Psychogeography," in M. Crang, P. Crang, and J. May (eds), *Virtual Geographies: Bodies, Space and Relations*, pp. 92–106. London: Routledge.

Jordan, T. (1999) *Cyberpower: The Culture and Politics of Cyberspace and the Internet*. London: Routledge.

Knights, D., Noble, F., Vurdubakis, T., and Willmott, H. (2002) "Allegories of Creative Destruction: Technology and Organization in Narratives of the e-Economy," in S. Woolgar (ed.), *Virtual Society? Technology, Cyberbole, Reality*, pp. 99–114. Oxford: Oxford University Press.

Latour, B. and Woolgar, S. (1986) *Laboratory Life: The Construction of Scientific Facts*, 2nd edn. Princeton, NJ: Princeton University Press.

Liff, S., Steward, F., and Watts, P. (2002) "New Public Places for Internet Access: Networks for Practice-based Learning and Social Inclusion," in S. Woolgar (ed.), *Virtual Society? Technology, Cyberbole, Reality*, pp. 99–114. Oxford: Oxford University Press.

Livingstone, S. (2003) "The Opportunities and Dangers of the Internet: A Young Users' Perspective," paper presented to the iCS/OII conference, Oxford, September 17–20.

Loader, B. (ed.) (1997) *The Governance of Cyberspace*. London: Routledge.

McGrail, B. (2002) "Confronting Electronic Surveillance: Desiring and Resisting New Technologies," in S. Woolgar (ed.), *Virtual Society? Technology, Cyberbole, Reality*, pp. 115–36. Oxford: Oxford University Press.

Mason, D., Button, G., Lankshear, G., and Coates, S. (2002) "Getting Real about

Surveillance and Privacy at Work," in S. Woolgar (ed.), *Virtual Society? Technology, Cyberbole, Reality*, pp. 137–52. Oxford: Oxford University Press.

Miller, D. and Slater, D. (2000) *The Internet: An Ethnographic Approach*. Oxford: Berg.

Nettleton, S., Pleace, N., Burrows, R., Muncer, S., and Loader, B. (2002) "The Reality of Virtual Social Support," in S. Woolgar (ed.), *Virtual Society? Technology, Cyberbole, Reality*, pp. 176–88. Oxford: Oxford University Press.

Schiller, D. (2000) *Digital Capitalism: Networking the Global Market System*. Cambridge, MA: MIT Press.

Shove, E. and Rip, A. (2000) "Users and Unicorns: A Discussion of Mythical Beasts in Interactive Science," *Science and Public Policy*, 27 (3): 175–82.

Smith, M. A. and Kollock, P. (eds) (1999) *Communities in Cyberspace*. London: Routledge.

Star, S. L. and Griesmer, J. (1989) "Institutional Ecology, Translations and Coherence: Amateurs and Professionals in Berkeley's Museum of Vertebrate Zoology, 1907–1939," *Social Studies of Science*, 19: 387–420.

Swann, G. M. P. and Watts, T. (2002) "Visualisation Needs Vision: The Pre-paradigmatic Character of Virtual Reality," in S. Woolgar (ed.), *Virtual Society? Technology, Cyberbole, Reality*, pp. 41–60. Oxford: Oxford University Press.

Toulouse, C. and Luke, T. W. (eds) (1998) *The Politics of Cyberspace*. London: Routledge.

Watt, S. E., Lea, M., and Spears, R. (2002) "How Social is Internet Communication? A Reappraisal of Bandwidth and Anonymity Effects," in S. Woolgar (ed.), *Virtual Society? Technology, Cyberbole, Reality*, pp. 61–77. Oxford: Oxford University Press.

Wellman, B. (2003) "The Mobilized Society in Theory and Practice," paper presented to the iCS/OII conference, Oxford, September 17–20.

— — and Gulia, M. (1999) "Virtual Communities as Communities: Net Surfers Don't Ride Alone," in M. A. Smith and P. Kollock (eds), *Communities in Cyberspace*, pp. 167–94. London: Routledge.

Wittel, A., Lury, C., and Lash, S. (2002) "Real and Virtual Connectivity: New Media in London," in S. Woolgar (ed.), *Virtual Society? Technology, Cyberbole, Reality*, pp. 189–208. Oxford: Oxford University Press.

Woolgar, S. (1999) "Analytic Scepticism," in W. D. Dutton (ed.), *Society on the Line: Information Politics in the Digital Age*, pp. 335–7. Oxford: Oxford University Press.

— — (2000) "The Social Basis of Interactive Social Science," *Science and Public Policy*, 27 (3): 165–73.

— — (2002) "Five Rules of Virtuality," in S. Woolgar (ed.), *Virtual Society? Technology, Cyberbole, Reality*, pp. 1–22. Oxford: Oxford University Press.

— — and Cooper, G. (1999) "Do Artefacts Have Ambivalence? Moses' Bridges, Winner's Bridges and Other Urban Legends," *Social Studies of Science* 29 (3): 433–49.

Wyatt, S., Thomas, G., and Terranova, T. (2002) "They Came, They Surfed, They Went Back to the Beach: Conceptualizing Use and Non-use of the Internet," in S. Woolgar (ed.), *Virtual Society? Technology, Cyberbole, Reality*, pp. 23–40. Oxford: Oxford University Press.

PART III

The Network Economy

6. Why information should influence productivity

Marshall Van Alstyne and Nathaniel Bulkley

Productivity isn't everything, but in the long run it is almost everything.

Paul Krugman (1994)

HISTORICAL CONTEXT

Economists have long recognized the importance of productivity: increases in living standards depend almost entirely on increasing the output a worker produces with a given amount of input, including time. Historically, sustained productivity increases have been associated with the development of technologies underlying economic revolutions, such as the steam engine and electricity (David, 1990). In the future, rates of productivity growth will determine whether living standards rise or fall as Third World economies mature and baby-boomers retire.

In the modern era, productivity growth in most industrialized countries proceeded at a moderate rate of about 2 percent from 1870 to 1950, increased to more than 2 percent from 1950 to 1973 and then slowed considerably from 1973 to 1993 (Castells, 2000). The combination of a productivity slowdown and rapidly increasing investments in information technology led to the "productivity paradox" of the 1980s and early 1990s (Roach, 1987; Brynjolfsson and Yang, 1996). After controlling for factors such as energy price shocks and inflation, correlations between information technology investments and productivity remained negative or non-existent. On the flip side, in the past decade productivity has surged, even after sharp declines in information technology investments (Yang and Brynjolfsson, 2003). A considerable literature aimed at unraveling the seeming contradictory statistical relationship between information technology investments and productivity provides context for this chapter.

Our inquiry, however, pursues a different course. We focus on explaining how information management practices influence white-collar productivity.

Examples from an ongoing study of executive recruiters illustrate our hypotheses and give them practical significance. Recasting Robert Solow's (1987) observation that "We see computers everywhere except the productivity statistics," we want to know *how* the information they gather, store, produce, and transmit makes us more effective.

At least four hypotheses have emerged to explain the productivity paradox (Brynjolfsson and Hitt, 1998). The "lag hypothesis" focuses on the time required for the development and diffusion of new technologies (David, 1990). Under the lag hypothesis, it is only after costly investments in re-engineering and other complementary organizational practices and strategies that productivity gains can be expected (Greenwood, 1997; Greenwood and Jovanovic, 1999; Hobijin and Jovanovic, 1999; Yang and Brynjolfsson, 2003). The "needle in a haystack hypothesis" emphasizes that, although information technology investments increased rapidly, until recently they constituted such a small share of the overall economy that their influence – positive or negative – was unlikely to be measurable in aggregate statistics at the level of industries or nations (Oliner and Sichel, 1994). The "competition hypothesis" focuses on instances in which new technologies make consumers better off without increasing profits, which occurs when technologies fail to offer a competitive advantage for any single company (for example, Internet banking). Finally, the "mis-measurement hypothesis" points out that productivity gains from information technology investments often lead to changes in timeliness, quality, convenience or variety or the introduction of new products; only when these intangibles are quantified can productivity gains be seen (Griliches, 1994; Brynjolfsson and Hitt, 1996, 2000). In addition, if the effects of information technology are uneven, productivity increases might be visible at the firm level, but hidden in larger aggregates.

Studies since the mid-1990s have argued that investments in information technology do influence productivity (Brynjolfsson and Hitt, 1996, 2000; Lehr and Lichtenberg, 1999, Oliner and Sichel, 2000; Jorgenson, 2001). These studies benefit from the passage of time required for investments in information technology and its complements to accumulate, as well as better measurement through more precise firm-level analyses. Taken together, they lend statistical support to all four hypotheses, suggesting an affirmative answer to the question of whether information technology influences productivity at all.

The result has been to open debate on the larger question of *how* information technology might influence productivity. Some economists argue that productivity gains are limited to IT producing industries, such as semiconductors (Gordon, 2000). Others argue that while gains are concentrated in IT producing industries, as much as half may come from IT users (Jorgenson, 2001). Statistical support for the influence of information technology on service and white-collar occupations remains weak. Measuring output as an increase in the number of widgets produced is typically far more straightforward than gauging increases in the value of white-collar labor. Managerial output, for example, is often remote from the bottom line. However, the question of how information technology might contribute to productivity remains central to understanding what is significantly different about the information age.

Current literature offers a starting-point. Productivity per information technology dollar varies widely, and may differ with clusters of technology, strategy, and organizational practice. Findings in the literature correspond with managers' conventional wisdom: it is not the presence of the technology itself that influences productivity, but how it is used. Our central question follows from this insight: specifically: how should information management practices influence white-collar productivity and what theories would explain these effects?

This analysis differs from earlier work on the relationship between computerization and productivity by focusing on how *information* and *connectivity* influence productivity as distinct from computer technology per se. The central question is approached from two distinct theoretical perspectives on information: the economics of uncertainty and computational complexity theory. Both theories are highly abstracted from social context and emphasize the thorough and rigorous development of results related to information and efficiency. But they ask different questions, use different tools, and, most importantly, conceptualize information in different ways. We apply them here intending to inform organizational theory and with the hope of moving theory into practice.

In adopting a Bayesian view, neoclassical economists consider only how information addresses the probabilistic "truth" of a proposition. Roughly stated, the neoclassical view of information and productivity is that if you could reduce uncertainty about the state of the world to zero then solutions to productivity puzzles would be obvious. In contrast, computational complexity theory asks first whether a problem can be solved, given an algorithm, encoding or heuristic. If so, theoretical interest then centers on determining an upper bound for the time it will take specific procedures to locate a satisfactory solution.

As the efficient use of information is unlikely to be independent of efficient structures for moving it, we combine these models with insights from network modeling. Hypotheses are extended such that topology and path length affect search and overload. Centrality and holes affect access.

The first section of this chapter seeks to develop a common theoretical understanding by posing and addressing three questions: (1) What is productivity? (2) What defines the Bayesian and computational perspectives? (3) What is the relationship between these perspectives and white-collar output?

The second section of the chapter develops a dozen broad hypotheses governing factors such as information search, coordination, risk, push, sharing incentives, know-how distribution, and network topology. The scope is limited to the consideration of theories explaining how information management practices might influence individual output. For clarity of focus, it does not address strategic uses of information in a game theoretic or political sense.[1] Such questions tend toward the distribution of surplus while our interest centers on how surplus is created. When information serves as an input, how does it connect to output?

To breathe life into theory and illustrate each hypothesis, practical examples are provided from an ongoing empirical study of output in the executive search industry.[2] Two firms are providing data that include six months of e-mail communications, one year of accounting data, online surveys, and personal interviews. A third firm also provided surveys, interviews, and modest accounting data but ceased operations as an independent entity during this investigation. Survey response rates exceed 85 percent at three firms, while e-mail coverage exceeds 87 percent at two firms.[3] The virtue of executive search as a point of inquiry is that recruiting efforts involve complex white-collar professional tasks in a context where output is measurable and where information networks matter. Output can be measured in terms of revenue, duration, completion rate, and ability to multitask. Social networks also help recruiters ascend industry learning curves as well as identify and vet viable candidates.

WHAT IS PRODUCTIVITY?

In this chapter, *productivity* refers to the definition of total factor productivity in economics: the difference between total real output product and total real factor input (Jorgenson, 1995). Changes in the values of product and factor input are separated into price and quality components. The definition is consistent with a summary measure of performance based on the ratio of the total value of output divided by the total value of input.

Following the economic theory of production, firms are assumed to possess a means of transforming inputs into outputs. Different combinations of inputs can be used to produce specific levels of output, and the production function is assumed to adhere to certain basic assumptions: Inputs and outputs are valued at market prices and investments in fixed factors of production are apportioned as shares of input across time.

Productivity increase is defined as an *outward shift* of feasible production (see figure 6.2b which shows *increased* production with the *same* resources). This is the difference between the rate of growth of real product and the rate of growth of real factor input (Jorgenson, 1995). The rates of growth of real product and real factor input are defined, in turn, as weighted averages of the rates of growth of individual products and factors. A productivity increase is differentiated from substitution of factors due to changes in the relative prices of inputs, which is identified with *movements along* the production function (see figure 6.1).

Economists also distinguish between productivity, profit, and increases in consumer welfare (for an empirical study, see Hitt and Brynjolfsson, 1996). Depending on who enjoys the resulting surplus, a productivity gain may lead to an increase in firm profit, an increase in consumer welfare, or a combination of both. In a perfectly competitive market, all surplus from a productivity gain goes to the consumer. Innovations copied by competitors lead to price wars, which transfer surplus to consumers or providers of scarce resources. Consumer welfare increases, but profit does not (Teece et al., 1997). For a productivity gain to generate profit, barriers to entry (Bain, 1956; Porter, 1980) or application (Barney, 1991) must exist that prevent another firm from appropriating the source of the productivity gain. In the case of information, firms may be able to appropriate a productivity gain to earn profits as the result of legal protection (for example, patents and copyrights) or knowledge of a process that others are unable to reverse-engineer or otherwise imitate (for example, trade secrets).

At the macro level of an economy, productivity may be roughly interpreted as a proxy for the standard of living. More precisely, productivity growth increases the potential for welfare, but is not an independent standard because it may be accompanied by positive or negative changes in the physical,

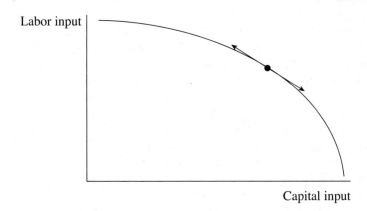

Figure 6.1   *Moving along the efficient production frontier (e.g. resource substitution). This radial line is a single iso-quantity level in figure 6.2*

economic, and political environments, as well as the relationship between work and leisure (Griliches, 1998; 368). At the micro level of the firm, productivity metrics are used to benchmark performance against standards of market value (Sudit, 1995). Growth in labor productivity has been characterized as the foundation of the new economy (Castells, 2001).

TWO VIEWS OF INFORMATION USE: *HOMO ECONOMICUS* AND *HOMO COMPUTICUS*

In adopting a Bayesian framework, neoclassical economics defines information as a change in uncertainty regarding the state of nature. Using the rational choice framework of decision theory, *Homo economicus* begins with a priori estimates over a description of possible states. News contains information if it alters this prior belief. In this context, the value contributed by information is the difference between informed and uninformed choice (Arrow, 1962b; Hirshleifer, 1973). For example, in choosing among job candidates, a successful recruiter's strategy may be conditional on the content of resumés she receives when maximizing the value of her placed candidates. Information on a resumé has value if it leads to a better choice.

On the other hand, computational complexity theory considers information in both declarative and procedural forms. Declarative information provides the facts, a minimum description, or "entropy" necessary to describe the conditions of interest. Procedural information provides the rules, the know-how, or instructions for changing the set of facts. Additionally, descriptions need not be finite and are typically orders of magnitude larger than those found in economics: for example, consider all of the possible permutations of values that could be stored in the memory of a modern PC. As a result, it is not uncertainty, but rather the complexity or computational costs of searching an enormous state space that concerns *Homo computicus*. The value contributed by procedural information is the difference in value between the results obtainable by invoking rules from one knowledge base and that of another (Van Alstyne, 1997). For example, successful recruiters have multiple methods for locating, evaluating, and placing job candidates. An information procedure has value if using it changes conditions for the better.

Intuitive notions that process knowledge contributes to productivity are widely recognized but rarely modeled. Hayek (1945) notes that "civilization advances by extending the number of important operations which we can perform without thinking about them"; evolutionary economics and organizational theory emphasize the contribution of "routines"; (March and Simon, 1958; Cyert and March, 1963; Nelson and Winter, 1982); corporate strategy speaks of "capabilities" or "competencies" (Wernerfelt, 1984; Prahalad and

Hamel, 1990; Barney, 1991; Kogut and Zander, 1992). When procedural information is recognized within economics, it is most frequently modeled as accumulating stocks of knowledge spillovers without processes for logical inference. Examples include the endogenous growth theory literature of macroeconomics (Romer, 1986, 1990; Adams, 1990; Rivera-Batiz and Romer, 1991; Aghion and Howitt, 1998) and the industrial organization literature (Griliches, 1986; Pakes, 1986).

In terms of our recruiting example, computerization of the executive search industry has dramatically increased not only the searchable resumés on file – the facts – but also the methods for finding candidates and sharing knowledge about them – the processes. Each improves output in a distinct fashion, one by improving the quality of a match, the other by matching with less effort. If the goal is to tie information, its flows, its value, and its navigation to productivity, then we need models of how it changes both quality of output and also the input/output ratio.

These perspectives can be visualized using an idea from the economic theory of production, in which a firm transforms inputs into outputs using the most efficient means at its disposal. In its most abstract form, this is represented by an efficient frontier – a production function boundary equating combinations of inputs that produce the same level of output (figure 6.1). Substituting inputs at efficient marginal rates only moves points along the frontier.

If risk and uncertainty lead to poorer decisions and hedging bets, then production lies away from the optimum. News and facts that reduce uncertainty move the firm toward increased efficiency. The best outcomes are increasingly achieved as present and future conditions are known with increasing certainty (figure 6.2a). Consider hiring recruiters in one period for uncertain projects in the next. With too few projects, excess labor hours are wasted. With too few recruiters, projects are dropped and recruiters spread thin. News that reduces inefficiency moves a firm to the frontier.

While the economic view of production is coarse grain – a black box transforms inputs to outputs – the computational view is finer grain – modular routines can be rearranged to rearrange results. If rearranging resources creates a new result or uncovers an unknown cost reduction, then technological possibilities change. As more real value output results from an equivalent amount of real value input, it corresponds to the neoclassical definition of a productivity increase: an outward shift of the efficient frontier (figure 6.2b). Across different recruiters, we found limited evidence of IT increasing the capacity to multitask projects and therefore carry a greater load. Multitasking is strongly associated with increased output. If process knowledge of how to effectively use IT changes the ability to multitask, it could change the production frontier.

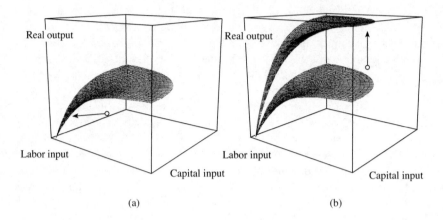

(a)   (b)

Figure 6.2   (a) Moving to the frontier (e.g. better decisions). Achieve the
*   same output with fewer inputs, say by reducing waste.*
*   (b) Shifting the frontier (e.g. new processes). Achieve greater*
*   output with the same inputs, say by new technology. Any point*
*   below or to the right of the frontier is attainable by being less*
*   efficient with the same inputs*

Drawing from a base of different theory, each perspective emphasizes
different aspects of how people use information. Economic models help
understand questions of value and information as facts. Computational
models help understand questions of efficiency and information as instructions. The former applies statistical inference to information problems. The
economic model employs decision theory and principal agency to characterize risk, search, and mechanisms for achieving efficient outcomes despite
incomplete information. Economists are also interested in how incentives
affect production and information sharing. The computational model, on the
other hand, applies rule-based logic to construct paths through a collection
of problems. The computational framework considers modularity, robust-
ness, search, and connectivity. It also extends logically to information flows
and social networks.

In each case, more effectively navigating a pattern of information connections can raise productivity. Core information concepts are mediated by
network structure so that topological models will inform our understanding of
effective organization as information flows along channels determined by
network structure.

DEVELOPMENT OF HYPOTHESES

Economic Perspectives on Organizational Productivity

A fundamental question that economists ask is what makes information more or less valuable? While a rising relationship between quantity and value is typically assumed for physical goods, this relationship does not generally hold for information in a Bayesian sense, which considers the value of information in terms of a specific decision problem. Changing the problem changes the value (Marschak and Radner, 1972. More troubling is that adding new information can invalidate old information. Consider, for example, a job candidate whose credentials and accomplishments make him appear highly desirable, then add news of indictment for fraud. There is, however, one sense in which information is always more valuable within a Bayesian framework: more precise information (i.e., more accurate or less noisy) is always at least as valuable as less precise (i.e., less accurate or more noisy).[4] By definition, an information structure that represents another information structure at a finer level of granularity is more precise.[5] More precise information may increase productivity when it leads to more accurate matching of supply and demand (for example, job candidates and clients) or reduces organizational slack and delay costs (Cyert and March, 1963; Feltham, 1968; Galbraith, 1973). This can be stated formally as:

Hypothesis 1: More precise information improves decisions by reducing waste.

In the executive search context, more precise information can refer to records that are updated monthly instead of quarterly or quarterly instead of annually. It can also refer to a candidate record that gives a specific department not just an organization.

Since the number of firms under study is small and all employees of a firm have access to the same records, we are unable to determine the exact effects of precision on performance. Differences in perceived accuracy, however, are observed in conjunction with increased employee happiness and also willingness to use the database. Both factors are observed in conjunction with increased performance.

More precise information also reduces risk. A risk-averse decision-maker will pay a premium to insure against an arbitrary risk (Pratt, 1964; Rothschild and Stiglitz, 1970). Risk aversion is normally assumed for investors – who seek insurance through diversification – and for employees – who prefer fixed to unsure wages (for a survey, see Eisenhardt, 1989). While firms and principals are traditionally assumed to be risk neutral, economists have increasingly recognized situations in which they may be risk averse as well, conditions that often relate to informational imperfections in capital markets, such as under-investment (Arrow, 1962b; Stiglitz, 2000).

In addition to risk reduction through risk pooling in insurance and stock markets, the economics of uncertainty focuses on the design of mechanisms that address risks arising from information asymmetry in market exchange, such as adverse selection (pre-contractual information asymmetry) or moral hazard (post-contractual information asymmetry). The underlying idea is that efficiency gains can be realized through information mechanisms that prevent poor transactions or unnecessarily waste resources in the course of establishing mutually beneficial transactions. These include signaling mechanisms established by the party with the private information (for example, the seller of a used car offering a guarantee) and screening mechanisms established by the party attempting to ascertain the truth of private information (for example, a potential employer requesting educational credentials from job applicants) (Akerlof, 1970; Spence, 1973). Economic literature further distinguishes between one-shot and repeated contracts. In the latter, factors such as reputation can encourage trading and mitigate the risk of opportunistic behavior (Tirole, 1988). More formally:

Hypothesis 2: Information that reduces risk aversion increases productivity when it leads to actions that are closer to true risk-neutral levels.

In executive recruiting, risk aversion could be associated with a preference for gathering as much information about a candidate as possible or a perception that there are severe costs from missing the right information. Recruiters who could "pull the trigger faster" on a candidate had weakly correlated higher completion rates but this was not statistically significant. We have not found significant relationships between these survey measures and output.

Economists' interest in the role of information frequently extends beyond a focus on the individual decision-maker to an interest in how the structure of exchange relationships affects the ability of self-interested people to jointly achieve efficient outcomes. For example, the principle that co-location of a right decision with the most complete information promotes efficiency underlies economic arguments for conditions under which competitive markets promote efficient outcomes.

Within organizations, the importance of global factors favors data *centralization* since it promotes coordination and consistency. Examples include decisions involving organization-wide processes (for example, accounting, finance, and legal services), integral aspects of design processes (Ulrich, 1995), and crises in which rapid coordination is essential (Bolton and Farrell, 1990). Additional layers of hierarchical review may also be favored when costs of bad projects are high relative to the benefits of good ones (Sah and Stiglitz, 1986). Economically, centralization limits the costs of redundant systems, in terms of construction, maintenance, and search. Technically, centralization is favored in terms of data integrity and enforcing a uniform standard (Van Alstyne et al., 1995).

On the other hand, *decentralization* favors data gathering and adaptation. The argument follows from contract theory economics: owning an asset boosts incentives for maintaining and improving that asset. Conversely, not owning it discourages investing in that asset by reducing expectations of future gains since these must be negotiated with the owner (Grossman and Hart, 1986; Hart and Moore, 1990). With pay-off uncertainty, then "to the *owner* go the spoils." Decentralized control is favored if disparate parties have indispensable information since they will be better positioned to use and maintain that information.

Applied to information management, contract theory offers the following results: (1) information systems that are independent of other parts of the organization should have decentralized control; (2) systems with complementary information should be combined under centralized control; (3) more indispensable agents should exercise greater control; (4) no distribution of control will induce optimal investment in situations involving both complementary information sources and more than one indispensable agent; (5) providing local copies may mitigate this problem at the risk of reintroducing fragmentation (Brynjolfsson, 1994; Van Alstyne et al., 1995). In case of conflicting design principles, a reasonable heuristic is to consider the investment motives of the party contributing both the greatest marginal and the greatest total value.

Hypothesis 3: Centralized decisions promote decision consistency, global perspective, and avoid wasteful duplication. Decentralized decisions promote data gathering, distributed incentives, and adaptation. Productivity increases to the extent that distributing control optimally balances these factors in light of complementarity and indispensability.

In a recruiting context, project teams consist of a mix of one to four partners, consultants, associates, and research staff with two as the team mode. As a rule, the party with final decision authority is the one who landed the business. This is usually the senior party but most importantly it is the one with the client relationship. Thus, ultimate authority is concentrated in the hands of the party with the client relationship, which can supersede seniority. Fact finding in teams, however, is decentralized.

Further, two firms decentralized the task of database entry for interview data to the recruiter who conducted it, while the third centralized this function in research staff. The former practice led to inconsistent data entry based on more individualistic behavior but increased perceptions of control. The latter practice frees more time and allows recruiters to contact more people per day. These provide competing benefits as both database control and higher contacts per day correlate with revenues.

While allocations of information access and decision rights suggest a policy framework, they do not specifically address the question of how organizations motivate self-interested individuals to proactively share information.

Another economic principle – aligning incentives with outcomes encourages proper behavior – suggests that when organizational information sharing is desired, absolute incentives may have an advantage over relative incentives.

The intuition follows from a classroom grading example: under an absolute incentive scheme, every student who scores 90 percent or higher gets an "A." One successful student does not displace another but group study can lower individual effort. Under a relative scheme, the top 10 percent of the students get an "A" regardless of the actual score. Students are ranked relative to one another and may work hard to beat out other students. Assuming self-interested behavior, the former policy promotes sharing, while the later discourages it. An axiomatic model of this phenomenon is developed in Van Alstyne and Brynjolfsson (1995), while the motivation follows from Orlikowski's (1992) case study of groupware use in a competitive up-or-out consulting firm. Orlikowski found that junior consultants refused to share information for fear of losing strategic advantage, while senior consultants, who were rewarded based on the absolute performance of the firm, willingly shared information. The optimal incentive policy is hypothesized to depend on the degree of task interdependence, which correlates with increased information sharing.

Hypothesis 4: Absolute incentives encourage information sharing, which promotes group productivity; relative incentives discourage information sharing, but promote individual productivity. The optimal incentive policy in terms of productivity becomes increasingly absolute with increasing task interdependence.

Evidence from recruiter surveys correlates well with incentive theory predictions. Employees of the firm reporting the greatest weight on individual performance reported sharing the least information. Those of the firm reporting the greatest weight on team performance reported moderate information sharing. Those reporting the greatest weight on whole company performance reported the most sharing. No firm in the study employs more than 150 recruiters so these positive benefits may be contingent on firm size.

Having information, firms and individuals must decide what to do with it. Hirshleifer (1971) emphasizes that one valuable technique is to use "information push" to arbitrage supply of and demand for a resource. By predicting or causing future changes and controlling a key resource, one can disseminate news widely in order to profit from the shift. Such news resolves uncertainty over market opportunities and benefits those who acted early to control undervalued assets. This represents a classic example of reduced inefficiency as in figure 6.2a and leads to:

Hypothesis 5: Information push benefits individuals and organizations that control undervalued assets (owners of overvalued assets incur losses). Efficiency increases when resource allocations rebalance to account for problems and opportunities.

Empirically, two factors shed light on this thesis. First, individual recruiters who send more e-mail and have more outbound contacts are weakly more successful in terms of revenues than those who send less e-mail and have fewer outbound contacts.[6] Second, all firms do engage in a form of "information push" in that each will market news of an employment opportunity to prospective candidates in their databases. Rather like advertising, these techniques do appear successful and firms continue to invest in them.

COMPUTATIONAL PERSPECTIVES ON ORGANIZATIONAL PRODUCTIVITY

Information Sharing and the Development of the Knowledge Base

While economic perspectives focus on the role of information in choosing between alternatives, computational complexity theory focuses on the efficiency with which procedural information is used to navigate through problem space. The value of an individual's knowledge base is assumed to be non-decreasing in the addition of new information, since procedures represent options that are only exercised when conditions are favorable (Van Alstyne, 1997). Existing procedures can also be used in the creation of new procedures. It follows that sharing procedural information increases individual productivity by increasing the range of functions a person can perform.

Examples of procedural information sharing include informal know-how trading in which non-proprietary information is routinely exchanged based on norms of reciprocity (Von Hippel, 1988); sharing through the networks of informal, professional, or industry associations (Crane, 1969; Saxenian, 1994); and diffusion when the information is offered at little or no cost as a complement that enhances the sale of a product (Griliches, 1958).

Hypothesis 6a: Know-how can increase productivity by creating new options for those who are unfamiliar with it. This includes options for recursively creating new process know-how. Sharing disseminates these options.

Initial observations in a recruiting context provide interesting conflicting evidence on sharing and on what is shared. On one hand, individual recruiters report learning a great deal from colleagues about how to handle difficult cases, especially when they join the firm. Examples include disclosing information on candidate sexual orientation and unsubstantiated claims of sexual harassment, where stakes for candidate privacy or client liability are high.

On the other hand, survey respondents who claimed to share predominantly factual information in lieu of process tips appeared to complete more projects. This raises numerous unresolved issues concerning whether (1) procedural information is more difficult and time-consuming to transfer, (2) experts have encoded rules tacitly making them harder to express, (3) people who withhold process knowledge benefit themselves at the expense of the firm, (4) differences are really between seeking tips and volunteering facts as between questioner and answerer, and (5) style differences between managers who tell subordinates what they want versus how to proceed.

Procedural information often involves a tacit component. Difficulties of sharing tacit information are widely recognized. Research on the learning of skills suggests that the transfer is greater the greater the overlap between components already acquired and those required for the performance of a new task (Singley and Anderson, 1989). Studies of technology transfer further suggest that when people are motivated to share information the difficulty is typically related to the complexity of the information (Hansen, 1999). Two relevant dimensions of complexity are the level of codification (Winter, 1987; Zander and Kogut, 1995) and the extent to which information to be transferred is an element of a set of interdependent components (Treece, 1986; Winter, 1987).

Efficiency gains accrue to the sharing of complementary information. If two people share no common understanding, each will be unable to connect information the other knows to anything he or she knows how to perform. Likewise, a person who knows everything another person knows gains nothing by exchanging information. Stated formally:

Hypothesis 6b: Optimal sharing occurs between partners with partial information overlap.

Within firms, interviews indicate that this would largely be true for peer-to-peer relations but self-reports of social network overlap show little correlation with performance. Rather, status distinctions govern sharing: "Facts are shared in all directions. Methods flow downward. A partner would never ask an associate [consultant] 'How would you do this?'" (interview data).

In moving from individual to organizational levels of analysis, connecting people holding different kinds of knowledge becomes important. Huber observes that organizations often do not know what they know. In economic terms, such missed opportunities often lead to failed economies of scale or scope.

Economies of scale arise because informational fixed costs (for example, learning, the investment in creating a first copy) are often high relative to the marginal costs involved in repeating a procedure (Arrow, 1974; Shapiro and Varian, 1999). Economies of scope arise when the joint cost of producing two different outputs is less than the cost of producing them separately. Informational economies of scope arise from indivisibilities in the application of a specialized knowledge base (Teece, 1980). Improvements may also take the form of either informing the uninformed or drawing new insights from bridging disciplines.

Divisions within an organizational knowledge base are termed "balkaniza-tion," which can be measured empirically using similarity and distance metrics from information theory and graph theory measures of social networks (Wasserman and Faust, 1994; Val Alstyne and Brynjolfsson, 1996a, b). Stated formally as a hypothesis:

Hypothesis 6c: Information sharing reduces "balkanization," increasing productivity by promoting economies of scope and scale.

In the firms studied, individual contact networks within offices are not at all "balkanized." Over any period longer than several weeks, contacts are dense and average e-mail distance rapidly falls below two links to reach most people. Information sharing is more concentrated within industry sectors and within geographically dispersed offices than across these groupings. Importantly, recruiters with more contacts inside the firm, as measured by unique e-mail correspondence, are observed in conjunction with higher output in terms of revenues, completion rates, and multitasking.

Utilizing the Knowledge Base

Organizational knowledge is a highly distributed resource. It can also be thought of as both a set of templates for action and a huge collection of facts. In this context, the productivity problem of allocating resources toward the highest value combination of actors, assets, and actions becomes one in which complexity overshadows uncertainty. Problem complexity increases so rapidly that answers become difficult even to enumerate.

Standards may increase productivity by reducing the range of complexity. They cut the costs of monitoring, deliberation, and search. They promote economies of scale or scope in information processing and foster network effects. At the same time, standards reduce information processing require-ments by constraining potential interpretations. Short-run costs include those of recognizing, formulating, and handling exceptions or the hidden costs of ignorance. In the long run, deference to a standard can mask environmental changes.

Once adopted, standards give rise to patterns of complementary invest-ment. Economic implications include: path dependency, increasing returns, switching costs, and network externalities (Katz and Shapiro, 1985; Arthur, 1989; David, 1990; Liebowitz and Margolis, 1990, 1994; Shapiro and Varian, 1999; Shy, 2001) Following organizational adoption of a standard, economists often assume productivity will increase over time, although at a decreasing rate, which corresponds with empirical regularities seen in learning curves or learning-by-doing (Arrow, 1962a; Epple et al., 1996) In the presence of learn-ing-by-doing effects, a central microeconomic question for productivity analy-sis involves timing the switch to a potentially more efficient standard

(Jovanovic and Nyarko, 1996). These factors highlight a trade-off inherent in the adoption of informational standards:

Hypothesis 7a: Information routines and standards reduce complexity. They foster interoperability and sharing, but limit adaptation and flexibility. Optimal information standardization increases with decision stability.

In executive recruiting, standardization examples include interview forms for capturing candidate data, generation of new business leads, and routinization of data-entry procedures by research staff. While the number of firms is too small for statistically meaningful firm-level conclusions, the firm with the most standardized practices on all three dimensions also had the highest per capita revenues, implying that such practices do matter.

While informational standards are applied to declarative information, standardization can also take place at the process interface. Modularity increases the number of independent processes, while standardizing interfaces between them. Dividing tasks into independent modules partitions the search space of potential designs, which can reduce the costs of experimentation and speed development by allowing design processes to operate in parallel (Fine, 1998; Baldwin and Clark, 2000).

Simon's (1996) parable of two watchmakers, Tempus and Hora, provides an illustration. Each watchmaker builds watches of 1,000 parts. Hora divides the task into sub-assemblies based on powers of ten, while Tempus does not. Interruptions by customers cause the watchmakers to lose any partially completed work – five steps on average in the case of a sub-assembly, but 500 steps on average otherwise. At the end of the day, Hora has built more than an order of magnitude more watches. The modular design proves significantly more robust. Stated formally as a hypothesis:

Hypothesis 7b: Modular designs can increase productivity by spreading the risk of process failure or enabling new combinations of processes that extend the efficient frontier.

In terms of executive recruiting, tasks are modularly distinct for partners, consultants, and recruiters. For example, researchers specialize in generating contacts, consultants typically perform the initial screening of candidates, while partners interact directly with clients and are responsible for generating new business. This allows individuals to specialize in certain tasks and is reflected in our survey as differences in how recruiters spend their time that vary significantly more across job types than across firms. For example, researchers spend the most time in front of computers, while partners spend twice as much time as consultants interacting face to face. Job specialization also allows teams to constantly re-form across engagements, which also encourages information spillovers across teams.

While informational standards and modularity both seek to limit the costs of transmitting information between processes, a more general trade-off often exists between the information considered in transitioning between processes and the flexibility of response. Contingency and coordination theorists consider the properties of specific coordination strategies by identifying and analyzing trade-offs that arise in managing the hand-offs or interdependencies between activities (Lawrence and Lorsch, 1967; Thompson, 1967; Galbraith, 1973; Malone and Crowston, 1994), while knowledge and resource-based theorists argue that the difficulty of replicating tacit aspects of coordination generates sustainable advantages in efficiency (Kogut and Zander, 1992, 1996; Conner and Prahalad, 1996; Barney, 2001). Stated formally as a hypothesis:

Hypothesis 7c: Coordinating information improves the efficiency of existing processes by reducing the number of bad hand-offs and improving resource utilization rates.

Data in the recruiting context are inconclusive. Survey responses for those who used technology principally for coordination, as measured by scheduling and calendaring, appeared weakly less successful in terms of completion rates than those who *also* used database and search technologies. An absence of data on those who barely used either technology prevents better comparisons. The group using neither is represented largely by a handful of the oldest and most senior partners who also had staff perform these activities on their behalf. Comparisons between those who use coordination technologies alone and those who do not are therefore difficult to construct.

An example of the importance of coordinating information is the bullwhip effect observed in the "beer game." This is a well-known supply-chain problem in which the volatility of demand and inventories becomes amplified the further one looks upstream from the consumer (Fine, 1998; Sterman, 2000). Knowledge of this effect suggests ways to increase efficiency by compensating for lags in feedback or investing in information gathering that provides missing links in the chain between the supplier and the customer.

Volatility problems and nonlinear systems provide examples in which simulation modeling is particularly effective in helping formulate strategies that are robust to system dynamics. In modeling, tacit conceptualizations of design problems are made explicit (Sterman, 2000). Simulations increase the potential for intra-organizational information sharing by acting as a boundary object between distinct communities of practice (Brown and Duguid, 1998; Wenger, 1998). Simulations also increase favorable conditions for learning about problem structure by lowering the costs of learning and promoting feedback (Conlisk, 1996). Better decisions may result from a better sense of complex interrelationships between factors or a sense of the distribution from which outcomes are drawn as opposed to a particular draw sampled from experience (March et al., 1991; Cohen and Axelrod, 2000). Stated formally as a hypothesis:

Hypothesis 8: Simulation and modeling help decision-makers more accurately identify leverage points within dynamic systems and reduce the cost of exploring alternative courses of action. They boost productivity by reducing wasted resources and creating new options.

No firm within the empirical study performed any simulation modeling. Data mining, to the extent that it happened at all (cf. hypothesis 9 on information search), was limited to market trend analysis. The firm performing the most trend analysis was also the firm having more routine information practices and had the highest per capita revenues.

INFORMATION FLOWS AND NETWORK TOPOLOGIES

Organizational information management practices can also be analyzed by considering information flows and topologies. A network perspective is not specific to either the Bayesian or computational models. However, it can complement these frameworks by focusing on the economic importance of information in contexts involving search and deliberation.

Search is a process of scanning for news of the unknown or generating courses of action that improve on known alternatives. Search grows in importance when actors cannot independently or through market mechanisms meet objectives in a cost-effective manner. *Deliberation* occurs when exchange is contemplated with unfamiliar partners or when evaluating untried courses of action. Deliberation grows in importance with the perception that potential downside effects of a decision miscalculation can be large and costly to reverse (Rangan, 2000).

Economic treatments of search typically focus on identifying optimal stopping points given uncertainty in parametric distributions (Stigler, 1961; Diamond, 1989), while computational treatments emphasize algorithmic efficiency. A third factor focuses on the role of information flows and network topologies when search or deliberation are problematic (Watts et al., 2002).

Structuring a solution space optimally involves grouping the possible choices into well-balanced groups or trees such that, starting from scratch, a set of well-asked questions can identify all choices in the lowest average time. In searching for job candidates, for example, criteria ought to cover all necessary attributes while not placing everyone in the same large pool. One would also not waste time by interviewing the weakest candidates first. If the criteria for search cannot be articulated in advance, then the problem itself is unstructured. Search then involves sampling broadly to discover important criteria before structuring the solution.

Hypothesis 9a: Efficient information search relies on structuring a solution to provide a balanced index, sorting choices to provide best options first, and stopping when the net expected value of the best unsampled choice no longer exceeds the best sampled choice.

In executive search, a recruiter establishes the set of search criteria in deliberation with the client. As the hypothesis suggests, the search then focuses on 4–6 sine qua non factors that are immediate deal breakers. The next half-dozen factors are important but less critical, and the next dozen are factors that most reasonable candidates already have. The best matches involving "horse trading" among these weighted factors.

As it is not possible to examine every viable candidate, search terminates at the point of "throwing good money after bad" (interview). This typically occurs after recruiters have established a clear picture of the specific candidate pool and interviewed enough candidates to defend their recommendations. No recruiter can "stand before God and claim to have contacted every conceivable candidate" (interview). In terms of search efficacy, it also appears that recruiters who actively seek information are weakly more successful in terms of completion rates than those who wait for automatic processes to distribute it (local "pull" versus central "push").

Globalization and technologies that reduce the costs of transmitting and manipulating information contribute to increasing rates of change in white-collar work. By definition, increasing rates of environmental change increase uncertainty and shorten windows of opportunity, placing a premium on the role of information in search and deliberation. Rates of environmental change or clockspeeds are generally thought of in terms of cyclical frequencies. Product cycles are the most familiar, but cyclical patterns of transition from integral to modular arrangements may also be observed in organizational processes and structures (Fine, 1998). Conditional on an ability to adapt, organizations that match their information gathering to environmental change rates are hypothesized to be more productive. Stated formally:

Hypothesis 9b: The optimal rate of information gathering and flow increases with the rate of environmental change.

Among the firms studied, the best example uncovered is a quasi-proprietary method for the automatic generation of new business leads. This process is tied to market factors that automatically generate more information as the market changes. It appears to be highly effective.

Information intensive strategies must inevitably contend with constraints on human information processing. Empirical research in psychology has led to a theoretical relationship between levels of arousal, which are typically influenced by information, and task performance. The Yerkes–Dodson Law considers two effects: an inverted "U"-shaped relationship between arousal and the efficiency of performance and an inverse relationship between the optimal level of arousal for performance and task difficulty (Broadhurst, 1959; Weick, 1984). Faced with overload, human coping mechanisms become more primitive in at least three ways: (1) reversion to more dominant, first learned behaviors; (2) patterns of responding that have been the most recently learned are the first to disappear; (3) novel stimuli are treated as if they are similar to older stimuli (Staw et al., 1981). In other words, overload focuses attention on preconceptions at a time when needs for accurate sensing of current conditions are perceived to be greatest. Chronic overload also decreases productivity through fatigue. Stated formally:

Hypothesis 9c: Optimal information gathering balances the costs of overload against the costs of ignorance.

Reports among recruiters of information overload are observed only very weakly in conjunction with reduced output factors such as completion rates. As measured in the limited sense of e-mail volume, perceived overload also has very low correlation with actual e-mail received. It is possible that recruiters experiencing less overload have developed better coping strategies that allow them to handle greater volume. At present, no clear connection between perceived and actual overload – with effects on performance – has been established.

When search or deliberation is problematic, organizations that are better able to address crucial informational gaps through the *structures* of their information networks may be more productive. One potential trade-off seeks to balance access to key information sources in times of urgent need against sources that may provide novel domain-specific expertise.

Empirical observations of organizational communication networks suggest some interpretations. In the context of innovation, sparse networks rich in weak ties may provide the latent links needed to spot new opportunities, while strong ties characterized by repeated interactions may be needed to transfer complex knowledge (Hansen, 1999). Focusing on key sources may be favored in contexts where deliberation takes precedence over search, in the sense that the trust needed to evaluate another's opinion depends on shared history. We state the trade-off formally as:

Hypothesis 10: The need for redundant links to critical information sources increases with the likelihood of agent incapacitation. Latent links are needed for occasions when novel domain-specific experience becomes essential. Redundant links conflict with the desire to use these links for new information.

When surveyed about having multiple sources for critical information, partners who disagreed were observed in conjunction with higher revenues and more completed searches. This appears to speak more to the novelty of sources than the novelty of links to a particular source. Not surprisingly, novel sources appear valuable. As measured by larger in-bound e-mail contact networks, those with more links were observed in conjunction with higher revenues and more completed searches.

Social network theorists have paid particular attention to relationships between social structure and economic opportunity (Granovetter, 1973, 1985; Burt, 1992, 2000). Granovetter emphasizes the importance of weak ties, while Burt focuses on the importance of bridging structural holes, defined as a gap between two communities with non-redundant information. Burt considers the return on investment from social capital flowing from three sources: access, referrals, and timing.

With respect to social networks, bigger is hypothesized to be better, since information about new opportunities is time dependent and flows through existing contacts. However, consideration of opportunity costs in the face of bounded rationality leads to Burt's suggestion that players optimize social networks by focusing on maintaining primary contacts within non-redundant communities so as to maximize access to information from secondary sources.

Burt's theory of structural holes is a theory of competitive advantage that follows from social capital. Although the emphasis is strategic, parties that occupy structural holes might theoretically increase productivity in two ways. The first explanation can be conceived in economic terms as a form of infor-mational arbitrage, in which profits or social status are realized through personal relationships, but the end result is a more efficient allocation of resources. For example, Baker (1984) documents the extent to which social network topologies of floor traders dampen the volatility of options prices within a national securities market. The second explanation can be conceptu-alized as realizing economies of scope and scale in the face of "balkanization." In this case, information about an opportunity is transmitted across a structural hole, while the actual creation of new value follows from subsequent infor-mation flows. Examples include: Hargadon and Sutton's (1997) ethnographic analysis of brainstorming practices that facilitated the brokering of technolog-ical expertise within a design firm; Powell et al.'s (1996) analysis of relation-ships between intra-organizational collaboration patterns, profitability, and growth in biotechnology; Saxenian's (1994) ethnographic account of regional differences between Route 128 and Silicon Valley; and Castells's (2000, 2001) portrait of a network society, in which productivity gains are attributed to the abilities of self-programmable human labor to continuously reconfigure around opportunities in a globally interconnected world.

Hypothesis 11: Network efficiency balances network size and diversity of contacts. Network effectiveness distinguishes primary from secondary contacts and focuses resources on preserving primary contacts. Individuals who are more central will be more effective.

In terms of e-mail communications, three contact measures, calculated on more than 40,000 messages for recruiters, included "betweenness," "central-ity," and "in-degree." These can be interpreted both for individual nodes and for their contacts' contacts. All three were correlated and all three were observed in conjunction with higher output as measured by revenues and completion rates at statistically significant levels.

Optimal network structure might balance efficient information sharing across strong ties and the identification of opportunities across structural holes. A network topology that theoretically combines these desired properties is the "small world" topology (Watts and Strogatz, 1998; Watts, 1999). The "small world" is defined by two measures: characteristic path length (the smallest number of links it takes to connect one node to another averaged over all pairs of nodes in the network) and the clustering coefficient (the fraction of neighboring nodes that are also collected to one another).

An explanation for this effect is that adding only a few shortcuts between cliques turns a large world into a small world. Using formal models, Watts and Strogatz (1998) shifted gradually from a regular network to a random network by increasing the probability of making random connections from 0 to 1. They found characteristic path length drops quickly, whereas the value of the clustering coefficient drops slowly. This leads to a small-world network in which clustering is high but the characteristic path length is short.

Importantly, however, we emphasize small worlds characterized by clustering and short paths apart from the randomness of connection that is only one way of shortening distance. Shortcuts can be intentional. Kleinberg (2000) points out that, although random graphs may have shortcuts, individual agents will typically have insufficient information to exploit them. Since the average person (node) is not directly associated with the key people (clique-linkers), it is impossible to determine whether you live in a small world or a large world from local information alone. However, the small-world hypothesis can be tested through the collection of network data. Stated formally:

Hypothesis 12: The small-world pattern of high local clustering and short average path lengths promotes productivity more than either hierarchical or fully connected networks.

Among recruiters, modal e-mail communications across nodes were highly interconnected over any time period longer than one month. It appears that, for most project teams, communications within the firm were many to many with respect to recruiters outside the team but within the organization. The firm with the shortest average path length (1.5 versus 1.9) generated the most revenue per recruiter. However, as no organization studied numbered more than 150 employees, relatively short path lengths may also imply that information overload is not yet a binding consideration.

CONCLUSIONS

Empirical evidence that investments in information technology positively influence productivity has renewed long-standing debate among economists over the sources of productivity growth. We argue that the complexity of the relationship between information and productivity necessitates approaches that transcend traditional disciplinary boundaries and acknowledge contributions from economics, complexity, and network theories.

Our argument begins by linking theoretical notions for valuing information as data and process to the economic definition of total factor productivity. Formally recognizing the economic value of information as process opens the door for integrating theory from multiple traditions.

A major contribution of this work is to codify predictions of various theories and connect them to white-collar productivity. One set of theories considers questions of value and information as facts. The economic tradition connects information to output via risk, precision, push, search, standards, and incentives. Another set of theories helps understand efficiency and information as instructions. Computational and network models connect information to output via topological efficiency, modular design, standards, centrality, modeling, and search.

While relationships between information and productivity are clearly complex, they should be amenable to testing and validation. Along this line, the second contribution of this work is to provide a glimpse of how each hypothesis might be interpreted and applied. In the specific context of executive search, absolute incentive systems track information sharing, larger social networks are observed with more revenues and higher completion rates, routines correlate with revenue, decentralized data entry parallels perceptions of information control, and centrality seems connected to revenue. Although anecdotal in nature, these illustrations from a continuing multi-year study point to the means of probing these predictions further.

Empirical verification of hypotheses will undoubtedly involve considerable ingenuity in generating suitable controls and translating predictions of theory into precise measures of information use and human interaction. This process is ongoing. The greater promise, however, lies in the potential not only to reflect on patterns of organization as they exist, but to generate new lines of research that actively informs business practice in light of the opportunities offered by continuing advances in information, network, and communication technologies.

ACKNOWLEDGMENTS

We gratefully acknowledge valuable suggestions from Manuel Castells, Michael Cohen, David Croson, Misha Lipatov, Brian Subirana, and Jun Zhang. Charles King III provided useful resources and helpful conversations.

This work has been generously supported by NSF Career Award #9876233 and by Intel Corporation. Interested readers may test precise interpretations of our theories in an online simulation environment of networked societies (the Information Diffusion and Growth Simulator available at www.IndigoSim. org).

NOTES

1. Strategic uses of information are covered in the literature on game theory and industrial organization. On political uses of information within organizations, there is a separate literature (cf. Markus, 1983; Davenport et al., 1992).
2. We emphasize that illustrations here are either bivariate correlations or anecdotes based on interviews. Subsequent research will seek to introduce appropriate statistical controls.
3. Participants were paid $25 and $100 for surveys and for permission to capture e-mail respectively.
4. Blackwell demonstrates a formal equivalence between increased precision and reduced noise.
5. Interestingly, precision also has a computational interpretation as the number of bits necessary to distinguish different cases (Cover and Thomas, 1991).
6. In-bound e-mail contacts are more important, which might indicate a stronger correlation with social networks than marketing per se (cf. hypotheses 11 and 12).

REFERENCES

Adams, J. D. (1990) "Fundamental Stocks of Knowledge and Productivity Growth," *Journal of Political Economy* 98 (4): 673–702.

Aghion, P. and Howitt, P. (1998) *Endogeneous Growth Theory*. Cambridge, MA: MIT Press.

Akerlof, G. A. (1970) "The Market for 'Lemons': Quality Uncertainty and the Market Mechanism," *Quarterly Journal of Economics* 84 (3): 488–500.

Arrow, K. J. (1962a) "The Economic Implications of Learning by Doing," *The Review of Economic Studies* 29 (3): 155–73.

— — (1962b) "Economic Welfare and the Allocation of Resources for Invention," in Richard R. Nelson (ed.), *The Rate and Direction of Inventive Activity: Economic and Social Factors*, pp. 609–25. National Bureau of Economic Research, Conference Series. Princeton, NJ: Princeton University Press.

— — (1974) *The Limits of Organization*. New York, W. W. Norton.

Arthur, B. W. (1989) "Competing Technologies, Increasing Returns and Lock-in by Historical Events," *The Economic Journal* 99 (394): 116–31.

Bain, J. (1956) *Barriers to New Competition*. Cambridge, MA: Harvard University Press.

Baker, W. E. (1984) "The Social Structure of a National Securities Market," *American Journal of Sociology* 89 (4): 775–811.

Balakrishnan, A., Kalakota, R. et al. (1995) "Document-centered Information Systems to Support Reactive Problem-solving in Manufacturing," *International Journal of Production Economics* 38: 31–58.

Baldwin, C. Y. and Clark, K. B. (2000) *Design Rules: The Power of Modularity*. Cambridge, MA: MIT Press.

Barney, J. (1991) "Firm Resources and Sustained Competitive Advantage," *Journal of Management* 17 (1): 99–120.

— — (2001) "Is the Resource-based 'View' a Useful Perspective for Strategic Management Research? Yes," *Academy of Management Review* 26 (1): 41–56.

Blackwell, D. (1953) "Equivalent Comparison of Experiments," *Annals of Mathematical Statistics* 24 (2): 265–72.

Bolton, P. and Farrell, J. (1990) "Decentralization, Duplication and Delay," *Journal of Political Economy* 98 (4): 803–26.

Broadhurst, P. L. (1959) "The Interaction of Task Difficulty and Motivation: The Yerkes–Dodson Law Revisited," *Acta Psychologica* 16: 321–38.

Brown, J. S. and Duguid, P. (1998) "Organizing Knowledge," *California Management Review* 40 (3): 90–110.

Brynjolfsson, E. (1994) "Information Assets, Technology, and Organization," *Management Science* 40 (12): 1645–62.

— — and Hitt, L. (1996) "Paradox Lost? Firm-level Evidence on the Returns to Information Systems Spending," *Management Science* 42 (4): 541–58.

— — and — — (1998) "Beyond the Productivity Paradox: Computers Are the Catalyst for Bigger Changes," *Communications of the ACM* 41 (8): 49–55.

— — and — — (2000) "Beyond Computation: Information Technology, Organizational Transformation and Business Performance," *Journal of Economic Perspectives* 14 (4): 23–48.

— — and Yang, S. (1996) "Information Technology and Productivity: A Review of the Literature," *Advances in Computers* 43: 179–214.

Burt, R. S. (1992) "Structural Holes: The Social Structure of Competition," in N. Noria and R. G. Eccles (eds), *Networks and Organizations*, pp. 57–91. Cambridge, MA: Harvard University Press.

— — (2000) "The Network Structure of Social Capital," in R. I. Sutton and B. M. Staw (eds), *Research in Organizational Behavior*. Greenwich, CT: JAI Press.

Castells, M. (2000) *The Rise of the Network Society*, 2nd edn. Oxford: Blackwell.

— — (2001) *The Internet Galaxy*. Oxford: Oxford University Press.

Cohen, M. D. and Axelrod, R. (2000) *Harnessing Complexity: Organizational Implications of a Scientific Frontier*. New York: The Free Press.

Conlisk, J. (1996) "Why Bounded Rationality," *Journal of Economic Literature* 34 (2): 669–700.

Conner, K. R. and Prahalad, C. K. (1996) "A Resource-based Theory of the Firm: Knowledge vs. Opportunism," *Organization Science* 7 (5): 477–501.

Cover, T. M. and Thomas, J. A. (1991) *Elements of Information Theory*. New York: John Wiley.

Crane, D. (1969) "Social Structure in a Group of Scientists: A Test of the 'Invisible College' Hypothesis," *American Sociological Review* 34 (3): 335–52.

Cyert, R. M. and March, J. G. (1963) *A Behavioral Theory of the Firm*. Malden, MA: Blackwell.

Davenport, T. H., Eccles, R. G. and Prusak, L. (1992) "Information Politics," *Sloan Management Review*, 53–65.

David, P. A. (1990) "The Dynamo and the Computer: A Historical Perspective on the Modern Productivity Paradox," *American Economic Review Papers and Proceedings* 1 (2): 355–61.

Diamond, P. (1989) "Search Theory," in J. Eatwell, M. Milgate and P. Newman (eds), *The New Palgrave: Allocation, Information and Markets*, pp. 273–9. New York: W. W. Norton.

Eisenhardt, K. M. (1989) "Agency Theory: An Assessment and Review," *Academy of Management Review* 14 (1): 57–74.

Epple, D., Argote, L. and Devadas, R. (1996) "Organizational Learning Curves: A Method for Investigating Intra-plant Transfer of Knowledge Acquired Through Learning by Doing," in M. D. Cohen and L. Sproull (eds), *Organizational Learning*, pp. 83–100. Thousand Oaks, CA: Sage.

Feltham, G. (1968) "The Value of Information," *Accounting Review* 43 (4): 684–96.

Fine, C. H. (1998) *Clockspeed*. Reading, MA: Perseus.

Fudenberg, D. and Tirole, J. (1991) *Game Theory*. Cambridge, MA: MIT Press.

Galbraith, J. R. (1973) *Designing Complex Organizations*. Reading, MA: Addison-Wesley.

Gordon, R. J. (2000) "Does the 'New Economy' Measure up to the Great Inventions of the Past?," *Journal of Economic Perspectives* 14 (4): 49–74.

Granovetter, M. (1973) "The Strength of Weak Ties," *American Journal of Sociology* 78 (6): 1360–80.

— — (1985) "Economic Action and Social Structure: The Problem of Embeddedness," *American Journal of Sociology* 91 (3): 481–510.

Greenwood, J. (1997) *The Third Industrial Revolution: Technology, Productivity and Income Inequality*. Washington, DC: AEI Press.

— — and Jovanovic, B. (1999) "The IT Revolution and the Stock Market," *American Economic Review, Papers and Proceedings* 86 (2): 116–22.

Griliches, Z. (1958) "Research Costs and Social Return: Hybrid Corn and Related Innovations," *Journal of Political Economy* 66 (5): 419–31.

— — (1986) "Productivity, R&D and Basic Research at the Firm Level in the 1970s," *American Economic Review* 76 (1): 141–54.

— — (1994) "Productivity, R&D, and Data Constraints," *American Economic Review* 84 (1): 1–23.

— — (1998) *R&D and Productivity: The Econometric Evidence*. Chicago: University of Chicago Press.

Grossman, S. J. and Hart, O. D. (1986) "The Costs and Benefits of Ownership: A Theory of Vertical and Lateral Integration," *Journal of Political Economy* 94 (4): 691–719.

Hansen, M. T. (1999) "The Search-Transfer Problem: The Role of Weak Ties in Sharing Knowledge across Organizational Subunits," *Administrative Science Quarterly* 44 (1): 82–111.

Hargadon, A. and Sutton, R. I. (1997) "Technology Brokering and Innovation in a Product Development Firm," *Administrative Science Quarterly* 42 (4): 716–49.

Hart, O. D. and Moore, J. (1990) "Property Rights and the Nature of the Firm," *Journal of Political Economy* 98 (6): 1119–58.

Hayek, F. (1945) "The Use of Knowledge in Society," *American Economic Review* 35 (4): 519–30.

Hirshleifer, J. (1971) "The Private and Social Value of Information and the Reward to Inventive Activity," *The American Economic Review* 61 (4): 561–74.

ó (1973) "Where Are We in the Theory of Information?," *American Economic Review* 63 (2): 31–9.

Hitt, L. and Brynjolfsson, E. (1996) "Productivity, Business Profitability, and Consumer Surplus: Three Different Measures of Information Technology Value," *MIS Quarterly* 20 (2): 121–42.

Hobijin, B. and Jovanovic, B. (1999) "The Information Technology Revolution and the Stock Market: Preliminary Evidence," mimeo. New York: New York University.

Huber, G. (1991) "Organizational Learning: The Contributing Processes and the Literatures," *Organization Science* 2 (1): 88–115.

Jorgenson, D. (1995) *Productivity.* Cambridge, MA: MIT Press.

— — (2001) "Information Technology and the US Economy," *American Economic Review* 91 (1): 1–32.

Jovanovic, B. and Nyarko, Y. (1996) "Learning by Doing and the Choice of Technology," *Econometrica* 64 (6): 1299–310.

Katz, M. L. and Shapiro, C. (1985) "Network Externalities, Competition and Compatibility," *American Economic Review* 75 (3): 424–40.

Kleinberg, J. (2000) "The Small-world Phenomenon: An Algorithmic Perspective," 32nd ACM Symposium on the Theory of Computing.

Kogut, B. and Zander, U. (1992) "Knowledge of the Firm, Combinative Capabilities, and the Replication of Technology," Organization Science 3 (3): 383–97.

— — and — — (1996) "What Firms Do? Coordination, Identity and Learning," *Organization Science* 7 (5): 502–18.

Lawrence, P. R. and Lorsch, J. W. (1967) "Differentiation and Integration in Complex Organizations," *Administrative Science Quarterly* 12 (1): 1–47.

Lehr, B. and Lichtenberg, F. (1999) "Information Technology and its Impact on Productivity: Firm-level Evidence from Government and Private Data Sources, 1977–1993," *Canadian Journal of Economics* 32 (2): 335–62.

Liebowitz, S. J. and Margolis, S. E. (1990) "The Fable of the Keys," *Journal of Law and Economics* 33 (1): 1–26.

— — and — — (1994) "Network Externality: An Uncommon Tragedy," *Journal of Economic Perspectives* 8 (2): 133–50.

Malone, T. W. and Crowston, K. (1994) "The Interdisciplinary Study of Coordination," *ACM Computing Surveys* 26 (1): 87–119.

March, J. G. and Simon, H. A. (1958) *Organizations.* New York: John Wiley.

— —, Sproull, L. and Tamuz, M. (1991) "Learning from Samples of One or Fewer," *Organization Science* 2 (1).

Markus, M. L. (1983) "Power, Politics and MIS Implementation," *Communications of the ACM* 26 (6): 430–44.

Marschak, J. and Radner, R. (1972) *Economic Theory of Teams.* New Haven, CT: Yale University Press.

Nelson, R. R. and Winter, S. G. (1982) *An Evolutionary Theory of Economic Change.* Cambridge, MA: Harvard University Press.

Oliner, S. D. and Sichel, D. E. (1994) "Computers and Output Growth Revisited: How Big is the Puzzle?," *Brookings Papers on Economic Activity* 2: 273–334.

— — and — — (2000) "The Resurgence of Growth in the Late 1990s: Is Information Technology the Story?," *Journal of Economic Perspectives* 14 (4): 3–22.

Orlikowski, W. J. (1992) *Learning from Notes: Organizational Issues in Groupware Implementation.* Proceedings of the ACM Conference on Computer-supported Cooperative Work, pp. 362–9.

Pakes, A. (1986) "Patents as Options: Some Estimates of the Value of Holding European Patent Stocks," *Econometrica* 54 (4): 755–84.

Porter, M. (1980) *Competitive Strategy.* New York: The Free Press.

Powell, W. W., Koput, K., et al. (1996) "Interorganizational Collaboration and the Locus of Innovation: Networks of Learning in Biotechnology," *Administrative Science Quarterly* 41 (1): 116–45.

Prahalad, C. K. and Hamel, G. (1990) "The Core Competence of the Corporation," *Harvard Business Review* 68 (3): 79–91.

Pratt, J. W. (1964) "Risk Aversion in the Small and in the Large." *Econometrica* 32 (1/2): 122–36.

Rangan, S. (2000) "The Problem of Search and Deliberation in Economic Action: When Social Networks Really Matter," *Academy of Management Review* 25 (4): 813–28.

Rivera-Batiz, L. and Romer, P. M (1991) "Economic Integration and Endogeneous Growth," *Quarterly Journal of Economics* 106 (2): 531–55.

Roach, S. S. (1987) "America's Technological Dilemma: A Profile of the Information Economy," Special Economy Study, Morgan Stanley and Co.

Romer, P. M. (1986) "Increasing Returns and Long-run Growth," *Journal of Political Economy* 94 (5): 1002–37.

— — (1990) "Endogenous Technological Change," *Journal of Political Economy* 98 (5): S71–S102.

Rothschild, M. and Stiglitz, J. E. (1970) "Increasing Risk. I: A Definition," *Journal of Economic Theory* 2 (3): 225–43.

Sah, R. K. and Stiglitz, J. (1986) "The Architecture of Economic Systems," *American Economic Review* 76 (4): 716–27.

Saxenian, A. (1994) *Regional Advantage: Culture and Competition in Silicon Valley and Route 128.* Cambridge, MA: Harvard University Press.

Shapiro, C. and Varian, H. R. (1999) *Information Rules.* Cambridge, MA: Harvard Business School Press.

Shy, O. (2001) *The Economics of Network Industries.* Cambridge: Cambridge University Press.

Simon, H. A. (1996) *The Sciences of the Artificial.* Cambridge, MA: MIT Press.

Singley, M. K. and Anderson, J. R. (1989) *The Transfer of Cognitive Skill.* Cambridge, MA: Harvard University Press.

Solow, R. (1987) "We'd Better Watch Out," *New York Times Book Review* (July 12): 36.

Spence, M. (1973) "Job Market Signaling," *Quarterly Journal of Economics* 87 (3): 355–74.

Staw, B. M., Sandelands, L. E., et al. (1981) "Threat-rigidity Effects in Organizational Behavior: A Multi-level Analysis," *Administrative Science Quarterly* 26: 501–24.

Sterman, J. D. (2000) *Business Dynamics: Systems Thinking and Modeling for a Complex World.* New York: McGraw-Hill.

Stigler, G. J. (1961) "The Economics of Information," *Journal of Political Economy* 69 (3): 213–25.

Stiglitz, J. (2000) "The Contributions of the Economics of Information to Twentieth Century Economics," *Quarterly Journal of Economics* 115 (4): 1441–78.

Sudit, E. (1995) "Productivity Measurement in Industrial Operations," *European Journal of Operational Research* 85 (3): 435–53.

Teece, D. J. (1980) "Economies of Scope and the Scope of the Enterprise," *Journal of Economic Behavior and Organization* 1: 223–47.

— — (1986) "Profiting from Technological Innovation: Implications for Integration, Collaboration, Licensing and Public Policy," *Research Policy* 15: 285–305.

— —, Pisano, G., and Shuen, A. (1997) "Dynamic Capabilities and Strategic Management," *Strategic Management Journal* 18 (7): 509–33.

Thompson, J. D. (1967) *Organizations in Action: Social Science Bases of Administrative Theory.* New York: McGraw-Hill.

Tirole, J. (1988) *The Theory of Industrial Organization.* Cambridge, MA: MIT Press.

Ulrich, K. (1995) "The Role of Product Architecture in the Manufacturing Firm," *Research Policy* 24: 419–40.

Van Alstyne, M. (1997) "A Proposal for Valuing Information and Instrumental Goods," chapter 2 in "Managing Information: Issues of Networks, Value, Policy, and Principles" unpublished PhD thesis, Massachusetts Institute of Technology, Cambridge, MA.

— — and Brynjolfsson, E. (1995) "Communication Networks and the Rise of an Information Elite: Do Computers Help the Rich Get Richer?," Proceedings of the International Conference on Information Systems, Amsterdam, pp. 93–6.

— — and — — (1996a) "Electronic Communities: Global Village or Cyberbalkans?," International Conference on Information Systems, December 16–18, Cleveland, Ohio.

— — and — — (1996b) "Internet: Could the Internet Balkanize Science?," *Science* 274 (5292): 1479–80.

— —, — — and Madnick, S. (1995) "Why Not One Big Database? Principles for Data Ownership," *Decision Support Systems* 15 (4): 267–84.

Von Hippel, E. (1988) *Sources of Innovation*. Oxford: Oxford University Press.

Wasserman, S. and Faust, K. (1994) *Social Network Analysis: Methods and Applications*. Cambridge: Cambridge University Press.

Watts, D. J. (1999) *Small Worlds: The Dynamics of Networks between Order and Randomness*. Princeton, NJ: Princeton University Press.

— — and Strogatz, S. H. (1998) "Collective Dynamics of 'Small-world' Networks," *Science* 393: 440–2.

— —, Dodds, P., and Newman, M. (2002) "Identity and Search in Social Networks," *Science* 296: 1302–5.

Weick, K. E. (1984) "Small Wins: Redefining the Scope of Social Problems," *American Psychologist* 39 (1): 40–9.

Wenger, E. (1998) *Communities of Practice: Learning, Meaning, Identity*. Cambridge: Cambridge University Press.

Wernerfelt, B. (1984) "A Resource-based View of the Firm," *Strategic Management Journal* 5: 171–80.

Winter, S. G. (1987) "Knowledge and Competence as Strategic Assets," in D. J. Teece (ed.), *The Competitive Challenge*, pp. 159–84. Cambridge, MA: Ballinger.

Yang, S. and Brynjolfsson, E. (2003) "Intangible Assets and Growth Accounting: Evidence from Computer Investments," discussion draft (available at: http://ebusiness.mit.edu/erik/itg01-05-30.pdf).

Zander, U. and Kogut, B. (1995) "Knowledge and the Speed of Transfer and Imitation of Organizational Capabilities: An Empirical Test," *Organization Science* 6: 76–92.

7. Labor in the network society: lessons from Silicon Valley

Chris Benner

During the dramatic Internet-driven boom of the 1990s, Silicon Valley was described as the home of "the greatest-ever legal creation of wealth in the history of the world."[1] For the young entrepreneurs, engineers, and computer professionals who benefited from abundant job offers, high wages, and sky-rocketing stock options during this time, Silicon Valley offered seemingly limitless opportunities for economic prosperity. By 2003, however, conditions for workers in the region had radically changed. Stock prices crashed, making most stock options worthless, while in the space of only two years, more than 18 percent of total jobs in the Valley disappeared and average pay declined by an astonishing 22 percent (JV: SVN, 2003; Sylvester, 2003).

A survey in June 2003 found that more than a quarter of all workers in the region had been laid off in the previous two years, and that nearly 35 percent of families had at least one person in their household out of work for more than three months during that time (Steen, 2003; Sylvester, 2003). Software programmers and web designers, who three years previously had been complacent in their secure futures at the core of rapidly expanding global software and Internet industries, were now found in the streets of San Francisco, protesting against the global outsourcing of their highly skilled jobs, which they feared threatened their future and very livelihood (Asaravala, 2003; Shinal, 2003).

Many workers and analysts in the region have been surprised at this rapid change of fortune. In reality, however, the volatility of the past three years merely continues (in perhaps a more extreme way) the pattern of insecurity and volatility that has characterized work and employment in Silicon Valley's information technology industries for at least the past thirty years. As the information technology industries that have dominated the region's economy for the past half-century have developed, evolved, and grown throughout the globe, rapidly changing technology, volatile competitive conditions, and constantly shifting skill requirements have led employers to place a high premium on labor flexibility. As a result, employment in the region over time has becoming increasingly unstable, with workers moving frequently from firm to firm, increasing levels of temporary workers, subcontracted employment relationships, self-employed workers, and independent contractors.

What are the social implications of this rise in labor flexibility? There is now general agreement that these contemporary labor patterns, which are not limited to Silicon Valley but are, in fact, fairly widespread, represent quite fundamental changes in work and employment. Despite an intense debate, however, there remains wide-ranging disagreement about how to characterize these changes in work and how to understand the implications for workers' livelihoods in contemporary labor markets. Silicon Valley provides useful lessons for contributing to these debates. Just like studying work in British textile mills of the early nineteenth century in order to understand the implications of the industrial revolution, or examining work in US auto plants of the early twentieth century in order to understand the implications of Fordist production systems, analyzing work in Silicon Valley at the turn of the twenty-first century provides useful insights into the ways in which the information revolution is transforming work globally.

In this chapter, I will discuss two fundamental features of labor markets in Silicon Valley that are particularly important for understanding broader patterns of work restructuring. First, Silicon Valley labor markets are characterized by a high degree of flexibility, but in analyzing this flexibility it is essential to make a distinction between flexible *work* and flexible *employment*. Flexible work practices are driven largely by competitive dynamics in knowledge-intensive industries, while flexible employment is shaped more by the legal and institutional framework that governs employment relations. Second, these high levels of flexibility are leading both employers and workers to turn to third-party intermediaries to help them navigate the complex and rapidly changing labor markets, and these intermediaries are, in turn, shaping regional labor-market dynamics in important ways.

After addressing both of these factors in turn, this chapter concludes with a discussion of the implications of these factors for social structures in the regional labor market, arguing that labor flexibility and intermediation contribute significantly to the high levels of inequality and insecurity that workers face in the regional labor market. In trying to understand the resulting social structure, however, it is essential to examine career trajectories, rather than simply the distribution of jobs, and recognize that people's outcomes in the labor market are shaped not just by their skill levels, but also by the strength and quality of their regional social networks and their regional bargaining power.

LABOR AND FLEXIBILITY

Flexibility can be defined as the ability to change or react to change with little penalty in time, effort, cost, or performance. The ability of Silicon Valley firms to be flexible – to be at the cutting edge of rapid change in information technology industries and rapidly take advantage of new opportunities associated with these changing technologies – has been a critical component of the region's long-term success. Yet change always entails some cost, and the benefits of flexibility to one actor in the economy may, and often do, come at the expense or loss of others. While some forms of flexibility are clearly important for firms to remain competitive in today's rapidly changing marketplace, all too often the drive of corporations for labor flexibility is simply a desire for decreased deregulation and the ability to hire and fire employees at will, which results in increased insecurity, declining wages, and deteriorating working conditions, while contributing little to economic competitiveness (Pollert, 1988; Standing, 1999). Thus understanding the nature of this labor flexibility, and how it does or does not contribute to economic competitiveness and workers' livelihoods, is critical in our efforts to understand contemporary labor markets.

The most common way of analyzing flexibility in the labor market and in production systems is to start with firms as the unit of analysis. In this framework, firms can pursue both *internal or functional flexibility* and *external or numerical flexibility*. Internal or functional flexibility involves a series of labor practices that increase the ability of workers inside the firm to adjust to changing demands, such as multi-skilling, broad job categories, redeployability, teamwork, and so on. External or numerical flexibility is a series of practices that allow firms to take advantage of external relations, either to access specialized skills and expertise or to adjust to fluctuating labor demands (Ozaki, 1999; Standing, 1999).

Using the firm as the primary unit of analysis clearly made sense during much of the post-World War II era, when large, vertically integrated firms dominated production in most major industries. Even today, a focus on firms provides important insights. The pressures on employers and their response shape much of the dynamics and structure of labor markets. Firms pay wages, determine hiring and firing decisions, and provide the bulk of training and career development opportunities. Public policy is most frequently centered on how to influence the behavior of firms and the consequences of particular policies on the ability of employers to compete (Osterman, 1999).

The emergence of a network economy, however, has led to the development of a wide range of conceptual frameworks that do not assume that the modern corporation is the most useful institution for understanding the organization of economy activity. Production networks, industrial clusters, "untraded interdependencies," milieux of innovation, learning communities, firm culture –

these are all analytical categories that have been developed in recent years that recognize the fluid boundaries of firms, while identifying sources of competitiveness that lie outside the activities of firms (Castells and Hall, 1994; Schoenberger, 1997; Simmie, 1997; Storper, 1997). Developing these alternatives to the firm as the fundamental unit of economic analysis has been widely accepted in the study of the organization of production, but is much less integrated into studies of work, employment, and labor markets. This limits our ability to understand contemporary labor dynamics. An assumption of strong firm boundaries neglects the increasing importance of non-firm specific knowledge, and work activities that cut across those firm boundaries, as workers communicate more regularly with customers, suppliers, and colleagues in other firms. Focusing on employment in single firms obscures the impact on employment conditions of temporary employment and subcontracting relationships, and minimizes the importance of career trajectories that cross multiple firms. Attention to internal and external flexibility leads to a core–periphery perspective that can miss the importance of work that may be peripheral to a single firm's efforts, but central to the functioning of an industrial complex. Thus an approach to labor-market flexibility that is rooted in the firm as the basic unit of analysis limits our understanding of many of the dimensions of flexibility.

A more useful framework for understanding labor flexibility is to make a distinction between flexible work and flexible employment, where *work* refers to the actual tasks performed by workers in the process of economic activity, and *employment* refers to the contractual relationship (both explicit and implicit) that shapes labor control and compensation. Making this distinction between *flexible work* and *flexible employment* – both of which may cut across firm boundaries – is particularly valuable in analyzing those aspects of labor flexibility that are driven by broad trends in the development of the information economy, versus those that are primarily driven by firms' human resource and management practices (see table 7.1).

Table 7.1   Dimensions of flexible labor

Work	Employment
The actual activities people do while engaged in the process of production	The informal and formal contractual relationship between worker and employer
Aspects of flexible work	*Aspects of flexible employment*
Rapid changes in quantity of work required	Rise in external employment relations (temporary, sub-contracted labor)
Rapid changes in skills, knowledge, information, and relationships required for work	Weakening of direct employment contract
Reflexivity in work tasks	Mediated management practices

Flexibility in Work

The term *work* refers to the actual activities people do while engaged in the process of production. It includes the physical skills and cognitive processes involved, the tools and technology used, and the relations with other people – customers, co-workers, colleagues from other firms, suppliers, and so on – that they engage in during the process of performing those activities. In this frame-work, *flexible* work – rapid change in the arena of work with little penalty in time, effort, or performance – refers in part to changes in the demand for labor in the way often described as numerical flexibility (i.e. fluctuating demand in the quantity of work needed in any particular enterprise). Flexible work, however, also refers to changes workers experience in their activities on the job, the changing value of their skills and experience in the marketplace, the changing social relationships and patterns of communication required to be effective in performing their work, and so on. Thus, in Silicon Valley, we can look at three components of flexible work that seem most salient: (1) rapid changes in the quantity of work required; (2) rapid changes in skill require-ments;[2] and (3) reflexivity in work tasks.

Quantitative change in work: Rapid change in the quantity of work required is evident through an examination of statistics on total employment. During the height of the 1990s' boom, total employment in Silicon Valley grew faster than 5 percent annually, with employment in the software industry growing 13 percent annually, and in computers and communication equipment, more than 25 percent annually between 1996 and 1999. By December 2000, unemploy-ment in Santa Clara County (the core of Silicon Valley) had reached a low of 1.3 percent, more than 3 percentage points below the national average. Employment decline during the economic downturn was even more rapid. In the space of just 13 months, unemployment jumped to 7.7 percent, and by early 2003 had reached 8.4 percent, more than 2 percentage points higher than the national average. Silicon Valley's driving industry clusters lost 22 percent of jobs in the space of a single year, between the second quarter of 2001 and 2002 (JV: SVN, 2003).

Yet even as dramatic as these changes are, they hide the even more dramatic job churning that lies behind these regional totals. These figures reflect *net* employment change, but net employment change is the result of some businesses expanding and some contracting, some new businesses form-ing and some dying. National figures suggest that this job churning can account for a full 15 percent of all jobs in the economy within a single quarter or 30 percent of all jobs within a single year (Pivetz et al., 2001). This figure is likely to be even higher in Silicon Valley, since there is significant evidence of rapid job decline amidst overall job growth, and signs of significant levels of firm formation and firm dying. As just an indicator, for example, in 1998 dozens of prominent Silicon Valley firms announced major lay-offs often amounting to more than 10 percent of their total workforce, and yet total employment grew by 5 percent. Or, as another indicator of firm churning, of the one hundred largest Silicon Valley companies in 1985, only 19 still existed and were in the top hundred in 2000 (Benner, 2002).

Rapid skill changes: Debates on the relationship between technological change and skill typically focus on relative levels of deskilling or skills upgrading over time (Braverman, 1975; Smith, 1994; Murnane et al., 1995; Handel, 2000) or the ways in which the value of skills is shaped by social struggles and power relationships (Derber et al., 1990; Gee et al., 1996; Wenger, 1998). More important from the perspective of flexible work, however, is the *pace of change in skill requirements.* This includes *both* deskilling and skill upgrading tendencies, as well as changing terrains in which social struggles over the value of skills are played out. In Silicon Valley, the pace of change in the skills workers need to be effective in their work is very rapid, and the pace seems to have quickened over time. Short product life-cycles, constantly shifting technological developments, wholesale shifts in the core subsectors of the region's information technology industries (evolving from defense, through integrated circuits, personal computers, Internet, bio-tech and nanotechnologies in the space of a generation) means that the skills that people may have learned in the past can quickly become obsolete. In the words of Michael Curran, director of the NOVA Workforce Investment Board, an award-winning training center and workforce development resource in the Valley: "The nature of industry in the Valley is constantly changing, and employers just can't tell you what skills they're going to need two years from now . . . In the past, the skills that employees had lasted longer, maybe 8–10 years. Now a current skill set might be valuable for only 18 months" (interview, June 1999).

The tendency toward rapid skills obsolescence in high-tech fields is further reflected in national earnings trends in high-tech industries, in which a study in 1996 (prior to the economic downturn) found that the earnings of engineers and managers actually started to decline for people with 24 years' experience or more (see Benner, 2002).

Reflexivity in work tasks: In addition to an unstable demand for work and rapidly changing skill requirements, work is becoming more volatile due to the increasing *reflexivity* of work tasks (Lash and Urry, 1994). This reflexivity requires workers at all levels to examine their own work activities in an effort to improve their work processes. The increasing importance of meeting rapidly shifting consumer demands in a range of information commodities and services means that a growing proportion of profitability is based on knowledge and accurate interpretation of shifting consumer tastes and cultural preferences. These interpretative tasks may be specialized amongst a group of design and marketing occupations, but in fact the "social life" of information in this context requires reflexivity in a large portion of the workforce (Brown and Duguid, 2000). Even in assembly-line, contract manufacturing facilities in the Valley continuous improvement systems based on input and reflexive activities of frontline workers are widespread (Gee et al., 1996).

In sum, numerical flexibility and volatility, rapidly changing skill requirements, and reflexivity in work are all aspects of greater flexibility in work activities. These various types of flexible work practices are largely driven by factors that operate at a fundamental level in the economy: widespread diffusion of information technology, the need for constant innovation for firms to remain competitive, the nature of competition in information-rich commodities and markets, and so on (Shapiro and Varian, 1998; Maskell and Malmberg, 1999). These work practices cut across firm boundaries and are shaped by forces that are more diffuse and less malleable than the forces that shape employment relations.

Flexibility in Employment

Work is distinct from *employment*. Employment refers to the nature of the relationship between worker and employer, the processes employers use in directing, motivating, and monitoring workers' activities, and the nature of compensation provided for the activities performed. Flexible employment, therefore, is rapid change in employment contracts with little penalty in time, effort, and performance. Temporary employment, part-time employment, self-employment, independent contractors, and various compensation schemes that link compensation to performance (such as stock options, performance evaluations, and so on) are all issues related to flexible employment, but may or may not be directly linked to flexible *work*. For example, temporary employees at an electronic manufacturing services firm doing routine assembly may be performing routine work while being engaged in flexible employment.

Changes in employment relations are more direct and more visible than many of the changes in the nature of work. Employment relations are more directly shaped by institutional factors, including the legal and regulatory framework, the organizational structure and dynamics of firms and their management practices. The implications of the employment relationship have a much more visible, immediate, and direct impact on the livelihoods of workers since it fundamentally shapes most people's primary source of income. There are three dimensions of flexible employment relationships that are particularly salient in Silicon Valley: (1) the growth in non-standard employment relationships; (2) shortened job tenures, reflected in high levels of job turnover; and (3) mediated employment relationships, in which the direct employee–employer relationship is mediated by additional institutions and external pressures.

Non-standard employment: This term generally refers to all employment that is not characterized by full-time, year-round employment for an indefinite period, working for a single employer who largely directs and controls the conditions of employment (Carré et al., 2000; Kalleberg, 2000). This includes temporary, part-time, contract employment, and self-employment. While estimates of non-standard employment vary, driven by ambiguities in definitions and difficulties in measurement, it seems to be high in Silicon Valley and growing quite rapidly (Benner, 2003d). Between 1984 and 1998, for example, employment in temporary help agencies in the Valley grew by 174 percent, compared to 26 percent in total employment (see table 7.2). Between 1990 and 1994, employment in temporary agencies actually increased by 30 percent, while overall employment declined.

Outsourcing has expanded in the past twenty years, first in service activities, manufacturing, and now increasingly in high-end design (Davis, 2003). The numbers of independent contractors and self-employed people have expanded as well: approximately 15 percent of tax returns in the region included some self-employment income in 1999 (JV: SVN, 2000). Depending on how one deals with potential double-counting, and definitions, an estimated 44–74 percent of all job growth in Santa Clara County between 1984 and 1998 was accounted for in the growth of non-standard employment (Benner, 2002). Using a somewhat broader definition of non-standard employment, a survey in 1999 estimated that a full 67 percent of workers in the state as a whole do not have "traditional employment" (Yelin and Trupin, 1999).

Job turnover: As described above, there are high levels of job turnover in Silicon Valley, as employees move more frequently from firm to firm. A 2001 survey of workers 25 years and older found a median job tenure of 30 months (about half the national median of 4.7 years),[3] with only 32 percent reporting having worked in their current job for at least five years, and only 20 percent longer than ten years (Pastor et al., 2003). Perhaps more important than increased turnover, however, is the short-term nature of the implicit employment contract, with many firms and workers not even presuming they will have a long-term relationship, even if workers are hired in "permanent" positions (Rousseau, 1995). There is widespread acceptance of people moving frequently from company to company; loyalty is typically owed more to project teams, particular technologies or industries, or the Valley as a whole, rather than to individual companies.

Table 7.2   Indicators of flexible employment in Silicon Valley

Growth in the non-standard workforce[a]	Workers		Change (%)	Increase (No.)
	1984	1998		
Temporary workers	12,340	33,850	174	21,510
Part-time workers	136,200	180,762	33	44,562
Business services	48,500	130,300	169	81,800
Self-employed	45,700	76,920	68	31,220
Upper estimate of size of non-standard workforce	242,700	421,832	74	179,132
Lower estimate of size of non-standard workforce	189,300	277,992	47	88,692
Total civilian employment	761,200	961,500	26	200,300

Signs of employment volatility	Employment growth of firms existing in 1990	Employment growth of new firms
Employment in high-tech industries (1990–2001)[b]	–120,559	258,796
	1999–2000	2001–2002
Employment change in high-tech industries[c]	+12%	–22%
Median job tenure (2001)[d]	30 months	

Sources: [a] Figures for temporary workers and business services come from the California Employment Development Department. Figures for self-employment are projections based on US Census data. Figures for part-time employment are from the Bureau of Labor Statistics, and assume Santa Clara County has the same percentage of part-time workers as the nation
[b] Junfu Zhang, *High-tech Start-ups and Industry Dynamics in Silicon Valley* (San Francisco: Public Policy Institute of California, 2003)
[c] Joint Venture: Silicon Valley Network, *2001 Index of Silicon Valley* and *2003 Index of Silicon Valley* (San Jose: Joint Venture: Silicon Valley Network, 2001, 2003)
[d] Manuel Pastor, Laura Leete, Laura Dresser, Chris Benner, Annette Bernhardt, Bob Brownstein, and Sarah Zimmerman, "Economic Opportunity in a Volatile Economy: Understanding the Role of Labor Market Intermediaries in Two Regions," report to the Ford Foundation (San Jose: Working Partnerships, 2003)

Mediated employment relationships: Another significant development in the nature of employment relations is the increasing mediation of that relationship by forces or institutions external to the firm. In some cases, this has been referred to as "market-mediated work arrangements" (Abraham, 1990; Cappelli, 1999) in which pressures from outside the firm boundaries are used as a management tool, which has become highly entrenched in Silicon Valley. This is reflected in the following description of electronic manufacturing services firm Solectron's shop-floor management system:

At the operational level, every customer and product has a focused team of people who essentially own that customer's product and own that service to that customer through the manufacturing process. If they feel that they need to do something, they have all the empowerment and all the authority for that particular customer. The managers manage between the customer-focus teams and different teams themselves, to make sure everything fits. There is no person at the operation saying, "You will do this. You will do that." (Suzik, 1999)

Another example of the growth in mediated employment relations lies in the way in which staffing services firms have increasingly entered into long-term contracts with their client firms, in which they are actually located onsite to provide a range of value-added management, accounting, and human resources services along with the provision of temporary personnel. Neuwirth (2004) describes this phenomenon as "institutional internalization," recognizing that these "external" organizations have become central actors "internal" to the firm, fundamentally shaping employment relations not only for their own employees, but, by shaping both explicit and implicit norms of employment, also affecting the employment relationship for permanent employees as well.

Thus, in sum, employment relationships have become increasingly tenuous and volatile, and mediated by a range of institutions external to firms themselves. These employment relations reflect the ways in which firms are trying to achieve greater flexibility in their relationships with workers, but it is important to keep in mind that it is primarily the work activities themselves, not employment relationships, that contribute to long-term economic competitiveness. Firms introduce flexible employment relations, in many cases, in an effort to promote flexible work, but firms *also* promote flexible employment practices in order to cut costs, shift economic risk, and improve labor control mechanisms. Such practices may have negative impacts on working conditions and compensation for employees, while doing little to promote long-term competitiveness in the economy. The rise in both flexible work and flexible employment, however, has led both workers and employers to turn to a variety of third-party intermediaries to help them navigate through these complex labor market dynamics.

LABOR MARKETS AND INTERMEDIARIES

Labor market intermediaries broker the relationship between workers and employers. Labor market intermediaries of all types provide services to both employers and to workers, related to both employment relations and to work practices. The most common service that intermediaries provide is to connect people to new employment opportunities and to help employers to find workers.

This service is often provided through a formal placement program, such as that provided by a temporary agency or contractor broker, in which the intermediary takes responsibility for ensuring the best match of skills, experience, and interests. The function may also be provided through more informal networking opportunities. In this context, the intermediary provides the organizational infrastructure that brings employers and workers together, but the employer and worker must still directly negotiate the conditions of employment. The role of some intermediaries may stop once a placement has been made – again, leaving the employment contract in the hands of the employer and worker to negotiate. In many cases, however, intermediaries will have some continuing involvement, such as in the case of temporary agencies and professional employer organizations.

Intermediaries can also play a critical role in shaping the work process, through facilitating rapid changes in work demand, shaping skills development over time, and shaping the reflexivity of work tasks. Clearly, the use of temporary agencies and contractor brokers by firms, for instance, allows them to rapidly ramp up or ramp down the number of workers in response to rapidly changing work demands. Some workers also use temporary agencies and brokers to find work fast. Intermediaries can play a critical role in shaping skills development. This may be done in a formal manner, through training and certification programs and responding directly to employer or worker demands. It may also proceed in more informal ways in which the intermediary provides the organizational infrastructure for building the social networks that are so essential for continuing learning. These learning networks fundamentally shape work practices on a day-to-day level, building communication across work sites. Intermediaries also provide important information on changing work demands in the labor market, amongst different firms and different industries, providing signals to both workers and firms of the need to respond to these changing work demands.

There are three broad types of intermediaries that operate in Silicon Valley: private sector, membership-based, and public sector (Benner, 2002).

Private-sector Intermediaries

Private-sector intermediaries, such as temporary agencies and contractor brokers, are the largest and most prominent category of labor market intermediary. They place workers with many different skill levels across a range of occupations and industries, and thus cannot be simply categorized as a cost-cutting strategy pursued by firms in an effort to shrink the size of their "core" workforce and reduce labor costs for non-core positions. Firms use intermediaries to find and employ people for many purposes, including many "core" functions within the region's high-tech industries. Temporary employees do include many assembly, shipping, light-industrial, and clerical positions, which, combined, still account for over half the employment in temporary agencies in the region. Temporary employees, however, also include highly skilled technicians, engineers, and computer professionals, who are the most rapidly growing segment in the temporary help industry and form the core of workers placed through many other types of private-sector intermediaries.

The four most prominent types of private-sector intermediary that exist in the Valley are the following:

Temporary help firms: These are the most visible and well-known type of intermediary, and the number of firms and the number of people employed in these firms have grown dramatically in recent years. Between 1984 and 1998, for example, employment in temporary agencies grew by 174 percent, while total employment grew by 26 percent. More importantly, temporary help firms have become increasingly integrated into the human resource practices of many high-tech firms, entering into long-term contracts, providing management and recruiting staff on the work site of client firms, and providing a variety of other value-added management and administrative services for a growing sector of the workforce.

Consultant brokerage firms: Though somewhat less well known, contractor or consultant brokerage firms play a critical role in the regional labor market, particularly at middle and upper levels of the occupational structure. Contractor brokers are very similar to temporary help firms in that they recruit professional contractors for temporary positions in firms in the area. They are distinct from typical temporary help firms in that they specialize in more skilled positions, they recruit often for permanent positions as well as contract positions, and will place contractors who are incorporated or prefer to remain self-employed. One of the most comprehensive directories of recruiting firms listed more than 800 firms in the Silicon Valley area in 1999.[4]

Web-based job sites: This category of private-sector intermediary has mushroomed since 1994. The largest job sites are general-purpose national sites, such as monster.com and hotjobs.com, which attempt to cover all occupational categories in regional labor markets across the country. Other sites are more specialized, such as dice.com (Data-processing Independent Consultants Exchange), or Jobs for Programmers (www.prgjobs.com). Many sites are stand alone, and only have a presence online. Other sites are linked to various industry associations and recruiting networks in which the web-based "cybermediary" work is an extension of their other activities.

Professional employer organizations (PEOs): These firms provide a variety

of human resource administrative services to firms. They are similar to temporary help firms in that they act as the legal employer of record for employees
who are doing work for a client firm. They are distinct from temporary help
firms in that their employees are "permanently" working for the client firm.
Typically, the PEO and the client firm have a joint-employer relationship to
the employee. PEOs do not generally actively recruit, but they do provide a
wider range of additional human resource administrative services for a more
comprehensive range of employees than temporary help firms typically
provide. This includes administering benefits packages, providing payroll
services, ensuring compliance with employment regulations, and sharing
responsibility for the management of employees. While PEOs are relatively
small as a category of intermediaries in Silicon Valley, they are growing very
rapidly. They act as labor market intermediaries in the employment sphere by
developing economies of scale in the "business of employment" for a range of
small and medium-sized firms.

Membership-based Intermediaries

A second broad category of labor market intermediaries includes those whose
organizational base is rooted in the membership of individual employees. This
category includes professional associations, guilds and guild-like associations,
and various union initiatives, which have become increasingly prominent in
recent years (Benner, 2003a). The intermediary activities of these organizations range from creating job listings and organizing networking opportunities
to providing skills training and building learning communities. Their strategies
help to build ties between workers and employers, and shape the nature of that
relationship in ways that aim to improve the labor market outcomes of their
members. Membership-based intermediaries are rooted in particular occupations. The skills, knowledge base, work practices, and labor market experiences associated with each occupation provide organizational coherence and
shape the structure and activities of the association. Many occupations in
Silicon Valley face rapidly changing skill requirements and high levels of
volatility in employment conditions. In response, these membership associations have arisen as a means to provide improved career opportunities for their
members.

   Membership-based intermediaries can be thought of as existing on a
continuum, based on the extent to which they actively advocate for their
members in the labor market. At one end of the spectrum are professional
associations, such as the Society for Technical Communication or the HTML
Writers Guild, that act primarily as an information intermediary, providing
networking opportunities and linkages between employers and workers in
particular occupations and helping to provide guidance on changes in skill

requirements and industry trends. In the middle are a range of professional associations and guild-type unions, such as the System Administrators' Guild or Graphic Artists' Guild, that also provide information to help their members advocate for themselves individually in the labor market. These associations may provide training in individual negotiating strategies, provide detailed salary information based on surveys of the profession, and ultimately try to empower workers through strengthening their information, knowledge, and skills in negotiating. At the other end of the continuum are organizations that play an active, direct role in advocating for their members. This may take the form of collective bargaining in a multi-employer relationship, as in the case of unions in the construction industry. It may also take the form of advocating for legislation or codes of conduct or developing corporate campaigns. Whatever the particular strategy, the goal of these organizations is to improve conditions of employment for their members *explicitly by altering the conditions of employment* of firms, not on an individual, but on a collective basis (Bernhardt et al., 2001.

Public-sector Intermediaries

There are a number of public sector programs and educational institutions that directly play an intermediary role in the labor market. In recent years, these programs have expanded their activities and grown more explicit in building their role as intermediaries. There are essentially three broad types. First are the range of institutions that make up the workforce development "system." In their efforts to link disadvantaged workers to employment opportunities these programs have always had some role as intermediaries in the labor market. In recent years, however, these frequently fragmented programs have become increasingly integrated into a "one-stop, career-center system" aimed at improving their effectiveness as intermediaries. Two components of these changes are particularly significant: first, these services are becoming more available to the entire workforce, rather than being reserved for specific sub-sectors of the labor market; and second, they are attempting to link training more closely with career mobility. Both these trends suggest the greater integration of these public-sector intermediary programs into the very structure of the regional economy and labor market (Kogan et al., 1997).

A second broad type of public-sector intermediary includes education-based institutions providing adult education and customized job training for employers. Historically, the education system has been distinct from the workforce development system, focusing on a broader set of education goals primarily oriented toward new entrants to the labor market. Employment training programs, in contrast, acted more as a "second-chance" system, providing occupation-based training for particular groups of people. In the past twenty years, however, education-based initiatives have played a greater role in retraining older workers and in expanding their ties with employers. This includes developing specialized curriculum development and training programs geared specifically for employers' needs, and providing a wide range of onsite custom training for employers. These trends blur the distinction between "education" and "job-training" programs, and position educational institutions as more active intermediaries in the labor market (Grubb, 1996).

The third category of publicly funded intermediaries is community and non-profit organizations that engage in job-training and placement activities. Most of the funding for these programs comes from federal and state workforce-development grants, and thus they are closely integrated into the growing one-stop, career-center system. Certain community-based organizations are exemplary, however, in the strength of their ties in particular communities of disadvantaged workers. Being strongly integrated into social networks in poor communities can be extremely valuable for improving the effectiveness of intermediaries in improving labor market outcome for disadvantaged workers (Harrison and Weiss, 1998).

All three types of intermediaries are quite widespread in Silicon Valley. A recent survey of workers' job-search experiences found that one in four people have held a job in the previous three years that they obtained through an intermediary, and that intermediary use was spread across the labor market (Pastor et al., 2003). This is a conservative estimate of the impact of intermediaries in the labor market since it does not include jobs found through web-based intermediaries, and does not examine the extent to which social networks, which account for the largest single means of finding a job, were built through intermediary activity. Furthermore, this only measures the extent to which intermediaries were successful in placing workers in a job, and does not measure "unsuccessful" attempts to use intermediaries, or the role intermediaries play in shaping work practices more broadly. Although most people still find work by contacting employers directly or through social networks, by directly touching at least 25 percent of the labor force in a three-year period, and indirectly probably touching a significantly larger portion, intermediaries are clearly important in shaping regional labor market dynamics (Benner, 2003b).

LABOR MARKET OUTCOMES

Flexible labor markets, at least certain aspects of them, are clearly a critical component of Silicon Valley's long-term economic success. The circulation of people and information from firm to firm has helped to foster creative innovation in product development and process improvements, and helped to ensure that those innovations quickly diffuse through the regional economy (Castells and Hall, 1994; Saxenian, 1994; Kenney, 2000; Lee et al., 2000). Intermediaries have also contributed to growth in the regional economy in important ways. As I argue in more depth elsewhere (Benner, 2003b), labor market intermediaries help to reduce transactions costs, help both firms and workers manage risk, and help to form the institutional infrastructure of the social networks and production relationships that have been such a critical part of the region's economic success. At the same time, however, flexibility and intermediation have also contributed to the high levels of insecurity and inequality that characterize labor markets in Silicon Valley.[5]

Flexible work and flexible employment relations clearly increase insecurity for workers. This has been made abundantly clear in the recent economic downturn, as tenuous and mediated employment relationships facilitated the rapid reduction in people employed in the region, with unemployment jumping from 1.3 to 7.7 percent in the space of thirteen months. The level of insecurity goes deeper than simple employment figures. In the highly volatile information-technology markets, workers have to continually upgrade their skills, through both formal training and informal learning. As the pace of technological change increases, workers frequently discover that their skills are valued less by employers, pushing them to return to school for significant retraining or to develop an entirely new career. Periods of unemployment, therefore, are not simply the result of cyclical patterns in the economy, but more a reflection of structural changes, and, as a result, people who experience unemployment often have a difficult time finding employment again, and face longer periods of unemployment while searching for new jobs (Baumol and Wolff, 1998).

Gaining the skills necessary to be successful in the labor market has also become more of an individual's responsibility, as the growth in flexible work and flexible employment relations has served to undermine the investment of firms in training. The intense pace of competition means that firms feel they have little "luxury" for providing training for people without readily identifiable valuable skills, and thus they expect to hire people with the exact match of skills for a particular job or project. Most employers are reluctant to invest in retraining their workforce for fear that the workers will leave and take the skills with them, or, if they do stay, that the demand for the skills will not last long enough to make the investment worthwhile. The lack of retraining exacerbates imbalances between supply and demand when markets shift because employers have to wait for employees to train themselves in the new skills, typically waiting for the next generation of graduates (Cappelli, 2000). Thus, rapidly changing work requirements can create significant labor market shocks for people, increasing the risk of serious misfortune.

The most negative impact of flexibility on workers' outcomes in the labor market, however, is primarily related to flexible employment, not flexible work (Masters, 1999). The growth of outsourcing and the increased use of temporary employees severely weakens the ability of workers to bargain over their employment relationships, making them more vulnerable to market downturns and less likely to demand higher wages from their current employer. This is clearly evidenced in statistics on the wages of temporary workers, which are significantly lower than the wages of "permanent" workers with similar educational and demographic characteristics (Barker and Christiansen, 1998; Hudson, 1999).

Temporary workers also face serious problems in relation to occupational health and safety issues. Their legal employer, the temporary agency, is responsible for paying workers compensation insurance and for ensuring the safety of the work site. The temporary agency, however, has little or no effective control over working conditions in the work sites where they place people. In one particularly poignant example in 1999, an assembly worker, who was employed by Manpower Temporary Services in a warehouse packing Hewlett-Packard printers, suffered respiratory problems due to poor ventilation and the carcinogenic chemicals used in the printers' ink cartridges. Yet, when he asked for an air-quality check to be conducted in the warehouse, he lost his job. He filed a complaint with the California Industrial Relations Board, which took more than 20 months to determine whether there was cause to fine Hewlett-Packard or Manpower or both. Ultimately, the California Labor Commissioner ruled that Manpower, as the legal employer, had violated the employee's right to express health safety concerns at work. In this case, however, Manpower had no power to order an air-safety check at the plant or to improve air-circulation systems in the facility (Jayadev, 2000).

The working conditions and employment contracts of temporary and contract employees of all types – particularly those in service jobs such as janitors, security guards, cafeteria workers, and landscape workers, but also to a certain extent those working in electronic assembly plants in the region – are often primarily determined by the clients of their legal employers, rather than the legal employers themselves. These client firms are frequently highly profitable, high-tech companies, while the legal employers are frequently marginally profitable firms. Yet the institutional framework governing employment relationships currently provides no mechanism for contract workers to demand better conditions from the client firms themselves. As contract employment relationships have proliferated in the Valley since the mid-1980s, wages and working conditions in many outsourced firms have declined significantly, though the work itself has largely remained the same (Zlolniski, 1994; Chun, 2001).

While it is fairly clear, therefore, that flexible employment has increased inequality and insecurity for workers in the region, it is much harder to understand the impact labor market intermediaries are having on labor market outcomes for workers. In the first ever quantitative study to try to measure the overall impact of labor market intermediaries in the region, for example, it did not appear that intermediaries had any significant direct impact on wages, though there was a very strong relationship between the use of temporary help agencies and lack of access to health insurance (Pastor et al., 2003). There was, however, a clear statistical relationship between the use of intermediaries and the character of people's social networks. Using a measure of "social connectedness," the study found that those who are more socially connected are less likely to use intermediaries. Furthermore, of those people who do use intermediaries, those with strong social connectedness are more likely to use "better" intermediaries – those intermediaries that provide a more comprehensive set of services, primarily community colleges, professional associations, and unions, rather than temporary agencies.

As qualitative studies of intermediaries in Silicon Valley have repeatedly pointed out, however, it is a mistake to assume that certain whole categories of intermediaries are "bad" and other categories are "good." In comparing a for-profit staffing services firm and a union-affiliated non-profit agency, for example, Neuwirth (2004) found surprising instances of the for-profit firm being *more* effective than the union-affiliated agency in advocating on behalf of their employees' rights and improving working conditions in their client firms, for temporary and permanent employees alike. Similarly, detailed studies of non-profit intermediaries find a wide array of effectiveness in improving outcomes for individuals in the labor market, with some agencies significantly improving long-term outcomes but many agencies having no measurable impact whatsoever (Harrison and Weiss, 1998; Benner et al., 2001).

Finally, though systematic qualitative research on labor market intermediaries is only beginning to emerge, it seems clear that intermediaries cannot be understood in isolation. Many staffing service firms are forming complex networking relationships with other staffing agencies, while intermediary networks bringing together public-sector, private-sector, and membership associations are also forming (Giloth, 2004; Neuwirth, 2004). Ultimately, it is the nature of these network relationships, and the relationships that intermediaries have with both the demand and supply side of the labor market, that shape labor market outcomes for workers.

Thus, in trying to understand the implications of the emerging social structures shaped by these complex labor market dynamics, one thing that is clear is that most labor market statistics provide very limited insights. Cross-sectional measures of the distribution of jobs by industry and occupation, or cross-sectional measurements of wage distributions, provide useful understandings of changes in the structure of the economy, but provide limited insights into the actual conditions individuals experience in the labor market.

Flexible labor markets are *risky* labor markets, and workers face high levels of uncertainty and volatility over time in their employment opportunities and working conditions – experiences that cannot be captured in cross-sectional data. To fully assess outcomes for workers in these flexible labor markets it is important to understand not just patterns of jobs and wages, but patterns of careers and earnings profiles over time (Arthur et al., 1989). The term *careers* in this context applies to all workers, not just those with neatly ordered patterns with consistent upward mobility. Studying careers requires that we incorporate a time-dimension into our analysis of labor market outcomes, trying to understand how work histories reflect employment stability and instability, skills and experience gained or made irrelevant, relationships nurtured or lost, risks or opportunities encountered. A focus on careers requires an understanding of relationships, both within and between firms, which cut across work and non-work activities (Arthur and Rouseau, 1996).

In developing this understanding of the implications of flexibility and inter-mediation on long-term labor market outcomes, particular attention needs to be paid to three key areas. First, it is critical to understand the nature and qual-ity of people's skills, information, and knowledge, how they gain these skills, and how these skills evolve over time. Clearly, formal education plays an important role in shaping labor market outcomes, but differences in formal education and experience can only explain roughly one-third of the variety in wage distribution, much less career outcomes (Gottschalk, 1997; Reed, 1999). We need a much better understanding of the factors shaping individuals' access to life-long learning opportunities, their incorporation into and effective participation in learning communities, and how growing flexibility and inter-mediation are shaping the evolution of those learning practices over time (Benner, 2003c).

Second, we need a better understanding of the ways in which flexibility and intermediation are shaping the nature and quality of people's social networks. Clearly, there is no shortage of research on social networks, and many studies have demonstrated that social networks are important not only in finding employment (Granovetter, 1995; Fernandez and Weinberg, 1997), but also in developing skills and learning over time, advancing and improving earnings across firms, coping with increasing lay-offs and job loss, and effectively deal-ing with a range of other issues that shape long-term employment outcomes (Lave and Wenger, 1991; Wial, 1991; Hull, 1997; Herzenberg et al., 1998; Saxenian, 2000). Yet it is important to recognize that social networks, though highly fluid, still shape patterns of exclusion and inclusion (Castells, 1998; Graham and Marvin, 2001). In the context of flexible labor markets, we need a better understanding of the patterns of inclusion and exclusion in cross-firm social networks, and, most particularly, the ways in which intermediaries shape both the strength and quality of people's social connectedness.

Finally, and probably most importantly, we need a greater appreciation of how power relations shape career outcomes, not simply within the context of the relationship between workers and their employer, but over time and space (Herod, 2001). As Osterman (1999) describes, employers have gained significant power over the past thirty years in the labor market, while workers have become increasingly vulnerable. Much of this loss of power is rooted in the growth of labor flexibility, and, in most cases, intermediaries seem to be also associated with a weakening of workers' power in the labor market, as they contribute to the "individualization" of employment relations that has helped to isolate individual workers, discourage collective organization, and increase workers' vulnerability to labor market risk (Benner, 2002). This situation creates opportunities for employers to use exploitative employment relations *simply because they can*, not because they are driven to by any competitive dynamics. Yet historical reflections of power relationships have been primarily rooted in the workplace and in the context of a clearly identified employer. Instead, we now need a greater appreciation of how capital–labor relationships play out in place and space, and why particular social actors engage in certain types of political praxis in particular places and times (Herod, 1998). Clearly, understanding how workers could wield greater power in a way that could simultaneously support flexible work practices and transform exploitative employment relationships would go a long way in helping to reconstruct flexible labor markets in ways that could simultaneously promote economic prosperity and minimize social insecurity.

NOTES

1. Venture capitalist John Doerr, quoted in Perkins and Nunez (2001).
2. I use the term "skill" in a comprehensive way to refer to the explicit and tacit skills, information, and knowledge workers require to perform their work activities.
3. See http://www.bls.gov/news.release/tenure.t01.htm
4. http://www.dice.com/recruiters/companies/regions/ncalif-ab.shtml accessed in May, 2000.
5. For a more detailed analysis of inequality and insecurity in the regional labor market, see Benner (2002).

REFERENCES

Abraham, Katherine (1990) "Restructuring the Employment Relationship: The Growth of Market-mediated Work Arrangements," in Katherine Abraham and Robert McKersie (eds), *New Developments in the Labor Market: Towards a New Institutional Paradigm*. Cambridge, MA: MIT Press.
Arthur, Michael and Rousseau, Denise (eds) (1996) *The Boundaryless Career: A New Employment Principle for a New Organizational Era*. Oxford: Oxford University Press.
— —, Hall, Douglas, and Lawrence, Barbara (eds) (1989) *The Handbook of Career Theory*. Cambridge: Cambridge University Press.

Asaravala, Amit (2003) "Protestors Mourn Tech Job Drain," *Wired.com*, September 17.

Barker, Kathleen and Christensen, Kathleen (eds) (1998) *Contingent Work: American Employment Relations in Transition*. Ithaca, NY: ILR Press.

Baumol, William and Wolff, Edward (1998) "Side Effects of Progress: How Technological Change Increases the Duration of Unemployment," Annandale-on-Hudson: Jerome Levy Economics Institute.

Benner, Chris (2002) *Work in the New Economy: Flexible Labor Markets in Silicon Valley*. Oxford: Blackwell.

— — (2003a) " 'Computers in the Wild': Guilds and Next Generation Unionism in the Information Revolution," *International Review of Social History* 48 (S11).

— — (2003b) "Labour Flexibility and Regional Development: The Role of Labour Market Intermediaries," *Regional Studies* 37 (6/7): 621–33.

— — (2003c) "Learning Communities in a Learning Region: The Soft Infrastructure of Cross-firm Learning Networks in Silicon Valley," *Environment and Planning* A 35 (10): 1809–30.

— — (2003d) "Shock Absorbers in the Flexible Economy," in Herbert Schaffner and Carl Van Horn (eds), *A Nation at Work: The Heldrich Guide to the American Workforce*, pp. 221–6. New Brunswick, NJ: Rutgers University Press.

— —, Brownstein, Bob, Dresser, Laura, and Leete, Laura (2001) "Staircases and Treadmills: The Role of Labor Market Intermediaries in Placing Workers and Fostering Upward Mobility," in Paula Voos (ed.), *Proceedings of the 53rd Annual Meeting of the Industrial Relations Research Association, January 5–7, 2001, New Orleans*. Champaign, IL: Industrial Relations Research Association.

Bernhardt, Annette, Pastor, Manuel, Hatton, Erin, and Zimmerman, Sarah (2001) "Moving the Demand Side: Intermediaries in a Changing Labor Market," in Paula Voos (ed.), *Proceedings of the 53rd Annual Meeting of the Industrial Relations Research Association, January 5–7, 2001, New Orleans*. Champaign, IL: Industrial Relations Research Association.

Braverman, Harry (1975) *Labor and Monopoly Capital: The Degradation of Work in the Twentieth Century*. New York: Monthly Review Press.

Brown, John Sealy and Duguid, Paul (2000) *The Social Life of Information*. Boston, MA: Harvard Business School Press.

Cappelli, Peter (1999) *The New Deal at Work: Managing the Market-driven Workforce*. Boston, MA: Harvard Business School Press.

— — (2000) "Is There a Shortage of Information Technology Workers?," Philadelphia: Wharton School, University of Pennsylvania.

Carré, Françoise, Ferber, Marianne, Golden, Lonnie, and Herzenberg, Stephen (2000) *Nonstandard Work: The Nature and Challenges of Changing Employment Arrangements*. Madison, WI: Industrial Relations Research Association.

Castells, Manuel (1998) *End of Millennium*. Malden, MA: Blackwell.

— — and Hall, Peter (1994) *Technopoles of the World: The Making of Twenty-first-century Industrial Complexes*. London: Routledge.

Chun, Jennifer (2001) "Flexible Despotism: The Intensification of Uncertainty and Insecurity in the Lives of High-tech Assembly Workers," in Rick Baldoz, Charles Koeber, and Philip Kraft (eds), *The Critical Study of Work: Labor, Technology and Global Production*. Philadelphia: Temple University Press.

Davis, Aaron (2003) "Software Developers Calling Shots," *San Jose Mercury News*, November 9, 2003.

Derber, Charles, Schwartz, William, and Magrass, Yale (1990) *Power in the Highest*

Degree: Professionals and the Rise of a New Mandarin Order. New York: Oxford University Press.

Fernandez, R. M. and Weinberg, N. (1997) "Sifting and Sorting: Personal Contacts and Hiring in a Retail Bank," *American Sociological Review* 62 (6): 883–902.

Gee, James Paul, Hull, Glynda, and Lankshear, Colin (1996) *The New Work Order: Behind the Language of the New Capitalism.* Boulder, CO: Westview Press.

Giloth, Robert (ed.) (2004) *Workforce Intermediaries for the 21st Century.* Philadelphia: Temple University Press.

Gottschalk, P. (1997) "Inequality, Income Growth, and Mobility: The Basic Facts," *Journal of Economic Perspectives* 11 (2): 21–40.

Graham, Stephen and Marvin, Simon (2001) *Splintering Urbanism: Networked Infrastructures, Technological Mobilities and the Urban Condition.* London: Routledge.

Granovetter, Mark (1995) *Getting a Job: A Study of Contacts and Careers.* Chicago: University of Chicago Press.

Grubb, Norton (1996) *Learning to Work: The Case for Reintegrating Job Training and Education.* New York: Russell Sage Foundation.

Handel, Michael (2000) "Is There a Skills Crisis? Trends in Job Skill Requirements, Technology, and Wage Inequality in the US," Annandale-on-Hudson: Jerome Levy Economics Institute.

Harrison, Bennett and Weiss, Marcus S. (1998) *Workforce Development Networks: Community-based Organizations and Regional Alliances.* Thousand Oaks, CA: Sage.

Herod, Andrew (ed.) (1998) *Organizing the Landscape: Geographical Perspectives on Labor Unionism.* Minneapolis, MN: University of Minnesota Press.

— — (2001) *Labor Geographies: Workers and the Landscapes of Capitalism.* New York: Guilford Press.

Herzenberg, Stephen, Alic, John, and Wial, Howard (1998) *New Rules for a New Economy: Employment and Opportunity in Postindustrial America.* Ithaca, NY: ILR Press.

Hudson, Ken (1999) "No Shortage of 'Nonstandard' Jobs," Washington, DC: Economic Policy Institute.

Hull, Glynda A. (1997) *Changing Work, Changing Workers: Critical Perspectives on Language, Literacy, and Skills.* Albany, NY: State University of New York Press.

Jayadev, Raj (2000) "Winning and Losing Workplace Safety on Silicon Valley's Assembly Line," *Pacific News Service,* San Francisco.

JV: SVN (2000) *2000 Index of Silicon Valley.* San Jose: Joint Venture: Silicon Valley Network.

— — (2003) *2003 Index of Silicon Valley.* San Jose: Joint Venture: Silicon Valley Network.

Kalleberg, Arne (2000) "Nonstandard Employment Relations: Part-time, Temporary and Contract Work," *Annual Review of Sociology* 26: 341–65.

Kenney, Martin (ed.) (2000) *Understanding Silicon Valley: The Anatomy of an Entrepreneurial Region.* Palo Alto: Stanford University Press.

Kogan, Deborah, Dickinson, Katherine, Redrau, Ruth, Midling, Michael, and Wolff, Kristin (1997) "Creating Workforce Development Systems that Work: A Guide for Practitioners. Organizing and Governing One-stop Systems," Menlo Park: Social Policy Research Associates.

Lash, Scott and Urry, John (1994) *Economies of Signs and Space.* London: Sage.

Lave, Jean and Wenger, Etienne (1991) *Situated Learning: Legitimate Peripheral Participation*. Cambridge: Cambridge University Press.

Lee, Chong-Moon, Miller, William, Hancock, Marguerite Gong, and Rowen, Henry (eds) (2000) *The Silicon Valley Edge: A Habitat for Innovation and Entrepreneurship*. Stanford: Stanford University Press.

Maskell, Peter and Malmberg, Anders (1999) "The Competitiveness of Firms and Regions: Ubiquitification and the Importance of Localized Learning," *European Urban and Regional Studies* 6 (1): 9–25.

Masters, Stanley (1999) "The Role of Flexible Production in Earnings Inequality," *Challenge* 42 (4): 102–17.

Murnane, R. J., Willett, J. B., and Levy, F. (1995) "The Growing Importance of Cognitive Skills in Wage Determination," *Review of Economics and Statistics* 77 (2): 251–66.

Neuwirth, Esther (2004) "Permanent Strategies: Staffing Agencies and Temporary Workers in the New Millenium," unpublished PhD dissertation, Department of Sociology, University of California, Davis.

Osterman, Paul (1999) *Securing Prosperity. The American Labor Market: How It Has Changed and What To Do About It*. Princeton, NJ: Princeton University Press.

Ozaki, Muneto (1999) *Negotiating Flexibility: The Role of the Social Partners and the State*. Geneva: International Labour Office.

Pastor, Manuel, Leete, Laura, Dresser, Laura, Benner, Chris, Bernhardt, Annette, Brownstein, Bob, and Zimmerman, Sarah (2003) "Economic Opportunity in a Volatile Economy: Understanding the Role of Labor Market Intermediaries in Two Regions," San Jose: Working Partnerships.

Perkins, Michael C. and Nunez, Celia (2001) "Why Market Insiders Don't Feel your Pain," *Washington Post*, March 15.

Pivetz, Timothy, Searson, Michael, and Spletzer, James (2001) "Measuring Job and Establishment Flows with BLS Longitudinal Data," *Monthly Labor Review* 124 (4): 13–20.

Pollert, Anna (1988) "Dismantling Flexibility." *Capital and Class* 34: 42–75.

Reed, Deborah (1999) "California's Rising Income Inequality: Causes and Concerns," San Francisco: Public Policy Institute of California.

Rousseau, Denise (1995) *Psychological Contracts in Organizations: Understanding Written and Unwritten Agreements*. Thousand Oaks, CA: Sage.

Saxenian, Anna Lee (1994) *Regional Advantage: Culture and Competition in Silicon Valley and Route 128*. Cambridge, MA: Harvard University Press.

— — (2000) "Networks of Immigrant Entrepreneurs," in Chong-Moon Lee, William Miller, Marguerite Gong Hancock, and Henry Rowen (eds), *The Silicon Valley Edge: A Habitat for Innovation and Entrepreneurship*. Stanford: Stanford University Press.

Schoenberger, Erica (1997) *The Cultural Crisis of the Firm*. Malden, MA: Blackwell.

Shapiro, Carl and Varian, Hal R. (1998) *Information Rules: A Strategic Guide to the Network Economy*. Boston, MA: Harvard Business School Press.

Shinal, John (2003) "Offshore Debate: Job Export Issue Pits Companies Against Workers," *San Francisco Chronicle*, September 17.

Simmie, James (ed.) (1997) *Innovation, Networks and Learning Regions?* London: Regional Studies Association.

Smith, Vicki (1994) "Braverman's Legacy: The Labor Process Tradition at 20," *Work and Occupations* 21 (4): 403–21.

Standing, Guy (1999) *Global Labour Flexibility: Seeking Distributive Justice*. New York: St Martin's Press.

Steen, Margaret (2003) "Pain from Layoffs Runs Deep in Valley," *San Jose Mercury News*, July 13.

Storper, Michael (1997) *The Regional World: Territorial Development in a Global Economy*. New York: Guilford Press.

Suzik, Holly Ann (1999) "Solectron Tells its Tale," *Quality* 38 (5): 53–9.

Sylvester, David (2003) "Valley's Bust More Severe than Other Regions' Fall," *San Jose Mercury News*, June 21.

Wenger, Etienne (1998) *Communities of Practice: Learning, Meaning, and Identity*. Cambridge: Cambridge University Press.

Wial, Howard (1991) "Getting a Good Job: Mobility in a Segmented Labor Market," *Industrial Relations* 30 (3): 396–416.

Yelin, Ed and Trupin, Laura (1999) "California Work and Health Survey: 2nd Year Results," University of California, San Francisco Institute for Health Policy Studies.

Zlolniski, Christian (1994) "The Informal Economy in an Advanced Industrialized Society: Mexican Immigrant Labor in Silicon Valley," *Yale Law Journal* 103 (8): 2305–36.

8. Time, space, and technology in financial networks

Caitlin Zaloom

Financial markets are central to arguments about the extent of global networks and the speed of transactions they support. They are noted for being the "most global" of forms working in "real time on a planetary scale" (Castells, 1996; see also Held et al., 1999; Sassen, 2001). These observations describe the significance of network forms in redefining time and space on a global scale. However, the era-defining observations of "time–space compression" or the breaking of life narratives that leads to "timeless time" leave a key level unexplored (Harvey, 1989; Castells 1996; see also Sennett 1998).[1] In technological networks, the constitution of time and space takes place, perhaps most significantly, at the scale of practice.[2] Analysts of networks need to take account of how technologies define the spatial and temporal environments of everyday labor. Network managers and designers plan and construct the global geography of financial markets.[3] However, at the same time, the traders who work with network technologies create competing notions of time and space that challenge technological design. Traders' daily work consists of gathering information and taking action in the marketplace. Market technologies shape and are shaped by these quotidian activities and their temporal and spatial dimensions.

Financial markets represent a critical research site for these technological and social network transformations. This chapter takes up an historic shift occurring in financial futures markets. It is a transition from the architectural technology of the trading pit – the nexus of financial futures – to electronic networks of dealers stretched over the globe. The reshaping of space and time shows that tensions between social and technological arrangements are key to the problems of centralization and decentralization of global networks.[4] The social forces that fragment the market along spatial and temporal lines drive forward the creation of new market forms.

This chapter examines the trading pit and an electronic trading network to analyze how material technologies and everyday practices shape financial time and space.[5] The chapter is based on fieldwork I conducted on the financial trading floor of the Chicago Board of Trade (CBOT) and in the digital dealing room of a London proprietary firm (LDF). I worked as a clerk at the CBOT for six months in 1998. I arrived at the exchange each morning at 6.45 a.m. to prepare for the day as a runner and a clerk, placing orders on paper and delivering them with hand signals to brokers inside the pits during trading hours. I learned to read the space and time of the market, as most CBOT traders do, by working within them.

My apprenticeship continued in London's electronic markets. I arranged to join LDF as a new recruit among ten new traders. Each morning before sunrise in the fall and winter of 2000, I arrived by tube in the heart of the City, London's financial district. Trading began at 7.00 a.m. and I arrived at my desk at 6.30 a.m., early enough for a cup of tea and to gather information about the overnight markets. I traded German treasury bond futures on an LDF account, spending nine hours a day in front of the trading screen working to glean profits from the differences in volatility between 10, 5 and 2-year German bond futures. To supplement my work and observations in these arenas of exchange, I interviewed officials at the exchanges and technology companies and attended meetings on the reorganization of the industry.

THE PIT

For the past 150 years, the CBOT has drawn participants and information together into the trading pit. The central location for trading, information gathering, and price discovery I call a "nexus market." The trading pit is the material technology that supports the nexus. Within the pit, the social network of traders gives definition to the whirl of speculation. The architecture of the pit defines the space where the relationships of obligation and reciprocity between traders are put to work and where information about financial commodities are evaluated and solidified into a price.[6]

The pit is a technology originally designed to configure traders in space and time. As the work of William Cronon (1991) has shown, the greatest achievement of the CBOT was the production of a centralized market in grain futures, which, at the time, utterly changed the grain trade and set the model for markets that later changed the face of global finance. The markets in grain futures that this organization developed were (and still are) run as auctions. The CBOT futures auctions produce prices for grain and bond futures, a single price for each commodity that fluctuates as information about the product changes the outlook for supply and demand.[7]

An auction is most efficient and effective when all those who want to buy and sell a product can see and hear the bids and offers of all the other participants. By the late nineteenth century, trading at the CBOT had become so popular and the trading area so crowded that the speculators could not see all the bids and offers available. Market reporters complained in the pages of their daily papers that traders in search of better sight lines were climbing onto their desks and obstructing the reporters' vision. In 1869, the CBOT installed trading pits to solve this problem. They introduced the eight-sided structure with three steps (Faloon, 1998). This basic arrangement, which is still in use today, allows traders to see each other and to match a bid to the particular person who shouted it. The structure integrates the market by making the information of each bid or offer available to all the participants.

The tiered steps of the pit organize the physical space of open-outcry trading. Most importantly, the stepped structure creates a unified field of financial competition where traders can make deals with the full range of market participants. Each speculator can trade with any other. This physical ordering of traders creates a market by drawing together the social network of traders in a single location. Even those traders who work off-site have to execute their trades in the pit. They, too, are connected to the trading floor.

In pit markets outside traders contact a clerk who "flashes" the order into the pit with hand signals or sends a paper order slip to a broker in the pit. If the trade must be executed right away, the outside speculator holds the phone line until his order has been completed and confirmed by the clerk. The clerk quickly reports the quantity and price that has changed hands inside the pit. The CBOT uses the pit to define both the temporal and spatial dimensions of trading. To be a legal trade, one recognized by the accountants of the CBOT and enforceable in a court, the exchange must occur within the confines of the pit and between the opening and closing bells of the trading day.

Space in the Pit

Physical and social space overlap in the pit. A pit market is a social network of traders. The intricate structure of favors, debts, and friendship establishes bonds of reciprocity and obligations. The network, forged over time in the pits, provides access to resources and jobs, and provides trading tips and informal training.[8] Ties of family, friendship, and neighborhood assist neophyte traders in acquiring entry-level positions, learning to interpret the market, finding an exchange member to sponsor admission to the CBOT, and often gaining the capital necessary to begin trading. But it is not only important for distributing resources among individuals. These actors do not deal with each other solely for individual utility. Their bonds are at once social and economic. Connections extend beyond, but the pit remains the network's spatial locus.

Although the Chicago pit grounds its markets, the CBOT has always been resolutely global. Futures markets have gathered information from around the world since the telegraph brought weather reports and harvest predictions from Russia, Argentina, and Europe to the trading floor (Morgan, 1979; Preda,

2002). There, in the pit, traders use this global information to identify a value for contracts for wheat and bond futures. The trading pit itself acts as a technology for arranging a local network of traders whose interdependence and mutual knowledge create the daily market at the CBOT.

Economic information is delivered directly to the pit. Traders orient their profit-making strategies around the information available to them within the legal space of trade. Some choose to read specialized market reports that chart historical trends in the market, others follow government agencies closely. All traders watch for significant new information from the Federal Reserve and the Treasury, such as changes in interest rates and the consumer price index. At the moment that these significant numbers are announced, the CBOT broadcasts them to the floor, posting them on the electronic screens that band all four walls of the hangar-like room. Alan Greenspan's reports to Congress play on the two-storey tall television screens that cut an angle across the south and west sides of the room.

However, many traders gather the most important information from within the pit itself. For these traders, the social network of the pit provides the informational materials for trading. Traders constitute the market by directly watching each other, observing the trading habits of the successful traders in order to emulate them and examining the failing strategies of others in order to exploit their weaknesses for profit.[9] Traders use their networks of friends and colleagues to gather information about the market, to find a profitable place in the pit to work, and to complete trades with their friends and long-time co-workers.

One strategy for profit-making relies on a "feel for the market" based on the collective effervescence on the CBOT trading floor. Listening to the rhythms of the changing bid and offer numbers brings on a sensation that leads traders to judge the market as "heavy" or "light," likely to rise or fall according to their sensory estimations. Beyond creating the basis for individual trader's economic judgments, the ambient noise affects the market as a whole. A feel for the market has concrete effects. Economists studying the CBOT found that increased sound levels lead to higher trading volumes and foreshadow periods of high volatility in the pits (Coval and Shumway, 1998). This affective information is possible only in a face-to-face market where traders experience the excitement of the market in the bodies and voices of their companions and rivals.

Traders utilize their knowledge of others' trading strategies to orient their own exchange tactics. This mutual exploitation is especially pointed in relationships between "locals," who are self-funded, independent traders, and brokers, who work on client commissions to complete trades. Brokers create relationships of reciprocity with local traders. The locals will accept trades that carry a potential loss. This allows for the client to complete the trade. In exchange, the broker is indebted to the local trader and will give him good trades in the future.

Brokers wield power to punish locals who are unwilling or unable to enter into these relationships of reciprocity. They can "dump" contracts on traders who cannot support the risk associated with large trades to test them. These tests can allow the local to enter into the neighborhood of a powerful broker or exclude him from these profitable relationships, requiring him to establish network connections with other traders. Each of these strategies creates a bond between the physical space of the pit and the social network of traders.[10]

Pit traders can exploit their place at the heart of the market to gain access to information about market players that firms intentionally obscure. Knowledge of brokers' customer trading habits can orient their own exchange strategies. Traders often track the trading patterns of certain large institutional players. It is common knowledge on the floor that certain firms work with particular brokers in the pit. Yet, it is unusual for a broker to work solely for a single institution. Exclusive use of one broker would give away too much information to pit traders with the potential to drive the price up or down. But traders gossip about the patterns of the Merrill Lynch and Goldman Sachs brokers in order to understand how the large institutional players are assessing current market conditions. If Nomura is selling large lots of contracts, local traders can understand that the Japanese firm is bringing selling pressure onto the market. This is called "knowing what the paper is doing." The institutional players are known as "paper" because of the slips that firms use to deliver their orders to brokers in the pit. This image of part for the whole shows how information is understood primarily in the context of the pit. The firms are "paper" because they make their appearance in the stacks of order slips that brokers hold in their pockets. The firms enter the pit as a series of paper orders.

The centrality of the market and the social networks among traders create this knowledge. It is there on the exchange floor that traders can see and hear what these large market players are doing and where they can solidify opinions around what this means in their daily gossip sessions.

Time in the Pit

The interplay between technology and social networks also shapes time in the pit. The pit's design centralizes the market in time as well as in space. Traders describe the market as existing at the moment of exchange. The market exists only in the pit since this is where exchange happens. Each market is made at the moment of agreement between buyer and seller. Once that moment has passed, even as the two traders write up the deal, the market has moved on. The fleeting temporal nature of the market makes physical presence in the pit even more necessary. If a trader is out of the pit, he is out of the market. Any information he receives will be seconds behind at best. That outdated information is a representation of a temporal market reality that no longer exists.

Social networks complicate this understanding of the market. These networks stretch the market over time. They create agreements between individuals about the shape of the market, even though the CBOT defines the market as a phenomenon confined to the daily trade. The formation of a defined social space within the pit creates problems for the designers and managers who are responsible for creating and maintaining an "efficient" marketplace. The social understandings of time and space in the market undermine the technological design of the market. The competing notions of space and time cannot be reconciled easily.

Splintering

Despite the temporal and spatial centrality of the pit, the physical proximity of traders creates splintering. Strategies for profit-making in the pit result in the spatial and social fragmentation of the market. The largest pit at the CBOT holds 600 traders. In an arena of such vast size, not all traders are available at a single time. Traders can use their own discretion when identifying their trading partners. Traders use this judgment to create protected spaces of exchange, or neighborhoods. In these enclaves, traders of similar skills and risk-taking tastes gather in a single area of the pit to support each other's labor. Brokers and individual traders of great influence encourage younger traders who show promise to stand close to them in the pit. This proximity allows the influential speculator to do business with the traders of his choice, establishing centers of profitability within the supposedly open marketplace.[11] Although the pit was created to centralize and unify the market, the social network of the pit is arranged in clusters that trade more with one another and less with those outside their "neighborhood."

The stepped structure of the pit also creates a problem for traders who practice a technique called spreading between contracts. These speculators – also called yield-curve traders – exploit fluctuations in the relationship between prices in the 30, 10, and 5-year treasury futures. For a spreader based primarily in the 10-year pit the key profit is to have instant access to trade in the 5-year notes. Spreaders dominate an area where these traders have an uninterrupted view of the 5-year pit. The pit is also divided into areas according to the expiration month of the contract. Traders who deal in "front month" contracts – the futures contract that will expire next – gather in one area of the pit. Traders who trade the middle and back month contracts gather in distinct areas. The shape of the pit and the arrangement of pits on the trading floor condition the physical arrangement of the social network of traders.

CBOT dealers have been plying their trade in pits for 155 years. Until recently, the logic of the trading nexus has been unchallenged. Changes to the pit technology have focused on the delivery of information to the pit and the distribution of commodity prices that are made there. From chalkboards and telegraphs to telephone, digital order books, and electronic screens, information technology has been used to augment the trading nexus.

FROM NEXUS TO NETWORK

After a century and a half of dominance, the pit is now giving way to online forms of trading. Digital markets are obviating the CBOT nexus by establishing electronic networks that stretch over the globe. This new market form links dispersed traders into a unified, but decentralized, market. This is not, however, a simple reproduction or rationalization of the marketplace. These digital platforms create new orientations to space and time that define the market environment and the information available to traders. Where the trading pit was designed to unify the market in space and time, electronic futures trading creates a technological network of traders that share time but neither space nor relationships.[12] These network technologies reconfigure the spatial and temporal relationships of the trader to the market, and, in turn, reshape their strategies for information gathering.

Space

Electronic technologies create a global scale for the marketplace. Instead of a nexus form, where information and traders converge in a central location, connections between traders are stretched into globe-spanning networks. In 1999, the CBOT and its partner, the German-Swiss exchange Eurex, launched a common trading platform on which any member of either exchange could trade the other's products. The exchanges distributed the new screens widely with particular concentrations in Chicago, London, and Frankfurt. A central server located in Chicago for American Treasury futures and Frankfurt for German Treasury futures matches trades and redistributes the profit and loss information to the traders' desks around the world.

The new electronic network reorganizes space and time in two important ways. First, the electronic network separates physical and social space. The rationale for creating electronic markets was built on the logic of efficiency. For clients of the exchanges, traders and their social networks are seen as a potentially costly impediment between the clients' strategies and the market. The technological possibility of more direct contact with the market drives managers and designers to create new technological platforms.[13] These platforms both unify and spread access to the market. The trading screen dissolves the personal relationships of the pit that mediate between individuals and the market. In electronic networks, the majority of competitors lie beyond the boundaries of any individual's dealing room. Electronic technologies separate traders from their strategies built on watching the actions of others. Distanced from their competitors, traders can also no longer draw on the "feel" of the market. The noise and collective excitement that traders used to index the strength or weakness of the market are unavailable. Second, the trading screen creates a new representation of the market. Replacing face-to-face with face-to-screen interaction allows seemingly direct access to the market. Traders no longer apprehend the market through the voices and bodies of their competitors. The screen presents the market as an object to be read: a digital market made material in bid and offer numbers.

Like the original pit design, electronic markets also face the challenge of unifying a fragmented market. Trading screens accomplish this by creating an integrated representation of the market. The design of the a/c/e, the formal name for the CBOT/ Eurex platform, represents the market as a single entity. It appears as a series of changing bids and offers on the screen. There are no identifications of individual traders. The screen is completely anonymous. Each individual strategy is masked. There is no indication of how many futures contracts any one trader is bidding for or offering to the market. There is only an aggregate number of bids and offers. These numbers confront the trader as a unified opinion of supply and demand. Rather than displaying the market as a collection of individual assessments of economic information, the a/c/e screen presents the market as a coherent force with which the individual trader contends. He is not in direct engagement with other competitors, but rather he is attempting to glean profit as an individual against the mass. This representational centrality focuses the traders on the supra-spatial entity of the market rather than on their competitors in locations around the globe. The physical representation of the market on the screen now mirrors a particular vision of the market: the market as a singular unit, rather than as a collection of individual players. Each trader now confronts the market as an individual against the unitary will of the market – an object without a place.

Time in Electronic Markets

Creating an efficient, liquid electronic market in futures requires drawing in participants from around the globe. Electronic markets reshape temporal conditions that effect the participation of traders. Traders in certain markets dominate trade in CBOT products and the work-hours in their time zones are the most active in the market. For dealing rooms far from Chicago and Frankfurt, managers must find traders who are willing to work hours that begin late and extend into the early hours of the morning. These night owls can take advantage of the hours when the greatest number of traders is operating in the market – the hours of maximum liquidity.

Electronic technologies and a commitment to 24-hour markets make trade possible at all hours of the day. However, the social density needed for a liquid market restricts the best hours of operation. The temporality of this global market is linked with time zones. The unity of the marketplace is created not through the technology, but in the working schedules when Chicago, London, and Frankfurt traders are all at their desks.

In the markets that the London office of LDF specialized in – the German bond futures – the most active hours were between 1.00 and 4.00 p.m. Most LDF traders arrived at their desks before 7.00 a.m. when the German traders entered the trading arena. Between 7.00 a.m. and 1.00 p.m., British and German traders constituted the bulk of the market. After 1.00 p.m. London time, traders in Chicago began to enter the market as their work hours commenced. The heaviest volume occurred between 1.00 p.m. and 4.00 p.m. when Chicago, London, and Frankfurt were all in the mix. At 4.00 p.m. London time, the German traders would mostly have withdrawn from the market for the day, leaving less business and diminished profitability for the London and Chicago traders.

As in the trading pits, futures exchanges design the spatial and temporal arrangement of the market, shaping the information available to traders. The designers of the a/c/e embedded key features of economic rationality on the formal design of the market. First, they created greater speed and direct contact between traders. The goal of distributing trading screens to dealing rooms around the world was to make the market available to the greatest number of participants. Creating an electronic market removes the CBOT nexus, which is now seen as an unnecessary middle agent. The designers of the market system sought to construct a trading field that would approximate perfect competition.[14]

Where the pit forged a central space for the social networks of traders to convene and a focal point for information gathering and processing, the network form of electronic trading forces traders to use new sources of information. In the LDF dealing room, traders garnered information from three key sources. First, the bid and offer numbers on the screen hold their primary focus. Because these traders can make use of each fluctuation in the market to make a profit, they constantly scrutinize their screens for profit opportunities. Second, the discussions among traders over the course of the day identify patterns and reasons for each movement of the market. These constantly changing explanations orient the traders within the flux of prices. Third, each trader keeps a stream of information at his desk. The screens of a CQG machine show charts that track the historical movement of the market over the course of the past week, day, or ten-minute period, set to the personal preference of the user.

Each of these sources has a complex relationship to the space and time of the market. Traders read the bid and offer numbers within the confines of a dealing room filled with the screens and bodies of other traders. The talk between traders also happens within the dealing room. There, traders can station themselves to engage with the will of the market. However, the market itself, as I have noted, is presented as a supra-spatial entity. The third element of information gathering derives more from understanding the market as a temporal entity. The CQG screen displays a number of charting techniques that traders can choose from. Many used a technique derived from Bollinger Bands, a framing device that predicts the movement of the market. The lines follow a moving average that provides definitions of high and low prices for futures contracts. The trader can than see where the price on the screen departs from this indicator and buy or sell accordingly. The bands illuminate how a price has moved out of alignment at any given moment. This helps the trader fix the market in time.

Many economists agree that the step-by-step movement of the market is unpredictable, a random walk that renders short-term fluctuations impossible to anticipate.[15] Although traders who make money from the fast-paced changes of market direction would disagree with this theory, they concur that gleaning coherent information from and orientation to the market is a critical and complex process.

AN ENGINEERED SOCIAL FIELD

The spatial and temporal conditions of the electronic market favor a certain kind of trader. Each market technology creates an environment that establishes the set of skills that will be most effective and yield the most profits. The trading pit favored the well connected. Traders who can take best advantage of the electronic field are masters of speed and prescience. The informational and social conditions forged in electronic markets assume that the profitable trader will be the fastest to see where the market is headed and the most able to react quickly. Electronic networks condition the competitive field to give advantage to traders who seem to operate as isolated individuals. The a/c/e is an anonymous system. Anonymity is not a property of the technology. It is rather a choice of representation – a market without the appearance of individual actors.

The CBOT's first electronic trading system, Project A, operated on the social principals of the pit. The screen created an image of a marketplace filled with individual traders. The Project A screen displayed a three-letter identifier for each trader participating in the market. In the pits, traders wear badges imprinted with these codes pinned to a lapel. Traders sometimes use these letters to form words, BUL, or RED, for instance, and use this tag as a pit persona. Project A made use of the already existing network of traders at the CBOT by recreating the possibility of knowing each trading partner and market participant. Because Project A was limited to members of the CBOT, it was quite likely that the traders operating on screen would be in regular exchanges in the pit. The first group of CBOT traders to try their skills on the screen brought this intimate knowledge of pit social conditions with them online. Personal and electronic interactions reinforced each other.[16] This representation creates a marketplace on each screen. Even though each trader sat at a desk separated from the others, the Project A screen created a visual image of the pit space projected onto an electronic network. Project A also did not change the temporal conditions of trading significantly. The majority of traders remained in Chicago. For most of the life of Project A, the system operated only during hours that the trading pit was closed. Since the bulk of trading volume remained in the pit, Project A traders worked without the advantage of liquidity that ran through the nexus of exchange.

When the CBOT developed the next generation of screens for electronic trading, the designers jettisoned the representation of the social network of traders and developed screens that excluded any personal information. As I have noted, they changed the representation of the market by altering its spatial and temporal dimensions. These new conditions set the stage for older traders, who relied on the space and time of the pit, to fade away. It was time for a new kind of trader to emerge.

CONCLUSION

Global financial markets are made up of networks, both technological and social. The interaction of these elements is a material force in the design and operation of financial markets. Specifically, the technological and social dimensions generate conflicting ideas and practices of space and time. These clashes surface in arguments over how to construct, govern, and act in efficient markets. From the nexus of the trading pit to the network of dealing screens, exchange technologies define the organization of financial competition, and in turn require new forms of economic conduct from traders. I would like to end with four observations about technology, space, and time in financial markets and the possibility for new actors to arise at their intersection.

(1) In the transition from nexus to network we see a transformation of the marketplace. Network designers advocate a desocialized marketplace that adheres to ideals of economic efficiency. However, creating such market technologies requires designers to construct a strategic social field. The new markets built around face-to-screen interactions divorce traders from social

networks and represent the market as a unified powerful entity apart from the individuals that compose it. Still, traders redefine the trading arena. Profit-making advantage lies in creating protected spaces within the temporally and spatially defined marketplace. Pit traders fragment the market into enclosed dealing spaces where ties of friendship and reciprocity deliver profit. As in the case of the trading pit, the ethics of efficiency demand further rationalization of the contradictions between the design and operation of the marketplace. New technologies offer materials to create the appearance of direct contact between trader and market.

(2) Electronic technologies can, in theory, extend to any area. But, in prac-tice, economic action is intertwined with specific, spatially defined networks. The information that traders need to make strategic decisions arises from the particular setting of the trading floor or dealing room. Saskia Sassen (2001) argues that certain cities remain key for global finance because of the concen-tration of high-level services, such as accounting and law. Global cities are important beyond connections between firms and the glamor of urban living. Cities and their financial institutions create cohorts of traders whose tech-niques of exchange and information-gathering practices are bound to their location.

(3) Liquid markets require dense participation. In the nexus market form, traders gather in a single space and circumscribed time to make exchanges. The pit arranges liquidity by concentrating trading. The global scale of elec-tronic networks creates a problem for organizing a liquid market. Because traders are located in widely dispersed time zones, market coordination through time management is a key element of global financial networks. Traders in different hubs must be engaged in the market at the same time, otherwise there is too little action to create easy exchange at high volumes. In the global financial marketplace, traders in certain locations, like Chicago, London, and Frankfurt, create nodes of liquidity for particular financial instru-ments. Traders in these locations work in the markets each day, generating possibilities to deal at a fair price for any number of contracts.

Although in theory liquid markets can spread over the surface of the globe, in practice global cities provide concentrations of traders that support liquid-ity. The time zones of these cities determine the peak times of financial activ-ity. In the absence of spatial concentration, the temporal dimensions of markets assume a heightened importance. In electronic networks, temporal coordination is crucial for maintaining liquid markets.

(4) The redesign of exchange technologies and the changes in time and space create the possibility for new kinds of traders to emerge. A technolog-ical form that favors actors with abstract analytical skills is replacing the nexus system based on relationships among locals and between locals and brokers. These are not, however, the skills of the "symbolic analyst" or

"reprogrammable labor" that require agile manipulation of complex information and an ability to learn new systems of analysis and research (Reich,
1991; Castells, 1996). Profitability in electronic markets lies in rapid identification of simple patterns in bid and offer numbers, the basic representation
of the market on the screen. The type of trader who entered the financial
futures markets at the time of their founding in the late 1970s and early
1980s is being replaced by more educated workers as screen-based trading
replaces face-to-face exchange. Banks are now placing financial trading
within a career trajectory. Dealing is no longer the domain of the savvy
trader whose life in finance is tied only to his trading skills. Yet these new
traders are not the same as their financial analyst counterparts. In the new
electronic dealing rooms, they are training in the new forms of time and
space that both separate and tie together competitors around the globe.

In financial networks, the ethical imperative for efficient markets drives
technological and social innovations. Time and space are key areas of
contestation in the elusive search for market efficiency. The transition from
nexus to network remakes the material infrastructure of exchange to create
the representation of a unified, liquid market. This market confronts traders
as individuals with disregard for their spatial and temporal location. In the
contest between technological and social configurations of time and space,
the shape of financial networks emerges.

NOTES

1. Miyazaki (2003) has observed that the position of social theorists as analysts in a rapidly
   changing world has generated a sense of "being behind" that is mirrored in Tokyo financial markets. Also, by connecting the temporal assumptions of arbitrage to the life strategies of Japanese securities traders, he shows us how the time dimensions of finance extend
   far beyond the market domain.
2. Claude Fischer (1992) has warned against confusing the properties of technology with the
   properties of society and also shown how users can change the trajectory of technological
   design. The potentials of the technology should not blind us to the ways in which actors
   appropriate devices. In the case of financial markets, this means considering how traders
   shape the time and space of the network in using it. This chapter adds to the growing body
   of work that examines how information technologies and daily practices shape new
   temporal and spatial dimensions in everyday life and labor (see Laurier, 2001; Green,
   2002).
3. When examined from inside market organizations, managers and designers of network
   technologies emerge as key to establishing particular configurations of "power geometry"
   (Massey, 1995). These managers and designers are the "specific intellectuals" of the
   network (Rabinow, 1989). As this chapter will show, they shape financial networks
   according to the ethics of market efficiency, a practice that sets patterns of inclusion and
   exclusion from the profits of the market.
4. Arguments about the spatial arrangements of financial networks have focused on the problem of physical centralization of command and control functions (Sassen, 1999, 2001).
   The infrastructure of these locations is also used as evidence of the centralization of
   highly skilled labor and global management functions (Graham, 2002). These analyses,

however, do not examine the significance or impact of technological change on the practices of actors or the structure of markets.

5. Urs Breugger and Karin Knorr Cetina (2002) have shown how electronic networks can establish a unified temporal platform that allows for global interchanges. They see this as establishing a new social system based on economic transactions. Breugger and Cetina work on markets where communications and relationships between individual traders are possible even at a global scale. In the markets examined here, traders work without this personal contact and instead interact with the market as a whole as their trading screen depicts it. This makes the issue of temporal coordination less crucial for the individual traders, although it remains critical for the electronic trading system.

6. In this way, the face-to-face trading pit is just as much a "system of connectivity and integration" as Breugger and Knorr Cetina (2002) have claimed for electronic platforms in currency markets.

7. See Smith (1989) for a detailed account of the social operation of auctions.

8. Granovetter (1973) is the foundation of a body of sociological research that explains how social networks support the distribution of resources.

9. Harrison White (1981) analyzes the way that mutual observation among competitors creates markets.

10. I use the masculine pronoun descriptively throughout. The CBOT trading floor and the LDF dealing room were staffed overwhelmingly by male traders.

11. Sociologist Wayne Baker (1984) has shown how this fragmentation of a centralized market affects volatility and price in the market.

12. Breugger and Knorr Cetina (2002) call this "temporal coordination," and point to the collectivities that develop from interacting within time when acting at a distance from competitors. I argue that this is in some ways specific to markets where actors are known to one another, such as the foreign exchange markets that Breugger and Knorr Cetina study. The "virtual society" that these foreign exchange traders form is anathema to the notions of efficiency that futures exchange managers seek to build into their systems. In futures exchanges, temporal coordination is the condition for creating a market. Yet, at the same time, action at a distance offers a way for eviscerating the social content of the market, at least at the level of representation.

13. This logic of creating direct market access I call "disintermediation," borrowing a term from the financial industry for bringing debt instruments directly to the market (Zaloom, 2003). However, from an analytic point of view, these interactions and communications are always mediated by technologies, relationships, and legal rules.

14. This feedback loop between economic theory and the marketplace Michel Callon (1998) has described as "the performativity of markets."

15. See Burton Malkiel (1999) for an accessible and thorough explanation of this theory.

16. Keith Hampton and Barry Wellman (2003) have observed similar reinforcement of personal and electronic ties in Netville. However, in this case there was an ethical commitment to participation in community and a fear that Internet involvement would dissolve local ties. In financial markets, the "efficiency" of electronic communications rests on the evacuation of personal interactions. The case of the futures markets shows that it takes aggressive intention to create an online arena devoid of personal interaction. From this perspective, anxiety over the loss of community in an Internet era is misplaced.

REFERENCES

Baker, Wayne E. (1984) "Floor Trading and Crowd Dynamics," in P. A. Adler and P. Adler (eds), *The Social Dynamics of Financial Markets*, pp. 107–28. Greenwich: JAI Press.

Breugger, Urs and Knorr Cetina, Karin (2002) "Global Microstructures: The Virtual Societies of Financial Markets," *American Journal of Sociology* 107 (4): 905–50.

Callon, Michel (1998) "Introduction," in Michel Callon (ed.), *The Laws of the Markets*. Oxford: Blackwell.

Castells, Manuel (1996) *The Information Age: Economy, Society and Culture*, vol. I: *The Rise of the Network Society*. Oxford: Blackwell.

Coval, Joshua D. and Shumway, Tyler (1998) "Is Noise just Sound?," CBOT Educational Research Foundation Papers.

Cronon, William (1991) *Nature's Metropolis*. New York: W. W. Norton.

Faloon, William D. (1998) *Market Maker: A Sesquicentennial Look at the Chicago Board of Trade*. Chicago: Board of Trade of the City of Chicago.

Fischer, Claude S. (1992) *America Calling: A Social History of the Telephone to 1940*. Berkeley, CA: University of California Press.

Graham, Stephan (2002) "Communication Grids: Cities and Infrastructure," in S. Sassen (ed.), *Global Networks, Linked Cities*, pp. 71–92. New York: Routledge.

Granovetter, Mark (1973) "The Strength of Weak Ties," *American Journal of Sociology* 78 (6): 1360–80.

Green, Nicola (2002) "On the Move: Technology, Mobility, and the Mediation of Time and Space," *The Information Society* 18: 281–92.

Hampton, Keith and Wellman, Barry (2003) "Neighboring in Netville: How the Internet Supports Community and Social Capital in a Wired Suburb," *City and Community* 2 (4): 277–311.

Harvey, David (1989) *The Condition of Postmodernity*. Oxford: Blackwell.

Held, David, McGrew, Anthony, Goldblatt, David, and Perraton, Jonathan (1999) *Global Transformations: Politics, Economy, and Culture*. Stanford, CA: Stanford University Press.

Laurier, Eric (2001) "Why People Say where They Are during Mobile Phone Calls," *Environment and Planning D: Society and Space* 19: 485–504.

Lee, Benjamin, and LiPuma, Edward (2002) "Cultures of Circulation: The Imaginations of Modernity," *Public Culture* 14 (1): 191–213.

Malkiel, Burton Gordon (1999) *A Random Walk Down Wall Street*. New York: W. W. Norton.

Massey, Doreen (1995) "Power Geometry and a Progressive Sense of Place," in Jon Bird et al. (ed.), *Mapping the Futures: Local Culture, Global Change*, pp. 59–69. London: Routledge.

Miyazaki, Hirokazu (2003) "The Temporalities of the Market," *American Anthropologist* 105 (2): 255–65.

Morgan, Dan (1979) *Merchants of Grain*. New York: Viking.

Preda, Alex (2002) "Of Ticks and Tapes: Financial Knowledge, Communicative Practices, and Information Technologies of Nineteenth Century Financial Markets," New York Conference on the Social Studies of Finance, Columbia University.

Rabinow, Paul (1989) *French Modern: Norms and Forms of the Social Environment*. Chicago: University of Chicago Press.

Reich, Robert (1991) *The Work of Nations*. New York: Vintage.

Sassen, Saskia (1999) "Digital Networks and Power," in M. Featherstone and S. Lash (eds), *Spaces of Culture: City, Nation, World*, pp. 49–63. London: Sage.

— — (2001) *The Global City*. Princeton, NJ: Princeton University Press.

Sennett, Richard (1998) *Corrosion of Character: The Personal Consequences of Work in the New Capitalism*. New York: W. W. Norton.

Smith, Charles W. (1989) *Auctions : The Social Construction of Value*. New York: Free Press.

White, Harrison (1981) "Where do Markets Come From?," *American Journal of Sociology* 87 (3): 517–47.

Zaloom, Caitlin (2003) "Ambiguous Numbers: Trading Technology and Interpretation in Financial Markets," *American Ethnologist* 30 (2): 258–72.

PART IV

Sociability and social structure in the age of the
Internet

9. Networked sociability online, off-line

Keith N. Hampton

THE NETWORK SOCIETY

The growth of the Internet and home computing has ignited a debate on the nature of community and how computer-mediated communication affects social relationships. Dystopians argue that in an information society where work, leisure, and social ties are maintained online, people could completely reject the need for social relationships based on physical location. Moreover, relationships that are maintained online are evaluated as less meaningful and complete than traditional, in-person social contacts. Utopians argue that by creating new forms of community online, "virtual community," the Internet offers a replacement for traditional public spaces, such as cafés, bars, and community organizations, which have atrophied over the past quarter century (Oldenburg, 1989; Putnam, 2000). It is argued that the electronic agoras of the Internet free the individual from the restraints of geography and unite people in new communities of interest free from place-based existence. What this debate – arguing that community is either lost or completely recreated online – fails to recognize is that community has long been freed from geography and that the Internet may hold as much promise for reconnecting people to communities of place as it does for liberating people from them.

THE RISE AND FALL OF COMMUNITY

Concerns about the decline of community are not confined to the network society. Since at least the 1800s, scholars have debated how societal change and technological innovation affects community (Tönnies, 1887; Durkheim, 1893). The transition from an agrarian preindustrial society to an urban industrial society was also accompanied by concerns for the changing structure of interpersonal relations. In the urban environment "bonds of kinship, neighbourliness, and sentiments arising out of living together for generations" were said to be "absent or, at best, relatively weak in an aggregate" (Wirth 1938: 11). Stanley Milgram (1970: 1465) described an "acceptance of noninvolvement, impersonality, and aloofness in urban life" that was accompanied by "blasé attitudes toward deviant or bizarre behaviour," descriptions that are remarkable in their similarity to what has been reported in the popular press about the Internet: "I see people developing a more blasé attitude toward the unthinkable as our information overload increases" (Lactis, 1999). "The Internet permits us to hide behind a screen rather than interact face to face with other humans. It is isolating individuals who forget what real community is … online communities are increasing the fragmentation of society" (Angsioco, 2003). Indeed, descriptions of cyber-life as impersonal, superficial, and transitory are motivated by the same concern for a loss of densely knit, broadly supportive, place-based interactions as those that motivated earlier debates about urban industrial society.

Like the rural to urban transition, the transition to the network society frees the individual from "the pettiness and prejudices" of traditional "organic" relations (Simmel, 1950). The Internet reduces the friction of space – the time and cost necessary to communicate across distances – from what could be achieved through the technologies of the urban environment (for example, the train, automobile, and telephone). A reduction in the friction of space, combined with access to a large, heterogeneous population, facilitates the ability of individuals to form relations that were previously inaccessible. No longer limited to those who are closest at hand, it is increasingly possible to seek out social ties based on shared interest and mutual identification, but not necessarily shared place. Freedom from the constraints of place provides Internet users with the opportunity to explore aspects of individual identity and interest that previously may have been repressed or lacked a critical mass of others.

While this extension of "community without propinquity" (Webber, 1963) does not exclude the possibility that people can form social ties based on shared place, it does suggest that similarity of interest is more important in forming relations than similarity of setting. Indeed, most of the social support that people require to function day to day comes from sources outside the local setting (Fischer, 1982; Wellman et al., 1988). The failure to consider the possibility that ties from outside the local setting could provide supportive resources led some to conclude that the urban setting was responsible for a decline of community (Wellman, 1979). When communities are defined as informal ties of sociability, support, and identity, they are rarely neighborhood solidarities or even densely knit groups of kin and friends. Communities consist of far-flung kinship, workplace, interest group, and neighborhood ties that together form a network of aid, support, and social control. Evidence from the study of social networks has shown that, while communities often consist of dispersed relations, people still have strong, supportive communities (for a review, see Wellman, 1999).

While concerns for the loss of community are not new, there is evidence to suggest that over the past thirty years there has been a significant decline of community in the form of what Robert Putnam (2000) calls "social capital." In *Bowling Alone: The Collapse and Revival of American Community*, Putnam finds that people are spending less time with friends, relatives, and neighbors; they are more cynical; and they are less likely to be involved in clubs and organizations. Putnam addresses numerous possible causes for this decline, including suburbanization, globalization, changing family structures, and financial and temporal pressures. Largely excluding these factors, Putnam focuses on television as the largest factor that has contributed to a decline of social capital. Time devoted to watching television is said to come at the expense of participation in other activities, primarily those that take place outside the home (Putnam, 2000: 238). Indeed, there has been a decline in the number of community organizations and other "third places" that provide opportunities for public interaction outside the domestic setting (Oldenburg, 1989). People are increasingly likely to socialize in small groups in private homes rather than with large groups in public spaces (Wellman, 1992, 1999: 31–2).

The decline is social capital observed by Putnam (2000) occurs too early to be associated with home computing or Internet use. While the Internet shares many characteristics with television, it also shares characteristics with technologies that are less passive, like the telephone. However, even the telephone has contributed to increased privatism. Claude Fischer (1975) argues that, although the telephone has allowed people to maintain a greater number of social ties, it has also shifted communication out of public spaces and into the home. The growth of mobile phones and wireless computing has brought computer-mediated communication out of the home and onto the street, but it can also be argued that, when engaging with mobile devices, people cut themselves off from public spaces by creating private spheres of mobile interaction. The fear of many pundits is that the Internet, mobile phones, and other forms of computer-mediated communication withdraw people from the public realm, exasperating the trend toward home centeredness and privatization observed by Putnam (2000).

VIRTUAL COMMUNITY: HOPE FOR TOMORROW?

The "virtual community" has done much to highlight the potential for communities to form beyond the confines of geographic space. Enthusiasts argue that electronic spaces, such as multi-user domains (i.e., MUDs, MOOs, and MUSHs) and graphical worlds (e.g., Sims Online and other MMORPGs), provide a new realm of public space (Mitchell, 1995), and there are seemingly endless accounts of how cyberspace can facilitate the formation of new communities of interest (Calhoun, 1998). Some even suggest that there is an erosion of the boundary between the "real and the virtual, the animate and the inanimate" (Turkle, 1997: 39).

Yet, by most accounts, online communities have not become a dominant component of most Internet users' regular Internet experiences. Telephone surveys of American Internet users, conducted by the Syntopia Project, found that in 1995, when 9 percent of the American population had access to the Internet (Taylor, 2000), only 25.5 percent of users reported being a member of an online community. In 2000, when the proportion of Internet users had grown to 59 percent of the American population (Taylor, 2000), the proportion of users who were members of at least one online community had shrunk to 10.4 percent. For the most part, it is only those who have used the Internet the longest and those who are the most technologically savvy, who regularly participate in online communities (Katz and Rice, 2002: 245–6). With such a small proportion of Internet users participating in the virtual agora, what can we say of the utopian promise that electronic spaces will substitute for the loss of public places in the Cartesian plain?

As with earlier concerns about the urban environment and loss of community, looking for community in only one place at one time (be it in neighborhoods or in cyberspace) is an inadequate means of revealing supportive community relations. Defining "virtual communities" as environments with clearly defined and discrete boundaries ignores the potential for social relations online to be maintained off-line, and privileges the Internet as a separate social system. Social networks are cross-cutting and multi-stranded. People use multiple methods of communication in maintaining their communities: direct in-person contact, telephone, postal mail, e-mail, chats, and other online environments. Relationships that originate on the Internet can move off-line, and existing friendship and kinship relations can be supported online. Only by looking at how the Internet is used in everyday life can we begin to understand how it is used along with existing means of social contact in the maintenance of community relations.

COMPUTER-MEDIATED COMMUNICATION IN EVERYDAY LIFE

Early Evidence

The Homenet study by Kraut et al. (1998) was one of the first and remains one of the most complete studies of Internet use in everyday life. Kraut and his collaborators interviewed participants from 93 households in eight neighborhoods in Pittsburgh, USA. Participants were provided with a free computer, telephone line, and dial-up Internet access. Only those households where no one had previous in-home Internet or computer experience were eligible to participate. Participants were interviewed twice, a pre-test before they received Internet access, and a post-test 12–24 months later. Kraut et al. (1998) concluded that the Internet was similar to the television in displacing time spent on more social activities. Internet use was associated with relatively small, but statistically significant declines in the amount of time family members spent communicating with each other, the size of participants' local social networks, and psychological well-being. Kraut et al. (1998) also found negative, although not statistically significant, relationships between Internet use and stress, the size of participants' distant social networks, and the number of people participants felt they could go to for social support.

Norman Nie and Lutz Erbring (2000) lent support to the findings of Kraut et al. (1998) in a panel survey of over two thousand Internet users. They found that 5 percent of Internet users reported spending less time at social events, 9 percent spent less time with friends and family, and 17 percent reported a drop in phone contact. Moreover, they found that those who spent the most time online were the most likely to report declines in social contact. Like Kraut et al, (1998), Nie and Erbring (2000) concluded that "the Internet could be the ultimate isolating technology that further reduces our participation in communities even more than did automobiles and television before it" (Norman Nie, as quoted in O'Toole, 2000). It should be noted, however, that the large majority of participants in Nie and Erbring (2000) reported that they experienced no change in social activities as a result of Internet use, and a proportion of users also reported an increase. Nie and Erbring did not report on the relationship between time spent online and increased or unchanged social contact.

There have been a number of criticisms of the methodology employed by Kraut et al. (1998) and Nie and Erbring (2000) (e.g., Caruso, 1998; Scheer, 2000). For example, the sample used by Kraut and co-workers was non-random. Participants were drawn from pre-existing community and school groups that may have experienced a decline in involvement and social contact unrelated to Internet use. The selection of participants with no previous Internet experience left open the explanation that the observed effect of Internet use on social contact and psychological well-being may have been the result of being new Internet and home-computer users, and not directly a result of Internet use. The frustration associated with learning to use the Internet and a new home computer, particularly if it did not meet with initial expectations, may have increased stress, affected family communication, and encouraged increased levels of isolation and depression. Nie and Erbring (2000), while using random sampling, employed an unusual and untested survey methodology. Participants were given WebTV, a system that allowed users to access the Internet through a set-top box connected through the television, and were asked to complete surveys online over their TVs. WebTV tends to be adopted by the least experienced Internet users, those who do not already own a home computer and do not expect all the functionality of a full Internet connection, and there is no way to measure how the use of this technology may have affected the results of the survey.

Every study has its methodological strengths and weaknesses. However, the biggest concern with the findings of Kraut et al. (1998) and Nie and Erbring (2000) is not in their methodology, but how they and most other Internet dystopians frame Internet use. Like virtual community enthusiasts, there is a tendency within these studies to privilege the Internet as a social system removed from the other ways in which people communicate. The use of computer-mediated communication in maintaining existing social networks, and in the formation of new social ties, are omitted or regarded as insignificant. Limiting the analysis to communication with network members outside of cyberspace neglects the possibility that computer-mediated communication could substitute for other means of social contact. It is impossible to determine if the size of people's social networks, or the frequency of contact, decreases as a result of Internet use, or if the Internet allows people to shift the maintenance of social ties to a new communication medium. Alternatively, the Internet may even allow people to reinvest time spent on in-person or telephone contact in the maintenance of a greater number of social network members online, as was the case with the adoption of the telephone (Fischer, 1992). Indeed, 90 percent of participants from Nie and Erbring's (2000) study used e-mail, 10 per cent used chat rooms to communicate with family members, 12 per cent used chat rooms to communicate with friends that they already had before going online, and 16 per cent reported using chat rooms to communicate with new friends they had met online.

It may be argued that the "social presence" (Short et al., 1976) or "media richness" (Daft and Lengel, 1986) of computer-mediated communication results in the exchange of fewer social cues online than people experience with face-to-face interactions, but there is little doubt that computer-mediated communication could be used in the exchange of aid and support (e.g., Haythornthwaite and Wellman, 1998). Explaining the affect of the Internet on social relations by peering into cyberspace and ignoring the network of social relations that extended to other social settings, or neglecting the value of online ties in supporting new and existing community relations, fails to consider the cross-cutting nature of community, including the many ways and the many places people interact.

One Form of Communication Amongst Many

More recently, a number of studies have been published that both recognize the value of computer-mediated communication – as a legitimate, supportive means of social contact – and holistically evaluate the impact of the Internet on ties, on- and off-line. As the proportion of total Internet users increases, more recent studies may also paint a more reliable picture of Internet use in everyday life. Just as the telephone could not be understood by observing the first few homes in town to purchase a phone, social uses of the Internet are dependent on the existence of a critical mass of users within one's social network. Indeed, the majority of recent studies, including a follow-up to the Homenet study by Kraut et al. (2002), have concluded with more optimistic results about the effects of Internet use on social ties.

Consistent with the hypothesis that participants in the Kraut et al. (1998) study experienced a decrease in the size of their social networks, a reduction in the frequency of communication with family members, and reduced psychological well-being as a result of being new Internet users, and not directly as a result of Internet use, a three-year follow-up study by Kraut et al. (2002) found that the negative effects originally attributed to Internet use dissipated over time. Kraut et al. (2002) found that more frequent Internet users increased the size of their social networks, had greater face-to-face interaction with friends and family, and became more involved in community activities (2002: 61). They also concluded that the Internet was particularly successful in helping those with pre-existing low levels of social support make new friendship ties (2002: 67).

Recognizing the cross-cutting nature of social ties – principally that relationships that start online do not necessarily remain online – the UCLA Internet Report (2000) found that roughly one-quarter of Internet users have met someone online (averaging 12.9 new ties each), and a full 12 percent of users have taken new online relationships off-line (averaging 5.6 new in-person friendships). Katz and Rice (2002: 263) report a similar finding from the Syntopia Project: that over 10 percent of Internet users reported making new friendships online that extend to in-person meetings, and 85 percent reported that their off-line experiences with online friends resulted in positive experiences.

Rejecting online social ties as insignificant can also exclude ties that would traditionally be considered central in a person's support network. In a random telephone survey, the Pew Internet and American Life Project found in 2000 that 79 percent of American Internet users reported e-mailing members of their immediate and extended family (Horrigan and Rainie, 2002: 9). Following the same sample over a period of one year, the percentage of Internet users who used e-mail to contact kinship relations grew to 84 percent; 31 percent of those who e-mailed family members started communicating with relatives with whom they previously had only limited contact (Howard et al., 2002: 68). Counter to the assumption that physical presence is required for sociability (see Nie et al., 2002), a large proportion of those who emailed family members did so to seek advice and social support. In fact, the proportion of Internet users who used e-mail to seek advice and support from family members increased between 2000 and 2001 (see table 9.1). The percentage who e-mailed family members to seek advice increased from 45 percent in 2000 to 56 percent in 2001; the percentage who e-mailed about something that worried them increased from 37 percent to 44 percent. Not only did the tendency to seek advice and raise worries with kinship relations increase with Internet experience, but it was particularly pronounced amongst the newest of Internet users. As a larger proportion of the population goes online, the proportion of Internet users in a person's social network generally increases, and it becomes increasingly easier for both new and more experienced users to use e-mail and other Internet technologies in the exchange of social support.

Internet studies that recognize the potential for computer-mediated communication to be used in maintaining social ties, and examine the network of people's social relations, on- and off-line, generally conclude with more optimistic results about the fate of social relationships in the network society. Still, in examining the role of this new technology in everyday life, few have directly addressed concerns about the relationship between Internet use and privatism. The Internet may be connecting people on- and off-line, but is it

Table 9.1   Seeking advice from family (% answering yes)

	Do you e-mail a family member for advice?	Do you e-mail a family member about something you are worried about?
All users 2001	56	44
All users 2000	45	37
Long-wired in 2001	60	46
Long-wired in 2000	49	41
Mid-range in 2001	51	45
Mid-range in 2000	42	37
Newcomers in 2001	58	45
Newcomers in 2000	45	33
Brand newbies	55	41

Note: Questions asked of all Internet users who e-mail family members.
$n = 862$ for March 2001; $n = 723$ for March 2000.
Long-wired = online > 3 years; mid-range = online 2–3 years; newcomers = online 1 year in 2000; brand newbies = came online between 3/00 and 3/01.

Source: Horrigan and Rainie (2002)

also shifting interaction out of the public realm and into homes and other private spheres of interaction?

LOCAL AFFORDANCES OF THE INTERNET

Concerns about the decline of community as a result of growing urbanization were only curtailed as it was accepted that supportive community relations could be found outside the neighborhood setting (Wellman, 1999). While this did not preclude the possibility that people could form close neighborhood attachments, it did suggest that the availability of a large, heterogeneous urban population allowed people to place similarity of interest over similarity of setting when selecting social ties (Fischer, 1975). The Internet radically expands on this earlier trend, providing access to an even larger, more heterogeneous population. However, there is a paradox in how the Internet shapes social relations. While computer-mediated communication further reduces the friction of space, it can also afford local interactions.

The availability of a large, diverse urban population and, more recently, a large, diverse online population, with subcultures that match every interest, is only part of the explanation as to why people tend to develop few strong neighborhood ties. Access is equally as important as social similarity in determining the likelihood of tie formation. The pattern of social relations known as "homophily" – the tendency for people to form social ties with those who are similar to themselves – has as much to do with people's desire to associate with similar others as it does with a tendency for similar people to participate in common activities (Feld, 1982; McPherson et al., 2001). North American neighborhoods generally lack institutional opportunities for social contact, and those institutions that do exist to promote local interaction (cafés, bars, community organizations, and so on) are in decline (Oldenburg, 1989; Putnam, 2000), and in many cases are absent from the suburban setting (Jacobs, 1961). There are simply too few opportunities for people to form local social ties.

What the Internet offers – that existing forms of communication do not – is a way of overcoming barriers to local tie formation. As neighborhood common spaces, such as parks and community centers, can be used to increase local tie formation and community involvement (Kuo et al., 1998), the provision of virtual common places can afford similar interactions. However, sophisticated online communities that require participants to engage in real-time conversations are generally not the answer (for example, chat rooms, virtual worlds, and so on). Online communities tend to be populated by only a small proportion of total Internet users and often require specialized knowledge and computer skills. The Internet's potential to afford local interaction comes from its ability to be used as an asynchronous form of communication that can engage others not only one-on-one, but as a broadcast of one-to-many.

Asynchronous communication facilitates temporal flexibility: people can read and respond to communication at individually convenient times and places. Similarly, the broadcast ability of computer-mediated communication removes the costs associated with having to travel door to door in organizing local activities and in seeking local support. "Like a habitually-frequented hangout, people show up at their email in-boxes and listen in on the happenings of their communities, interjecting when appropriate, but often just observing" (Hampton and Wellman, 2003: 286). In fact, there is a growing body of empirical evidence to suggest that the Internet supports "glocalization," the adoption of global technologies like the Internet for local use. A survey of 4,500 Internet users in nine countries by KRC Research (2003), commissioned by the Oracle Corporation, found that in France, Germany, Italy, and the US, one in every four e-mails never leaves the building in which it originated. At the residential level, it is the ability to observe the social happenings of a local community, the ability to broadcast information to others, and the potential to coordinate off-line activities through online interactions, where there exists the potential for IT-mediated, place-based community.

IT-MEDIATED, PLACE-BASED COMMUNITY: NETVILLE

"Netville" is one example of how computer-mediated communication can be used to facilitate local involvement.[1] Indistinguishable in appearance from most Canadian suburbs, what made this suburban neighborhood of detached, single-family homes notable in comparison to others in the Greater Toronto Area was that it was one of the first developments in the world to be built from the ground up with a broadband high-speed local network. Residents with access to the local computer network had free use of high-speed Web surfing (10 Mbps), a videophone, an online jukebox, online health services, a series of online entertainment and educational applications, and an e-mail discussion list that allowed residents to broadcast messages to other neighborhood residents. While the intention of the housing developer was to connect all homes in Netville to the local computer network, of the 109 homes that comprised the community, only 64 were ever connected. The remaining 45 households were never connected to the network, despite assurances that they would be connected, made at the time residents purchased their new homes.

Netville was also unique in that it was the site of one of the first long-term investigations of how online communities influenced local place-based community. In an effort to recognize that online interactions where a subset of the total interactions that could take place within Netville, and that online ties could play an important role in supporting relations both on- and off-line, it was desirable not only to conduct detailed interviews with residents, but to conduct an ethnography and observe everyday life in the wired neighborhood. From October 1997 to August 1999, an ethnography was conducted from a basement apartment in Netville. This apartment provided access to the same information and communication technologies available to other "wired" Netville residents and made it possible to work from home, participate in online activities, attend all possible local meetings (formal and informal), and walk the neighborhood, chatting and observing. The relationship between online, virtual interactions and "real-life," place-based encounters was observed on the screen, on the streets, and through a survey of local residents.

Netville's wired and non-wired residents were found to be remarkably similar in terms of lifestyle, stage in the life-cycle, and the length of time they had lived in Netville (Hampton, 2001: 64–5). What was remarkably different about wired residents was the structure of their local social networks. Residents were presented with a list of all other adult residents within Netville and were asked to identify those they recognized by name and their frequency of interaction. This survey confirmed what was revealed on the computer screens of neighborhood homes. "I have walked around the neighborhood a lot lately and I have noticed a few things. I have noticed neighbors talking to each other like they have been friends for a long time. I have noticed a closeness that you don't see in many communities" (quote from the Netville neighborhood e-mail list, 1998).

Compared to non-wired residents, wired residents recognized three times as many of their neighbors (averaging 25.2 neighbors), talked to twice as many neighbors on a regular basis (averaging 6.4 neighbors), and in the previous three months had visited 50 percent more of their neighbors (averaging 4.8 neighbors) (Hampton and Wellman, 2003). Not only were they communicating over the Internet and in person, but wired residents also sent an average of four personal e-mails to their neighbors in the previous month, and made four times as many local phone calls as their non-wired counterparts.

While wired Netville residents averaged greater name recognition, visiting, and frequency of communication with their neighbors, when statistical controls were introduced for demographic characteristics, such as age, gender, education, and tenure of residence, it became apparent that access to Netville's virtual domain had the greatest effect on relatively weak neighborhood ties (Hampton, 2003). Indeed, most North Americans do not have a large number of strong ties at the neighborhood level (Wellman, 1979; Fischer, 1982). It is simply more convenient to form social relations with similar others outside of the neighborhood setting. Access to computer-mediated communication in Netville was primarily successful in affording frequent social contact with a high number of what were comparatively weak social ties. What might not be immediately apparent is that weak ties have been shown to be a valuable form of social capital. They provide access to diverse social circles that are separate from more "homophilious" strong tie networks. At an individual level, they provide a bridge to resources that would otherwise be unavailable, such as job information (Granovetter, 1995). At a group level, they are an important factor in the ability of communities to mobilize collectively (Granovetter, 1973).

Wired Netville residents were very successful in their ability to organize for collective action, on- and off-line. When faced with concerns about the quality of construction of their new homes, and the rate at which the housing developer was addressing problems, residents organized and discussed strategies online, and met off-line to pressure the developer into addressing their problems and concerns (Hampton, 2003). When the telecommunications consortium that provided their broadband local computer network decided to end access to their free Internet services and remove the technology from residents' homes, wired residents again took to their screens and sidewalks in an attempt to pressure the consortium into reversing their decision. While they were ultimately not successful in reversing the consortium's decision to end the trial, residents did organize two community meetings, one at a local school and another at a nearby community center, and exchanged nearly a hundred e-mail messages through the neighborhood e-mail list in the first four weeks of organizing (compared to 260 messages during the previous 16 months). Residents were also successful in preserving the two features of their "wired neighborhood" that they valued the most: high-speed web access (offered at a slight discount from a competing telecommunications company) and the neighborhood e-mail list. (For a complete discussion and examples of collective action in Netville, see Hampton, 2003.)

When computer-mediated communication is used to facilitate local interactions neighborhood community may flourish. Indeed, as much as the Internet may afford local place-based interactions, the opposite may also be true: off-line neighborhood relationships may facilitate new online relations (Matei and Ball-Rokeach, 2001). Still, there are barriers that reduce widespread Internet affordances of new neighborhood interactions. Low Internet adoption rates, particularly in neighborhoods of lower socioeconomic status, and an inability to locate local information (such as a directory of neighborhood residents; see Resnick and Shah, 2002) impedes local interaction, on- and off-line. The community networking movement (see Kretzmann and McKnight 1993; Beamish 1999) and websites such as *UpMyStreet.com* in the UK, and *i-neighbors.org* in North America, provide forums that introduce neighbors, local e-mail directories, and other services to help overcome the initial constraints to IT-mediated interactions. This does not mean that the Internet can facilitate place-based community in all neighborhood settings. Some neighborhoods are involved to the point that the Internet bridges no barriers to local interaction, and there are others where the barriers are simply too big to be overcome through technology or another intervention (see, for example, Banfield, 1967).

CONCLUSION: NETWORKED SOCIABILITY IN THE NETWORK SOCIETY

In the network society it is unlikely that people will reject the need for social relationships based on physical location. As evidence from Netville, the Syntopia Project, Pew Internet and Everyday Life, and an increasing number of other projects suggests, many relationships with origins online move off-line and vice versa. When social ties are examined in terms of networks and not groups, and when the Internet is considered as one form of communication amongst many, computer-mediated communication tends to support the formation of larger, more diverse, social networks, community organizing, and public participation. It is a misnomer to label online ties as insufficient and incomplete in comparison to ties from the "real world" as they are part of the same social system.

As public spaces, online communities may become the street corners of the twenty-first century, but as yet there is no evidence that the Internet will reduce the importance of existing public places or "third places" such as cafés and bars (Oldenburg, 1989). The reduction in the friction of space enabled by the Internet has not made geography or place irrelevant. In fact, the opposite appears even more likely. Most computer-mediated communication is local, affording and reinforcing connections within existing realms of activity: the home, neighborhood, and workplace. Computer-mediated communication helps overcome obstacles to interaction within existing patterns of relations. Rather than dramatically altering our way of life, the new technologies of the network society are more subtle in their impacts, facilitating interaction and coordination. The Internet can break down barriers to local involvement, coordinate public participation, and provide new opportunities for place-based interactions. If we accept the evidence of Putnam (2000) and others – that there has been an increase in privatism and a decline in public participation over the past quarter-century – then the Internet may become a central force in reversing this established trend.

NOTE

1. "Netville" is a pseudonym adopted to protect the identity and privacy of the residents of the wired suburb.

REFERENCES

Angsioco, Leonceo (2003) "Addiction to Virtual Connections Can Have Heavy Toll on Real Communities," *The Seattle Times*, Opinion Section, August 24, C4.

Banfield, Edward (1967) *The Moral Basis of a Backward Society*. New York: Free Press.

Beamish, A. (1999) "Approaches to Community Computing: Bringing Technology to Low-income Groups," in D. Schon, B. Sanyal, and W. Mitchell (eds), *High Technology and Low-income Communities*, pp. 351–67. Cambridge, MA: MIT Press.

Calhoun, C. (1998) "Community without Propinquity Revisited: Communications Technology and the Transformation of the Urban Public Sphere," *Sociological Inquiry* 68 (3): 373–97.

Caruso, Denise (1998) "Critics are Picking Apart a Professor's Study that Linked Internet Use to Loneliness and Depression," *The New York Times*, September 14, C5.

Daft, R. L. and Lengel, R. H. (1986) "Organizational Information Requirements, Media Richness and Structural Design," *Management Science* 32 (5): 554–71.

Durkheim, E. (1893) *The Division of Labour in Society*. New York: Free Press, 1964.

Feld, Scott (1982) "Social Structural Determinants of Similarity among Associates," *American Sociological Review* 47: 797–801.

Fischer, Claude (1975) "Toward a Subcultural Theory of Urbanism," *American Journal of Sociology* 80: 1319–41.

— — (1982) *To Dwell Among Friends*. Berkeley, CA: University of California Press.

— — (1992) *America Calling: A Social History of the Telephone to 1940*. Berkeley, CA: University of California Press.

Granovetter, Mark (1973) "The Strength of Weak Ties," *American Journal of Sociology* 78: 1360–80.

— — (1995) *Getting a Job: A Study of Contacts and Careers*, 2nd edn. Chicago: University of Chicago Press.

Hampton, Keith (2001) "Living the Wired Life in the Wired Suburb: Netville, Glocalization and Civil Society," unpublished PhD Dissertation, Department of Sociology, University of Toronto.

— — (2003) "Grieving for a Lost Network: Collective Action in a Wired Suburb," *The Information Society* 19 (5): 417–28.

— — and Wellman, Barry (2003) "Neighboring in Netville: How the Internet Supports Community and Social Capital in a Wired Suburb," *City and Community* 2 (4): 277–311.

Haythornthwaite, Caroline and Wellman, Barry (1998) "Work, Friendship and Media Use for Information Exchange in a Networked Organization," *Journal of the American Society for Information Science* 49 (12): 1101–14.

Horrigan, John and Rainie, Lee (2002) *Getting Serious On-line*. Washington, DC: Pew Internet and American Life Project.

Howard, Philip, Rainie, Lee, and Jones, Steve (2002) "The Place of the Internet in Everyday Life," in Barry Wellman and Caroline Haythornthwaite (eds), *The Internet in Everyday Life*, pp. 45–73. Oxford: Blackwell.

Jacobs, Jane (1961) *The Death and Life of Great American Cities*. New York: Vintage Books.

Katz, James and Rice, Ronald (2002) *Social Consequences of Internet Use: Access, Involvement, and Interaction*. Cambridge, MA: MIT Press.

Kraut, Robert, Patterson, Michael, Lundmark, Vicki, Kiesler, Sara, Mukhopadhyay, Tridas, and Scherlis, William (1998) "Internet Paradox: A Social Technology that Reduces Social Involvement and Psychological Well-being?," *American Psychologist* 53 (9): 1017–31.

— —, Kiesler, Sara, Boneva, Bonka, Cummings, Jonathon, Helgeson, Vicki, and Crawford, Anne (2002) "Internet Paradox Revisited," *Journal of Social Issues* 58 (1): 49–74.

KRC Research (2003) "Email Use Survey: Survey of 'Professional Email Users' in the UK, France, Germany, Italy, Spain, Denmark, Sweden, the United States and Canada," report to Oracle, July. London: Weber Shandwick.

Kretzmann, J. P. and McKnight, J. L. (1993) *Building Communities from the Inside Out: A Path Toward Finding and Mobilizing a Community's Assets*. Chicago, IL: ACTA.

Kuo, Frances, Sullivan, William, Coley, Rebekah, and Brunson, Liesette (1998) "Fertile Ground for Community: Inner-city Neighborhood Common Spaces," *American Journal of Community Psychology* 26 (6): 823–51.

Lactis, Eric (1999) "Shock Absorption: In the Info Age, We've Become Blasé," *The Seattle Times*, February 7, L2.

McPherson, Miller, Smith-Lovin, Lynn and Cook, James (2001) "Birds of a Feather: Homophily in Social Networks," *Annual Review of Sociology* 27: 415–44.

Matei, Sorin and Ball-Rokeach, Sandra (2001) "Real and Virtual Social Ties: Connections in the Everyday Lives of Seven Ethnic Neighborhoods," *American Behavioral Scientist* 45 (3): 550–63.

— — and — — (2002) "Belonging in Geographic, Ethnic, and Internet Spaces," in Barry Wellman and Caroline Haythornthwaite (eds), *The Internet in Everyday Life*, pp. 404–30. Oxford: Blackwell.

Milgram, Stanley (1970) "The Experience of Living in Cities," *Science* 167: 1461–8.

Mitchell, William (1995) *City of Bits: Space, Place and the Infobahn*. Cambridge, CA: MIT Press.

Nie, Norman, and Erbring, Lutz (2000) "Internet and Society: A Preliminary Report," Stanford Institute for the Quantitative Study of Society, Stanford University, retrieved May 24, 2001 (http://www.stanford.edu/group/siqss/Press_Release/ Preliminary_Report-4-21.pdf).

— —, Killygus, D. Sunshine, and Erbring, Lutz (2002) "Internet Use, Interpersonal Relations, and Sociability," in Barry Wellman and Caroline Haythornthwaite (eds), *The Internet in Everyday Life*, pp. 215–43. Oxford: Blackwell.

Oldenburg, Ray (1989/1999) *The Great Good Place: Cafés, Coffee Shops, Community Centers, Beauty Parlors, General Stores, Bars, Hangout, and How They Get You Through the Day*. New York: Paragon House.

O'Toole, Kathleen (2000) "Study Offers Early Look at How Internet is Changing Daily Life," February 16. News Release, Stanford, CA: Stanford Institute for the Quantitative Study of Society, retrieved May 24, 2001 (http://www. stanford.edu/group/siqss/Press_Release/press_release.html).

Putnam, Robert (2000) *Bowling Alone: The Collapse and Revival of American Community*. NewYork: Simon and Schuster.

Resnick, Paul and Shah, Vishant (2002) "Photo Directories: A Tool for Organizing Sociability in Neighborhoods and Organizations," Working paper, retrieved July 4, 2003 (http://www.si.umich.edu/~presnick/papers/whothat/WhoThat021303.pdf).

Scheer, Robert (2000) "Stanford Internet Study Paints the Wrong Picture," *Online Journalism Review*. Annenberg School for Communication at the University of

Southern California, retrieved August 29, 2003 (http://www.ojr.org/ojr/ethics/1017965944.php).

Short, J., Williams, E., and Christie, B. (1976) *The Social Psychology of Telecommunications*. London: John Wiley and Sons.

Simmel, Georg (1950) "The Metropolis and Mental Life (1903)," in *The Sociology of Georg Simmel*, pp. 409–24. New York: Free Press.

Taylor, Humphrey (2000) "Internet Access Continues to Grow but at a Slower Pace," The Harris Poll, no. 60, retrieved August 8, 2003 (http://www.harrisinteractive.com/harris_poll/index.asp?PID=122).

Tönnies, Ferdinand (1887) *Community and Organization*. London: Routledge and Kegan Paul, 1955.

Turkle, Sherry (1997) *Life on the Screen: Identity in the Age of the Internet*. New York: Simon and Schuster.

UCLA Internet Report (2000) "Surveying the Digital Future," Los Angeles: UCLA Centre for Communications Policy.

Webber, Melvin (1963) "Order in Diversity: Community without Propinquity," in Lowdon Wingo, Jr (ed.), *Cities and Space: The Future Use of Urban Land*, pp. 23–54. Baltimore, MD: The Johns Hopkins University Press.

Wellman, Barry (1979) "The Community Question," *American Journal of Sociology* 84 (March): 1201–31

— — (1992) "Men in Networks: Private Communities, Domestic Friendships," in Peter Nardi (ed.), *Men's Friendships*, pp. 74–114. Newbury Park, CA: Sage.

— — (1999) "The Network Community," in Barry Wellman (ed.), *Networks in the Global Village*, pp. 1–47. Boulder, CO: Westview Press.

— —, Carrington, Peter, and Hall, Alan (1988) "Networks as Personal Communities," in Barry Wellman and S. D. Berkowitz (eds), *Social Structures: A Network Approach*, pp. 130–84. Cambridge: Cambridge University Press.

Wirth, Louis (1938) "Urbanism as a Way of Life," *American Journal of Sociology* 44: 3–24.

10. Social structure, cultural identity, and personal autonomy in the practice of the internet: the network society in Catalonia

Manuel Castells, Imma Tubella, Teresa Sancho, Maria Isabel Díaz de Isla, and Barry Wellman

The uses of the Internet in everyday life are a good indicator of the diffusion, shape, and cultural specificity of the network society in a given social context. The interplay between social structure, social behavior, and the construction of meaning, as mediated by the Internet, expresses the process of social transformation that results from the interaction between technology, culture, and society. In this chapter we will analyze this interaction on the basis of the data obtained from a survey of a sample of 3,005 people, statistically representative of the population of Catalonia older than 15 years. A significant feature of this survey is that it was conducted by face-to-face interview on a sample of the entire population, of which almost two-thirds were not Internet users at the time of the survey, in the spring of 2002. This allows us to draw conclusions about the overall dynamics of the social structure, as we can compare users and non-users in their demographics, social practices, and attitudes on a wide range of dimensions, while avoiding the biases introduced by an exclusive focus on Internet users. Indeed, the study covered the entire set of behaviors in everyday life, and not just the use of the Internet. It is a comprehensive study of Catalan society at the dawn of the twenty-first century, in which we have emphasized the role of the Internet in the process of social structuration and social change.

We will examine, in sequence, the differential use of the Internet according to position in the social structure; the interaction between networked sociability and the patterns of sociability in society at large; the uses of the Internet in everyday life; the construction of cultural identity and the role that the Internet plays in the production of meaning; and we will conclude with an empirical analysis of the role of the Internet in the construction of autonomy as it is manifested through the subjective projects of social actors. We must emphasize that this study is not based on a comparative approach because we have not defined our observations to be equivalent to those of other studies in other contexts. Thus, the analysis presented here is specific to Catalonia. Yet, it is no more or less specific than a study of America or of England is beyond its social setting. By studying different societies with a common set of analytical questions, and recording and interpreting the data that relate to these questions, the international research community may elaborate on the contrasts, similarities, and differences that characterize the development of the network society throughout the world.

THE HISTORICAL CONSTRUCTION OF THE DIGITAL DIVIDE

The diffusion of the Internet among people is highly differentiated by their position in the social structure. Catalan society is no exception to this rule. However, there are some features that allow further analysis of general relevance. At the time of our survey, in February–May 2002, Catalonia was in the middle range in terms of its percentage of Internet users, in relation to other countries: slightly over one-third (33.5 percent) were Internet users at least once a month, although the number of people connected from their home was lower (29.8 percent). This was significantly lower than in North America, Scandinavia, or Korea, and lower than the average for the European Union (40 percent), although higher than Spain as a whole, and significantly higher than the world at large (about 8 percent at that time).

The digital divide, in terms of education and income, exists in Catalonia, as elsewhere. Thus, 77.4 percent of college graduates are Internet users, in contrast to 46.8 percent of those who have only secondary education, and 16.7 percent of those who have primary education or less. Income levels also condition access to the Internet: 63.8 percent in high-income groups are users, but only 15.4 percent of those with low incomes, and 53.7 percent of those with middle incomes. There is in Catalonia, unlike the United States or Scandinavia, a gender gap: 39 percent of men are users versus 30.5 percent of women. But the influence of one's position in the occupational structure on Internet use presents a more complex picture. To be sure, only 17 percent of manual workers are users. But there is a surprising contrast between managers and executives (37.8 percent of users) and the high frequency of use among professionals and technicians (70.4 percent) and clerical personnel (55.5 percent). This reveals an occupational structure in which the information-processing labor force is largely on the Internet, but the corporate leaders remain anchored in old-fashioned practices, certainly in technological terms, but most likely also in organizational terms.

So, the digital divide is not only between the top and the bottom of the social structure, but also within managerial groups between those working on information and those directing their work on the basis of their positions of power. We suspect that the technological conservatism of the managerial elites may be a relevant feature in other societies as well. The implications are that the decision-makers in the moment of transition to the network society are relatively distant from the technological system of the new society, and of its organizational correlates. As a result, their decisions will be dependent on technological practices in other societies, unless they develop applications specific to their own social context.

However, the most important factor in explaining the differential diffusion of the Internet is age. Thus, between 15 and 19 years, 72.8 percent are Internet users, and between 15 and 29, 64.7 percent, but the percentage falls to 39.3 percent for those in the age group 30–49, and drops to 8.4 percent for those over 50, with less than 4 percent of users among those over 60. Age also conditions the effect of all other variables on the use of the Internet. Thus, in the younger group (15–29 years) the gender gap works in favor of women: 67 percent are Internet users in contrast to 62.5 percent of men, while in the group over 50 years of age, only 4.3 percent of women are users, versus 13.3 percent of men. Income and occupational status are also largely conditioned by age in their effect on Internet use. Among young people (15–29 years) of low income, 49.8 percent are Internet users, a higher proportion than those of high income over 50 years old (41.3 percent are users in this case). Similarly, 41.7 percent of young workers are Internet users in contrast with managers and executives over 50 (28.3 percent users). When age and education combine, the percentage of Internet use is the highest: 93 percent of college and high-school students are Internet users. The same pattern of social structuration of Internet practice by age and education appears when we analyze, beyond mere use, the frequency and intensity of use.

The meaning of these findings is less obvious than it appears to be. Catalonia is a society in the process of rapid historical change. The cultural backwardness and economic exploitation of Franco's dictatorship (1939–1976) led to massive migration to industrialized Catalonia by the huddled masses of peasants and workers from southern, central, and western Spain. These "new Catalans" made a decisive contribution to the economic growth and social diversity of Catalonia, and were at the forefront of the social struggles that led to democratic Spain in 1977, and to the new, autonomous Catalan nationality in 1980. Yet, their educational background was minimal, and their ability to adapt to an informational society somewhat limited. Thus, in 2002 our study revealed that 62.3 percent of the Catalan population over 15 had not completed secondary education, and only 12 percent were college graduates. The data are similar for Spain as a whole, in sharp contrast to France, Germany, the UK, and Scandinavia.

On the other hand, we defined a "Young Catalonia" segment of the population, using as an indicator those people who started their primary education in 1980, the year that the Catalan Statute was approved that enshrined the autonomy of Catalonia in the new, democratic Spain. We also included in this group, of course, those who entered school subsequently. This is equivalent to the 15–29-year age group in our study. When we consider this group, the percentage of current and future high-school graduates and college graduates is close to the European Union average, and similar to that of France. And so is the percentage of Internet users, and the demographic distribution of frequency and intensity in Internet use. Thus, Catalonia is experiencing an extraordinary change in cultural and educational terms, to the point that the digital divide is in fact an educational–age divide, as a result of the history of Catalonia and the heritage of Francoism, an historical period characterized by educational and cultural backwardness. The challenge for the new Catalonia will be to avoid social fracture by age, given the high life expectancy of the population and the fact that more than 22 percent of Catalans are over 60 years old. In fact, not only are 39 percent of Catalans not connected to the Internet, but they are also determined never to use the Internet because they see no use for it in their lives. As we will analyze below, the critical matter for the majority of the population is the lack of any appealing offer of Internet use that fits into their lives.

In broader terms, while the age gap in terms of education and use of the Internet is less dramatic in North America and Northern Europe, we suspect that, worldwide, Catalonia is more representative of what is taking place in the diffusion of the Internet, and its associated culture, than, let us say, Scandinavia. That is: in most societies, the new generations are growing up in an Internet-based world, in a culture of multimedia and global communication, and in a new technological paradigm, and find that all around them is a society whose institutions and organizations are in the hands of elites and managers with little openness to technology and great reluctance to cultural and organizational change. Thus, the digital divide is not only a matter of social inequality but of a differential openness to the Internet and its organizational correlates. If we understand the Internet as a culture of autonomy based on a technology of freedom, our findings suggest that social conservatism and technological stalemate go hand in hand in Catalonia, and, probably, in most of the world.

NETWORKED SOCIABILITY IN A HYPER-SOCIAL CULTURE

We know, from the available evidence, that sociability, in the age of the Internet, neither dwindles nor surges, but transforms itself, under the form of networked sociability that connects people online and off-line, building on their elective social networks (see chapter 9 in this volume). Our study of Catalonia, while broadly confirming these general findings, adds an interesting twist. What happens to Internet-based sociability in a context of high density and frequency of face-to-face social relationships? Indeed, for a non-traditional society, meaning a society that is fully part of the advanced global economy and of the modern European world, Catalan society is characterized by an extraordinary level of territorially based community, persistence of strong family ties, a wide network of face-to-face friendships, and an active practice of neighborliness.

This specific pattern of sociability seems to be determined by a low level of geographical mobility in the life cycle. Indeed, 66.9 percent of people in our sample were born in Catalonia (a country of relatively small territorial size), and for those between 15 and 29 years, the percentage increases to 92.6 percent. This is in sharp contrast with the parents of those we interviewed, who were born in the majority in the rest of Spain (52.3 percent). Here again, history and culture interact. The mass migrations to Catalonia in the 1960s and 1970s were fully integrated into Catalonia, and, once there, migrants and their children remained territorially stable. The picture for the future is less clear, as rapid immigration from outside Spain has taken place since the 1990s, bringing the proportion of non-Spanish born population in just five years from 2 percent to at least 7 percent of the Catalan population. It is highly doubtful that the integration of these immigrants in the coming years will proceed as smoothly as the previous one. But, for the time being, and for the analytical purposes of our study, Catalans are territorially rooted and highly sociable.

In the five years preceding our study, 76 percent of our sample were already living in Catalonia. And their family is nearby: 53.3 percent of their fathers and 55.6 percent of their mothers dwell in the same municipality, and about another 25 percent of their parents live somewhere else in Catalonia. This helps us understand the stunning finding that about one-third of our sample see their parents every day, and two-thirds at least once a week. Furthermore, 61 percent of people in our sample live in a family in which all the members of the family have dinner together every day, and another 17.7 percent at least four times a week. Outside the family, when they have friends who live in the same municipality, 32 percent of our sample see these friends every day, and about 45 percent at least once a week. Some 40 percent see their neighbors every day, and an additional 30 percent every week.

Under these conditions it is not surprising that the use of the Internet for the purpose of sociability is very limited. But we have analyzed, nonetheless, the effects of the use of the Internet on sociability patterns. In this regard, we confirm the results of international research: the use of the Internet adds to sociability rather than subtracts from it. Internet users have a larger number of friends and family members in their network in comparison with non-users. We also investigated the effects on personal psychology after one year of Internet use, compared with the evolution of non-users during the same year. Catalans appear to be a very emotionally stable lot: when asked if they felt depressed or more isolated than one year earlier, 85 percent of our sample reported no change in sociability, and 79 percent reported that they were not more or less depressed. But among the minority that felt more isolated and more depressed, the non-users had a higher frequency than the users of the Internet. The only significant change among users of the Internet was a higher proportion than among non-users of the experience of stress: 31.5 percent of users versus 20.3 percent of non-users. Thus, the use of the Internet does seem to be related to a higher level of intensity in people's life, but not at the expense of isolation or depression.

Indeed, among Internet users, time spent in conversations with the family and being with the children increased over the preceding year in a higher proportion than among non-users. Here, again, the intensity associated with the Internet seems to take a toll not on real interaction with family and friends, but in relation to the perception of non-availability for the family: a small minority (6.4 percent) of Internet users are faced with complaints from the family about their activity, in a much higher proportion than among non-users. So, overall, the Internet does have a small effect of increasing sociability and reducing feelings of isolation, in the context of a population that does not need the Internet to relate to family, friends, and neighbors and that, as a result of their full social life, does not use the Internet much for this purpose.

However, we have observed a rapid rise in the practice of Internet chats among the younger population, particularly in the 15–19-year age group. It may well be the harbinger of a new kind of networked sociability, connecting online and off-line in people's lives, in accordance with observed patterns in other countries. Yet, the intensity of social life in the street, in cafés, in public places, and the quasi-universal use of the cell phone by the younger population to arrange their meetings on the move, and to keep in touch, seem to emphasize the specificity of the pattern of sociability in Catalonia. And beyond Catalonia, it would be wise not to extrapolate on patterns of sociability from the early studies of the Internet, dealing mainly with the puritan cultures of Northern Europe and North America and with the geographically mobile populations of the United States and Canada. Indeed, these cultures and practices have made the Internet a privileged medium of communication to maintain ties at a distance because they are more geographically mobile and have less dense networks of family and friends. The history and culture of each society shape the actual uses of the Internet, thus specifiying the network society.

THE USES OF THE INTERNET IN EVERYDAY LIFE

Studies on the uses of the Internet have shown that people adapt the Internet to their needs and projects, rather than submitting to the logic of the technology. Thus, the uses of the Internet are an extension and specification of what people do, want, and feel in their everyday lives (Haythornthwaite and Wellman, 2002). Our own study in Catalonia has tried to test this hypothesis by asking people to report the activities they regularly perform on the Internet. Table 10.1 shows the findings. Let us emphasize the main results before briefly elaborating on their meaning.

As in all other studies, electronic mail is the most frequent activity: the Internet is, above all, a medium of communication for all kinds of purposes. There are two leading activities: one is what we could call leisure-oriented activities, such as surfing without a precise goal or downloading music; the other is searching for information for practical uses, such as consulting libraries, travel information, or looking for information concerning public services or shows in town. A third level of frequency concerns participation in chats.

Uses for sociability are less diffused, and shopping on line is minimal. Teleworking or distant education concerns a very small proportion of the user population. It is interesting to observe that the proportion of users looking at pornography is rather moderate (8.8 percent), and sharply differentiated by gender (3 percent of women versus 13 percent of men), and by age (it is highly concentrated in the male age group of 20–29 years). On the other hand, uses for sociability (such as reaching out to friends when people feel "low") are less frequent, and the use of the Internet to organize children or family activities is rare. So are uses of the Internet for political purposes.

This pattern of Internet use is differentiated by the social characteristics of the users. Simplifying our observations, young users (up to 29 years old) display a higher proportion of leisure-oriented activities and participation in chats. Mature professionals tend to use the Internet for their work and for information searches, including searching for news. The use of the Internet for practical purposes, such as accessing public services, increases with age. And the youngest users (15–19 years) are those who are most interested in video games and chats.

There are therefore few surprises in our findings: Internet use follows people's dominant patterns of behavior, derived from their social characteristics. Teenagers play and chat. Young people are more leisure-oriented than work-oriented. The opposite trend is perceived among professionals and highly educated people. And the older the user, the more important the Internet becomes as a source of help in managing the practical matters of everyday life. There are few political uses of the Internet because there is a

Table 10.1 *Distribution of Internet users according to Internet use (ordered from greater to lesser frequency of each use) (percentage against Internet user total)*

	User interviewee	
	No.	%
Sending and receiving e-mail messages	921	88.6
"Net-surfing" (navigation without a specific objective)	597	57.5
Consulting libraries, encyclopaedias, dictionaries, atlases	547	52.6
Searching for travel information	483	46.5
Downloading music from the web	389	37.4
Searching for information on programmed shows	380	36.6
Searching for information on public services	378	36.4
Searching for information on your city	375	36.1
Participating in chat channels or news groups	367	35.3
Finding out news in the general press	356	34.3
Sending electronic greeting cards	312	30.0
Arranging or confirming meetings with friends	311	29.9
Downloading software from the web	300	28.9
Searching for information on training programs	299	28.8
Sending photos of you or your family	265	25.5
Searching for information on your professional association	247	23.8
Carrying out banking operations	234	22.6
Finding out sports news	232	22.3
Contacting friends when you are feeling down	223	21.5
Searching for information on your own health or that of others	204	19.6
Playing video games on the Internet	193	18.6
Searching for work	171	16.5
Reserving trips and accommodation, hiring a car	166	16.0
Working from home	135	13.0
Buying or reserving tickets to shows	119	11.5
Searching for recipes	116	11.2
Buying books or music	97	9.3
Searching for political or union information	93	9.0
Looking at pornography	91	8.8
Searching for an apartment	70	6.7
Making telephone calls via the Internet	68	6.5
Buying other things	60	5.8
Participating in online courses	54	5.2
Buying computer products	51	4.9
Buying food or cleaning products	43	4.1
Searching for information on gays and lesbians	30	2.9
Participating in or buying at an auction	28	2.7
Organizing children's activities	27	2.6

Note: The percentages correspond to affirmative answers against the total of persons responding.

low level of political participation in Catalonia as everywhere else. True, there is a mobilized minority (for example, anti-globalization militants) for whom the Internet is very important, but this is only a fraction of the population.

The specificity of Internet use in Catalonia underscores the specificity of Catalan society. The use of the Internet for sociability is not widespread because face-to-face sociability is very intense and facilitated by a strong localization of family and friendship ties in the territorial vicinity. Work-related activities are limited, except for students and professionals, because use of the Internet in the business world is not extended to the majority of the workforce. The potential demand for the facility to manage public services on the Internet is frustrated by the lack of a sufficient offer of online services from the public sector.

In sum, the uses of the Internet, and their social structuration by the characteristics of Internet users, reflect, at the same time, the values and practices of people in their lives and the organizational and cultural framework that characterizes Catalonia in contrast to other societies.

CULTURAL IDENTITY AND THE CONSTRUCTION OF MEANING IN THE INTERNET

One of the most debated themes in international research is the potential value of the Internet as a medium for the expression of cultural identity (Castells, 2001). Catalonia offers a particularly interesting field of study because national identity (in contrast to the dominant officialdom of Spain) is an entrenched feature of Catalan society, a society that has preserved its own language and culture throughout history in spite of suffering centuries of linguistic and cultural repression from the Spanish government, at least between 1714 and 1980. Therefore, we studied the current expression of identity in Catalan society in order to assess the specific role of the Internet in the construction and development of this identity.

However, we differentiated multiple dimensions of identity and tried to assess the relative weight of national identity as a source of cultural meaning. Indeed, according to our data, when people are confronted with a choice of self-definition in terms of national-cultural belonging, only 19.7 percent feel predominantly Spanish, whereas 37.5 percent feel predominantly Catalan, with 36.2 percent feeling equally Catalan and Spanish, and 6.6 percent who do not feel either Catalan or Spanish. But this predominant feeling of being Catalan, or as much Catalan as Spanish, does not become the primary source of construction of meaning for people. We asked our sample to opt for *one primary identity* from a long, detailed list of possibilities. The majority of people (56 percent) identified themselves primarily with their family. A long

Manuel Castells et al.

Manuel Castells et al.

way behind, in second position, came those who asserted "themselves" as the primary source of meaning for them (8.7 percent). Identification with country was only recorded as the choice of 2.5 percent, and with the culture of the country as the choice of 4.7 percent. Professional identity was chosen by 5.1 percent, and age group was the primary identity for only 4.9 percent. In other words, family relationship and individualism appear to be the primary sources of meaning for people, in line with recorded observation in other European countries. Religion, in contrast to the United States, is the primary source of meaning for a mere 2.5 percent of respondents.

Our findings are reinforced by an analysis of linguistic practice. While practically everybody understands Catalan, and the younger generation is fully trained in Catalan, 44.3 percent of the population consider Spanish their primary language, versus 41.1 percent who consider Catalan as their language, with 14.6 percent declaring themselves bilingual.

Our data also show that the younger group, which is the one group fully fluent in Catalan because it has been educated in Catalan, is the group that most often uses Spanish at home and with friends. So, in other words, while the majority of the population of Catalonia consider themselves either Catalan or as much Catalan as Spanish, this is not their primary source of identity, and the use of the Catalan language is still second to Spanish, particularly among the younger generation. Thus, we observe a bilingual society in which most people, and particularly the younger generation, do not attach symbolic importance to the matter of speaking Catalan. What does this finding mean?

Our interpretation requires the distinction between what we call "resistance identity" and "project identity" (Castells, 2004: ch. 1). Resistance identity refers to the construction of autonomous meaning with the materials of historical experience to counter social–cultural domination. By project identity, we mean the affirmation of a collective project to achieve certain social goals as the expression of a cultural community of shared experience. Catalonia, having suffered the political and cultural domination of Spain from the seventeenth and eighteenth centuries, built a resistance identity that found its expression in modern Catalan nationalism between the end of the nineteenth century and the end of the twentieth. With the coming of democracy in Spain in 1977, Catalonia achieved recognition of its identity in a Statute of Autonomy approved in 1980, which made some self-government possible and the widespread use of the Catalan language in education, in public administration, and in the media owned by the Catalan government, such as radio and television. Therefore, to speak Catalan, to assert Catalan specificity, and to live in Catalonia became normal practice, particularly for the generation born into democracy.

Resistance identity faded by and large because it was no longer needed as a collective Catalan identity: an identity that was now acknowledged and institutionalized. The majority of people feel Catalan, and a substantial proportion feel different from being Spanish, but they do not have to assert it every day because it is now accepted as a fact of life, although recent attacks (in 2003) on Catalan autonomy from the conservative government in Madrid may ignite resistance identity again. At the same time, since Catalan nationalism, in its diverse political expressions, did not articulate a collective project, but dwelt instead on the defense of resistance identity as its political argument, people, and particularly young people, in their majority, did not feel part of a nation on the move. Rather, they followed the example of other Europeans, constructing meaning from and for their own individual lives. Given the importance of family life in Catalonia, this actually meant rooting meaning in the family as the way of asserting one's meaning.

However, we also investigated in our study the possibility of a project identity based on a strong feeling of Catalan identity. We constructed an indicator of strong Catalan identity (based on uses of language, media preferences, and special sensitivity to Catalan nationalist themes). Only 19.4 percent of the population could be associated with this strong Catalan identity. However, this identity is particularly intense in certain groups. It is concentrated among professionals and executives of the middle age group. Furthermore, it is also strongly present in the 20–29-year age group for those individuals who are politically active and socially entrepreneurial. This is where the role of the Internet becomes essential. We found a significant association between strong Catalan identity and use of the Internet, and a relationship between the group of young professionals, active users of the Internet, interested in individual and collective projects for themselves and for society, and the presence of a strong Catalan identity. Thus, while Catalan resistance identity is mainly present in the older generations, particularly in small towns and rural areas, Catalan project identity, a feature of a minority of people, is concentrated in the upcoming professional class, which is specially active on the Internet. Not that the Internet is the source of this identity, but it becomes a privileged medium for the expression of alternative projects of social organization, including the manifestation of a renewed Catalan identity as a collective national project adapted to the conditions of the twenty-first century. On the other hand, for the majority of the population the use of the Internet is predominantly in Spanish (with only 11 percent visiting websites in English), a direct consequence of the limited offer of Catalan language websites on the Internet.

We have also analyzed the role of the Internet in the construction of meaning in the framework of practices of communication with reference to other media. As in other societies, television is the predominant medium of communication and the most important source of cultural influence, followed by radio. Because the Catalan government television (broadcasting only in Catalan) is the main television network in Catalonia, the dominance of television reinforces the feeling of a cultural, national community. What is specific to Catalan society vis-á-vis Europe is a lower percentage of readers of newspapers and magazines. But it is significant that, while most newspapers are in the Spanish language, the newspapers based in Catalonia have a much larger readership than the main Spanish newspapers, such as the leading newspaper in Spain, *El Pais*, which is based in Madrid. So, national cultural identity, in this case, is not expressed in language preference (since there is not much choice in Catalan) but in the focus on the Catalan-oriented press.

In this context, the main effect of the Internet is that intense activity on the Internet reduces time spent watching television, and this is particularly the case for young viewers, a phenomenon that replicates trends in other countries, such as the United States. So, in terms of national identity, television and radio in Catalonia, and the mass media as a whole, seem to convey a sentiment of resistance identity, while the Internet appears associated with an emerging Catalan project identity, built in relative autonomy vis-á-vis the mass media. Indeed, the Internet has been associated in some analyses to the construction of autonomy from the point of view of social actors (Katz and Rice, 2002). We now turn to this analysis.

THE INTERNET AND THE CONSTRUCTION OF AUTONOMY

The Internet is a technology of freedom. It allows the construction of self-directed networks of horizontal communication, bypassing institutional controls. It also allows information to be retrieved, and recombined in applied knowledge at the service of purposive social action. Thus, the hypothesis has often been put forward of the role of the Internet in stimulating project-oriented activities by individuals or collective social actors. In our study of Catalonia we tested the relevance of this hypothesis. To do so, we built a typology of projects of autonomy, each one expressed by empirical indicators defined in the population of our survey. We used factor analysis to obtain the clustering of these indicators in six different factors, statistically independent, which constitute the empirical basis of our analytical typology. We then studied the relationship between the differential presence of the social characteristics in each type and the use of Internet. Table 10.2 presents the results of the factor analysis, whose methodology can be consulted in the book cited as the general source for our study (Castells et al., 2003).

Table 10.2   Results of factor analysis of variables indicative of projects of autonomy

Variables	Component					
	1	2	3	4	5	6
Would prefer to be self-employed even if this meant earning less money	8.239E–02	0.358	0.811	–6.429E–02	–0.146	–3.872E–03
Would prefer to be self-employed even if this meant less job security	6.858E–02	0.366	0.817	–7.461E–02	–0.127	–5.982E–02
Would prefer that children were business owners rather than tenured civil servants	–8.399E–02	–0.255	–0.498	3.222E–04	8.554E–02	–0.243
Agree with statement that what you make in life depends on your own efforts	0.185	–7.818E–02	0.121	2.389E–02	0.300	–0.445
Besides consulting a doctor, he/she tries to learn about the illness when he/she or a close person is seriously ill	0.272	–5.703E–02	0.153	0.538	0.410	0.269
Reads written instructions included with medication carefully before taking it	0.177	–2.840E–02	0.154	0.600	0.393	0.295
Index of citizen activism	0.391	–4.560E–02	–6.983E–02	0.249	–0.424	4.512E–02
Index of sociopolitical mobilization	0.318	–4.226E–02	–0.121	0.376	–0.439	–0.105
Index of sociopolitical participation	0.358	1.034E–03	–8.016E–02	0.366	–0.464	–0.156
Scale of personal autonomy (constructed on the basis of answers to 10 questions)	–0.315	1.959E–03	–0.120	–0.233	–0.102	0.584
Index of personal belief in the capacity to influence the world	–7.187E–02	–6.780E–02	0.135	0.147	0.256	–0.433
Trust in information received from television	3.211E–02	0.748	–0.261	0.117	7.715E–02	–1.685E–02
Trust in information received from radio	–4.474E–02	0.756	–0.317	1.569E–02	5.336E–02	4.678E–02
Trust in information received from newspapers	–0.108	0.733	–0.263	7.540E–02	5.043E–02	–6.012E–02
Trust in information received from the Internet	8.049E–02	–0.377	0.154	–5.849E–02	–1.414E–02	0.170
Follows an educational course	0.551	–1.192E–02	–0.142	6.952E–02	–0.102	0.135
Visits web pages related to his/her profession	0.740	3.278E–02	–3.889E–02	–0.281	0.172	–2.577E–03
Consults professional documentation	0.850	5.990E–02	–6.681E–02	–0.283	0.117	3.775E–02
Reads books related to his/her profession	0.837	4.361E–02	–8.664E–02	–0.284	0.102	5.220E–02

245

The six types of projects of autonomy observed in the Catalan population are the following:

Component 1   Project of professional development, related to the self-promotion and initiative of the person in his/her work-related career.

Component 2   Project of communicative autonomy, characterized by the individual's distance vis-à-vis the mass media.

Component 3   Entrepreneurial project, expressed in a predisposition to business initiatives.

Component 4   Project of autonomy of the body, manifested in a predisposition to control information concerning his/her own health.

Component 5   Project of sociopolitical participation (including participation in political institutions, social movements, and civil society activities).

Component 6   Project of individual autonomy, characterized by the self-affirmation of individual personality.

Of course, the large majority of our population does not display any project of autonomy. However, there is a minority (between 10 and 20 percent of the population depending on which type) that ranks high in the values of the variables indicative of each type of autonomy. Therefore, we can analyze the relationship between these indicators of the different types of autonomy and the use of the Internet. In a nutshell, what we find is that the higher the level of autonomy, for each project, the higher the proportion of Internet users, as well as the frequency and intensity of Internet use. Furthermore, in the one case in which we can measure a temporal sequence – the project of professional development – we find that the use of the Internet does have a positive effect on the practice of the project of professional development. On the other hand, there is statistical independence between the different groups engaging in specific projects of autonomy. So that those who have a high level of sociopolitical project are not the same as those with an entrepreneurial project; or, alternatively, those with a project of individual autonomy are not the same as those displaying a project of communicative autonomy.

These findings are highly relevant because they mean that the Internet is, indeed, a tool for the expression of autonomy, and in the cases in which we can observe a feedback effect it reinforces this autonomy. But the content of the autonomy is independent of the use of the Internet: it is linked to the social characteristics of the actors, underlying each project of autonomy. The Internet seems, indeed, to be a technology of freedom and a medium for the construction of autonomy, but the content of this freedom and the horizon of this autonomy are determined by the social structure, as well as by the dynamics of the actors in the process of their self-affirmation.

CONCLUSION: TECHNOLOGY, COMMUNITY, AND CULTURE IN THE TRANSITION TO THE NETWORK SOCIETY

The study of the network society in Catalonia confirms the need to understand the Internet, and information technology-powered social networks, in the specific social and cultural context in which they operate. There is no network society, but network societies. At the same time, there are some common features that specify the social structure characteristic of the network society, as argued in chapter 1 of this volume. In our analysis of Catalonia we observed both these common trends, and the variations produced by history, culture, and institutions.

Among the commonalities, we found the role played by the Internet and by the networking logic in the construction of social autonomy for those social actors capable of articulating their individual and collective projects. We also discovered how social structure shapes social networks and conditions the uses of the Internet, so that the processes of domination and inequality, present in the social structure, are amplified by the new communication technology. We confirmed, as well, the findings of researchers around the world that show how people adapt technologies to their needs and values, so that their patterns of behavior in everyday life are reproduced on the Internet: children play, the young explore, the mature work and manage, the elderly run after the process of social change, while trying to keep in control of their lives. Identity building is, by and large, primarily rooted in individual projects, as the process of individuation of meaning characterizes Catalonia as much as other developed societies in the world.

On the other hand, we also discovered how the specific structural conditions, history, and culture of Catalonia influence the uses of the Internet and their social and organizational correlates. A territorially rooted culture, family-oriented, and with highly dense networks of strong ties in social relationships, builds networked sociability on top of community and kinship as the predominant mode of social interaction. National identity is still significant, and when, in a minority of the population, it appears linked to a collective project of cultural transformation, it finds in the Internet a strong element of support and connectivity. The generation gap that characterizes societies in a process of rapid social change takes a dramatic dimension in Catalonia, as the young Catalans, heavy users of the Internet and network-oriented in their social practice, contrast sharply with a majority of poorly educated people, often resistant to technological change.

Yet, the social cohesion provided by strong communities, built on territorially based families, friends, and neighbors, reunites the segments of society that belong to different cultural-technological galaxies in the sharing of every-day life. The Internet Galaxy of "Young Catalonia," the McLuhan Galaxy (based on the mass media) of traditional working-class society, and the Gutenberg Galaxy of the aging cultural elite coexist peacefully without actu-ally merging in the practice of individuals. These are, indeed, three different socio-technical cultures. Thus, the Catalan network society offers, in a certain sense, a striking example of a transition from a traditional, industrialized soci-ety to a network society: a transition that is made possible without major disruption by the social cohesion of the territorial community and the cultural dynamism of the Internet-powered projects of autonomy.

ACKNOWLEDGMENTS

The analysis presented in this chapter is based on a study conducted within the framework of the Project Internet Catalonia (PIC), a research program of the Internet Interdisciplinary Institute (IN3) of the Open University of Catalonia (UOC), under the general direction of Manuel Castells and Imma Tubella, and sponsored by the Government of the Generalitat of Catalonia. This particular study was conducted by the authors of this chapter. The authors wish to thank the Government of the Generalitat of Catalonia, and President Jordi Pujol for their generous support.

For a full presentation of this study we refer to our book: Manuel Castells, Imma Tubella, Teresa Sancho, Maria Isabel Diaz de Isla, and Barry Wellman, *La societat xarxa a Catalunya* (Barcelona: Random House/Mondadori, Series Rosa dels Vents with Edicions UOC, 2003). For a full presentation in English of the tables and methodology of the original survey, see the original research report, published online in August 2001 (http://www.uoc.edu/in3/pic/eng/pic1.html).

REFERENCES

Castells, Manuel (2001) *The Internet Galaxy*. Oxford: Oxford University Press.
— — (2004) *The Power of Identity*, 2nd edn. Oxford: Blackwell.
— —, Tubella, Imma, Sancho, Teresa, Diaz de Isla, Maria Isabel, and Wellman, Barry (2003) *La societat xarxa a Catalunya*. Barcelona: Random House/Mondadori, Series Rosa dels Vents with Edicions UOC.
Haythornthwaite, Caroline and Wellman, Barry (eds) (2002) *The Internet in Everyday Life*. Oxford: Blackwell.
Katz, James E. and Rice, Ronald E. (2002) *Social Consequences of Internet Use: Access, Involvement, and Interaction*, Cambridge, MA: MIT Press.
Levy, Pierre (1997) *La cibercultura: el segon diluvi*. Barcelona: Proa with Edicions UOC.

11. Racial segregation and the digital divide in the Detroit metropolitan region

Wayne E. Baker and Kenneth M. Coleman

The city of Detroit and its suburbs comprise one of the most racially segregated regions in the United States. Does the digital divide mirror this fundamental fact about the social structure and culture of the area? Past research has demonstrated a social network diffusion effect: generally, people are more likely to own and use computers, as well as use the Internet, if their friends and neighbors already do so (for example, Lenhart, 2000; Goolsbee and Klenow, 2002; DiMaggio et al., 2004). If computer and Internet usage varies by location and race, then the racial divide could be the basis of a persisting digital divide. Using data from the 2003 Detroit Area Study, we examine this hypothesis by analyzing computer and Internet usage in the city of Detroit and the three counties that make up the metropolitan region.[1]

After a brief description of the Detroit region, we focus on patterns of computer and Internet usage by the key variables included in the National Telecommunications and Information Administration (NTIA) studies of the digital divide: location, employment status, income, education, race, age, gender, and family structure (NTIA, 2000, 2002; DiMaggio et al., 2004). We conclude by analyzing the impact of computer and Internet usage on overcoming social and geographic barriers, focusing on two key indicators of social capital: whether a respondent has been in the home of someone of a different neighborhood (or had them in his or her home) in the past twelve months, and whether a respondent has been in the home of someone of a different race (or had them in his or her home) in the same time frame (Putnam, 2000; Social Capital Benchmark Survey, 2000).

THE DETROIT METROPOLITAN REGION:
BACKGROUND

Detroit is a quintessentially North American city. As Farley and co-authors (2000) describe, the explosive growth of automobile manufacturing in the twentieth century transformed Detroit from just another large Midwestern town in 1908 to the fastest growing city in the United States by 1920. A series of sequential, but overlapping, developments underpinned this growth: Henry Ford's pioneering of assembly-line production techniques in 1908, the growth of demand for trucks in World War I, extensive public investment in road building in the postwar era, the need for aircraft in World War II, and even greater public investments in road building via the interstate-highway system after the Second World War. For some decades, Detroit was the fourth largest city in the United States, following New York, Chicago, and Los Angeles. While racial tensions periodically erupted between Euro-Americans and African Americans in Detroit, the eventual unionization of the automobile and ancillary supplier industries eventually created a situation where African Americans profited from the manufacturing economy. For many, including African Americans lured from the American South in search of employment, Detroit represented opportunity.

Yet Detroit has always been a divided city. And race has always mattered to one's life chances in Detroit. As the twentieth century wound down, Detroit looked more and more like the quintessentially troubled American city. Symbolic of Detroit divided was the riot of 1967, among the first of a series of American urban disturbances that seemed contagious in 1967 and 1968. But the signs of trouble were more widespread than that particular manifestation of rebellion against urban stratification and racism. The auto industry was already in trouble by the 1960s. As Farley et al. (2000: 8) note:

> Automobile firms and their suppliers shifted jobs, sometimes to the suburbs, some-times to other parts of the United States or other countries. Because wage rates in Detroit were so high, plants that remained were retooled and modernized. Employment opportunities for unskilled workers declined dramatically, and by the mid-1960s, in-migration from the South had ceased.

Given racial tension after the 1967 riot and longer-term economic trends, Detroit became a city transformed. Its white population fell from 1.5 million in 1950 to 220,000 in 1990, and in the 1990s Detroit even lost population. In an informal sense, Detroit came to represent an American-style racial apartheid. Few laws held populations apart, but racial fears and attitudes, as well as the unequal distribution of skills and opportunity in a rapidly changing economy, conspired to produce an equally devastating set of apartheid-like effects.

In 1990 the city's population was 76 percent African American; the suburban ring was only 5 percent African American. The poverty rate for the city was 32 percent; for the ring, 6 percent. The economic disparity is even greater among children, with just under half (47%) of the city's population under the age of eighteen living in impoverished households, compared to 10 percent in the surburban ring. (Farley et al., 2000: 2–3)

While the 1990s were a decade of remarkable economic growth in the United States, they were also a decade of wealth concentration. Consequently, local trends were not reversed but accelerated. By 2003, the city of Detroit was now 82 percent African American, 5 percent Hispanic, and 1 percent Asian. The white population of Detroit had decreased from 33 percent in 1980 to 11 percent in 2000. According to the 2000 US Census, Detroit has a racial segregation index of 85, making it the most segregated major metropolitan area in the nation (table 11.1). Moreover, Detroit's African American population is the most isolated black population in the country.

Segregation statistics for the three counties covered in the Detroit Area Study – Wayne, Oakland, and Macomb – reveal the racial divide in the larger region. The index of residential segregation at the block group level for these counties is 87, 73, and 58, respectively. At the individual block level, the index is 89, 77, and 72, respectively. Racial groups are highly segregated into different neighborhoods in each of these counties. But there is some variation, with the highest segregation occurring in Wayne County (where Detroit is located) and the lowest in Macomb County.

A DIGITALLY DIVIDED DETROIT?

Social and spatial divisions are likely to coincide with, but need not necessarily imply, digital division. To what extent are the racial and geographic divisions of the Detroit area mirrored in the distribution of access to and use of computers and the Internet? To what extent does a digital divide exist in the area? To what extent does it replicate, extend, or even narrow existing socioeconomic and racial divisions represented in an economy now focused on information processing? Answers are critical because exclusion from the Internet and computer networks "is one of the most damaging forms of exclusion in our economy and in our culture" (Castells, 2001: 3). In the context of the urban metropolis, one prospect of exclusion is the development of what Castells (1999: 27–8) calls the "dual city":

> an urban system socially and spatially polarized between high value-making groups and functions on the one hand and devalued social groups and downgraded spaces on the other hand. This polarization induces increasing integration of the social and spatial core of the urban system, at the same time that it fragments devalued spaces of groups, and threatens them with social irrelevance.

Table 11.1   Black–white segregation and black isolation in top metropolitan areas in the United States (2000 census)

Area	Black–white segregation index	Black–white segregation rank	Black isolation index	Black isolation rank
Detroit, MI	85	1	79	1
Milwaukee–Waukesha, WI	82	2	67	8
New York, NY	82	3	60	18
Chicago, IL	81	4	73	3
Newark, NJ	80	5	67	9
Cleveland–Lorain–Elyria, OH	77	6	71	6
Cincinnati, OH–KY–IN	75	7	58	21
Nassau–Suffolk, NY	74	8	41	41
St Louis, MO–IL	74	9	65	12
Miami, FL	74	10	62	17

The index of residential segregation is also called the index of dissimilarity (D), defined as measuring "whether one particular group is distributed across census tracts in the metropolitan area in the same way as another group. A high value indicates that the two groups tend to live in different tracts. D ranges from 0 to 100. A value of 60 (or above) is considered very high. It means that 60 percent (or more) of the members of one group would need to move to a different tract in order for the two groups to be equally distributed. Values of 40 or 50 are considered a moderate level of segregation, and values of 30 or below are considered to be fairly low" (Lewis Mumford Center for Comparative Urban and Regional Research, University of Albany at http://mumford1.dyndns.org/cen2000/WholePop/CitySegdata/2622000City.htm). The Mumford Center defines the isolation index as "the percentage of same-group population in the census tract where the average member of a racial/ethnic group lives. It has a lower bound of zero (for a very small group that is quite dispersed) to 100 (meaning that group members are entirely isolated from other groups). It should be kept in mind that this index is affected by the size of the group – it is almost inevitably smaller for smaller groups, and it is likely to rise over time if the group becomes larger."

Source: Adapted from tables provided by the Lewis Mumford Center for Comparative Urban and Regional Research, University at Albany (2003)

BASIC PATTERNS OF COMPUTER AND INTERNET USE IN THE DETROIT REGION

We examined three indicators of computer and Internet usage – use of a computer, use of the Internet, and, if the Internet is used, connection from home – by race, gender, age, education, household income, employment status, family structure, and city/suburb location. Overall, about 75 percent of area residents report using a computer. For a rough comparison, note that the September 2001 Current Population Study (CPS) finds that 66 percent of Americans nationwide used a computer (NTIA, 2002: 24). This is a rough comparison because the CPS includes Americans aged 3 and up, while the Detroit Area Study covers adults aged 18 and older. Since Americans aged 3–17 are more likely than any other age group to use computers (NTIA, 2002: 24), the comparable proportion of Americans aged 18 and older who uses computers is lower.

Sixty-eight percent of residents in the Detroit region say they use the Internet. For a rough comparison, note that 54 percent of Americans aged 3 and older used the Internet in September 2001 (NTIA, 2002: 26), with 55–58 percent of Michigan residents aged 3 and up reporting that they used the Internet (NTIA, 2002: 8). Among those who use the Internet in the Detroit three-county area, 87 percent connect from home.

Rates of use vary for different groups in the Detroit region in about the same way as they vary in the American population (NTIA, 2002). For example, African Americans in the Detroit area, like African Americans nationwide (NTIA, 2002: 24, 26), are less likely to use a computer or use the Internet. Nonetheless, two-thirds of African Americans in the Detroit area aged 18 and older report using a computer (table 11.2). The NTIA reports 56 percent for the nationwide population aged 3 and up (NTIA, 2002: 24). And, the majority of African Americans in the Detroit region (54 percent) use the Internet. Nationwide, only 40 percent of African Americans aged 3 and older reported using the Internet in 2001 (NTIA, 2002: 26). Gender differences have virtually vanished nationwide (NTIA, 2002) and in the Detroit region (table 11.2).

There is essentially no difference between the young (ages 18–25) and the middle-aged (26–54) in computer usage and in Internet usage, but those 55 and older are far behind on both indicators. As before, the odds ratios in table 11.2 are comparable to national level data reported by DiMaggio et al. (2004). Defining our age cohorts exactly as they did, we find that the odds ratio between youngest and oldest age cohorts on computer usage is 4.400, whereas DiMaggio and associates report an odds ratio of 4.173 for national data in 2001. If those 55 and older do use the Internet, however, they are more likely than younger residents to connect from home.

A huge gap exists between those with college degrees and all others (table 11.2). More than 90 percent of college graduates use computers, use the Internet, and connect from home. Forty percent of those with a high-school education or less use a computer or the Internet. Clearly, college education generates computer and Internet usage in Detroit, as it does elsewhere. However, the gap narrows for use of the Internet at home, if one uses the

Table 11.2 Patterns of computer and Internet use by race, gender, age, education, household income, employment status, family structure, and location

	Use a computer	Use the Internet	If use the Internet, connect from home
All (%)	74.9	68.3	86.7
Race			
White and other (%)	77.9	72.8	88.0
African American (%)	65.5	53.4	79.7
Odds ratio: white/other to African American	1.851	2.339	1.874
Gender			
Women (%)	71.8	66.3	82.8
Men (%)	78.7	70.6	91.0
Odds ratio: men/women	1.454	1.223	2.094
Age (years)			
18–25 (%)	83.3	80.6	75.9
26–54 (%)	83.4	78.3	87.2
> 55 (%)	53.2	40.4	94.7
Odds ratio: youngest to oldest age groupings	4.400	6.121	0.175
Education			
Less than high school (%)	40.3	40.3	74.1
High school degree (%)	54.5	45.9	82.1
College graduate (%)	92.5	90.3	93.4
Odds ratio: college grad to less than HS degree	12.776	13.789	4.944
Household income			
Less than $20,000 (%)	34.8	22.9	50.0
$20,000–49,999 (%)	75.5	64.9	76.0
$50,000 or more (%)	84.2	80.8	93.6

	Use a computer	Use the Internet	If use the Internet, connect from home
Odds ratio: highest group to lowest	9.986	14.163	14.667
Employment status			
Working now (%)	85.2	77.7	86.9
Not working now (%)	59.6	54.2	85.5
Odds ratio: working now to not working	3.900	2.947	1.131
Family structure			
Children at home (%)	80.1	74.9	90.2
Children not at home (%)	70.4	62.5	83.3
Odds ratio: children at home to no children at home	1.691	1.793	1.835
Location			
City of Detroit (%)	66.1	56.3	70.3
Suburbs (%)	77.5	71.5	90.1
Odds ratio: suburbs to city of Detroit	1.771	1.948	3.860

Internet. Nearly three-quarters (74.1 percent) of those with less than a high-school degree use the Net from home, if they use the Net at all, while the comparable figure is 93.4 percent among college graduates. These findings are also comparable to national patterns.

Income is the single biggest predictor of computer and Internet usage in the Detroit area, consistent with findings from other studies (Castells, 2001; DiMaggio, et al., 2004). From the lowest income category (under $20,000) through the highest ($50,000 and more), the growth in computer and Internet usage is astonishing – from roughly 23–35 percent to over 80 percent. For example, more than three times as many in the highest income group connect to the Internet, compared to those in the lowest income group. Odds ratios greatly favor those with high income.[2]

As in other studies, employment has a large impact on computer and Internet use, although over half of those who are not working now use a computer and use the Internet. Nonetheless, 85 percent of those who are employed now use a computer and 78 percent use the Internet. Employment status does not have an effect on the proportion of Internet users who connect from home.

Having children under the age of 18 at home, surprisingly, has only a modest impact on computer usage in the Detroit metropolitan area (an increase from 70.4 percent to 80.1 percent), a roughly comparable impact on use of the Internet (an increase from 62.5 percent to 74.9 percent), and, again, a minor impact on connecting to the Internet from home (an increase of 7 percentage points).

Location of residence appears, in this bivariate analysis, to have an influence on computer and Internet usage. Those who live in the city of Detroit are less likely to use a computer, to use the Internet, and to connect from home if they use the Internet. For these indicators, there is an 11–20 percentage point difference between Detroit and its suburbs.

These basic findings suggest that a digital divide continues to exist in the Detroit metropolitan area in 2003. Income, education, age, and employment status appear to be the main sources of this division in the digital world; race, location, and family structure are secondary determinants. Since some of these factors vary together, we now turn to multivariate analyses to assess the relative impact of each of these sources of the digital divide.

EXPLAINING PATTERNS OF COMPUTER AND INTERNET USE IN THE DETROIT REGION

We analyze the effects of race, gender, age,[3] education, household income, employment status, family structure,[4] and place of residence on the three indicators of computer and Internet usage discussed above, plus two more indicators: number of computers in the household and frequency of computer use. As shown in table 11.3, the three best predictors are income, education, and age, controlling for the other variables. Higher income is positively and significantly related to all five indicators of computer and Internet usage, controlling for multiple other variables. Education is positively correlated to four of the dependent variables in table 11.3. Note that there are independent contributions of income and education to explaining computer usage and Internet usage (models 1 and 4 in table 11.3). Similarly, youth is a significant predictor of four of these variables in the multivariate analysis, although being young makes one *less likely* to use the Internet at home. The middle-aged cohort (ages 26–54) exhibits exactly the same pattern as does the youth; that is, a significant predictor of four of these variables, and less likely to connect to the Net from home. Similarly, those who are currently employed are both more likely to use computers and to use them more frequently, compared to those who are unemployed. However, employment status does not predict the other three dependent variables.

Table 11.3 *OLS and logistic coefficients from the regression of computer and Internet use on income, education, age, race, gender, employment status, location, and family structure*

Variables	(1) Do you use a computer? (logistic)	(2) No. of computers used at home (OLS)	(3) Frequency of computer use (OLS)	(4) Do you use the Internet? (logistic)	(5) Do you use the Internet at home (logistic)
Income	0.350***	0.216***	0.242***	0.394***	0.430***
	(0.070)	(0.030)	(0.035)	(0.071)	(0.112)
Education	0.676***	0.152**	0.412***	0.745***	0.286
	(0.124)	(0.050)	(0.058)	(0.121)	(0.175)
Youth (18–25)	1.811***	0.237	0.853***	2.495***	−1.677*
	(0.442)	(0.187)	(0.218)	(0.441)	(0.736)
Middle-aged (26–54)	1.309***	0.337*	0.696***	1.799***	−1.439*
	(0.342)	(0.152)	(0.177)	(0.334)	(0.735)
African American	−0.285	0.081	−0.011	−0.737*	0.349+
	(0.381)	(0.180)	(0.210)	(0.368)	(0.641)
Gender (female)	−0.031	−0.059	−0.080	0.173	−0.759*
	(0.259)	(0.110)	(0.129)	(0.251)	(0.384)
Currently employed	0.553*	0.170	0.409**	0.098	−0.461
	(0.268)	(0.124)	(0.144)	(0.266)	(0.437
Lives in suburbs	−0.218	0.201	−0.202	−0.409	1.859**
	(0.392)	(0.187)	(0.218)	(0.383)	(0.609)
Children at home	−0.276	0.248*	−0.189	−0.270	1.117**
	(0.313)	(0.124)	(0.144)	(0.291)	(0.396)
Constant	−3.977***	−1.066***	−0.782*	−4.878***	−1.738
Adjusted r^2 or Nagelkerke r^2*	0.396	0.237	0.328	0.454	0.298
Correctly classified (%)	80.8	n.a.	n.a.	80.8	86.9
Weighted n of observations	508	508	507	508	346

*** $p <0.001$; ** $p <0.01$; * $p <0.05$; + $p <0.10$ (two-tailed test).
Adjusted r^2 is reported for OLS; Nagelkerke r^2 is reported for logistic regression.
$n = 507$ for model 3 due to missing data from one partial interview.
n.a. = not applicable.

African Americans are not significantly less likely than others to use a computer; similarly, race does not predict the number of computers used at home or the frequency of computer use, after controlling for the effects of household income, education, and other factors. African Americans are significantly less likely to use the Internet, compared to non-blacks, but the effects of income, education, and age are stronger than the effect of race on Internet use. If African Americans do use the Internet, they are *more* likely to use it from home, once other predictors are controlled. While some analysts of the digital divide might expect otherwise, race appears *not to be* the crucial variable in structuring Detroit's digital divide.

It is reasonable to suppose that computer use is a phenomenon of affluent social strata and, therefore, it might be structured in part by where one resides in a metropolitan area. Sheer propinquity to other computer users might have a social influence effect (for example, Lenhart, 2000; Goolsbee and Klenow, 2002; DiMaggio et al., 2004). Consequently, suburban residents might be higher computer users. The multivariate analyses suggest otherwise (table 11.3), with one exception. Most patterns of computer and Internet usage are not significantly different for residents of the suburbs versus residents of Detroit. Only use of the Internet at home distinguishes suburban residents from those who live in the city of Detroit, with suburbanites more likely to connect from home.

Overall, gender is not a significant factor: men and women do not differ in their patterns of computer and Internet usage, controlling for other factors, with one exception – connecting to the Internet from home, which women are less likely to do. Moreover, having children under the age of 18 at home is significantly associated only with the number of computers in the household and with connecting to the Internet from home.

While not shown in table 11.3, a good way to judge the relative impact of various independent variables on a dependent variable is to compare Betas, or standardized regression coefficients. Comparing Betas for all variables in models 2 and 3,[5] we find that the Beta for income is the largest one in each equation and education is second. That is, household income produces the greatest amount of change in each indicator of Internet and computer usage, with education accounting for the second largest change in each indicator. These findings suggest that, to the extent that there is a digital divide in Detroit, it is structured primarily by income and education, age and work status, and to a much lesser extent by other variables, such as race or inner-city location. For example, returning to table 11.2, we see the odds ratios for whites and others versus African Americans represent an increase of only 1.9 to 2.3 times the probabilities of given computer-use outcomes. But the income variable produces an increase in probabilities of certain outcomes by 10.0 to 14.7 times, while the effects of education change the odds by 4.9 to 13.8 times. A variety of indicators suggests that income, education, and age are the key determinants of computer and Internet use.

Thus, there *does* appear to be a digital divide in Detroit, but one structured primarily by income, education, age, and, to a lesser extent, by employment status. Race and inner-city location are far less important than might have been expected, though they still matter on selected uses. Differentiated use of the Internet is as important as differences in access (DiMaggio et al., 2004). Next, we consider what Detroiters use the Internet for, taking up part of the agenda for research on digital inequality proposed by DiMaggio et al. (2004).

WHAT DO DETROIT AREA RESIDENTS DO ON THE INTERNET?

Residents of the city of Detroit and the three counties of Wayne, Oakland, and Macomb use the Internet for a variety of purposes (table 11.4). The most popular activities (done by over 50 percent of Internet users) are getting information about a product or service, learning more about something that has to be done for work or school, getting information about a health concern, actually making a purchase online, and going to a website to find information about government services, public policy issues, or world events. The least popular activities (done by fewer than 20 percent of Internet users) are participating in chat rooms and interactively discussing political or social issues with others.

Some of the activities that people do on the Internet vary by race and location but many do not, according to the results of multivariate analyses using race, gender, age, education, household income, employment status, family structure, and place of residence to predict the likelihood of doing each of the ten Internet activities (tables not shown here). For example, there are no significant differences between African Americans and others, or between Detroit and suburban residents, for six of the ten activities we examined: getting information about a product or service, getting information about a health concern, actually making a purchase, going to a website to find information about government services, public policy, or world issues, locating contact information, or getting help with home finances or doing banking online. The *only* significant difference between Detroiters and suburbanites is learning about something a respondent had to do for work or school, with residents of Detroit more likely to do so. Significant racial difference appears for three Internet activities: looking for a new job or exploring career opportunities, participating in chat rooms, and interactively discussing political or social issues with others (table 11.4). Compared to non-blacks, African Americans are almost four times as likely to use the Internet to look for employment or career opportunities, and almost five times as likely to use it to interactively

Table 11.4   Activities done on the Internet in the past 12 months by race and location

Activity	Use the Internet (%)	Race and location of Internet users (%)			
		African American	Non-black	Suburbs	Detroit
Got information about a product or service	83.7	88.3	82.6	83.3	85.0
Learned more about something for work or school	73.3	82.0	71.2	71.2	83.3
Got information about a health concern	65.5	57.4	67.3	66.3	61.7
Made a purchase, incl. travel reservations	60.9	51.7	63.0	63.5	48.3
Got information about government services, public policy issues, or world events	58.0	58.3	58.0	58.5	55.0
Located someone's phone number, e-mail, or mailing address	47.2	43.3	48.0	47.5	46.7
Looked for a new job or explored career opportunities	47.0	65.6	43.1	44.5	58.3
Help with home finances or did banking	40.9	34.4	42.3	42.3	33.3
Participated in chat rooms	14.3	11.5	14.9	13.8	16.7
Interactively discussed political or social issues with others	10.9	16.7	9.6	10.7	11.7

discuss political and social issues. African Americas are less likely than non-blacks to participate in chat rooms.[6] (Note, however, that interactive discussions and chat-room participation are low-volume activities on the Internet.)

Overall, these findings suggest that the Internet may be a means to overcome racial and residential barriers. Many activities, where racial prejudice or residential segregation could interfere with access to important information or to the consumer market, do not exhibit significant differences by race or residence. Moreover, African Americans may be using the Internet to overcome barriers in the labor market. Not only do the majority of African Americans who use the Internet use it to access information about employment and career opportunities, but they are much more likely to do so than non-blacks. Of course, African Americans who are excluded from using the Internet do not enjoy these informational advantages.

THE EFFECT OF COMPUTER AND INTERNET USE ON SOCIAL INTERACTION ACROSS SPACE AND RACE

Most research on Internet use documents positive effects on social interaction, sociability, community participation, and political involvement (for reviews, see Castells, 2001: 118–25; DiMaggio et al., 2004). We consider the impact of computer and Internet usage on two key indicators of social capital: whether a respondent has been in the home of someone of a different neighborhood (or had them in his or her home) in the past twelve months, and whether a respondent has been in the home of someone of a different race (or had them in his or her home) in the same time period. These items are replicated from the Social Capital Benchmark Survey (2000) "short form."

Neither race nor residence is a significant predictor of either form of socializing, controlling for gender, education, household income, employment status, family structure, and computer and Internet usage (see table 11.5). African Americans are not more or less likely than non-blacks to have been in the home of someone of a different neighborhood (or to have had them in their homes) or to have been in the home of someone of a different race (or to have had them in their homes). Similarly, Detroiters are not more or less likely than suburbanites to have been in the home of someone of a different neighborhood (or to have had them in their homes) or to have been in the home of someone of a different race (or to have had them in their homes). Similarly, gender does not have significant effects on inter-neighborhood or inter-racial socializing.

Age is a big predictor of both forms of social interaction. The young (ages 18–25) are always much more likely than the old (ages 55+) to have engaged in both types of socializing. Those who are middle-aged (ages 26–54) are much more likely than the old to have been in the home of someone of another

Table 11.5 *Logistic coefficients from regression of inter-neighborhood and inter-racial socializing on income, education, age, race, gender, employment status, location, family structure, and computer and Internet usage*

Variables	Been in the home of someone from a different neighborhood (or had them in your home) in the past 12 months			Been in the home of someone of a different race (or had them in your home) in the past 12 months		
	(1)	(2)	(3)	(4)	(5)	(6)
Income	0.228** (0.080)	0.205** (0.080)	0.193* (0.079)	0.059 (0.057)	0.052 (0.057)	0.051 (0.056)
Education	0.368** (0.143)	0.343* (0.144)	0.289* (0.147)	0.199 (0.363)	0.184+ (0.095)	0.072+ (0.096)
Youth (18–25)	1.685* (0.804)	1.465+ (0.812)	1.470+ (0.807)	1.439*** (0.363)	1.368*** (0.370)	1.383*** (0.364)
Middle-aged (26-54)	-0.287 (0.419)	-0.429 (0.428)	-0.416 (0.420)	0.802** (0.272)	0.748** (0.278)	0.777** (0.272)
African American	0.545 (0.469)	0.622 (0.474)	0.604 (0.470)	0.296 (0.326)	0.334 (0.329)	0.314 (0.327)
Gender (female)	-0.380 (0.312)	-0.397 (0.313)	-0.415 (0.315)	-0.310 (0.202)	-0.319 (0.202)	-0.312 (0.202)
Currently employed	0.654* (0.339)	0.669* (0.340)	0.652+ (0.341)	0.355 (0.220)	0.374+ (0.219)	0.363+ (0.220)

Lives in suburbs	0.449 (0.465)	0.464 (0.468)	0.439 (0.466)	0.462 (0.335)	0.476 (0.336)	0.476 (0.336)
Children at home	0.187 (0.371)	0.230 (0.373)	0.237 (0.376)	0.134 (0.229)	0.137 (0.229)	0.135 (0.229)
Use a computer	0.409 (0.342)			0.264 (0.254)		
Use the Internet		0.718* (0.352)			0.354 (0.248)	
Use e-mail			1.044** (0.393)			0.387+ (0.233)
Constant	-1.391	-1.264	-1.080	-2.022***	-1.955***	-1.917***
Nagelkerke r^2	0.220	0.229	0.245	0.167	0.169	0.171
Correctly classified (%)	88.3	88.4	88.8	68.5	69.0	69.0
Weighted n of observations.	508	508	508	507	507	507

*** $p < 0.001$, ** $p < 0.01$, * $p < 0.05$, + $p < 0.10$ (two-tailed test).
$n = 507$ for models 4–6 due to missing data from one partial interview.

race (or had them in their homes). Employment has a positive effect on both forms of social interaction. Education, too, has a positive effect on both forms. Compared to respondents with less formal education, those with more education are more likely to have socialized with someone from another neighborhood and to have socialized with someone of a different race. Household income influences the likelihood of inter-neighborhood socializing but not inter-racial socializing. Respondents from households with higher incomes are more likely than those from households with lower incomes to have socialized with someone from a different neighborhood.

Simply using a computer does not increase or decrease the chances of inter-neighborhood socializing or inter-racial socializing (see models 1 and 4 in table 11.5). Using the Internet has a positive effect on the likelihood of inter-neighborhood socializing but not inter-racial socializing (models 2 and 5). Using e-mail, however, significantly increases the probability of both types of social interaction (models 3 and 6). Compared to respondents who do not use e-mail, those who do are 2.8 times as likely to have socialized with someone from a different neighborhood, and 1.5 times as likely to have socialized with someone of a different race.

These findings suggest that the new information and communication technologies may help to overcome the barriers of race and space, even in an urban system that is as severely segregated as the Detroit region. In contrast, the "old" communication technologies do not appear to have an influence. The number of telephone numbers in a household, for example, does not have a significant effect on either form of social interaction (tables not shown here). Those who use the new technologies are more likely to engage in both inter-neighborhood and inter-racial socializing, even when controlling for race, gender, education, household income, employment status, family structure, and place of residence.

CONCLUSION

The "new American dilemma," argues Castells (2000: 128–9), is the combination of inequality, urban poverty, and social exclusion in the information age. If ever there were an urban system that illustrates this dilemma, it is metropolitan Detroit. Inequality is vast, urban poverty is high, and, as we have documented here, segregation, isolation, and social exclusion are as severe as anywhere in the United States. However, this view of "Detroit divided" should not be overstated. As Farley and colleagues (2000) note, many manufacturing jobs moved to the suburbs in recent decades, and some blacks managed to follow those jobs. The percentage of African Americans in the Detroit suburban ring is now 7 percent and in certain suburbs, such as Southfield, the percentage is much higher, with employment in high-paying manufacturing jobs available to some African Americans.

Additionally, in an effort to revitalize the city – which stayed stagnant for some decades after the 1967 riot – major new investments have been made. Not the least of these is the signature urban redevelopment project, the Renaissance Center, now home to the headquarters of General Motors. Additionally, an entertainment complex is growing in downtown Detroit, including an opera house, Ford Field (for football's Detroit Lions), Comerca Park (for baseball's Detroit Tigers), various casinos, and other theaters (such as a remodeled Fox Theater). Perhaps most symbolic of the passing of one economic era and the advent of another is that a major new office tower in downtown Detroit is home to Compuware, a leading developer and provider of software applications for business, which opened in 2003 and brings hundreds of high-tech jobs back from the suburbs to downtown Detroit. To the extent that Detroit has a local symbol of the informatics economy, the physical presence of that entity has just moved to the city center, a site emptied out by racial tension, socioeconomic division, and the collapse of the old economy.

Might, in fact, the informatics economy be an agency for the rebirth and reconstruction of one of America's quintessentially troubled manufacturing cities? And are there any potentially "leveling" consequences of Internet usage in metropolitan areas as polarized as Detroit's? Our data suggest cautious optimism. First, the digital divide that exists in Detroit is not primarily structured by race; rather, it is structured mainly by income, education, age, and work status. Young, educated, and employed African Americans are vastly more likely to be frequent computer and Internet users than are older, less well educated and retired or unemployed African Americans. Education is generating opportunity among the young. Second, a revealing datum in table 11.4 pertains to the use of the Internet by African Americans. Sixty-six percent of African American Internet users used the Internet to "look for a new job or explore career opportunities" versus 43 percent for non-black Internet users. This fact is crucial in a city that lacks an effective public transportation system to connect suburbs and inner city.[7] Knowing where the jobs are is essential to pursuing jobs. A significant part of social exclusion is employment based. The Internet appears already, in metropolitan Detroit, to be affording a tool with which to attack this dimension of social exclusion.

Finally, and perhaps most hopefully, our multivariate analysis in table 11.5 suggests that using the Internet and using e-mail helps to break down isolation and exclusion. E-mail users in the metropolitan Detroit region are significantly more likely than non-users to visit the homes of people living outside their neighborhood (or have them visit their homes), and they are significantly more likely to visit the home of someone of a different race (or have them visit their own homes). This contribution is statistically independent of income, education, age, suburban versus inner-city residence, and other possible determinants of these social interactions.

There is a public policy implication here. Metropolitan Detroit is the most racially segregated and isolated city in the United States. Recent budgetary crises in state government have led to cutbacks in public investments in computers for classrooms. This may be precisely the kind of decision that reinforces, rather than reduces, social exclusion in a manufacturing state trying to adjust to the informatics economy. Public investments (via tax subsidies) have lured major industries back to downtown Detroit. But the presence of high-tech jobs will not suffice to erode social exclusion until public investment in educational opportunity for the young subverts a digital divide that persists on the basis of education, income, and employment.

ACKNOWLEDGMENTS

The data reported in this study come from 2003 Detroit Area Study (principal investigator, Wayne Baker), which was funded in part by the Russell Sage Foundation. We are grateful to Jim Lepkowski, Director of the Institute for Social Research Survey Methodology Program, for technical advice and assistance with the construction of sample weights, and to Sang Yun Lee for assistance with data imputation.

NOTES

1. $n = 508$, based on a multi-stage area probability sample of residents living in the Detroit three-county region (Wayne, Oakland, and Macomb). Sampling weights were constructed to account for variation in probabilities of selection and non-response rates, and to adjust sample results to match known US Census totals for the Detroit three-county region for age, gender, and race. The probabilities of selection varied because a single adult was selected from each household, in effect over-representing in the sample persons who live in households with fewer adults. Non-response rates were higher in some areas than others, and the inverse of the response rates in sample areas was used as an adjustment factor. Post-stratification weights were developed so that the final weighted estimates agreed with census distributions by age, gender, and race for the metropolitan area. A rescaled final weight, which is the product of all three adjustments, was computed which sums to the unweighted sample size of 508. All analyses employ the final rescaled weight in computation. Missing data for key variables were imputed using IVEware, which performs imputations of missing values using the sequential regression imputation method (Raghunathan et al., 2001).
2. Our odds ratios on the effects of income are higher than those derived from national level data reported by DiMaggio et al. (2004) because our lowest income category (under \$20,000) is lower than the \$20,000–\$20,999 category employed by the Current Population Study. Hence, the contrast is greater.
3. In analyzing the effects of age, we have created two dummy variables for youth (18–25) and middle-age (26–54). Their coefficients should be interpreted as the effect of an individual

falling into one of these groups versus being of age 55 and above, which constitutes the "excluded" group used as a baseline.
4. Family structure is a dichotomous variable, which = 1 if a household has one or more residents under the age of 18 (0 = otherwise).
5. These equations have interval-level dependent variables, thereby allowing the use of OLS procedures, which permit the calculation of standard parameter estimates. A Beta coefficient is essentially the amount of change in standard deviation units in the dependent variable for each change in a standard deviation unit of the independent variable, holding other predictor variables constant.
6. Norris (2003) suggests that participation in online communities can affect two forms of social capital: "bonding social capital" and "bridging social capital" (Putnam, 2000). Participation can deepen connections among similar people ("bonding social capital") and it can increase linkages of different sorts of people ("bridging social capital").
7. And, as Farley et al. (2000: 253) suggest, metropolitan Detroit lacks such an integrated system of public transport in part precisely so as to enforce barriers of racial isolation.

REFERENCES

Castells, Manuel (1999) "The Informational City is a Dual City: Can it be Reversed?," in Donald A. Schon, Sanyal Bish, and William J. Mitchell (eds), *High Technology and Low-income Communities: Prospects for the Positive Use of Advanced Information Technology*, pp. 25–41. Cambridge, MA: MIT Press.
— — (2000) *End of Millennium*, 2nd edn. Oxford: Blackwell.
— — (2001) *The Internet Galaxy: Reflections on the Internet, Business, and Society*. Oxford: Oxford University Press.
DiMaggio, Paul, Hargittai, Eszter, Celeste, Coral and Shafer, Steven (2004) "From Unequal Access to Differentiated Use: A Literature Review and Agenda for Research on Digital Inequality," in Kathryn Neckerman (ed.), *Social Inequality*. New York: Russell Sage Foundation.
Farley, Reynolds, Danziger, Sheldon, and Holzer, Harry J. (2000) *Detroit Divided*. New York: Russell Sage Foundation.
Goolsbee, Austan and Klenow, Peter J. (2002) "Evidence on Learning and Network Externalities in the Diffusion of Home Computers," *Journal of Law and Economics* 45: 317–44.
Lenhart, Amanda (2000) *Who's Not Online? 57 Percent of Those without Internet Access Say They Do Not Plan to Log On*. Washington, DC: Pew Internet and American Life Project.
National Telecommunications and Information Administration (NTIA) (2000) *Falling Through the Net: Toward Digital Inclusion*. Washington, DC: US Department of Commerce.
— — (2002) *A Nation Online: Americans are Expanding their Use of the Internet*. Washington, DC: US Department of Commerce.
Norris, Pippa (2003) "The Bridging and Bonding Role of Online Communities," in Philip N. Howard and Steve Jones (eds), *Society Online: The Internet in Context*. Thousand Oaks, CA: Sage.
Putnam, Robert D. (2000) *Bowling Alone: The Collapse and Revival of American Community*. New York: Simon and Schuster.
Raghunathan, T. E., Lepkowski, James M., Van Hoewyk, John, and Solenberger, Peter W. (2001 "A Multivariate Technique for Multiply Imputing Missing Values Using a Sequence of Regression Models," *Survey Methodology* 27: 85–95.

Social Capital Benchmark Survey (2000) (http://www.cfsv.org/communitysurvey/index.html).

University of Albany, Lewis Mumford Center for Comparative Urban and Regional Research (2003) (http://mumford1.dyndns.org/cen2000/WholePop).

PART V

The Internet in the public interest

12.   The promise and the myths of e-learning in post-secondary education

Tony Bates

E-LEARNING AND CHANGE IN EDUCATION

The Internet and, in particular, the World Wide Web have had a remarkable impact on education at all levels. In the past, new technologies such as the telephone, radio, television, cassettes, satellites, and computers were all predicted to bring about a revolution in education. However, after the initial hype, these new technologies left a marginal impact on the general practice of education, each finding a niche, but not changing the essential process of a teacher personally interacting with learners.

However, the Internet and, especially, the World Wide Web are different, both in the scale and the nature of their impact on education. Certainly, the web has penetrated teaching and learning much more than any other previous technology, with the important exception of the printed book. Indeed, it is possible to see parallels between the social and educational influence of both mechanically printed books and the Internet on post-secondary education, and these parallels will be explored a little further in this chapter.

The application of the Internet to teaching and learning has had both strong advocates and equally strong critics. Electronic learning has been seized upon as the next commercial development of the Internet, a natural extension of e-commerce. John Chambers, the CEO of the giant American Internet equipment company, Cisco, described education as the next Internet "killer application" at the Comdex exhibition in Las Vegas in 2001 (Moore and Jones, 2001). Chambers linked several concepts together: e-learning is necessary to improve the quality of education; e-learning is necessary to improve the quality of the workforce; and a highly qualified technology workforce is essential for national economic development and competitiveness.

It is perhaps not surprising that the CEO of a company that makes its living through the Internet would be supporting the use of the Internet for education and training. However, there are also strong advocates of e-learning within the

education profession. Their arguments tend to be based primarily on pedagogical issues. For instance, Harasim and co-workers (1995) have argued that
e-learning represents a paradigm shift in education. Both Harasim et al. and
Jonassen and colleagues (1995) claim that e-learning facilitates a more
constructivist approach to learning, thus encouraging knowledge construction
and critical thinking skills. Collis (1996: xxi) predicted that "two of the most
important changes to education involving tele-learning will be the importance
of virtual communities to complement face-to-face relationships in learning,
and the increasing use of 'knowledge utilities,' particularly through hyper-
linked distributed environments such as the WWW."

Peters (2002) is one of many commentators who believe that e-learning will
force a radical restructuring of our educational institutions. For universities,
Peters argues that "the only treatment available is a bold wave of modernization
such as never before in the history of academic . . . institutions" (2002: 158). Both
the pedagogical and organizational issues will be explored later in the chapter.

The heady mixture in electronic learning of commercialization, technology,
and challenge to institutions and traditions has not surprisingly resulted in an
active body of critics. Noble, over a series of articles (1997, 1998a, b, 1999,
2001), ironically available initially only on the Internet, has associated e-learning with the commercialization and automation of education: "Here faculty
. . . are transformed into mere producers of marketable instructional commodities which they may or may not themselves 'deliver'" (1997). Noble argues
that such automation and commercialization is coercive in nature, being forced
upon professors as well as students, with commercial interests in mind. He
argues that online learning is not a progressive but a regressive trend, toward
the old era of mass-production, standardization, and purely commercial interests. According to Noble (1998a):

> the primary commercial impulse has come from non-academic forces, industrial
> corporations seeking indirect public subsidy of their research needs and private
> vendors of instructional hardware, software, and content looking for subsidized
> product development and a potentially lucrative market for their wares. In both
> cases also, there has been a fundamental transformation of the nature of academic
> work and the relationship between higher educational institutions and their faculty
> employees.

Others have suggested that the use of the Internet for education increases the
divide between the wealthy and the poor, and that the Internet acts as a form of
Western cultural dominance, with its predominant use of English and primarily
American programs and materials (see, for example, Wilson et al., 1998).

On a more pragmatic level, many instructors are worried about the extra
workload and skills needed to teach effectively through e-learning, and
administrators are concerned with what appear to be the high investment and

maintenance costs of e-learning. Others (for example, Bates, 2000) have criticized institutional managements and governments which, while exhorting institutions and teachers to do more e-learning, have failed to provide the necessary resources. In particular, there is criticism that institutions and governments are not doing enough to prepare managers, teachers, instructors, and students for the organizational, institutional, and cultural changes needed to make e-learning successful (for example, see COIMBRA Group of Universities, 2002). Lastly, a number of critics have questioned the costs and benefits of e-learning. In particular, there is a dearth of evidence of improved performance, and some evidence to suggest increased costs, at least in the initial stages of an e-learning program (for instance, Bartolic-Zlomislic and Bates, 1999).

The rhetoric on some of these issues has changed over the years, as more experience of e-learning has been acquired. In particular, the belief that e-learning is somehow a totally new educational phenomenon is becoming increasingly untenable. At the same time, e-learning is becoming a major component of post-secondary education and training, and therefore deserves careful attention. Consequently, the rest of the chapter explores the issues raised in more depth.

WHAT IS E-LEARNING?

We need to start with some definitions because, as always with a new phenomenon that is emerging and developing over time, terminology is not always well defined or used consistently. From about 1996 onwards, when the World Wide Web was first applied to teaching on a consistent basis, regular classroom teachers started to incorporate the Internet into their teaching. This occurs in a variety of forms. Web pages may be used as illustrations in face-to-face classes or lectures. Online discussion forums can be used to continue discussion after class or the lecture. Students may be asked to do web searches or use recommended websites as part of their studies, either in or outside class. Textbooks have started to appear with dedicated websites, which provide student activities and tests based on the textbook. The development of software platforms such as WebCT and Blackboard has encouraged instructors and teachers to create their own web-based learning materials. "Hybrid," "blended," or "mixed mode" are all terms used for integrating the web into classroom teaching, though I prefer to call this type of application "web-enhanced" or "Internet-enhanced" classroom teaching.

In general, these Internet-based activities have been incorporated into regular face-to-face classes. However, in still a few rare cases, instructors have reduced (but not eliminated) the number of face-to-face classes to allow for more online learning: hybrid, blended, mixed mode, and distributed learning are all terms used for this form of teaching. "Distributed learning" is a term that usually encompasses both on-campus and distance courses delivered online (from the computer term "distributed intelligence;" Twigg, 2001). However, I prefer to use the term "mixed mode" in the specific context of a reduction in class time to accommodate more time spent studying online, whereas hybrid or blended could mean just adding online teaching to regular class time. However, there is no consistency yet in terminology in this field.

It would not appear to be a big step, then, for a classroom instructor to move to a class that is entirely delivered online, that is, to create a distance education course as an extension of their classroom teaching. Some teachers also call a fully online course "distributed learning" because they do not want to confuse it with print-based distance education via correspondence course. However, from my experience, there are significant differences in a class delivered entirely at a distance, whether online or print-based, compared with a face-to-face or mixed-mode class with online elements.

At the same time as classroom teachers were moving to online components of their teaching, so too were many print-based "correspondence" distance education operations. Many institutions started adding e-mail, online web articles, and online discussion forums to their already existing print-based correspondence courses. Often, these additional online activities were optional, so as not to reduce access to students without Internet or computer facilities. However, institutions with such online enhancements also claimed to be offering e-learning courses. Bates and Poole (2003) have described these developments graphically (see figure 12.1).

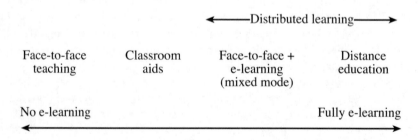

Figure 12.1   The continuum of e-learning in formal education

The OECD has extended these definitions. In a new study (OECD, 2004), it offers the following categories of e-learning:

Online learning: For the purpose of this survey, the following categories are used to define different types of online learning:

(i)   *Web supplemented* (e.g. course outline and lecture notes online, use of email, links to external online resources)

(ii)   *Web dependent*: students are required to use the Internet for key "active" elements of the programme, e.g. online discussions, assessment, online project/collaborative work, but without significant reduction in classroom time.

(iii) *Mixed mode*: classroom time has been reduced but not eliminated. The reduced classroom time is replaced by online activities, e.g. online discussions, assessment, online project/collaborative work.

(iv)   *Fully online*

The terms "online learning" and "e-learning" are used synonymously throughout the survey.

Thus the OECD study subdivides Bates and Poole's (2003) classification of "classroom aids" into "web supplemented" and "web dependent," further reinforcing the notion of a continuum of e-learning.

So far I have described forms of Internet-based learning in the formal post-secondary education sector. However, e-learning is also growing rapidly in the corporate sector, and, indeed, in some aspects, e-learning has a unique function in this sector. The more conventional application of e-learning is to move more traditional training from a face-to-face mode to one delivered into the workplace, and often to the desk or workstation of the employee. In this sense, it is similar to the use of e-learning in the formal education sector, except that the learning tends to be more modular, more skill-specific, and delivered "just-in-time," that is, on demand at the moment when the employee needs the training or information.

However, there is a more fundamentally different view of e-learning in the corporate sector, and that is in the sense of the learning organization (see, for example, Senge, 1990). In this sense, e-learning is far more encompassing than the conventional application of the Internet to study or training. In a learning organization, the aim is to use the Internet and access to integrated company databases to empower employees across the organization to learn more about the operations of the organization, and to use that knowledge and information to improve the products and services of the organization. In other words, it is about knowledge management (see Rosenberg, 2001).

Thus, defining e-learning is not straightforward. Institutions often claim that they are offering e-learning when all they have done is merely added an online component to what is basically a face-to-face, print-based, or video-based course. However, even courses designed from scratch as "online" courses will often contain printed readings, either in the form of required textbooks or collections of printed articles distributed to students by mail. Some mainly online courses require attending an institute in the summer or weekend classes. These are not just issues of terminology. There is a tendency by many

institutions to over-inflate their claims to be an e-learning institution, so terms
need to be defined and used consistently.

HOW BIG IS E-LEARNING?

Since the first appearance of the World Wide Web in education around 1995,
we have seen the emergence of fully online universities in both the public and
private sectors, university for-profit, spin-off companies, public and private
partnerships, national and international consortia, extensive penetration of e-
learning into the corporate training market, and the development of virtual
schools. In addition, there has been a large penetration of e-learning into traditional campus-based teaching.

   Given the issues around definitions of e-learning, it is not surprising that
there are few reliable sources of data about the extent of e-learning in post-
secondary education (a comprehensive survey by the OECD, UNESCO, or a
similar body would be extremely timely). I will try to give a rough indication.
I have drawn data from multiple sources, but in particular from Cunningham
et al. (2000), Dirr (2001), Allen and Seaman (2002), and many articles from
the *Chronicle of Higher Education*. And, above all, I have used the search
engine Google and the web to go to institutional and corporate websites to
ensure that data for 2002–2003 were accurate. This rough-and-ready survey
produced the following results. Figures refer to course enrolments, not individual students.

e-Learning on Conventional Campuses

In terms of e-learning on university and college campuses, figures from the
major learning resource management system (LRMS) companies give some
guidance. The two major LRMS companies for higher education are WebCT
and Blackboard Inc. WebCT and Blackboard cover about 80 per cent of the
market, with the rest made up of a number of different proprietary LRMSs and
open-source systems. In 2002–2003, WebCT had approximately 2.5 million
student licenses and Blackboard about 1.5 million. WebCT estimates that
approximately 80 percent of the applications of WebCT are to support on-
campus courses. If we make the same assumption for other LRMS providers,
we get an estimate of approximately four million on-campus e-learners in
higher education in 2002–2003. The vast majority of these, though, will be
supplementing their face-to-face classes with e-learning. These students are
spread throughout the world (WebCT has licenses in over 80 different countries), but the majority will be in North America.

Public Dual-mode Institutions

Public universities and colleges that are primarily campus-based but also offer distance courses as well (dual-mode institutions) are particularly difficult to analyze in terms of student numbers and mode of delivery. In terms of institutions that offer distance education programs they are by far the most numerous (I counted just over a thousand institutions with at least some distance programs as well as campus-based operations), although the numbers of students in dual-mode distance education programs are in total less than those in autonomous distance teaching universities (one million compared to four million).

The great majority of dual-mode institutions are in transition from print-based to online teaching for their distance courses. Because of the backlog of print-based inventory, it appears that at least two-thirds of distance courses being offered are still primarily print-based. However, this figure is changing rapidly, at roughly 15 per cent a year being moved to fully online delivery. In addition, there are some institutions that have no print-based inventory that are going straight to online distance delivery. I estimate that there are probably about 250,000 students taking fully online courses in these institutions, mainly in North America, Britain, and Australia. (Not included in this category are blended or mixed-mode courses; that is, courses requiring regular campus attendance. The 250,000 students taking fully online courses in conventional universities would be in addition to the estimate of four million e-learners supplementing their campus-based courses in higher education institutions.)

Commercial Post-secondary Institutions

Particularly in the United States, but also in Malaysia, China, and India, there have been a number of attempts to develop private or commercial forms of e-learning in higher education. Although some of these new initiatives have been clearly successful in terms of sustainability and market penetration (for example, University of Phoenix Online, with 22,000 students in 2002–2003), others have been nothing short of a disaster. In particular, some very prestigious universities got it badly wrong in their attempts to cash in on the e-learning bonanza. Columbia University, New York University, Temple University, the University of Chicago, the University of Melbourne, and the UK Open University were all involved in operations that lost a minimum of US$10 million each in trying to set up for-profit e-learning operations. Thus the number of students in private e-learning universities is probably no more than 50,000 in 2002–2003 (mainly at the University of Phoenix Online and Jones International University).

Consortia

Also, e-learning consortia of public (and sometimes private) universities such as Western Governors University, Cardean, and Fathom seem too cumbersome to work. The numbers enrolled in 2002–2003 in such consortia (under 5,000 in total) are pitiful, given the publicity and level of investment. If we include some of the public university consortia, such as the Canadian Virtual University and NextEd in Asia, the total number is unlikely to exceed 50,000 enrolments, many of which will already be included in the figures for e-learners in dual-mode institutions.

Distance Universities

Autonomous distance education institutions are those that teach solely at a distance. These tend to be very large institutions operating on a national basis, often on an open-access basis. There are currently about fifty such universities globally with a total of over four million students worldwide (Daniel, 1998). Most are primarily print and broadcast based, but many have what the British Open University calls "Internet-enhanced courses." Thus there are many students (probably half a million) in these institutions using online teaching to supplement other forms of distance education, but the Open University of Catalonia in Spain is one of the few public universities dedicated to teaching entirely online. Thus the number of students studying entirely online in autonomous distance teaching universities in 2002–2003 is probably no more than 150,000. These students are quite widespread (for example, Spain, Britain, Mexico, India, China, and Canada) but few in the United States, which has very few autonomous distance teaching universities.

Corporate Training

The number of students in workplace and distant corporate training is another difficult figure to estimate. Meister (1998) stated that there were approximately two hundred genuine corporate universities, in the sense of offering in-house training. Some of these have several hundred thousand employees taking programs. However, many corporate university programs are primarily classroom-based. In addition, there are thousands of small training companies who offer online programs. For corporate training, a module may be as short as two minutes, so that counting "learner sessions" can be very misleading. The figure of four million is an estimate of the number of individuals who would have used e-learning as part of their employment in one year. Much more focused and detailed research is needed in this sector.

Thus, there appear to be about nine million e-learning course enrolments worldwide in post-secondary education and training (see table 12.1). This is a snapshot taken in 2003. I have tried to be conservative in estimating numbers, and will have missed many small e-learning education operations, so the actual numbers are probably higher. What I am concerned with, though, are the trends, and the relative size of the different categories of e-learning providers.

What has grown relatively rapidly over the past eight years is the use of e-learning both in company training and on university and college campuses, and I see this continuing. Fully online courses form a minority of all e-learning enrolments (probably less than 10 percent). Europe seems to be lagging behind the USA, Canada, Mexico, Australia, Singapore, and Korea in the application of e-learning in post-secondary education, although in the past few years some European countries (especially Britain, Scandinavia, and The Netherlands) have started to pick up speed.

Despite the pressure toward privatization in the United States, I do not see a rapid expansion in North America of private e-learning post-secondary institutions, as long as the public universities remain adequately funded. However, private e-learning universities and colleges such as the University of Phoenix Online will expand slowly. On the other hand, I anticipate that private sector university and college e-learning will grow rapidly in countries such as Mexico, Brazil, Chile, China, Malaysia, Korea, India, and other newly emerging economic powerhouses, where powerful and impatient middle classes are increasing faster than the provision of good-quality public sector post-secondary education. In poorer countries, and for the poor in rapidly developing countries, post-secondary e-learning will remain the

Table 12.1   Rough estimate of e-learners globally, 2002–2003

Higher education	
Web-supplemented classroom teaching (public)	4,000,000
Fully online (dual-mode)	250,000
For-profit online universities	50,000
Public and private consortia	50,000
Distance teaching universities	
Web-supplemented	500,000
Fully online	150,000
Corporate sector	
e-Learning in the workplace	4,000,000
Total	9,000,000

privilege of a small minority, and for such target groups the large public sector print and broadcast-based autonomous open universities will continue to be important.

PEDAGOGICAL ISSUES: A NEW PARADIGM OR OLD WINE IN NEW BOTTLES?

Is e-learning a fundamentally different approach to teaching and learning, as some have argued, or is it merely a more convenient and flexible way of teaching in the same manner as in a face-to-face situation? Does it lead to the automation of teaching, as Noble has claimed, or is it an emancipation of learners, freeing them from institutional constraints?

These are difficult questions to answer. The use of the web for teaching is still less than ten years old, and hence its application to teaching and learning is still evolving. As a result, there are few convincing evaluative studies based on student learning outcomes that allow for widespread generalization. Furthermore, the actual applications of e-learning are highly dependent on the way in which teachers choose to teach, and, above all, on their epistemological preferences. What is clear is that e-learning enables a wide range of approaches to teaching and learning to be accommodated. At the same time, greater attention or promotion has been given to certain teaching methods over others.

For instance, those teachers who take a more behaviorist approach can give students tasks that are broken down into small units of work. Using a course platform such as WebCT or Blackboard, each unit of activity can be accompanied by immediate feedback on the learner response. As Bates and Poole (2003) describe:

> Feedback can take the form of test results or automated responses, such as mouse clicks against the multiple choice answer options on the screen, accompanied by the words "correct" or "wrong," or sounds such as cheering or boos. Feedback can include remedial activities to be repeated until the student has mastery over the item (defined usually as 100% correct performance). The use of technology is particularly valued by behaviorists, as it allows for repetition, for "objective" assessment, and for tight control and management of the learning activities. (Bates and Poole, 2003: 199–200)

This is an example of the automation of teaching criticized by Noble. However, this form of teaching is mostly used in empirical sciences or engineering, and is also just as likely to be found in campus-based teaching, where graduate students act as the automated markers of multiple-choice tests. Bates and Poole (2003: 200) argue that:

teachers taking a more cognitive approach are more likely to give students activities, exercises and assignments that facilitate or test analysis or synthesis of learning materials, application of principles to real world examples, and an evaluation or a critique of different situations, viewpoints, or processes. Media can be particularly useful for providing student activities and exercises of this kind, since text or video can be used both to model and to test cognitive processing.

If comprehension is the main learning outcome, common student questions can be collected, and an area of the Web site created called "Frequently asked questions," with the response to the questions. This limits the number of one-on-one communications between student and instructor . . . Some course development software such as WebCT allows instructors through the use of tests to identify specific parts of the course where students are having difficulties.

However, these more objectivist approaches to teaching are not, in fact, the ones where the most interest has been shown in e-learning in colleges and universities. Bates and Poole (2003: 200–1) point out:

It is no co-incidence that online learning arrived at a point in time when constructivist approaches to teaching were at the height of their popularity (in North American higher education). For constructivists, reflection and discussion are key activities through which knowledge is constructed by the learner. The asynchronous nature of online teaching, enabling students to control to some extent the pace and timing of their learning, allows for and encourages reflection. Online forums provide the opportunity for students to test ideas, and build and construct knowledge through collaborative learning.

Most publications on moderating online discussion forums focus on helping learners to develop their own meanings of concepts and ideas presented in the course or offered by other learners (a constructivist approach to learning). Scardamalia and Bereiter (1999) and MacKnight (2001) provide some guidelines on facilitating critical thinking skills and knowledge construction online within school settings.

Another major trend in education is the move to problem-based learning, and this is an area where online learning has been used successfully. At the University of British Columbia, the Faculty of Medicine has moved entirely to a problem-based learning approach. In general, program content is provided entirely through the web and printed readings. Classroom time is used for developing clinical skills, laboratory work, and the setting, discussion, and analysis of problems. Students work on problems mainly online.

In some cases, the whole of a problem-based course is delivered online. For instance, two instructors at the University of British Columbia, Dr Niamh Kelly and Dr Elisabeth Bryce, have developed a fourth-year undergraduate course on microbial infections (Pathology 417). The course explores human bacterial infections focusing on both the virulence factors of the micro-organism and the patho-physiology of the host response. Students in small online groups work through case scenarios. The groups discuss each case, and answer questions posed to them by the instructors. Then the multiple groups share their answers with each other, after which the instructors give online feedback to the whole class on their answers. Students work to a tightly scheduled process, completing one problem set each week (see Bates and Poole, 2003, for further details).

Bates and Poole (2003: 236) also identify collaborative learning as a strength of e-learning:

> One great advantage of online learning is the opportunity for students separated by time and place to work together on a common task. Learning to work together online is an increasingly important work-place skill, but it also provides opportunities for students to share experiences, to learn how to work collaboratively, and to test and develop their own ideas, without being physically present. It is particularly valuable for courses where students are from different countries or cultures, and for continuing professional development, where participants have relevant professional experiences to share and draw from.

Market Demand

Electronic learning is also attractive to collections of individuals sharing similar interests who cannot or do not want to be attached to a particular institutional approach to teaching and learning. For instance, they may want to pick and choose courses from different institutions, or may not want to study for credit or formal qualification. They may wish to share professional experience with other professionals. They may have come together through an institutional course or program, but wish to continue their collective learning in an informal way (with or without a formal instructor). The aim here is to build a self-sustaining community of learners.

In particular, the area of continuing professional education is proving to be particularly appropriate for e-learning. For instance, the University of British Columbia has developed several graduate programs aimed at those who already have bachelor or even postgraduate degrees who need to update or develop new areas of expertise. Usually in partnership with another institution, the University of British Columbia has developed both postgraduate certificates (consisting of five one-semester online courses) and fully online masters degrees, where students can incorporate the certificate courses within the masters program. These programs have several distinct features that separate them from traditional graduate programs:

- they are aimed at working professionals who study part-time;
- students can take single courses, or combine five courses toward a certificate, or ten courses toward a masters degree;

- the courses are delivered globally, often with an international partner, and in two languages;
- the program is available almost entirely online;
- the students themselves contribute extensively to the knowledge base, through collaborative online discussion;
- there is no research dissertation, but the programs are often project-based, drawing on the experience of diverse professionals working collaboratively online;
- the courses are entirely self-funded through tuition fees, allowing the university to hire additional tenured faculty;
- the programs are self-sustainable because they meet a market demand.

Lastly, in a corporate training environment, e-learning may be used for "just-in-time" learning, allowing employees to develop skills as and when they need them. A typical example would be an employee wishing to develop a graph from an Excel data spreadsheet for a company presentation. The company has arranged with an external e-learning company access for its employees to short modules of training for Excel. Using a pre-assigned identification and password, the employee goes online and chooses a module on creating graphs, and has on-demand and continuous access to that module until mastery of the task is achieved.

Stability and Change

Returning, then, to the questions posed at the beginning of this section, e-learning in general does *not* change the fundamental processes of *learning*. Students need to read, observe, think, discuss, practice, receive feedback, be assessed, and accredited. These requirements are not changed by e-learning. Furthermore, e-learning does not really transform the traditional methods of face-to-face teaching. Indeed, face-to-face methods transfer very easily to technology. Information can be transmitted over the web probably more effectively and just as easily as in a lecture theater. Online discussion forums replicate most of the features of face-to-face seminars, although there are some losses, such as visual cues, and some gains, such as the opportunity for reflection before participating. Problem-based learning and project work can be just as easily replicated online as in class, with probably greater access to resources. Even a great deal of laboratory work can be simulated, at a cost.

In this sense, then, I do not share the view of Harasim et al. (1995) or Peters (2002) when they argue that e-learning is a "paradigm shift." Rather, it is old wine in new bottles, at least at present. But one needs to be careful here. Developments in computer-based expert systems, simulations, learning objects, virtual reality, and the vast resources available over the Internet, are likely to result in a greater emphasis on methods that are not so prevalent in face-to-face teaching, and may lead eventually to radically new formats for teaching.

As a result, there is already a shift to more project work and problem-based learning, the creation by students of multimedia projects and assignments, and more student choice in learning and the curriculum, through e-learning. Radically different ways of structuring learning materials may be developed to support new forms of learning, and innovative teachers will discover and create new methods of teaching that better exploit the potential of e-learning. E-learning opens up new markets for higher education; indeed, it is meeting needs in professional continuing education that have otherwise been largely ignored by universities. Nevertheless, the old methods have well served the basic processes of learning for over 800 years. It would be surprising if they disappeared entirely from e-learning applications, although they may be continuously adapted as the technology changes.

Where e-learning is having an effect is by facilitating and making more efficient or more effective the learning *process*. Electronic learning no more automates learning than traditional large classes and multiple-choice testing. What it can do, though, is to shift the balance of work from teacher to student. By providing self-controlled activities, student time on task can be increased. Electronic learning can provide more opportunities for practice, and more flexible access to a wider range of materials.

Electronic learning also enables teachers to offer alternative approaches to learning that suit the needs of different kinds of learners. It can offer access to resources that would not otherwise be available in a traditional classroom. Thus while not changing the fundamental ways in which students learn, e-learning can *add value* to the process of teaching and learning, by creating richer or more authentic learning environments, and by providing more options to meet individual needs in learning.

ORGANIZATIONAL ISSUES

Where e-learning *can* lead to fundamental change in education is in the *organization* of teaching. Electronic learning provides teachers and students with opportunities to organize teaching and learning in radically different ways. Neither teachers nor students have to be (always) present in the classroom. They can be freed from the requirement to be at a specific place at a specific time in order to teach or to study. Electronic learning allows for access to materials that would otherwise not be available in a classroom, and allows teachers and students to structure learning materials in a variety of ways. It enables different preferences for learning to be more easily accommodated, and makes it easier for part-time or working students to access learning. In particular, e-learning provides lifelong learners with a flexible and convenient way to continue to study and learn throughout their lives.

The biggest impact, though, is in the work organization of the teacher. There are many different ways in which a course can be developed and delivered. The choice of model will depend on the scale and complexity of the course, and the centrality of the use of technology. By far the most common model of e-learning course development is what I have called the "Lone Ranger" approach, after an old Hollywood cowboy film and subsequent television series (Bates, 2000). Teachers work on their own, usually using a course management system or platform such as WebCT or Blackboard. This fits well with the autonomy of the classroom teacher. Furthermore, Lone Rangers are essential for getting innovation started, for demonstrating the potential of technology for teaching, and for ensuring e-learning is used when there is no systematic support from the institution. Usually, Lone Rangers are dedicated teachers who put a great deal of time and effort into experimenting with technology for teaching. However, there are considerable limitations of the Lone Ranger approach to the use of e-learning. The main problems are workload and quality.

For a teacher to work alone, the Lone Ranger has to deal with all the activities associated with the use of technology, as well as choosing and organizing content and learner interaction. Consequently, the Lone Ranger model usually results in a great deal more work for the teacher compared with a regular face-to-face class. Furthermore, quality in teaching with technology requires expertise not just in content, but also in course or program planning, instructional design, media production, online moderating, student support, and course or program evaluation and maintenance. It is very difficult for teachers to become experts or even experienced in all these areas without their workload increasing to unsustainable levels. Therefore, a number of alternative approaches to the Lone Ranger model are being developed

Hartman and Truman-Davis (2001) describe the *boutique* approach to e-learning course development. A teacher approaches an instructional support unit for professional assistance on an individual, one-to-one basis from an instructional designer or technology support person. As Hartman and Truman-Davis (2001) explain, this is a satisfying experience for both teacher and support person and works well when there are relatively few instructors needing help. However, the model starts to become unsustainable as demand increases because of the resources needed. It causes particular difficulties for the instructional support unit or person, as there is no obvious way to determine priorities between multiple requests for help, and there is no boundary around the support commitment. Furthermore, because the teacher usually initiates the process, the wrong kind of assistance may be requested. For instance, the request may be limited to purely technical assistance, when what may be required is a different approach to course design for the technology to be used effectively. Nevertheless, the boutique model can be useful in helping individual teachers to get started in using technology in a systematic and professional way.

Another model that is beginning to emerge is the *collegial materials development* model. In this model, several teachers work collaboratively to develop e-learning materials. The teachers may be from the same department or from different departments in the same institution, or subject experts from different institutions. By working collaboratively, they can share ideas, jointly develop or share materials, and provide critical feedback to each other. In collegial materials development, each participant in the project is free to decide what materials to include in his or her own courses, and what materials to share with other colleagues. Often, the material is made public.

Another feature of collegial materials development is that rarely is a whole course produced. The focus is usually on developing materials that other teachers and students may find useful within their own courses. However, at some stage, even collegial development approaches are likely to reach a point where there is a need for more formal management of the process, some form of evaluation or peer review of the materials, and the need for professional design and graphics. At this point, a project management approach is needed.

Project management is common in creative media areas, especially where the project is complex, such as film and television production, advertising, video and computer games design, and also in many building, engineering, and information technology-based projects. Project development and delivery involves a team of individuals each contributing different skills, and the process is managed by a team leader or project manager. There is a defined set of resources, usually determined at the outset of the project, a timeline, and a clear "deliverable," that is, it is clear what the project has to achieve and it is obvious when it is completed. Project management has been used for many years in education for course development and delivery. However, it has tended to be restricted to distance teaching and educational television. Nevertheless, as the use of e-learning in regular teaching becomes more complex, project management will become increasingly important as a means of controlling workload and quality.

The decision whether to adopt a Lone Ranger, boutique, collegial materials development, or project management approach depends on a number of factors. The most critical are the size, complexity, and originality of a project, and the resources available. Thus, a teacher thinking of adding PowerPoint presentations to her classroom teaching will not need project management for this. However, if a whole course is to be delivered online and at a distance, or if a multimedia expert system is to be developed, or if a large lecture class is to be completely re-designed, then project management becomes essential. It is more difficult to determine whether mixed-mode courses, which combine a reduced face-to-face teaching load with substantive online learning, require a project management approach, but they would certainly benefit from collegial materials development. In general, though, the more important the role of e-learning becomes in a course, the more important it becomes to use a full project management approach.

Lastly, successful boutique, project management, and collegial materials development require access to resources, such as instructional designers, graphics designers, web programmers and, above all, someone who understands and is experienced in project management. Project management and collegial materials development therefore require a significant shift in management strategies and approaches to teaching, as well as resources dedicated to funding staff other than teachers. However, even a Lone Ranger can use many of the principles of project management when developing courses using e-learning.

LEARNER SUPPORT

Support for e-learners is perhaps the most important and least understood aspect of e-learning. Noble's fear of the automation of teaching has not proved a reality in most cases because, without adequate support for learners, programs collapse. Learner support covers a wide range of topics, but the most important are:

- marketing/course information;
- registration and tuition-fee payment;
- course admission/passwords/technical help;
- ordering and delivery of materials;
- online moderating;
- student counselling;
- student assessment and feedback.

With the possible exception of online moderating, these issues are not any different from those of regular campus-based learners where e-learning is merely used as a classroom aid. However, as the proportion of time devoted to e-learning compared with regular classroom teaching increases, then so does the importance of equivalent online learner support services. The more time students spend on e-learning, the more they need and expect other services, such as online admission and registration, online counselling, online payment of tuition fees, and online ordering of materials to be available. For students who study entirely online (that is, distance students), the provision of these services online becomes essential. This means that administrative systems need to change alongside teaching systems.

One of the big mistakes that many institutions made in setting up for-profit e-learning operations was to underestimate the importance and the resulting high cost of these learner support systems. This is particularly true with respect to online moderating. It is the ability of students to interact not only with a teacher but also with each other over time and distance that gives e-learning its pedagogical advantage. Experience and research have shown quite clearly that, for quality learning to take place in most subject areas, the ratio of teachers to students in online classes has to be carefully controlled and managed (see Salmon, 2000; Paloff and Pratt, 2001; Bates and Poole, 2003, for more on online moderating).

THE DIGITAL DIVIDE AND OTHER SOCIAL AND CULTURAL ISSUES

The same pattern of Internet development found in economically advanced countries seems to be spreading to other less economically developed countries. The first locations are institutional, in universities, large multinational companies, and select areas of government, such as the military and ministries. Services then spread to community centers, schools, and public cybercafés, smaller companies, and local government. At the same time, home access is gradually increasing, initially in the homes of the more wealthy, then spreading to middle-income and, later, relatively low-income homes. The very poor, though, may never get access at home. In Canada, only 32 percent of homes with incomes in the lowest quartile used the Internet, compared with 87 percent in the highest income quartile (Statistics Canada, 2003). Access to the Internet, then, will spread, and high speed access will increase. The only question is the rate at which this will happen, and this will depend primarily on economic factors in different countries.

The post-secondary sector tends to be more privileged with regard to Internet access, with universities often being pioneers within a country for providing access for students on campus. It is difficult to separate cause and effect with regard to the digital divide. The digital divide can be seen as yet another manifestation of inequalities between the rich and the poor. Indeed, a comparison of Canada with the United States suggests that where the wealth gap is wider, so is the digital gap. However, it is a moot point as to whether the Internet increases or reduces inequalities in itself. What is clear is that strong policies at governmental level can help reduce some of the digital divide by ensuring that schools and local community centers enable all students to have access to the Internet, irrespective of home conditions. Post-secondary institutions, in particular, can play an essential role in developing countries in providing at least a presence in the information society.

Although a great deal of attention is given to the digital divide in educational circles, less attention has been paid to other social and cultural issues. An OECD study (2001) noted the trend toward private and public partnerships in managing the costs and complexity of e-learning in the face of global competition, and raised questions about the public interest of such partnerships. The potential also for cultural imperialism and economic exploitation is high when programs emanating from more economically advanced countries start attracting the more wealthy students from less-developed countries. For instance, students from some countries find the approach to learning based on social constructivism alien, at least initially, compared to more traditional teacher-focused and information-based courses offered in their own country. Thus, as well as the disadvantage of working in a second language, students from foreign countries also have to overcome cultural barriers to learning online. Nevertheless, for many students in less-developed countries, the prestige and opportunities to learn from well-established Western institutions without the cost of leaving home more than compensate for the extra difficulty. (For more on the cultural issues of international e-learning programs, see Bates and Escamilla de los Santos, 1997; Mason, 1998; and *Distance Education*, 2001, vol. 22, no. 1: the whole edition is devoted to this topic.)

CONCLUSIONS

Underlying this debate is the critical issue of who benefits most from e-learning. As access to computers and the Internet is not equal, and because students differ in their learning needs, it is important not to treat e-learning as a panacea for post-secondary education. It is a useful method that serves some groups better than others. It is particularly appropriate for students who need to work and study at the same time. This might include students who have to work part-time to cover living costs or tuition fees, and especially lifelong learners who have families and jobs, and have probably already been through a conventional state higher education institution once already. It is also appropriate for students in rural areas or areas without good local post-secondary education institutions. It is appropriate for employees who need to learn continually in the workplace.

Electronic learning is less appropriate for immature students, for students unable or unready to learn independently, and for students in need of close and personal interaction with other students (although an introduction to e-learning under controlled conditions is probably beneficial even for this group of students). In particular, given the cost of developing and sustaining high-quality e-learning, governments and institutions need to pay careful attention to cost–benefit analysis. For some groups, more conventional educational provision may be a better investment; while for others, e-learning will be the best option.

There is certainly strong pressure, particularly from some American interests, to commercialize post-secondary education, and e-learning was seen as a major means by which this could be achieved. The initial optimism around this strategy crashed with the dot-com bust of 2001, although it is unlikely that pressure to use e-learning to privatize higher education will disappear.

Electronic learning can and perhaps should change the nature of teaching and the relationship between teacher and learner in post-secondary education, but to date its applications in general have been quite conservative, replicating, either virtually or at a distance, many of the traditionally valued approaches to teaching, such as seminars, testing, and searching, analyzing, and applying information. However, as the technology improves, allowing for both synchronous and asynchronous interaction, video as well as text, and as instructors begin to understand the power and potential of e-learning, it is likely that we will see new and more powerful approaches to teaching and learning emerging.

This is unlikely to happen, though, without some fundamental changes in the way in which faculty work. The technology raises the skill requirements of faculty, and, in particular, successful applications of e-learning depend on harnessing the skills of other professionals, such as instructional designers and media producers. This means that faculty will need to pay more attention to instructional design and to teamwork if they are to use e-learning cost-effectively.

Lastly, e-learning has suffered as much from over-exaggeration of its benefits as it has from fear and resistance to change in very conservative institutions. Nevertheless, there is growing evidence that e-learning is a useful tool for post-secondary education, as long as it is used with skill and discrimination.

REFERENCES

Allen, I. E. and Seaman, J. (2003) *Sizing the Opportunity: The Quality and Extent of Online Education in the United States, 2002 and 2003*. Wellesley, MA: The Sloan Consortium.

Bartolic-Zlomislic, S. and Bates, A. (1999) "Investing in Online Learning: Potential Benefits and Limitations," *Canadian Journal of Communication* 24: 349–66.

Bates, A. W. (2000) *Managing Technological Change: Strategies for College and University Leaders*. San Francisco: Jossey-Bass.

— — and Escamilla de los Santos, J. (1997) "Crossing Boundaries: Making Global Distance Education a Reality," *Journal of Distance Education* 12 (1/2): 49–66.
— — and Poole, G. (2003) *Effective Teaching with Technology in Higher Education: Foundations for Success*. San Francisco: Jossey-Bass.
COIMBRA Group of Universities (2002) *European Union Policies and Strategic Change for e-Learning in Universities* (HECTIC Report). Brussels: European Commission (available at: http://www.flp.ed.ac.uk/HECTIC/HECTICREPORT .PDF).
Collis, B. (1996) *Tele-learning in a Digital World*. London: International Thomson Computer Press.
Cunningham, S. (2000) *The Business of Borderless Education*. Canberra: Commonwealth of Australia, Department of Education, Training and Youth Affairs.
Daniel, J. (1998) *Mega-universities and Knowledge Media: Technology Strategies for Higher Education*. London: Kogan Page.
Dirr, P. (2001) "The Development of New Organizational Arrangements in Virtual Learning," in G. Farrell (ed.), *The Changing Faces of Virtual Education*. Vancouver, BC: The Commonwealth of Learning.
Harasim, L., Hiltz, S., Teles, L., and Turoff, M. (1995) *Learning Networks: A Field Guide to Teaching and Learning Online*. Cambridge, MA: MIT Press.
Hartman, J. and Truman-Davis, B. (2001) "The Holy Grail: Developing Scalable and Sustainable Support Solutions," in C. Barone and P. Hagner (eds), *Technology-enhanced Teaching and Learning*. San Francisco: Jossey Bass.
Jonassen, D., Davidson, M., Collins, M., Campbell, J., and Haag, B. (1995) "Constructivism and Computer-mediated Communication in Distance Education," *American Journal of Distance Education* 9 (2): 7–26.
MacKnight, C. (2001) "Supporting Critical Thinking in Interactive Learning Environments," in C. Maddux and D. Lamont Johnson (eds), *The Web in Higher Education*, pp. 17–32. Binghamton, NY: The Haworth Press.
Mason, R. (1998) *Globalising Education: Trends and Applications*. London: Routledge.
Meister, J. (1998) *Corporate Universities*. Columbus, OH: McGraw-Hill.
Moore, C. and Jones, M. (2001) "Comdex: E-Learning Takes Stage as Next Killer App.," *InfoWorld*, November 15 (http://archive.infoworld.com/articles/hn/xml/ 01/11/15/011115hnelearnmantra.xml).
Noble, D. (1997) *Digital Diploma Mills, Part I: The Automation of Higher Education* (http://communication.ucsd.edu/dl/ddm1.html).
— — (1998a) *Digital Diploma Mills, Part II: The Coming Battle over Online Instruction* (http://communication.ucsd.edu/dl/ddm2.html).
— — (1998b) *Digital Diploma Mills, Part III: The Bloom is off the Rose* (http://communication.ucsd.edu/dl/ddm3.html).
— — (1999) *Digital Diploma Mills, Part IV: Rehearsal for the Revolution* (http://communication.ucsd.edu/dl/ddm4.html).
— — (2001) *Digital Diploma Mills, Part V: Fool's Gold* (http://communication. ucsd.edu/ dl/ddm5.html).
OECD (2001) *E-Learning: The Partnership Challenge*. Paris: OECD.
— — (2004) *E-Learning Case Studies in Post-secondary Education and Training*. Paris: OECD.
Paloff, R. and Pratt, K. (2001) *Lessons from the Cyberspace Classroom*. San Francisco: Jossey-Bass.

Peters, O. (2002) *Distance Education in Transition*. Oldenburg, Germany: Biblioteks-
und informationssystem der Universität Oldenburg.

Rosenberg, M. J. (2001) *e-Learning*. New York: McGraw-Hill.

Salmon, G. (2000) *E-Moderating*. London: Kogan Page.

Scardamalia, M. and Bereiter, C. (1999) "Schools as Knowledge-building
Organizations," in D. Keating and C. Hertzman (eds), *Today's Children, Tomorrow's
Society: The Developmental Health and Wealth of Nations*, pp. 274–89. New York:
Guilford Press.

Senge, P. (1990) *The Fifth Discipline: The Art and Practice of the Learning
Organization*. New York: Doubleday.

Statistics Canada (2003) (http://www.statcan.ca/english/Pgdb/arts56a.htm).

Twigg, C. (2001) "Quality Assurance for Whom? Providers and Consumers in Today's
Distributed Learning Environment." New York: The Pew Learning and Technology
Program, Rensselaer Polytechnic Institute (available at: http://www.
center.rpi.edu/PewSym/mono3.html).

Wilson, M., Qayyum, A., and Boshier, R. W. (1998) "World Wide America: Think
Globally, Click Locally," *Distance Education* 19 (1): 109–23.

13. e-health networks and social transformations: expectations of centralization, experiences of decentralization

James E. Katz, Ronald E. Rice, and Sophia K. Acord

We subtitled our edited volume, *Internet and Health Communication* (Rice and Katz, 2001), "Experience and Expectations" to suggest that, by reflecting on early experiences with e-health, leaders in academic research and healthcare planning might have more temperate expectations. In this chapter, we reverse the order of the terms, identifying not only where historical expectations concerning e-health have been fulfilled but also where they have missed the mark, and suggesting areas where additional progress might make the strongest contributions to public and individual health.

The chapter is organized around four analytical themes, all of which stem from the fact that the Internet has given a large portion of the general public and most healthcare professionals an opportunity to gain medical and health information and communication resources. Anticipatory of and reactive to the opportunity that is created by the social interaction between health information technology and participant desires, (1) there has been substantial resource commitment, resulting in the creation of many useful centralized services (some commercial, some governmental); (2) however, despite their utility, perceived and actual inadequacies of these services have stimulated disparate groups to organize their own compensatory, decentralized and local networks of health information resources. In both centralized and decentralized Internet health resources, though, there are still many issues to be resolved, such as (3) reconfiguring physician/patient relationships in the light of new technology, and (4) creating socially sensitive e-health services that are also socially equitable in terms of accessibility.

Each of the above four analytical themes implies both an original problem, which gives rise to specific forms of Internet use, and subsequently to contradictions, which suggest potential, often novel, solutions. A reciprocal consideration, then, is to examine some of the ways in which people try to use the Internet to serve their own needs, and how, when doing so, they bump against the logic and vested interests of health institutions and information systems. Hence, we strive to locate structural constraints that, if successfully addressed, could improve e-health systems in networked societies.

Inescapable questions underlie these themes. First is the inherent bureaucratic logic of one-way information flow. This logic governs traditional relations of healthcare organizations with their clients (as it does in other topical domains as well), even as these operations are extended to their online operations. Further, as this process unfolds, it often includes within it a market logic of packaging information for profit. This packaging is sometimes done in ways that are anything but clear to the consumer. Second, to survive, organizations must attend to their vested interests. These yield some inherent limitations for organizations. Moreover, the specific area of health is further complicated by considerations of (and conflicts among stakeholders over) value orientations toward the rules governing commercial free speech, access to markets, legal and medical regulations, and effectively informing, protecting, and enabling patients as well as physicians and other healthcare workers. Thus, responses to identified problems that do not address these limitations are unlikely to be viable.

Before delving into the themes, we should mention our perspective, which we dub "syntopian" (Katz and Rice, 2002). The syntopian perspective rejects both dystopian and utopian perspectives on the social uses and consequences of information and communication technology. Rather, it emphasizes how people use and reinvent (Johnson and Rice, 1987; Katz, 1999, 2003; Rice and Gattiker, 2000) technologies to make meaning for themselves relative to others. Hence, while possibilities are limited by the nature of the given technological tools, systems and their uses are (potentially) surprisingly flexible. Thus technology becomes altered by individual needs and social contexts. The perspective also highlights that the internal logic of both formal organizational systems and personal social systems are fully extensible to the Internet (Castells, 2000). Finally, although we do cite examples from many countries, most of our analysis focuses on the United States.

The following sections place our four analytic themes within the context of the growing magnitude and intensity of Internet use in the US for medical and health information.

A POPULAR SOURCE OF HEALTHCARE INFORMATION

The Internet makes it much easier for people to seek health information and become more competent concerning their own healthcare (Hardey, 1999). As early as 1997, in what appears to be the first national random survey comparing users to non-users regarding healthcare, 41 percent of US Internet users had gone online to access healthcare information resources (Aspden and Katz, 2001). By 2002, surveys commonly reported that in the region of 60 percent of online users in America have sought healthcare resources on line, notably for other people besides themselves (Pew, 2002). (Some research, however, suggests that this percentage is exaggerated; for example Tu and Hargraves, 2003.)

Table 13.1 shows the percentage distribution of the US population in terms of Internet use, and various types of medical and health information seeking behaviors, in 1997, 2000, and 2002. Over half of the population uses the Internet; of that half, two-thirds use it to seek healthcare information, with perhaps one out of 20 using it for that purpose within any given day. Clearly, then, at least in the US, the populace has embraced the online world as an important health resource. Those with more education are dispropor-tionately more likely to be health seekers than just Internet users. Concerning race, whites and "other" use the Internet more than blacks, but are even greater health information seekers than Hispanics and blacks.

Table 13.1   *Use of the Internet and Internet healthcare resources by the US public, 1997–2002*

Date	All respondents (%)	Internet users (%)			
	Internet user	Ever seek online health info	Sought online health info yesterday	Ever go to health websites	Went to health website yesterday
December 2002	57	66	6	54	4
September 2002	59	62	6	47	5
June 2000	47	55	5	36	3
November 1997	30	41	n.a.	n.a.	n.a.

Health website = a site that provides information or support for specific conditions or personal situations.

Source: Katz and Aspden (2001); Pew Internet and American Life Project (2003b)

Those with higher income are more likely to be Internet users, and more likely to be health seekers.

People with a specific question or issue they need addressing are often motivated to access the web for health information. One study found that 77 percent of patients did this (Boston Consulting Group, 2001). Understandably, people engage in wide-ranging search behavior in order to meet these specific aims (Malin, 2002). In 2001, 65 percent of health seekers used general search engines and banner ads to find information, 24 percent used general health portals, and 11 percent used disease-specific websites (Boston Consulting Group, 2001). Whether searching for more information on clinical diagnoses or alternative treatments, 80 percent of health seekers say that they found most or all of the information they were looking for the last time they logged on (Pew, 2002). Of those in the September 2002 survey ($n = 2092$ respondents, 1318 Internet users) who do seek healthcare information online, 58 percent reported that they would first go online for reliable healthcare information, while 35 percent said they would first contact a medical professional. Percentages for all Americans were 31 percent turning to the Internet and 59 percent contacting a medical professional.

We will now turn to our four analytical themes to explore the issues and conundrums regarding healthcare in a network society.

THEME 1: CENTRALIZED ONLINE VENTURES HAVE STRENGTHS, BUT THEIR WEAKNESSES CREATE NEEDS FOR SELF-ORGANIZED LOCAL SYSTEMS

Centralization Failures

Centralized medical initiatives dominated the early Internet expectations for health resources. Government resources such as Healthfinder.com, academically oriented databases such as The National Library of Medicine's PubMed for Medline, · commercial offerings such as drkoop.com or Pointcastnetwork.com, institutional sites such as the Healthscout or American Medical Association, and search engines such as the Medical World Search all had an early presence online. Those centralized sources that have survived play an important role in distributing quality health information. Indeed, their technological infrastructures make health seeking accessible to the larger population, and a bridge to span various digital divides. They also have the strategic location, if not the resources, to engage in vigorous website certification and verification roles for quality information. Medical documents that were conventionally out of reach in terms of patient access and circulation are now being made accessible by the Internet. For example, Wikgren (2001) found that the bulk of citations in discussion group postings came from abstracts of professional journals, such as the Medline database.

However, despite the fact that centralized sources could (and in many cases do) provide up-to-date and individualized assistance, too often they do not. Few take advantage of website certification services. Varieties of helpful services, which are technologically feasible, are also often not available from leading institutions of centralized medical care (discussed below). Despite the impressive promise of Internet technology, substantial numbers of these top-down initiatives have been weak (though many have valuable and timely information and have been a success). For instance, a surprising number of sites have out-of-date or misleading information; and many of those that do not are but little visited, which often means closure. Six factors may account for poor performance.

- Nonprofit, centralized sources may not be widely promoted to the relevant audiences – online or offline. Sigouin and Jadad (2002) studied cancer patients, their general practitioners, and all oncologists and oncology nurses at the Hamilton Regional Cancer Center in Ontario. They found that few patients were aware of local, official cancer information websites (3 percent) or Medline (13 percent). While oncologists reported high levels of awareness, less than a third of family practitioners had used any online sources other than Medline.
- To use centralized sources, training is often required. Even if users of systems do not require training, they invariably have to face a learning curve. Further complicating matters is the fact that different protocols are usually required for each e-health resource. For instance, Surgerydoor.com (a British commercial health website) offers a specialized search engine linked to high-quality medical information. However, Williams et al. (2002) note that even deft users had difficulty using it as they were accustomed to generic search engines.
- Old habits die hard. Bamford et al. (2003) implemented a country-wide network of physician webcams throughout 35 histopathology departments in the UK. A year after installation, they found that 71 percent had not been used, due to the physicians' excessive workloads and IT staff reluctance, but above all, because of negative attitudes toward the technology. Technology in general, and centralized systems in particular, do not seem to fit in with the "social side" of how people – whether physicians, nurses, technicians, administrators, or patients – gain and evaluate health information and participate in medical service (Rice, 2004).
- While centralized sources use peer-reviewed literature, which tends to have the highest quality, this literature is also the most difficult to read.

As a partial solution, Till (2003) proposes that "e-prints" be marked by commissioned reviews as well as unsolicited comments.

- Centralized sources lack local representation. Mendelson and Salinsky (1997) found that the failure of many community health management information systems (CHMIS) (similar to CHINS or community health information networks) was due to the lack of local and private sector support for integrated, state-wide systems.

- Centralized sources often lack emotional, personalized, and subjective aspects. Many potential users want this quality.

Commercialization of Health Websites

Much of the health information on the Internet is commercialized, either directly or indirectly. Most patients end up using commercial web-health portals such as WebMD.com for information, followed by other commercial and pharmaceutical sites. Many fewer patients go to educational and academic sites (Boston Consulting Group, 2003). Suarez-Almazor et al. (2001) searched for "rheumatoid arthritis" using WebCrawler, a popular search engine. Of the 388 unique and functioning websites out of the 537 returned hits, 51 percent were posted by a for-profit industry, one-third carried educational (nonprofit or university) sponsorship, and 17 percent were posted by an individual.

Although some people may judge the quality of online health information based on nontraditional or even misleading criteria such as a commercial brand or logo (Eysenbach and Kohler, 2002), other users may even be unaware of the commercial aspects of a health site. The late 1990s' revelation that the drkoop.com site, founded by the former Surgeon General of the US, failed to disclose financial ties and the fact that hospitals paid to be listed on the site, led to the resignation of its executive team, as well as a plummet in its market capitalization (Charatan, 1999a, b, 2000; the site has now closed entirely). More generally, those who report reading online commercial health information are more likely to report reading unreliable health information; thus, overt commercialism may be a turn-off to health seekers (Aspden and Katz, 2001).

Commercial health sites are, indeed, noticeably different from nonprofit or governmental sites. A content analysis of commercial and government health website features found that academic materials, search methods and tools, and topic headings were more frequently available on government than on commercial sites, while commercial health websites provided more interactivity among users, such as chat rooms and newsgroups (Rice et al., 2001). Street and Rimal (1997) note that the interactivity of the Internet provides a modicum of control to users; they can modify content and respond to prior actions and other participants, for example. A more radical form that this interaction can take may be shown in the case of MedicineOnline.com, which even offers an auction service in which patients can elicit physician bids for surgeries (Baur et al., 2001). More typical is HealthCentral.com, which allows users to create their own health profiles and provide personal feedback (Allen, 1999). However, such interactive websites are not without problems.

One particularly sensitive area is that of privacy. An online pharmacy, drugstore.com, sold information it collected from visitors to its website to a pharmaceutical marketing company. Thus, if someone purchased or asked about drug X from drugstore.com, that person might find herself solicited or "couponed" by the maker of drug Y, a competitor of drug X. The web company drkoop.com sold, as part of its bankruptcy liquidation, some of the personal information about site visitors that it had collected. These data included personal medical and financial information on many consumers who collected or shared information via interactive chat rooms or used interactive tools for searching the web (Health Data Management, 2003).

Other types of e-health privacy abuses are more subtle. Companies including Doubleclick.com and Amazon.com work with their partner sites to collect individually identifiable data on web surfers through "cookies," which serve to draw ever-more precise pictures of an Internet user. So, for instance, a surfer who reads an Amazon.com review about a book on depression and later clicks on a bulletin about a Hollywood star's suicide could potentially have data on his book-buying and news-reading habits, his name, address, and phone number, and much else besides, sold to a life insurance company (who might cancel his policy), a drug marketer (who would send him product solicitations), or even a cemetery (offering "pre-planning"). The more participating sites a user visits, the more detailed and inter-related becomes the personal portrait. Privacy-abusive practices are disturbing to privacy advocates, and alarming to e-health seekers, and in some cases are deterring surfers from using Internet resources. Ultimately, these practices could erode the ability of the Internet to provide services to precisely those who would most benefit from the web.

Quality of Online Health Information

The prospect of easily accessible, high-quality health information was another early appeal of the Internet. The hope was that, by having quality certification (such as is offered by the "Health on the Net" [HON] Foundation [www.hon.ch], created in 1995), users would patronize certified cites, and inaccurate medical information or practices would be disputed and diminished. Yet researchers consistently find problems with the quality of online health information, in commercial sites as well as discussion lists, usenet newsgroups, and online support groups (Kassirer, 1995; Jadad and Gagliardi, 1998; Consumers International, 2003).

Eysenbach et al.'s (2002) analysis found that the quality of information on the web was noted as a problem in 70 percent of the articles reviewed, while the 9 percent of articles that did not indicate a problem scored significantly lower in search and evaluation methodology. Internet health and medical information, Eysenbach et al. conclude, deviates from recognized safety standards, is seldom updated, does not offer advice on avoiding drug interactions, and promotes unconventional medicine (see also Rice, 2001; Currò et al., 2003). Veronin (2002) collected data in 1998–9 on 184 websites with health information, and attempted to assess the same sites in 2002. By then, the majority of the original sites (59 percent) had disappeared, one in six (17 percent) had moved to a new URL address, and only about a quarter (24 percent) of the sites could be found from their original URLs. Of the 45 websites still in existence at their original locations, only a minority (38 percent) provided information that was updated from the original posting. Rose et al. (1998) noted that of 5,947 retrieved pages in a search for fever in young children, only 7 percent were actually relevant to the condition. Wikgren (2001) found that no health-oriented personal home pages offered citations of references to other sources of data. In an online survey of 800 web-using doctors in the UK (94 percent response rate), only 20 percent believed Internet health information to be "usually" or "sometimes" (48 percent) reliable (Potts and Wyatt, 2002).

The high ideals of the initial claims about improved online health information have also struggled as ludicrous health conspiracy theories and implausible "alternative" health sites thrive. To cite but one recent study demonstrating the problem, physicians analyzed 443 popular websites involving the eight most widely used herbal products. Of those, 273 sites boasted health claims for the herbs. The majority of those (149) held that these products could "treat, prevent, diagnose or cure specific diseases." Moreover, 39 percent of the 62 kava retail sites made no mention of a US Food and Drug Administration (FDA) advisory connecting that herb to liver toxicity (Morris and Avorn, 2003: 1506).

Yet users overall tend to be quite positive, or, possibly, quite unaware of accuracy and validity criteria. While 28 percent of health seekers note that they have seen some bad information, 69 percent report seeing no wrong or misleading data online (Pew, 2002). And although 73 percent of health seekers say they have rejected data at some time or another, 72 percent of health seekers think that "almost all" or "most" of the health information they find on the Internet is credible, a 20 percent rise from 2000 (Pew, 2000, 2002). Clearly, then, many Internet offerings are fraught with problems of quality and conflict of interest. At the same time, consumers seem to prefer the empty promises over the careful, limited (and limiting) offerings available through careful and conservative systems of that involve hierarchies of approval, peer review, evaluations of conflicts of interest, and re-verification.

As noted above, there were many enthusiastic expectations about the provision of health information through centralized and commercial Internet websites, and indeed such sites have many advantages. We can ask how much difference these technologies are actually making in practical terms. One way to assess this is to ask if they allow providing organizations to be more efficient. If one considers samplings of success stories from hospitals and medical practices, the answer would clearly be that, if the innovations are well considered and implemented, they save money for the practitioner and the supporting organization (Landro, 2003). Does it make a difference in terms of quality of care for the patient? The answer would seem to be, in many cases, yes. The information resources of the Internet have enabled many to find solutions to their needs and take greater responsibility for their health. (This conclusion is supported by anecdotal as well as survey data of both health-seekers and physicians as shown below.) There is much to be proud of in this record of achievement.

However, despite enormous progress on the technological front, most large, high-quality sites still fall far short of what might be offered that would serve the needs and convenience of patients qua individuals. A review of major sites shows that, while they have much that benefits patient-clients, they remain incomplete successes since they have not offered a wide variety of possible services. As table 13.2 shows, despite the fact that some of these premier sites have seemingly interactive features, most have not addressed users' needs for more social interaction with healthcare providers (which, in turn, would also increase the burdens on the care providers). As this is the situation not only for

Table 13.2   Comparison of features of Internet patient decision-support tools of some leading providers

	Patient video interviews	Online social or community network support tools	Offers user-specific outcomes data	Free public access on the web
FIMDM	No	No	No	Subscribers only
CHESS	Yes	Yes	No	Limited to consortium member groups
NexCura	No	No	Yes	Access through co-branded partner site; registration required
DIPEx	Yes	No	No	Yes
MayoClinic.com	Yes	No	No	Yes

Source: Adapted from Schwitzer (2002)

the identified sites, but is characteristic of centralized e-health services generally, it is understandable (as the next section argues) that users have applied and reinvented features of the Internet to try to resolve some of these problems themselves. That is, the Internet has provided the potential for self-organization among many kinds of social networks, especially along the lines of personal and group identities.

THEME 2: STRAIN TOWARD SELF-ORGANIZATION

Online Support Group Communities

Groups and networks of interacting participants use technology to decentralize health information and unite global networking and information flow with the human experience of their own illness or suffering (Izenberg and Lieberman, 1998, cited in Napoli, 2001). The developing complex network society is one in which distant, global edges are combined with many local, organizational clusters (Castells, 2000: 369). Networking thus becomes a self-organizing human activity, as health seeking is based primarily upon information sharing and development (Wellman, 1995).

The Internet has the capabilities to support virtual health communities (Wynn and Katz, 1997; Patsos, 2001; Katz and Rice, 2002). Such communities (as well as mediated relationships between physicians and patients, discussed in the following section) possibly represent a transforming relationship between lay and medical knowledge (Hardey, 2001, 2002; Loader et al., 2002). Such communities are particularly useful for patients with rare diseases, as these people are by definition relatively few in number; they are usually also dispersed geographically, lack specialized care or even acceptance in their local environment. Social distance offers the opportunity for having expertise available while (seeming) anonymity reduces the reluctance to discuss sensitive topics; these, of course, are characteristics of the Internet, which enable users to manage their interactions with respect to expressiveness and stigma. Access is readily available at any time and from many places (Rice, 2001). As a quick illustration of these processes in action, we note that individuals with depression, diabetes mellitus (a gastrointestinal disorder), or a gynecological condition were more likely to use online groups than those suffering from other illnesses (Millard and Fintak, 2002).

Centralized medicine typically works to treat the individual patient, often ignoring the suffering or therapeutic contributions of their loved ones. Online websites and support groups provide information, support, acceptance, and a sense of real-time understanding to patients and their families and friends (Wellman, 1995; Till, 2003), and, in conjunction with physical communities, apply cultural or generational norms and customs (Burhansstipanov et al., 2001; Hanson et al., 2002). Empathy is stronger in online support and patient groups, especially in moderated ones, than in other kinds of discussion groups (Preece and Ghozati, 2001). As many online support groups are peer-moderated rather than professionally moderated, Till (2003) suggests that veteran members or survivors often function as tacit but highly effective peer navigators. Partially because of the lack of moderation by medical experts, however, Culver et al. (1997: 471) concluded that online support groups are a mixture of "snake oil" and "self-help," preventing appropriate diagnosis and treatment (see Rice, 2001).

Aspden and Katz (2001) note that 73 percent of health seekers discuss their Internet information with others. For example, online users report medical data from the *Journal of the American Medical Association* and Medline to each other as persuasive techniques in support groups (Wikgren, 2001). Paterniti et al. (1999) evaluated postings on breast cancer-focused computer bulletin board systems, and found that participants discussed strategies for health seeking and worked together to make decisions on clinical recommendations and treatment options. Sharf (1997) studied an online breast-cancer discussion group and concluded that it was a powerful force in information exchange, social support, and personal empowerment.

While support groups appear to heal the soul and feed the mind, there is some evidence about the crucial question of whether they help to heal the body as well. While, at most, only 9 percent of health seekers have participated in an online support group of any sort, those that have do report notable benefits (Celio et al., 2000; McKay et al., 2001; Pew, 2002). These benefits may include reductions in depression, cancer-related trauma, and perceived stress; these were the benefits that accrued among 72 women with primary breast carcinoma participating in a 12-week web-based support group (Winzelberg et al., 2003). McKay et al. (2001) found that patients taking part in an online diabetes education and support group saw their blood glucose levels lowered more than those in the control group. Likewise, in a randomized controlled trial, participants in a back pain e-mail discussion group noted significant improvements in pain, disability, role function, and health distress, compared to a control group (Lorig et al., 2002). In a controlled experiment comparing Internet and classroom-delivered psychoeducational interventions for eating disorders, Celio et al. (2000) found that measures of body image and eating disorders were significantly reduced in the Internet group in comparison to the classroom group. These studies suggest that the Internet is not only an equal to face-to-face support groups, but may produce beneficial and unique results. Overall, online support groups had some benefits not found in face-to-face relations, including seeming anonymity, which moderated inhibitions toward discussing sensitive topics, and around-the-clock access (Rice, 2001).

Taking Care of One's Own Care

Whereas centralized top-down Internet based initiatives have not delivered as promised, localized applications have indeed produced successful results. The Internet can be used not only to find new health information, but also to disseminate health knowledge to monitor conditions. Using the Interactive Multimedia Program for Asthma Control and Tracking, patients saw their asthma symptom days decrease from 81 to 51 a year, and their emergency room visits decrease from an annual mean of 1.93 to 0.62 (Krishna et al., 2003).

In another example, patients with access to their medical records primarily used the system to review their laboratory results, resulting in enhanced under-standing on the part of the patients and improved communication with their physicians (Cimino et al., 2001). These expert-run cases of health seeking on the Internet seem successful because they are based on the self-service and convenience aspects that empower patients (93 percent of health seekers value convenience according to the Pew 2000 survey), while providing quality infor-mation. (There are also manifold reports of abuse and exploitation via these technologies as well, however.)

Thus, users are accessing the Internet not only to obtain health information that they could not otherwise easily obtain, but also to create contexts for social interaction, empathy, and emotional support. As with other human activ-ities, this self-organization has both benefits and disadvantages. Among the disadvantages is the tremendous amount of mis-information, disinformation, and duplicity that is propagated by these unregulated forums. However, due to their many advantages, it remains likely that online interfaces between the centralized and decentralized, such as between physicians and patients, could possibly become valuable sites for transforming social relations in the pursuit of health.

THEME 3: EXPECTING/RESISTING TRANSFORMATIONS OF PHYSICIAN/PATIENT RELATIONSHIPS

As part of the widening use of the Internet for obtaining information, and, as we noted above, communicating with other patients and supporters, patients are also pushing for online communication with their physicians. Some 90 percent of Americans would like to be able to contact their physician online or by e-mail, and 40 percent of respondents would be willing to pay for this service (CyberAtlas, 2002). Indeed, 26 percent of medical practices were engaging in online communication with patients in 2001, with another 13 percent planning to start in the following 18 months (Harris Interactive, 2001).

The incursion into centralized care by a decentralized medium has the potential to affect social relations among multiple stakeholders. Anderson et al. (2003), in a study of unsolicited patient e-mails at a university dermatological hospital, observed that, over time, the tenor of e-mail content shifted from patients' self-perception as passive recipients of medical care to active consumers and demanders of health information. Anderson et al. (2003) attribute this shift to at least four factors.

- Both patients and physicians perceive greater dissatisfaction with medical services due to the limited time patients have with physicians. In all, 93 percent of physicians believe that many serious problems could be avoided with more discussion, according to a 1997 Harris study. However, 67 percent of the same physicians note that not having enough time to spend with patients is a very serious problem (cited in Rice, 2001). Hence, the Internet may provide a way to increase communication with one or more medical sources.
- People feel the cost-saving pressures of healthcare plans, and thus take quality control into their own hands. Surveys suggest that about 43 percent of US adults are not satisfied with their doctor's accessibility, while the Internet is available around the clock, every day (Reents and Miller, 1998, cited in Anderson et al., 2003).
- Increasingly, legal and ethical standards require patients to make informed choices. Yet it is difficult for them to be as informed as they wish. For instance, in a 2002 survey of Canadian cancer patients, only 54 percent who wanted information about their disease felt that they had obtained an adequate amount of information from their healthcare providers (Chen and Siu, 2001). Given this perceived need, many will be turning to the Internet in order to meet their information needs as well as their perceived responsibilities.
- There is simply a new wealth of accessible and inexpensive sources of information. Thus, there is a reluctance to accept one physician's discouraging prognosis or to rely solely on a single traditional source. On a typical day, 6 million Americans seek health information online, more than the number who visit or contact a physician (Pew, 2002), and 48 percent of health seekers have looked for information about alternative or experimental treatments and medicines. Although 83 percent of patients continue to rely on their doctor as the main source of information, 71 percent search elsewhere.

Health seekers are increasingly bringing Internet information with them to their doctor visits. Their motivations include seeking to increase their (1) time with the doctor, (2) level of informed decision-making, and (3) individualization of case and needs. One study reported that over 90 percent of physicians and nurses in one hospital said that patients had shown them information from the Internet (Jadad et al., 2001). Overall, 41 percent of health seekers who got Internet information prior to a visit discussed this information with their doctors, and those that did rated the quality of the information higher (Diaz et al., 2002). While 79 percent noted that the physician was "very interested" or "somewhat interested," 13 percent felt that they were given the "cold shoulder" (Pew, 2002). Patients empowered by the Internet say that they are more likely to ask informed questions of their physicians and to comply with prescribed treatment plans because they feel that they are taking part in the decision and understanding the reasoning behind it (Harris Interactive, 2001).

Expectations of the Internet were that it would provide an informational resource to aid patients, but not replace the physician's role in diagnosis and treatment. Although a third of health seekers in one survey reported that the Internet affected a decision about their healthcare (Baker et al., 2003), the great majority of patients trust their doctor above all; in a 2003 survey, 62 percent of respondents reported this view (Tu and Hargraves, 2003). A 2002 survey found that 83 percent continued to rely on their doctor as the main source of information despite advances in online services (*Impact*, 2002). It may well be that a primary reason for such faith is the personalized nature of the service that physicians deliver via their interaction with patients and the physicians' seemingly individualized response concerning the patients' reports of health problems.

PHYSICIANS' USE OF THE INTERNET

Physicians are positive about using the Internet for their own work. A survey of primary care practitioners in Scotland found that 67 percent use the Internet, with 54 percent of those users rating the Internet as "useful" or "very useful" for work-related purposes (Moffat et al., 2001). A 2001 survey of 1,043 US physicians found that 62 percent used the Internet for their practice, and of those who did only about 15 percent said they communicated with at least some frequency with patients via e-mail. However, physicians are less positive about the role of the Internet in providing their patients with quality information, support, and communication. Only 14 percent of the representatives of online practices in one study felt that it helped to deliver better care (Harris Interactive, 2001). As table 13.3 shows, while 60–90 percent of physicians indicate that they use the Internet to obtain journal information or to interact with colleagues, the use of e-mail and Internet communication technologies falls off dramatically when it comes to their interaction with patients. Almost two-thirds say that they never have any e-mail contact with patients.

Table 13.3   Use of online resources by physicians in the United States

	Often	Sometimes	Hardly ever	Never
Obtain professional information resources (treatment guidelines, journal articles)	34.2	54.0	10.2	1.5
E-mail and communication with colleagues	23.2	39.7	19.5	17.6
Obtain patient clinical information, test results	13.6	14.4	17.1	54.9
E-mail and communication with patients	3.7	11.6	20.1	64.6

n = 1022.

Source: Adapted from The Robert Wood Johnson Foundation data (2001)

The possible tools for helping patients are not being widely adopted. This is shown by the example of what is known as remote disease management (RDM), which includes the collection, analysis, and reporting back of data on patients, as well as physician-initiated communication to help patients manage disease, including lifestyle recommendations. A 2003 study reported that a mere 7 percent of doctors who were already online use RDM technology (mainly for monitoring patient blood glucose levels), an insignificant growth from 5 percent two years earlier (Boston Consulting Group, 2003).

Physicians and their Patients' Use of the Internet

Although healthcare seekers may be using the Internet avidly, and claim to be discussing their findings with physicians (Aspden et al., 2001), physicians do not notice substantial proportions of their patients discussing their findings with them. This is suggested by table 13.4, which shows the results of a Robert Wood Johnson Foundation survey of 1,050 physicians in 2001. One out of six physicians reported that, over the prior year, none of their patients had discussed anything concerning information they had seen on the Internet with them. About half reported that a few of their patients had done so. Less than 10 percent reported that more than half of their patients had done so. A small survey of New Jersey physicians, also supported by The Robert Wood Johnson Foundation, found physicians reporting somewhat higher rates of patients discussing Internet information with them (Aspden et al., 2001). About 30 percent of 201 physicians said patients had discussed Internet information with them within the last week, though 10 percent reported that few or none of their patients had ever discussed such information with them. It seems, then, that even if many patients are using the Internet to get healthcare information, relatively little of it is being discussed with their physicians.

Nonetheless, the majority of physicians have positive views toward patients

Table 13.4   Physician reports of the percentage of their patients who talked to them in person about information that the patient has obtained from the Internet

Almost all (81–100%)	0.2
Most (61–80%)	1.9
About half (41–60%)	6.3
Some (21–40%)	25.6
Few (1–20%)	48.7
No discussion of Internet material with any patient in past 12 months	14.7

n = 1022.

Source: Adapted from The Robert Wood Johnson Foundation data (2001)

presenting them with information from the Internet (see table 13.5). The substantial majority finds the information accurate, feels that this use of online information shows that patients are taking responsibility for their healthcare, and that such presentations are not challenges to physician authority. (Notably, positive attitudes seem inversely related to physician's age.) Those who considered such presentations as challenging physician authority were less likely to view the experience positively, but this still only amounted to a third of those who viewed matters in this light.

In sum, there is little to support the notion that physicians, especially younger ones, discourage patients from bringing healthcare information from the Internet to the attention of their physicians. Despite the fact that there is apparently a great deal of health information seeking on the part of patients, large proportions of patients do not seem to bring such material to the attention of their physicians. One possible explanation for this conclusion is that patients are investing their new-found knowledge in non-traditional, or at least non-physician, relationships, such as the support groups noted above or family and friends.

Physician Interaction with Patients via E-mail

One expectation was that patients would be able to have ready contact with physicians via the Internet. Similar expectations accompanied the adoption of an earlier technology, the telephone (Spielberg, 1998). For the same reasons, in neither the case of the telephone nor the Internet have these technologies led to substantially more open access to the physician. In various e-mail surveys of physicians, the majority noted a low response rate from their subjects. Schmidt et al. (2003) reported a 38 percent response rate when a fictitious patient e-mailed members of the Association of Reflexologists. In a similar

Table 13.5 *Physician assessment of effect on physician/patient relationship of patient presenting Internet-derived information*

	Effect on physician/patient relationship (%)			No. of physicians responding to question
	Improved	No difference	Worsened	
How accurate was the information?				
Very / somewhat	44	52	5	298
Not very / not at all	22	59	19	106
Did you feel the patient was taking responsibility for his/her health?				
Yes	43	51	6	313
No	23	62	15	89
Did you feel the patient was challenging your authority?				
Yes	24	40	35	68
No	41	56	3	337

All questions p (chi-square) <0.001; $n = 405$.

Source: Adapted from Murray et al. (2003)

study, Oyston (2000) received a 54 percent response rate from anesthesiologists in Canada. In most cases, the health professional responded by advising the patient to go to a medical professional: 85 percent (Schmidt et al., 2003) and 83 percent (Oyston, 2000). Few attempted to make a diagnosis or suggest underlying causes: 29 percent (Schmidt et al., 2003) and 41 percent (Oyston, 2000). Thus, even in those cases where the physician responds, no new information is usually communicated over the medium.

A report from Forrester Research (cited in Schachtman, 2000) notes that 72 percent of healthcare professionals would not personally respond to patient e-mail, while an additional 19 percent said that they would only if compensated. Similar findings are reflected in our analysis of The Robert Wood Johnson Foundation-sponsored data reported above. Some medical societies discourage the use of e-mail by physicians to communicate with patients. "On the whole, it's not a good idea," according to Linda Millington, a spokesperson for the British Medical Association (BMA). In addition to putting patient confidentiality at risk, among the reasons she cited are that it is difficult to ascertain exactly with whom physicians are communicating and that there is no personal contact which is necessary for picking up crucial diagnostic clues (Pincock, 2003). (The BMJ's discouraging views are presented at bma.org.uk/ap.nsf/Content/Consultingmodernworld.) On the other hand, the American Medical Association is more moderate. While it does urge caution and mandates follow-up in-person visits, it does see substantial benefit to e-mail communication. Indeed, it has undertaken a joint venture in this area. Private firms, for example, WebMD, also are seeking to turn small-scale experiments into full-fledged profit centers.

Physician Websites

Health seekers are increasingly requesting reliable websites and recommendations from their local medical practitioners. Over two-thirds of patients consider websites recommended by their physicians to be the most reliable, 61 percent consider their physician's website to be most reliable, and over half of patients trust health sites affiliated with other local medical authorities (LaurusHealth survey, cited in Pastore, 2000). One survey found that nearly two-thirds of consumers would change to a doctor who provided a website with credible content, appointment scheduling capabilities or secure communication (Pastore, 2001). However, according to another survey, only 40 percent of physicians had a web page, and the majority of such sites lack the sort of depth sought by patients (Pastore, 2000). Sanchez (2002) notes that the vast majority of physician websites focus on practice enhancement tactics, rather than concrete patient service.

Hence, we suggest that, just as the Internet is providing a context for reinventing or renegotiating the relationships between centralized and decentralized sources of health information, it is doing so also for actors within traditional small practices of "street-level" healthcare. As individuals and groups are becoming more active, seeking out and creating their own information and communication resources, they are increasingly, though not dramatically, turning to physicians as expert guides and interpreters of the information they find as well as seeking reassurance or innovative steps from them. While patients still think of their physician as their trusted medical agent, they are turning to other sources, even those that question traditional Western medicine, and using that information as part of interactions with their physician.

Physicians, for their part, are attempting to maintain as well as extend their ambit to include a virtual side. They do this by becoming more involved in Internet communication, drawing on the Internet for information, extending patient communication to include Internet information resources, and developing their own websites. However, for reasons of professional role definition, not to mention practicality and legality, they are reluctant to become a node in the patients' self-organized network. Instead, they seem more inclined, but only slightly so, to make patients part of their own organized system of health delivery. Ultimately, as was the case with the professionalization of healthcare in earlier times, the logic of information networks, combining expertise and economics, leads them to look for ways to retain centrality and efficiency in an environment where authority is increasingly challenged and constrained.

THEME 4: POTENTIALS OF NEW TECHNOLOGY NOT MET

Overcoming Access Inequities

Internet health information, as with other Internet resources, remains inaccessible to large and specific parts of the population (Katz and Rice, 2002). Least likely to have the tools to seek health information online are those with preventable health problems or without health insurance (Eng et al., 1998). Race, at first blush, appears to be an important factor in determining potential access as 87 percent of health seekers are white (Houston and Allison, 2002), and gender is also correlated with access behavior (Nicholson et al., 2003). However, statistically speaking, both race and gender gaps in general Internet use is closing, if they have not disappeared entirely, once other demographic factors such as income are controlled for (Katz and Rice, 2002). Our studies (Katz and Aspden, 1997; Katz and Rice, 2002), as well as others (Kakai et al., 2003; Mead et al., 2003; Peterson and Fretz, 2003), show that educational achievement and income, not race or gender, are the primary drivers of inequality in Internet access in the US. That is, little or no inequality exists in terms of Internet access among these groups at any particular income level. It is, of course, the case that the mix of groups in terms of percentages varies greatly by income level, but it remains the case that the income level is the driving factor in terms of statistical variation. Indeed, a "reverse" gender gap may emerge, as women and older people are more likely to use the Internet for healthcare than are men or younger people.

Physically impaired and disabled people, though, are clearly still at a disadvantage despite the shift toward a networked society. In an evaluation of 500 websites representing common illnesses, only 19 percent were accessible to visually impaired readers using automated screen readers (Davis, 2002). Pew (2002) found that only 38 percent of Americans with disabilities go online, versus 58 percent of all Americans; and, of disabled health seekers, one-fifth reported that their disability makes it difficult for them to go online (Pew, 2003a). While deplorable, these findings are not unexpected. As we wrote during the early days of the Internet, the physical and visual demands of computer use are substantial barriers to the very people who were most expected to benefit from the Internet (Katz and Aspden, 1997). This observation seems as valid today as when we first evaluated the results of our 1995 survey. Finally, as noted above, Internet-based services fail to offer many existing technologies that could tangibly improve matters for the ill and their caregivers. This gap is even more profound for those who are, even under the best of circumstances, beset with physical limitations.

CONCLUSION

The Internet has made prior health information tools more available, allowing those with initiative to use the technology get information (but also mis-information) and obtain emotional and local support. The Internet makes novel approaches possible. Yet, despite some dramatic changes, startlingly little has altered in some areas. In fact, a surprising – and perhaps even widening – gap exists between what could be and what is available using the ever-rising capabilities of "off-the-shelf" technology.

Thus, in spite of the most utopian expectations, experiences are not only a product of individual and group choices and interactions, but also of institutional, infrastructural, social, and economic constraints. This may be seen not only in the absence of readily available and extremely helpful technologies that could serve the patient, but also in the persistent inequities, based on education and lifestyle, in the way in which new technologies are made available to various socio-demographic groups, and the growth and use of uneval-uated alternative-style health models.

The perceived need for emotional support and personal relevance has mobi-lized the creation of "the people's Internet," a loosely connected (or entirely isolated) set of self-organized networks, offering expertise and assistance. This move toward a degree of self-care is, nonetheless, not independent of physi-cians or the medical establishment; rather it grows alongside, complementing these systems even while challenging them. Yet a bulwark of expertise and professional support, which can be made available by centralized systems, is necessary as quality control against a rising tide of bogus and exploitative pseudo e-health activities on the Internet.

Perhaps the biggest need is to help centralized systems, which have many other strengths, to include resources at the level of individualized patient, care-giver, and counselor; resources that are grounded in local and other social contexts and networks. There is a great need for increased sensitivity to cultural norms as well as truly individualized applications. The problem, though, is at its core less financial than sociological. This is because the institutional dynamic is powerful and often threatens to eclipse the nominal purpose of a web-based health initiative. Earlier expectations of centralization in mediated health information continue to affect program planning and deployment, perhaps diminishing positive experiences that might grow from community produced and locally consumed mediated health information.

ACKNOWLEDGMENTS

We thank The Robert Wood Johnson Foundation for a grant that allowed us to conduct the initial work for this chapter and for the use of survey data that they have sponsored. We thank the Pew Internet and American Life Foundation, especially Lee Rainie and Susannah Fox, for use of survey data that they have sponsored. We also thank Elizabeth Murray, Lance Pollack, Bernard Lo, and Martha White for their collegial assistance.

REFERENCES

Allen, J. (1999) "Surgical Internet at a Glance: Healthcentral and drkoop," *American Journal of Surgery* 178 (5): 359.

Anderson, J. G., Rainey, M. R., and Eysenbach, G. (2003) "The Impact of Cyberhealthcare on the Physician–Patient Relationship," *Journal of Medical Systems* 27 (1): 67–84.

Aspden, P. and Katz, J. E. (2001) "Assessments of Quality of Health Care Information and Referrals to Physicians: A Nationwide Survey," in R. E. Rice and J. E. Katz (eds), *The Internet and Health Communication*, pp. 99–106. Thousand Oaks, CA: Sage.

— —, Katz, J. E., and Bemis, A. (2001) "Use of the Internet for Professional Purposes: A Survey of New Jersey Physicians," in R. E. Rice and J. E. Katz (eds), *The Internet and Health Communication*, pp. 106–19. Thousand Oaks, CA: Sage.

Baker, L., Wagner, T. H., and Singer, S. (2003) "Use of the Internet and Email for Health Care Information: Results," *Journal of the American Medical Association* 289: 2400–6.

Bamford, W. M., Rogers, N., Kassam, M., Rashbass, J., and Furness, P. N. (2003) "The Development and Evaluation of the UK National Telepathology Network," *Histopathology* 42 (2): 110.

Baur, C., Deering, M. J., and Hsu, L. (2001) "E-health: Issues and Approaches," in R. E. Rice and J. E. Katz (eds), *The Internet and Health Communication*, pp. 355–83. Thousand Oaks, CA: Sage.

Boston Consulting Group (BCG) (2001) "Vital Signs Update: The e-Health Patient Paradox" (retrieved July 30, 2003 from www.bcg.com/publications).

— — (2003) "Vital Signs: E-health in the United States" (retrieved July 30, 2003 from www.bcg.com/publications).

Burhansstipanov, L., Gilbert, A., Lamarca, K. and Krebs, L.U. (2001) "An Innovative Path to Improving Cancer Care in Indian Country," *Public Health Reports* 116: 424–33.

Castells, M. (2000) *End of Millennium*, 2nd edn. Oxford: Blackwell.

Celio, A. A., Winzelberg, A. J., Wilfley, D. E., Eppstein-Herald, D., Springer, E. A., Dev, P. and Taylor, C. B. (2000) "Reducing Risk Factors for Eating Disorders: Comparison of an Internet- and a Classroom-delivered Psychoeducational Program," *Journal of Clinical Psychology* 68 (4): 650–7.

Charatan, F. (1999a) "Drkoop.com Criticised for Mixing Information with Advertising," *British Medical Journal* 319: 727 (18 September) (retrieved August 21, 2003 from http://bmj.com).

— — (1999b) "AMA Launches New Internet 'supersite'," *British Medical Jornal* 319: 1217 (6 November) (retrieved August 21, 2003 from http://bmj.com).

— — (2000) "Executives Fly the Koop.com," *British Medical Journal* 321: 257 (retrieved July 29, 2003 from http://bmj.com).

Chen, X. and Siu, L. L. (2001) "Impact of the Media and the Internet on Oncology: Survey of Cancer Patients and Oncologists," *Canada Journal of Clinical Oncology* 19: 4291–7.

Cimino, J. J., Patel, V. L., and Kushniruk, A. W. (2001) "What Do Patients Do with Access to their Medical Records?," *Medinfo* 10 (2): 1440–4.

Consumers International (2003) "Websites Providing Misleading Information," *NUA Internet Surveys* (retrieved July 16, 2003 from www.nua.com/surveys).

Culver, J., Gerr, F., and Frumkin, H. (1997) "Medical Information on the Internet: A Study of an Electronic Bulletin Board," *Journal of General Internal Medicine,* 12 (8): 466–71.

Currò, V., Buonuomo, P. S., De Rose, P., Onesimo, R., Vituzzi, A., and D'Atri, A. (2003) "The Evolution of Web-based Medical Information on Sore Throat: A Longitudinal Study," *Journal of Medical Internet Research* 5 (2): e10 (retrieved on August 13, 2003 from www.jmir.org).

CyberAtlas (2002) "Americans Want Online Access to Doctors: A Report from Harris Interactive," *NUA Internet* Surveys (retrieved July 15, 2003 from http://cyberatlas.Internet.com).

Davis, J .J. (2002) "Disenfranchising the Disabled: The Inaccessibility of Internet-based Health Information," *Journal of Health Communication* 7 (4): 355–67.

Diaz, J. A., Griffith, R. A., Ng, J. J., Reinert, S. E., Friedmann, P. D., and Moulton, A. W. (2002) "Patients' Use of the Internet for Medical Information," *Journal of General Internal Medicine* 17 (3): 180–5.

Eng, T. R., Maxfield, A., and Gustafson, D. (1998) "Access to Health Information and Support: A Public Highway or a Private Road?," *Journal of the American Medical Association* 280 (15): 1371–5.

Eysenbach, G. and Kohler, C. (2002) "How Do Consumers Search for and Appraise Health Information on the World Wide Web? Qualitative Study Using Focus Groups, Usability Tests, and In-depth Interviews," *British Medical Journal* 324 (7337): 573–7.

— —, Powell, J., and Kuss, O. (2002) "Empirical Studies Assessing the Quality of Health Information for Consumers on the World Wide Web: A Systematic Review," *Journal of the American Medical Association* 287 (20): 2691–700.

Hanson, E., Andersson, B. A., Magnusson, L., Lidskog, R., and Holm, K. (2002) "Information Centre: Responding to Needs of Older People and Carers," *British Journal of Nursing* 11 (14): 935.

Hardey, M. (1999) "Doctor in the House: The Internet as a Source of Lay Health Knowledge and the Challenge to Expertise," *Sociology of Health and Illness* 21(6): 820–35.

— — (2001) " 'E-Health': The Internet and the Transformation of Patients into Consumers and Producers of Health Knowledge," *Information, Communication and Society* 4 (3): 388–405.

— — (2002) " 'The Story of my Illness': Personal Accounts of Illness on the Internet," *Health* 6 (1): 31–46.

Harris and Associates (1997) "Take Time to Talk: A Survey of Primary Care Physicians and the Public," Study no. 728320/1. New York: Louis Harris and Associates.

Harris Interactive (2001) "The Increasing Impact of E-health on Physician Behavior: Report by the Boston Consulting Group," *Health Care News* 1 (31): 1–14.

Health Data Management (2003) "Koop Clients' E-mail Addresses for Sale," September 30 (retrieved September 30, 2003 from www.healthdatamanagement. com).

Houston, T. K. and Allison, J. J. (2002) "Users of Internet Health Information: Differences by Health Status," *Journal of Medical Internet Research* 4 (2): e7 (retrieved August 16, 2003 from www.jmir.org).

Izenberg, N. and Lieberman, D. A. (1998) "The Web, Communication Trends, and Children's Health. Part 3: The Web and Health Consumers," *Clinical Pediatrics* 37 (4): 215–21.

Jadad, A. R. and Gagliardi, A. (1998) "Rating Health Information on the Internet," *Journal of the American Medical Association* 279: 611–14.

— —, Sigouin, C., Cocking, L., Whelan, T., and Browman, G. (2001) "Internet Use among Physicians, Nurses, and their Patients," *Journal of the American Medical Association* 286: 1451–2.

Johnson, B. and Rice, R. E. (1987) *Managing Organizational Innovation: The Evolution from Word Processing to Office Information Systems.* New York: Columbia University Press.

Kakai, H., Maskarinec, G., Shumay, D. M., Tatsumura, Y., and Tasaki, K. (2003) "Ethnic Differences in Choices of Health Information by Cancer Patients Using Complementary and Alternative Medicine: An Exploratory Study with Correspondence Analysis," *Social Science and Medicine* 56 (4): 851–62.

Kassirer, J. P. (1995) "The Next Transformation in the Delivery of Health Care," *New England Journal of Medicine* 332: 52–4.

Katz, J. E. (1979) *Presidential Politics and Science Policy.* New York: Holt, Rinehart.

— — (1999) *Connections: Social and Cultural Studies of the Telephone in American Life.* New Brunswick, NJ: Transaction.

— — (2003) *Machines that Become Us: The Social Context of Personal Communication.* New Brunswick, NJ: Transaction.

— — and Aakhus, M. (2002) *Perpetual Contact: Mobile Communication, Private Talk and Public Performance.* New York: Cambridge University Press.

— — and Aspden, P. (1997) "Motives, Hurdles, and Dropouts: Who is On and Off the Internet and Why," *Communications of the ACM* 40 (4): 97–102.

— — and — — (2001) "Networked Communication Practices and the Security and Privacy of Electronic Health Care Records," in R. E. Rice and J. E. Katz (eds), *The Internet and Health Communication,* pp. 393–416. Thousand Oaks, CA: Sage.

— — and Rice, R. E. (2001) "Concluding thoughts," in R. E. Rice and J. E. Katz (eds), *The Internet and Health Communication,* pp. 417–30. Thousand Oaks, CA: Sage.

— — and — — (2002) *Social Consequences of Internet Use.* Cambridge, MA: MIT Press.

Krishna, S., et al. (2003) "Internet-enabled Interactive Multimedia Asthma Education Program: A Randomized Trial," *Pediatrics* 111 (3): 503–10.

Landro, L. (2003) " 'Most Wired' Hospitals Embrace Technology to Boost Patient Care," *Wall Street Journal* (July 15): D4.

Loader, B. D., Muncer, S., Burrows, R., Pleace, N., and Nettleton, S. (2002) "Medicine on the Line? Computer-mediated Social Support and Advice for People with Diabetes," *International Journal of Social Welfare* 11 (1): 56–65.

Lorig, K. R., Laurent, D. D., Deyo, R. A., Marnell, M. E., Minor, M. A., and Ritter, P. L. (2002) "Can a Back Pain E-mail Discussion Group Improve Health Status and Lower Health Care Costs? A Randomized Study," *Archives of Internal Medicine* 162 (7): 792–6.

McKay, H. G., King, D., Eakin, E. G., Seeley, J. R., and Glasgow, R. E. (2001) "The Diabetes Network Internet-based Physical Activity Intervention: A Randomized Pilot Study, *Diabetes Care* 24 (8): 1328–34.

Malin, B. A. (2002) "Correlating Web Usage of Health Information with Patient Medical Data," *Proceedings of the AMIA Symposium*, 484–8.

Mead, N., Varnam, R., Rogers, A., and Roland, M. (2003) "What Predicts Patients' Interest in the Internet as a Health Resource in Primary Care in England?," *Journal of Health Services Research and Policy* 8 (1): 33–9.

Mendelson, D. N. and Salinsky, E. M. (1997) "Health Information Systems and the Role of State Government," *Health Affairs* 16 (3): 106–20.

Millard, R. W. and Fintak, P. A. (2002) "Use of the Internet by Patients with Chronic Illness," *Disease Management and Health Outcomes* 10 (3): 187–94.

Moffat, M. O., Moffat, K. J., and Cano, V. (2001) "General Practitioners and the Internet: A Questionnaire Survey of Internet Connectivity and Use in Lothian," *Health Bulletin (Edinburgh)* 59 (2): 120–6.

Morris, C. A. and Avorn, J. (2003) "Internet Marketing of Herbal Products," *Journal of the American Medical Association* 290: 1505–9.

Murray, E., Lo, B., Pollack, L., Donelan, K., Catania, J., Lee, K., Zapert, K., and Turner, R. (2003) "The Impact of Health Information on the Internet on Health Care and the Physician–Patient Relationship: National US Survey among 1,050 US Physicians," *Journal of Medical Internet Research* 5 (3): e17 (retrieved September 19, 2003, from http://www.jmir.org/2003/3/e17).

Napoli, P. M. (2001) "Consumer Use of Medical Information from Electronic and Paper Media: A Literature Review," in R. E. Rice and J. E. Katz (eds), *The Internet and Health Communication*, pp. 79–98. Thousand Oaks, CA: Sage.

Nicholson, W. K., Grason, H. A., and Powe, N. R. (2003) "The Relationship of Race to Women's Use of Health Information Resources," *American Journal of Obstetrics and Gynecology* 188 (2): 580–5.

Oyston, J. (2000) "Anesthesiologists' Responses to an Email Request for Advice from an Unknown Patient," *Journal of Medical Internet Research* 2 (3): e16 (accessed on October 6, 2003 from http://yi.com/jmir).

Parker, L. (2003) "Medical Privacy Law Creates Wide Confusion," *USA Today*, October 17 (retrieved October 17, 2003 from www.usatoday.com).

Pastore, M. (2000) "Customers Choose Health Sites with Doctors' Input," April (retrieved July 30, 2003, from http://cyberatlas.Internet.com).

— — (2001) "Physicians' Web Sites, eHealth Plans Mark Future of Healthcare," February (retrieved July 3, 2003 from http://cyberatlas.Internet.com).

Paterniti, D. A., Price, M. D. and Goodman, T. (1999) "Trajectories of Health, Illness, and Care: Women and Breast Cancer," American Sociological Association (ASA) Annual Meeting, August 9, Washington, DC.

Patsos, M. (2001) "The Internet and Medicine: Building a Community for Patients with Rare Diseases," *Journal of the American Medical Association* 285 (6): 805.

Peterson, M. W. and Fretz, P. C. (2003) "Patient Use of the Internet for Information in a Lung Cancer Clinic," *Chest* 123 (2): 452–7.

Pew Internet and American Life Project (2000) "The Online Health Care Revolution: How the Web Helps Americans Take Better Care of Themselves" (retrieved July 16, 2003 from www.pewInternet.org).

— — (2002) "Vital Decisions: How Internet Users Decide What Information to Trust When They or their Loved Ones are Sick" (retrieved July 17, 2003 from www.pewInternet.org).

— — (2003a) "Internet Health Resources: Health Searches and Email Have Become More Commonplace, But There is Room for Improvement in Searches and Overall Internet Access" (retrieved July 25, 2003 from www.pewInternet.org).

— — (2003b) *December 2002 Tracking Survey* (November 25–December 2002). Washington, DC: Pew Internet and American Life Project.

Pincock, S. (2003) "UK Doctors Still 'Out of Office' to Patients Online: E-health-media.com (retrieved October 2, 2003, from www.e-health-media.com).

Potts, H. W. and Wyatt, J. C. (2002) "Survey of Doctors' Experience of Patients Using the Internet," *Journal of Medical Internet Research* 4 (1): e5 (retrieved August 16, 2003 from www.jmir.org).

Preece, J. J. and Ghozati, K. (2001) "Experiencing Empathy Online," in R. E. Rice and J. E. Katz (eds), *The Internet and Health Communication*, pp. 237–60. Thousand Oaks, CA: Sage.

Reents, S. and Miller, T. E. (1998) "The Health Care Industry in Transition: The Online Mandate to Change," *Cyber Dialogue* (retrieved August 16, 2003 from www.cyber-dialogue.com).

Rice, R. E. (2001) "The Internet and Health Communication: A Framework of Experiences," in R. E. Rice and J. E. Katz (eds), *The Internet and Health Communication*, pp. 5–46. Thousand Oaks, CA: Sage.

— — (2004) "Social Aspects of Implementing a Hospital Information System: Cure or Symptom?," in P. Whitten and D. Cook (eds), *Understanding Health Communications Technologies: A Case Study Approach*. San Francisco: Jossey-Bass.

— — and Gattiker, U. (2000) "New Media and Organizational Structuring," in F. Jablin and L. Putnam (eds), *New Handbook of Organizational Communication*, pp. 544–81. Newbury Park, CA: Sage.

— — and Katz, J. E. (2001) *Internet and Health Communication: Experience and Expectations*. Thousand Oaks, CA: Sage.

— —, Peterson, M., and Christine, R. (2001) "A Comparative Features Analysis of Publicly Accessible Commercial and Government Health Database Web Sites," in R. E. Rice and J. E. Katz (eds), *The Internet and Health Communication*, pp. 213–32. Thousand Oaks, CA: Sage.

Robert Wood Johnson Foundation, The (2001) "Dataset: The Impact of Internet and Advertising on Patients and Physicians Survey." Princeton, NJ: The Robert Wood Johnson Foundation.

Rose, S., Bruce, J., and Maffulli, N. (1998) "Access the Internet for Patient Information about Orthopedics," *Journal of the American Medical Association* 280 (15): 1309.

Sanchez, P. M. (2002) "Refocusing Website Marketing: Physician–Patient Relationships," *Health Marketing Quarterly* 2 (1): 37–43.

Schachtman, Noah (2002) "Why Doctors Hate the Internet," *Wired News* (April 10) (retrieved March 29, 2004 from http://www.wired.com/news/culture/ 0,1284,35516,00.html).

Schmidt, K., White, A., and Ernst, E. (2003) "Reflexologists' Responses to a Patient with Abdominal Pain: A Survey on Internet Advice," *Complementary Therapies in Medicine* 11 (2): 98–102.

Schwitzer, G. (2002) "A Review of Features in Internet Consumer Health Decision-support Tools," *Journal of Medical Internet Research* 4 (2): e11 (retrieved on August 13, 2003 from http://www.jmir.org/2002/2/e11/).

Sharf, B. F. (1997) "Communicating Breast Cancer On-line: Support and Empowerment on the Internet," *Women and Health* 26 (1): 65–84.

Sigouin, C. and Jadad, A. R. (2002) "Awareness of Sources of Peer-reviewed Research Evidence on the Internet," *Journal of the American Medical Association* 287 (21): 2867–9.

Spielberg, A. R. (1998) "On Call and Online: Sociohistorical, Legal, and Ethical Implications of E-mail for the Patient–Physician Relationship," *Journal of the American Medical Association* 280 (15): 1353–9.

Street, Jr, R. L. and Rimal, R. (1997) "Health Promotion and Interactive Technology: A Conceptual Foundation," in R. L. Street, Jr, W. Gold, and T. Manning (eds), *Health Promotion and Interactive Technology: Theoretical Applications and Future Directions*, pp. 1–18. Mahwah, NJ: Lawrence Erlbaum.

Suarez-Almazor, M. E., Kendall, C. J., and Dorgan, M. (2001) "Surfing the Net: Information on the World Wide Web for Persons with Arthritis: Patient Empowerment or Patient Deceit?," *Journal of Rheumatology* 28 (1): 1–2.

Till, J. E. (2003) "Evaluation of Support Groups for Women with Breast Cancer: Importance of the Navigator Role," *Health and Quality of Life Outcomes* 1 (1): 16.

Tu, H. T. and Hargraves, J. L. (2003) "Seeking Health Care Information: Most Consumers Still on the Sidelines," *Issue Brief Center for Studying Health System Change* 61: 1–4.

Veronin, M. A. (2002) "Where Are They Now? A Case Study of Health-related Web Site Attrition," *Journal of Medical Internet Research*, 4 (2): e10 (retrieved August 13, 2003 from www.jmir.org).

Wellman, B. (1995) "Lay Referral Networks: Using Conventional Medicine and Alternative Therapies for Low Back Pain," in J. J. Kronenfield (ed.), *Research in the Sociology of Health Care 12*. Greenwich: JAI Press (retrieved July 25, 2003 from www.utoronto.ca).

Wikgren, M. (2001) "Health Discussions on the Internet: A Study of Knowledge Communication through Citations," *Library and Information Research* 23: 305–17.

Williams, P., Nicholas, D., Huntington, P., and McLean, F. (2002) "Surfing for Health: User Evaluation of a Health Information Website. Part two: Fieldwork," *Health Information and Libraries Journal*, 19 (4): 214–25.

Winzelberg, A. J., Classen, C., Alpers, G. W., Roberts, H., Koopman, C., Adams, R. E., Ernst, H., Dev, P., and Taylor, C. B. (2003) "Evaluation of an Internet Support Group for Women with Primary Breast Cancer," *Cancer* 97 (5): 1164–73.

Wynn, E. and Katz, J. E. (1997) "Hyperbole over Cyberspace: Self-presentation and Social Boundaries in Internet Home Pages and Discourse," *The Information Society* 13 (4): 297–328.

14. Narrowing the digital divide: the potential and limits of the US community technology movement

Lisa J. Servon and Randal D. Pinkett

Information technology (IT) has wrought fundamental changes throughout society. IT has been instrumental in the shift from an industrial age to a network age. We now live in a society in which the production, acquisition, and flow of knowledge drive the economy and in which global information networks represent key infrastructure. How have these changes affected existing power relations and patterns of inequality? Does IT benefit or hinder progress toward social and economic justice?

Clearly, it has the power to do both. In addition to altering commerce, education, government, and communications, IT affects the construction of and response to social problems such as poverty and inequality. The very existence of the "digital divide" – or lack of access to IT for certain segments of the population – is evidence of the ability of technology to exacerbate existing inequality. At the same time, technology can bring education to people living far from good schools. It can promote organizing efforts in disadvantaged communities and it can connect people to a wide range of opportunities. The community technology movement – a grassroots social movement that employs IT to empower historically disadvantaged individuals and communities – demonstrates the potential of IT to serve as a tool of social change.

The digital divide is now recognized as an international issue. High-income OECD countries account for over three-quarters of the world's Internet users (United Nations Development Programme, 2001). In virtually all countries, Internet users tend to be young, urban, male, and relatively well educated and wealthy. In short, the diffusion of technology both within and between countries has been extremely uneven. Current and historical patterns of access to IT illustrate a significant separation between information "haves" and information "have-nots" along lines of race, socioeconomic status, education level, household type, and geographic location (Doctor, 1994; US Department of Commerce, 2000). Why has the technology gap emerged as such a prominent issue nationally and internationally? Does it warrant this recent attention?

Undoubtedly. IT affects how we work and what we work toward, how we connect with each other and with whom we connect, and how we make decisions and with what information. Living on the wrong side of the digital divide, as do the persistent poor, means being cut off from these changes and disconnected from the information society.

This chapter makes two arguments. First, that in order to narrow the digital divide we must redefine it. And, second, that we must look to community technology centers (CTCs) as key innovators. In the process of making these two arguments, we will discuss the importance of technology literacy and lay out the context in which CTCs work. This chapter is based on a literature review of the community technology field, a 1999 survey of the 336 affiliates of the Community Technology Centers Network (CTCNet), and extensive fieldwork at CTCs in East Palo Alto, Seattle, Austin, Pittsburgh, and New York City.

WHY TECHNOLOGY?

When community technology activists talk about the need to narrow the digital divide, they are often met with skepticism. Is IT something people really need, or is it more accurate to think of it as a luxury? Why would people on low incomes use computers to contact elected officials? They can write letters now, but they seldom do. They can vote now, but the poor are one of the groups with the lowest voter turnout rates. Was the cable access movement not supposed to give people a voice? Why has it not made the kind of impact many hoped that it would make? Perhaps the Internet, the IT medium of communication, is just the next in a long succession of over-hyped media.

These questions and doubts are legitimate. However, the Internet possesses key attributes that make it differ from these other media in significant ways. First, the Internet is an open medium that allows broad participation: the shorthand for this characteristic is "many to many." Unlike other media used to deliver information – television and newspapers, for example – the Internet allows users both to respond to what exists and to produce their own material relatively inexpensively *if* they possess the skills and access necessary to do so. This "many-to-many" aspect of the Internet is one of its key cultural features. The Internet's interactive nature creates the conditions necessary "for learning, confidence-building, and self-empowerment" (Sanyal, 2000: 146). In short, the Internet provides "the capacity for anyone to find his/her own destination in the net, and if not found, to create and post his/her own information" (Castells, 2001: 19).

Second, the Internet enables the creation and support of networks. These networks are organized and maintained for social and economic purposes. The value of networks increases as the number of people who belong to and actively participate in the network increases (Brock, 1994; Civille, 1995). The Internet makes joining and remaining engaged much easier, and enables participation across space, thereby increasing the potential for a greater number of users to join. More importantly, online networks have the capacity to strengthen and enhance place-based community networks, extending the reach of existing community-based organizations and institutions.

These two attributes – the openness of the Internet and its capacity to support networks – are revolutionizing the way in which individuals, communities, firms, governments, and other institutions and organizations engage with the rest of the world. To ensure that all people have the skills and access to participate in the information society is a matter of utmost importance. But before attempting to achieve consensus that this issue must be addressed, we must first agree on the specific nature of the problem

REDEFINING THE PROBLEM

What exactly is the digital divide? Policy-makers and the media have thus far defined the digital divide narrowly and incompletely. In short, the technology gap has been defined as a problem of access in the narrow sense of possession or permission to use a computer and the Internet.

This chapter challenges the current popular conception of the digital divide. Access to information technology is increasing at a rapid rate. Although some groups of people, namely, African Americans, Latinos, and the disabled, remain persistently and disproportionately on the wrong side of the digital divide, the gaps between those who have access to IT and those who do not are rapidly closing. Groups that have traditionally been digital "have-nots" are now making dramatic gains. Gaps between rural and non-rural households and between seniors and younger people have begun to narrow. Some divides, such as that between women and men, have disappeared altogether. Indeed, some have proposed thinking about the problem as the digital continuum rather than the digital divide (Lenhart et al., 2003; see table 14.1).

And yet the larger problem persists. Inequities remain between those who possess the resources, education, and skills to reap the benefits of the information society and those who do not. Persistent gaps remain between different racial and ethnic groups, people with and without disabilities, single and dual parent families, the old and the young, and people with different levels of income and education. People on low incomes, and minorities, particularly when they reside in inner cities, are among the groups being left behind.

Clearly, the digital divide is much more complex than merely a lack of computers. Simplistic solutions have therefore masked, and perhaps even exacerbated, the larger problem. When we provide people with computers, we

Table 14.1 Dimensions of the digital divide

	Households with computers (June 2001) (%)	Individuals with Internet (June 2001) (%)		
		Dial-up	Broadband	Any type
General population	56.3			50.5
Gender				
Male	65.5			53.9
Female	65.8			53.8
Geography				
Urban	56.7			51.1
Central city	51.5			45.7
Rural	55.6			50.5
Income				
Under $15000		83.4	16.7	
$15,000 – 19,999	31.8	86.4	13.7	
$20,000 – 24,999	40.1	86.2	13.8	
$25,000 – 34,999	49.7	85.4	14.6	
$35,000 – 49,999	64.3	84.1	15.9	
$50,000 – 74,999	77.7	82.4	17.7	
$75,000+	89.6	74.9	25.1	
Education[a]				
Less than high school	18.2			5
High school	39.6			23
Some college	60.3			34
Bachelors	74.0			
Postgraduate	79.0			
Race				
White	70.7			59.9
Black	55.7			39.8
Asian American/ Pacific Islander	71.2			60.4
Hispanic	48.8			31.6

[a] Data as of August 2000.

Sources: Pew Internet and American Life Project Tracking surveys (March 2000 to present) and "The Ever-shifting Internet Population" (April, 2003); NTIA and ESA, US; US Department of Commerce, using US Bureau of the Census Current Population Survey supplements (February, 2001)

find that not much changes. IT on its own does not function as a ladder out of poverty. This chapter defines the digital divide in a broader and more complex way, and suggests similarly broad solutions to deal with the problem. More comprehensive responses, based on a more finely textured and nuanced understanding of the problem, can be employed to enable disadvantaged groups to participate in today's economy and society, in effect providing the kind of boost necessary to exit poverty. To redefine the problem, we need to shift the primary question from "who has access?" to "what are people doing, and what are they able to do, when they go online?" (DiMaggio and Hargittai, 2001).

If the digital divide is not simply a problem of access, what is the appropriate definition? Access is one dimension of the issue. Clearly, people need the basic IT tools – computers and Internet access – at their disposal. But access is only the first component. The second dimension of the digital divide concerns training or IT literacy: the ability to use IT for a range of purposes, and the knowledge of how and why IT can be used as a key resource. The training issue extends from schools to disadvantaged workers who cannot find work that pays a living wage because they do not have the appropriate skills to work in the information economy. As with any tool, users of IT must understand it and have the facility to fully exploit its potential in order to benefit completely from it.

The third dimension of the digital divide has to do with content, both content that meets the needs and demands of disenfranchised groups and content that is created by them. The Internet, like most media, is shaped by the first people to occupy its territory, in this case middle- and upper-income white males. When disadvantaged groups do log on, they often find that there is no content there for them. The kind of information they seek – information that is directly related to their lives and communities and cultures – does not exist. If and when it does, they often lack the skills to find it. Language and literacy issues create additional barriers for these groups (Lazarus and Mora, 2000). This content dimension is clearly related to the training dimension; IT skills are needed in order to access and create content.

Redefining the digital divide, then, requires broadening the concept beyond access to include training and content issues. Access is a necessary precondition but this engenders a need for training in order to use the tools. Once people have facility with the tools, they demand content that serves their interests and meets their needs.

THE COMMUNITY TECHNOLOGY MOVEMENT: A BRIEF OVERVIEW

The community technology movement has been instrumental in closing the digital divide. Before discussing the second argument of this chapter – that community technology centers (CTCs) are key innovators in this effort – it is necessary to establish the context in which these organizations work. The genesis of the community technology movement arguably dates back to 1968 when the National Urban League established a training program in Los Angeles, California, for adults in COBOL programming using a mainframe computer. More than two decades passed before the movement reached its next major milestone.[1]

In 1980, Antonia Stone, a former public school teacher, started a non-profit organization called Playing2Win (P2W) (Mark and Briscoe, 1995; Stone, 1996). P2W's mission was to address computer access inequities in the low-income community of Harlem, New York. Consequently, P2W opened the Harlem Community Computing Center in a public housing development in 1983, where it enjoyed tremendous success. In 1990, P2W and six similar technology centers created an informal network as a means of sharing their collective experiences in the use of computing in under-served communities, thus helping to formalize the concept of "community technology." In 1990 and 1992, P2W secured a planning grant and a subsequent three-year commitment from the National Science Foundation (NSF) to establish and develop P2WNet – a network of community technology centers (CTCs) primarily based in the north-east United States. Finally, recognizing the need for additional organizational infrastructure to bring the network to a national scale, the Education Development Center (EDC) proposed and received a five-year grant from NSF to expand P2WNet into the independent, nationally based Community Technology Centers Network (CTCNet). Today, CTCNet is largest network of community technology centers in the United States, representing more than 650 CTCs across the country.

The evolution of CTCNet signified one of a number of developments occurring during the early to mid-1990s that significantly advanced the field of community technology. In July 1995, the National Telecommunications and Information Administration (NTIA) of the US Department of Commerce, under the leadership of Secretary Ron Brown and Assistant Secretary Larry Irving, released its first statistical report of computer and Internet use in the United States entitled, *Falling Through the Net: A Survey of the "Have Nots" in Rural and Urban America* (US Department of Commerce, 1995). This survey represented the first in a series of reports released in 1998, 1999, and 2000 by the NTIA examining the gap between the so-called "haves" and "have-nots" with respect to information and communication technology, and popularizing this phenomenon under the term "the digital divide."

The movement reached a peak in 2000–2001, during President Bill Clinton's final year in office. In January 2000, Clinton announced his plan to narrow the digital divide during his State of the Union address. This high-profile statement placed the issue at the forefront of the nation's consciousness. One month later, the Clinton–Gore administration released its comprehensive proposal, *From Digital Divide to Digital Opportunity* (The White House, 2000), which outlined specific strategies and budget initiatives for addressing the problem. In April 2000, President Clinton led a "new markets" tour to mobilize public and private partnerships to address what he referred to as the "key civil rights issue of the 21st century" (The White House, 1999). The tour included stops at CTCs such as "Plugged In" in East Palo Alto, California. Clearly, the community technology movement had come of age.

In 2001, dramatic changes occurred in the community technology landscape as the Bush administration assumed office. As early as February 7, 2001, Michael Powell, the newly appointed chair of the Federal Communications Commission (FCC) likened the digital divide to a "Mercedes divide" (*The New York Times*, February 7, 2001), arguing that it was not the government's responsibility to provide everyone with access to the latest technologies. That same month, the Bush administration released its first study of computer and Internet penetration under the revealing title *A Nation Online: How Americans Are Expanding their Use of the Internet* (US Department of Commerce, 2002), wherein they suggested that the gap had closed significantly in recent years.

CTCS AS KEY INNOVATORS

The community technology movement works to foster the positive benefits of the information revolution, while combating problems associated with the digital divide (Hecht, 1998). This movement was initiated primarily by people who had access to technology, usually through their jobs, and who foresaw the potentially negative externalities of leaving large segments of the population behind as socioeconomic systems were undergoing transformation. Like many community-based movements, community technology initiatives were developed to fill a gap unfilled by the public, private for-profit, or private non-profit sectors. The majority of existing community-based organizations (CBOs) did not have the capacity to extend their missions to encompass the technology gap issue. For the most part, then, CTCs were initiated by community-minded people with some understanding of technology. Most were started as independent efforts without strong ties to the existing community development infrastructure.

Community technology centers (known as telecenters in other countries) have emerged at an increasing pace in the past several years to try to narrow the digital divide in various ways. CTCs are locally based non-profit organizations that link community residents to IT resources. Thousands of organizations are currently working to disseminate IT to local communities. CTCs work to foster the potentially positive benefits of the information revolution, while combating its associated problems. CTCs address the digital divide comprehensively and advance larger social, political, and economic goals in the process.

THE CTC UMBRELLA

The term "community technology center" covers a wide range of organizational types with a broad range of missions. CTCs differ along three dimensions: their organizational type, their programmatic orientation, and their target population. The latter two dimensions shape and are shaped by program missions. There are three primary organizational types of CTCs: stand-alone centers; CTCs housed in multi-service agencies; and networks of CTCs (which may comprise one or both of the previous two types). Stand-alone CTCs are centers that were created explicitly to address information technology and digital divide issues, which include access, training, and content. Other CTCs are part of multi-service agencies, which means that they are part of organizations or institutions such as a public library, a YWCA, or a community development corporation (CDC) that offer a variety of services and programs to the community. A third model is a network of CTCs connected by a larger organization. The Austin FreeNet (which has 34 locations, including schools, libraries, community centers, churches, and housing projects) is an example of this type of CTC.

CTCs also differ in terms of their IT programming. Some centers focus on providing access to technology. A public library, for example, may simply provide a space for computers with Internet access, but offer no training. Other CTCs offer either general or specialized classes. Many CTCs, for example, offer basic classes in keyboarding, how to use e-mail, and popular software applications such as Word and Photoshop. Others are more oriented toward providing specific training that can help participants obtain jobs in IT-related fields. The Bay Area Video Coalition (BAVC) in San Francisco and Per Scholas in the Bronx are two examples of CTCs oriented toward workforce development. Some CTCs use technology more indirectly. For example, the mission of Street-Level Youth Media in Chicago,[2] which uses technology as part of a comprehensive program plan, much like a number of other CTCs, is as follows:

> Street-Level Youth Media educates Chicago's inner-city youth in media arts and emerging technologies for use in self-expression communication, and social change. Street-Level programs build self-esteem and critical thinking skills for urban youth who have been historically neglected by policy makers and mass media. Using video production, computer art and the Internet young people address

community issues, access advanced technology and gain inclusion in our information-based society.

Finally, CTCs differ with respect to their target populations. Although most CTCs aim to help people on low incomes in urban areas, they tend to serve different segments of that larger population. Some programs target youth, while others target unemployed and under-employed workers, and still others serve senior citizens, the disabled, the homeless, and/or a particular neighborhood.

How do CTCs bridge the digital divide? One way to answer this question is to understand the ways in which these organizations confront the three dimensions of the problem laid out above: access, training, and content.[3]

Access

Despite the trend toward expansion of CTC missions beyond access, the most common function of CTCs remains providing unstructured computer access to people who might otherwise have little or no opportunity to use computers and information technologies. General computer access is offered by 87 percent of CTCs, and more than three-quarters use technology as a communication tool (i.e., offering access to e-mail). As access providers, CTCs allow community members to drop in and surf the Internet, work on homework, prepare résumés and cover letters, use e-mail, or engage in a variety of other activities. The Hill House Community Access Network (HHCAN), a CTC in Pittsburgh, Pennsylvania, offers some structured workshops to provide participants with the skills necessary to use computers, but its emphasis is on providing access to neighborhood residents. Carl Redwood, former associate director of HHCAN emphasizes the importance of providing unstructured access:

> The free aspect of these centers . . . is very important. I think there is a danger in the technology center movement, particularly as it relates to low-income communities, to assume that we're doing something for people . . . I think what we have to do is just make resources available to the community and the community will figure out what, when, and how to use them. And they may not use them the way the mayor's office or someone else thinks they should use them . . . But I think it just needs to be open like that.

Redwood and others essentially argue that those who support IT initiatives in low-income communities must remain open to the multiple ways in which these communities may use these tools. Narrow, prescriptive interventions can cut off potentially rich applications of IT resources.

At the same time, most CTCs (including HHCAN) have a broader definition of access than Redwood's statement implies. They not only provide the necessary tools, they also show low-income communities how and why IT tools might be useful to them. A great deal of learning occurs during the open access hours of the CTC – it simply occurs informally. CTC staff circulate among users, offering assistance and showing people new websites and software applications. In addition, much learning occurs among drop-in users. CTCs are a new form of community institution where people meet, exchange ideas, and learn.

Literacy/Training

Many CTCs focus on developing the IT skills of program participants. Those that grew out of the workforce development tradition directly address the problem of the jobs/skills mismatch. Literacy and training programs range from basic courses in which participants learn how to use e-mail and develop keyboarding skills, to advanced courses in building computers, HTML, web development, and media production.

There is a strong emphasis among CTCs on education and job preparedness. Some of these CTCs use IT as a tool to deliver traditional material, such as GED and ESL curricula. Others focus more specifically on computer literacy and IT skills. One example of a CTC that is training people for IT jobs is the Bay Area Video Coalition (BAVC) in San Francisco. BAVC's JobLink program maintains close working relationships with a range of Bay Area employers who recognize the quality of the program and are eager to hire its graduates. The relationships with employers also enable BAVC to understand and respond to the quickly changing skill needs of these employers. BAVC keeps current with new programs and continually modifies its curriculum. The JobLink program places 95 percent of its participants in jobs, such as web developers, HTML coders, and designers, which have an average hourly wage of $30. Employers hiring BAVC graduates range from high-profile IT companies such as Oracle to a wider range of service companies such as Charles Schwab and TravelSmith.

Content

Finally, some CTC programming employs IT as a mechanism to create and deliver content. CTCs that focus on the creation and delivery of content work to address the social impacts of the technological revolution. The goals of these CTCs may include: providing information to the community; fostering a sense of community or personal effectiveness; encouraging collaboration; developing problem-solving and strategic-thinking skills. CTCs that emphasize content have three distinct purposes: creating material that constituents can use; teaching community members to create this content; and helping community members connect to important information that already exists on the Internet. Not all content-oriented CTCs do all three. Those CTCs that actively foster the creation of new content believe that people should not be passive consumers of information but rather actively shape the Internet by producing content that reflects and represents their lives and communities.

Content-oriented CTCs begin their work from the recognition that the Internet is not currently oriented to low-income communities and that these communities face several content-related barriers. According to Chapman and Rhodes (1997: 3):

> The Internet reflects the culture of its principal inhabitants – upper middle-class white males. Thus the global network is dominated by the culture, tastes, preoccupations, styles, and interests of the affluent. A network isn't much good if you don't know anybody who has email, an online shopping mall holds little allure to someone lacking money or credit cards.

Content-oriented CTCs focus on providing stimulating content about local issues and an opportunity for users to talk with one another. They connect residents to resources and provoke discussion about issues that people care about (Shapiro, 1999: 5).

A 2000 report distributed by the Children's Partnership identifies four significant, content-related barriers that affect large numbers of Americans: lack of local information; literacy barriers; language barriers; and lack of cultural diversity (Lazarus and Mora, 2000). Residents of low-income communities "seek 'life information,' . . . practical information about their local community" (Lazarus and Mora, 2000: 19). Specifically, adult users wanted information about jobs and housing in their communities. Few sites provide this information. Even when this information is available, researchers have found that it is often "still out of reach to users because it is so difficult to find."

At Project Compute, a volunteer-run CTC in Seattle, volunteers incorporate computers and information technology into their learning programs by teaching participants how to create content. As Anthony Williams, long-time volunteer and sponsor of Project Compute, stresses, "We don't want people to believe that a computer is a computer. We really want people to believe that a computer is a tool." This philosophy manifests itself in Project Compute's Life-Web Journalist Project, the first phase of which was completed in March 1999. As part of the initiative, Project Compute loaned twenty-five hand-held computers equipped with Windows, an audio-recorder, and a digital camera to participants for a six-month period. Participants were to go out into the community, capture stories of interest, and create an Internet website. In addition to helping participants hone their journalistic and computer skills, the Life-Web Project provides participants with the opportunity to tell their stories. Project Compute also offers various classes for school-age children, adults, and senior citizens, and provides open-lab time for all community members.

Project Compute is deeply rooted in its community. This connection ensures that projects reflect the interests and concerns of the community. According to Lazarus and Mora, 2000: 28): "inclusion helps ensure that online content incorporates what the community wants and will use, that content acknowledges residents' methods of acquiring information, and that the look and feel of the content works with the user's literacy and linguistic levels." One advantage of the Internet is that it allows for two-way communication in a way that print media and television do not. Users can respond quickly and directly to the information posted and communicate with each other about topics of interest. Content-oriented CTCs exploit this many-to-many attribute of the Internet, creating space for community members to shape what is available to them.

WHAT WE KNOW ABOUT OUTCOMES

To what extent are CTCs narrowing the technology gap? Many CTCs continue to experiment with programming, and most of the existing research that has attempted to evaluate the work of these new institutions is exploratory. Given the range of goals and organizational types of CTC, it is important not to judge all CTCs by the same standards. A small access lab in a housing project will have different goals from a dedicated training organization. In addition, most CTCs are small, neighborhood-based institutions that have not achieved scale. A clear problem is that these initiatives tend to be fragmented, under-resourced, and reliant on a charismatic leader (Graham and Marvin, 2001).

Despite these issues, existing research does indicate that CTCs are filling a critical need for populations that do not have access to computers and other technologies at home or work. The 1999 NTIA study reports that "households with incomes less than $20,000 and Black households ... are twice as likely to get Internet access through a public library or [CTC] than are households earning more than $20,000 or White households" (NTIA, 1999: 78). In a survey of users of CTC services, CTCNet found that CTCs have been a valuable resource for obtaining job skills and learning about employment opportunities, have had a positive effect on participants' goals and experiences, and have fostered a sense of community and personal effectiveness (Chow et al., 1998).

A 1997 study indicated that most CTC users do not have access elsewhere. Those that do have access elsewhere go to CTCs to use applications and equipment they do not have access to, for social interaction, and for the learner-centered atmosphere. Evaluations of the California-based Computers in our Future Project, which studied member centers, show that these centers "are reaching groups who have normally been intimidated by technology, and people who have been difficult to attract to the computer-using world" (cited in Lazarus and Mora, 2000: 28).

Given the networking that community technology facilitates – both physically, at CTCs, and virtually – it seems reasonable to assume that CTCs are promoting the creation of weak ties among participants. Weak ties are connections between acquaintances rather than family members or good friends. Weak-tie theory argues that weak ties are more helpful in the labor market than are strong ties (Granovetter, 1973). According to Civille (1995: 181): "electronic mail appears to significantly reduce the costs of acquiring and maintaining new acquaintances beyond community boundaries, an ability that those with discretionary time and money tend to take for granted." It is important, then, that some groups that are on the wrong side of the digital divide – for example, African Americans and Latinos – are using public computer centers more than other groups for job-related purposes.

CTCs are performing critical functions that help bridge the digital divide. These include providing disadvantaged workers with the skills necessary to work in the IT economy, exposing youth to IT careers and opportunities, and extending the work of traditional CBOs to address issues of social and economic justice.

The high cost of evaluation, coupled with the newness of these programs, have kept CTCs from doing much evaluation of their own. When asked what they see happening in the programs in which they work, staff members are likely to tell stories rather than to produce numbers. These stories are about connecting people who previously did not know each other; helping people stay in touch with faraway friends and relatives; watching people learn how to use new technology and create things with it. Ana Sisnett of the Austin FreeNet has observed:

Age groups working together that did not work together before. For a while antagonistically – looking at each other suspiciously, but then over time they get familiar with each other and they're able to collaborate and help each other out, even if it's something as simple as helping to reload a page, you know? And I've seen people find out as they talk about what their interests are, as they do searches. For example, in a class – "Oh, I didn't know that" – and then they might end up walking out of class talking to each other about something.

Roxanne Epperson, the director of the New Beginnings Learning Center (NBLC) points to other evidence of success.

Kids won't leave. At 5:30 when it's time for them to go, you have to make sure there are none hidden in the basement. They hide under the desks . . . I don't know how their little bodies can fold up, but down in the library there's an opening under one of the shelves, they're all up under there. So that tells me we're doing something right, you know?

CTCs are incredibly diverse in terms of both their organizational structures and their missions. The relationships between these differences and program outcomes merit closer examination to determine how successful CTCs are in meeting their goals. This recommendation is particularly tricky to operationalize given the diversity of community technology programs and the range of goals they pursue. Despite the great potential of CTCs, they also face a range of challenges which must be addressed if these organizations are to realize their potential.

THE COMMUNITY TECHNOLOGY MOVEMENT: CURRENT CHALLENGES

The community technology movement is now at a crossroads. On one hand, the significant momentum established during the 1990s has produced a well-established infrastructure, which includes the following: CTCs such as the Department of Education grantees; networks of CTCs such as CTCNet and the Intel Computer Clubhouse Network; technology training programs such as the Cisco Networking Academy; web resources such as DigitalDivideNetwork.org, Contentbank.org and TechSoup.org; technology programs akin to the TOP funded initiatives; and intermediary and capacity-building organizations such as the America Connects Consortium. On the other hand, this momentum has been noticeably affected by recent and proposed federal budget cuts, the realities of the current economic downturn, and the resulting diminished support from the philanthropic and private sectors. In addition to these setbacks there are other challenges and opportunities facing the community technology movement.

First, there have been *difficulties in capturing the "late majority"* (Rogers, 1983),[4] or significant members of the movement's target population (for example, low to moderate income or rural communities) who are often the hardest to engage. Some argue that community technology efforts have only been successful in reaching the "early adopters" (Rogers, 1983), those already inclined to embrace computers and the Internet. Recent studies at MIT, *The Camfield Estates–MIT Creating Community Connections Project: Strategies for Active Participation in a Low- to Moderate-Income Community* (Pinkett, 2001; Pinkett and O'Bryant, 2001), and the University of California, San Diego, *Beyond Access: Qualifying the Digital Divide* (Stanley, 2002), examined the factors that inhibit residents' use of community technology programs. Both reports concluded that a lack of relevance, fear, and cultural considerations in addition to the lack of relevant content cited earlier, all contribute to this obstacle.

Second, *difficulties in distributing lessons learned and forming partnerships locally and regionally* have caused redundancy and prevented the movement from leveraging its collective experience nationally. In 2000, the University of Michigan released a study of CTCs and their efforts to share lessons learned, aptly titled *Surely Someone Knows How To Do This: Organizing Information Flows of Community Technology Centers* (Sandor and Scheuerer, 2000). Their findings included the need for more networking opportunities and better access to documentation of others' practices.

Third, *the community technology movement currently faces huge challenges of achieving scale and sustainability*. How should we address the digital divide in the many places that do not benefit from the existence of CTCs? Should we devise a way to create CTCs in these places? Replication of those models that have demonstrated success is one possibility, but has always seemed better in theory than it has worked in practice. Locally based organizations work because they are rooted in their local context; this makes such models difficult to transfer. Or should we construct mechanisms that enable existing CBOs and other local organizations to build the capacity necessary to address the technology gap? One vision is that of CTCs playing key roles as the community institutions of the future, functioning as gathering places, training institutions, and family learning centers. Another vision would position CTCs as stopgap measures, functioning to fill a present void only until existing institutions can gain sufficient capacity to address the technology gap themselves.

The most realistic way for CTCs to achieve scale and sustainability is through partnerships with existing institutions such as CBOs, schools, and libraries. Such partnerships will help to institutionalize the goals of the community technology movement and enable it to reach many more people. The community technology movement is also mature enough to have generated a set of intermediary organizations and trade associations. These organizations can help to create scale by documenting and disseminating best practices, educating funders about the problem of the digital divide and community-based solutions, and connecting with other community-based movements that have complementary goals.

Fourth, *the community technology movement has yet to fully align its efforts with the community building movement*, an interrelated and parallel movement, which seeks to revitalize distressed communities, that has emerged over the past half-century. Many community technology practitioners are only beginning to situate their work within the context of much broader efforts to catalyze community change. Analogously, many community building practitioners are only now considering how to incorporate information and communications technology into their community outreach activities. In *Bridging the Organizational Divide: Toward a Comprehensive Approach to the Digital Divide* (Kirschenbaum and Kunamneni, 2001), researchers at PolicyLink coined this disconnect, the "organizational divide," and highlighted programs across the US that are integrating community technology and community building successfully. As a recent Seedco (2002) study found, however, these CBOs remain the exception.

Fifth, and finally, as the original funding sources for community technology programs continue to diminish, *it will become increasingly incumbent on program directors to identify alternative sources of support as well as new and innovative approaches to service delivery*. Scale and sustainability are critical current issues for the community technology movement. These are perhaps the movement's greatest challenges as well as its greatest opportunities as they may force practitioners to wrestle with each of the aforementioned issues of capturing the late majority, disseminating best practices, moving beyond access to outcomes, and facilitating greater alignment with community builders. In other words, the strategies needed to sustain the movement could serve to elevate those programs that have utilized resources effectively and necessitate changes among those that have not.

Naturally, there are a number of CTCs that have overcome these hurdles to play a significant and effective role in the communities they serve. In some respects, they could be considered models for the future of the community technology movement, serving as new "public spaces" or places that engage diverse groups of people and contribute to positive local change.

CONCLUSIONS

The community technology movement has grown up at the edges of established institutional arrangements, in the interstices between traditional policy spheres and existing community-based movements. It has incorporated aspects of community development, economic development, education, and organizing. This movement is a response to the larger socioeconomic transformation that has created the information society. The response has resulted in a new set of locally based institutions and programs – community technology centers – that act to diffuse technology, engage people in civil society, and connect traditionally disadvantaged groups to the opportunities offered by the new economy.

In the short time that they have existed, CTCs have helped countless individuals and communities to harness the power of the information society and reap its benefits. But CTCs are too small, scattered, and vulnerable to the vicissitudes of the funding world to be the answer for society at large. On their own, they are unlikely to make a significant dent in the problem of the digital divide or to substantially narrow other longstanding divides.

CTCs are a growing, new form of community organization. Although small and unevenly distributed across the US and around the world, they fill an important niche, delivering the benefits of the information age to those who have been passed by. At present, the community technology movement is at a critical juncture, when many of the pieces are in place to bring technology to those regions that do not currently benefit from it. First, a key group of mature CTCs has existed for several years; these organizations have amassed an important body of collective experience. Second, policy-makers and funders have begun to recognize the importance of confronting the digital divide. And, third, a range of traditional institutions – schools, libraries, CBOs, and community colleges, for example – understand that they have a role to play. Cities and regions that decide to take on the digital divide can now benefit from the experiences of others that have already traveled this route.

The digital divide is one manifestation of an enormous shift currently underway in our society. This shift has made us more global, and our progress more dependent on the facility with which information can be moved and applied. The move to an information society increases our ability to connect to each other, to share information, and to open up access to education and the labor market. At the same time, the digital divide reveals and repeats patterns of inequality that long pre-existed the current problem. These patterns exist not only in the United States but also throughout the world, in developed and developing countries alike. These old divides, which continue to fall out along the familiar lines of race, class, gender, and location, will not be narrowed by a simple "tech" fix. Rather, addressing persistent poverty and inequality requires a new generation of efforts characterized by greater integration, coordination, and, most of all, a willingness to question and change the structures that maintain existing power relations.

Although the potential of IT to create opportunities for disadvantaged groups must be pursued aggressively, we must also assess pragmatically what it can and cannot do. Technology alone will not level deep historical inequalities. Technology, then, is one tool, not "the" answer. Deployed wisely, it can significantly advance important human development goals. Without support to make it equally available, and without integrating it into a more comprehensive solution, it will likely aggravate existing inequalities (Rogers, 1983; Markusen, 1999; Graham and Marvin, 2001). Technology can be a tool of inclusion or exclusion. The question that needs to be answered is: how can we employ technology as a tool of inclusion in a society that is not structured to be fully inclusive? In the end, it is futile to think about either policy or technology in the abstract. Both are driven by people. Both are tools with the potential to create a global society that is more just, more open, and more inclusive – if we can muster the political will to make it so.

NOTES

1. See Servon (2002) for a history of the community technology movement.
2. Interestingly, Street-Level Youth Media obtains the majority of its funding from non-technology sources such as youth and arts funders.
3. Data presented here are from a survey conducted by one of the authors in 1999 (see Servon, 2002).
4. Rogers's "Diffusion of Innovations" is a theory concerning the "process by which an innovation is communicated through certain channels over time among the members of a social system." The theory is an extension of the work of two sociologists, Bryce Ryan and Neal Gross, who "published their seminal study of the diffusion of hybrid seed among Iowa farmers" in the 1940s. In this work, they classified the segments of Iowa farmers in relation to the amount of time it took them to adopt the innovation; in this case, the hybrid corn seed. The five segments were as follows: (1) innovators, (2) early adopters, (3) early majority, (4) late majority, and (5) laggards.

REFERENCES

Brock, Gerald (1994) *Telecommunications Policy for the Information Age*. Cambridge, MA: Harvard University Press.

Castells, Manuel (2001) *The Internet Galaxy: Reflections on the Internet, Business, and Society*. Oxford: Oxford University Press.

Chapman, Gary and Rhodes, Lodis (1997) "Nurturing Neighbourhood Nets: Technology Review" (accessed July 21, 1999 from http://www.techreview.com/articles/oct97/chapman.html).

Chow, Clifton, Ellis, Jan, Mark, June, and Wise, Bart (1998) *Impact of CTCNet Affiliates: Findings from a National Survey of Users of Community Technology Centers*. Newton, MA: Community Technology Centers' Network (CTCNet), Education Development Center.

Civille, Richard (1995) "The Internet and the Poor," in Brian Kahin and James Keller (eds), *Public Access to the Internet*. Cambridge, MA: MIT Press.

DiMaggio, Paul and Hargittai, Eszter (2001) "From the 'Digital Divide' to 'Digital Inequality': Studying Internet Use as Penetration Increases," unpublished manuscript.

Doctor, Ronald D. (1994) "Seeking Equity in the National Information Infrastructure," *Internet Research* 4 (3): 9–22.

Graham, Stephen and Marvin, Simon (2001) *Splintering Urbanism: Networked Infrastructures, Technological Mobilities, and the Urban Condition*. New York: Routledge.

Granovetter, Mark (1973) "The Strength of Weak Ties," *American Journal of Sociology* 78: 1360–80.

Hecht, Lawrence (1998) "Community Networking and Economic Development: A Feasibility Assessment" (accessed February 2, 1999 from http://home.earthlink.net/~hechtl/Communities).

Kirschenbaum, Josh and Kunamneni, Radhika (2001) *Bridging the Organizational Divide: Toward a Comprehensive Approach to the Digital Divide*. Oakland, CA: PolicyLink.

Lazarus, Wendy and Mora, Francisco (2000) *Online Content for Low-income and Underserved Americans: The Digital Divide's New Frontier*. Santa Monica, CA: The Children's Partnership.

Lenhart, Amanda, Horrigan, John, Rainie, Lee, Allen, Katherine, Boyce, Angie, Madden, Mary, and O'Grady, Erin (2003) *The Ever-shifting Internet Population: A New Look at Internet Access and the Digital Divide*. Washington, DC: Pew Internet and American Life Project.

Mark, June and Briscoe, Kimberly (1995) *The PTW Network: History, Change, and Opportunities*. Newton, MA: Education Development Center.

Markusen, Ann (1999) "Sticky Places in Slippery Spaces: A Typology of Industrial Districts," in T. Barnes and M. Gertler (eds), *The New Industrial Geography*, pp. 98–123. London: Routledge.

Pinkett, R. D. (2001) "The Camfield Estates–MIT Creating Community Connections Project: Strategies for Active Participation in a Low- to Moderate-income Community," paper presented at the Second Kyoto Meeting on Digital Cities, Kyoto, Japan, October 18–20 (http://www.media.mit.edu/~rpinkett/papers/).

— — and O'Bryant, R. L. (2001) "Building Community, Empowerment and Self-sufficiency: Early Results from the Camfield Estates–MIT Creating Community Connections Project," paper presented at Digital Communities 2002: Cities in the Information Society, Chicago, IL, November 4–6 (http://www.media.mit.edu/~rpinkett/papers/).

Rogers, E. M. (1983) *Diffusion of Innovations*, 3rd edn. New York: The Free Press.

Sandor, Laurel and Scheuerer, Karen (2000) *Surely Someone Knows How To Do This: Organizing Information Flows of Community Technology Centers*. Ann Arbor, MI: School of Information, University of Michigan (available at http://www.si.umich.edu/community/connections/findingsreport.html).

Sanyal, Bish (2000) "From Dirt Road to Information Superhighway: Advanced Information Technology and the Future of the Urban Poor," in James O. Wheeler, Yuko Aoyama, and Barney Warf (eds), *Cities in the Telecommunications Age: The Fracturing of Geographies*. New York: Routledge.

Seedco (2002) *The Evolving Role of Information Technology in Community Development Organizations*. New York: Seedco.

Servon, Lisa J. (2002) *Bridging the Digital Divide: Technology, Community, and Public Policy*. Oxford: Blackwell.

Shapiro, Andrew L. (1999) "The Net that Binds: Using Cyberspace to Create Real Communities," *The Nation* (June 21).

Stanley, L. (2002) *Beyond Access: Qualifying the Digital Divide*. San Diego, CA: UCSD Civic Collaborative (available at http://www.mediamanage.net/Beyond_Access.pdf).

Stone, A. (1996) "CTCNet: History, Organization, and Future," *Community Technology Center Review* (Fall/Winter) (available at http://www.ctcnet.org/new6toni.html).

United Nations Development Programme (2001) *Human Development Report 2001: Making New Technologies Work for Human Development*. New York: United Nations Development Programme.

US Department of Commerce (1995) *Falling Through the Net: A Survey of the "Have Nots" in Rural and Urban America* (Full Report, July, available at http://www.ntia.doc.gov/ntiahome/digitaldivide/).

— — (1998) *Falling Through the Net II: New Data on the Digital Divide* (Full Report, July, available at http://www.ntia.doc.gov/ntiahome/digitaldivide/).

— — (1999) *Falling Through the Net III: Defining the Digital Divide* (Full Report, July, available at http://www.ntia.doc.gov/ntiahome/digitaldivide/).

— — (2000) *Falling Through the Net IV: Toward Digital Inclusion* (Full Report, October, available at http://www.ntia.doc.gov/ntiahome/digitaldivide/).

— — (2002) *A Nation Online: How Americans Are Expanding their Use of the Internet* (Full Report, February, available at http://www.ntia.doc.gov/ntiahome/dn/index.html).

The White House (1999) *Remarks by the President on Bridging the Digital Divide.* Washington, DC: Office of the Press Secretary, The White House, December 9 (available at http://clinton4.nara.gov/WH/New/html/19991209.html).

— — (2000) *From Digital Divide to Digital Opportunity.* Washington, DC: The White House.

PART VI

Networked social movements and informational
politics

15. Networked social movements: global movements for global justice

Jeffrey S. Juris

Facilitated by the greater speed, adaptability, and flexibility afforded by new information technologies, decentralized network forms are out-competing more traditional vertical hierarchies. Nowhere has this trend been more apparent than within the realm of collective action, where transnational social movements reflect the broad decentered networking logic of informationalism, even as they attack the roots of informational capitalism. Since bursting onto the scene in Seattle in 1999, and through subsequent direct action protests against multilateral institutions and alternative forums around the world in places such as Prague, Quebec, Genoa, Barcelona, and Porto Alegre, anti-corporate globalization movements have challenged global inequalities, while making new struggles visible. The more aptly named "movements for global justice" – activists are actually building alternative globalizations from below – involve a politics of articulation, uniting a broad network of networks in opposition to growing corporate influence over our lives, communities, and resources. Movements for global justice can thus be viewed as signs indicating a democratic deficit within emerging regimes of transnational governance, as well as social laboratories for the production of alternative codes, values, and practices.

Inspired by the *Zapatistas* and previous struggles against free trade, structural adjustment, and environmental destruction, global justice activists have made innovative use of global computer networks, informational politics, and network-based organizational forms. Theorists have pointed to the rise of global "Netwars" (Arquilla and Ronfeldt, 2001) or the emergence of an "electronic fabric of struggle" (Cleaver, 1995), but such broad descriptions tell us very little about concrete networking practices or how such practices are generated. Manuel Castells (1997: 362) has identified a "networking, decentered form of organization and intervention, characteristic of the new social movements, mirroring, and counteracting, the networking logic of domination in the information society." However, scholars have yet to explore the specific mechanisms through which this decentered networking logic is actually produced, reproduced, and transformed by concrete activist practice within particular social, cultural, and political contexts.[1]

Following Fredric Jameson (1991), who refers to postmodernism as the cultural logic of late capitalism, and Aihwa Ong (1999), who explores a specific type of late capitalist cultural logic, transnationality, I introduce the term "cultural logic of networking" as a way to conceive the broad guiding principles, shaped by the logic of informational capitalism, which are internalized by activists and generate concrete networking practices.[2] This logic specifically involves an embedded and embodied set of social and cultural dispositions that orient actors toward: (1) building horizontal ties and connections among diverse, autonomous elements; (2) the free and open circulation of information; (3) collaboration through decentralized coordination and directly democratic decision-making; and (4) self-directed or self-managed networking (Castells, 2001: 55). The cultural logic of networking reflects the values and practices associated with "open source" software development, incorporated in operating systems such as LINUX, or the World Wide Web. It thus forms part of a broader "hacker ethic" explored by Himanen (2001), which is rooted in the values of free information, decentralized coordination, collaborative learning, peer recognition, and social service. However, this networking logic represents an ideal type: it is unevenly distributed, and always exists in dynamic tension with other competing logics, often generating a complex "cultural politics of networking" within particular spheres.[3]

This chapter explores the dynamics of networking within movements for global justice along three main analytical planes – networks as computer-supported infrastructure (technology), networks as organizational structure (form), and networks as political model (norm) – and the complex interrelationships among them.[4] Global communication networks constitute the basic infrastructure for transnational social movements, providing arenas for the production, contestation, and dissemination of specific movement-related discourses and practices (Diani, 1995). These networks are, in turn, produced and transformed through the discourses and practices circulating through them (see Mische, 2003). Moreover, above and beyond the level of social morphology, networks are increasingly associated with values related to grassroots participatory democracy, self-management, horizontal connectedness, and decentralized coordination based on autonomy and diversity. The network has thus become a powerful cultural ideal, particularly among more radical global justice activists, a guiding logic that provides both a model of and a model for emerging forms of directly democratic politics on local, regional, and global scales.[5]

THE RISE OF GLOBAL JUSTICE MOVEMENTS

Nearly 50,000 people took to the streets to protest against corporate globalization at the World Trade Organization (WTO) meetings in Seattle on

November 30, 1999. A diverse coalition of environmental, labor, and economic justice activists succeeded in shutting down the meetings and preventing another round of trade liberalization talks. Media images of giant puppets, tear gas, and street clashes between protesters and the police were broadcast throughout the world, bringing both the WTO and a novel form of collective action into public view. Seattle became a symbol and a battle cry for a new generation of activists, as anti-corporate globalization networks were energized around the globe. Diverse networks and historical processes converged in Seattle, producing a new model of social protest, involving direct action, NGO-based forums, labor marches and rallies, independent media, and the articulation of economic justice, environmental, feminist, labor, and international solidarity activism.

Global justice activists alternatively trace their genealogy back to the *Zapatista* uprising, campaigns against the North American Free Trade (NAFTA) and Multilateral Investment (MAI) Agreements, student-based anti-corporate activism, and radical anarchist-inspired direct action, bringing together traditions from the United States, Great Britain, Italy, and Germany, among others. Indeed, Seattle was the third Global Day of Action loosely coordinated through the People's Global Action (PGA) network, which was founded in 1998 by grassroots movements that had taken part in the second *Zapatista*-inspired Intercontinental Encounter for Humanity and Against Neoliberalism organized in Spain the year before.[6] However, when these diverse historical trajectories came together, the result was an entirely new phenomenon bigger than the sum of its parts.

On the one hand, the "Battle of Seattle," packaged as a prime-time image event (Deluca, 1999), cascaded through global mediascapes (Appadurai, 1996), capturing the imagination of long-time activists and would-be post-modern revolutionaries alike. On the other hand, activists followed the events in Seattle and beyond through Internet-based distribution lists, websites, and the newly created Independent Media Center.[7] New networks quickly emerged, such as the Continental Direct Action Network (DAN) in North America,[8] or the Movement for Global Resistance (MRG) in Catalonia,[9] where my own field research was based, while already existing global networks such as PGA, the International Movement for Democratic Control of Financial Markets and their Institutions (ATTAC), or Via Campesina also played crucial roles during these early formative stages. Although more diffuse, decentralized, all-channel formations (Arquilla and Ronfeldt, 2001), such as DAN or MRG, proved difficult to sustain over time, they provided concrete mechanisms for generating physical and virtual communication and coordination in real time among diverse movements, groups, and collectives.

Global justice movements have largely grown and expanded through the organization of mass mobilizations, including highly confrontational direct actions and counter-summit forums against multilateral institutions. The anti-WTO protests were a huge success, and everywhere activists wanted to create the "next Seattle." Mass mobilizations offer concrete goals around which to organize, while they also provide physical spaces where activists meet, virtual networks are embodied, meanings and representations are produced and contested, and where political values are ritually enacted. Public events can broadly be seen as "culturally constituted foci for information-processing" (Handelman, 1990: 16), while direct actions, in particular, generate intense emotional energy (Collins, 2001), stimulating continuing networking within public and submerged spheres. Activists organized a second mass protest against the World Bank and International Monetary Fund (IMF) in Washington, DC on April 16, 2000, and went truly global during the subsequent mobilization against the World Bank/IMF in Prague on September 26, 2000. Protesters came from around Europe, including large contingents from Spain, Italy, Germany, and Britain, and other parts of the world, including the United States, Latin America, and South Asia. Solidarity actions were held in cities throughout Europe, North and South America, and parts of Asia and Africa.[10]

The first World Social Forum (WSF), organized in Porto Alegre, Brazil, in late January 2001, coinciding with the World Economic Forum, represented an important turning point, as movements for global justice began to more clearly emphasize alternatives to corporate globalization.[11] The unexpected success of the first WSF was magnified during the subsequent two editions, which drew 70,000 and 100,000 people from around the world, respectively. Much more than a conference, the WSF constitutes a dynamic process, involving the convergence of multiple networks, movements, and organizations. Whereas PGA remains more radical, horizontal, and broadly libertarian,[12] the WSF is a wider political space, including both newer decentralized network-based movements and more hierarchical forces of the traditional left. Meanwhile, mass actions continued to intensify and expand during the spring and summer of 2001, including the anti-FTAA (Free Trade Area of the Americas) protests in Quebec and increasingly militant actions against the European Union in Gothenburg, the World Bank in Barcelona, and the G8 summit in Genoa, where widespread police violence culminated in the death of an Italian activist and a brutal night-time raid on the Independent Media Center. Mass marches and rallies the following day brought 350,000 protesters onto the streets of Genoa, and hundreds of thousands more around Italy.

US-based global justice movements, which were severely shaken by the September 11 attacks, re-emerged when activists shifted their attention from the war in Iraq back toward corporate globalization, leading to mass mobilizations against the WTO in Cancun and the FTAA summit in Miami during the fall of 2003. In the rest of the world, mobilizations continued to grow after

9/11, including a march of half a million people against the European Union in Barcelona in March 2002, and a mass protest involving more than 30,000 people against the FTAA in Quito, Ecuador during October 2002. Movements for global justice and those against the war in Iraq soon converged, leading to an anti-war protest of more than a million people during the European Social Forum in Florence in November. Meanwhile, the third edition of the World Social Forum in Porto Alegre drew 100,000 participants during January 2003. The following June, hundreds of thousands of global justice and peace activists descended on the border of France and Switzerland to protest against the heavily militarized G8 summit in Evian.

THE DYNAMICS OF OPPOSITION IN THE INFORMATION AGE

In *The Power of Identity*, Manuel Castells (1997) points to the emergence of powerful communal resistance identities that have arisen in opposition to economic globalization, capitalist restructuring, and the disruption caused by global financial and cultural flows, all important features of the information age. He also holds out another possibility: that from the midst of communal resistance, the seeds of a proactive project identity might emerge, capable of producing alternative cultural codes and sowing the seeds for a global civil society. In this sense, movements for global justice represent the (re)-emergence of an alternative political project based on the articulation of diverse local/global struggles against the disjuncture wrought by corporate globalization. Beyond creating alternative cultural codes, however, activists are generating new networking forms and practices that allow for the production of global webs of resistance, while providing diverse models for building an alternative, more directly democratic and globally networked society. Global justice movements can thus be characterized according to three specific features, which are more broadly associated with the nature of informational capitalism.

First, global justice movements are *global*. Coordinating and communicating through transnational networks, activists have engaged in institutional politics, such as global campaigns to defeat the MAI or abolish the external debt, and extra-institutional strategies, including coordinated Global Days of Action, international forums, and cross-border information sharing. Perhaps most importantly, activists *think* of themselves as belonging to global movements, discursively linking their local protests and activities to diverse struggles elsewhere. Global justice movements have thus emerged as transnational fields of meaning, where actions, images, discourses, and tactics flow from one continent to another via worldwide communication networks in real time.[13] Some have objected that these movements are restricted to middle-class youths with Internet connections and resources to travel. This is largely true for direct action-oriented sectors, which tend to be youth-based and located in major or secondary "global cities" (Sassen, 1991), along important transnational trajectories of power. Even so, radical youth sectors should not be mistaken for the whole. Sizable contingents from Southern indigenous and peasant networks have taken part in anti-globalization actions, while movements such as the Brazilian MST or the Indian Karnataka State Farmers have played key roles within both PGA, whose global conferences have been held in India and Bolivia, and the WSF, which has taken place in Brazil and India. Moreover, Southern movements have organized against free trade, structural adjustment, environmental devastation, and corporate exploitation for decades.

Second, global justice movements are *informational*. The various protest tactics employed by activists, despite emerging in very different cultural contexts, all produce highly visible, theatrical images for mass-mediated consumption, including: giant puppets and street theater, mobile street carnivals (Reclaim the Streets), militant protesters advancing toward police lines with white outfits, protective shields, and padding (White Overalls), and black-clad, masked urban warriors smashing the symbols of corporate capitalism (Black Bloc).[14] The general blockade strategy, where diverse formations "swarm" their target (Arquilla and Ronfeldt, 2001), inscribing meanings into urban terrains of resistance (Routledge, 1994) through alternative forms of embodied political praxis, produces high-powered social drama indeed. Whether broadcast images depict roving samba dancers dressed in pink and silver, thousands of Michelin Men advancing toward a "red zone," or skirmishes between robocops and hooded stone-throwers, mass actions are powerful image events. Militant protest violence becomes yet another form of symbolic communication, while tactics circulate through global networks, where they are reproduced, transformed, and enacted in distant locales. Moreover, the horizontal, directly democratic process through which direct actions are organized, involving decentralized coordination among autonomous affinity groups, as well as the prevailing "diversity of tactics" ethic among many activists, embody the broader cultural logic of networking itself.

Finally, global justice movements are organized around flexible, decentralized *networks*, reflecting the dominant organizational logic of informational capitalism. In practice, they are composed of a multiplicity of diverse network forms, including more hierarchical "circle" patterns, intermediate "wheel" formations and the more decentralized "all-channel" configurations (Kapferer, 1973: 87).[15] Alternative network models imply divergent cultural logics, often leading to a complex cultural politics of networking when different logics interact within broad convergence spaces. In addition, real-time global activist networking is made possible by the emergence of new information technologies, particularly the Internet, which allows for a "politics of scale" based on direct coordination and communication among small-scale, autonomous units without the need for hierarchical mediating structures such as traditional political parties or labor unions. Diverse, locally rooted struggles can now directly link up, articulating around common objectives without compromising their autonomy or specificity, which is precisely what global justice activists mean when they talk about "unity through diversity." Moreover, as we shall see, the network is also emerging as a widespread cultural ideal among certain sectors, implying new forms of decentralized, directly democratic politics, reflecting both the traditional values of anarchism and the logic of computer networking.

COMPUTER NETWORKS AND GLOBAL JUSTICE MOVEMENTS

By significantly enhancing the speed, flexibility, and global reach of information flows, allowing for communication at a distance in real time, computer networks provide the technological infrastructure for the operation of contemporary network-based organizational and social forms. With regard to social networks more generally, Barry Wellman has argued that "computer-supported social networks" (CSSNs) are profoundly transforming the nature of communities, sociality, and interpersonal relations (Wellman, 2001; cf. Castells, 2001: 129–33). Although the proliferation of increasingly individualized, loosely bounded, and fragmentary community networks predates cyberspace, computer-mediated communications have reinforced such trends, allowing communities to sustain interactions across vast distances.[16] Moreover, the Internet is being incorporated into more routine aspects of daily social life (Wellman and Haythornthwaite, 2002), as virtual and physical activities become increasingly integrated (Miller and Slater, 2000; Wellman, 2001). Despite the shrinking, yet still formidable, digital divide, the Internet facilitates global connectedness, even as it strengthens local ties within neighborhoods and households, leading to increasing "glocalization" (Wellman, 2001: 236; cf. Robertson, 1995).

Similar trends can be detected at the level of political activity, where Internet use, including electronic distribution lists and interactive web pages, has broadly facilitated new patterns of social engagement. Global justice movements thus belong to a particular class of CSSN: *computer-supported social movements*. Using the Internet as technological infrastructure, such movements are increasingly "glocal," operating at both local and global levels, while seamlessly integrating both online and off-line political activity. The

Zapatistas were important forerunners in this regard: although locally rooted among Mayan Indian communities in Chiapas, the *Zapatistas* used the Internet to communicate with a global network of solidarity collectives (Cleaver, 1995; Castells, 1997: 72–83; Ronfeldt et al., 1998; Routledge, 1998).

Building on the pioneering use of the Internet by the *Zapatistas* and early free-trade campaigns, such as the successful battle against the MAI, global justice activists have employed computer networks to organize direct actions, share information and resources, and coordinate campaigns through communication at a distance in real time. For example, the flurry of electronic activity that accompanied the organization of the Seattle protests quickly moved to a new nationwide list-serve after the WTO action to coordinate the mobilization against the World Bank/IMF in Washington, DC in April 2000, while new distribution lists were created shortly thereafter to plan for the summer 2000 mobilizations against the Republican and Democratic National Conventions in Philadelphia and Los Angeles, respectively. Meanwhile, European-based activists set up a series of English-language list-serves in early May 2000 to prepare for the September 26 actions against the World Bank/IMF in Prague. The first Spanish-language anti-globalization list-serve was also established around the same time to coordinate local solidarity actions throughout Latin America, mainly involving anarchists and radicals from Mexico, Brazil, and Argentina. Later that month, activists in Barcelona established the first distribution list in the Spanish state to organize for Prague. Since then, global justice list-serves have sprung up in nearly every country around the world, particularly where local actions and campaigns have been organized. Internet use has complemented and facilitated face-to-face coordination and interaction, rather than replacing them. Activists use list-serves to stay informed about activities and to perform concrete logistical tasks, while more complex planning, political discussions, and relationship building occur during physical settings, where virtual networks become embodied.

Although global justice activists have primarily used e-mail lists to facilitate planning and coordination, interactive web pages are becoming more widespread. Particular activist networks and processes – such as PGA, WSF, or ATTAC – have their own home pages, while temporary web pages are created during mobilizations to provide information, resources, and contact lists, to post documents and calls to action, and, increasingly, to house real-time discussion forums and chat rooms.[17] Activist networking projects, such as the "Infospace" in Barcelona, have also begun to collectively produce and edit documents online using new "wiki" open-editing technology, reflecting a more general growth in computer-based networked collaboration.[18] Similarly, independent media centers, which have been established in hundreds of cities around the world, provide online forums for activists to post their own news stories, constituting a self-managed communications network that bypasses

the corporate media.[19] Moreover, activists have created temporary convergence centers, media spaces, and communication hubs during mobilizations
and forums, providing physical spaces for the practice of "informational
utopics," involving the production of alternative media, experimentation with
computer and video technologies, and the sharing of ideas and resources.[20]
Activists are thus using new technologies to physically manifest their political
ideals, both within temporary and more sustained spheres.

NETWORK-BASED PRACTICES AND ORGANIZATIONAL FORMS

The Internet does not simply provide the technological infrastructure for
computer-supported social movements, its reticulate structure reinforces their
organizational logic. Decentralized, flexible, local/global activist networks
constitute the dominant organizational forms within global justice movements,
reflecting the broader logic of informational capitalism. New Social
Movement (NSM) theorists have long argued that, in contrast to the centralized, vertically integrated, working-class movements, newer feminist, ecological, and student movements are organized around flexible, dispersed, and
horizontal networks (Cohen, 1985). Mario Diani (1995), on the other hand,
defines social movements more generally as network formations. In a similar
vein, anthropologists Luther P. Gerlach and Virginia H. Hine (1970) argued
years ago that social movements should be characterized as decentralized,
segmentary, and reticulate. Gerlach (2001: 295–6) has more recently
suggested that: "The diverse groups of a movement . . . form an integrated
network or reticulate structure through nonhierarchical social linkages among
their participants . . . Networking enables movement participants to exchange
information and ideas and to coordinate participation in joint action."
However, the introduction of new information technologies has significantly
enhanced the most radically decentralized all-channel network configurations,
greatly facilitating transnational coordination and communication among
contemporary social movements.

Network designs are diffusing widely, as new technologies power the
expansion of globally connected, yet locally rooted computer-supported social
movements. These are increasingly organized around highly flexible all-channel patterns rather than more traditional top-down political formations. Global
justice movements in Catalonia, for example, initially grew and expanded with
the emergence of highly diffuse, flexible, and decentralized activist networks.
The Movement for Global Resistance (MRG), which mobilized around the
protests in Prague and subsequently became a major anti-globalization refer-
ent in the Spanish state, was initially conceived as "a network of people and

collectives against economic globalization and unitary thinking . . . a tool for providing local struggles with global content and extension."[21] Activists wanted to create a flexible mechanism for communication and coordination among diverse local struggles, including environmentalists, squatters, *Zapatista* supporters, solidarity and anti-debt activists, and opponents of the European Union. Rather than top-down, centralized command, activists preferred loose and flexible coordination among autonomous groups within a minimal structure involving periodic assemblies, logistical commissions surrounding concrete tasks, such as finances or media, and several project areas, including a social movement observatory and a resource exchange. In practice, the MRG often dissolved into broader campaigns, but it remained an effective space for sharing resources and information, generating analysis and discourse, and inspiring more broadly what activists considered to be a new form of political action based on "working as a network, through horizontal assemblies, and with local autonomy in order to reach people with a more open, less dogmatic style" (interview, May 30, 2002). In contrast to traditional leftist forces, open participation was favored over representation: "MRG is a movement 'without members;' membership ... leads to static, non-dynamic structures and to a clear and distinct, rather than a more diffuse sense of belonging."[22]

Moreover, many MRG participants were active in broader regional and global networks, particularly PGA, which itself represents a highly diffuse, all-channel network design involving communication and coordination among diverse local struggles around the world. Given the lack of resources and cultural differences, transnational coordination around concrete campaigns has proved difficult within PGA, yet global conferences and distribution lists have facilitated the exchange of experiences and information, while inspiring many Global Days of Action. There has been much more effective grassroots participation at the regional level, particularly in Europe, where the MRG served as a continental "co-convenor." Like the MRG, PGA has no formal members, seeking to provide an instrument of coordination and to help "the greatest number of persons and organizations to act against corporate domination through civil disobedience and people-oriented constructive actions."[23] Any person or collective can participate so long as they agree with the basic hallmarks, which include: a clear rejection of capitalism and all systems of domination, a confrontational attitude, a call to direct action and civil disobedience, and an organizational philosophy "based on decentralization and autonomy."[24] Rather than a centralized coordinating committee, each continent selects its own rotating "convenors" to organize regional and global conferences, assume logistical tasks, and facilitate communication mechanisms along with the help of various support groups. In September 2002, the European PGA assembly decided to organize a decentralized network of PGA "Infopoints" in order to give more visibility to the network and promote the struggles, activities, and values of participating collectives.

Within movements such as the MRG or PGA, the cultural logic of networking has given rise to what grassroots activists in Barcelona call the "new way of doing politics." By this they mean precisely those network-based forms of political organization and practice based on non-hierarchical structures, horizontal coordination among autonomous groups, open access, direct participation, consensus-based decision-making, and the ideal of the free and open circulation of information (although this is not always conformed to in practice). While the command-oriented logic of traditional parties and unions is based on recruiting new members, developing unitary strategies, political representation through vertical structures, and the pursuit of political hegemony, network-based politics involves the creation of broad umbrella spaces, where diverse organizations, collectives, and networks converge around a few common hallmarks, while preserving their autonomy and identity-based specificity. Rather than recruitment, the objective becomes horizontal expansion and enhanced "connectivity" through articulating diverse movements within flexible, decentralized information structures that allow for maximal coordination and communication. Guided by this networking logic, key activists become relayers and exchangers, generating concrete practices involving the reception, interpretation, and relaying of information out to the diverse nodes within and among alternative movement networks.

Following Diane Nelson (1999), who employs the term "Maya-hacker" to characterize Mayan activists engaged in cultural activism and transnational networking, global justice activists can be similarly viewed as "activist-hackers," generating innovative networking practices guided by the cultural logic of networking. Like computer hackers, activist-hackers receive, combine, and recombine cultural codes, in this case, political signifiers, freely sharing and circulating information about projects, mobilizations, strategies, tactics, and ideas through global communication networks. As with computer hackers, activist-hackers seek to enhance the connectivity of social movements, widening and diversifying networks through the open sharing and circulation of information. For example, a member of the PGA network support group, the son of Chilean exiles who grew up in Germany near the French border, stressed the value of "proficiency in multiple languages" and "cultural flexibility" for contributing to the group, signaling both the importance of recombining codes and connecting people through diversity and difference. In addition, a Barcelona-based activist, widely recognized as a key social relayer and exchanger, developed a system for instantly sending messages to hundreds of list-serves around the world.

Visibly impassioned, he once remarked, "Now I can reach thousands of activists at the touch of a button every time we want to communicate something important!"

This networking logic is unevenly distributed within global justice movements, however, and often generates fierce resistance. Network-based forms and practices are more prevalent among certain sectors, while the discourse of open networking can also serve to conceal other forms of domination and exclusion based on unequal access to communication technologies or control of information flows. Indeed, these issues often emerge as crucial points of contention among activists. As a grassroots activist from India commented in Porto Alegre: "It is not enough to talk about networks, we also have to talk about democracy and the internal distribution of power within them." A given cultural logic thus always exists in dynamic tension with other competing logics, and even when specific cultural practices become dominant within a concrete social space, they never achieve complete hegemony. What many observers view as a single, unified global justice movement is actually a congeries of competing, yet sometimes overlapping, social movement networks that differ according to issue addressed, political subjectivity, ideological framework, political culture, and organizational logic.

Social movements are complex cultural fields shot through with internal differentiation and contestation. Struggles within and among different movement networks largely shape the way specific networks are produced, how they develop, and how they relate to one another within broader social movement fields. Cultural struggles surrounding ideology (anti-globalization versus anti-capitalism), strategies (summit hopping versus sustained organizing), tactics (violence versus non-violence), as well as organizational form and decision-making (structure versus non-structure, consensus versus voting) – what I call the cultural politics of networking – have become enduring features of the global justice landscape. Indeed, the ubiquity of movement-related debates and discussions within physical and online forums, including the incessant production and circulation of documents, reflections, editorials, and calls to action, reflects the highly "reflexive" nature of contemporary social movement networks (see Giddens, 1991; Beck et al., 1994). Some of the most intense conflicts revolve around political culture and organizational form. Newer movements, such as the MRG and PGA, are characterized by a networking logic, while more traditional movements involve command logics and vertical structures, such as political parties and trade unions. Discrepant logics often lead activists into heated struggles within the broad umbrella spaces characteristic of global justice movements, such as the "unitary" campaigns against the World Bank or the European Union in Barcelona or the World Social Forum process at local, regional, and transnational scales.

THE SELF-GENERATED NETWORK AS EMERGING POLITICAL IDEAL

Expanding and diversifying networks is much more than a concrete organizational objective; it is also a highly valued cultural goal in itself. The self-produced, self-developed, and self-managed network becomes a widespread cultural ideal, providing not just an effective model of political organizing, but also a model for re-organizing society as a whole. The network ideal is reflected in the proliferation of decentralized organizational forms within global justice movements, as well as the development of new self-directed communication and coordination tools, such as Indymedia, the European Social Consulta, a process for generating information exchange among local assemblies coordinated at regional and global levels, or the countless Internet distribution lists established over the past several years. The dominant spirit behind this emerging political praxis can be broadly defined as anarchist, or what activists in Barcelona refer to more broadly as libertarian.[25] Classic anarchist principles, such as autonomy, self-management, federation, direct action, and direct democracy, are among the most important values among radical sectors of the movement, while activists are increasingly identifying themselves as anti-capitalist, anti-authoritarian, or left-libertarian.

I would argue, however, that these emerging political subjectivities are not necessarily identical to anarchism in the strict ideological sense; rather, they share specific cultural affinities which revolve around the broader values associated with the network as an emerging cultural and political ideal: open access, the free circulation of information, self-management, as well as coordination based on diversity and autonomy. Despite widespread popular belief, anarchism does not mean complete disorder. One of the important threads uniting the many diverse strands of anarchism involves precisely the importance of organization, although of a distinctly different kind: organization based on grassroots participation from below rather than centralized command from above. As Bakunin (1872) once wrote, "We want the reconstruction of society and the unification of mankind to be achieved, not from above downwards by any sort of authority, nor by socialist officials, engineers, and other accredited men of learning – but from below upwards" (cited in Ward, 1973: 22). After the Bolshevik Revolution, another Russian-born anarchist, Voline (1955),[26] similarly posited that: "The principle of organization must not issue from a center created in advance to capture the whole and impose itself upon it but, on the contrary, it must come from all sides to create nodes of coordination, natural centers to serve all these points" (cited in Guerin, 1970: 43).

The networking logic within contemporary globally linked social movements involves precisely this conception of horizontal coordination among autonomous elements. Colin Ward, a contemporary British anarchist, specifically views anarchist federations as decentralized networks, explaining that communes and syndicates would "federate together not like the stones of a pyramid where the biggest burden is borne by the lowest layer, but like the links of a network, the network of autonomous groups" (1973: 26). In many ways, anarchism resembles the decentered networking logic of informational capitalism, as Ward (1973: 58) further explains: "The anarchist conclusion is that every kind of human activity should begin from what is local and immediate, should link in a network with no center and no directing agency, hiving off new cells as the original ones grow." From this vantage point, it is not surprising that anarchism, or left-libertarianism more generally, would become the prevailing ethos of opposition within an age characterized by decentralized network forms. The "autopoietic" or self-produced network (see Luhmann, 1990) thus becomes a powerful model, reflecting an open-source development logic, based on a multitude of autonomous components coordinating and interacting without mediating structure or central command.

Kropotkin (1905) similarly argued that in a society without government, social order and harmony would be produced through "an ever-changing adjustment and readjustment of equilibrium between the multitudes of forces and influences" (cited in Ward, 1973: 52). Whereas neoliberalism revolves around the ideal of the self-regulating market, anarchism does away with mediation altogether, positing completely self-managed, self-regulating networks. The important point, though, is not whether networks are autopoietic in a strict sense, but, rather, that the self-generating network becomes a broader cultural and political model for organizing society based on horizontal connectedness, direct democracy, and coordination through autonomy and diversity – among hackers, anarchists, and more radical global justice activists alike.[27]

This emerging network ideal was particularly pronounced among the Catalan and Spanish activists I worked with during my field research in Barcelona. For example, the Citizens Network to Abolish the External Debt (RCADE), which helped give rise to and continued to work alongside the MRG, self-consciously employed the terminology of computer networks to characterize its organizational structure. The "Network," as it is popularly known, is thus composed of various local, regional, and statewide "nodes." The organizational and political base of the Network is constituted by local nodes, which are "self-defined, self-managed and self-organized spaces." Broader coordination is carried out through periodic meetings of regional and statewide nodes, as well as annual gatherings. The Network was specifically forged to organize a statewide consultation to ask citizens if they were in favor of abolishing the external debt owed by developing nations to the Spanish government. As one activist explained:

> We organized ourselves as nodes, using the nomenclature of the Internet. It was completely new because we were thinking in network terms. The nodes were the spaces where information was produced and made public, the physical embodiment of the Internet, what we might call affinity groups today. We took the idea, not of a platform – we didn't want to work as a platform – but rather of a network. (interview, June 12, 2002)

Moreover, the broader political goal was not just abolishing the external debt, but rather expanding the Network itself, along with its directly democratic modus operandi, as an RCADE document explains, "The Network is a tool for creating social fabric, and we do this in our local contexts . . . Participatory democracy is not only a transversal theme in our work; it constitutes our model of . . . operation."[28] This network ideal emerged among many activist sectors around the Spanish state during the latter half of the 1990s, ultimately becoming an important part of the broader ethos within global justice movements, as an MRG activist explained: "For me, the twenty-first century, with the discourse of postmodernity, people are always talking about the 'network of networks of networks,' but for me building these networks represents the world we want to create" (interview, June 11, 2002). She went on to define her ideal world as composed of "small, self-organized and self-managed communities, coordinated among them on a worldwide scale." When asked about networks, another global justice activist and squatter responded: "The revolution is also about process; the way we do things … is also an alternative to capitalism, no?" (interview, June 2, 2002). Specifically contrasting traditional politics with the network ideal, another MRG-based activist described networks as the best way to "balance freedom with coordination, autonomy with collective work, self-organization with effectiveness" (interview, May 30, 2002). Networking tools – such as Indymedia, electronic distribution lists, interactive web pages, the European Social Consulta, or the Barcelona Infospace – are thus specifically designed to help people "construct networks at whatever rhythm possible."

CONCLUSION: BUILDING LABORATORIES FOR DEMOCRACY

In the process of using new networking technologies and practices to communicate, coordinate, and (self-)organize, global justice activists are building new organizational forms that are network-based, and which express and reflect the network as an emerging political and cultural ideal. Eric Raymond (1999: 224) has characterized a popular folk theorem among software engineers in the following terms: "Organizations which design systems are constrained to produce designs which are copies of the communication structures of these organizations." There is indeed something to this. Emerging network norms and forms within global justice movements (and within the academy as well) thus not only mirror one another, they also reflect underlying technological transformations mediated by concrete human practice, pointing to a much broader dialectic among cultural norms, organizational forms, and technological change.

Global justice movements are extremely diverse phenomena. While some Marxist and social democratic sectors promote a return to the nation-state as the locus for democratic control over the global economy, others support an internationalist "globalization from below" (Brecher et al., 2000), where transnational movements represent an emerging global civil society. Activists within more libertarian networks, however, increasingly view social movements as concrete political alternatives in and of themselves. Many ecologists, squatters, and militant anti-capitalists emphasize the local sphere, while others share a broad vision for a decentralized, yet globally coordinated network of autonomous, self-managed communities. What brings all these different visions together involves a commitment to help people establish democratic control over their daily lives. Alberto Melucci (1989: 75–6) argues that social movements are signs that announce to society the existence of a conflict and render power visible. In this sense, global justice movements highlight the increasing social and economic polarization, environmental devastation, and cultural domination that activists associate with the current regime of corporate globalization, where the market has become disembedded from society (Polanyi, 1957).

Moving from resistance toward alternative political projects often generates heated micro-political struggles among activists, which largely revolve around two distinct forms of practicing democracy: one based on political representation within permanent structures and another rooted in flexible coordination and direct participation through decentralized network formations. Political parties, unions, and formal organizations of civil society operate according to a representative logic, where social movements function as lobby groups, applying grassroots pressure to institutional actors, who ultimately process and implement political proposals. On this view, movements, parties, and unions should work together, each filling distinct, yet complementary roles, as a labor delegate from Barcelona explained: "Social movements carry out grassroots work, raising awareness among citizens, but they cannot substitute for political parties ... Each one has to know what role they play, and in which social and political space they operate" (interview, June 12, 2002).

On the other hand, radical network-based movements have articulated a more sweeping political project: transcending both the market and the state. During a debate between Catalan activists and their more institutional counterparts in May 2002, for example, an activist from XCADE (the Catalan version of RCADE) strongly criticized the logic of electoral representation, suggesting that very few people identify with political parties: "We are thus creating a new political culture, a new way of doing politics, based on grass-roots citizen participation." An MRG-based militant later confided that he stopped voting after becoming involved with grassroots movements, explaining that "I am building an alternative political system, and that is much more important." When I specifically asked another activist from XCADE what might replace representative democracy, he was unsure, but thought it was important to create a more directly democratic system from below:

> One of the things that most motivates me these days is trying to figure out how to organize democracy at the beginning of the twenty-first century given the new technological infrastructure at our disposal. How do we deepen our local democratic practices – at work and in our neighborhoods – and transfer that spirit to the global level?

Whereas directly democratic forms of participation have historically been tied to local contexts, new networking technologies and practices are facilitating innovative experiments with grassroots democracy coordinated at local, regional, and global scales. Among the more radical global justice activists, networks represent much more than technology and organizational form; they also provide new cultural models for radically reconstituting politics and society more generally. In this sense, grassroots, network-based movements can be viewed as democratic laboratories, generating the political norms and forms most appropriate for the information age.

ACKNOWLEDGMENTS

This chapter is based on fieldwork conducted in Barcelona from June 2001 to August 2002, including travel to Brussels, Genoa, Leiden, Madrid, Porto Alegre, Seville, Strasbourg, and Zaragoza, as part of my doctoral dissertation entitled "Digital Age Activism: Anti-Corporate Globalization and the Cultural Logic of Transnational Networking," completed in May 2004. Previous fieldwork was also carried out in San Francisco, Prague, and Seattle between November 1999 and June 2001. Barcelona-based research and subsequent writing were supported by a Dissertation Field Research Grant from the Wenner-Gren Foundation for Anthropological Research, Inc., a Dissertation Field Research Fellowship from the Social Science Research Council (with Andrew W. Mellon Foundation funding) and a Simpson Memorial Fellowship from the Institute for International Studies at the University of California, Berkeley. I would like to thank Manuel Castells and Aihwa Ong for their valuable comments on previous drafts.

NOTES

1. Moving beyond much of the recent anthropological literature on networks (cf. Latour, 1987, 1993; Riles, 2000), I employ a practice-based approach, which explores the construction of concrete social networks by human actors within specific locales. Riles's (post)-structural analysis remains largely formal, while Latour sheds light on how resources are mobilized, alliances negotiated, and ideas translated within actor-networks, but obscures the specific practices through which networks are built within broader social, political, and economic contexts. Bockman and Eyal (2002) provide a much more socially and historically grounded use of actor-network theory. Similarly, recent sociological approaches have explored network structure, resource mobilization, and the circulation of meaning within local and transnational activist networks (cf. Smith et al., 1997; Keck and Sikkink, 1998; Diani and McAdam, 2003), but have yet to examine the specific practices through which such networks are generated. However, Mische's (2003) discussion of how conversational practices constitute activist networks represents an important exception.
2. Like Bourdieu's *habitus*, my use of cultural logic implies a set of internalized dispositions, shaped by social, economic, and political conditions, which generate concrete practices. However, unlike habitus, they are not so mechanical or deeply embedded, and can thus be contested and transformed through cultural struggle, innovation, or interaction within diverse social fields.
3. Andrew Barry (2001: 15) has recently criticized the network metaphor, suggesting that it "may convey an illusory sense of rigidity, order and of structure; and it may give little sense of unevenness of the fabric and the fissures, fractures and gaps that it contains and forms." By shifting the emphasis from network structure toward networking practices, however, involving myriad micro-level political struggles, my work specifically elucidates the fluid, uneven, and contradictory nature of the process of network formation. Moreover, as we shall see, grassroots activists in Barcelona often directly contrast highly diffuse, decentralized networks with what they consider to be more rigid and structured organizational forms.
4. Barry (2001: 102) also introduces a distinction between the political and technological, urging caution when using the network metaphor to characterize both politics and technology. Although his point regarding the danger of analytic conflation is well taken, I specifically explore how networks operating within multiple domains mutually shape one another, mediated by concrete logics and practices.
5. Barry (2001: 87) makes a similar point based on research within the European Union (EU), pointing out that, "Networks do not so much reflect social, political and technological reality; they provide a diagram on the basis of which reality might be refashioned and reimagined: they are models of the political future." For EU officials, networks represent a mode of government beyond the opposition between market and state. For many radical global justice activists, on the other hand, networks represent a directly democratic form of self-management that transcends the market and state altogether.
6. The first Intercontinental Encounter was held in Chiapas in 1996. For more information about PGA, see: http://www.nadir.org/nadir/initiativ/agp/. For more information regarding the First and Second Intercontinental Encounters for Humanity and Against Neoliberalism, see http://www.geocities.com/CapitolHill/3849/gatherdx.html and http://www.eco.utexas.edu/faculty/Cleaver/dailyreports.html.

7. The Independent Media Center (IMC), or Indymedia, was initially launched in Seattle as an alternative source of news and information for activists. The network has since expanded along with global justice movements, and there are now hundreds of autonomous sites throughout the world.

8. The Continental DAN process came to a standstill during the year following Seattle.

9. MRG-Catalonia proved more sustainable, coordinating activities, meetings, and actions from shortly before the Prague mobilization to January 2003, when activists "self-dissolved" the network as both a response to declining participation and a political statement against the reproduction of rigid structures.

10. See http://www.nadir.org/nadir/initiativ/agp/s26/index.htm.

11. For more information regarding the World Social Forum, see http://www.wsfindia.org/.

12. This brand of left-wing "libertarianism" should be distinguished from the variety prevalent in the United States. The former involves a radical critique of both the market and the state, while the latter is oriented toward limiting the role of the state in order to unleash the dynamic potential of the free market.

13. For scholarly analyses of transnational social movements, transnational advocacy networks, and global social movements, see Smith et al. (1997), Keck and Sikkink (1998), and Cohen and Rai (2000), respectively.

14. US-based political art collectives, such as Art and Revolution or the Bread and Puppet Theater, have specialized in the use of large, colorful puppets and dynamic street theater during mass protests. British-based Reclaim the Streets (RTS) emerged in the 1990s, when activists began organizing impromptu street parties and festivals of resistance as part of a broader cultural critique of corporate dominated consumer society. RTS street parties have since been organized in cities around the world. Black Bloc refers to a set of tactics employed by loosely organized clusters of affinity groups, often involving targeted property destruction against capitalist symbols. Based on the aesthetics of German autonomen, Black Bloc militants wear black bandanas, ragged black army surplus pants, black hooded sweatshirts and shiny black boots. Finally, the White Overalls tactic, which was developed by Milan-based Ya Basta!, involves a form of action where large, orderly groups of activists advance behind large plastic shields toward police lines where they initiate bodily contact, involving pushing and shoving.

15. Broadly, networks can be defined as sets of "interconnected nodes" (Castells, 1996: 469), which can assume any number of structural shapes according to the specific pattern of connections that adhere.

16. Wellman (2001) argues that the shift toward personalized relations, where the individual becomes the basic unit of connection, constitutes a new form of "networked individualism" (cf. Castells, 2001: 129).

17. See the following websites: www.agp.org, www.wsfindia.org, and www.attac.org.

18. For more information, see http://c2.com/cgi/wiki.

19. See www.indymedia.org.

20. Kevin Hetherington (1998: 123) refers more broadly to "utopics" through which "a utopian outlook on society and the moral order that it wishes to project, are translated into practice through the attachment of ideas about the good society onto particular places." "Informational utopics" specifically refers to the embodiment of utopian visions through innovative networking practices involving experimentation with new information technologies.

21. Cited in an article written by an MRG activist called "La Organización del

MRG,' which was published in the February–March 2001 edition of *EIMA*, a Catalan activist journal.

22. Cited in a document produced by MRG activists regarding the identity, structure, and functioning of the network that circulated on the global@ldist.ct.upc.es list-serve (October 18, 2000).
23. See PGA Network Organizational Principle no. 1: www.nadir.org/nadir/initia-tiv/agp/cocha/principles.htm.
24. See PGA Hallmarks: www.nadir.org/nadir/initiativ/agp/gender/desire/nutshell.htm.
25. See note 12.
26. "Voline" was the pen name used by V. M. Eichenbaum.
27. Although Varela (1981) maintains that autopoiesis cannot be directly transposed to society, other theorists have also used autopoiesis to characterize social systems (Benseler et al., 1980; Luhmann, 1990).
28. Cited in an organizational proposal presented at the Fifth RCADE Encounter (October 12–14, 2001).

REFERENCES

Appadurai, Arjun (1996) *Modernity at Large: Cultural Dimensions of Globalization*. Minneapolis, MN: University of Minnesota Press.
Arquilla, John and Ronfeldt, David (2001) *Networks and Netwars*. Santa Monica, CA: Rand.
Bakunin, Michael (1872) "Letter to the Internationalists of the Romagna," January 28.
Barry, Andrew (2001) *Political Machines: Governing a Technological Society*. London: The Athlone Press.
Beck, Ulrich, Giddens, Anthony, and Lash, Scott (1994) *Reflexive Modernization: Politics, Tradition and Aesthetics in the Modern Social Order*. Stanford: Stanford University Press.
Benseler, Frank, Hejl, Peter M., and Kock, Wolfram K. (1980) *Autopoiesis, Communication and Society: The Theory of Autopoietic Systems in the Social Sciences*. Frankfurt and New York: Campus.
Bockman, Johanna and Eyal, Gil (2002) "Eastern Europe as a Laboratory of Economic Knowledge," *American Journal of Sociology* 108 (2): 310–52.
Brecher, Jeremy, Costello, Tim, and Smith, Brendan (2000) *Globalization From Below: The Power of Solidarity*. Cambridge, MA: South End Press.
Castells, Manuel (1996) *The Rise of the Network Society*. Oxford: Blackwell.
—— (1997) *The Power of Identity* (2nd edn, 2004). Oxford: Blackwell.
—— (2000) "Materials for an Exploratory Theory of the Network Society," *British Journal of Sociology* 51 (1): 5–24.
—— (2001) *The Internet Galaxy: Reflections on the Internet, Business, and Society*. Oxford: Oxford University Press.
Cleaver, Harry (1995) "The Zapatistas and the Electronic Fabric of Struggle" (http://www.eco.utexas.edu/facstaff/Cleaver/zaps.html).
Cohen, Jean L (1985) "Strategy or Identity: New Theoretical Paradigms and Contemporary Social Movements," *Social Research* 52: 663–716.
Cohen, Robin and Rai, Shirin M. (eds) (2000) *Global Social Movements*. New Brunswick: The Athlone Press.

Collins, Randall (2001) "Social Movements and the Focus of Emotional Attention," in Jeff Goodwin, James M. Jasper, and Francesca Polletta (eds), *Passionate Politics: Emotions and Social Movements*, pp. 27–44. Chicago: University of Chicago Press.

Deluca, Kevin Michael (1999) *Image Politics: The New Rhetoric of Environmental Activism*. New York: Guilford Press.

Diani, Mario (1995) *Green Networks: A Structural Analysis of the Italian Environmental Movement*. Edinburgh: Edinburgh University Press.

— — and McAdam, Doug (eds) (2003) *Social Movements and Networks: Relational Approaches to Collective Action*. Oxford: Oxford University Press.

Gerlach, Luther P. (2001) "The Structure of Social Movements: Environmental Activism and its Opponents," in John Arquilla and David Ronfeldt (eds), *Networks and Netwars*, pp. 289–310. Santa Monica, CA: Rand.

— — and Hine, Virginia H. (1970) *People, Power, Change: Movements of Social Transformation*. Indianapolis: Bobbs-Merril.

Giddens, Anthony (1991) *Modernity and Self-identity: Self and Society in the Late Modern Age*. Stanford: Stanford University Press.

Guerin, Daniel (1970) *Anarchism: From Theory to Practice*, trans. Mary Klopper. New York: Monthly Review Press.

Handelman, Don (1990) *Models and Mirrors: Towards an Anthropology of Public Events*. Cambridge: Cambridge University Press.

Hetherington, Kevin (1998) *Expressions of Identity: Space, Performance and Politics*. Thousand Oaks, CA: Sage.

Himanen, Pekka (2001) *The Hacker Ethic and the Spirit of the Information Age*. New York: Random House.

Jameson, Fredric (1991) *Postmodernism, or the Cultural Logic of Late Capitalism*. Durham, NC: Duke University Press.

Kapferer, Bruce (1973) "Social Network and Conjugal Role in Urban Zambia: Towards a Reformulation of the Bott Hypothesis," in Jeremy Boissevain and J. Clyde Mitchell (eds), *Network Analysis*. The Hague: Mouton.

Keck, Margaret and Sikkink, Katherine (eds) (1998) *Activists Beyond Borders: Transnational Advocacy Networks in International Politics*. Ithaca, NY: Cornell University Press.

Kropotkin, Peter (1905) "Anarchism," in *Encyclopaedia Britannica*, 11th edn.

Latour, Bruno (1987) *Science in Action: How to Follow Scientists and Engineers Through Society*. Philadelphia: Open University Press.

— — (1993) *We Have Never Been Modern*. Cambridge, MA: Harvard University Press.

Luhmann, Niklas (1990) *Essays on Self-reference*. New York: Columbia University Press.

Melucci, Alberto (1989) *Nomads of the Present: Social Movements and Individual Needs in Contemporary Society*. Philadelphia: Temple University Press.

Miller, Daniel and Slater, Don (2000) *The Internet: An Ethnographic Approach*. Oxford: Berg.

Mische, Anne (2003) "Cross-talk in Movements: Reconceiving the Culture–Network Link," in Mario Diani and Doug McAdam (eds), *Social Movements and Networks: Relational Approaches to Collective Action*, pp. 258–80. Oxford: Oxford University Press.

Nelson, Diane (1999) *A Finger in the Wound: Body Politics in Quincentennial Guatemala*. Berkeley, CA: University of California Press.

Ong, Aihwa (1999) *Flexible Citizenship: The Cultural Logics of Transnationality*. Durham, NC: Duke University Press.

Polanyi, Karl (1957) *The Great Transformation*. Boston: Beacon Press.

Raymond, Eric (1999) *The Cathedral and the Bazaar: Musings on Linux and Open Source by an Accidental Revolutionary*. Cambridge, MA: O'Reilly.

Riles, Annelise (2000) *The Network Inside Out*. Ann Arbor: University of Michigan Press.

Robertson, Roland (1995) "Glocalization: Time–Space and Homogeneity–Heterogeneity," in Mike Featherstone, Scott Lash, and Roland Robertson (eds), *Global Modernities*, pp. 25–44. London: Sage.

Ronfeldt, David, Arquilla, John, Fuller, Graham E., and Fuller, Melissa (1998) *The Zapatista "Social Netwar" in Mexico*. Santa Monica, CA: Rand.

Routledge, Paul (1994) "Backstreets, Barricades, and Blackouts: Urban Terrains of Resistance in Nepal," *Environment and Planning D: Society and Space* 12: 559–78.

— — (1998) "Going Globile: Spatiality, Embodiment and Mediation in the Zapatista Insurgency," in Simon Dalby and Gearoid O'Tuathall (eds), *Rethinking Geopolitics*, pp. 244–60. London: Routledge.

Sassen, Saskia (1991) *The Global City: New York, London and Tokyo*. Princeton, NJ: Princeton University Press.

Smith, Jackie, Chatfield, Charles, and Pagnucco, Ron (eds) (1997) *Transnational Social Movements and Global Politics*. Syracuse: Syracuse University Press.

Varela, Francisco J. (1981) "Describing the Logic of the Living," in Milan Zeleny (ed.), *Autopoiesis: A Theory of Living Organization*, pp. 36–48. New York: North Holland.

Voline (1955) *The Unknown Revolution*. New York: Libertarian Book Club.

Ward, Colin (1973) *Anarchy in Action*. London: Freedom Press.

Wellman, Barry (2001) "Physical Place and Cyberplace: The Rise of Personalized Networking," *International Journal of Urban and Regional Research* 25(2): 227–52.

— — and Haythornthwaite, Caroline (eds) (2002) *The Internet in Everyday Life*. Oxford: Blackwell.

16. From media politics to networked politics: the Internet and the political process

Araba Sey and Manuel Castells

THE INTERNET AND DEMOCRACY: UTOPIAS AND DYSTOPIAS

Never in history has democracy been more pervasive throughout the world. Yet, available evidence points to a growing, widespread crisis of legitimacy of governments, parliaments, political parties, and politicians in most countries, including the United States and Western Europe (Castells, 2004: ch. 6). Because the Internet is seen as the ultimate technology of freedom, its diffusion among citizens has been hailed as a potential savior for the political ills of representation and participation. At the same time, critics have sounded an alert on the dangers of electronic democracy, not the least being the potential fragmentation of citizenship and the capture of public attention by elites and demagogues (Anderson and Cornfield, 2003).

A symbolic manifestation of both utopian and dystopian views is apparent in the work of one of the world's leading political theorists, Benjamin Barber. In 1984, in his pioneering essay *Strong Democracy*, he foresaw the possibility of using new information and communication technologies to energize citizen information and political participation. Fourteen years later, having observed the actual practice of democracy under the new technological paradigm, Barber himself called attention to the deteriorating quality of public debate and democratic decision-making in the biased space of the new media (Barber, 1998). In principle, both of his arguments are plausible and not contradictory. The Internet can, indeed, be an appropriate platform for informed, interactive politics, stimulating political participation and opening up possible avenues for enlarging decision-making beyond the closed doors of political institutions. On the other hand, any technology – and this is particularly true of the Internet – is shaped by its uses and its users. Thus, bureaucratic politics will tend to use the Internet as a billboard for one-way communication. Cynicism and individualism from disaffected individuals will translate into the use of the

Internet to deride politicians and call for insurgent expressions of alternative political values. Alternatively, an active citizenry may find in the Internet a medium of communication to bypass the filters of mass media and party machines, and to network itself, asserting its collective autonomy. The actual influence of the Internet on politics, and on the quality of democracy, has to be established by observation, not proclaimed as fate.

This is not to say that we are in the dark on the issue of democracy in the network society. We already know a number of things. First, we know that the Internet is a powerful tool of autonomous political expression outside the formal political system (Hague and Loader, 1999; Norris, 2001). Thus, grass-roots groups from all ideologies find in the Internet their medium of communication of choice, and social movements and collective action are greatly enhanced in their capacity to influence society and government by using computer networks, as the study by Jeff Juris in chapter 15 of this volume documents. Second, the well-crafted research conducted by Bruce Bimber (2003) on the impact of the use of the Internet on political behavior shows that there is no significant effect in increasing political engagement in formal politics, such as voting, although there is a positive correlation with donations of money to political candidates, a key finding that we will use later in constructing our analysis. Bimber does show a positive association between use of the Internet and level of political participation, but this is explained by other variables, primarily by education. Third, we know that there is a positive correlation between exposure to the media and political participation (Norris, 2000), and that the use of the Internet for political information adds to this media effect, instead of substituting for it (Bimber, 2003). Fourth, the futuristic schemes of e-democracy and electronic voting have been discarded, in America and elsewhere, by several blue-ribbon panels, which have shown the dubious constitutionality and blatant social discrimination implicit in the procedure (California Internet Voting Task Force, 2000; Internet Policy Institute, 2001).

However, we know much less about the actual effect of the Internet on the transformation of the formal political process. Does the Internet play a role in changing the process of political campaigns, and in creating new forms of political debate, political choice, political representation, and political decision-making? Bimber argues that the effects of the Internet are more significant on the structure of the process of representation than on individual behavior. The most important effect may be the fact that "The flow of information is central to political structure and political behavior. Not only is information a tool and resource used by political actors in a strategic or psychological sense, its characteristics and qualities help define political actors themselves" (2003: 231). In other words, by changing the direction and the content of the flow of information through the use of the Internet, the range of political actors is broadened, new avenues of collective mobilization may appear, and a different format of debate may take place, transforming the political scene that had been framed by the one-way communication systems of the mass media era. This is the hypothesis that we will try to explore in this chapter, grounded on observation of political trends and on available literature on the topic.

In view of the analytical purpose of our study, we will be focusing only on the United States and on the United Kingdom (the societies in which most studies on the matter are available) in the hope that our approach can be usefully applied to other contexts. As an additional caveat, we do not imply that all politics can be reduced to formal politics. For us, politics includes all social processes that relate to the exercise of power relationships in society, regardless of their institutional and organizational context. Formal politics refers to the processes of representation, deliberation, and decision-making in the constitutionally designated institutions of political authority. We also focus on the process of accessing institutions of governance (leaving aside issues of so-called e-government); that is, the management of public administration and the practice of government under the networked paradigm. Our concern in this chapter is to investigate the emerging interaction between people and democracy in the process of political representation in the new form of networked public space constituted by the Internet.

THE USES OF THE INTERNET IN THE POLITICAL PROCESS

Well into the twenty-first century, the Internet is no longer an exotic political medium. The first thing most political candidates do upon declaring their candidacy is to set up a website. Parliaments and government agencies around the world are gradually moving their activities online. However, despite this expansion of online political communication, there has been little real change in the structure and conduct of formal politics. Expectations of increased deliberation and interaction between citizens and politicians have not been met, as the Internet has been used largely to facilitate a one-way flow of information from politicians to the public (Norris, 2002; *The Economist*, 2003; Johnson, 2003; Levine, 2003; Pew Internet and American Life Project, 2003; Ward et al., 2003).

Like the traditional media, the Internet is most valued by politicians as a tool for disseminating information to the media and the public at large, although it is also uniquely effective in mobilizing voters and enhancing interaction. Even so, Internet users are often unable to find the kind of political information they want, such as comparative information, explanation of voting records, and campaign finance (Browning, 2001; Pew Internet and American Life Project, 2003). Available information may be superficial (Levine, 2003), non-analytical (Wolfensberger, 2002), or, in some cases, high quality but not user friendly (Coleman, 1999). Studies of online political campaigns in the US and UK conclude that most campaigns use the Internet as an "electronic brochure" (Kamarck, 2002: 89).

Despite indications of the Internet's effectiveness in mobilizing voters (for example, Jesse Ventura's success in the 1998 Minnesota gubernatorial election), by 2002 there was still limited mobilization online. Internet users were more energized by websites offering political humor than by those of official campaigns (Coleman, 2001; Pew Internet and American Life Project, 2003). In the UK, only 38 percent of political sites allowed visitors to join up online, and this usually involved using off-line methods such as mailing downloaded applications (Ward et al., 2003).

Politicians are also generally reluctant to engage actively with their publics on- or off-line (Browning, 2001; Gibson et al., 2003; Levine, 2003). For example, less than a third of UK political sites examined by Ward and co-workers (2003) had interactive capabilities, and during the 2002 US elections, Internet portals such as Yahoo!, AOL, and MSN provided more tools for analysis and interaction than campaign sites did (Pew Internet and American Life Project, 2003). Where politicians have tried to interact with Internet users, the openness of such forums is questionable (Gibson et al., 2003). Although closure of the US House and Senate offices after the September 11 attacks spurred a more central role for the Internet in Congress, members still have an ambivalent attitude toward the medium (Wolfensberger, 2002). Overall, widespread acceptance of the Internet as a tool for political campaigns and programs has not translated into a more open and participatory political process.

THE POLITICAL LIMITS OF INTERNET-BASED POLITICS

The limited exploitation of the democratic capabilities of the Internet by politicians can be attributed to perceptions of the Internet or to the characteristics, preferences, and motivations of politicians. Generally speaking, few politicians see the Internet as a force to be reckoned with. They perceive the Internet as "little more than a big electronic auditorium where millions of people gather to spout off much like high-school kids in a civics class – but nonetheless have little actual impact on the crafting of policies that govern them" (Browning, 2001: 13), thus underestimating the democratizing potential of the medium.

On the flipside of this is a general distrust of public engagement in politics. Increasing use of direct political methods, such as protest politics, direct balloting, and opinion polling, have not erased concerns about the limits of direct democracy (Wolfensberger, 2002; *The Economist*, 2003). Taking advantage of the benefits of Internet technology is particularly problematic for parliamentary bodies. As Wolfensberger (2002: 91) notes, "just because the information super-highway and deliberation are both two-way streets does not mean that they are perfectly integrated and compatible systems. In reality, they operate at radically different speeds." Politicians recognize the usefulness of the Internet, but fear that depending on a public ill equipped to deliberate and make decisions on complex issues will consume too much time and erode representative democracy.

Experiences such as frequent hacking of candidates' sites, inaccurate online polls, and low-quality or extreme discussions in chat rooms have turned both politicians and the public away from political websites (Coleman and Hall, 2001; Thompson, 2002). Distrust of the Internet is not helped by past flops such as Steve Forbes's elaborate online presidential candidacy in 2000, which did nothing to prevent his dismal performance as a candidate. Adoption of new information and communication technology by the UK central government has also been less efficient and influential than anticipated (Chadwick and May, 2003).

The above reasons explain why politicians are skeptical about using the Internet for serious political communication. But the successful use of the medium by politicians such as Jesse Ventura, as well as the incorporation of Internet components into most political operations and programs, suggests that there are other, deep-rooted reasons for the current patterns of limited use. Some observers have pointed to the fact that politicians are unfamiliar with the technology (Coleman, 1999; Johnson, 2003). However, this argument has less strength after almost a decade of Internet use in politics and the availability of a pool of trained Internet professionals.

Rather, the problem may be the inability to understand what Internet politics really is and how it works. There is a great deal of uncertainty about which models of political communication are most effective on the web. The communication model chosen is influenced by perceptions of the role of the Internet in politics. The predominance of a given communication model can be partially explained by the perception of Internet politics as dealing mainly with acquiring information to make decisions during campaigns and elections (Agre, 2002; Anderson, 2003). Hence, online political campaigns focus more on the provision of the candidate's position on issues and less on other types of participation, such as organizing demonstrations, contacting officials, and building relationships around individuals and organizations (Anderson, 2003). This is in line with the dominant political paradigm (managerial model of state/citizen interaction), which prioritizes efficiency of internal organizational activities and linear provision of information to citizens, in contrast to models that prioritize consultation or participation (Chadwick and May, 2003). Thus, although Coleman (2001) identifies three possible e-campaigning models in UK politics, he concludes that, while the campaigns concentrated on the "e-marketing" model, and Internet users focused on the "voter empowerment" model, the "e-democracy" model, based on interactive participation, was conspicuously absent.

It is not unusual for old models of political communication to linger while politicians get used to, and find effective ways to work with, emerging methods (Kamarck, 2002; Katz and Rice, 2002). However, the primary reason for the continued dominance of traditional communication models is not the gradual easing in of a new model, but the reluctance on the part of politicians to lose control over the political process. "Control of the message in a campaign is as much an obsession as is money and candidates fear this loss of control," which is likely to happen in an open Internet campaign (Kamarck, 2002: 98). Not only can Internet users exchange information that may not be "on-message," but both supporters and opponents also have the capacity (thanks to hypertext and other Internet capabilities) to produce new messages using campaign information without approval from the official campaign, what Foot and Schneider (2003) call "unilateral coproduction." Furthermore, politicians anticipate "burdensome exchange among candidates, campaign staffs, and citizens, which would entail . . . losing the ability to remain ambiguous in policy positions" (Stromer-Galley, 2000: 112). Consequently, political institutions consciously develop only those aspects of Internet campaigning that are less subject to manipulation and input from users and more in tune with how they believe politics should be conducted.

In sum, if the added value of the Internet is its interactivity and its potential for autonomous communication, a political system predicated on the control of messages and the gatekeeping of access to institutions of representation and governance is unlikely to use the medium to its fullest potential. On the other hand, the more a political process is based on the building of citizens' autonomy, the more the Internet may play a role as an enhancing medium of political mobilization and influence. Let us explore this hypothesis.

THE INTERNET AS A MEDIUM OF POLITICAL AUTONOMY

While politicians seek to retain control over the political process, some segments of the electorate seek to attain greater autonomy in political engagement. The Internet potentially offers two levels of autonomy to the online electorate. First, users can access more campaign information without being dependent on the mass media. The Internet frees users to construct their own information sets, limiting the role of news editors. Table 16.1 shows that the percentage of the US public getting information online because they consider that the other media do not provide enough information increased from 29 percent in 2000 to 43 percent in 2002. This suggests that people turn to the Internet for political information when they are dissatisfied with traditional media content. Bimber's (2003) analysis of US election data indicates that people who use the Internet for political purposes are more likely to be skeptical of media information, and may be more independent and self-reliant.

Second, the Internet enables users to communicate without intervention by politicians. The Internet thus provides channels of action for people disenchanted with traditional politics but desiring some political activity (Coleman and Hall, 2001). This certainly appeared to be the case in past elections where online citizens ignored campaign websites and engaged in "anti-establishment" activities such as forwarding campaign jokes and vote-

Table 16.1   Internet use for political purposes in the US, 1998–2002

Internet use	1998 (%)	2000 (%)	2002 (%)
For election news	6	18	13
Reasons for going online for election news			
Information more convenient	–	56	57
Not enough information from other media	–	29	43
News sources reflect personal interests	24	6	8
Activities performed by online election news consumers			
Research candidates' position on issues	–	69	79
Research candidates' voting record	30	33	45
Participate in online polls	26	35	39
Join discussion/chat groups	13	8	10
Contribute money to candidate	–	5	5
Visit political websites	–	19	32

Source: Pew Research Center for the People and the Press and Pew Internet and American Life Project (2003) "Modest Increase in Internet Use for Campaign 2002" (available at www.pewinternet.org)

swapping (Browning, 2001; Coleman and Hall, 2001; Pew Internet and American Life Project, 2003). The question, then, is whether such political tendencies can be turned to more formal political activity, such as deliberating on policy and supporting candidates for office, which seems to be receptive to activists online.

While some critics have warned of the tendency for citizen participation to excessively quicken the political process (for example, Levin, 2002), evidence from various initiatives suggests that citizens can make careful choices under the right conditions. Experiments in the US, Britain, Denmark, Australia, and Bulgaria brought together a few hundred ordinary voters to question experts on an issue and then debate among themselves. Polling before and after the debates showed that citizens could deliberate on complex issues and make difficult trade-offs. Such juries, convened and monitored by the public with Internet technology, may be an adequate substitution for professional politicians (*The Economist*, 2003). Similar projects in Japan have yielded positive results, especially showing that "Japanese voters have a great deal of appetite for engagement in policy discourse with politicians" (Ishikawa, 2002: 342).

Conversely, Internet politics may be rejected by people who want strong links with the formal organizations of the political system, such as party chapters. In the UK, Gibson and Ward (2003) found that many grassroots party members preferred a structure that fostered more member-to-party rather than member-to-member communication. This may explain why only 17 percent of the UK online population are politically active, compared to 30 percent of the US online population (Gibson and Ward, 2003). The difference in the type of political engagement that citizens want may be a critical factor contributing to the shape of politics on- and off-line. People who want autonomous political activity may turn to the Internet because it facilitates autonomous participation. However, whether this will influence formal politics or foster alternative politics depends on the willingness of politicians to give citizens full access to the political infrastructure.

In sum, it is not that the Internet makes people want autonomy. It is that people searching for autonomy turn to the Internet as their medium of choice. If the political system is based on subordination to the party structure, the Internet becomes simply a billboard to post messages and process requests. If citizens are either disaffected from politics or find themselves searching for autonomy within an unresponsive political system, then the Internet is used by political activists without directly aiming at the process of political representation. It is only under the conditions of an autonomous citizenship and an open, participatory, formal political channel that the Internet may innovate the practice of politics. Let us examine one such political experience that appears to yield interesting analytical lessons.

A TURNING POINT? THE HOWARD DEAN PRESIDENTIAL CAMPAIGN IN 2003

The 2004 US presidential race provides a striking example of how willingness to cede control can transform a campaign. Howard Dean's run for the Democratic nomination illustrates the interplay between political organizations, political messages, technologies of freedom, and an electorate that wants to increase its autonomy. Dean, one of nine candidates in the Fall of 2003, made the Internet an integral part of his strategy, running an online campaign that surpassed the others in online fund-raising, grassroots mobilization, and interactivity (Drinkard and Lawrence, 2003; Getlin, 2003; Giegerich, 2003; Kessler, 2003a; Scheiber, 2003; Schulte, 2003). Dean's campaign uniquely allowed full autonomy for supporters to engage with the campaign in their own ways, particularly through the web log (blog) and a range of participation options.

The effectiveness of this campaign was not simply an outcome of using the Internet: it grew out of a strategic convergence of political issues, political Internet users, and the Internet itself. Specifically, Dean's campaign message, advocating universal health care and opposition to the Iraq war, resonated with the liberal and left-wing electorate, who tend to be both disillusioned with mainstream politics and Internet savvy. The point here is that a segment of the electorate, who happen to be active Internet users, found Dean's message appealing; and, because the campaign was open to letting them participate in new ways, it found a loyal following that could communicate and organize itself using the Internet as a tool.

Dean's Internet success prompted other candidates to beef up their online campaigns, although, by November 2003, they had been unable to achieve similar results (Bolton, 2003). The most established candidate, Joe Lieberman, who used the Internet in his 2000 campaign (Mosquera, 2000), was running a fairly traditional campaign. Interactivity and autonomy were not strong components of his online strategy, which emphasized information provision, although there were some unique applications, such as a fund-raising challenge, capitalizing on the symbolic value of the number 18 to a segment of the electorate (CNN, 2003; Kessler, 2003b). The other front-running candidate (Wesley Clark) decided to "capitalize on the Internet" partly because his late entry made it difficult for him to catch up using traditional methods (*Associated Press*, 2003). The Clark campaign used online mobilization and fund-raising tools similar to the Dean campaign but did not show the same commitment to using the Internet intensively (Clough, 2003; Scheiber, 2003).

Dean's campaign, in contrast, capitalized on the three strengths of Internet communication – information dissemination, mobilization, and interactivity – not just separately but in combination, and in ways that enhanced autonomous

participation by supporters. Using the unique capabilities of Internet communication, the campaign shaped an effective strategy, combining motivational
information, grassroots mobilization and fund-raising, and freedom to organize. The result was a powerful, low-cost, person-to-person recruitment force
that brought thousands of zealous people to the Dean campaign.

Information provision on election 2004 campaign websites was not
unusual, neither was the availability of mobilization tools such as forwarding
e-mails. Less common was the Dean campaign's use of information to motivate and mobilize. The website provided daily updates on new online recruits,
fund-raising totals, as well as recruitment and fund-raising challenges. For
example, in a four-day fund-raising challenge, the campaign successfully
exceeded the amount a rival candidate was raising at a luncheon (NPR, 2003).
September 2003 was designated a "September to Remember," during which
online supporters were challenged to help the campaign reach a target of
450,000 recruits and $40 million in donations, and send a message to America
about the efficacy of grassroots politics.

Grassroots fund-raising was a unique feature of the Dean campaign, which
focused on obtaining small amounts from a lot of people. About half of the $25
million raised by the end of November 2003 was raised online, with contributions averaging less than $100. The campaign's confidence in this fund-rais-
ing strategy was tested when, in an unprecedented move, Dean invited
supporters to vote on the critical question of whether or not to receive public
matching funds. The strategic question was that, at that time, Bush, who had
opted out of federal funding, had already raised about $85 million, and was
aiming to raise $200 million. Accepting public matching funds, under the
federal regulations, meant that Dean could not spend in excess of the cap limit
of $45 million. In spite of the lack of financial support from major donors,
Dean decided to take the chance of relying on his grassroots effort to be financially competitive with Bush. However, this was a hard question in terms of
political ideology, since Dean, and most of his followers, were critical of
private funding of political campaigns. He argued that principles had to be
bent somewhat in order to have a realistic prospect of beating Bush in the
general election, something that was difficult anyway but that seemed out of
reach without increasing the amount of total funding above the limit determined by the rules of public funding.

Thus, for both ideological and tactical reasons, Dean decided to put to an
open electronic vote the most important decision of his campaign.
Acknowledging that rejecting public funding would be difficult, Dean assured
his supporters:

> Declining federal money and funding a campaign with grassroots support has never
> been done before, and if you choose this option it will be a challenge – but with your

commitment, your dedication and your hard work, we can do it. This decision is no longer mine to make. This is a campaign of the people, by the people and for the people. Your successful effort of raising a historic amount of money through small contributions has made this choice possible. This is why I am putting this decision in your hands. (Dean, 2003)

The two-day vote online, involving about 20 percent of supporters, returned an 85 percent result in favor of declining matching funds. This freed the campaign from the spending cap associated with public funding, but left it with the challenge of raising $200 million – the amount Bush expected to mobilize. The Dean campaign planned to achieve this funding target by getting 2 million Americans to contribute $100 each. The striking thing here is the campaign's confidence in its strategy, and commitment to involving supporters in crucial decision-making.

The campaign was also very successful in mobilizing grassroots support, partly through MeetUp.com, a non-partisan Internet resource that enables people to connect with other like-minded people in their community. This resource came to be a part of the campaign when MeetUp executives were testing the market for political gatherings and found a significant demand among Dean supporters (Scheiber, 2003). Joe Trippi, a consultant and later Dean campaign manager, seized on the idea when it was presented to him, recognizing the potential to identify hundreds of supporters without spending much on organizing activities. Over 140,000 Dean supporters had signed up with MeetUp by the end of November 2003, compared with between 140 and 47,000 for other candidates. And over half a million people had provided their e-mail addresses to the website of the campaign.

Furthermore, without regard to loss of control, Dean's campaign gave supporters free rein to organize their activities (NPR, 2003). Visitors to Dean's official website were given several options for participation, ranging from setting the official website as a homepage to joining the fund-raising team. Supporters could decide for themselves how involved they wanted to be. *The New York Times* wrote: "Staffers no longer flinch when a donor suggests to other potential givers that Dean backers eat ramen noodles for dinner once a week and forward the savings to the campaigns. Or when an obituary asks mourners to send contributions to the Dean campaign in lieu of flowers" (Justice, 2003). Dean's campaign manager explained: "You have to have a campaign that's willing to let go" (Joe Trippi, quoted in Malone, 2003). Unofficial support groups were a valued resource for Dean's campaign, unlike the Clark campaign, which slowly dismantled unofficial structures once Clark decided to run and the media campaign was under way (Franke-Ruta, 2003).

Perhaps the most talked about aspect of Dean's campaign, along with fund-raising, was the blogging phenomenon (Lessig, 2003), which, together with the MeetUps, helped both to mobilize and instill a sense of ownership among supporters. The campaign website linked to one official and several unofficial blogs, daily discussion forums where Internet users and campaign staff could share ideas. The blog was not only "a constant conversation between campaign headquarters and Dean loyalists" (NPR, 2003), but also, "peer-to-peer politics – voters connecting to other voters – without the middleman of official campaign sanction" (*Slate*, 2003). At least three other candidates had blogs. None generated as much attention as Dean's, apparently because Dean's blog community was allowed to function without campaign interference (Lessig, 2003). An example of how this facility promoted autonomy can be seen in a posting where one supporter asked for advice on how to respond to possible arguments against Dean (open thread posting by Cat.M, August 31, 2003). Rather than refer Cat.M to the official campaign, respondents either gave their own opinion or suggested other unofficial sources. Indeed, the official campaign dealt with the overflow of enquiries by encouraging people to visit the blog for answers from other users.

In addition to effective use of the Internet, the energy of Dean's campaign could be attributed to his charismatic and rebellious characteristics (*Pioneer Press*, 2003). The Internet has been shown to have the greatest impact with anti-establishment candidates (Kamarck, 2002) and Dean's blatant anti-war stance endeared him to like-minded Americans, especially middle-class male youth, who are precisely those that dominate the Internet and online politics (Coleman and Hall, 2001; Clough, 2003; Pew Internet and American Life Project, 2003; Ward et al., 2003). Apart from having grown up with the Internet as their primary information source, this group is also more likely to be seeking autonomous avenues for political participation, making the Internet an appropriate tool to reach them with targeted messages.

Whether the Dean campaign knowingly capitalized on this characteristic of the Internet audience is arguable. Some commentators have suggested that the campaign was heavily Internet focused because Dean could not afford to use relatively expensive traditional campaign strategies (*CBS News*, 2003) and had nothing to lose by venturing into the unknown (Bolton, 2003). Nevertheless, this strategy proved effective for Dean, and his campaign's willingness to cede control to the electorate, in order to reap the benefits of Internet politics, stood in stark contrast to the other Democratic campaigns.

Of course, the innovative Dean campaign, which epitomized a new kind of networked politics, could not necessarily amount to a formula for success in the presidential election. Indeed, by the time you are reading our analysis, you will know the results of the 2004 election. Our feeling, in November 2003, is that there are too many factors influencing the presidential election outside the dynamics of the campaign itself, not the least being the politics of fear on which the Bush administration has based its influence over an American society still traumatized by the attacks of September 11, 2001, and ready to give absolute priority to the global war on terror, a conservative specialty. However, since our purpose is analytical, the study of the first phase of the Dean campaign, up to December 2003, provides useful lessons to understand, in general terms, the relationship between the political process and the networks of interaction constructed around the Internet.

Power dynamics tends to limit the democratization of politics. Politicians expect uncontrolled citizen participation to lead to problematic campaigns and processes. However, the experience of the Dean campaign shows that this is not necessarily the case. The Internet does not by itself create an effective political campaign or increase civic-mindedness. Rather than causing radical transformation, its impact on politics is incremental, contextual, and amplifying (Agre, 2002; Katz and Rice, 2002), working with factors such as the nature, motivations, and message of candidates and the desires of citizens, with access to the Internet, to produce different outcomes (Anderson, 2003; Johnson, 2003; Levine, 2003). Thus, the key to using the Internet in politics is not the technology per se, but the use of the technology to promote, as the Dean campaign did, a message and a style of political participation that resonate with the electorate.

THE RISE OF NETWORKED POLITICS

In the past decades, the mass media have become the main political space. Citizens receive most of their information from the media, particularly from television, and they largely form their opinion, and enact their political behavior, with the materials provided by the media (Dahlgren and Sparks, 1997; Davis and Owen, 1998). This is not to say that people follow blindly what the media say. For one thing, the media are relatively diverse, although current trends toward concentration of ownership are restricting their plurality. But, more importantly, communication scholars established long ago that media audiences are not passive recipients of messages. Rather, people react and counter-react to the images, sounds, and text that they access through the media. And they do it on the basis of their own perceptions, values, interests, and projects (Neuman, 1991; Norris, 2000). This complex process of communication is largely undetermined, and any politician or ideologue trying to ride the tiger of manipulation of public opinion ends up confronting unforeseen surprises. However, the fact that the media frame the political debate has substantial consequences on the political process. Messages or faces that are not present in the mainstream media have little chance of reaching a significant proportion of citizens, so that they become structurally marginalized.

Media politics has its own language and rules: simplification of the message, image-making, the personalization of politics, and story-telling and character assassination as a means of promoting or demoting political candidates. There is, for instance, a direct connection between media politics and the widespread use of the politics of scandal; that is, the use of damaging information (true, false, or halfway) to undo political adversaries in the public mind (Thompson, 2000). Furthermore, media politics is expensive, particularly when it is considered that it runs well beyond the periods of political campaigning. It is expensive in money and resources to be present in the media with a favorable spin, and this activity becomes a key mechanism in ensuring the dependence of politicians on donors and their lobbyists. In the United States, the repeated failure of congressional efforts to legislate on campaign financing derives from an obvious obstacle: the majority of the representatives in congress are elected by their skillful use of the very mechanism that they are expected to restrict. So, unless a large majority decides simultaneously that it is in its interest to disarm, there is little chance of obtaining the unilateral disarmament of politicians, with some honorable exceptions who are either above the fray or choose to keep their integrity and lose their seat.

Overall, media politics has transformed political practice and affected political behavior. The net result is not that people are less politically active because of the media. Indeed, the contrary seems to be the case, as Pippa Norris (2000) has demonstrated: media exposure and political interest correlate positively, although the causal relationship may work both ways.

However, there are reasons to believe that there is a connection between media politics and its consequences (personalization, image-making, financial dependence on interested donors, scandal politics) and the crisis of political legitimacy (Fallows, 1996; Dautrich and Hartley, 1999). In other words, it is not that people withdraw from politics, but that they tend to disbelieve formal politics and politicians and engage in a number of alternative political practices, including voting for third parties, abstaining, engaging in referendum politics, or exploring political mobilization outside the traditional party system.

There are, of course, many reasons for the crisis of legitimacy, as has been analyzed elsewhere (Castells, 2004), but the prevalence of media politics may be counted among them because it makes the relationship between representatives and the represented even more indirect. Party structures were, and are, subjected to nepotism and bureaucracy, but there is a direct connection between the institutions of power and the different forms of aggregation of civil society; for example, labor unions, party chapters, churches, neighborhood associations, groups of women voters, and the like. Media politics comes between this organic relationship, and establishes a quasi-market relationship between the producers of political messages and their clients/citizens, who watch/read the media and buy their political option with their votes in a fully individualized relationship. This mechanism works efficiently as long as the clients/citizens are satisfied. But when public affairs turn sour, there is no feedback system until the next election. Furthermore, come the election, the offer is still articulated through the media, so that the actual ability to control and process the information is largely removed from the hands and minds of individual citizens, with little access to the media on their own. At most, they can react through opinion polls, if they are lucky enough to be sampled. When, for reasons linked to the process of broader structural transformation (for example, globalization), citizens feel lost and disfranchised, media politics does not offer the possibility of readjusting the relationship between politicians and citizens, except in the few instances when journalists place themselves in the position of defenders of the public interest.

The crisis of political legitimacy, associated to some extent with the practice of media politics, is at the origin of new forms of politicization in our societies. While a substantial proportion of citizens give up hope in the political system, many others undertake alternative forms of political expression, sometimes in the form of social movements, at other times in the shape of insurgent politics within the political system, and often trying to connect civil society to new leaders in the political process. This is the privileged terrain of the Internet as a political medium. As long as the Internet is used as a reproduction of top-down politics controlled by the political machines in a market-like relationship to its citizens, its added value is limited and its ability to reach out to public opinion vastly inferior to the mass media. However, when, and if, individual citizens, grassroots organizations, and political entrepreneurs engage in an autonomous project to redesign the political process, the Internet becomes the platform of choice. This is because of its potential to build up, with little cost in resources, very large networks on the basis of individual connections that are multidirectional. The network can expand endlessly, as long as it has an open-ended program, which implies the lack of central control and the configuration of the network around some general themes whose specification results from the interactive, recurrent process inside the network. Such was the key mechanism, as we have seen, behind the unexpected success of the Dean campaign in 2003.

However, these political networks are not chat rooms, they are not just expressive: they are instrumental. They are geared toward accomplishing political goals. This is why it is so important that their dynamics materializes in the two levers that move the political system: money and activists, which both lead to votes. The ability to generate tens of thousands of small, individual donations was key in the Dean campaign. And Bimber's (2003) data showed, as we saw above, that one of the few variables of political behavior that was influenced by Internet use was the willingness to donate money to a candidate. Thus, while media politics costs money, networked politics is a source of funding, not because of the technology, but because involvement in an interactive political network is an expression of commitment toward a personal political option. Media politics is mass politics. Networked politics is individualized politics, which tries to connect to many other individuals, suddenly identified as recognizable citizens. In the same way that media politics disrupted traditional party machines, networked politics is disrupting media politics.

The potential consequences are vast as formal politics is nowadays generally predicated on the client/citizen model of consumption of one-way political messages. The consequences include the fragmentation of politics, the spread of referendum politics, the unpredictability of political opinion, the whirlwind of political leadership that results from the emergence of insurgent political entrepreneurs, and, ultimately, the erosion of the stable system of political representation that characterized democracies in the past half-century. The dilemma seems to be between the continuation of traditional party politics, enacted through media politics and increasingly delegitimized, and the emergence of networked politics in a process characterized by the production of new actors and new issues against or around the political establishment, thus leading to systemic instability.

REFERENCES

Agre, P. E. (2002) "Real-time Politics: The Internet and the Political Process," *The Information Society* 18: 311–31.

Anderson, David M. (2003) "Cautious Optimism about Online Politics and Citizenship," in D. M. Anderson and M. Cornfield (eds), *The Civic Web: Online Politics and Democratic Values*, pp. 19–34. Lanham, MD: Rowman and Littlefield.

— — and Cornfield, M. (eds) (2003) *The Civic Web: Online Politics and Democratic Values*. Lanham, MD: Rowman and Littlefield.

Associated Press (2003) "Wesley Clark Enters Crowded Presidential Race," September 17 (retrieved October 1, 2003 from www.katv.com).

Barber, Benjamin (1984) *Strong Democracy*. Berkeley, CA: University of California Press.

— — (1998) "The New Telecommunications Technology: Endless Frontier or End of Democracy," in Roger G. Noll and Monroe Price (eds), *Communications Cornucopia*, pp. 72–98. Washington, DC: Brookings Institution.

Bernstein, D. (2003) "Campaign Dot-com," *Boston Phoenix*, September 5–11 (retrieved October 3, 2003 from www.bostonphoenix.com).

Bimber, B. (2003) *Information and American Democracy: Technology in the Evolution of Political Power*. New York: Cambridge University Press.

Bolton, A. (2003) "Dean Presidential Rivals Suffer 'Growth Pains' Chasing Dean," *The Hill*, October 8 (retrieved October 25, 2003 from www.thehill.com).

Browning, Graeme (2001) *Electronic Democracy: Using the Internet to Transform American Politics*, 2nd edn. Medford, NJ: CyberAge Books.

California Internet Voting Task Force (2000) *A Report on the Feasibility of Internet Voting*. Sacramento: Office of California Secretary of State, January.

Castells, Manuel (2004) *The Power of Identity*, 2nd edn. Oxford: Blackwell.

CBS News (2003) "Dean Raises $1m via Internet," May 23 (available at www.cbsnews.com).

Chadwick, A. and May, C. (2003) "Interaction between States and Citizens in the Age of the Internet: "E-government" in the United States, Britain, and the European Union," *Governance: An International Journal of Policy, Administration and Institutions* 16 (2): 271–300 (available at www.rhul.ac.uk).

Clough, M. (2003) "New Way to Win, or Cyber-hype?," *Los Angeles Times*, October 26: M2.

CNN (2003) "Web Changing Presidential Politics," August 18 (retrieved October 5, 2003 from www.cnn.com).

Coleman, S. (1999) "Westminster in the Information Age," *Parliamentary Affairs* 52: 371–87.

— — (2001) "The 2001 Election Online and the Future of E-politics," in S. Coleman (ed.), *2001: Cyber Space Odyssey. The Internet in the UK Election* (retrieved October 31, 2003 from www.hansardsociety.org.uk).

— — and Hall, N. (2001) "Spinning on the Web: E-campaigning and Beyond," in S. Coleman (ed.), *2001: Cyber Space Odyssey. The Internet in the UK Election* (retrieved October 31, 2003 from www.hansardsociety.org.uk).

Dahlgren, Peter and Sparks, Colin (1997) *Communication and Citizenship*. London: Routledge.

Dautrich, Kenneth and Hartley, Thomas (1999) *How the News Media Fail American Voters: Causes, Consequences, and Remedies*. New York: Columbia University Press.

Davis, Richard and Owen, Diane (1998) *New Media and American Politics*. New York: Oxford University Press.

Dean, H. (2003) "A Message from Governor Howard Dean to his Supporters on November 5, 2003 (available at www.deanforamerica.com).

Drinkard, J. and Lawrence, J. (2003) "Online, Off and Running: Web a New Campaign Front," *USA Today*, July 15 (retrieved October 5, 2003 from www.usatoday.com).

The Economist (2003) "Power to the People (Political Effects of the Internet)" (January 25) 366: 8303.

Fallows, James (1996) *Breaking the News: How the Media Undermine American Democracy*. New York: Pantheon.

Foot, K. A. and Schneider, S. M. (2002) "Online Action in Campaign 2000: An Exploratory Analysis of the US Political Websphere," *Journal of Broadcasting and Electronic Media* 46 (2): 222 (electronic version).

Franke-Ruta, G. (2003) "Fan Friction," *Prospect*, September 25 (retrieved October 1, 2003 from www.prospect.org).

Getlin, J. (2003) "Web-savvy Staff Helps Dean Weave his Way Up," *Los Angeles Times*, September 24 (retrieved October 5, 2003 from www.latimes.com).

Gibson, R. K. and Ward, S. J. (2003) "Participation, Political Organisations and the Impact of the Internet," ESRC end of award report L215252036. Salford: ESRI (available at www.ipop.org.uk).

— —, — —, and Lusoli, W. (2003) "The Internet and Political Campaigning: The New Medium Comes of Age?," *Representation* 39 (3): 166–80 (retrieved October 31, 2003 from www.esri.salford.ac.uk).

Giegerich, S. (2003) "Dean Uses Internet and Word-of-mouth to Expand Base among

College Students," *San Francisco Chronicle*, October 1 (retrieved October 5, from www.sfgate.com).

Hague, Barry and Loader, Brian (eds) (1999) *Digital Democracy: Discourse and Decision Making in the Information Age*. London: Routledge.

Internet Policy Institute (2001) "Report of the National Workshop on Internet Voting: Issues and Research Agenda" (avaliable at www.netvoting.org).

Ishikawa, Y. (2002) "Calls for Deliberative Democracy in Japan," *Rhetoric and Politics* 5 (2): 331–45.

Johnson, Deborah G. (2003) "Reflections on Campaign Politics, the Internet and Ethics," in D. M. Anderson and M. Cornfield (eds), *The Civic Web: Online Politics and Democratic Values*, pp. 9–18. Lanham, MD: Rowman and Littlefield.

Justice, Glen (2003) "Mix of Donors Adds to Dean Coffers," *The New York Times*, October 2 (retrieved October 2, 2003 from www.nytimes.com).

Kamarck, E. C. (2002) "Political Campaigning on the Internet: Business as Usual?," in E. C. Kamarck and J. S. Nye, Jr (eds), *Governance.com: Democracy in the Information Age*, pp. 81–103. Washington, DC: Brookings Institution.

Katz, J. E. and Rice, R. E. (2002) *Social Consequences of Internet Use: Access, Involvement, and Interaction*. Cambridge, MA: MIT Press.

Kessler, E. J. (2003a) "Joe Pulls in Cash, but Howard Dean Hits the Jackpot," *Forward*, July 4 (retrieved October 5, 2003 from www.forward.com).

— — (2003b) "Internet Invitation," *Forward*, August 8 (retrieved October 5, 2003 from www.forward.com).

Lessig, L. (2003) "The New Road to the White House: How Grassroots Blogs are Transforming Presidential Politics," *Wired Magazine* 11: 11 (retrieved October 22, 2003 from www.wired.com).

Levin, Y. (2002) "Politics after the Internet," *Public Interest* (Fall): 80 (available from www.web6.infotrac.gale.com).

Levine, Peter (2003) "Online Campaigning and the Public Interest," in D. M. Anderson and M. Cornfield (eds), *The Civic Web: Online Politics and Democratic Values*, pp. 47–62. Lanham, MD: Rowman and Littlefield.

Malone, J. (2003) "Dean Shows How to Catch Cash with Net: New Trend in Politics May be Clicking," *Atlanta Journal-Constitution*, July 4: A12.

Mosquera, M. (2000) "Gore, Bush Scramble for Undecided Voters," *Techweb News*, November 3 (retrieved October 5, 2003 from www.techweb.com).

Neuman, W. Russell (1991) *The Future of the Mass Audience*. Cambridge: Cambridge University Press.

Norris, Pippa (2000) *A Virtuous Circle: Political Communications in Postindustrial Societies*. Cambridge: Cambridge University Press.

— — (2001) *Digital Divide: Civic Engagement, Information Poverty, and the Internet Worldwide*. Cambridge: Cambridge University Press.

— — (2002) "Revolution, What Revolution? The Internet and US Elections, 1992–2000," in E. C. Kamarck and J. S. Nye, Jr (eds), *Governance.com: Democracy in the Information Age*, pp. 59–80. Washington, DC: Brookings Institution.

NPR (2003) "Howard Dean Campaign's Successful Internet Exploitation (Interview Transcript)," July 28 (retrieved from www.npr.org).

Pew Internet and American Life Project and Institute for Politics, Democracy, and the Internet (2003) "Untuned Keyboards: Online Campaigners, Citizens, and Portals in the 2002 Elections" (available at www.pewinternet.org).

Pioneer Press (2003) "Web Site Reels in Political Newbies," September 29 (retrieved October 1, 2003 (available at www.twincities.com).

Scheiber, N. (2003) "Joe Trippi Reinvents Campaigning: Organization Man," *The New Republic*, November 17 (retrieved November 27, 2003 from www.tnr.com).

Schulte, G. (2003) "Dean's 'Net Money Success Goes On," *Washington Times* (July 30) (retrieved October 5, 2003 from www.washingtontimes.com).

Slate (2003) "Peer-to-peer Politics: Should Howard Dean be a Little Bit Afraid of the Internet?," July 14 (retrieved October 5, 2003 from www.slate/msn.com).

Stromer-Galley, J. (2000) "Online Interaction and Why Candidates Avoid it," *Journal of Communication* 50 (4): 111–32.

Thompson, John (2000) *Political Scandals*. Cambridge: Polity Press.

Thompson, N. (2002) "Machined Politics: How the Internet is Really, Truly – Seriously! – Going to Change Elections," *Washington Monthly* (May) 34 (5): 27 (electronic version).

Ward, S. J., Gibson, R. K., and Lusoli, W. (2003) "Online Participation and Mobilization in Britain: Hype, Hope and Reality," *Parliamentary Affairs* 56: 652–68.

Wolfensberger, D. R. (2002) "Congress and the Internet: Democracy's Uncertain Link," in L. D. Simon, J. Corrales, and D. R. Wolfensberger (eds) *Democracy and the Internet: Allies or Adversaries?*, pp. 67–102. Washington, DC: Woodrow Wilson Center Press.

PART VII

The culture of the network society

17. Television, the internet, and the construction of identity

Imma Tubella

COMMUNICATION AND CULTURAL IDENTITY: A COMPLEX WORLD

We live in a complex world where communication media and cultural flows extend more and more across boundaries. Accordingly, one of the characteristics of communication media in the network society is that they take place on a scale that is increasingly global. Concepts like time, space, and distance obtain new meanings because of the proliferation of networks of electronic communication, which, as Castells (1996) has pointed out, represent the new social morphology of our societies. The end of distance involves the reordering of time and space, and a set of processes that are transforming modern societies. These processes are described today as globalization, a growing interconnectedness producing complex forms of interaction and interdependency.

The globalization of culture has a long history. Development and implantation of religions, for instance, show how ideas cross continents and influence societies. Nowadays, the concept of globalization is used to refer mainly to two processes: the globalization of the world economy, and the global diffusion of cultural forms and meanings. Information and communication technologies have opened up a vast number of communication channels that cross national borders and create a massive quantity of new images and new cultural habits, moving very fast, even if there remain significant differences in information density and velocity in different zones of the world. Globalization is about growing mobility across frontiers, mobility of goods, information, and people. Will this mobility affect collective identities? In this chapter, I will focus on the global diffusion of cultural forms through communication media, the local appropriation of these forms, and the impact of this process of globalization and localization of meanings on collective identity.

At the same moment that communication is settling at the heart of transformations in the network society, cultural and collective identities are taking a central place in the debates in contemporary communication theory and in cultural and sociological theory in general. Although the reshaping of cultural identity by communication processes is increasingly discussed around the world, the debates remain local and largely overlooked outside their cultural boundaries. For instance, the dependency model or the dependency framework has highly influenced Latin American theory. Latin American scholars are concerned about the role of the media and popular culture in society and their relationship to the process of the construction of identity (Martin Barbero, 1993; Garcia Canclini, 2001). European scholars are worried about North American influence in popular culture through cinema and television (Mattelart et al., 1984; Thompson, 1995). American scholars (Nye, 1990) concentrate their thinking and intellectual output about influence in a more positive way. Their simple question is how communication can be used to influence. Some of them are engaged in a more critical approach to American cultural colonialism around the world (Said, 1981; Chomsky and Herman, 1988; Schiller, 1992; Martin Barbero, 1993; Mowlana, 1996; Befu, 2000; Garcia Canclini, 2001).

However, in general and with some exceptions, at the present moment we face a highly complex set of communication and identity problems equipped only with the theoretical and analytical tools of the nineteenth century. There is a critical need for comparative research about the impact of media on identity.

If we are not capable of generating a language that is sufficiently clear to be able to take account of our world, we will not be able to understand what is going on. In addition to generating a new language (network society, for instance), new tools, and, above all, new attitudes, there is a need to re-establish and give new meanings to a multiplicity of social ties and social relations. As Roland Barthes (1970) has already pointed out, in order to formulate new connotations you have to develop a new language.

The development of information and communication technology (ICT) and the span of globalization are changing the very nature and meaning of cultural identity. At the same time, ICT has transformed the way in which we create and communicate and this has transformed us. The empirical and imaginary space between the individual and the collective is where much theoretical work must be accomplished.

> We live in a time of fractures and heterogeneity, of segmentations inside each nation and of fluid communications with transnational orders of information, style and knowledge. In the middle of this heterogeneity, we find codes that unify us, or at least permit us to understand ourselves. These codes are less and less of ethnicity, class or the nation into which we were born. (Garcia Canclini, 2001)

As Castells (1997: 359) suggests, these codes are codes of information and representation: "The new power lies in the codes of information and in the images of representation around which societies organize their institutions, and people build their lives, and decide their behavior. The sites of this power are people's minds." If we understand this, we will understand the role of communication in the construction of individual and collective identity.

To sum up, cultural and collective identities are constructed in new ways that signal a fundamental transformation of human experience. Especially for the global middle class, construction of cultural identity increasingly reflects exposure to abundant symbolic resources and discourses broadcast through information and communication technologies. In this context, community building and connectivity are deeply linked.

IDENTITY FORMATION IN A GLOBAL COMMUNICATION ENVIRONMENT

Theorists of identity are divided between those who see cultural identity as a flexible and constantly changing construction and those who see it as an immemorial and unchanging essence. Smith (1991) shows that the central question that has divided theorists is the place of the past. Theorists such as Kedourie (1960), Deutsch (1966), and Gellner (1983) define collective identity as a real community of culture and power, circumscribed, potent, unifying, and constraining. Smith (1991) explains the process of identity building as a piece of engineering which tries to connect history, symbols, myths, and languages.

But, in the context of the information society, the definition that I think best fits is the old definition of free will by Renan (1882: 12). He used this definition to build an idea of French nationhood that negated diversity in favor of reinforcing centralism: "The existence of a nation is a daily plebiscite." If we abstract the centralistic considerations and just take the definition, I think that we shall be on the way to rethinking the identity-building process and that we will be able to find systems of integration rather than ideas of exclusion. According to Renan, what counts is the desire and the will to live together, to form together a collective consensus that is renewed daily. I find this definition useful for our times because it reminds us not only of the importance of willpower, but also of the need for constant connection, consensus, and negotiation between community members, and, in some way, the role of the mass media to build this connection and consensus.

Benedict Anderson (1983) writes about the nation as a formalized, relatively stable, homogenizing social space that citizens encounter every moment of their everyday lives, but also as an imagined community, a cultural space that they share in common. Cultural identity gives people a shared sense of difference that is reinforced through the routines and rituals of everyday life, and through symbolic displays of their values and traditions. Collective identity is much more than a collection of individuals who share history and space and speak the same language. Collective identities are complex and distinctive cultural narratives, mythical stories that people tell themselves. In this context, the role of the mass media is clear as an instrument for creating an image of the collective identity for insiders and for outsiders, and in doing so, they contribute to the construction of the identity itself.

In the information society, the symbolic character of cultural identity, increasingly built, represented, and promoted by the media, stimulates levels of emotional involvement that contribute to the viability of any individual country. The nation-states understand this premise very well, and they do their best to control the mass media. Indeed, the mass media have long played an important role in the process of identity building, creating, ritualizing, and broadcasting who we are, and who the other is.

American anthropologist Conrad Kottak (1990) argues that soccer, television, and carnival create a democracy in Brazil that is lacking in most areas of Brazilian life. Television provides, in general, an equality of access, except in Africa where radio plays a cohesive role for people in ways that the political powers cannot achieve. Events like the death of Princess Diana or the September 11 disaster constitute symbolic displays of common feelings and purpose. Anti-war demonstrations around the world broadcast by the media in the winter of 2003 created a sense of global citizenship unknown before this moment.

European theorists are still very influenced by the classic Marxist concern about the role of ideology. New theories coming from South America offer a broad conception of communication and identity which proposes that mediation should be a central category for analysis. Martin Barbero (1993) suggests that, for South America, the syncretic nature of popular practices contributes both to the preservation of cultural identities and to their adaptation to new demands. One implication of this analysis for the processes of construction of cultural identity is that "the culture industry, by producing new hybrids resulting from the erasing of boundaries between high and popular culture, traditional and modern, and domestic and foreign is reorganizing collective identities and forms of symbolic differentiation."

If we consider cultural identity a symbolic construction rather than a thing already there to be described, we shall understand that identity formation in a global communication environment is highly influenced by the media, which construct our everyday perceptions of the other and ourselves. People live in a symbolic environment, a world of meaning, and it is clear that the mass media play a critical role in people's perceptions and attitudes in industrial societies and even more so in the information society where they play a central role.

COMMUNICATION AND CULTURAL IDENTITY: AN OLD DEBATE

Thompson (1995) examines the beginning of the globalization of communication by focusing on three key developments of the late nineteeth and early twentieth centuries: the development of underwater cable systems by the European imperial powers; the establishment of international news agencies and their division of the world; and the formation of international organizations concerned with the allocation of the electromagnetic spectrum. I would add a fourth development: the speed of information and communication technologies and the birth of the Internet during the 1960s.

In the 1970s, concern about cultural imperialism underpinned a growing perception across the Third World of imbalances in international news reporting and worldwide media flows. In 1977, UNESCO sponsored an international commission for the study of communication problems known as the McBride Commission after its chairman, the Irishman Sean McBride. The Commission spent two years examining questions about the communication gap between the developed and the developing worlds. Concern that most countries in the developing world were merely passive receivers of news and fiction from the developed world inspired calls for the creation of a "new more just and more efficient world information and communication order" known as NWICO. In fact, the demand for a new international economic order and the quest for a new world information and communication order of the 1970s have been transformed into a new global economic competitiveness. Since the McBride Report, both the world and the communication flows have changed. In Latin America, Brazil and Mexico have built strong audiovisual industries and have become successful exporters of media products (specially soap operas), but they still import an average of more than 30 percent of their broadcasts from the United States.[1]

The 1993 North America Free Trade Agreement (NAFTA) between the United States, Canada, and Mexico worried Mexican identity scholars because of the cultural impact of a free trading zone. Moreover, controversy about whether to include audiovisual products in the GATT Treaty indicates that variants of arguments about cultural imperialism have continued to be put forward. These arguments have been displaced by the notion of globalization and a recognition that the concept of globalization suggests interconnection and interdependency and that it is not exactly a synonym for imperialism. Neither does globalization mean universalism.

It is interesting to observe that European intellectuals and politicians used the same discourse of dependency deployed and used by Latin American intellectuals in the 1970s during the concluding phase of the GATT negotiation in 1993, trying to protect European audiovisual production from the United

States. During the concluding phase of the GATT negotiations, the European Union insisted upon a cultural exception for audiovisual products, refusing to consider them just as any other commercial product or to accept that globalization must mean Americanization.

The problem is that these debates were based on the primacy of the sovereignty of the state. A French minister wrote at this time that if he had to renounce being French or being European he would prefer to renounce being European. It has been a typical French problem: imposing a quota of French production to protect French identity and, at the same time, rejecting such cultural identities as Corsican, Catalan, or Basque. Another example is that, although the French state forbids the use of anglicisms in the mass media, people include them in their everyday language; for instance, the use of "Bye" is general.

So far, in the field of media and culture, the dependency model has concluded that the communication interests of the United States conditioned communication systems and that the result has been destructive to cultural identities. The cultural imperialism argument holds that imported media products (usually from the United States) contain ideas that will lead to the decline of traditional lifestyles and values: "By importing a product we are also importing the cultural forms of that society" (Mattelart et al., 1984). The contention that imported cultural forms will weaken a country's sense of itself and erode national identity has not been unique to Latin America. France has been a leader in promulgating this view. Mitterrand affirmed the right of every country to create its own images, saying that a society that abandons the means of representing itself would soon be an enslaved society, though when he said country, he meant state.

Constructing identity is both a matter of disseminating symbolic representations and forging cultural institutions and social networks. We catch the meaning of a collectivity through the images it casts, the symbols it uses, and the fictions or narratives it evokes. It is about a system of collective imaginings and symbolic representations. The United States has used the cinema, and audiovisual production in general, to spread an image of itself both across the world and within its own borders. The Japanese mass media have used the concept of *kokuminshugi* or "civic national consciousness" to strengthen the social construction of the Japanese and the Japanese self-image. *Nihonjinron*, theories of Japaneseness, have been used by the mass media inside the country to recover Japanese self-esteem. The first product for television in Japan was: *Watashi wa kai ni naritai* (I will become an oyster), a model of behavior for the people of post-war Japan, and a bet on a positive future. Authors like Muruyama (1963) use concepts such as "healthy civic national consciousness" (*kenzen na kokuminshugi*), which combines democracy with civic nationalism, to theorize behaviors broadcast by cinema and television.

In short, in a changing world, experiencing the double process of globalization and localization, collective identities are a stable point of reference, even if we consider identity as something that is never finished, never being, always becoming. Moreover, in this context, we find the role of the mass media as active creators of meaning, and the political aim of some collectivities with a strong cultural identity to consolidate their own media system with a double strategy: projecting their local culture as global and, at the same time, reinventing themselves. This is the case of Euskal Telebista in the Basque Country, Radio Québec in Quebec, or Teilifís na Gaeilge in Ireland, among others.

In order to proceed with a grounded analysis of my theoretical approach, I will use the development of Catalan Television as an exemplary case of national identity building in the field of communication.

THE CASE OF CATALAN TELEVISION

The political process of transformation in Spain, from the dictatorship toward democracy between 1975 and 1980, ended with the reform of the centralized state and the creation of the "State of the Autonomies," which reorganized the state into seventeen autonomous communities. These autonomous communities gained control over powers that were in the hands of the central state during the dictatorship. Among these powers, the autonomous communities won the right to own and operate their own independent television systems as a condition for the extension of democracy and, on the other hand, as a corrective to the centralized, state-controlled media. In addition, in the so-called "Historical Communities" (Basque Country, Galicia, and Catalonia), these systems had the main purpose of strengthening cultural and collective identity and their own language, other than Spanish.

During the first years of democracy, there was a long succession of deadlocked resolutions, compromises, and pacts among the major political parties to establish the media policies to build a legal framework for autonomous television. At the same time, these parties had serious difficulties in understanding the changes in the structure of the centralist state. These difficulties provoked the autonomous parliaments of the Basque Country and Catalonia into approving their own television systems, without approved legislation from the central state, and building their own parallel technical infrastructures as a result of a misunderstanding with central government, which owned the technical infrastructure of Spanish television and was reticent to lend them, fearing competition, but, more importantly, the fragmentation of the centralist national discourse. Basque Television (ETB)[2] began broadcasting on January 1, 1983 and Catalan Television (TVC) in September 1983. These actions constituted the first major institutional change in broadcasting since the appearance of Spanish Television (TVE) in the 1950s.

In Galicia, autonomous television (TVG) appeared later than in Catalonia and the Basque Country. Broadcasting began in July 1985. As the two other channels, Galician Television began as an instrument to normalize the use of Galician culture and language in addition to serving as the sociocultural backbone for community cohesion.

The Third Channel Law came into force at the end of 1984, months after the Basques and Catalans had begun broadcasting, believing that their right to broadcast was not dependent on the state and maintaining that their own statutes of autonomy, in combination with relevant clauses in the Constitution, protected their action in this area.

By 1990, eleven autonomous broadcasting organizations were approved, seven of which had already begun broadcasting on a daily basis. In 1989, these systems agreed to merge into a national federation of autonomous broadcasters, known as FORTA,[3] creating a network of public broadcasters, a confederation more than a federation with the aim of buying programs and negotiating with major American production companies, such as Metro, Orion, and Columbia, jointly rather than individually. Participating in FORTA are autonomous systems from the Basque Country, Catalonia, Andalusia, Galicia, Valencia, Madrid, Castilla la Mancha, and Murcia.

Autonomous television broke the monopoly of television in Spain and ran as a duopoly for several years before the emergence of private television in 1990. By the late 1980s, with only three autonomous TV networks and one state-based network (commercial TV had not yet started) the total investment in TV advertising had been pushed up to more than 1,000 percent of investment in 1975. In the first few months, the audiences of these autonomous networks reached 50 percent. The transition to democracy in Spain must be understood in relation to the media transition that helped stage the difficult changes in state structure and the debate on the role of media; in particular, the role of television helped social cohesion and the construction of cultural and collective identity.

To understand the present media space and the building of national public spheres in Europe, to understand the quest for a European identity and how public television is positioned within the global commercial culture, we have to take into consideration this kind of identity building through the media. For this purpose, the autonomous television networks broadcasting in the Spanish state provide a clear case study. In this chapter, therefore, I am going to look in depth at the case of Catalan Television.

Catalan Television (TVC) is a public enterprise created on September 11, 1983 to run and operate the television channels of the Catalan Broadcasting Corporation. Since its inception, TVC has sought to reflect the identity of a country and has helped to build and rebuild this identity.

TVC broadcasts in the Catalan language with a global vision. It has two terrestrial stations, TV3 and Canal 33, two satellite channels, TVCSat and TVC International, a twenty-four hour news channel, 3/24, and a terrestrial digital television service. This variety of channels offers a choice of programming for both general and specific audience segments. TVC was the first network in Spain to establish a site on the Internet.[4] The number of TVC programs on the Internet has grown rapidly, with the medium taking its place as part of the network's communication philosophy and strategy.

The Catalan Radio and Broadcasting Corporation set up TVC Multimedia in 1998 with the aim of commercially exploiting production in the information technology field. As part of this strategy, TVC set up a production center called SAM for audiovisual meteorology services. SAM's multimedia output employs sophisticated production methods and cutting-edge technology. It produces thematic channels for other TV stations, interactive services and applications for digital channels, and production services for the Internet.

From the beginning, TVC has contributed significantly to the development of the Catalan audiovisual industry, encouraging production, creativity, and new talent, centered, up until now, around Spanish television. TVC's two terrestrial channels broadcast 300 hours a week of high-quality programs in Catalan, covering all genres and areas of interest. TV3 is a general interest channel with top ratings in most genres: news, in-house fiction, entertainment with variety and creative humor, sporting events such as FC Barcelona, professional soccer league play-offs, and the Olympic Games. It devotes 1,600 hours of broadcasting a year to sport. The ranking of the most widely viewed programs in the Spanish state is usually headed by American films or by football. In Catalonia, the Spanish-speaking population follows TV3 football, broadcast usually in Catalan.

Canal 33, the second channel, is both an alternative and a complement to TV3, and offers more culturally oriented and innovative programs. During the daytime it covers children's programming with the name of K3. Half a million children in Catalonia under the age of 16 belong to Club Super 3. This program, on the air since 1991, is much more than just a standard children's program. It has more members than any other club in Catalonia. On the program and via Super 3 publications and its Internet website, Club members are kept abreast of recreational and cultural activities available to them and are often invited to attend free of charge. The majority of members are from Catalonia but there are members in other Catalan-speaking areas, such as the Balearic Islands, the autonomous community of Valencia, French Catalonia, and Alguero, a Catalan-speaking city in Sardinia.

Catalan Television is located on a 15-acre site close to Barcelona. Its premises comprise five buildings with eight studios with a total of 2,600 m^2 of floor space; thirty-four post-production video suites, including two digital suites and seven non-linear digital editing suites; eight audio post-production rooms, including five digital rooms; three sound studios and seventeen voice-over recording cabins; thirty-five ENG/EFP units; two mobile microwave links and a third one equipped with a satellite uplink dish (SNC); eight fully equipped outside broadcast vans, one capable of producing in 16 x 9 format; a large number of microwave links with more than twenty reception and trans-mission dishes, including a 6-m steering dish and a growing number of fibre-optic connections; a meteorological radar system as a result of an agreement between the Catalan Government and the University of Barcelona; twenty beauty shot cameras throughout Catalonia, and several regional facilities located in different parts of the country.

Within a few years Catalan viewers identified with TVC. They see it as "their" television. Both channels have a larger viewing audience than any other in Catalonia, with between 25 and 30 percent of total audience share. Its daily news programs have maintained their lead day after day from the very first days of broadcasting. News programs represent the backbone of the station's programming and provide a reference point for the viewers, a matter of loyalty. On the other hand, news bulletins not only contribute to an audi-ence's structured perception of the world, but they contribute decisively to the constitution of communication spaces, which give a public presence to collec-tive identities.

In a recent research project, Project Internet Catalonia (PIC),[5] carried out at the Open University of Catalonia (UOC), we found that, even by understand-ing the concept of communication practice in the widest possible sense, frequencies showed us that the most common daily communication practice in Catalonia is watching television (90.8 percent), followed by talking to people at home, playing with children, or similar (80.8 percent). Watching television is the most common communication practice even if it has suffered the most from the use of the Internet: 16.6 percent of people watch television less since they have gone online, and of this 16.6 percent, 61.7 percent are under the age of 30.

To construct the variable of communication practices we used news programs as a reference point because we considered that they represented an approximation of people's loyalty to the channel. Television is still the refer-ence communication medium for keeping people informed, but people do not trust it. People trust the radio more. The Internet, in spite of the possibilities for contrast that it contains, or the possibility of receiving information in real time, is only used as a source of regular information by 1 percent of the popu-lation and only for international events.

The meaningful finding is that almost 50 percent (47.6 percent) of Catalans watch TV news in Catalan, which means, fundamentally, TV3, but also Canal 33, BTV (the local television of Barcelona), City TV (a local private channel), some other local channels and some programs on the Spanish second channel,

La2. It is interesting to observe that Catalan-speakers watch television in Catalan (83.4 percent), Spanish-speakers watch it in Spanish (83.4 percent), and bilingual viewers adopt a bilingual behaviour: 48.2 percent watch in Catalan and 51.8 percent in Spanish.

But, in considering the influence of Catalan Television in identity building, we observe that, on one hand, knowledge of the language has grown from 50 percent to almost 100 percent from the beginning of TVC broadcasting until now. On the other hand, we also observe that, even though knowledge of the language has increased a lot, its normal use is still low in proportion. Some 43.2 percent of Catalans still consider their own language to be Spanish; 50.3 percent speak Spanish at home, and 41 percent speak Spanish with friends. These percentages of Spanish use are higher among young people (Castells et al., 2002).

We can conclude that TVC has been an important instrument in normalizing Catalan culture, recovering knowledge of the language, and strengthening the country's cohesion. However, there is still a long way to go in the construction of Catalan representation. Perhaps, a key differential factor in Catalonia, as a network society, could be a search for a collective strategy of adaptation to the change produced by structural globalization, a search to find new ways to present and represent itself.

TVC has been a powerful and successful instrument for the recuperation of the language, but, just as important as language is content, which is the creator of the imaginary, the builder of meaning, and of a specific type of discourse. Catalonia, in spite of the great leap forward that TVC represents, has had and still has a serious deficit in the control of its own representation, its meaning, caught between the global content and the Spanish imaginary. That is one of the main challenges that Catalonia has to face.

GLOBALIZATION AND THE DIALECTICS OF THE LOCAL: *DALLAS* AS INSTRUMENT OF LINGUISTIC NORMALIZATION IN CATALONIA

The programming choice for the opening night of the new Catalan channel, TV3, in an effort to promote the language and culture of Catalonia to the widest possible audience, was the hit episode of *Dallas*, "Who Shot JR?" dubbed, of course, into Catalan. All the autonomous broadcasters have followed similar programming strategies, choosing to dub the most popular imported series into their own language rather than pursue a strategy based on subtitling or on broadcasting in-house production, without the prestige to capture mass audiences.

For an important part of the Catalan population it has been difficult to understand the choice of *Dallas*, "the perfect hate symbol, the cultural poverty against which one struggles" (Mattelart et al., 1984) as a strong point of the Catalan television schedule. The feeling of Mattelart et al. (1984) was the general feeling in Europe against American programs at this time. Ang (1985) had another vision: "People watch *Dallas* for pleasure and the ideology of mass culture fails to recognize this. The high-minded defenders of national cultural identities in Western Europe have focused on the wrong level when they decry American Imperialism." In fact, she talks mainly about the French, the leaders of the European normative "Television Without Frontiers" by that time. She possibly did not know the case of the Catalans and Basques, who were much more worried by Spanish imperialism than by American cultural dominance.

Arjun Appadurai (2001: 19) introduces an interesting argument into the debate: "It is worth noticing that for the people of Irian Jaya, Indonesianization may be more worrisome than Americanization, as Japanization may be for Koreans, Indianization for Sri Lankans, Vietnamization for the Cambodians, Russianization for the people of Armenia or for the Baltic Republics." On the other side of the coin, France is extremely worried by Americanization at the same time as it does not allow the expression of their own cultural identity to Bretons, Catalans, or Corsicans, to mention some of the different cultural identities cohabiting inside the French state.

In this sense, Schlesinger (1991) suggests that, rather than starting with communication and its supposed effects on collective identity and culture, we should begin by posing the problem of collective identity itself, asking how it might be analyzed and what importance communicative practices play in its construction. We find a good example in the People's Republic of China where people interpret and use foreign cultural materials quite differently depending on their perspective of different civilizations (Lull, 1991). While Chinese television viewers enjoy and learn from programs imported from North and South America and Europe, because they offer new vistas, new life styles and new ways of thinking, they are less enthusiastic about Japanese productions. The Chinese government has even imported certain Japanese programs, hoping to inspire the Chinese to work hard and succeed like the Japanese, but Chinese viewers interpret Japanese programs in ways that differ from their involvement with cultural materials that are imported from other civilizations more distant in both in terms of geography and lifestyle, with a kind of symbolic distancing. Moreover, Chinese consumers prefer Japanese commercial products to American goods.

Coming back to the *Dallas* example, at the beginning people did not feel comfortable hearing JR speaking Catalan. For Catalans, the "normal" language of *Dallas* characters was Spanish. Nevertheless, very soon they felt proud to hear JR speaking their own language. The Disney strategy "Think global, act local" works the same way. Children are used to thinking that Disney characters are local because they always speak local languages. Thompson (1995) describes this situation as globalized diffusion and localized appropriation.

The vast majority of audiovisual products circulating across borders are from the United States, but the evidence suggest that national cultures remain strong, and foreign cultural products are read and reinterpreted in new and different ways by local audiences. *Dallas*[6] and Disney products are good examples of this local reinterpretation. There are others where the translation has not been enough. MTV, the global music television service, began to differentiate its content around the world and incorporate local music and local programs in addition to local languages. They adopted this strategy after the campaign to establish a Pan Asian TV service failed for lack of cultural specificity. They forgot that India and Japan and Malaysia have little in common.

Moreover, the lesson of the 1990s has been that, although American films, music, and culture have considerable following worldwide, this acceptance has its limits. In Western Europe during the 1980s, prime time was American. In the 1990s, it began to be domestically produced and, in many cases, audiences often prefer in-house programs to Hollywood productions. In the case of cinema, this has happened later, after multiple precedent windows: pay per view, pay channels, and DVD.

CONCLUSION

Collective identity refers to the sense of oneself as a member of a social group or collectivity. It is a sense of belonging, a sense of being part, an action system, a mode of praxis that makes sense of the world and one's place within it. What is the relevance of communication media to the construction of this identity? The media provide some of the important symbolic materials for the construction of identity, both at the individual and the collective level: beliefs, assumptions, and patterns of behavior. The construction of identity can never start anew; it always builds on a pre-existing set of symbolic materials which form the foundation of identity. But with the development of communication media, the very nature of this construction has been reshaped in significant ways, and not always in a negative way.

The experience of Catalan television shows us that the media can be used not only to challenge traditional values and beliefs but also to extend and consolidate a sense of belonging and to incorporate new patterns of behavior, called by Thompson (1995) "cultural migrations," due partly to the globalization of media products. The development of the media has transformed identity and, above all, identity building, a process increasingly dependent on forms of interaction which involve media products such as books, television, cinema, and the Internet.

The increasing importance of communication media in a changing and dynamic society and the development of information and communication technologies have created a new situation where communication and identity need to be rethought. Such development belies any idea of culture or identity as a monolithic force and reinforces the idea of community and connectivity, a community that has its own cultural specificity but is open to explore distant worlds. The construction of identity has to be shaped in relation to the rapidly changing circumstances of social life on a local and global scale where the individual and the collectivity must integrate information and knowledge from a diversity of communication-mediated experiences. The Internet, and its association with globalization, can have a "pluralizing impact" (Hall, 1997) on the construction of collective identity, producing a less fixed identity because communication flows and interconnection promote cultural encounters and interactions.

Today, classical elements of collective identity definition, such as language, territory, religion, common past or common culture, are still relevant but there are other important factors to be considered, like the capacity for connectivity, cooperation, and interaction. In other words, individuals and collectivities have, on the one hand, the ability to network, and, on the other hand, the ability to present and represent themselves. Using Castells's terminology, we can speak about the space of places and the space of flows. These two different spaces coexist and the Internet is the instrument able to connect them. The new approach to identity building works through the interaction of places and flows, through the interaction of language, culture, history, and territory, with the ability of integration, cooperation, and networking.

Clear evidence of the Internet as an identity builder does not exist. However, in Catalonia, our research for the Project Internet Catalonia (2002) shows us that, once we have analysed the different dimensions of projects of personal autonomy, such as entrepreneurial, sociopolitical, psychosocial, or personal projects, we see that the more autonomous people are, the more Catalan identity they have, and, on the other hand, the more autonomous people are, the more they use the Internet and with more intensity.

Evidence for the influential role that the media play in societies is overwhelming. Perhaps most significant of all is the fact that people attach central importance to the media as critical contributors to the way in which they think and live their lives. In this way, it is very important to remember that collective identity is collective consensus, a symbolic project, and shared interests, and that the media in general and the Internet in particular are powerful tools to actively build it.

NOTES

1. The United States imports 2 percent of its broadcasts and Japan no more than 5 percent.
2. Like Catalan Television, *Euskal Telebista* was created basically to promote the normalization of Basque culture and language, which had an extremely low level of knowledge among the Basque population. For this reason, in 1986 the Basque government created a second channel, ETB2, mainly in Spanish, except for children's programs, in order to reach the whole of the population and to offer a specific vision of the world and their own country accessible to the whole population.
3. Federación de Organismos de Radio y Televisión autonòmicos (Federation of Autonomous Organizations of Radio and Television).
4. http://www.tvcatalunya.com.
5. See Castells et al. (2002). This research analyzes Internet use and its relationship to social and communicative practices within the framework of the social structure and social practices of the whole Catalan population. It is based on a survey with a sample of 3,005 people representative of the population of Catalonia. It includes both Internet users and non-users, allowing comparison of the specific effect of Internet use on social practices.
6. See the very interesting study of Liebes and Katz (1993) on the local reception of *Dallas*.

REFERENCES

Anderson, B. (1983) *Imagined Communities: Reflections on the Origin and Spread of Nationalism*. London: Verso.
Ang, I. (1985) *Watching Dallas: Soap Opera and the Melodramatic Imagination*. London: Methuen.
Appadurai, A. (2001) *Globalization*. Durham, NC: Duke University Press.
Barker, C. (1999) *Television, Globalization and Cultural Identities*. Buckingham: Open University Press.
Barthes, R. (1970) *Mythologies*. Paris: Seuil.
Befu, H. (2000) "Globalization as Human Dispersal: From a Perspective of Japan," in J. S. Eades, T. Gill, and H. Befu (eds), *Globalization and Social Change in Contemporary Japan*. Melbourne: Trans Pacific Press.
Bertz, C. R. (1983) "Cosmopolitan Ideals and National Sentiment," *Journal of Philosophy* 80: 591–600.
Castells, M. (1997) *The Information Age: Economy, Society and Culture*, vol. II: *The Power of Identity*. Oxford: Blackwell.
— — and Himanen, P. (2001) "The Finnish Model of the Information Society," Sitra Reports, no.17. Helsinki: Sitra.
— —, Tubella, I., and Sancho, T. (2002) "The Network Society in Catalonia: An Empirical Analysis" (available at http://www.uoc.edu/in3/pic/eng/pic1.html).
Chomsky, N. and Herman, E. (1988) *Manufacturing Consent: The Political Economy of the Mass Media*. New York: Pantheon.
Connolly, W. E. (1991) *Identity/Difference: Democratic Negotiations of Political Paradox*. Ithaca, NY: Cornell University Press.
Curran, J. and Gurevitch, M. (eds) (1991) *Mass Media and Society*. London: Edward Arnold.
Deutsch, K. (1966) *Nationalism and Social Communication: An Inquiry into the Foundation of Nationality*. Cambridge, MA: MIT Press.
Eley, G. and Suny, R. G. (eds) (1996) *Becoming National: A Reader*. New York: Oxford University Press.

Ferguson, M. (1995) "Media Markets and Identities: Reflections on the Global–Local Dialectic," *Canadian Journal of Communication* 20: 439–59.

Garcia Canclini, N. (2001) *Consumers and Citizens, Globalization and Multicultural Conflicts*. Minneapolis, MN: University of Minnesota Press.

Gellner, E. (1983) *Nations and Nationalism*. Oxford: Blackwell.

Hall, S. (1992) "The Question of Cultural Identity," in S. Hall, D. Held, and A. McGrew (eds), *Modernity and its Features*. Cambridge: Polity Press.

— — (1997) "Encoding/Decoding," in Paul Marris and Sue Thornham (eds), *Media Studies: A Reader*, pp. 41–9. Edinburgh: Edinburgh University Press.

Held, D. and McGrew, A. (eds) (2001) *The Global Transformations Reader*. Cambridge: Polity Press.

Hobsbawm, E. (1996) "Language, Culture, and National Identity," *Social Research* 63: 1065–80.

Kedourie, E. (1960) *Nationalism*. London, Hutchinson.

de Kerckhove, D. (1995) *The Skin of Culture*. Toronto: Somerville House.

Kottak, C. (1990) *Prime Time Society: An Anthropological Analysis of Television and Culture*. Belmont, CA: Wadsworth

Liebes, T. and Katz, E. (1993) *The Export of Meaning: Cross-cultural Readings of Dallas*. Cambridge: Polity Press.

Luke, C. (1990) *Constructing the Child Viewer: A History of the American Discourse on Television and Children, 1950–1980*. New York: Greenwood.

Lull, J. (1991) *China Turned On: Television, Reform and Resistance*. London: Routledge.

— — (2000) *Media, Communication and Culture: A Global Approach*. Cambridge: Polity Press.

Mackinnon, N. J. and Alison, L. (2002) "Changes in Identity Attitudes as Reflections of Social and Cultural Change," *Canadian Journal of Sociology* 27: 299ff.

Mankekar, P. (1999) *Screening Culture, Viewing Politics: An Ethnography of Television, Womanhood, and Nation in Postcolonial India*. Durham, NC: Duke University Press.

Martin Barbero, J. (1993) "Latin American Cultures in Communication," *Media Journal of Communication* 43 (2): 18–30.

Mattelart, A., Delcourt, X., and Mattelart, M. (1984) *International Image Markets: In Search of an Alternative Perspective*. London: Comedia.

Meech, P. and Kilborn, R. (1992) "Media and Identity in a Stateless Nation: The Case of Scotland," *Media, Culture and Society* 14 (2): 245–59.

Morley, D. and Robins, K. (1995) *Spaces of Identity: Global Media, Electronic Landscapes and Cultural Boundaries*. London: Routledge.

Mowlana, H. (1996) *Global Communication in Transition: The End of Diversity?* London: Sage.

Muruyama, M. (1963) "The Ideology and Dynamics of Ultranationalism," in *Thoughts and Behavior in Modern Japanese Politics*. London: Oxford University Press.

Noam, E. (1991) *Television in Europe*. New York: Oxford University Press.

Nye, Jr, J. S. (1990) "Soft Power," *Foreign Policy*, 80.

Robins, K. and Asu, A. (2001) "From Spaces of Identity to Mental Spaces: Lessons from Turkish-Cypriot Cultural Experience in Britain," *Journal of Ethnic and Migration Studies* 27 (4): 685–711.

Renan, E. (1882) *Qu'est ce qu'une nation?* Paris: Calman Levy, 1908. Reprinted Paris: INALF, 1961.

Said, E. (1981) *Covering Islam: How the Media and the Experts Determine How We See the Rest of the World*. London: Routledge.

Schiller, H. (1992) *Mass Communication and American Empire*. Boulder, CO: Westview Press.

Schlesinger, P. (1991) *Media, State and Nation: Political Violence and Collective Identities*. London: Sage.

— — (1993) "Wishful Thinking: Cultural Politics, Media, and Collective Identities in Europe," *Journal of Communication* 43: 6–17.

Slevin, J. (2000) *The Internet and Society*. Cambridge: Polity Press.

Smith, A. (1980) *The Geopolitics of Information: How Western Culture Dominates the World*. London, Faber.

— — (1991) *National Identity*. Harmondsworth: Penguin.

Thompson, J. B. (1995) *The Media and the Modernity: A Social Theory of the Media*. Cambridge: Polity Press.

18. Globalization, identity, and television networks: community mediation and global responses in multicultural India

Anshu Chatterjee

The widespread adoption of reform in the media sector has permitted the development of global communication networks that are organized around cultural communities. These networks encompass community enterprises operating at a global level in addition to transnational enterprises whose use of local culture and resources extends beyond expected operations in a secondary market. Several public enterprises also continue to operate in this media space, targeting national communities residing both within and outside their national territories to deliver messages shaped by their national objectives. The aggregation of these various enterprises operating at different levels provides an impression of *localization*, which, as several observers indicate, constitutes a crucial element of the post-industrial processes (Giddens, 1990; see also Hall, 1997).

What causes the commercially oriented transnational enterprises to function in this manner, especially in locations where commercial television is comparatively underdeveloped? The answer to this is of considerable significance to communication theories of cultural and economic domination that point to problems associated with the dissemination of externally developed programming to less-developed countries. The consequences, these theories indicate, include the delivery of out-of-context messages that impress upon community culture and local aspirations as well as bringing extraneous agendas into the public sphere reserved for domestic discussions (Herman and McChesney, 1997: 3).

A comparative study of the expansion of commercial television among different language communities in India illustrates the contextualized outcomes of widespread restructuring of the media space. Here we examine the reorganizing of competitive structures in a developing country with a history of state-controlled television. The rapid appearance of several community enterprises prompted unexpected strategies among transnational media and caused the national media to decentralize along community lines, shifting from a long-standing national policy of control. Ironically, the decentralization occurred at a time when nationalism occupied crucial space in the media due to the mobilization strategies of the Hindu nationalist party. Media enterprises, including external players, responded to this in various forms, illustrating a continued association between media activities and the domestic setting.

The television sector in India is studied utilizing an institutional analysis that places the media within the context of the social and political framework of democracy and its institutions.[1] As an embedded institution, the media reflect the dominant norms and trends in society. The media may also play an important role in providing space for communicative action among community members. According to Jürgen Habermas (1996: 360–3), the public sphere provided by the media serves as a link between institutions seeking to address social and political issues. Although Habermas does not address representational inequalities in the public sphere, an historical consideration of communities, their popular movements, and the political institutions that impress upon production and distribution may help delineate the asymmetry in representation. Furthermore, the recent use by transnational media of selected domestic symbols and themes in framing programs also underscores the need to study institutions that emphasize selected symbols.

A discussion of dominance requires us to approach these new television networks from the reception aspect as well. The processes of communication, as several scholars illustrate, do not flow in one direction. John Thompson (1999) argues that there is a structured break between production and reception, which allows spectators to determine messages in their own context. Although the relationship is not equal, the audience brings specific preferences to the viewing setting (see Hall, 1980; Morley, 1980). An examination of the political relationships at the reception setting delineates these preferences.

LIBERALIZING INDIAN TELEVISION

In 1991, restructuring processes initiated by the Indian state deregulated the state-dominated television sector. The entry of the foreign media into the region instituted a transformative decade. CNN and Star TV, initially owned by Hutchinson-Wampoa of Hong Kong, and later by Rupert Murdoch's News Corporation, began their transmission immediately after the announcement of expected reform. In 1992, Star TV included BBC and MTV segments which targeted English speakers in the Asian sub-continent. In 1995, Sony Entertainment entered the region using Hindi-only programs. During this phase of transnational expansion, the Indian government made no serious attempt to re-regulate this media space.

Indian entrepreneurs located across the nation also received a tremendous boost in the reform-oriented environment, gaining access to external sources that enabled them to broadcast into their own communities. Previous restrictions surrounding the television industry had barred local entrepreneurs from the television sector. The lowered cost of access to new technologies at the global level, combined with regional expertise and associations, provided these enterprises with an unexpected advantage. Within a decade of the deregulatory moves, the Indian television sector consisted of 40–50 new players affiliated with a diversity of channels directed at community audiences. In 1990, 27 million households in the country had television. By comparison, in 2001, over 60 million households, comprising more than 31 percent of the country's one billion residents, contained televisions sets.[2]

In comparison to other developing nations, the expansion of commercial television in India occurred among the nation's multiple cultural communities, challenging the larger players seeking a national audience. Historically, the state-owned Doordarshan controlled this space, transmitting mainly Hindi and English programs despite the nation's language diversity. Although, Doordarshan's reach extended across the nation by 1990, no clear reception figures exist. However, only 42 percent of Indians are Hindi speakers. Over 106 language communities reside in India, of which twenty retain the official status of a national language. Reception among these communities remained limited.

From Doordarshan's inception in 1959, the state had utilized television to promote selected developmental, social, and political objectives. In 1983, Rajiv Gandhi's reform-oriented administration extended Doordarshan's entertainment segment to include programs with a possible national appeal. New cultural programs, such as Hindu mythology programs, gained an immediate viewership. Some scholars detect a link between the appearance of Hindu mythology programs and Rajiv Gandhi's attempts at mobilizing the Hindu vote (Rajagopal, 2001; see also Mitra, 1993). They argue that the increasing popularity of the Hindu Nationalists, the Bharatiya Janata Party (BJP) in the northern and western parts of the nation caused Rajiv Gandhi to introduce religious programs into state television which had previously followed a secular policy.

However, the proliferation of religious programs in the 1980s may be better understood in the light of the state's new commercial agenda. India consists of 83 percent Hindus. Under Rajiv Gandhi, the objectives of the national media developed under the Nehruvian state confronted the new commercial objectives that responded to popular preferences. In addition, no apparent links exist between audience programming preferences and their political choices. Rajiv Gandhi lost the following 1989 elections and, although the Hindu mythology programs continued to be popular across the country, the BJP's vote base remained limited to the northern and western parts of India. In comparison, business logic dictates that programs are designed to reach the largest number of Indians. Since then the policy preferences of the BJP-led coalition, which came to power in 1998, also indicate the significance of commercial objectives. In 2001, it further deregulated the communication space by permitting foreign investment in the press sector. Interestingly, external players have yet to contradict the BJP's cultural preferences.

COMMUNITY CHANNELS: REORGANIZING INDIAN TELEVISION

Following liberalization, the challenge to the state's television monopoly was expected to come from well-resourced external players. Instead, the more significant challenge to the national commercial policy has come from community channels allied to regional political groups. The diverse language communities provided an existing set of audiences with historically determined consumption patterns. These community channels were able to successfully target language communities establishing a lead for others to follow. Table 18.1 delineates the expansion of the media across selected language communities since 1991.

Table 18.1   Community language channels, 1990–2002

Targeted language group	Foreign-owned channels	Domestically owned channels	Domestic ownership with foreign investors (including expatriate investors)
Hindi	Sony, MTV (1995) Star Plus (1998)	Doordarshan 1 and 2 (1959, 1982)	Zee TV (1993–2000)
Punjabi	Star/Tara Punjabi (2001)	Doordarshan 18 (1997)	Lashkara (1999) Alpha Punjabi (2000)
Telugu	–	Doordarshan 8 (1995) Eenadu (1995) Gemini (1995)	–
Malayalam	–	Doordarshan 4 (1993)	Asianet (1993)
Bengali	ATN Bangla (1997) Tara Bengali (2001)	Doordarshan 7 (1994) ETV Bangla (2000)	Alpha Bangla (2000)
Gujarati	Tara Gujarati (2001)	Doordarshan 11 (1994) Alpha Gujarati (2000)	Gujari (2000)

These enterprises cut into Doordarshan's national audience by providing community-relevant programs. Mythology-based programs among community channels, for instance, were in regional languages and were adaptations based on regional variations of Hindu culture. In response, the state was compelled to address competition at diverse levels, initiating regional language programs across the country and reinforcing programming on its nationally televised channels. Soon after Doordarshan's regional response, the transnational media followed suit.

The appearance of Hindi channels in the northern parts of the country presented the initial challenge to the larger players seeking a national audience. In 1992, when the transnational media began to broadcast English programs into India, Subhash Chandra, the founder of Zee TV, launched an entertainment-oriented Hindi channel. The immediate success of Zee Telefilms was an indication of the challenge that would confront Doordarshan's administration in the coming years. It also compelled the transnational media to restructure their programming toward specific communities. Zee's productions paralleled Doodarshan's entertainment segments based upon northern Indian culture and social norms. The popularity of Bollywood-style programs on Doordarshan in the past ensured a positive reception for Zee. The channel also re-ran several of Doodarshan's mythology programs. Its new productions borrowed game and talk shows from the Western media. Within a year, Zee had captured large segments of the Hindi/Urdu-speaking cable and satellite audience. Its success attracted the interest of News Corporation, which purchased 49 percent of Zee in 1994 with a contract stipulation that divided the Indian language market exclusively into English and Hindi. Star was not to venture into the Hindi market. In 1999, Zee was watched in 22 million homes, mainly located in Hindi speaking areas.[3] Zee's success established the importance of a localized strategy for transnationals initially seeking a national audience.

By 1997 Star TV had been operating in the country for four years, but it had yet to show profit. In comparison, companies operating in local languages were expanding rapidly. For example, SET, a late comer in 1995, gained high ratings within two years of operating in India. MTV India, also having changed its language of transmission into *Hinglish*,[4] was successfully reaching young urban Indians. In 1997, Star began to challenge its contract with Zee by introducing Hindi programs into Star channels. In 1999, Zee and Star ended their relationship. Subsequently, Star Plus began transmitting Hindi productions.

However, Zee Telefilms and its transnational competitors are notably limited to the Hindi/Urdu communities as are Doordarshan's Hindi channels. Table 18.2 compares the limited appeal of Hindi channels in three of the non-Hindi regions. In Kerala, Zee captures an insignificant 0.5 percent of the view-

Table 18.2   Audience share of major channels in three states, 1999

	Punjab (10,222)[a] (%)	Kerala (15,631)[a] (%)	Andhra Pradesh (28,113)[a] (%)
Star Plus (in Hindi)	10.7	3.5	4
Star Sports (English/Hindi)	3.5	3	4.5
Star Movies (English)	2.5	<1	3
Zee TV (Hindi)	35	<1	2
Asianet (Malayalam)	–	24	–
Eenadu (Telugu)	–	–	70
Gemini (Telugu)	–	–	68
Doordarshan (Punjabi)	73	–	–
Doordarshan (Malayalam)	–	18	–
Doordarshan (Telugu)	–	–	40

[a] Estimated TV-watching adults in thousands (MARG Survey, August 1999).

ers compared to regional Asianet's 24 percent or even bilingual Star Plus's 3.5 percent. Similar trends are apparent in Andhra Pradesh where people prefer regional Telugu channels to the Hindi or English channels. In Punjab, Zee is watched by 35 percent of the television audience because of a significant number of bilingual Punjabi/Hindi speakers in the state.[5] Furthermore, the region's proximity to the Hindi belt translates into an exchange of labor between the two communities. Meanwhile, in other language regions that constitute over 58 percent of the population of India, several community channels have appeared to challenge the state's monopoly.

The states of Andhra Pradesh and Kerala provide parallel examples of the rapid development of non-Hindi channels in a liberalized space. After 1991, several southern Indian entrepreneurs responded to the reforms. Although national resources were yet to be made available for the private sector, new access to global technology and capital permitted transmission into previously restricted areas. More significantly, the local and state governments, who were denied access to national television in the past, encouraged these channels. By 1994, private regional channels, operated by an alliance between Indian businesses and external players, were transmitting into southern India, targeting specific language communities. Similar to Zee TV, these channels formed the first layer of competition for the state and the transnational media companies.

In Andhra Pradesh, the *Eenadu* newspaper group, owned by Ramaji Rao, a Telugu media mogul, established ETV using a Russian satellite to transmit into the community. His television venture was supported by the regional pro-liberalization Telugu Desam Party, in power from 1984. The relationship between *Eenadu* and the political party was established at the time of the founding of the party in 1983. When N. T. Rama Rao established the regional Telugu Desam Party to compete with Indira Gandhi's Congress Party, *Eenadu*'s editors candidly endorsed the party. Although Rama Rao's initial popularity derived from his acting career in Telugu films, *Eenadu* played a significant role in promoting his political career (see Pandian, 1992). Indira Gandhi's administrative style in the post-emergency era raised a red flag for the community. When Rama Rao declared that the self-respect of the Telugu people was "mortgaged" in Delhi by the state's Congressmen, *Eenadu*'s editors backed his portrayal of the Congress as an outsider.

This relationship continued throughout the 1990s. The state supported *Eenadu* by providing it with advertising revenues or presenting it with awards and loans. When *Eenadu* launched its television venture, ETV, the distinct pattern of media involvement in the region's sociopolitical activities was apparent. While the national administration debated the extension of liberalization measures, the new TDP leader, Chandrababu Naidu, invited global capital into the state to form partnerships with regional businesses.[6] The state's openness allowed *Eenadu* executives to take advantage of the availability of global resources and the amenability of the state's ruling party to new technologies and capital. The paper and the channel also endorsed the policies of Naidu that opened up the state's economy. The founding of Gemini TV also provides evidence of a similar pattern of association between the political and economic elites in the region. Gemini TV is owned by a regional business house, the Prasad family, and Kalanidhi Maran, the son of a prominent politician in the neighboring Tamil Nadu and the owner of Tamil Sun TV.

From a state governmental perspective, the relationship between such media ventures and the state's economic elite could only be beneficial. Hence, in Kerala, when Sashi Kumar, a former executive officer of the Press Trust of India, launched Malayali Asianet, the government of Kerala provided the initial infrastructure.[7] In 1993, Kerala had yet to develop a cable infrastructure, unlike other Indian states consisting of larger urban areas. Therefore, Asianet also won the state contract to establish the cable system network utilizing pre-existing telegraph poles owned by the government. Sashi Kumar launched Asianet with initial funding from a Moscow-based Indian, Raji Menon. A Russian satellite provided the initial transponder. By 1995, Asianet claimed viewership of 14 percent of the state's TV audiences, which translated into all of Kerala's cable and satellite homes. Currently, cable and satellite connections are found in 24 percent of the state's households. Asianet continues to dominate this space (Page and Crawley, 2001: 103). Such rapid developments in the south prevented external players from venturing into the region dominated by media embedded in their community's political system.

These developments caused national Doordarshan to establish regional television centers for producing specific language programs. Initially, Doordarshan's origin as part of the national administration and its dependency upon central government for finance kept it aloof from regional institutions and insensitive to preferences among diverse communities. However, its commercialization compelled it to consider audience preferences at regional levels. In Kerala, Asianet was launched in 1993; Doordarshan Malayalam followed in the same year. In Andhra Pradesh, two private Telugu channels, ETV (Eenadu) and Gemini TV were launched in 1995. Doordarshan Telugu expanded its Telugu programming to four hours on a daily basis. Doordarshan's regional channels currently form the secondary layer of competition (see table 18.2 for Doordarshan's audience share).

LANGUAGE PROMOTION AND MEDIA INSTITUTIONS: EXPLAINING THE VARIATIONS

Television in Punjab provides a contrasting example to the southern channels that emerged immediately to take advantage of the resources available at the global level. Punjabi channels did not appear until 1998. As a result of this slower development, the Punjabi community presented a different market structure for external players seeking regional audiences. By 2000, several external players, including several transnational companies, were operating in Punjab. Although Punjab consists of only 2 percent of India's population, Punjabi audiences also include Punjabi communities in other parts of North India, such as Haryana and Delhi. In addition, a large number of Punjabi speakers in neighboring Pakistan augment the Punjabi audience market. Punjabi speakers in Pakistan consist of 48 percent of the nation's population.[8]

The slow progress of private Punjabi language television is not necessarily a reflection of Punjabi audiences' lack of preference for Punjabi programming. For instance, Doordarshan's Punjabi channel, started in 1998, claimed the attention of 73 percent of Punjabi audiences in 1999. Nor is it a reflection of the state's economy, which ranks as the wealthiest in the country.[9] The cable penetration rate of 35 percent is the highest in the northern parts of the country, and a rate of 82 percent of homes with television is the highest in the nation.[10] In comparison, Andhra Pradesh, with its larger population of 67 million, is a mid-level economy, and Kerala, with 29 million inhabitants, is considered a low-ranking economy. Economic explanations also do not adequately address audience choices. Instead, a process of identifying some of the institutional players and enterprises at the community level generally provides a more realistic picture of a necessary collaboration that causes global processes to mold to the domestic environment.

Unlike Zee TV, which had the advantage of a pre-existing Hindi audience base, the southern enterprises had to create a television audience base. The presence of community institutions that encourage production along community lines and advocate the consumption of cultural goods among its community members provided a critical supportive role. In return, these institutions gained a communication channel, which augmented the community sense of unity and autonomy. Such alignment of interest was not replicated in Punjab, leading to the faltering pace of television development.

The mutually beneficial nexus between community institutions, the media, and the elite found among the South Indian communities was established historically in the early part of the twentieth century. It emerged as a consequence of widespread social movements that appeared in reaction to the British claim to superiority. These movements, in different forms, some as caste movements and others as religious movements, adopted distinct languages as differentiating symbols and transformed them into icons for collective mobilization against the prevailing sociopolitical order. Their association with different regional political movements produced variations in objectives that had an effect upon the development of media institutions.

The Telugu language movement, for example, became associated with the lower-caste movement that sought to establish a politically autonomous region of Andhra Pradesh in order to differentiate from other politically important lower-caste communities. The spread of press and cinema technology in India at the time assisted in diffusing the ideals of the movement, establishing a priority in the media for promoting the community and its language. Telugu cinema, for instance, reflected both the autonomy movements as well as the nationalist movement simultaneously. The current association between the political and media elites in Andhra Pradesh is embedded in this history.

Similarly, in Kerala, the language movement became a vehicle for the development of an autonomous region for Malayalam speakers. Interestingly, it provided the unifying element in a notably diverse community, which confronted not only the British but also the domination of "foreign" upper castes in running the princely administration. Currently, Kerala's diversity consists of 57.28 percent Hindus, 23.33 percent Muslims, and 19.32 percent

Christians, proportions that have not altered drastically in the past century.[11] The relationship between the media and the community social and political institutions developed at the time. Several founders of Malayali vernacular newspapers were members of the newly formed Malayali political associations as well as the Indian National Congress, linking their drive for autonomy with the nationalist movement for independence. Correspondingly, involvement in the region's movements by several of cinema's prominent personalities formed a link between the region's film sector and the political institutions. This relationship was later institutionalized when the new state utilized its resources to encourage Kerala's media sector.

After independence, these language affinities remained resolute in confronting the attempt by the nation-state to unify modern India through homogenizing policies. The manner in which Hindi was promoted to replace English in post-colonial India raised concerns of discriminative policies among other language communities, producing widespread opposition and the suspension of the sole language policy (Dasgupta, 1970: ch. 2). The combination of enhanced awareness of distinct language communities, promoted by the elite and the state, and the regional threat of discrimination further enhanced affinity toward language collectivities. Community media institutions participated in this process by diffusing these objectives, supporting the community elite, as well as becoming cultural symbols whose consumption was critical for community cohesion.

The success of these movements and the formation of states strengthened the alliance between the media and the new elite. For Andhra Pradesh and Kerala, territorial reorganization initiated in the 1950s provided spatial symbols for further enhancement of their language identities. The new political boundaries strengthened their language community, legitimized their differences, and presented an opportunity to institutionalize the objectives of the community movements. Simultaneously, the national and state governments instated coordinating institutions to promote regional language resources such as the Central Institute of Indian Languages and the Sahitya Akademy (literary academy) to develop Indian languages.

The film sectors in the two language communities reflect this relationship. Andhra Pradesh ranks as the largest film production center in the country. In 1995, it produced 168 films. During the same period, Kerala produced a total of 83 films, which ranked it as the fourth largest film industry. The Hindi film industry in Mumbai provides the only other corresponding figure with the production of 157 films in 1995 (Rajadhyaksha and Willemen, 1999: 33). Comparatively, the Punjabi film industry produced 12 films in 1995, further emphasizing the importance of the historical link between media institutions and the state during the language movements. In Punjab, the presence of three language movements, each associated with a politico-religious movement, produced institutions which did not encourage collaboration between the community's religiously diverse social and political elites. Whereas the language movement in Kerala was able to provide a unifying symbol, the movement in Punjab became secondary due to political competition among the three Punjabi communities.

As part of historical democratization and social reform processes, Punjabi Muslims, Hindus, and Sikhs sought to differentiate themselves through the use of religious symbols. Urdu became a political symbol for the Muslims as they associated themselves with the elite culture of pre-colonial Mughal administration, which utilized Urdu as an official language. Meanwhile, Hindu reform movements seeking cultural symbols chose Hindi in order to differentiate themselves from British and Muslim cultural symbols. Consequently, large sections of Punjabi-speaking Hindus and Muslims turned away from their mother tongue in order to rally behind Hindi and Urdu, leaving few resources for the promotion of Punjabi or its cultural industries, including its media sector. In the post-independence phase, this linkage between the region's political and religious organizations continued. The Punjabi religious communities developed their exclusive media after the partition, reflecting their political language preferences and, thus, dividing up resources and audience in the process.

The history of the Punjabi press reveals the consequences of social and political competition between the three religious communities (see Jeffrey, 1997b). Urdu's previous status meant that many of the Muslim, Hindu, and Sikh elites were educated in the language. Punjabi, on the other hand, was the language of the home for these communities, the marketplace, and Sikh religious activities. As a result, Punjab's press was predominantly Urdu or English, avoiding the major vernacular. Promotion of Punjabi, meanwhile, became the limited domain of some scholars and the Sikh religious community for religious services. After the partitioning of India, in which the western parts of Punjab became a part of Pakistan, the Urdu press continued to operate in India's Punjab because it still enjoyed a large non-Muslim Urdu readership. Punjabi remained the language of the home and the marketplace. The status of Punjabi changed in 1966 after the region was reorganized along language lines. The new state instituted an educational system which promoted Punjabi and encouraged literary societies and programs that were also assisted by a central policy of support for regional languages.

Consequently, the Punjabi press did not emerge until the 1960s. The history of two newspapers in Punjab reveals the consequences of these movements on the region's media. In the newly structured state, *Ajit*, initially established as a Urdu newspaper in the pre-independence Punjab, transformed into a Punjabi paper in 1960. Its founder, Sadhu Singh Hamdard expected an increase in Punjabi readership due to the change in the education system. His motivations were also political, since the state was to be reorganized in 1966 as a Punjabi state providing the Sikhs with a majority in the state. The paper deeply supported the Sikh community politically and socially. After Operation Blue Star in 1984 in which Indira Gandhi sent troops into the Golden Temple to drive out Sikh extremists, *Ajit* spoke out bitterly against the central government's actions. Throughout the 1980s and early part of the 1990s, the paper remained sympathetic toward Sikh separatism (Jeffrey, 1997b). Barjinder Singh, the current editor, became a Member of Parliament in 1999, and adopted a more moderate stance.[12] Currently, *Ajit* has the highest circulation among Punjabi newspapers.

The continued presence of Hindi advocates after the re-division of Punjab is also reflected in Punjab's media development. Despite the restructuring of Punjab that made it primarily a Punjabi-speaking area, the state continues to accommodate the largest circulating Hindi paper in the country. The *Punjab Kesari*, launched by the Hind Samachar group, boasts the third largest circulation among the vernacular newspapers in the country with a circulation of over 700,000 daily. A large readership in Delhi and Haryana account for over half of its circulation figures. In Punjab, this paper is associated with the Hindu business community. In the 1980s, *Punjab Kesari* openly opposed Sikh extremists. Consequently, the paper's editor-owners paid a heavy price. Its founder, Lala Jagat Narain, was killed in 1981 by Sikh extremists. His son, Ramesh Chandra, was similarly assassinated in 1984. Such direct connection between media organizations and the tense politics of Punjab affects investment in the media and divides its audience along sectarian lines.

The Punjabi film industry also suffered as a consequence of the divided objectives of the Punjabi community. After the partition, several prominent actors and directors migrated from a thriving Punjabi film industry to Mumbai to the rapidly developing Hindi film industry. These Punjabi film personalities participated in Hindi and Punjabi films before the partition and, then, primarily in Hindi films following the partition. The result was the transfer of capital and expertise from Punjab. This left a vacuum in the Punjabi cinema, influencing media development for many years thereafter. Not surprisingly, Punjabi media lags behind their southern counterparts despite the high consumer propensity of the region.

In modern-day Punjab, religious and language differences continue to rear their heads, influencing the region's social and political institutions. Initial media enterprises, such as Punjabi TV, struggled to survive due to shortage of investment capital. Punjabi TV's association with the Shiromani Gurudwara Prabhand Committee (SGPC), a sociopolitical organization in charge of managing the Sikh religious bodies, may have excluded the Punjabi Hindu audience. Also, the less-developed Punjabi film industry was unable to play the supportive role played by the Telugu and Kerala film sectors. Soon,

Punjabi TV faced competition from other enterprises, the Lashkara channel, started by a non-Punjabi corporation, Reminiscent TV, based in England. Subsequently, Doordarshan's Punjabi channel also expanded its programming to become a primary player. The launching of two Punjabi channels, Alpha Punjabi (Zee) and TARA Punjabi (Star TV) in 2001 indicates a more differentiated development of competitive structures than in the south.

Hindi television also forms considerable competition for Punjabi channels. Many Punjabis continue to be educated in Hindi as well as Punjabi. Channels such as Zee TV, Sony, and Star Plus operate successfully in the region, whereas in the southern states their presence is negligible. The presence of the BJP, with its primary support base in North India, contributes to the continued association of Hindi with Hinduism in the region. The members of the older generation who were educated in Urdu are also fluent in Hindi, as the two languages are verbally similar. Close proximity to the Pakistani border delivers Pakistani TV (in Urdu) to many Punjabi homes.

TRANSNATIONAL MEDIA: LOCALIZED RESPONSES

Initially, several transnationals hoped to use pan-Asian, English-speaking audiences, as a secondary market for the distribution of programs designed for their home audiences. Their expectations were based on a previous relationship between state-operated television systems and First World media exporters. In India, productions such as *I love Lucy*, and *Yes, Prime Minister* entertained large numbers of television audiences through the state television which focused its own productions on development and political issues.

After 1995, transnational media sought to establish themselves as Indian companies with external links, focusing on communities with a higher potential of consumption and success. For instance, Star TV (News Corporation) sought out Indian audiences using localized material produced by Indian producers and companies.[13] It was unable to do so immediately because of contract stipulations with Zee Telefilms, which required it to stay away from the Hindi market. Along with its English channels, it therefore focused on a news channel that relied on an Indian production company for news and news broadcasts. When the contract ended in 2000, it immediately launched Hindi Star Plus, followed by Tara Punjabi and Tara Bengali in regions were media competition was less developed.

An examination of Star's content follows a pattern established by its local competition. The focus of Zee TV's and Doordarshan's Hindi channels on conservative traditions, themes, and religious programming is also apparent on Star. For instance, it recently aired *Gurukul*, a visual magazine that addresses topics related to Hinduism under the category of "ancient wisdom of India."

In 1998–2000, Star introduced *Jai Mata Di*, focusing on different *avatars* of the goddess Durga, and *Sanskruti* (Tradition) where the characters were derived from the Hindu god, Krishna.

Star TV's focus on Hindu themes may be a response to criticism by Indian media observers who denounced the corporation as a symbol of foreign challengers. During contractual disagreements with Zee, the latter lobbied for state support in fighting the transnational media. The press also aided by representing the dispute as that of a small Indian corporation against a large transnational corporation (Chatterjee, 1997). Following the dissolution of the partnership, Star undertook reorganization aimed at gaining acceptance from the state. New Delhi Television (NDTV), the news production house of Star TV till 2002, was directed to follow Doordarshan guidelines.[14] In this effort, Star also recruited staff previously employed by the state media.[15]

In 1995, MTV also changed its strategy toward localization. Viacom's initial reluctance to customize MTV for local audiences led to its separation from Star in 1994. MTV and Star's contract ended when MTV refused to comply with Star's Indianization strategy. Subsequently, MTV struggled for the next year to find a new route into Asia. In 1996, it re-established itself and, by 1997, reinvented itself as an Indian music television with an additional objective of providing Indians with western music. This reorganization instated a domestic office operated by management from India.

Currently, up to 70 percent of MTV programs are Indian productions. The objective of the MTV strategy after 1999 was to "Indianize, humanize, and humorize" its programming.[16] In 1999, MTV's estimated reach was 10.3 million households.[17] Reprogramming its software to include local hosts and slang, the channel was to re-establish itself as a pop cultural leader for a young urban audience. In the 1998 national elections, MTV India launched the campaign "Rock the Vote" to get young audiences to vote and participate in social and environmental issues, including women's rights and pollution. More recently, Indian outrage at MTV US's portrayal of Mohandas Gandhi as a rock fan wearing an earring caused MTV India to claim it played no part in the production which originated at its American headquarters. This demonstrates that global media organizations might not be as cohesive as the previous generation of transnational media.[18]

Dennis McQuail and his associates present essential guidelines for delineating the structure of media development and the organizational framework of transnational media in the global context (McQuail et al., 1991: 17–19). They provide five indicators that help differentiate between ownership reality and the level of control. First, they state, the level at which the action occurs is important in determining the organization's relationship to its headquarters. Second, the type of actors that participate in the production deeply influences the process. Third, the location of decision-making may affect the nature of the decisions. The fourth and fifth elements follow from this as the decision-making forum and the type of decision taken also impress upon the organizational structure.

In tracking these elements in the Indian context, transnational media management appears to internally decentralize by shifting domestic control over productions to high-level management from the region. Star TV and MTV's management at the Indian headquarters come from a domestic media background and continue to operate with some of the objectives defined in their previous positions. The regional management furnishes these corporations with their expertise and their professional and political networks at domestic levels. Meanwhile, other corporations, such as Sony, form alliances with Indian partners who participate in their daily operations. This ownership actuality exerts influence upon production by guiding the images and messages promoted in the content. Because of such actors, regional branches often differ in organizational and operational manner from their founding headquarters.

THE QUESTION OF DOMINANCE IN THE COMMUNICATION SECTOR

The restructuring of television in India suggests a new direction for research on the consequences of liberalized media space. Without doubt, domination by the transnationals of the developed world remains a critical element of the new communication debate. Imperial theories that appeared in the 1960s and 1970s expressed their concerns regarding the exportation of media into secondary markets that had yet to sufficiently develop their television systems. They warned of the threat of cultural hegemony and new value systems by the flow of Western models into non-Western systems (see Schiller, 1979; Sussman and Lent, 1991). These frameworks placed the world system in the context of a dependency relationship between developed and less-developed nations with the latter relying on the former for economic sustenance (see Evans, 1979). However, the gradual importation of media products into developing countries was mitigated by the state's control over television, limiting the contradictions surrounding the creation of independent systems that relied on the West. The opening up of several developing economies to foreign media enterprises appears to make these propositions increasingly relevant.

Yet, the unexpected emergence of community media indicates some interesting possibilities. The new liberalized environment unexpectedly introduces new sources for expression for the community elite in a multicultural environment at the national and global level. The majority of the local television sites have appeared outside what are commonly understood as the dominant cultural sites on the national scene. The Dravidian language communities in the south, for instance, who were excluded from the national communication space in the past, were able to take advantage of the global resources. Their presence further helps reinforce the multicultural nature of the Indian social and political scene. This may suggest changing fields of dominance at the national level as these communities participate in restructuring the nation's communication channels.

At the sub-regional level, however, the opportunities introduced by the liberalizing efforts present themselves mainly to the regional elite, pointing to sociopolitical continuity at the regional level. The control of communication channels by the sub-regional elite may reinforce existing social positions. For example, the elite caste communities in the south dominate the community television sector, whereas the Hindi channels in the north may reflect the religious concerns of Hindu nationalists. Transnationals such as Star and Sony also appear to respond to the cues offered by the successful Hindi competition. However, Hindu concerns are by no means homogeneous and, in a complex democracy, conservative religious politics has to compete with reformist religious and secular voices of compelling numbers. When the Hindu conservatives' cause dominates in segments of programming, it reduces the space of minorities and the underprivileged groups within the Hindu community as well. Over time, this offers an opportunity for competing media enterprises to gain access to these deprived publics.

The southern channels and their alliance with the regional political elite can be understood along these lines. They respond to the new access to communication channels that were denied them in the past. Therefore, the implications of the globalized setting of the media sector have to be investigated as having differentiated consequences for communities situated at different levels. The question of domination of information channels requires an historical context as different communities, their institutions, political players, enterprises, and audiences appear to impress upon the competitive structures in diverse ways.

ACKNOWLEDGMENT

This chapter is based on research for my dissertation "Global Communication and Television Development: Community Mediation in Multicultural India," University of California, Berkeley, which is an interdisciplinary work that links the different strategies of transnational corporations in a global economy to domestic social and political processes.

NOTES

1. For more recent work, see Norris (2000), who provides an analysis that places the media within the structural framework of democracy. See also Deutsch (1966b); Connor (1970–1); Blumer and Gurevitch (1995).
2. See Government of India, Ministry of Human Affairs, at www.censusindia.net/2001housing/S00-020.html. The former figure is from Government of India, Ministry of Information and Broadcasting, *Doordarshan 1996*, p. 44.
3. *Zee Telefilms Annual Report*, 1999. Zee's popularity extended into Pakistan and Nepal with proximate language communities.
4. *Hinglish* is a mix of Hindi and English often utilized by urban youth.
5. Zee TV's figure is an average derived from three of the Zee channels, Zee TV, Zee Cinema, and Zee Music.
6. Chandrababu Naidu is often referred to as the lap-top minister. He has pushed for liberalizing polices in the center as part of the BJP-led ruling coalition (see www.chandrababunaidufanclub.org).
7. The Press Trust of India is a central state-sponsored news agency.
8. Pakistan's population is estimated at 145 million.
9. Punjab ranked second in the country in per capita net state domestic product at Rs 23,040 for the year 1999–2000. It has maintained the high ranking of the previous two decades. See Government of India, Ministry of Finance, *Economic Survey, 2000–2001*, Appendix, table 1.7, S-11.
10. Audience Research Unit, Ministry of Information and Broadcasting, Government of India, *Doordarshan 2002*.
11. Government of India, Ministry of Human Affairs, *Census 1991*, state profiles (available from www.censusindia.net/data/ke.pdg).
12. Barjinder Singh, Managing Editor, *Ajit*, interview with the author, June 25, 1999.
13. "Murdoch in Asia: Think Globally, Broadcast Locally," *Business Week,* June 6, 1994.
14. Indira Mansingh, News Director, Star TV, New Delhi, interview with the author, July 12, 1999.
15. Rathikanta Basu, the CEO of Star India division was Doordarshan Director General in 1990. Indira Mansingh, who originally worked at Doordarshan from 1985 to 1997, became Star's News Director in 1997.
16. Natasha Malhotra, Marketing Director at MTV office, interview with the author, March 30, 1999.
17. Figures are from National Readership Survey, 1997, Marketing and Research Group (India), Audience Survey, August 1999, and INTAM Study.
18. See "MTV and Gandhi" at www.Indiantelevision.org (February 3, 2003). See also Rajan and O'Brien (2003: 17).

REFERENCES

Blumer, Jay G. and Gurevitch, Michael (1995) *The Crisis of Public Communication.* London: Routledge.

Castells, Manuel (1997) *The Network Society.* Oxford: Blackwell.

Chatterjee, Saibal (1997) "How Zee is Shooting Star," *Outlook* (September 22), 72–4.

Connor, W. (1970–1) "Nation-building or Nation Destroying?," *World Politics* 24: 319–55.

Dasgupta, Jyotirindra (1970) *Language Conflict and National Development.* Berkeley, CA: University of California Press.

Deutsch, Karl (1966a) *Nationalism and Social Communication: An Inquiry into the Foundations of Nationality.* Cambridge, MA: MIT Press.

— — (1966b) *Nation-building*. New York: Atherton Press.

Evans, Peter (1979) *Dependent Development: The Alliance of Multinational, State, and Local Capital in Brazil*. Princeton, NJ: Princeton University Press.

Giddens, Anthony (1990) *The Consequences of Modernity*. Cambridge: Polity Press.

Habermas, Jürgen (1996) *Between Facts and Norms*, trans. William Rehg. Cambridge, MA: MIT Press.

Haggard, Stephan (1995) *Developing Nations and the Politics of Global Integration*. Washington, DC: The Brookings Institution.

Hall, Stuart (1980) "Encoding and Decoding," in Stuart Hall, Dorothy Hobson, Andrew Lowe, and Paul Willis (eds), *Culture, Media, Language*. London: Hutchinson.

— — (1997) "The Local and the Global: Globalization and Ethnicities," in Anthony D. King (ed.), *Culture, Globalization and the World System*. Minneapolis, MN: University of Minnesota Press.

Herman, Edward S. and McChesney, Robert W. (1997) *The Global Media: The New Missionaries of Global Capitalism*. London: Cassell.

Jeffrey, Robin (1976) *The Decline of Nayar Dominance*. New York: Holmes and Meier.

— — (1997a) "Malayalam: Day-to-day Social Life of the People," *Economic and Political Weekly* 32 (1/2) (January 4–11).

— — (1997b) "Punjabi Press: Subliminal Change," *Economic and Political Weekly* 32 (9/10) (March 1–7/8–14).

— — (1997c) "Telugu Press: Ingredients of Success and Failure," *Economic and Political Weekly* 32 (5) (February 1–7).

Kohli, Atul (1989) "Politics of Economic Liberalization in India," *World Development* 17 (3).

McQuail, Dennis, de Mateo, Rosario, and Tapper, Helena (1991) "A Framework for Analysis of Media Change in Europe in the 1990s," in Karen Siune and Wolfgang Treutschler (eds), *Dynamics of Media Politics: Broadcast and Electronic Media in Western Europe*. London: Sage.

Mitra, Ananda (1993) *Television and Popular Culture in India*. New Delhi: Sage.

Morley, David (1980) *The Nationwide Audience, Structure and Decoding*. London: British Film Institute.

Norris, Pippa (2000) *Virtuous Circle: Political Communications in Postindustrial Societies*. Cambridge; Cambridge University Press.

Page, David and Crawley, William (2001) *Satellites over South Asia*. New Delhi: Sage.

Pandian, M. S. S. (1992) *The Image Trap*. New Delhi: Sage.

Rajadhyaksha, Ashish and Willemen, Paul (1999) *Encyclopedia of Indian Cinema*. New Delhi: Oxford University Press.

Rajagopal, Arvind (2001) *Politics after Television: Hindu Nationalism and the Reshaping of the Public in India*. Cambridge: Cambridge University Press.

Rajan, Sujeet and O'Brien, Irene (2003) "Reworking Gandhi," *Indian Express*, North American Edition (February): 17.

Sachs, Jeffrey, Varshney, Ashutosh, and Bajpai, Nirupam (1999) *India in the Era of Economic Reforms*. New Delhi: Oxford University Press.

Schiller, Herbert I. (1979) "Transnational Media and National Development," in Karle Nordernstreng and Herbert I. Schiller (eds), *National Sovereignty and International Communication*, pp. 21–33. Norwood, NJ: Ablex.

Sussman, Gerald and Lent, John (1991) *Transnational Communications: Wiring the Third World*. Newbury Park, CA: Sage.

Thompson, John (1999) "The Media and Modernity," in Hugh Mackay and Tim O'Sullivan (eds), *The Media Reader: Continuity and Transformation*. London, Sage.

19. The hacker ethic as the culture of the information age

Pekka Himanen

THE CULTURE OF THE INDUSTRIAL ECONOMY

In his famous essay, "The Protestant Ethic and the Spirit of Capitalism," Max Weber described how the "Protestant ethic" formed the culture of capitalism. His analysis extended from the beginnings of modern capitalism in the seventeenth century to the industrial economy of his own time in the early twentieth century. Three elements constitute the core of Weber's concept of the culture of capitalism in this period. First, the Protestant ethic and the spirit of capitalism include the notion of work as a duty:

> this peculiar idea, so familiar to us today, but in reality so little a matter of course, of one's duty in a calling, is what is most characteristic of the social ethic of capitalistic culture, and is in a sense the fundamental basis of it. It is an obligation which the individual is supposed to feel and does feel towards the content of his professional activity, no matter in what it consists, in particular no matter whether it appears on the surface as a utilization of his personal powers, or only of his material possessions (as capital). (Weber, 1904–5: 54)

A second element of the Protestant ethic and the spirit of capitalism is temporal discipline. Weber cites Benjamin Franklin's "remember that time is money." Time must also be subjected to a temporally regularized lifestyle. In this culture, "irregular work, which the ordinary laborer is often forced to accept, is often unavoidable, but always an unwelcome state of transition. A man without a calling thus lacks the systematic, methodical character which is . . . demanded by worldly asceticism" (Weber, 1904–5: 161). The third element in Weber's definition of the Protestant ethic and the spirit of capitalism is the earning of money as an end in itself: "the summum bonum of this ethic," Weber writes, is "the earning of more and more money" (Weber, 1904–5: 53). Maximizing money becomes an imperative.

Weber's analysis of the Protestant ethic and the spirit of capitalism has been questioned in many ways (for some of the main ways, see, for example,

Giddens, 1992). Most importantly, it has been pointed out that there is no necessary historical relationship between the Protestant religion and modern capitalism. The modern spirit of capitalism also emerged in non-Protestant environments like Venice. However, for the purposes of this chapter, the exact historical relationship between Weber's two distinct concepts of the "Protestant ethic" and the "spirit of capitalism" is not central because Weber emphasized the above three elements in both. In fact, in the common use of language, the "Protestant ethic" is used as a synonym for the "spirit of capitalism." The expression "Protestant ethic" has become somewhat similar to the expression "Platonic love": when we say that people have a Platonic relationship we do not mean that they are Platonists (holding Plato's views on metaphysics, epistemology, and so on) and even less that Platonism is the reason for their love! The same goes for the "Protestantism" in the Protestant ethic.

In this chapter, the expression "Protestant ethic" will be used in a way that does not include any historical claims about the relationship between Protestantism and capitalism. There are additional advantages in this approach. It makes sense also to talk about the "Protestant ethic" in the economy of non-Christian cultures. For example, the above three elements have been very strongly present in Japan's rise as a powerful industrial economy. In this context, the expression "Protestant ethic" means the culture of industrial capitalism, which had the three key elements listed above in otherwise different cultural and political environments.

In the same sense, this chapter intends to formulate the key characteristics of the culture of the new informational economy. Again, the analysis will express elements that are shared in otherwise different cultural and political settings wherever there is an informational economy. I called this culture the "hacker ethic" in my book *The Hacker Ethic and the Spirit of the Information Age* (Himanen, 2001). The reasons for the choice of this expression are presented below.

To be sure, the current form of the informational economy is still capitalist. Manuel Castells has presented the theory of the informational economy in his trilogy *The Information Age: Economy, Society and Culture* (Castells, 2000a,b, 2004). In this context, *informational* refers to a trend in which operations become (1) based on the use of information technology, (2) organized (globally) like computer networks, and (3) focused on information (symbol) processing. The resultant *informational capitalism* is one in which the *dominant* operations are – with the help of information technology – organized (globally) as networks and based on information (symbol) processing. (I use these concepts here along the lines of Castells and Himanen, 2002.)

It should not be necessary to add that this development is very different from the hype of the "dot-com economy" or the "new economy." But, as there is so much hype surrounding it, it is useful to emphasize that the emergence of

the informational economy is not about the Internet but about the basic structures of companies and labor markets, and production – developments that
have been happening for a couple of decades now. For the present analysis,
there are three especially important features in the development of the informational economy.

First, enterprises are developing into informational enterprises (for empirical background to the "network enterprise" in both the West as well as Asia,
see Imai, 1990; Castells 1996, 2000a, 2001). That is, companies are organizing themselves as *networks* that increasingly create products based on information (symbol) processing. All of this is done with the help of information
technology. Internally, the companies are decentralized into relatively
autonomous units that network together for projects. Externally, the companies coordinate a changing network of suppliers. They also network with their
competitors on an ad hoc basis for certain large projects. In general, projects
that consist of a varying network of actors become an important organizing
unit for companies. The growing importance of information (symbol) processing products means that research and development, as well as other forms of
symbol creation (such as marketing), become increasingly important functions
in companies.

Second, labor markets are becoming informational. This means that
network enterprises organize their labor as ever-changing networks of workers in which the role of information (symbol) processing work grows. Basic IT
skills are required in almost all jobs. The emergence of "flexible work
markets" has been documented both in the West and in Asia (Castells, 1996,
2000a, 2002; Carnoy, 2000). In a sense, work becomes more and more *project-
based*, whether it is information creation work defined by deadlines or routine
work available for temporary periods. This is reflected in the rise of "non-
traditional" jobs: more and more workers belong to the categories of the self-
employed, temporary, and part-time workers.

Third, growth is based on innovation. This is a critical difference between
the concept of the informational economy and ideas about the "dot-com economy" or the "new economy." The informational economy is about *growth
based on innovation*. It is not just about the Internet. And it is not just about
growth in market value but, more importantly, about productivity growth
based on innovation. This growth derives from innovation in technology,
process (the network form of organization), and products, as Castells and
others have shown (Castells, 1996, 2000a, 2002; for empirical data, see
Brynjolfsson and Hitt, 2000). The role of organizational change should be
emphasized here because empirical studies show that the mere introduction of
information technology does not increase productivity if it is not combined
with re-organization (ibid.).

The central role of innovation as the foundation of economic growth is also what distinguishes the informational economy from the industrial economy. Innovation was, of course, also one of the sources of growth in the industrial economy, but the primary means of growth was increasing the energy input into the process. A bigger output was the result of a bigger input in energy (time). In the informational economy, companies increasingly compete on the basis of innovation, and more and more workers have moved from routine executing work, such as classic assembly-line work, to jobs that involve innovating (Castells, 2002).

THE CULTURE OF THE INFORMATIONAL ECONOMY

Together, the above three developments (the change in company structure, the change in labor market structure, and the change in the role of innovation for growth) constitute an economy that is very different from the industrial economy. The culture of this economy can be approached in an illuminating way through the work ethic of the builders of the technological foundation of the informational economy. This group originally called themselves "hackers," meaning by this, not computer criminals but, in the words of the hacker *Jargon file* compiled on the Net, people who "program enthusiastically" and who believe that "information-sharing is a powerful positive good" (Raymond, 2000b). This formed the "hacker ethic" (see also Levy, 1994).

This creative impulse, combined with the idea of sharing information, was behind the creation of the Internet and the World Wide Web and the software used to run it, such as the Linux/Unix operating system (Abbate, 1999; Berners-Lee, 1999; Himanen, 2001). Eric Raymond, who has been one of the most visible participants in this hacker culture, has formulated its work ethic well. In the following extract, Raymond speaks of the "Unix philosophy" because of context, but his description applies to the larger hacker culture. For "Unix philosophy," read "hacker ethic":

> To do the Unix philosophy right, you have to be loyal to excellence. You have to believe that software is a craft worth all the intelligence and passion you can muster . . . Software design and implementation should be a joyous art, and a kind of a high-level play. If this attitude seems preposterous or vaguely embarrassing to you, stop and think; ask yourself what you've forgotten. Why do you design software instead of doing something else to make money or pass the time? You must have thought software was worthy of your passions once . . . To do the Unix philosophy right, you need to have (or recover) that attitude. You need to *care*. You need to *play*. You need to be willing to *explore*. (Raymond, 2000a)

The same kind of philosophy is repeated in the descriptions of the founders of key IT companies, and their work culture. For example, Andy Bechtolsheim, one of the founders of Sun Microsystems, describes the passion that drove the company: "We were twenty-something-year-olds running a company and we had just met, but we certainly shared the passion" (Southwick, 1999; see also Alahuhta and Himanen, forthcoming).

It is a creative passion that is referred to here. In their work, hackers realize their creativity and constantly develop themselves. Hackers play with new ideas and are enthusiastic about this work. And this creativity takes place together with other hackers, either virtually or physically: hacker creativity is based upon an open and shared development of ideas. It is about belonging to a group whose members have the same creative passion, give recognition to each other's contributions, and develop ideas further together.

A significant additional feature of the hacker ethic is that the archetypal hacker works to the rhythm of his or her creativity. This is the image of the hacker sometimes programming into the small hours of the night and then waking up in the afternoon, or mixing work and leisure in their daily lives in other ways. They take advantage of the possibilities of IT to manage their time more freely.

Together, these features make up the two core elements of the hacker relationship to work: (1) a networked creative passion; and (2) a flexible relationship to time. What is important here is that, although information technology hackers were the first to become self-conscious about this new work ethic, they realized that the work ethic is not limited to information technology professionals. In fact, from the beginning, the hacker *Jargon file* said that a hacker can be "an expert or enthusiast of any kind."

It was in this general sense that I proposed in my book, *The Hacker Ethic and the Spirit of the Information Age*, the expression the "hacker ethic" to describe the work culture of the informational economy, as a counterpart to Weber's "Protestant ethic" in the industrial economy. I still prefer this expression because it was the first "real-life" expression for the new general work ethic. Nowadays, however, the "hacker ethic" has problematic connotations that are not meant here. First of all, to many people it immediately brings computer criminals to mind. Second, for other people it conjures up only the most idealist version of the work ethic, such as the ideology of the most extreme forms of the open-source software movement (everything is "fun" and everything must be open).

To avoid these misunderstandings, expressions such as the "culture of innovation," the "innovation work ethic," or the "creative work ethic" can be used as alternatives for the "hacker ethic" (I would recommend using the "culture of innovation" in most contexts). Outside academic circles and those of the information technology hackers themselves, these alternative expressions better convey the idea of a more general new work ethic, which is not limited to information technology jobs. They also link the new work culture explicitly to its structural basis in the informational economy: the role of innovation as the source of growth.

This structural connection also clarifies the sense in which the concept of the hacker ethic or the culture of innovation is presented here. One of the first questions invoked about the meaning of the concept is: "But is there anything new about this? Have there not always been innovators like this, such as scientists or artists?" The first answer is, of course, that the hacker ethic is not completely new: people with the "hacker ethic" existed before the informational economy. But a second response must be that it still makes sense to limit the primary meaning of the expression to our age. It is the new, structurally dominant role that innovation has in our economy that makes it valid to talk about the "hacker ethic" or the "culture of innovation" as the culture of the informational economy. There were, of course, innovators before the informational age but they formed a small group that was not at the center of the economy. In the informational economy, the innovators are the dominant, and fast-growing, group at the core of the economy.

Again, it is necessary to clarify the claim. A relevant question here would clearly be: "But how can one have the hacker ethic in such and such a job? The concept seems to be limited only to some workers." Of course, this is true. There are many jobs – for example, routine jobs – where there is no hacker ethic; I do not mean that everyone now has the hacker ethic. However, it is not a marginal group that has the new work ethic, it is the dominant (and large) group. Even Weber did not mean that in the industrial economy everyone had the Protestant ethic; this was clearly not true. What mattered was that it was the dominant culture. (Richard Florida has also approached the subject with the interesting concept of the "creative class," which is very much the same as the group I call "hackers." The hacker ethic / culture of innovation / creative work ethic is the core that constitutes this "class"; see Florida, 2002.)

The role and nature of innovative work in the informational culture gives the concept of the hacker ethic or the culture of innovation a specific meaning. First, the *growth based on innovation* requires creative passion. In the industrial economy, many jobs consisted of executing routines that were not only uninteresting in themselves but gave little room for the use of individual creative capabilities. In this kind of setting, the Protestant ethic made a lot of sense: work should be regarded as a duty where one just needs to do one's allotted task.

However, in an increasing number of jobs in the informational economy, the Protestant ethic does not make sense but even works counterproductively. When the success of companies depends on innovation a different work culture is needed: the culture of innovation. Workers who feel that their work is just an unavoidable obligation, in which they just do what they are told, do not act creatively. This is why the world's leading companies now emphasize a work culture in which new ideas and creative achievements are encouraged and rewarded (see Alahuhta and Himanen, forthcoming, on how this is changing management culture).

This is related to another feature that differs from the industrial economy. In the informational economy, there is very little work that can be done alone. In particular, most innovative work is based on working together with other innovators, in networks of innovation. This is why it must be called *networked* creative passion. This is the case both on the level of the company and the individual. Within companies, people work as teams, which is a form of operation that requires an open flow of information. This flow is supported by IT systems that make the information available to all participants, as well as by the culture of open communication within the company.

But a new openness of information is also very important on another level. The openness that is meant here does not exclude proprietary information, of which there is plenty in the informational economy. But the enormous efforts needed for innovation are not possible even for the biggest companies on their own because, in global competition, the required resources are so huge. This is why big companies network even with their competitors to develop the most basic-level innovations, such as the Net standards or the standards for mobile phones. The history of technology has shown that a closed approach has difficulties in competition with open networks: for example, Apple's closed architecture, which was originally technically superior, lost out to IBM's open PC architecture; Sony's closed Betamax video standard lost out to the open VHS standard; and in the history of the Net and mobile telecommunication, the open Internet/Web and GMS architectures got the better of their closed alternatives. So, in the global informational economy, maintaining one's leading position in the most fundamental areas of innovation requires networking. It is critical for companies to get others to join in their revolution; otherwise, even great innovations become outdated secrets buried within the company. Of course, this network of innovation is only possible with a sufficiently open flow of information.

It is the *network* structure of our global economy that advances networked creative passion as the culture of the informational economy. This is also related to one of the reasons why the closed, communist societies lost in competition with the open, capitalist societies: when innovation became central to economic growth an open flow of innovations became crucial. Scientists in the Soviet Union were as well educated as those in the United States, but new innovations remained closed in secret military laboratories, whereas in the West military innovations were allowed to flow into civil innovations (some examples being the computer and computer networking).

THE FLEXIBLE RELATIONSHIP TO TIME

The second element of Weber's concept of the Protestant ethic is its relationship to time. Weber describes the ideas of systematic work time and of optimizing time. In the informational economy, time is still money. Time is optimized to an even greater extent than in the industrial age. This is clear in the global financial markets where the speed of change is unprecedented. Companies have to be more and more agile in reacting to developments in their environment. And, for individuals, there is even a sense of continuous emergency in their work where everything has to happen faster and faster. The present optimization of time continues the trend that started in the industrial economy.

But there is also a new feature of the informational age that can be seen in its culture. Information technology makes it possible to transcend time and place. It makes both global real-time operation and operation in "un-real" time possible. The latter refers to the fact that IT systems facilitate a way of doing things, in which contributions to a process do not have to be made in synchronous time. This means a new, more flexible relationship to time, which breaks the mold of everyone working in the same sequential time. This results in the possibility of organizing one's own time and of living one's life in a new way.

The informational economy's structural equivalent to this flexible relationship to time is *project-based* work. This is why few people any longer have the industrial economy's paradigmatic life-long career in the same job, a development that has both its bright side and downside: while it means that many workers are able to enjoy new challenges, if there is no social protection to match the new flexible labor market, it also generates uncertainty for many workers.

More positively for most involved, the fact that work is increasingly organized around projects means that people are given more power to self-manage time. As work is increasingly defined by results, workers get more freedom to customize the ways in which they can achieve these results. Workers can use IT to give them more freedom in relation to time and place and to combine their work and leisure lives more flexibly.

This development is again linked to innovation: not everyone's creative rhythm (not to mention other aspects of life) runs from 9 a.m. to 5 p.m. every day, so it makes sense for companies to allow individual patterns of creativity. In addition, the work produced is not primarily a function of the time taken (as it was in the industrial economy, for example, on the assembly line), but the product of work is primarily a function of innovation.

All of this does not mean any idealistic relationship to time. It certainly does not mean anything like the hype of "telecommuting," which has not become a significant part of real working life. (This is another example of hype in which the focus is on the technical surface of the Internet, while the much more important structural changes of the economy are missed.) There are many creative jobs that require a lot of physical presence at particular times. Furthermore, there are a lot of routine jobs where the workers have practically no control over time. Again, the development has both a positive and a negative side: for many workers it provides a real opportunity to pattern work and other aspects of life in a way that better suits one's own situation, but at the same time there is the risk that flexibility remains only an elitist possibility or that flexibility is misused at the cost of leisure time so that the balance between work and family life becomes unsustainable.

However, these reservations do not change the fact that there is now a new structural flexibility. And Weber's description of the Protestant ethic's relationship to time clearly does not fit the observed dominant trend in the development of the informational economy. The relationship to time has to be redefined because work is now primarily defined by projects and results rather than fixed hours in a certain location, and because the line between work and leisure has been made more flexible by the new information technology.

THE MONEY ETHIC

As for the third element in Weber's analysis of industrial capitalism, its relationship to money, here informational capitalism continues its spirit in an important way. As in the industrial economy, money is still a goal in itself. The informational age is at least as money-centered as the industrial age. The growing role of the financial markets – where money is made from money – is a good symbol of this.

But, at the same time, this symbol of the informational economy also reveals that there has been an important shift in the relationship to money in the new economy that is different from industrial capitalism and yet continues to be *capitalist*. In the Protestant ethic, both work and maximizing money are described as goals in themselves. However, these goals can come into conflict. If one really puts work first as the highest value, one is ready to work even if it does not maximize one's income (it is a duty). And if one really puts money as the highest value, work becomes only one means to that goal. Making money without working would be the ideal. But the idea of living idly on an income from stocks investments is the very opposite of the Protestant ethic's ideal. So, at bottom, the Protestant ethic resolves the conflict between work and money as goals in themselves by placing work as the higher goal.

This is where there is a difference between informational and industrial capitalism. On a societal level, money has become the higher goal. In fact, the idea of making money directly from money in the stock markets is idolized.

The meaning of this for the general economy is that the value of a company's or an individual's work becomes more and more based not on the value of that work (measured in itself) but on the movements of money made out of money in the financial markets. To be sure, pay and profits definitely remain fundamental measures for workers and companies, but market value and market value-related rewards (stocks, options) are acquiring a new significance that further shifts the balance between work and money toward money as the weightier value. In addition, individuals are increasingly moving their money from traditional savings in the bank to investments in the financial markets. The informational economy is permeated with the idea of betting on the movements of money – while the very idea of betting was abhorred by the Protestant ethic. The informational economy is far removed from the asceticism of the Protestant ethic. In its more moderate form, this means a culture where people want to enjoy their money; in its extreme form, it is a consumer culture where people expect immediate self-gratification.

This is the answer – for better or worse – of the informational economy to the old tension in the Protestant ethic between work and money as supreme values. However, a new, unsolved tension has been created by combining money as the highest value with increasingly tight intellectual property laws. There is now a tension between the current extremely money-oriented informational capitalism and the basic tendency of the culture of innovation. Money-centeredness leads to the closing off of information. Innovation lives on the open flow of information. If information is owned too tightly, the global innovation process suffers. This has both an economic and an ethical dimension: it keeps a large part of the world's population structurally outside the informational economy, thus limiting both the markets and the sources of innovation, as well as exacting a great human price through exclusion.

It also limits the culture of innovation within the informational economy. Tight intellectual property laws make it very hard for new innovators to enter the market. Money-centeredness also blinds us from seeing how there might be room to develop a stronger culture of innovation or the hacker ethic outside the private sector. In fact, it stops us from seeing that, in the information age, the sustainability of the public sector will also depend on the release of a work culture of innovation based on networked creative passion and a more flexible relationship to time – something that is possible only through a conscious change in the culture of public management. It is only through such an innovation-based improvement in productivity that the public sector will be able to continue to provide a sustainable basis for the global information age, and not be eliminated as outdated. (This can be called the idea of the "e-welfare state" or "the welfare state in the information age" or "the creative welfare state," the "e" referring not to the Internet but to the informational structure and culture as described above.)

Without renewing the basis for trust in the public systems, the informational economy risks falling into a cycle of fear which blocks innovation: people who fear do not innovate or want to try new things as consumers. When our thinking is freed from an over-emphasis of money, we can both support and benefit from the opportunities afforded in the public sector of mobilizing in the hacker manner (see Feldman et al., 2004).

The information age, as all new societal systems, provides both benefits and challenges. A sufficiently open culture of innovation carries a great deal of economic and human promise: a culture of people fulfilling themselves with creative joy both in their work and leisure lives, but this requires that we do not build our societies in a way that is too centered on money.

REFERENCES

Abbate, Janet (1999) *Inventing the Internet*. Cambridge, MA: MIT Press.
Alahuhta, Matti and Himanen, Pekka (forthcoming) *Managing the Creative Work Culture*.
Berners-Lee, Tim (1999) *Weaving the Web: The Original Design and the Ultimate Destiny of the World Wide Web by its Inventor*. New York: HarperCollins.
Brynjolfsson, Erik and Hitt, Lorin M. (2000) "Computing Productivity: Firm-level Evidence," Cambridge, MA: MIT–Sloan School Center for E-business, working paper.
Carnoy, Martin (2000) *Sustaining the New Economy: Work, Family, and Community in the Information Age*. Cambridge, MA: Harvard University Press.
Castells, Manuel (1996) *The Information Age: Economy, Society and Culture*, vol. 1: *The Rise of the Network Society*. Oxford: Blackwell.
— — (1997) *The Information Age: Economy, Society and Culture*, vol. 2: *The Power of Identity*. Oxford: Blackwell.
— — (1998) *The Information Age: Economy, Society and Culture*, vol. 3: *End of Millennium*. Oxford: Blackwell.
— — (2000a) *The Information Age: Economy, Society and Culture*, vol. 1: *The Rise of the Network Society*, 2nd edn. Oxford: Blackwell.
— — (2000b) *The Information Age: Economy, Society and Culture*, vol. 3: *End of Millennium*, 2nd ed. Oxford: Blackwell.
— — (2001) *The Internet Galaxy: Reflections on the Internet, Business, and Society*. Oxford: Oxford University Press.
— — (2004) *The Information Age: Economy, Society and Culture*, vol. 2: *The Power of Identity*, 2nd edn. Oxford: Blackwell.
— — and Himanen, Pekka (2002) *The Information Society and the Welfare State: The Finnish Model*. Oxford: Oxford University Press.
Feldman, Jerome, Himanen, Pekka, and Weber, Steven (2004) "The Social Web," Berkeley, CA: Berkeley Center for Information Society.
Florida, Richard (2002) *The Rise of the Creative Class*. New York: Basic Books.
Giddens, Anthony (1992) "Introduction," in Max Weber, *The Protestant Ethic and the Spirit of Capitalism*, trans. Talcott Parsons (1930). London: Routledge, 1992.
Held, David, McGrew, Anthony, Goldblatt, David, and Perraton, Jonathan (1999)

Global Transformations: Politics, Economics and Culture. Stanford, CA: Stanford University Press.

Himanen, Pekka (2001) *The Hacker Ethic and the Spirit of the Information Age*. New York: Random House.

Imai, Ken'ichi (1990) *Joho netto waku shakai no tenbo* [The Information Network Society]. Tokyo: Chikuma Shobo.

Levy, Steven (1994) *Hackers: Heroes of the Computer Revolution*. New York: Delta.

Raymond, Eric (2000a) "The Art of Unix Programming," draft manuscript.

— — (ed.) (2000b) "The Jargon File" (www.tuxedo.org/~esr/jargon).

Southwick, Karen (1999) *High Noon: The Inside Story of Scott McNealy and the Rise of Sun Microsystems*. New York: John Wiley and Sons.

Weber, Max (1904–5) *The Protestant Ethic and the Spirit of Capitalism*, trans. Talcott Parsons (1930). London: Routledge, 1992.

Afterword: an historian's view on the network society

Rosalind Williams

THE TRADING ZONE OF SOCIAL SCIENCE AND HISTORY

After this *tour du monde*, this *mappa mundi*, this astounding overview of today's world – its economics, politics, communications, cultures, institutions, social movements – how can there possibly be anything more to say? What can an historian add to this rich, fertile, expansive survey?

Historians think in time. As the title of this volume suggests, the contributors are primarily thinking across space: a cross-cultural perspective of the world as it now exists, not presuming to cover the entire globe, but ranging far and wide enough to give a sense of the whole. When I was asked to join this party, at first I assumed my presence would add a vertical dimension, adding the depth of time to the view of the network society, saying a few words about where it comes from and proposing how it resembles or does not resemble earlier societies. It did not take me long, however, to realize that I would not add much to the party if I begin with concepts and issues as they are laid out here (beginning with the concepts of "network" and "society") and simply project them backwards. Instead, I need to suggest how historians construct things differently in the first place.

Social scientists and historians engage with the same reality – our common world – but in different ways. The differences arise in part from professional training and institutions, but they go much deeper. One of the fascinating complexities of the human mind is the persistent coexistence of two very different modes of structuring human experience: through logic and through narrative. Whether or not this coexistence will endure as long as humanity does, it apparently goes back to the dawn of what we like to call civilization. Most of the earliest examples of writing encode logical analysis, usually in the form of what we would now call "business records": lists of goods, reckonings, tallies, counting (Robinson, 1995). The earliest examples of poetry encode stories about where people come from, what their identity is, what their collective experience means.

432

Both modes of organizing experience provide structures for thinking about the significant realities of human life. The quest for understanding now institutionalized as the history profession certainly depends upon logical analysis and theories of causality and agency, but it still seeks to understand origins, purposes, and meanings. Social science, on the other hand, gives priority to logical analysis in its quest for understanding; while a story line is often implied, or embedded, it is not the main purpose of the enterprise. Both "mind sets," despite their vast differences, are apparently necessary for human beings to understand their experience. As scholars, one of our most exciting challenges is to see how they can overlap and interact in intriguing ways.

This is not always easy to do. As an historian of technology, I have looked at many books on the recent "information technology revolution" and today's "information society," which breathlessly explain the present and predict the future, while lacking any sense of the past. But it can be done. I was happily surprised to open Manuel Castells's *The Rise of the Network Society* (1996) some years ago and to discover, as early as page 5, citations of some of the leading lights in the history of technology (Merritt Roe Smith, Leo Marx, Melvin Kranzberg), along with those of historically inclined social scientists (Wiebe Bijker, Joel Mokyr), all supporting a sophisticated discussion of the major issues relating to "Technology, Society, and Historical Change": technological determinism, the social construction of technology, sources of innovation, technological revolutions, technological paradigms, and much more. This dialogue between history and sociology continues throughout the three volumes of Castells's *The Information Age: Economy, Society, and Culture* (1996–8). Its purpose is to understand contemporary society, but always in the context of the much longer story of the efforts of human beings to shape their physical and social environment.

As demonstrated in *The Information Age*, social scientists and historians can develop a robust "trading zone" where they invent ways of communicating to accomplish a common project, even though they come at it from different professional cultures. This metaphor self-reflexively illustrates the point: I am borrowing it from historian of science Peter Galison, who in turn has borrowed from linguistics (specifically from studies of pidgins and Creoles) to explain how physicists and engineers have developed techno-scientific trading zones (Galison, 1997: 46, 48). I could just as well have cited Castells, who proposes "protocols of communication between different cultures" as "the cornerstone of the network society" (p. 39).

In this comment, I want to engage in some "protocol development" and "trading-zone building" between social scientists and historians around the project of understanding our common world. Since this volume defines the essential character of contemporary society as one of "networks," as an historian I begin by asking about the relation between networks and history: what does it mean to identify a stage of history with a stage of technology? I will begin by commenting on the ways in which historians try to connect the past with the present, and vice versa, and then will reflect on the introduction of the concept of "technology" to accomplish such connections. This leads to a discussion of the way the concept of "technology" entered the study of history, beginning in the seventeenth century, leading to a new understanding (in the eighteenth century) of history as the record of progress. The chapter will conclude with a consideration of the ways in which technological activities have altered the conditions of human existence and therefore of history.

CONNECTING PAST AND PRESENT

The major contribution so far of historians of technology to the current discussion of "network society" may be summarized in two words: context matters. In Castells's somewhat longer formulation: "Studies on the uses of information and communication technologies demonstrate, again, what historians of technology established long since: that technology can only yield its promise in the framework of cultural, organizational, and institutional transformations" (pp. 41–2).

In order to demonstrate how context matters, historians of technology have concentrated on case studies that show the "social construction of technology," both in design and in use, in a particular context of material, political, and economic constraints and actors (individual, institutional, and networked). Many of these studies are models of fine-grained archival research presented in a nuanced and sophisticated analysis. For all their virtues, however, contextual studies may promote an untenable distinction between a technological core and a social environment, when a deeper understanding of "context matters" demonstrates that social relationships are embedded in technological relationships and vice versa. Case studies of social construction tend to focus attention on contemporary (to the study) players and issues rather than on ones deeper in the past. Such types of case study beg the question of how the actors and forces that are the agents of "social construction" have themselves been shaped by technological forces and events, as is inevitably the case in a reflexive world.

Historians of technology need to make the transition from "context matters" to "history matters." We need to deploy case studies to develop higher-order generalizations about history and technology, and to explain to ourselves and to our readers the relevance of history to the present. Most historians want their work to have some degree of generalizability and relevance, but historians of technology seem to want this more than most. The drive to generalize is strong because the question of the relationship between technological and historical change is one of the deep problems of historical theory:

any historian wants to contribute to clarifying such a central problem. The drive to be relevant is especially strong in a self-proclaimed "technological age." When the past, present, and future of technology is the subject of so much popular and semi-popular speculation, the "so what" question keeps poking historians of technology in the ribs, so to speak. We feel that we should have something special to say to our own times, and complain when we are not listened to.[1]

In wanting to demonstrate generalizability and relevance, however, we confront an inner conflict. On the one hand, we feel a sense of civic responsibility to remind our readers that history matters, that the present world is rooted in past worlds, and that past experience offers some useful analogies and lessons for the present. Since the eruption of whole new species of technologies – computers, networks, the web, biotechnology – is well within the historical lifespan of most readers, for historians it is an almost automatic professional reflex to write that there is a longer story here, that these things did not appear just yesterday, that purposes of the past have shaped the present. On the other hand, we feel a sense of scholarly responsibility to remind our readers that "the past is a foreign country," that the world today is very different from that of the past, and that analogies and lessons are always highly limited. The past is present and it is also past.

These conflicting responses and responsibilities are what make history such an interesting profession. History itself is a trading zone between past and present. History establishes communication between storytellers and actors, between what happened and what is remembered, between the dead and the living. The subject matter of history is by definition weighted toward those who have come before us, their deeds and actions and agendas. By writing history, the living try to push off some of the dead weight of the past, giving themselves a little breathing room, protesting that they are not doomed to carry on with the past because it was so very different. If tyranny breeds resistance (Castells's first law), the tyranny of the dead is no exception (Harrison, 2003).

On the other hand, if resistance to the past is too extreme, it leads to the fallacy of "presentism," in which the reality of the past (not to mention that of death) is denied. Presentism can take several forms. In today's most commonplace version, the past is simply ignored: the present is taken as it appears, as a self-contained reality, as if there were no past realities that have shaped it. Another version connects past with present, but in the manner of what in the historical trade is called "Whig history": constructing the record of the past as a track to the present, a narrative of events leading to the triumph of whatever is deemed most commendable today. So, for example, among the Whig politicians of nineteenth-century England, history was a record of the gradual emergence of democratic, liberal politics, as defined by the then-current principles of the Whig party. In current versions, technology stands in for the Whig party. The "information society" is the apogee of the continuum from nomadic to agricultural to industrial societies, so that human history is then the record of "the long march of progress under the guidance of reason" (p. 42). Similarly, the "network society" is hailed as the climax of inevitable technological progress toward more ubiquitous, more rapid, more portable, more miniaturized, more power-ful communication.

Another version of presentism, already alluded to, involves taking the cate-gories and concerns of the present, shaking (or stirring) them with history, and adding the dimension of time to inquire into their origins. This is an obvious temptation in dealing with the concept of "network society." As Castells has cautioned, this concept, as he uses it, cannot be freely floated through the waves of history to far and distant shores. It relates to a specific technological paradigm, based on microelectronics; a specific type of technological system, that of linked computers; a specific form of globalization, acting in real time; and other very specific types of information, employment, and other social behaviors. So it is quite possible and helpful to look back, as Castells does, on the emergence of contemporary network society in the unanticipated conflu-ence of three originally independent processes: "the crisis of industrialism, the rise of freedom-oriented social movements, and the revolution in information and communication technologies" (p. 22). But once one moves further back in time, very quickly the gap between the concept of a network society and the specifics of networks in that historical situation grows ever wider.

One can readily see this gap, for example, in the standard work on electri-cal networks in the early twentieth century – Thomas P. Hughes's classic *Networks of Power* (1983) – where both the specific content of the network system and the context in which it operated are markedly different from that of contemporary computer systems. If one looks back even further – at the Roman Empire, for example – to ask how it might be analyzed as a "network society," the mismatch becomes even more striking. If the network is composed of roads and aqueducts, and the labor force is based on slavery, and the social goals are focused on the maintenance and extension of imperial power, this is an entirely different "network society" from the one based on the development of computer networks in a job-holding, market-oriented econ-omy. Concepts, too, have a history, and when one from the present is anachro-nistically imposed on the particularities of the past, the effort to generalize can quickly become absurd.

That is why historians of technology have to be particularly careful. We have been outspoken in rejecting the types of presentism that would deny the very reality of the past or read the historical record as the grand narrative of technological progress. However, in our very self-definition, we are indulging in presentism of the last sort, by applying the concept of "technology" to the past, especially the distant past. In this respect, the history of technology is one grand exercise in anachronism.

TECHNOLOGY AND PRESENTISM

"Technology" can be a thing, a concept, and a word. These are easily confused. As a word, technology was almost unknown until a century ago. As a thing, "technology" has always been a central and necessary human activity: the reworking of the given world in order to provide the material basis for human life. The concept that these activities are central and necessary in human life goes back at least to the Greek term *techne*, and in English has long been expressed in terms such as "the material arts" or, more lately, "the industrial arts." But collecting them under the singular, abstract word "technology" is a very recent development. First introduced into English in the early seventeenth century, "technology" was rarely used until it was appropriated by Jacob Bigelow in 1828 to describe the study of industrial activities. The term first achieved some public prominence when it was used to name the Massachusetts Institute of Technology in 1861 (Bigelow was one of its founders), but even at the end of the century its use was uncommon.

Only in the 1920s and 1930s did "technology" became a commonplace term, in large measure because social scientists found it so useful to describe current trends (for example, William Ogburn's "technological gap," or, even more widely, "technological unemployment"). Only after World War II did it become identified as a semi-autonomous, dominant agent of historical and social change, the force with the most "impact" on our lives, the one that defines our historical period: "our technological age." "Technology" emerged as an historical concept when new technological "things" made it necessary to rethink how history worked – above all, the construction of large technological systems, not always visible in their entirety, but understood as the abstract ensemble of coordinated tools, machines, symbolic representations, material infrastructure, social systems, and human beings (Marx, 1997).

The emergence of the history of technology is therefore an inherently presentist application of a category of current importance back into history where technological activities abounded, but where the concept of technology as an historical agent was absent. As such, the history of technology demonstrates the positive role of presentism. Applied retrospectively, the concept of technological history has revealed elements of the past that were undetected, or underdetected, due to limits either in historical imagination or in the historical record. So, for example, the habit of thinking in terms of technological systems encourages historians to relate a whole set of historical artifacts – tools, settlements, and structures of all sorts – to the systems of transportation and communication that may be less visible in the record but that were necessary to connect and support the artifacts. Because a technological system is always also a social one, the systems perspective leads the historian to infer labor relations, legal codes, education and training, weights and measures,

governance structures, and the like, all of which can be analyzed in their relationships to lead to a much richer view of history writ large, especially the
social, political, and economic record of the past.

The concepts of "technology" and especially of "technological systems"
have therefore helped historians notice and retrieve large parts of the historical record that would otherwise have been neglected. In this respect they have
participated in one of what Castells calls the "freedom-oriented social movements" (p. 22) of the postwar years: the movement of historians to liberate
retrospectively whole categories of actors and activities so long ignored.
Women, children, laborers, sexual outcasts, and many others were not deemed
worthy of historical significance in their own times, but have been accorded
this dignity by ours.

In the case of the history of technology, however, this retrospective liberation is particularly radical. By giving "technology" a place of honor in historical studies, we are not just bringing new actors onto the historical stage, but
redefining the stage itself. What we now call "technology" has not just been
neglected as part of history, but has been deliberately omitted as unworthy of
historical remembrance. And what is most intractably presentist about the
whole enterprise of the history of technology is not the temptation to compose
a Whiggish narrative of technological progress, not the temptation to impose
current concepts (such as the "network society") back into times where they
do not fit, but the assumption that "technology" has any place in history at all.

For the Greeks and Romans, history was the record of great deeds and great
words; for the Christians of the Middle Ages, it was the record of God's revelation in the world; for both, the practical arts were the background against
which these significant dramas, whether human or divine, were played. For
historians until the seventeenth century, technological activities – technology
as a "thing" – were self-evidently necessary to provide biological support for
life and to construct a world for human dwelling. Historical activities were a
different thing altogether: they were rare words and deeds that stood apart
from the everyday, that rose above the level of repetitious life-sustainment and
material world-building (Arendt, 1998: 42). The idea that technology has a
role in history, much less that it has a leading role – or even becomes the
measure of history – was unthinkable. "Prehistory" could be defined by technology – early stone age, late stone age, bronze age, iron age – but history
begins where epochs cease to be defined primarily by tools.

Have we come full circle, returning to technology as the way to categorize
phases of human activity, so that prehistory and post-history reconnect now
after a long interlude of history defined as great deeds and words? How has
"technology" come to dominate the historical consciousness? How did technological innovation and organization come to dominate the reading of the
past and predictions of the future?

TECHNOLOGY ENTERS HISTORY

The assertion that technology deserves a leading role in the historical record was first articulated long before the cluster of events normally called the Industrial Revolution of the late eighteenth century. The historiographical revolution that brought technology into the writing of history began in the seventeenth century, with two declarations of independence from the past. The first declaration was that of René Descartes, who, in *Discourse on Method*, "takes his stand against tradition the moment he decides to doubt its authority and to rely upon his own personal resources in the quest for truth" (Harrison, 1992: 111). Descartes detaches himself from the past in order to become "methodically self-reliant in matters of action and knowledge" and also in order to achieve "the mastery and possession of nature" (Harrison, 1992: 108).

The second declaration of independence came from the moderns in the so-called "battle of the books" between the moderns and the ancients, which demonstrates how supposedly literary quarrels – or, as we might say now, "culture wars" – can raise fundamental conflicts with meaningful implications for more than just intellectual elites. The seventeenth-century "moderns" might concede equality or even superiority to the ancients in philosophy and the arts, but they felt they clinched their arguments for the superiority of modernity in pointing out that only their age possessed the compass, the printing press, and gunpowder. Furthermore, the moderns claimed, they could be confident that such technological achievements would continue because the modern age possessed the experimental method: not a body of knowledge, such as the ancients had bequeathed, but a method for acquiring and improving knowledge that no longer depended on individual genius (Jones, 1936).

Descartes and the moderns converged, then, in claiming a break in history through the discovery of a method that would enable them to defy the tyranny of the past and open the way to the development of a new mastery over nature through reason. They redefined history as the record of increasing superiority in areas where the moderns had an advantage. In a move that would be repeated over and over again, Europeans shifted the ground of the debate to "machines as the measure of men" to proclaim to others and to assure themselves of their own superiority (Adas, 1990). The value system emerges in response to a perceived advantage and becomes the basis of further development of that advantage.

The historian-philosophers of the eighteenth century went even further. Because enlightened Europeans claimed superior methods of advancing knowledge and attaining power over the natural world, they proposed that history itself would begin to work differently. The first important statement of this claim was the *Discours sur les progrès successifs de l'esprit humain* (A Philosophical Review of the Successive Advances of the Human Mind), a speech delivered by Anne Robert Jacques Turgot at the Sorbonne in 1750, when he was only 23. In it, Turgot advanced three novel assertions about history. First, he redefined its scope: history is global, he claimed, the story of "the human race," which to the "eye of a philosopher" appears as "one vast whole." Second, Turgot redefined its content: history is not the record of political or diplomatic events (which he dismissed as motivated by "self-interest, ambition, and vainglory"), but the gradual and enduring enlightenment of the human mind. Third, Turgot redefined the direction of history. The past was composed of cycles, countless rounds of routine and repetition, as each successful civilization succumbed to internal vices and external invasion, and as individual genius was swamped by waves of mediocrity or buried in obscurity. Hereafter, thanks to the power of reason as expressed in scientific inquiry and technological achievements, history would move forward in a linear track.

In his *Discours* Turgot reviews crucial turning points in history, ones that have decisively changed circumstances so that not only can humanity innovate, but it can also accumulate its innovations. These turning points are technological ones: Turgot rewrites history as a sequence of great inventions, all of them vastly increasing humanity's ability to communicate. The first is language: the sounds which "have made of all the individual stores of knowledge a common treasure-house" (Meek, 1973: 41); the next is writing, which lifts humanity from the surface of the earth, seeming "to give wings to those people who first possessed it" (Meek, 1973: 44); the climactic invention is that of printing, the art which makes it possible to "wing to every corner of the earth the writings and glory of the great men who are to come" (Meek, 1973: 57). This slow process of enlightenment, Turgot says, proceeds to the extent that, through these inventions, human beings are in contact with other social groups, and especially as "separate nations are brought closer together" (Meek, 1973: 40–1). Henceforth discoveries will accumulate, in a universal library, available to all: progress in time depends upon the extension of knowledge in space.

If Turgot's 1750 speech marks the opening of the high age of Enlightenment, the death in 1794 of Marie Jean Antoine Nicolas Caritat, marquis de Condorcet (b. 1743) marks its end. After the deaths of his mentors and heroes Voltaire, d'Alembert, and Turgot, the younger Condorcet saw himself as carrying on their political and intellectual legacy. Its implications for historical theory he expressed in the most influential summary of the Enlightenment ideal of historical progress, the *Esquisse d'un tableau historique des progrès de l'esprit humain* (Sketch for an Historical Picture of the Progress of the Human Mind), written in 1793–4, at the height of the Terror, when he was in hiding from the Jacobins, just before his capture and apparent suicide.

Like Turgot, Condorcet defines history as the global extension of knowl-

edge among humanity as a whole. Also like Turgot, he is a technological determinist. The titles of the ten chapters of the *Esquisse* correspond to major steps
in technological progress, beginning with the invention of the alphabet, and
culminating in the invention of printing, when for the first time the human
mind was truly freed from spatial limits: "Men found themselves possessed of
the means of communicating with people all over the world . . . The public
opinion that was formed in this way . . . operated with equal strength on all
men at the same time, no matter what distances separated them" (Condorcet,
1955 [1795]: 100). Condorcet reaffirms Turgot's conviction that progress will
now continue indefinitely because, for the first time in history, technical innovations prevent regression and decline (see Williams, 1993):

> The strength and the limits of man's intelligence may remain unaltered; and yet the
> instruments that he uses will increase and improve, the language that fixes and
> determines his ideas will acquire greater breadth and precision and . . . the methods
> that lead genius to the discovery of truth increase at once the force and the speed of
> its operations. (Condorcet, 1955 [1795]: 185)

According to these historian-philosophers of the Enlightenment, the historical
record traces the evolution of an intellectual world system, based on rational
thought, and expressed through the logical, nonmetaphorical articulation of
universally valid information. The global system has a hierarchical though
dynamic arrangement of cores and peripheries, linked together by lines of
transportation and communication: this spatial organization of history makes
historical progress possible. There is a tendency for the global system to keep
expanding in scope and for the rate of circulation to become more rapid. The
inventions that make this system possible – speech, the alphabet, writing,
printing – also make a new mode of history possible. Technology not only
enters history, but redefines what history is. Instead of great words and deeds
that achieve immortality for individuals but fail to interrupt the cycles of
history, history becomes the accumulation of great discoveries and inventions
that permit a linear development of ever-increasing knowledge and mastery of
nature.

HISTORY ENTERS TECHNOLOGY

Anyone reading these predictions in the twenty-first century does so with a
mixture of déjà vu, wistfulness, and irony. Déjà vu, because this historical
vision sounds so familiar: the belief that history has reached a point of major
discontinuity due to unprecedented technological capabilities, especially capabilities that make it possible, for the first time, for information to be quickly
and easily communicated around the globe. Wistfulness, because the Internet

incarnates as technological reality the means of which Turgot and Condorcet dreamed to advance human civilization. Irony, because the technological means now at our command are so disconnected from the civilizing ends that they believed in.

To be sure, elements of the Internet approximate their vision of a universal library of text, images, and sounds, globally and instantly available, and endlessly empowering through providing new forms for creativity and social participation. But the Internet is also the site of spam, snooping, child porn, and property rights, and far from being globally available it highlights vast disparities of opportunity generally summarized as the "digital divide." The way in which the web has evolved in the past generation is a dramatic illustration of the "social construction of technology" in a society of economic and political disparities. Context matters.

And so does history: what is striking here is the way in which belief in technological progress has parted company with belief in historical progress. In current raptures about the Internet, we still hear the echoes of the Enlightenment and its conviction that a new phase of history is nigh, thanks to the universal circulation of information accumulated through reason-based inquiry. The echoes are faint, however. Belief that technological progress will inevitably lead to general historical progress has faded as events have repeatedly demonstrated otherwise. A quick capsule history of the twentieth century – the Great War, the collapse of the world financial structure, the rise of fascism, the Second World War, the Holocaust, the use and proliferation of atomic weapons, the economic and public health collapse of Africa – is enough to undermine belief in inevitable historical progress.

But events do not necessarily subdue beliefs: the narrative of progress is too important to the identity of the West to collapse entirely in the face of these events. When the concept of technology was brought into the study of history beginning in the 1600s, and confirmed as a revolutionary agent in history in the 1700s, history became redefined as the record of human progress. The idea of progress, based on scientific and technological evidence, was extrapolated to history in general. Since the Enlightenment, the idea of progress has retreated from history in general, where evidence is lacking, back to the more restricted realms of science and technology, where it can be marshaled. The Great War may have mocked any notion of historical progress, but all the time Henry Ford's assembly lines were turning out cheap cars. Earthly cities may be appalling, but men have walked on the moon.

At the beginning of the twenty-first century, historical change and technological change have diverged. Old-fashioned political, military, and diplomatic history continues, as difficult and as painful as ever. Technological progress also continues, making money for some, improving medical care for others, churning out consumer products for many. The belief persists that if we can somehow avert environmental or military catastrophe, technology may make life better for most people. Technology has not transformed history as we have known it, but has set up a parallel track of development that seems "progressive" on its own terms, without apparently altering the course of history. This is not a logical conclusion, but it does allow people to maintain a conviction in scientific and technological progress, while accounting for the evidence that history seems to go on without discernible improvement.

Given this state of confusion, it is worth returning to the question that engaged the *philosophes* of the Enlightenment: how has human-generated technology changed the conditions of human life and therefore, possibly, the way history operates? Without necessarily signing up to their optimistic answer, we can accept the importance of this question. Will technological change alter history as we have known it – not necessarily by creating a new kind of history (linear progress rather than cyclical stagnation) but by changing how history as we have known it works? If historians of technology address this question, we may achieve a level of generalizability and relevance above that of discrete contextual case studies. We may also do the case studies better, by showing how the society that largely forms the "context" and does the "constructing" is itself evolving as a result of technological change. The best way to proceed is to focus on the large but answerable question of how technological activities have altered the conditions of human existence.

In her extraordinary book on the subject, *The Human Condition* (first published 1958, 2nd edition 1998), Hannah Arendt proposes that there are three elements of "the human condition": labor, work, and action. She uses these categories to survey human experience from antiquity to the present. The categories remain constant, but in each case she shows how technological change has profoundly altered the human experiences of labor, work, and action – in short, has altered "the human condition" and therefore the conditions of historical change. What follows is a much too brief summary of and gloss upon her rich contemplation of the ways in which the human condition has been transformed through human-generated technological conditions. As she says, " 'What we are doing' is indeed the central theme of this book" (Arendt, 1998: 5).

First and foremost, new sources of energy and new modes of production have vastly multiplied the productivity of human labor. This unprecedented increase, primarily in the past two centuries, is a new fact in human history – something new under the sun, as it were. In the nineteenth century, despite all the tragedies and miseries that accompanied industrialization, the possibility of universal abundance and opportunity was central to historical, political, and utopian thought of all varieties.[2] In the twentieth century, despite continued tragedies and miseries and ever-growing anxiety about environmental limits, the possibility of globalizing abundance and opportunity, made possible by exponentially greater labor productivity, is still an article of faith for many elites (who do not hesitate to exploit the deep hope it inspires) and, more important, for people around the world (who cling to this hope).

Second, technology has rebuilt the world – the relatively durable, objective, shared world of things, produced by work, which houses individual lives and which "is meant to outlast and transcend them all" (Arendt, 1998: 7). In Arendt's analysis, work is not the same as labor. While labor arises from the body, in never-ending life cycles of production and consumption, the world is constructed by humans through fabrication from what nature gives us (Arendt, 1998: 136). The world is therefore always to some degree "artificial," but what has changed in the past two centuries is the dominance of the human-built world in relation to the natural or given one. The world is now a hybrid environment – part nature, part technology, with no one able any longer to tell where one ends and the other begins.[3]

The challenge of managing this environment is even more complicated than that of controlling nature. Its scale, scope, complexity, and pace of change are all unprecedented, as well as the consequences of mismanagement. The transformation of the world from one that is primarily given to one that is primarily human-constructed is, like the increase in labor productivity, a dramatic and concretely measurable transformation of the human condition. Many of the measures are provided in the study of twentieth-century environmental history by J. R. McNeil (2000), the title of which succinctly summarizes the evidence: "something new under the sun."

Third, more difficult to measure, but arguably most important of all, is the transformation of action because of technological change, or in this case more properly because of techno-scientific change. Like the productivity of labor and the dominance of the human-made world, the fueling of human actions by natural forces is "something new under the sun." Arendt begins her analysis by reminding her reader that processes of change are now being inserted into the world, formerly the site of durability and stability:

> we no longer use material as nature yields it to us, killing natural processes or inter-rupting and imitating them . . . Today we have begun to "create," as it were, that is, to unchain natural processes of our own which would never have happened without us, and instead of carefully surrounding the human artifice with defenses against nature's elementary forces, keeping them as far as possible outside the man-made world, we have channeled these forces, along with their elementary power, into the world itself. (Arendt, 1998: 148–9)

Writing in the late 1950s, Arendt used automated manufacturing, scientific research in general, and atomic energy in particular as examples of humanity channeling natural forces into the world. We would now add two even more powerful examples: irreversible environmental processes (especially those associated with global warming) and all the techniques of biotechnology that remove the quotation marks from her reference above to the human ability to "create." The elementary forces of creation and reproduction now being harnessed through biotechnology only underscore her argument that human action is redefining the boundaries of what we think of as history. "Only because we are capable of acting, of starting processes of our own, can we conceive of both nature and history as systems of processes" (Arendt, 1998: 232). As techno-scientific action becomes part of history, the line between history and nature becomes blurred: acting into nature becomes part of acting in history.

As already noted, Arendt admired the Greek understanding of history as the record of heroic action in great words and great deeds. With this new variety of action, however – "acting into nature" by starting processes – outcomes are uncertain, responsibility is diffused, and possibilities for starting anew are diminished. In this new type of historical action, "uncertainty rather than frailty becomes the decisive character of human affairs" (Arendt, 1998: 232).

Humanity may have hoped that technology and science would enable it to "tak[e] charge of the conditions for its own existence," in Castells's words (p. 8). If anything, however, the opposite seems to be happening. The uncertainty of science and technology is being leveraged into new forms of action. For example, what are usually called acts of terrorism may be defined as the exploitation of unpredictability for political ends. Historical action has always been tied to deeds of violence, but those deeds have typically been reserved for special groups of people acting in special circumstances. Now, the conditions for large-scale violence are available to many more people, in many more situations. This democratization of violence, as it were, is also "something new under the sun," and it is one of the most troubling novelties of our age. (Perhaps because it is so troubling, it is the aspect of network society that is relatively absent from the pages of this book.) Networks alter conditions of labor, work, and action – all three. In all of them, networking starts processes that alter the context of further technological change, and, by starting processes, networks therefore "act" as well as "build" and "labor."

CONCLUSION: MAKING HISTORY AS WELL AS TECHNOLOGY

Technological change has not made history jump onto a new track. However, by massively altering the human condition, technological change has intensified the processes of historical change. History has always been a web of circumstances into which we are born, a web of relationships that involve a multiplicity of selves and conditions. The historical condition is one of multiplicity, complexity, and unpredictability. Because human beings have created a technological world of tremendous inertia, its multiplicity and complexity seem more daunting than ever. The ability of any one person to affect the larger situation seems more constrained than ever. Because of "what we are doing," it is tempting to let technology become the narrative, the story line, the process that drives human affairs. When hope for progress is invested in technology, then humanity looks not to great deeds and actions but to great inventions as the basic story line. Technology becomes the substitute for history itself.

But the possibility of effective historical action diminishes as people assume that the story is about technology, not them. Historical consciousness is a source of habits such as responsibility, trust, and forgiveness, which are essential for effective historical action. In a collective life dominated by large technological systems, each of these habits becomes less useful and less practiced. When the systems are so large and complex, personal responsibility is increasingly less evident. When they are so unpredictable, trust among people becomes at once more important and more difficult to maintain. And when the technologies are so unforgiving, the human possibility of starting anew by forgiving mistakes seems increasingly remote and strange.

Jean-Paul Sartre reflected on the need for historical consciousness when he recalled his experiences in the French Resistance during World War II. There the events that mattered involved courage and physical endurance, which in retrospect seemed to him a myth, a false experience:

> After the war came the true experience, that of society. But I think it was necessary for me to pass via the myth of heroism first. That is to say, the prewar personage who was more or less Stendhal's egotistical individualist had to be plunged into circumstances against his will, yet where he still had the power to say yes or no, in order to encounter the inextricable entanglements of the postwar years as a man totally conditioned by his social existence and yet sufficiently capable of decision to reassume all this conditioning and to become responsible for it.

> For the idea which I have never ceased to develop is that in the end one is always responsible for what is made of one. Even if one can do nothing else besides assume this responsibility. For I believe that a man can always make something out of what is made of him. This is the limit I would today accord to freedom: the small movement which makes of a totally conditioned social being someone who does not render back completely what his conditioning has given him. (Sartre, 1970: 22)

The necessity of a "myth of heroism," even if it is not "real," returns us to the apparently irreplaceable need of humanity to structure our experience through narrative as well as through logic. Because historical narrative is always grounded in experiences of time and place, I wish to conclude these comments by speaking from my own historical experience as a citizen of the United

States at the beginning of the third millennium. From here, I observe a deep fear of history: the wish for the historical story to stop, here and now, at the pinnacle of American power. The American empire appears designed not so much to increase its power in the world as to maintain a world where it is safe from the change, safe from the future, safe from history. At the same time, I observe a deep desire for the technology to continue, with indefinite expansion of devices and systems that promise enjoyment, security, health, and wealth. These irreconcilable wishes – wanting history to stop, wanting technology to continue – can be summarized as an extreme form of presentism: fear of the past, fear of the future, longing for the present to continue indefinitely, as the eternal moment that alone seems to favor us. They can also be the most extreme form of regression: a desire to return to prehistory, defined by technological stages, so that technological change rather than historical change defines civilization.

But technology and history cannot be separated, and we are destined to create history as well as technology. History cannot be transcended or avoided. It has no pause, mute, or reset button. On the other hand, while it never entirely disappears or begins anew, history is always starting again in more modest ways. People die, babies are born, children grow up, things change. Acting historically means making decisions in ever-changing, highly constrained situations, clearing a pathway through the thicket of circumstances. Thinking historically means reflecting on the thicket and making a narrative out of the pathway. By acting and thinking, we make history.

NOTES

1. For example, the 1996 Presidential Address of the Society for the History of Technology by Alex Roland (1997).
2. "The various historical systems of the nineteenth century with their 'laws' – whether progressive, evolutionist, dialectical, positivist, or not – were all, in spite of their endless deficiencies, efforts to cope with this new history" (Shklar, 1966: 107).
3. In the words of historian of technology Elting Morison (1966: 16): "We are well on the way, in our timeless effort to bring the natural environment under control, to replacing it by an artificial environment of our own contriving. This special environment has a structure, a set of tempos, and a series of dynamic reactions that are not always nicely scaled to human responses. The interesting question seems to be whether man, having succeeded after all these years in bringing so much of the natural environment under his control, can now manage the imposing systems he has created for the specific purpose of enabling him to manage his natural environment."

REFERENCES

Adas, Michael (1990) *Machines as the Measure of Men: Science, Technology, and Ideologies of Western Dominance*. Ithaca, NY: Cornell University Press.

Arendt, Hannah (1998) *The Human Condition*, 2nd edn. Chicago: University of Chicago Press.

Castells, Manuel (1996) *The Information Age: Economy, Society and Culture*, vol. 1: *The Rise of the Network Society*. Oxford: Blackwell.

— — (1997) *The Information Age: Economy, Society and Culture*, vol. 2: *The Power of Identity*. Oxford: Blackwell.

— — (1998) *The Information Age: Economy, Society and Culture*, vol. 3: *End of Millennium*. Oxford: Blackwell.

de Condorcet, Antoine-Nicolas (1955 [1795]) *Sketch for a Historical Picture of the Progress of the Human Mind*, trans. June Barraclough. New York: Noonday Press.

Galison, Peter (1997) *Image and Logic: A Material Culture of Microphysics*. Chicago: University of Chicago Press.

Harrison, Robert Pogue (1992) *Forests: The Shadow of Civilization*. Chicago: University of Chicago Press.

— — (2003) *The Dominion of the Dead*. Chicago: University of Chicago Press.

Hughes, Thomas P. (1983) *Networks of Power: Electrification in Western Society, 1880–1930*. Baltimore, MD: The Johns Hopkins University Press.

Jones, Richard Foster (1936) *Ancients and Moderns: A Study of the Background of The Battle of the Books*. St Louis: Washington University Studies, New Series in Language and Literature, no. 6.

McNeil, John Robert (2000) *Something New under the Sun: An Environmental History of the Twentieth-century World*. New York: W. W. Norton.

Marx, Leo (1997) "Technology: The Emergence of a Hazardous Concept," *Social Research* 64 (3): 967–8, 974–5, 977.

Meek, Ronald L. (ed.) (1973) *Turgot on Progress, Sociology, and Economics*. Cambridge: Cambridge University Press.

Morison, Elting (1966) "Introductory Observations," in *Men, Machines, and Modern Times*. Cambridge, MA: MIT Press.

Robinson, Andrew (1995) *The Story of Writing: Alphabets, Hieroglyphs and Pictograms*. London: Thames and Hudson.

Roland, Alex (1997) "What Hath Kranzberg Wrought? Or, Does the History of Technology Matter?," *Technology and Culture* 38 (3): 697–713.

Sartre, Jean-Paul (1970) "An Interview with Sartre," *The New York Review of Books*, March 26.

Shklar, Judith (1966) "The Political Theory of Utopia: From Melancholy to Nostalgia," in Frank E. Manuel (ed.), *Utopias and Utopian Thoughts*. Boston: Houghton Mifflin.

Williams, Rosalind (1993) "Cultural Origins and Environmental Implications of Large Technological Systems," *Science in Context* 6 (2): 377–403.

Index

Note: page numbers in italics refer to figures or tables

Adams, Barbara 36
adult education 187, 324
Advanced Micro Devices 55
age factors
    Catalonia 236
    digital divide 235
    education 236
    Internet 256, 258, 261, 264, 266–7n3
    mobile phones 238
    see also youth factors
Ajit newspaper 412–13
Allen, J. E. 276
American Medical Association 296, 310
anarchism 353–4
Anderson, Benedict 387
Anderson, J. G. 305
Andhra Pradesh 407–8, 409, 410
Ang, I. 396
anti-globalization movement 23, 35, 341,
    342–3, 348
Appadurai, Arjun 396
Apple 55, 61, 426
arbitrage 156
Arendt, Hannah 438, 443–5
ARPAnet 7, 57
art collectives 359n14
Asianet 407, 409
Aspden, P. 303
Association of Reflexologists 308
asthma 304
Austin FreeNet 326, 331
automobile manufacturing 250
autonomy
    Catalonia 242, 391
    individual 18, 19, 21
    Internet 233–4, 244–6, 247
    labor 26
    voters 368–70

back pain information 303

Bakardjieva, M. 128
Baker, W. E. 165
Bakunin, Mikhail 353
Bamford, W. M. 297
banking 138–9
Barber, Benjamin 363
Barbero, Martin 388
Barcelona Infospace 355
Barry, Andrew 358n3
Barthes, Roland 117, 386
Basque Country 391, 392
Bates, A. W. 274–5, 280–81, 282, 285
Bay Area Video Coalition 326, 328
Bechtolsheim, Andy 57, 59, 423–4
Belgrade Chinese embassy 113, 116
Bell Laboratories 21, 56
Benner, Chris 192
Bereiter, C. 281
Berkeley 56, 57, 60, 64
Berlusconi, Silvio 33–4
Berners-Lee, Tim 10, 11
Bharatiya Janata Party 404–5
Bigelow, Jacob 437
Bimber, Bruce 364, 369, 377
biotechnology 7, 56, 445
Black Bloc 346
Blackboard 273, 276, 280–81, 285
blat (exchange of favors) 85
blogging 373–4
Brazil 388
Breugger, Urs 211n5, n12
Britain 126, 129, 136–7, 278
British Columbia University 281,
    282–3
British Medical Association 310
Brown, Ron 324
Bryce, Elisabeth 281
Brynjolfsson, E. 156
Burt, R. S. 165
Bush, George W. 325, 372

California, University of: *see* Berkeley
California Industrial Relations Board
    190
Campbell, H. 128
Canada 288, 305
Canadian Virtual University 278
Canal 33 393–4
cancer information 297, 303, 305
capitalism 22, 428–9
    capital accumulation 24
    global 25, 31
    Keynesian economics 15–16, 20
    power 32
    Protestant ethic 420–21, 428
    self-programmable 29
    time 37
Capra, Fritjof 4, 13
Carnoy, Martin 27
Castells, Manuel
    Catalonian study 241, 246
    China 99
    exclusion 251, 264
    The Information Age 39, 421, 433
    information codes 386–7
    innovation 56
    Internet 255
    legitimacy 106, 363, 376–7
    network society 14, 84, 165, 302, 436
    networks 385
    The Power of Identity 345
    The Rise of the Network Society 433
    social movements 341, 438
    statism 17
    technology 445
Catalan Television (TVC) 391–5, 397–8
Catalonia
    age 236
    autonomy 242, 391
    collective identity 398
    cultural identity 241–2
    Dallas 395–7
    digital divide 234–6
    global justice movements 349–50
    language 242, 392–3, 395–7
    media 243–4
    mental health states 238
    migrant labor 235, 237
    MRG 359n9
    nationality 235, 242, 243
    network society 233–4

Open University 278, 394
    religion 242
    sociability 236–8, 239, 241
Celio, A. A. 303
censorship on Internet 109–14
Central Institute of Indian Languages
    411
Cerf, Vint 14
Chambers, John 271
Chandra, Ramesh 413
Chandra, Subhash 406
Chapman, Gary 329
Chen, Winston 59
Chicago Board of Trade 198–201, 203,
    204–7, 208
Chicago School 17, 30
Chicago Street-Level Youth Media
    326–7
Children's Partnership 329
China, People's Republic of
    consumerism 115–16
    FDI 108
    gender gap 103, 119n15
    high-technology industry 99–100
    informationalism 99–102
    Internet 101–6, 117–18
    Internet cafés 105–6, 112–14, 119n19
    Internet censorship 109–14
    Linux 108, 115
    media 115, 396
    Ministry of Public Security 110–11,
        120n31
    modernization projects 101, 106, 107
    People's Liberation Army 110
    space of flows 107–8, 118
        State Council Informatization
        Steering Group 106, 110
    State Secrecy Bureau 110, 111
    student demonstrations 116
    and West 109
    WTO 103, 108
China Internet Network Information
    Center: *see* CNNIC
ChinaNet 100
Chinese Academy of Social Sciences
    105
Chinese Communist Party 18, 99,
    109–14
Chinese embassy bombing 113, 116
Chinese expatriates 108–9

Cisco Networking Academy 332
Cisco Systems 55, 61, 76, 271
Citizens Network to Abolish the External
    Debt (RCADE) 354–5
citizenship 370, 388
Civille, Richard 331
Clinton administration 324–5
CNN 403
CNNIC 100, 103, 104–5
COBOL 324
Coleman, S. 367–8
Collis, B. 272
communication
    asynchronous 226
    culture 32–3, 39–40, 402
    globalization 389
    network society 29–30, 385–6
    transport 5, 437
    see also computer-mediated
        communication
community
    computer-mediated communication
        228–9
    connectivity 398
    institutions/media 410–11, 416–17
    Internet 211n16
    locality 37–8
    online 220, 225–6, 267n6, 302–4
    social cohesion 247–8
    urban environment 217–18
    virtual 217, 219–20, 302–4
community technology centers 320, 324
    access 327–8
    IT 325–6, 328–30
    Michigan University 333
    outcomes 330–34
Community Technology Centers
    Network 320, 324, 332
community technology movement
    319–20, 323–5, 332–4
computational models 150, 152
computer networks 55, 347–9
computer-mediated communication
    community 228–9
    everyday life 220–25
    and face-to-face 131
    Netville 226–9
    social relationships 224–5
Computers in our Future Project 330–31
Concept of Building the Information
    Society in Russia 94

Concept of State Information Policy 94
Condorcet, M. J. A. 440–41
connectivity 147, 351, 398
consultant brokerage firms 185
consumerism 115–16, 117, 179–80
consumers 29, 149, 300–301
Contentbank.org 332
continuing professional education 282
contract employment 181, 190
Contractor, Noshir S. 3, 4
contractor brokers 184–6
Cooper, G. 134
creative accounting 65
creativity 424, 425–6, 427–8
Cronon, William 199–200
cultural logic 342, 358n2
culture
    Americanization 386, 389–90, 396
    communication 32–3, 39–40, 402
    dominance 416–17
    globalization 385
    imperialism 389–91
    industrialism 38
    of innovation 40, 74–7, 424–5
    network society 32–3, 38–40
Culver, J. 303
Cunningham, S. 276
Curran, Michael 179
Current Population Study, Detroit 253

Dallas 395–7
Dani, Mario 349
data management 128, 154–5
David, Paul 10
Dean, Howard 371–5
decision-making 31–2, 153, 155–6
democracy 42, 355–6, 363
    see also e-democracy
Deng Xiaoping 106–7, 114
Denmark 78
dependency model 386, 389–90
Dertouzos, Michael 57
Descartes, René 439
deskilling 179
Detroit
    background 250–51
    Current Population Study 253
    digital divide 251–2, 256, 259–61
    e-mail 265–6
    race 250–51

Detroit Area Study 249, 253
Deutsch, K. 387
developmental state model 106
diabetes information 303
Diaoyu Island protest 116
digital divide 138, 321, *322, 323*
  age 235
  Catalonia 234–6
  community technology movement
    320
  Detroit 251–2, 256, 259–61
  gender gap 235
  income 234–5
  information society 335
  Internet 24, 442
  IT 319
  race 249
DigitalDivideNetwork 332
DiMaggio, Paul 253, 259
Direct Action Network (DAN) 343
Dirr, P. 276
disadvantaged people 311–12, 319
Disney films 396–7
distance universities 278
DNA 12, 20, 50, 56
DNA-chips 10
Doordarshan 404, 406, 409–10, 414–15
dot-com economy 42, 65, 134, 290, 421
drkoop.com 296, 298

eating disorders information 303
Economic and Social Research Council
    126, 129, 135
The Economist 108, 370
e-democracy 42, 127, 363, 364, 368
education
  age 236
  computers 42
  digital divide 234–5
  Finland 49, 70
  Internet 253, 255, 256, 271–2
  sociability 264
  women 27
  World Wide Web 276
Education Development Center 324
Eenadu media 408, 409
e-learning 271–2, 273–6, *279,* 283–4
  corporate training 278–82
  course development models 285–7
  learner support 287–8, 289–90

OECD 274–5
  organizational issues 284–7
  teachers 273, 290
electronic technologies 131–2, 137–8
  banking 138–9
  Chicago Board of Trade 204–7, 208
  globalization 132–3, 204–5
  profitability 210
  research 125–6
  traders 207–9
  Virtual Society? program 129–30
Elisa 66, 67, 77
elites 86, 94, 95, 235
e-mail 11, 129–30, 239
  Detroit 265–6
  family 223–4
  networks 164
  physicians/patients 308–10
  recruiters 157, 165–6
  social relations 132, 331
Emerson, Ralph Waldo 118
employment 176
  flexibility 175, 177, 180–83
  Internet 255–6, 259, 261
  non-standard 180–81
  Russia 87
  Silicon Valley 178, 180–81, *182*
  sociability 264
  training 187–8
  see also labor; work
encryption, Internet 71, 76
endogenous growth theory 151
energy sources 8, 443–4
English language 90, 272–3
entrepreneurialism 61–3, 69, 77–80, 81,
    109
environmental movement 19, 34
Epperson, Roxanne 331
Erbring, Lutz 221–2
Eurex 204, 205
European Social Consulta 353, 355
European Social Forum 345
European Union 352, 358n5
exclusion 4, 23, 24, 251, 264, 429
executive search industry 148, 151, 160,
    163
Eysenbach, G. 300

Faggin, Federico 55, 59
Fairchild Semiconductors 54–5, 63

Falun Gong 111, 113
family relations 27, 223–4
Farley, Reynolds 250, 264
feminism 18–19
financial markets
    global 24, 28, 31, 37, 198–9, 208–9
    money 428–9
    reverses 65
    social networks 211n4
    see also trading pit
Finland
    education 49, 70
    entrepreneurialism 69, 77–80
    global networks 80–81
    hacker culture 71–2, 76–7
    ICT 66–7
    immigration 80
    inclusion 52–3
    information society *68*
    informationalism 50
    innovation 67–70, 72–3, 74–7
    IT 66–7
    mobile telecommunications 67, 69,
        74–5
    national identity 82
    Science and Technology Policy
        Council 67, 69, 70
    start-up activity 79–80
    state support 49, 67, 69, 72–3, 79–80
    UN Technology Achievement Index
        49, 51
    universities 70, 74, 77, 81
    venture capital 72
    welfare state 49, 67, 69–70, 79–80,
        81, 82
    World Economic Forum 49, 51
Fischer, Claude 210n2, 219
flexibility
    employment 175, 177, 180–83
    ICT 9, 11
    labor 63, 175, 176–83
    networks 5–6
    risk 192
    work 27, 177, 178–80
Florida, Richard 425
Foot, K. A. 368
Forbes, Steve 367
Ford, Henry 27–8, 442
Foresight exercises 129–30, 139
Forrester Research 309

FORTA 392
France 387, 390, 396
Franklin, Benjamin 420
Freeman, Christopher 8
Friedman, Milton 17
FTAA (Free Trade Area of the Americas)
    344
fundamentalism 34
futures 199–201

G8 Genoa summit 344
Galicia 391, 392
Galison, Peter 433
Gandhi, Indira 413
Gandhi, Mohandas 415
Gandhi, Rajiv 404
Garcia Canclini, N. 386
Garfinkel, Harold 127–8
GATT 389–90
GDP *64*
Gellner, E. 387
Gemini TV 408, 409
gender gap
    China 103, 119n15
    digital divide 235
    Internet 89, 103, 253, 258
    online health information 311–12
genetic engineering 7, 12–13
Gerlach, Luther P. 349
German fixed-term bonds 206
Gibson, R. K. 370
Giddens, Anthony 36, 352, 402
global justice movements 342–5
    Catalonia 349–50
    computer networks 346–9
    diversity 356
    global 345–6
    Internet 347
globalization 16, 18
    communication 389
    culture 385
    electronic technologies 132–3, 204–5
    ICT 386
    information flows 163
    Internet 226
    localization 391
    network society 39–40
glocalization 347
Gorbachev, Mikhail 17
Gordon, Richard 59

Gore, Al 99
Gould, Stephen J. 8
Graham, Stephen 36
grain futures 199–200
Granovetter, Mark 165, 228
Graphic Artists' Guild 187
grassrooting 38, 102, 364
gratification, instant 40, 114, 429
Greeks, ancient 438, 445
Greenspan, Alan 201
Grove, Andy 55, 59
Guangdong Province 107
guanxi 100
Gulia, M. 134
Gurukul magazine 414–15

Habermas, Jürgen 30, 403
hacker culture 71–2, 76–7, 82, 115,
     351
hacker ethic 40, 342, 421, 423, 424–5
Hall, S. 398
Hamdard, Sadhu Singh 412–13
Hampton, Keith 211n16
Harasim, L. 272, 283
Hargadon, A. 165
Harlem Community Computing Center
     324
Hartman, J. 285
Harvey, David 25, 36
Hayek, F. 150
health conspiracy theories 300
health information, online 293–6, 298
     access 311–12
     centralization 296–8, 310, 313
     commercialization 298–9
     consumers 300–301
     disabilities 311–12
     nonprofit 297
     physician/patient relationships 304–6,
        307–8, *309*
     privacy 299
     quality 299–302
Health on the Net Foundation 299
HealthCentral.com 299
Healthscout 296
Helsinki University 74, 77
herbal medicines 300
Hetherington, Kevin 359n20
Hewlett, William 54
Hewlett-Packard 53–4, 190

hierarchies 5, 341
high-technology industry 65–6, 86,
     99–100
Hill House Community Access Network
     327–8
Himanen, Pekka 40, 421, 424
Hindi film industry 411
Hindi television 406, 414–15
Hindu nationalist party 403, 404
Hinduism 414–15
Hine, C. 128
Hine, Virginia H. 349
Hinglish 406, 418n4
Hirshleifer, J. 156
history
     Christians 438
     Greeks/Romans 438, 445
     sociology 432–4
     technology 439–43
     time 432
     Whig 435–6
Hoerni, Jean 59
Hoff, Ted 55, 59
home networks 91–2
Homebrew Computer Club 56
Homenet study 220–22, 223
HTML Writers Guild 186–7
Huges, J. A. 138
Hughes, Thomas P. 436
Human Genome Project 12, 13
hypertext 10–11, 30

IBM 426
identity
     collective 385, 387–8, 390–91, 397,
        398
     cultural 38–9, 241–2, 387–8, 390,
        396
     national 82, 243
     nation-states 39
     netizens 114
     resistance 242–3, 345
IMF 31, 344
immigration 60, 80, 81–2
inclusion 4, 23, 24, 52–3, 69–70, 335
income
     digital divide 234–5
     health information 296
     Internet 255, 256, 288–9, 330
     sociability 264

Independent Media Center 343, 344,
    359n7
India
    grassroots activism 352
    language communities 402–3, 405–6,
        411–14, 417
    newspapers 412–13
    religious programs 404–5, 406
    television 403–5
India, South 410, 417
individuals 18, 19, 21, 218
Industrial Revolution 5, 439
industrialism
    capitalist accumulation 17
    crisis of 17, 20, 436
    culture 38
    energy sources 8
    Fordism 27–8
    restructuring 15
Indymedia 353, 355
information 41, 147, 150, 153–7, 161,
    201–2
information and communication
        technologies xvi, 9, 10–11
    anti-globalization movement 35
    collective identity 385
    Finland 66–7
    globalization 386
    informationalism 20
    investment 60–61, 65
    network society 3, 6, 7
    politics 363
    race 264
    as revolution 15
    space 133, 264
    time 37
information flows 3, 36, 152, 162–3,
    364–5
information processing 9, 163–4
information sharing 156, 157, 158–9
information society 6–7, *68,* 335
Information Superhighway rhetoric 99,
    107
information technology
    access 321, 323
    content 328–30
    digital divide 319
    Finland 66–7
    inclusion/exclusion 335
    language 323

literacy 323
    multitasking 151
    network enterprises 422
    productivity 145, 146–7, 166–7
    Russia 90–91, 94–5
    Silicon Valley 55, 174–5
    time/place 427
    worldwide slowdown 100
    see also community technology
        centers; information and
        communication technologies
informationalism 41, 50
    Castells 7, 421
    China 99–102
    exclusion 429
    ICT 20
    labor market 422
    network enterprises 27
    network society 8–9, 13
    space of flows 11–12
    welfare state 429
innovation 20, 61, 430
    culture of 40, 74–7, 424–5
    diffusion 336n4
    Finland 67–70, 72–3, 74–7
    funding 64–6, 69, 72–3
    hacker ethic 424–5
    military 426
    openness 426
    productivity growth 29, 422–3
    Silicon Valley 56–60, 64–6
integrated circuits 57
Intel 55, 58, 59, 61, 108
Intel Computer Clubhouse Network 332
intellectual property rights 58, 429
intelligentsia 87, 90, 93
intermediaries, labor market 183–8, 189,
    191, 193
International Monetary Fund 31, 344
Internet 23, 233, 238, 329
    access to 91, 102–6, 138, 288, 330
    age 256, 258, 261, 264, 266–7n3
    autonomy 233–4, 244–6, 247
    as boundary object 126
    censorship 109–14
    China 101–6, 117–18
    communities 211n16
    digital divide 24, 442
    education 253, 255, 256, 271–2
    employment 255–6, 259, 261

encryption 71, 76
gender gap 89, 103, 253, 258
global justice movements 347
globalization 226
income 255, 256, 288–9, 330
language 90, 95, 96, 105, 272–3
media 218
mis-information 312
networks 10–11, 320–21
origins 14, 57
physicians 306–11
pluralizing impact 398
politicians 367
politics 93–4, 95, 239, 241, 363–6,
    368–70
race 253, 258
Russia 86–96, 256, *260,* 261, 265,
    330
Silicon Valley 55
sociability 237–8
social actors 233–4
social capital 249
social relationships 217, 222, 225
Soviet Union 87–8
Trinidad 138
users 104–5, 220, 221–2, 223,
    319
uses 239, *240,* 241, *254–5,* 256–61,
    265, 288
see also health information
Internet and Health Communication
    (Rice and Katz) 293
Internet cafés 105–6, 112–14, 119n19
Internet relay chat 71, 76
Internet studies 126–8
Irving, Larry 324

Jadad, A. R. 297
Jameson, Frederic 342
Japan 28, 370, 390, 396, 421
Jiang Zemin 101, 113
job specialization 160–61
job turnover 178, 181
Jobs, Steve 55
Johnson, Chalmers 106
Jonassen, D. 272
*Journal of the American Medical
    Association* 303
Joy, Bill 57, 59
Jubilee Movement 34

Kahn, Robert 14
Kao, John 109
Katz, James E. 223, 293, 303
Kedourie, E. 387
Kelly, Niamh 281
Kennedy, Edward 16
Kerala 406–9, 410–11
Keynesian economics 15, 16, 20
Khosla, Vinod 59, 63
Kiselyova, Emma 17, 84
Kleinberg, J. 166
Kleiner, Eugene 55
Kleiner, Perkins, Caufield and Byers 55,
    63
Knorr Cetina, Karin 211n5, n12
know-how trading 157
knowledge 41, 58, 151, 180
knowledge base 157, 159–62, 165
knowledge processing 150–51
knowledge society 6–7
Korean *chaebol* 28
Kottak, Conrad 388
Kraut, Robert 220–22, 223
Kropotkin, Pyotr 354
Kuhn, Thomas 8, 11
Kumar, Sashi 408, 409
Kusumoto, Roy 59

labor
    autonomy 26
    discrimination 27
    energy sources 443–4
    feminized 27
    flexibility 63, 175, 176–83
    generic 26–7, 29
    migrants 235, 237
    productivity 150
    unionized 67
    white-collar 146, 147
    see also employment; work
labor divisions 26–7
labor market 175, 176
    informationalism 422
    intermediaries 183–8
    outcomes 188–93
    social structures 191–2
Lactis, Eric 218
languages
    anti-globalization movement 348
    Catalonia 242, 392–3, 395–7

English 90, 272–3
  India 402–3, 405–6, 411–14, 417
  IT 323
  Russia 90, 95, 96
  television 395–6, 409–10
Lash, Scott 36, 37, 179
Latin America 386
Latour, Bruno 32, 358n1
Lazarus, Wendy 330
LDF study 199, 206
learner support 287–8
learning 274, 282
  see also e-learning
learning institutions 277
learning resource management system 276
learning-by-doing 159–60
Lefebvre, Henri 30
Lenin, V. I. 28
Lieberman, Joe 371
Life-Web Journalist Project 329
Linux 49, 71, 72, 74, 76, 423
  China 108, 115
literacy 323, 328
living standards 87, 91, 145
locality 37–8, 225
localization 391, 402, 414–16

Ma, Lawrence 108
McBride Commission 389
McKay, H. G. 303
McKenna, Regis 55
McKenna Group 55, 59
MacKnight, C. 281
McNealy, Scott 59
McNeil, J. R. 444
McQuail, Dennis 415–16
Malayali Asianet 408
Manpower Temporary Services 190
Mao Zedong 99, 114–15
Maoism 18
Maran, Kalanidhi 408
Marvin, Simon 36
Marx, Leo 437
Marxism 388
Mason, D. 131–2
Mattelart, A. 396
media
  Americanization 389–90
  Catalonia 243–4
  China 115, 396

  community institutions 410–11, 416–17
  cultural dominance 416–17
  Internet 218
  localization 402, 414–16
  nationalism 403
  politics 30, 31–2, 33–4
  public space 30, 403
  Russia 88
  transformation of minds 24
  transnational 414, 416
media politics 375–6
medical information: *see* health
  information
MedicineOnline.com 298–9
Medline 296, 297, 303
Meek, Ronald L. 440
MeetUp.com 373
Meister, J. 278
Melucci, Alberto 356
Mendelson, D. N. 298
Michigan University 333
microbial infections example 281–2
microchip producers 108
microprocessors 55
Microsoft 21
migrant labor 235, 237
Milgram, Stanley 217–18
military sector 20, 24, 31, 58, 81, 426
Miller, D. 138
Millington, Linda 309–10
Ministry of Public Security 110–11, 120n31
Ministry of Telecommunications and
  Informatization 94
MIT studies 332
Mitchell, William 6, 11
Mitterrand, François 390
Miyazaki, Hirokazu 210n1
mobile telecommunications 67, 69, 74–5, 92, 219, 238
Modern Times (Chaplin) 28
modular designs 160–61
money 428–9
Monge, Peter R. 3, 4
Moore, Gordon 55
Mora, Francisco 330
Morison, Elting 447n3
Movement for Global Resistance (MRG) 343, 349–50, 352, 359n9

MTV 403, 415
MTV India 406
Mulgan, Geoff 23
Multilateral Investment Agreements 343, 348
multimedia systems 30
multitasking 151
Muruyama, M. 390

NAFTA (North America Free Trade Agreement) 343, 389
Naidu, Chandrababu 408
nanotechnology 6, 12
Narain, Lala Jagat 413
National Computing and Networking Facility of China (NCFC) 99, 100
National Library of Medicine 296–8
National Science Foundation 324
National Telecommunications and Information Administration (NTIA) 249, 324, 330
National Urban League 324
nationalism 117, 242, 403
nationality 235, 242, 243, 387–8
nationhood concept 387–8
nation-states 23, 25, 39, 388
NATO (North Atlantic Treaty Organization) 116
NEC 108
Nelson, Diane 351
Nelson, Ted 10
neoclassical economics 147, 150
netizens 102, 114, 118
Netscape web browser 55, 61, 77
Nettleton, S. 134
Netville case 226–9
network economy 176–7
network enterprises 27, 422
network society xvi–xvii, 3, 24–6, 38–9
    Britain 136–7
    Castells 14, 84, 165, 302, 436
    Catalonia 233–4
    communication 29–30, 385–6
    context 434
    culture 32–3, 38–40
    global 22–4
    globalization 39–40
    ICT 3, 6, 7
    individual 218
    informationalism 8–9, 13

power 34–5
Russia 84–5, 96–7
sharing 43
Silicon Valley 49
social movements 49–50
switchers 32, 33–4
technology 14
networks 3, 4, 5–6
    Castells 385
    efficiency 165–6
    e-mail 164
    global 80–81, 198–9, 208–9
    hierarchies 5, 341
    Internet 10–11, 320–21
    power 31–4
    self-generating 353–4
    social movements 35–6, 353–4
    software development 10
    Virtual Society? program 133–4
    see also social networks
Neuwirth, Esther 183, 191
New Beginnings Learning Center 331
New Delhi Television 415
new social movements 22, 349
The New York Times 113, 373
News Corporation 406
newspapers, India 412–13
NextEd 278
Nie, Norman 221–2
Nieminen, Jorma 74
NK Cables 66
NMT (Nordic Mobile Telephone) 74, 75
Noble, D. 272, 280, 287
nodes 3, 4
Nokia 66–7, 70–73, 74, 76
Nokia Research Center 75–6
nomenklatura 85
Norris, Pippa 376
NOVA Workforce Investment Board 179
Noyce, Bob 55

occupational health and safety 190
OECD 70, 274–5, 289, 319
Ogburn, William 437
Oikarinen, Jarkko 71–2
oil price shock 15
Ollila, Jorma 75
Ong, Aihwa 342
open source software 10, 49, 50, 342
Open University

Britain 278
Catalonia 278, 394
Operation Blue Star 413
Opium War 100
Oracle Corporation survey 226
organizational theory 150
Orlikowski, W. J. 156
outsourcing 181, 190
ownership, concentrated 35, 375
Oyston, J. 309

Packard, David 54
Paterniti, D. A. 303
patients 304–6, 307–10
patriarchy 19, 27
peace movement 18, 19
Pearl River Delta 107, 108
People's Bank of China 106
People's Global Action (PGA) 343, 346,
    348, 350–52, 358n6
People's Liberation Army 110
Per Scholas 326
perestroika 17
Perez, Carlota 8
performance-related pay 180
personal computers 14, 55
Peters, O. 272, 283
Pew Internet and American Life Project
    223, 229
Phoenix Online University 277, 279
physicians
    Internet 306–11
    patients 304–6, 307–10
    websites 310–11
PISA 70
Playing2Win organization 324
Pointcastnetwork.com 296
PolicyLink 333–4
political campaigns, online 367–8, 371–5
politics
    decision-making 31–2
    hypertext 30
    ICT 363
    Internet 93–4, 95, 239, 241, 363–6,
        368–70
    media 30, 31–2, 33–4
    networked 375–6, 378
    of protest 366–7
    Runet 92–6
    of survival 106

Poole, G. 274–5, 280–81, 282
Powell, Michael 325
Powell, W. W. 165
power
    capitalism 32
    network society 34–5
    networks 31–4
    switchers 33
presentism 435–6, 437–8
privacy/health information 299
productivity growth 145–6, 148–50
    consumers 149
    information 153–7
    innovation 29, 422–3
    IT 145, 146–7, 166–7
    living standards 145
    modular designs 160–61
    Silicon Valley 60–61
    simulation modeling 161–2
    Solow 41
    USA 51–2
professional employer organizations
    185–6
profitability 180, 210
programmers 32, 34
Project Compute 329–30
Project Internet Catalonia 394, 398
Protestant ethic 420–21, 428
public space 30, 334, 403
PubMed 296
Punjab 407, 409–10, 411–13, 414
Punjab Kesari 413
Punjabi film industry 411–12, 413
Punjabi television 413–14
Putin, V. 25
Putnam, Robert 219, 229

al-Qaeda 35
Qian Tianbai 99
Qianguo Luntan 116

race
    Detroit 250–51
    digital divide 249
    health information 295, 311–12
    ICT 264
    Internet 253, 258, 259, *260,* 261, 265,
        330
    sociability 261, *262–3*
    USA *252*
Rama Rao, N. T. 408

Rambler 95
Raymond, Eric 355–6, 423
RCADE (Citizens Network to Abolish
    the External Debt) 354–5
Reagan, Ronald 16, 17
Reclaim the Streets 346, 359n14
recruiters
    e-mail 157, 165–6
    evaluating candidates 150–51
    information searching 163
    information sharing 157–8
    social networks 148
Redwood, Carl 327–8
religion 242
religious programs 404–5, 406
Reminiscent TV 414
Renan, E. 387
research and development 57–8, *64*,
    70–71, 73, 125–6
resistance 19, 34, 35–6, 356, 435
rheumatoid arthritis information 298
Rhodes, Lodis 329
Rice, Ronald E. 223, 293, 303
Rimal, R. 298
risk 153, 154–5, 189, 192
Robert Wood Johnson Foundation survey
    307–8, 309
Robin, K. 94
Rock, Arthur 54, 55
Rogers, E. M. 336n4
Romans 436, 438
Rose, S. 300
Rostelecom 91
Runet
    humor 95–6
    politics/leisure 92–6
    Russian language 87
    subcultures 95–6
    users 88–90
Russia
    Concept of Building the Information
        Society in Russia 94
    Concept of State Information Policy
        94
    economic restructuring 86
    elites 86, 94, 95
    employment 87
    high-technology industry 86
    home networks 91–2
    informal networks 85

intelligentsia 87, 90, 93
Internet 86–96, 256, *260*, 261, 265,
    330
IT 90–91, 94–5
language 90, 95, 96
living standards 87, 91
media 88
Ministry of Telecommunications and
    Informatization 94
mobile telecommunications 92
network society 84–5, 96–7
nomenklatura 85
statism 85

Sahitya Akademy 411
Salinsky, E. M. 298
Salora 74
Sanchez, P. M. 310
Santa Fe Institute 13
Sartre, Jean-Paul 446
Sassen, Saskia 209
Saxenian, Anna Lee 59, 60, 165
scale economies 158
Scardamalia, M. 281
Schlesinger, P. 396
Schneider, S. M. 368
Science and Technology Policy Council
    67, 69, 70
scientific management 28
scope economies 158
Scotland 306
Seaman, J. 276
Seattle meetings of WTO 342–3
security networks 35
self-employment 180, 181
semiconductors 55, 57, 59, 61, 146
Sennett, Richard 30
service jobs 190
SET 406
Shanghai 108
Sharf, B. F. 303
sharing 21, 40, 43, 76–7
Shiromani Gurudwara Prabjand
    Committee 413–14
Shockley, William 54, 56
Sigouin, C. 297
Silicon Valley xvii, 23
    biotechnology companies 56
    development model 53–6
    employment 178, 180–81, *182*

entrepreneurialism 61–3, 81
hacker culture 82
immigration 81–2
informationalism 50
innovation milieu 56–60
Internet 55
IT 55, 174–5
military 81
multiethnicity 59–60
network society 49
new economy model *62*
productivity growth 60–61
start-up activity *63*
unemployment 174, 178–9, 189
universities 56, 57, 58, 60, 64, 81
venture capital 57–8, 64–5
Simon, H. A. 160
simulation modeling 161–2
Sisnett, Ana 331
Sitra 72
Slater, D. 138
small and medium businesses 28
Smith, A. 387
SMS (short messaging system) 11, 115
sociability
    Catalonia 236–8, 239, 241
    education 264
    employment 264
    income 264
    Internet 237–8
    inter-racial 261, *262–3*
social actors 23, 40, 84, 233–4
social capital 165, 219, 228, 249, 267n6
Social Capital Benchmark Survey 261
social cohesion 247–8
social connectedness 191, 192
social movements
    Castells 341, 438
    cultural 15, 18–19, 21
    network society 49–50, 353–4
    networks 35–6
    new 22, 349
    struggles within 352
    transactional 341
social networks
    computer-supported 347
    economic opportunity 164–5
    financial markets 211n4
    intermediaries 191
    Internet user surveys 223

recruiters 148
trading pit 200–2, 203
social relationships
    computer-mediated communication
        224–5
    e-mail 132, 331
    face-to-face 237
    Internet 217, 222, 225
    locality 225
social structures 3
    economic opportunity 165
    informationalism 41
    labor market 191–2
    networks 4, 5
Society for Technical Communication
    186–7
sociology 432–4
software development 10, 11
    open source 10, 49, 50, 342
Solectron 59, 182–3
Solow, Robert 41, 146
Sony Entertainment 403
Soros Foundation 90
South America 388
Soviet Union 17, 84, 87–8
    see also Russia
space
    ICT 133, 264
    online trading 204–5
    time 198, 218
    trading pit 200–202
    virtual community 219–20
space of flows 11–12, 36, 107–8, 118,
    398
Spain 391, 392–3, 395
    see also Catalonia
Sputnik 57
staffing services firms 183
Stanford Industrial Park 54
Stanford University 56, 57, 58, 60, 64
Star Plus 407
Star TV 403, 414, 415
start-up activity *63,* 79–80
State Council Informatization Steering
        Group 106, 110
State Secrecy Bureau 110, 111
states
    power 25, 32
    social expenditure 16
    support 49, 67, 69, 72–3, 79–80
    see also nation-state; welfare state

statism 15, 17–18, 22, 84, 85
Stone, Antonia 324
strategic alliances 28
Street, R. L. Jr. 298
Street-Level Youth Media 326–7
Strogatz, S. H. 166
Suarez-Almazor, M. E. 298
subcultures 95–6, 106
Sun Microsystems 55, 57, 59, 61, 63,
    424
Sun Yat-sen 100–101
Surgerydoor.com 297
surveillance technologies 131–2
Sutton, R. I. 165
Suzik, Holly Ann 183
Swann, G. M. P. 131
switchers 32, 33–4
Sykes, Richard 139
Syntopia Project 220, 229
System Administrators' Guid 187

Taiwan 108
Taylorism 28
technological determinism 126–7, 135,
    433
technology xvi, 5–6, 8
    Castells 445
    computerization 21
    emergent properties 10
    and history 439–43
    history of 433, 434–5, 436, 447n3
    information processing 9
    military funding 20
    miniaturization 7, 20
    network society 14
    presentism 437–8
    products into brands 58–9
    progress 442–3
    and science 445
    social construction 210n2, 434
    see also innovation
technology transfer 158
TechSoup.org 332
Tekes 72–3
telecommunications 84
    see also mobile telecommunications
television
    India 403–5
    languages 395–6, 409–10
    Spain 391, 392–3, 395

TeliaSonera 66, 67, 77
Telugu language movement 410
temporary agencies 184–6
Terman, David 54
terrorism 25, 35, 445
Thatcher, Margaret 16, 17
Thompson, J. B. 389, 397, 403
Thrift, Nigel 36
Tian, Edward 109
Tianenman Square 106
Till, J. E. 298, 303
time 37
    creativity 427–8
    history 432
    Internet 221
    IT 427
    online trading 205–7
    space 198, 218
    timeless 36, 37, 198
    trading pit 202–3
    Weber 427
Tokyo financial markets 210n1
Torvalds, Linus 71–2, 74, 76–7
Touraine, Alain 39
traders 198, 203–4, 207–9, 211n12
trading, online 204–7
trading pit 198–9, 200–203
    see also Chicago Board of Trade
training 187–8, 273, 278–82, 328
transistors 21, 54, 56
transnationality 342
transport 5, 21, 437
Trinidad 138
Trippi, Joe 373
Truman-Davis, B. 285
Turgot, A. R. J. 439–40

UCLA Internet Report 223
unemployment 174, 178–9, 189
UNESCO 389
United Nations Technology Achievement
    Index 49, 51
United States of America
    Americanization 386, 389–90, 396
    Defense Department 14, 57
    Federal Communication Commission
        35
    Federal Reserve Board 31, 60–61,
        201
    Internet user surveys 220

physicians 306, *307*
productivity growth 51–2
race *252*
social inequality 53
Treasury Department 31, 201
United Nations Technology
    Achievement Index 51
war against terrorism 25
World Economic Forum 51
universities
Finland 70
Nokia 70–71, 74, 81
sharing 21
Silicon Valley 56, 57, 58, 60, 64, 81
UNIX 50, 57, 423
Urdu 412, 414
Urry, John 36, 37, 179

Valentine, Donald 55, 63
Van Alstyne, Marshall 156
Ventura, Jesse 367
venture capital 54–5, 57–8, 63, 64–5, 72
Veronin, M. A. 300
Viacom 415
video standards 426
Vietnam War 18
virtual community 217, 219–20
virtual health communities 302–4
virtual society 130–33, 211n12
Virtual Society? program 128
    electronic technologies 129–30
    networks 133–4
    rules of virtuality 137
    title 135–6
Voline 353
voters 364, 368–70

wages 180, 190
Ward, Colin 354
Ward, S. J. 365–6, 370
watchmakers parable 160
Watt, S. E. 131
Watts, D. J. 166
Watts, T. 131
web-based job sites 185
WebCT 273, 276, 280–81, 285
Weber, Max xviii, 420–21, 427
WebMD.com 298
Webster, F. 94
WebTV 221–2

Wei Bu 103
welfare state
    Denmark 78
    Finland 49, 67, 69–70, 79–80, 81–2
    informationalism 429
Wellman, Barry 134, 211n16, 347
White Overalls 346
Wikgren, M. 297, 300
Williams, A. 329
Williams, P. 297
Williams, R. 95, 441
Wilson, Sonsini, Goodrich, and Rosati
    58
Winston, B. 95
wireless communications 11–12, 219
Wolfensberger, D. R. 367
women 18–19, 26, 27
    see also gender gap
Woolgar, Steve 130
work
    automation 444–5
    flexibility 27, 177, 178–80
    money 429
    paid/unpaid 26
    part-time 27, 180, 181
    project-based 427
    reflexivity 179–80
    self-employment 27, 180, 181
    temporary 27, 180, 181, 190
    see also employment; labor
workers
    creativity 425–6
    disadvantaged 188
    employers 180
    insecurity 190–91
    intermediaries 193
    loyalty 181
    women 26, 27
working hours 26
World Bank 344, 352
World Economic Forum 49, 51, 344
World Social Forum 344, 345, 352
World Trade Organization 16, 34, 103,
    108, 342–4
World Wide Web 11, 271–2, 273,
    276
Wozniak, Steve 55
Wyatt, S. 131

XCADE 356–7

Yahoo! 55, 59, 61
Yang, Jerry 59
Yangtze Delta 108
Ylonen, Tatu 71
youth factors 106, 256

Zapatistas 341, 343, 348
Zee Telefilms 406–7, 414
Zee TV 406
Zook, Matthew 57–8